CRC Press Reference Books in Computer Science

CRC Press Reference Books in Computer Science series offers advanced and authoritative resources for students, researchers, and professionals across the field of computer science. Books in this series serve as indispensable references which present rigorously researched and innovative approaches to current and complex issues.

Reimagining Literacy in the Age of AI: Theory and Practice
Edited by Jason D. DeHart, Suriati Abas, Raúl Alberto Mora, and Damiana Gibbons Pyles

Generative AI in Higher Education: Guiding Principles for Teaching and Learning: Volume 1
Dr Emmanuel K Nartey

Governing the Future: Digitalization, Artificial Intelligence, Dataism
Henning Glaser and Pindar Wong

Generative AI in Higher Education: Ethical Governance, Skills, and Employability: Volume 2
Dr Emmanuel K Nartey

Generative AI in Higher Education: Ethical Governance, Skills, and Employability

Volume 2

Dr Emmanuel K Nartey

CRC Press
Taylor & Francis Group
Boca Raton London New York

CRC Press is an imprint of the
Taylor & Francis Group, an **informa** business

Designed cover image: Shutterstock

First edition published 2026
by CRC Press
2385 NW Executive Center Drive, Suite 320, Boca Raton FL 33431

and by CRC Press
4 Park Square, Milton Park, Abingdon, Oxon, OX14 4RN

CRC Press is an imprint of Taylor & Francis Group, LLC

ISBN: 978-1-032-81798-9 (hbk)
ISBN: 978-1-032-82011-8 (pbk)
ISBN: 978-1-003-50251-7 (ebk)

DOI: 10.1201/9781003502517

Typeset in Minion
by SPi Technologies India Pvt Ltd (Straive)

Contents

Preface

THIS SECOND VOLUME, *GENERATIVE AI IN HIGHER EDUCATION: ETHICAL GOVERNANCE, Skills, and Employability*, has been written from the conviction that education remains, at its core, a human endeavour concerned with dignity, fairness, and the flourishing of persons and communities. Although the technologies that shape our world evolve at speed, the ethical responsibilities of educators, students, employers, and governments do not recede; if anything, they sharpen. Volume I set out the principles and institutional scaffolding for engaging responsibly with generative AI. It argued that transparency, accountability, inclusivity, and academic integrity must guide any adoption. The present volume moves from principles to practice. It asks what kinds of capabilities higher education must now cultivate, how those capabilities are formed in relation to AI, and why an inclusive and innovative approach is the only defensible route if employability is to serve not merely markets, but human beings.

My philosophical motivation is simple to state and difficult to enact: education must be both inclusive and innovative. Inclusive, because opportunity in the 21st century is inseparable from access to the literacies, tools, and networks that confer voice and agency; innovation, because standing still is not a neutral act when the world is moving. To insist on inclusion without innovation risks preserving inequities under a comforting rhetoric of goodwill. To insist on innovation without inclusion risks accelerating advantages for those already ahead. The argument of this book is that the two belong together in an explicit ethic of justice and responsibility and that this ethic should shape the very meaning of employability in an AI-mediated world.

I have written this book not as a technologist, though I value the technical craft, nor as a policy evangelist, though I recognise the place of strategy. I write as an educator and scholar who has watched many students discover capacities they did not believe they possessed, and who has seen others, equally gifted, blocked by structures they did not design. In the age of AI, we must not reduce education to short-term technical training, even while we refuse nostalgia for forms of learning that no longer meet the conditions of life and work. We need a capacious understanding of employability that preserves human judgement, cultivates ethical awareness, and makes space for creativity, leadership, and solidarity. This is the spirit in which the pages that follow have been composed.

Two ideas thread their way through the volume. The first is a justice–responsibility framework for thinking about human flourishing with AI. Justice here is not an abstract slogan; it is a concrete test for whether our systems distribute opportunities fairly, especially to those least advantaged. Responsibility names the anticipatory work of designing, governing, and using technologies in ways that reduce harm, surface bias, and honour human rights. Between these two poles sits the pair that animates much of the book: awareness and preparedness. Awareness is the cultivated understanding of how AI reshapes knowledge, work, and social relations; preparedness is the translation of that understanding into personal, institutional, and policy action. The second idea is skills dynamics: the claim that employability now emerges from the evolving interplay between foundational personal and interpersonal capacities, specialised technical expertise, and the digital infrastructures through which learning and labour are mediated. Skills are not coins to be collected; they are living patterns formed by practice, context, and relationship.

The context for these arguments is not theoretical alone. Governments make large promises for AI-driven productivity and public service reform. Universities are asked to supply a workforce that is adaptable and digitally fluent. Employers seek graduates who can collaborate across disciplines, communicate across cultures, and navigate uncertainty with integrity. At the same time, structural inequalities—within and between nations—shape who can access the benefits of these developments. Connectivity, infrastructure, policy capacity, and institutional cultures differ markedly. In some places, the new tools are amplifiers for creativity and participation; in others, they risk becoming instruments that reinforce exclusion. A philosophy of inclusive innovation insists that we design for those differences and that we measure success by the extent to which learners at the margins find meaningful pathways into learning and work.

In the pages ahead, the reader will encounter familiar debates—about creativity, collaboration, communication, and critical thinking—reframed through the lens of AI. The familiar is not discarded; it is deepened. Creativity is not simply the generation of ideas; it includes the skilled use of digital tools to refine, test, and communicate those ideas. Collaboration is not merely group work; it is the demanding practice of working across distance, time, and difference through platforms that both enable and constrain human connection. Communication is not solely eloquence; it is a reflective practice that understands data, interfaces, translation, and the ethics of representation. Critical thinking is not an academic ornament; it is the disciplined examination of systems whose workings are often hidden. Each of these capacities becomes more, not less, necessary as AI systems advance.

The book also challenges a habit that has persisted in educational discourse: the separation of skills from technology. It is no longer adequate to speak as though one might teach a timeless set of competencies and then add a thin layer of digital literacy. Technology now shapes the conditions under which knowledge is created, shared, and applied. The question is not whether to integrate technology; it is how to do so in ways that preserve human agency, enlarge capability, and protect the public good. That is why this volume engages directly with frameworks that have shaped discussions of 21st-century skills. I acknowledge their contributions, and I push them to think with AI at the centre rather than at the edge.

Because this is a companion to Volume I, a few words about continuity are appropriate. The earlier volume asked institutions to build governance capable of saying both 'yes' and 'no'—'yes' to innovation where it serves learning, equity, and integrity; 'no' where risks cannot be mitigated or where values are compromised. This volume assumes that institutional readiness and ethical guardrails are in place and then asks what a curriculum oriented around inclusive innovation should look like when employability is understood as a dynamic and relational practice. It is a move from architecture to habitation, from blueprint to lived space. Readers may wish to know how the book is organised. Although the chapters stand on their own, they are intended to be read as a sequence that moves from framing to analysis to synthesis. Each chapter summary is written to welcome readers into the distinctive work undertaken in that part of the book while showing how the argument develops.

Introduction opens with an account of why this volume is necessary now. It revisits the central claims of Volume I and sets out the justice–responsibility framework that orients the whole. The chapter articulates the need for awareness and preparedness as mutually reinforcing dispositions for life with AI. Awareness involves understanding how AI participates in decision-making, creativity, and collaboration; preparedness involves building skills, institutions, and regulations capable of guiding those processes in line with public values. The chapter situates these themes within current policy developments and reminds the reader that universities, governments, and employers have distinct yet overlapping responsibilities. It introduces the diagram that places human flourishing at the centre, with opportunities at the apex and challenges at the base, held in balance by justice and responsibility. The aim is not balance for its own sake, but a principled alignment that ensures innovation serves inclusion and that inclusion is pursued imaginatively.

Chapter 1 redefines employability for an AI-mediated world. It begins by showing the limits of traditional accounts that equate employability with a list of technical proficiencies or with credentials that may no longer track the realities of work. The chapter develops the core notion of skills dynamics: the adaptive interplay between technical expertise, cognitive agility, interpersonal capability, and the digital systems that structure learning and labour. Far from displacing human capacities, AI can increase the reach of human creativity, provided that learners are taught to use it critically. The chapter argues that employability is not a static state achieved upon graduation; it is an ongoing practice of integrating knowledge, values, and tools in evolving contexts. This redefinition gives universities a positive task: to design learning that forms judgement, nurtures imagination, and encourages lifelong adaptation without surrendering educational purpose to the shifting demands of any single industry.

Chapter 2 subjects widely used skills frameworks to scrutiny. It acknowledges the enduring value of the '4Cs' while showing that their fullest meaning becomes visible only when the role of technology is taken seriously. The chapter engages with authors who have mapped important terrain on personal development, problem-solving, and creativity, and it marks where these maps need to be redrawn. The text argues for a comprehensive understanding of capability that integrates ethical reasoning, intercultural awareness, and digital fluency. It considers the risks of over-reliance on platforms that can narrow attention or flatten complexity, and it cautions against narratives that promise effortless improvement simply through tool adoption. Throughout, the reader is invited to see skills not as isolated attributes but as interdependent practices that take their shape within technological ecosystems. The chapter concludes by setting out why comprehensive capability must include the courage to interrogate systems that produce bias or diminish human agency.

It then builds the positive model in detail. It presents the skills dynamics framework explicitly, showing how foundational personal and interpersonal qualities—self-control, social competence, higher-order reasoning, and a resilient self-concept—form the ground upon which specialised expertise and digital infrastructures can be integrated. The argument is practical as well as philosophical: curricula should be designed so that students encounter real problems, experiment with AI-enabled tools, and reflect on the ethical stakes of their decisions. The chapter provides international illustrations. One finds national strategies that embed AI literacy at scale; one finds initiatives that use adaptive learning to support underserved communities; one finds dual systems that pair vocational formation with ethical reasoning for Industry 4.0. These cases are not offered as perfect models but as invitations to institutional imagination. They demonstrate that there are many routes to inclusive innovation, each requiring attention to context, culture, and capacity.

Chapter 2 gathers the argument into a call for an integrated, ethically grounded approach to employability. It emphasises that universities must neither retreat into defence of older forms that no longer serve learners nor submit uncritically to technological determinism. The chapter returns to the justice–responsibility framework and to the pairing of awareness and preparedness, and it insists that policy must be judged by its practical effects on equity and opportunity. It discusses lifelong learning as a principle and a practice, framing it not as a burden of permanent remediation but as a dignifying account of human development across the life course. It urges collaboration between universities, employers, and governments that is candid about risks, disciplined about evaluation, and bold about designing structures that expand access to high-quality learning and meaningful work. The closing pages set an agenda that aligns employability with sustainability, social responsibility, and the capabilities people need to live well.

Throughout the book, philosophical lenses help clarify what is at stake. A conception of human flourishing inherited from Aristotle reminds us that education is for more than economic utility. A concern for fairness, informed by traditions of justice, reminds us that educational systems are accountable for how they distribute benefits and burdens. A resistance to the reduction of persons to data points, inspired by humanistic critiques of technological domination, reminds us that every system can obscure the human faces it affects. These are not abstract gestures. They are anchors for decisions about curriculum, assessment, governance, and partnership. The book addresses, directly and indirectly, a set of tensions that every university now lives with. There is the tension between depth and agility: how to cultivate rigorous knowledge and judgement while preparing students to move across domains. There is the tension between personal formation and platform logic: how to form habits of attention, empathy, and critical reflection in environments that encourage speed and surface. There is the tension between local responsibility and global competition: how to serve particular communities while remaining open to the world. Facing these tensions honestly is part of preparedness. Refusing to allow one side to win by default is part of responsibility.

In proposing an inclusive and innovative agenda, I am mindful of the risk of aspiration without traction. That is why the volume is concrete. It asks that AI be taught not only as a topic but also as a context for doing work that matters. Students should build, test, and critique tools; they should see where those tools help and where they hinder; they should learn to ask who benefits and who bears the cost. They should practise leadership that is collaborative and ethical, and they should encounter entrepreneurship as the disciplined search for value that advances the common good, not simply as a route to personal gain. They should be invited to imagine professions transformed by automation and augmentation, and to locate their own agency in those transformations. The book also addresses meritocracy with care. It recognises the appeal of systems that promise reward according to effort and ability, and it records how such systems can overlook the ways in which resources, networks, and bias structure opportunity. AI can either compound or illuminate these patterns. Recruitment algorithms can entrench old preferences under the appearance of objectivity; equally, they can be used to detect disparities and drive reform. Employability education must prepare graduates to navigate and challenge these realities. Fairness is not a topic to be visited once; it is a criterion that should shape how we teach, assess, partner, and build.

Readers will notice that the volume speaks frequently of lifelong learning. This is not a fashionable add-on. It is the corollary of understanding employability as a dynamic practice. When technology changes what counts as knowledge and skill, it is not only students who must learn; academics, administrators, and employers must also cultivate habits of renewal. A university worthy of the name is a community that learns in public, that shares what works and what fails, and that treats humility as a professional virtue. The best evidence of preparedness may be an institutional willingness to change course when the evidence demands it, and to do so in ways that protect students and staff from unnecessary harm.

The global orientation of the book is deliberate. I have tried to ensure that examples do not merely rehearse familiar stories from a few wealthy systems. There are initiatives on every continent that illuminate parts of the inclusive innovation agenda. Some demonstrate how to scale AI literacy without sacrificing ethical reflection. Some show how to use technology to reduce educational inequality rather than widen it. Some show the importance of embedding ethical and civic reasoning in vocational education. None is a universal template. Each is a lens through which universities might see their own possibilities more clearly.

A word too about the style of argument. The pages that follow combine analysis with invitation. Where the scholarship is thin or the evidence mixed, I say so, because candour builds trust. Where policy ambition outpaces delivery, I note the gap, because clarity is a precondition for improvement. Where institutions underestimate their own agency, I name the opportunities that remain within reach. And where hope is warranted, I do not apologise for expressing it. Students have a right to be taught by people who believe that education can make a difference. Although this volume is forward-looking, it is written with gratitude for those who have taught me most: students who asked difficult questions and refused easy answers; colleagues who noticed where my arguments needed strengthening; communities that reminded me that learning is not only for the privileged; and family and friends who sustained the patience this work requires. The personal is never far from the professional in education. It could not be otherwise, for we teach and learn as whole people.

Let me return, finally, to the two ideas with which I began: inclusive innovation and skills dynamics under a framework of justice and responsibility. If readers take only a few things from this book, I hope they are these. First, that employability worthy of the name is about forming people who can use their knowledge and tools for the benefit of others as well as themselves. Second, that the most powerful learning experiences are those in which students encounter complexity, practise discernment, and experience the dignity of contributing something real. Third, that AI will magnify the best or the worst of our systems depending on the quality of our governance, the wisdom of our pedagogy, and the seriousness of our ethical commitments. These are not slogans; they are choices, to be made over and over, in curriculum committees, in classrooms and labs, in partnerships with employers, and in the design of regulation.

The summaries of the chapters offered above are signposts rather than substitutes. Introduction provides the scene and the moral centre of gravity. Chapter 1 reframes employability as a dynamic practice. Chapter 2 interrogates existing frameworks and argues for comprehensive capability and develops the skills dynamics model with international illustrations and practical curricular consequences. Chapter 3 calls the community of higher education to an integrated, ethical, and global programme that aligns employability with human flourishing. Readers may start anywhere, but those who follow the order will see how the argument builds.

I do not claim that this volume resolves every question it raises. It is more faithful to the realities of education to admit that we are always between inheritance and invention, carrying forward what is still good while building what we lack. Yet I am persuaded that higher education has the resources, and the responsibility, to lead in shaping futures where AI is enrolled in the service of justice rather than the other way round. The students who walk through our doors deserve nothing less than an education that forms their character as it extends their capability, that introduces them to the exhilaration of discovery and the discipline of care, and that sends them into the world prepared both to excel and to serve.

If you are a student, I hope these pages recognise your hopes and anxieties and offer you tools worthy of your courage. If you are an educator, I hope you find here arguments and examples that support the changes you already sense are necessary. If you are a policymaker or employer, I hope you encounter an invitation to partnership that is ambitious, honest, and grounded in evidence. And if you are any combination of these, as many of us are, I hope you come away with renewed confidence that inclusive and innovative education is not a slogan but a programme capable of guiding the next decade of institutional practice.

The measure of this book will not be how elegantly it speaks of inclusivity and innovation, but whether it helps readers undertake specific acts of design, teaching, governance, and collaboration that make those words true in the lives of learners. That is the work ahead. May we do it with patience, imagination, and resolve.

Dr Emmanuel K Nartey

Reader (Associate Professor) of International Law and Artificial Intelligence

Programme Leader for LLM Programmes | Chair of Staff and Black Academic Network

Bath Spa University

Acknowledgement

THIS BOOK IS FIRST AND FOREMOST DEDICATED TO THE MEMORY of my late father, Richard Kwame Nartey, whose values, guidance, and example continue to inspire me. I also dedicate it to the wider Nartey family and Mum Enyonam Glawu, whose support has been a constant source of strength throughout my journey. My heartfelt gratitude extends to Lydia Akosua Boateng Darko and her family, whose encouragement and kindness have been invaluable. I wish to express my sincere thanks to my line manager, Steve Goulton, for his steady guidance and encouragement, and to Professor John Strachan, Pro Vice-Chancellor for Research and Enterprise at Bath Spa University, whose leadership and vision have been a source of inspiration. I am also grateful to my colleagues and friends across the sector, particularly the Pro Vice-Chancellors at the Open University, including Professor Ian Pickup, Pro Vice-Chancellor for Students, for their collegiality and support. Beyond academia, I am indebted to my judo family, whose friendship, discipline, and camaraderie have played a vital role in sustaining both my personal and professional life. Finally, I extend my thanks to my friends and colleagues at Bath Spa University, whose collaboration and encouragement have enriched both this project and my wider academic journey.

Dr Emmanuel K Nartey
Reader (Associate Professor) of International Law and Artificial Intelligence
Programme Leader for LLM Programmes | Chair of Staff and Black Academic Network
Bath Spa University Research Cluster Lead

Acknowledgement of the Use of Generative AI

The author declares that ChatGPT version 4.0 (OpenAI, San Francisco, CA, USA) was employed exclusively to assist with correcting typographical and grammatical errors in the manuscript. The tool was not used for generating content, developing arguments, interpreting findings, or contributing to the intellectual or scholarly substance of the work. Full responsibility for the accuracy, originality, and integrity of the manuscript rests with the author.

Introduction

In *Volume I: Generative AI in Higher Education – Guiding Principles for Teaching and Learning*, the groundwork was laid for understanding how higher education institutions (HEIs) can engage with Generative AI (GenAI) in principled and responsible ways. That volume argued that AI itself is neither inherently threatening nor inherently beneficial; its impact depends on how institutions adopt, govern, and integrate it into their core practices. Volume I traced the broader discourse surrounding GenAI, situating it within historical patterns of technological change, from industrialisation to digitalisation, and emphasised the importance of ethical reflection and institutional readiness. Central to Volume I was the articulation of guiding principles tailored to HEIs, with particular reference to the United Kingdom but with wider global resonance. These principles emphasised transparency, accountability, inclusivity, and academic integrity, framing GenAI not merely as a tool for efficiency but as a catalyst for reshaping the purposes and practices of higher education. The concluding chapter synthesised these arguments into actionable recommendations, urging HEIs to adopt adaptive and ethically grounded strategies that balance technological innovation with the cultivation of human-centred values. In doing so, Volume I provided the conceptual and institutional scaffolding necessary for a reflective engagement with AI.

Building upon that foundation, Volume II turns its attention more directly to the question of skills, employability, and professional preparedness in an AI-mediated world. While Volume I addressed the why and how of institutional engagement with GenAI, Volume II focuses on the what and who: what kinds of skills are now required, and who must be prepared to develop and apply them in an evolving professional landscape. Volume II explores the dynamics of employability in greater depth, examining how technical proficiency, ethical awareness, adaptability, and creativity intersect with AI to redefine professional competency for the 21st century. In this way, the two volumes are deliberately interlinked. Volume I established the principles of engagement, while Volume II advances the conversation into practice—connecting institutional strategies to the lived realities of students, educators, and employers. Together, they form a comprehensive framework for reimagining higher education in the age of AI, ensuring that technological innovation is guided not only by efficiency but also by justice, responsibility, and human flourishing.

For humans to flourish in the age of AI, justice and responsibility must remain central to how employability is conceptualised. This requires more than narrow discussions about

DOI: 10.1201/9781003502517-1

skills; it calls for institutions, employers, and governments to engage critically with the values underpinning graduate employability and the ways in which universities prepare students for complex professional realities. In this respect, higher education carries both an ethical and a practical duty: to equip learners with the competencies required in a changing labour market, while ensuring that such preparation is guided by principles of fairness, accountability, and social responsibility. Recent developments in policy illustrate the urgency of this challenge. On 13 January 2025, the British Government announced a £14 billion investment to establish the United Kingdom as a global leader in AI. According to the NCC Group (2025), the initiative seeks to stimulate economic growth and improve the delivery of public services through AI-driven innovation. While such ambitions signal recognition of AI's transformative potential, they also raise questions about timing, governance, and direction. It is striking that only now, in the mid-2020s, has a comprehensive investment of this scale been advanced, despite years of evidence pointing to AI's pervasive societal implications.

This development invites careful reflection on the evolving relationship between human progress and technology. It is increasingly evident that AI will not only shape industrial productivity but also influence the ethical fabric of education, employability, and civic life. The central empirical challenge lies in ensuring that society is adequately equipped to use AI both responsibly and legally, within the framework of established governance structures. Addressing this challenge requires engagement with two interconnected dimensions: the cultivation of skill sets and the establishment of robust regulatory systems. These elements cannot be understood in isolation, as each informs and shapes the other. This volume focuses primarily on the former—skills—examining them through the lens of employability in an AI-mediated world. Preparing individuals for the workforce now involves equipping them to thrive in contexts where AI is embedded in processes of decision-making, creativity, and collaboration. Yet this is inseparable from wider societal responsibilities, since technological systems are deeply interwoven with structures of governance, ethics, and accountability.

It is within this context that the following framework (Figure 0.1) is presented. The figure illustrates how human flourishing in the age of AI depends upon a balanced relationship between justice and responsibility. On one side lies the need to develop adaptable skill sets, underpinned by awareness and preparedness. On the other lies the requirement for effective regulation, governance, and accountability. These are complemented by the roles of universities, governments, and employers, each of which has a responsibility to contribute to a learning ecosystem that equips individuals for the demands of the future. Opportunities for innovation, employability, and inclusivity are positioned at the apex of this framework, while the potential challenges—ethical risks, bias, and gaps in preparedness—are acknowledged as ever-present considerations. Together, these elements depict a holistic model in which education, policy, and practice converge to support human flourishing. The framework highlights the argument that employability in the 21st century is not solely about acquiring technical proficiency, but about cultivating a reflective, ethical, and adaptable capacity to navigate a rapidly transforming world (Figure 0.1).

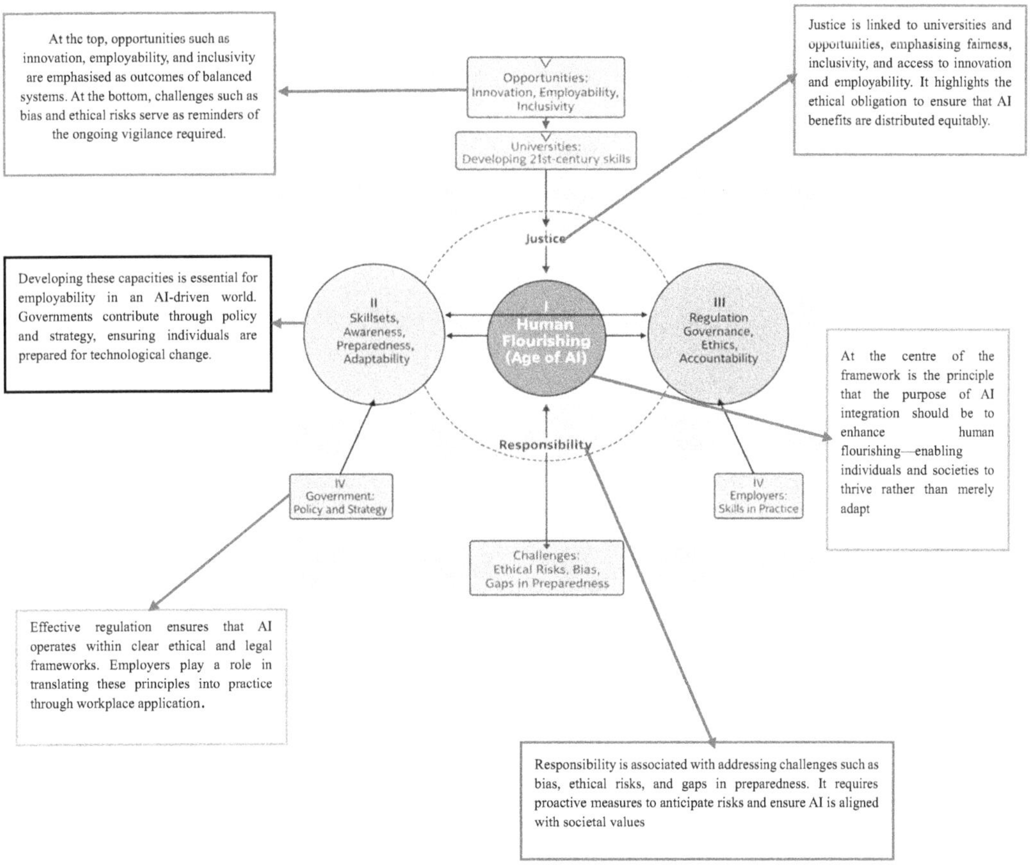

FIGURE 0.1 A justice–responsibility framework for human flourishing in the age of AI.

This framework illustrates the interdependence of skill development, regulation, and institutional roles in supporting employability and ethical practice. It highlights how justice, responsibility, and preparedness converge to enable innovation, inclusivity, and human flourishing in an AI-mediated society.

The phrase 'highlighting the need for both awareness and preparedness' in this book reflects a critical examination of how society must approach the integration of AI. It conveys a dual responsibility: to recognise AI's transformative potential and to ensure that individuals and institutions are equipped to engage with it ethically and effectively. This idea is central to the book's wider analysis of how AI is reshaping employability, social structures, and human interaction with technology. In this context, awareness refers to a reflective understanding of AI's impact on work, governance, education, and personal relationships. It requires recognition of how AI challenges established ideas of human agency and responsibility, while also raising pressing ethical questions of fairness, accountability, and potential misuse. Yet awareness alone is insufficient. Preparedness builds upon it by emphasising the translation of knowledge into action. Within the scope of this book, preparedness involves developing the skills, regulatory frameworks, and institutional

BOX 0.1 EXPLANATION NOTE—A JUSTICE–RESPONSIBILITY FRAMEWORK FOR HUMAN FLOURISHING IN THE AGE OF AI

The figure presents a conceptual framework for understanding human flourishing in the age of AI. At its centre is the proposition that the ultimate purpose of technological integration should be to advance human well-being. This requires a careful balance between justice and responsibility, both of which underpin the ethical and practical dimensions of employability in the 21st century. On the left-hand side of the framework lies the theme of skill-sets, encompassing awareness, preparedness, and adaptability. These qualities are essential for enabling individuals to navigate an AI-mediated workforce in which decision-making, problem-solving, and creativity are increasingly shaped by technological systems. The role of government, through policy and strategy, is positioned as a supporting element in this process, ensuring that education and training align with national and global demands.

On the right-hand side, the framework highlights the significance of regulation, which is concerned with governance, ethics, and accountability. Robust regulatory structures are necessary to ensure that AI is deployed in ways consistent with societal values and legal standards. Employers play a complementary role by embedding these principles into professional practice, thereby connecting regulatory frameworks with workplace realities. At the top of the figure, justice is represented through the role of universities and the opportunities generated by inclusive, innovation-driven, and employability-focused education. Universities are tasked with developing 21st-century skills and cultivating learning communities that foster a sense of belonging, collaboration, and fairness. The outcomes of such endeavours—innovation, employability, and inclusivity—are positioned as aspirational markers of success.

At the bottom of the framework, responsibility is linked to the challenges that inevitably accompany the adoption of AI, including ethical risks, systemic bias, and gaps in preparedness. These issues must be confronted openly, with a commitment to transparency and accountability, in order to prevent them from undermining human flourishing. Responsibility here denotes not only individual preparedness but also institutional and collective readiness to anticipate and mitigate the risks associated with technological transformation. Taken together, the framework demonstrates that human flourishing in the age of AI cannot be reduced to either technical proficiency or regulatory oversight alone. Rather, it emerges from the interplay between skill development, governance, and institutional responsibility, supported by governments, universities, and employers. By recognising both the opportunities and challenges that AI presents, the model advocates for a holistic approach in which education, policy, and practice converge to equip individuals and societies for an ethically grounded and sustainable future.

capacities necessary to engage with AI responsibly. It encompasses both equipping individuals for participation in an AI-driven workforce and ensuring that systems of governance align AI's application with societal values. Preparedness is not reactive but anticipatory, requiring foresight to address future developments and emerging risks. Together, awareness and preparedness form the foundation of the book's central argument: that society must adopt a balanced and proactive approach to AI. Awareness enables critical reflection on AI's ethical and social consequences, while preparedness ensures this reflection results in practical measures. Their interplay is essential for ensuring that AI supports employability, advances equity, and upholds ethical principles, consistent with the book's assessment of how technology is reshaping contemporary society.

From this perspective, the evolution of humanity may be understood as inseparable from the processes of knowledge creation and the continual deepening of understanding. Human progress has never been achieved in isolation from technological change; rather, it has emerged through our capacity to adapt to, engage with, and shape such developments in response to shifting societal needs. In the present age, this dynamic requires not withdrawal but a conscious elevation of both awareness and preparedness in relation to AI and its potential benefits and risks. Critical reflection on AI's integration into society is therefore indispensable. It is not sufficient to treat AI as an external or exceptional phenomenon; rather, it must be recognised as part of a broader continuum of technological and social transformation. This interdependence highlights the necessity of equipping individuals and institutions with the intellectual and practical resources to navigate AI's complexities ethically, effectively, and responsibly. Crucially, preparedness cannot be reduced to a narrow focus on technical upskilling alone. While digital competencies are necessary, they must be complemented by critical literacies, ethical reasoning, intercultural awareness, and adaptability.

This challenge is compounded by the reality that preparedness and awareness are unevenly distributed across global contexts. Structural inequalities—such as limited access to reliable internet, weaker policy infrastructures, and resource constraints in parts of the Global South—create barriers to equitable participation in the AI-driven economy. Thus, preparedness must be conceived not only as an individual responsibility but also as a collective and institutional duty, requiring governments, universities, and employers to embed foresight and inclusivity into their strategies. The implications for education are profound. If employability is to remain meaningful in an AI-mediated world, it cannot be confined to narrow technical proficiencies. Instead, it must be framed as a repertoire of diverse and substantive skills—technical, critical, creative, and adaptive—that enable individuals to respond to the uncertainties and opportunities generated by technological change. This diversity must be embedded within the very fabric of educational frameworks rather than appended superficially. Only then can universities cultivate graduates who are not merely reactive to change but capable of actively shaping the future of work and society. Embedding such an approach ensures that education contributes to human flourishing by aligning learning with both technological innovation and social responsibility. It situates employability not simply as a matter of labour-market readiness, but as a transformative practice that prepares students to engage meaningfully with the interplay between human knowledge, technological advancement, and societal progress (Nartey, 2025).

Although the importance of AI for education and employability is now widely acknowledged, the existing literature remains fragmented and partial in its treatment of preparedness and awareness. Much of the scholarship is weighted towards technical innovation or labour-market responsiveness, while relatively little has examined the conceptual underpinnings of preparedness or the ways awareness might operate as a reflective and critical capacity. Empirical studies of these ideas are particularly scarce, with most accounts either anecdotal or policy-driven rather than grounded in longitudinal or comparative research. Moreover, the literature tends to privilege Western and Global North perspectives, leaving underexplored how preparedness and awareness are differently constituted across diverse cultural, economic, and geopolitical contexts. Future research must therefore address these gaps by developing robust theoretical frameworks, gathering cross-cultural empirical evidence, and interrogating how preparedness and awareness can be systematically embedded into pedagogy, institutional governance, and employability practices.

Future scholarship could engage with a range of theoretical perspectives to deepen and enrich the debate. Preparedness, for example, might be understood through the lens of anticipatory governance, which highlights the importance of foresight and adaptability in conditions of uncertainty. Awareness could be framed as a form of critical digital literacy, emphasising the capacity for reflective engagement with the ethical, cultural, and political dimensions of AI. The capability approach also offers a valuable framework for rethinking employability: not as narrow labour-market responsiveness, but as the expansion of human freedoms, with preparedness and awareness serving as key enablers. In addition, intersectional perspectives can reveal how these concepts are unevenly distributed, exposing the structural inequalities that shape who can, and cannot, benefit from AI-driven opportunities. Taken together, these theoretical directions suggest ways in which the literature might move beyond descriptive accounts of technological change towards a more critical, justice-oriented, and transformative understanding of AI's role in education and work.

Building on this analysis, the British government's recent policies (2025) on advancing AI may be regarded as both timely and appropriate. By acknowledging the transformative potential of AI, these policies are aligned with the broader need to equip society with a substantive and diverse repertoire of skills that can support navigation through an increasingly dynamic technological landscape. Importantly, such an approach reflects an understanding that education must evolve to cultivate not only the technical proficiencies required for engaging with AI but also the critical, creative, and adaptive capacities essential for meaningful participation in societal and technological progress. Embedding this dual emphasis within educational frameworks has the potential to nurture a generation capable of responding to the complexities of an AI-driven world. In doing so, the United Kingdom would not only strengthen its position as a leader in technological innovation but also advance the development of a forward-looking and resilient workforce (Nartey, 2025).

Nevertheless, a degree of caution is warranted. Policy initiatives in this area often place disproportionate emphasis on technical training and economic competitiveness, sometimes at the expense of cultivating ethical awareness, intercultural understanding, and the socio-emotional skills necessary for democratic participation. Without careful balance, there is a risk that employability may be framed in narrowly instrumental terms, overlooking the wider purpose of education in supporting justice, equity, and human flourishing. Furthermore, there is little empirical evidence to suggest that current UK strategies are achieving this balance in practice. While government discourse highlights inclusivity and ethical responsibility, independent evaluations of how such principles are enacted within curricula, institutions, and labour markets remain limited. This gap raises questions about whether the ambition of policy translates into meaningful outcomes, or whether the rhetoric of preparedness risks masking persistent inequalities and uneven opportunities. Future policy development should therefore ensure that the promotion of technical expertise is complemented by a sustained commitment to ethical literacy and social responsibility, underpinned by robust evidence of impact.

At the same time, it is crucial to recognise that technological change is not confined to government initiatives alone. Technology has already reshaped the ways we live, work, and interact, spanning fields as diverse as autonomous aviation, advanced medical treatments, and industrial production. Consequently, universities and training organisations are equally implicated in this transformation, since the cultivation of intelligence and skills is increasingly mediated by technological systems (Eryandi and Nuryanto, 2020). In this respect, Chalkiadaki (2018) provides a helpful framework for conceptualising the skills required to thrive in the 21st century. These include personal development, critical thinking, creativity, and problem-solving—competencies that extend beyond instrumental applications to address deeper questions of human autonomy, decision-making, and our capacity to navigate complexity. Creativity, in particular, serves as a bridge between existing knowledge and emergent possibilities, encouraging imaginative thinking and opening new horizons. In parallel, critical thinking and problem-solving enable individuals to approach complex challenges with both rigour and innovation, ensuring that engagement with technological change remains both reflective and transformative (Joynes et al., 2019).

While technological innovation expands possibilities for creativity, adaptability, and problem-solving, it also unsettles traditional conceptions of learning in ways that are not uniformly positive. Proponents argue that digital tools foster flexible, self-directed learning and broaden access to knowledge (Ra et al., 2019). Yet sceptics caution that such claims risk overstating the benefits while neglecting the challenges of over-reliance on technology. The assumption that digital integration automatically enhances skills may obscure the erosion of foundational competencies, such as sustained attention, critical reasoning, or interpersonal communication, which remain essential in both professional and social contexts. The question of how learning itself is defined becomes central in this debate. If algorithms increasingly shape not only the content of learning but also its form, there is a risk of privileging efficiency and standardisation over depth and critical engagement. While conceptualising knowledge as fluid and contextually embedded provides a counterbalance, this ideal is difficult to realise in practice. Technological mediation can inadvertently narrow intellectual horizons by encouraging surface-level engagement or privileging information retrieval over synthesis. Thus, the challenge lies in negotiating the tension between the affordances of technology and the preservation of human agency and reflective judgement.

In this contested landscape, Chalkiadaki's emphasis on interpersonal skills acquires renewed weight. Advocates of digital progress often highlight global connectivity, yet the mere presence of communication platforms does not guarantee meaningful interaction. Without empathy, cultural awareness, and critical listening, technological connection risks degenerating into superficial exchange. Leadership, similarly, cannot be reduced to managing digital systems; it must remain grounded in relational practices that inspire and mobilise collective agency. In this respect, distributed and participatory models of leadership offer an important corrective to narratives that position technology as the primary driver of collaboration, reminding us that it is human relationships that sustain trust and cooperation. Equally significant is the challenge of navigating an environment oversaturated with information. Supporters of digital learning emphasise the opportunities for self-directed exploration and collaborative construction of knowledge, yet such opportunities presuppose access, autonomy, and motivation that are not evenly distributed. Critics point out that the celebration of adaptability and reflexivity risks overlooking structural inequalities, particularly for learners with limited digital resources or insufficient critical literacy. Moreover, an emphasis on constant adaptability may contribute to cognitive overload and diminish the capacity for deep, sustained learning. These perspectives suggest that skills development in the digital age must be understood as both dynamic and contested. Technology undoubtedly extends human capability, yet it also generates new dependencies, inequalities, and vulnerabilities. A critical approach requires resisting technologically deterministic narratives and instead recognising that skills are cultivated through a delicate balance of technological affordances and human capacities. Ultimately, the value of skills development lies not in efficiency or novelty alone but in its capacity to sustain meaningful, reflective, and ethically informed engagement with an increasingly complex world.

Chalkiadaki's framework rightly underlines the significance of human-centred skills. Yet it appears to treat skills development as distinct from the role of technology. I adopt a different standpoint. In this book, and in alignment with the volume III *Generative AI in Higher Education: Principles for Learning, Employability, and Ethics*, I maintain that technology is not simply an adjunct but rather an integral enabler of skills development. It provides the tools through which such competencies can be refined, applied, and embedded in both organisational settings and wider societal contexts. As mentioned previously, at the heart of these competencies lies the broader challenge of flourishing in an increasingly globalised and complex world. In this regard, adaptability and agility emerge as indispensable. They enable individuals to navigate constant change, embrace risk and uncertainty, and in turn cultivate innovation and growth. These qualities signal a resilient and open mindset—one that allows challenges to be approached with creativity and confidence. Within this spectrum, the integration of technology, and particularly AI, becomes vital in fostering innovation and sustaining progress. Chalkiadaki's analysis, therefore, while pragmatic, also prompts reflection on the deeper purposes of education and human development. The skills in question extend beyond immediate functional demands; they compel individuals to think critically, act ethically, and engage meaningfully with their world. Such a perspective inevitably connects to the ethical and societal implications of technology. Embedding these competencies within both educational and technological frameworks allows us not only to address present demands but also to contribute to shaping a more inclusive and reflective future.

It is at this juncture that the work of Voogt (2010) and Voogt and Roblin (2012) becomes particularly instructive. Like Chalkiadaki, they recognise the need for learners to cultivate competencies that transcend narrow academic knowledge—collaboration, communication, creativity, and critical thinking among them. Their analyses capture the urgency of preparing students for a rapidly changing world. Yet, much like Chalkiadaki, their frameworks inadvertently reproduce a limited vision of technology's role. By positioning digital tools primarily as instruments to enhance existing pedagogical practices, they risk reinforcing outdated models of education that remain tied to incremental improvement rather than transformative change. This limitation is not trivial. In overlooking technology's capacity to reconfigure how skills are developed, applied, and valued, Voogt and Roblin implicitly endorse a view of education that struggles to meet the demands of a technology-driven world. Their approach risks constraining learners within models that privilege subject-specific expertise while neglecting the integration of knowledge across domains. In contrast, this book advances the concept of comprehensive skills—a more expansive and future-oriented vision. These skills demand the ability to adapt to shifting contexts, synthesise insights across disciplinary boundaries, and apply ethical reasoning in navigating real-world challenges. While Voogt and Roblin acknowledge the importance of digital literacy and ICT, their narrow framing of technology as supportive rather than transformative leaves underexplored its potential to cultivate precisely these multidimensional competencies.

Moreover, the incremental perspective adopted by Voogt and Roblin runs the danger of underestimating how profoundly AI, data analytics, and digital collaboration tools are reshaping learning itself. Technology no longer operates at the margins; it defines the very conditions under which knowledge is created, shared, and applied. To treat it as peripheral is to risk preparing students for a world that no longer exists. Instead, comprehensive skills arise precisely from the integration of human capacities with technological affordances. Learners must therefore engage with technology not as passive recipients but as critical and active participants capable of using it to tackle complexity, innovate solutions, and drive progress (Hutson and Ceballos, 2023). From this standpoint, the central argument advanced in this book is that technology should not be conceived as a neutral medium for knowledge transfer. It should be recognised as a transformative element in education—one that empowers learners to respond to uncertainty, exercise ethical awareness, and embrace global opportunities. Skills development must therefore move decisively beyond subject-bound competencies, prioritising adaptability, employability, and reflective practice. Through personalised learning pathways, technology can equip students with the flexibility, creativity, and collaborative capacity demanded by contemporary and future workplaces. Without such a reorientation, educational frameworks risk leaving learners ill-prepared for the realities of an interconnected, rapidly evolving world.

Also, the discussions of 21st-century skills cannot be divorced from the ethical and social implications of technology in education. Comprehensive skills, as understood here, extend beyond technical proficiency to encompass the capacity for ethical judgement and engagement with societal concerns such as equity, privacy, and sustainability. Embedding these dimensions within educational practice transforms learning into more than a vehicle for immediate employability; it becomes a process that equips students to contribute to a more inclusive, responsible, and reflective future. In this light, the book critiques the persistent tendency in educational discourse to separate skills development from technology. Instead, it advances an integrated approach in which technology is not viewed as an optional enhancement but as a central framework within which comprehensive skills are nurtured. Such an approach has the potential to bridge the long-standing gap between academic knowledge and its practical application, enabling learners to thrive in an increasingly complex, dynamic, and globalised world. This vision, consistent with the purpose of this book, seeks to position technology as a vital enabler of adaptable, holistic, and future-ready education systems.

Within this discussion, Voogt's emphasis on the potential of digital tools to foster innovation offers an important contribution, yet it remains somewhat limited. His analysis gives insufficient attention to the ways in which such tools allow learners to navigate, integrate, and connect diverse bodies of knowledge. The interplay between technical proficiency, interpersonal understanding, and ethical awareness has become indispensable in an era shaped by AI, data analytics, and digital collaboration platforms. Skills development in the 21st century should therefore move beyond the notion of learners as passive consumers of technology, requiring instead that they become active agents capable of leveraging its potential to address complex challenges, promote inclusivity, and drive societal progress. This perspective disrupts traditional boundaries of skills development and employability, extending beyond the conventional parameters that universities have historically associated with preparation for the labour market (Bridgstock, 2017).

What is striking in Voogt's framing is not what is included but what is left underexplored. By positioning digital tools largely as mechanisms for pedagogical enhancement, his account risks confining higher education to incremental reforms that do little to disrupt entrenched practices. Such a stance overlooks the extent to which technological change is reconstituting the very conditions of learning and work. Universities that adopt this limited view may inadvertently prepare students for yesterday's challenges rather than tomorrow's uncertainties. A more ambitious approach is required—one that treats technology not as an auxiliary support but as a structuring force capable of reshaping curricula, learning environments, and graduate attributes. From this standpoint, integrating technology into skills development does more than provide marginal gains. It equips students with just-in-time skills and fosters the adaptability required to respond to the rapid transformations of the modern workplace. To emphasise this, however, is not to suggest that traditional approaches to skills development are redundant or fundamentally flawed. As this book demonstrates, such approaches remain valuable. Yet they are no longer sufficient on their own. What is required is a reimagined model in which technology acts as a complementary and, at times, catalytic force, ensuring that learners are prepared not only for immediate occupational demands but also for sustained participation in shaping a complex and uncertain future (Okolie et al., 2019). Ultimately, the critique of Voogt highlights a broader point: the discourse on 21st-century skills must evolve from incremental adjustments to systemic rethinking. Comprehensive skills can only be cultivated when ethical, social, and technological dimensions are understood as interdependent rather than separate. This integrated perspective ensures that education not only supports employability but also empowers students to engage critically, act ethically, and contribute constructively to the global challenges of the 21st century.

Voogt and Roblin's framework for 21st-century skills highlights valuable competencies such as creativity, collaboration, and critical thinking. Nevertheless, it gives limited attention to the transformative role of technology in shaping and extending these capacities. In contemporary contexts, creativity extends beyond the generation of ideas to include the capacity to employ digital tools in order to realise, adapt, and communicate those ideas in ways previously unimaginable. Collaboration has likewise been reshaped through digital platforms, which enable communication, negotiation, and knowledge co-creation across cultural and disciplinary boundaries, often unconstrained by geographical location. Critical thinking, too, now entails not only the interrogation of arguments and evidence but also the ability to evaluate, interpret, and ethically engage with technological systems and the vast amounts of information they produce.

To consider these competencies in isolation from technology risks marginalising the role of digital tools rather than recognising their centrality in the formation of comprehensive skills. For instance, digital platforms do more than facilitate collaboration; they redefine the very processes by which individuals and groups interact, problem-solve, and innovate. In this respect, the integration of technology into skills development should not be conceived as an additive layer but as a fundamental dimension of how such skills are developed, applied, and adapted in the modern era. Universities and education systems, therefore, must approach technology not as an optional enhancement but as an essential element of a holistic framework for skills development. While Voogt and Roblin's framework provides a useful foundation, its full potential is only realised when combined with a recognition of how technology mediates, transforms, and, at times, disrupts the competencies it identifies. This expanded perspective calls for skills development to be understood as a dynamic and integrative process—one that leverages the possibilities of technology to respond to the challenges and opportunities of the 21st century.

This limitation becomes even more apparent when considering the ethical and adaptive dimensions of skills. Comprehensive skills require a sophisticated engagement with the ethical implications of technology, including concerns about algorithmic bias, data privacy, and equitable access (Hanna et al., 2024). Although Voogt and Roblin acknowledge the importance of critical thinking, their frameworks do not fully address how technology shapes ethical reasoning and decision-making in educational and societal contexts. Yet these dimensions are essential if learners are to participate responsibly and reflectively in a digitally interconnected world (Stahl, 2021). Similarly, adaptability, which is frequently cited as critical for success in globalised and unpredictable environments, is often conceptualised in generic terms, with insufficient attention given to its technological dimensions. Comprehensive adaptability involves more than the ability to respond to external change; it requires the capacity to anticipate and influence technological developments. For example, engaging with the implications of machine learning or the ethical challenges posed by automation demands more than technical expertise alone. It reflects a deeper form of adaptability, enabling individuals to critique, shape, and direct technological trajectories, positioning them as active participants rather than passive recipients of change. From this perspective, these observations point to the need for an expanded conception of 21st-century skills—one that integrates the ethical, social, and technological dimensions of learning. This book builds on existing frameworks while critically challenging their limitations, arguing for a more comprehensive approach that positions technology as central to both the development and enactment of skills. By doing so, it seeks to reframe employability and education as interdependent processes that prepare learners not only for the demands of contemporary workplaces but also for meaningful engagement in an increasingly complex and uncertain world.

Thus, the omission of comprehensive skills from Voogt (2010) and Voogt and Roblin's (2012) frameworks suggests a broader issue within educational theory: the tendency to separate skills from technology. This division fails to recognise that, in contemporary contexts, skills are inherently mediated and shaped through technological ecosystems. Addressing this requires an integrated approach that sees technology not only as a subject of study but also as a dynamic context for skill application. From this perspective, comprehensive skills become a cohesive framework, connecting cognitive, interpersonal, and ethical dimensions to prepare learners for the complexities of modern life. To move this discussion forward, it is necessary to move beyond viewing technology as a supplementary tool and instead place it at the heart of skills development. Therefore, education's transformative potential may lie not only in building individual competencies but also in developing learners' broader ability to critique, navigate, and shape the digital and social landscapes they encounter. This integrated vision aligns with the objectives of this book, which seeks to redefine the relationship between skills development, technology, and education. It advocates for a paradigm that prepares students not only to address present challenges but also to imagine and contribute to a more inclusive and reflective future.

In a rapidly evolving society, preparing university students for future challenges requires the development of a broad spectrum of intelligence and qualities. Importantly, it also involves understanding the role and potential of technology. Students must develop digital literacy, navigate technological systems, and critically engage with their ethical implications. The integration of human and technological intelligences is now essential, fostering innovation and equipping graduates to thrive in dynamic environments. Therefore, in the 21st century, these skills represent the ultimate element of employability, bridging knowledge, adaptability, and technological proficiency. These attributes must not only be identified but also clearly articulated and embedded within educational practices that address the realities of a digitally interconnected world. This book argues for the centrality of comprehensive skills—those that integrate cognitive, interpersonal, and ethical dimensions—underpinned by technology's transformative role in shaping these competencies. Universities bear the responsibility of creating learning environments that enable the development of these skills in ways that align with the demands of contemporary workplaces. Therefore, traditional educational models, with their emphasis on foundational knowledge and critical thinking, remain essential for equipping students with the intellectual tools to analyse and evaluate complex ideas. However, as previously discussed, these models often fall short when isolated from the technological contexts that increasingly mediate how knowledge is created, shared, and applied. The dynamic nature of the modern workforce requires a rethinking of how traditional and modern approaches to education can work together to foster comprehensive skills, ensuring students are not only prepared for immediate employability but also capable of shaping the rapidly evolving landscapes they inhabit.

In a rapidly changing society, universities hold a pivotal responsibility in preparing students for the complexities of modern life and work. Their role extends beyond transmitting subject knowledge to cultivating qualities that enable graduates to thrive in an interconnected, technology-driven world. In this book, the notion of foundational knowledge refers not simply to the acquisition of principles and core concepts, but to the development of deeper capacities such as critical reasoning, intellectual curiosity, and reflective inquiry. These provide the framework through which learners can analyse, question, and apply ideas in diverse contexts. By grounding students in such fundamentals, universities equip them with adaptability and intellectual resilience to navigate uncertainty and complexity. This requires a shift from static educational models towards dynamic approaches that integrate problem-solving, ethical judgement, and resilience (Chapple and Tolley, 2013).

When situated in contemporary workplaces, these capabilities form the basis of what this book identifies as comprehensive employability (Stoica, 2010). Employability in this context goes beyond technical proficiency, encompassing the ability to operate within collaborative, culturally diverse, and technologically mediated environments. Global communication tools now reshape collaboration entirely, requiring professionals to manage teams across time zones, negotiate intercultural differences, and co-create solutions in virtual spaces—skills increasingly indispensable in the global job market. A further dimension of employability in the age of advanced technologies, including AI, is leadership and initiative. Modern leadership is less about hierarchical authority and more about influence, innovation, and the capacity to inspire collective action. Within AI-mediated contexts, leadership entails guiding teams in applying technological tools, fostering innovation, and addressing the ethical dilemmas inherent in their use (Segbenya et al., 2023). Universities can support this by creating opportunities for students to lead projects, experiment with AI-driven problem-solving, and design initiatives that reflect professional realities. Such experiences instil purpose, accountability, and the ability to navigate organisational complexity.

Furthermore, entrepreneurial thinking also requires redefinition in an era shaped by automation and data-driven processes. Entrepreneurship here is not restricted to launching new ventures but involves recognising opportunities within technological disruption, assessing risks, and innovating within fluid environments. Universities should encourage students to harness AI and related technologies to identify unmet needs, prototype solutions, and design scalable strategies. This prepares them to innovate within established industries while also equipping them to succeed in more flexible, technology-driven contexts such as the gig economy. The evidence presented in this book shows that skills development at universities cannot be separated from the technological transformations shaping society. A holistic perspective is required—one that integrates technology with employability, acknowledging technology as both a driver and an enabler in preparing graduates for the demands of contemporary professional life.

Academically, the integration of technology with employability offers a means to confront systemic barriers and biases that restrict career progression. By embedding technological tools capable of analysing hiring trends and workplace dynamics, universities can illuminate disparities in recruitment and promotion, enabling more inclusive approaches to employment. For example, AI-driven platforms can expose inequalities in recruitment processes, allowing students both to refine their skills in response to labour market realities and to recognise the structural inequities that persist within them. This approach challenges traditional notions of meritocracy, which assume that career progression depends solely on talent, effort, and achievement. While meritocracy is often presented as a neutral principle, it frequently ignores the influence of social background, ethnicity, or gender on opportunities for advancement. Technology both complicates and clarifies this picture: recruitment algorithms, if poorly designed, may entrench bias, yet the same tools can be deployed to reveal and counter such inequities. Thus, employability education must go beyond preparing students to succeed within an ostensibly meritocratic framework; it should also equip them to interrogate and address the inequities that distort genuine merit-based achievement. This perspective situates graduates not only as job seekers but also as potential advocates for systemic change. By engaging critically with technology, students can contribute to more equitable workplace practices and help develop alternative career pathways that emphasise transferable skills beyond narrow job roles. Universities, therefore, play a dual role: preparing students for the immediate demands of employment while empowering them to shape more inclusive organisational cultures.

The wider discourse on 21st-century skills—critical thinking, collaboration, digital literacy, and adaptability—illustrates these tensions. These skills are often presented as universally accessible markers of merit, yet in practice their acquisition is shaped by socio-economic and cultural conditions. Access to quality education, technological infrastructure, and social capital often determines who can acquire and apply them effectively. This raises questions about whether so-called meritocratic systems reward talent or reinforce privilege. Philosophically, this resonates with Rawls' theory of justice, particularly the difference principle, which holds that inequalities are only justifiable if they benefit the least advantaged (Rawls, 2020). When applied to 21st-century skills, the principle challenges employability systems that fail to address barriers to skill acquisition. For instance, if digital literacy is positioned as a prerequisite for employability, those from under-resourced backgrounds are disadvantaged regardless of their abilities or motivation. Addressing these inequities requires universities not only to provide access to technological skills but also to frame employability education in ways that explicitly recognise and mitigate the structural conditions that undermine fairness.

The integration of technology into 21st-century skills complicates the narrative of meritocracy. Algorithms and automation mediate access to opportunities, yet they are not neutral mechanisms. Biases embedded within recruitment systems or educational platforms can advantage some groups while marginalising others, undermining the notion of a level playing field. Hannah Arendt's critique of modernity, which cautions against the dehumanising tendencies of technological determinism, is pertinent here (Antaki, 2006). When technology reduces individuals to data points, assessments of merit risk losing their human dimension. The current emphasis on transferable skills—such as creativity, adaptability, and emotional intelligence—marks a shift from older conceptions of merit tied to fixed credentials or narrowly defined expertise. This evolution resonates with existentialist thought, particularly Sartre's claim that identity is fluid and self-determined (Webber, 2009). Yet the evaluation of such skills is often subjective, introducing the risk of inconsistency and bias. The tension between subjective judgements of merit and objective measures of achievement remains a persistent challenge in aligning skills development with the principles of fairness.

Education, as the primary means of fostering 21st-century skills, is central to navigating these tensions. The Aristotelian notion of eudaimonia—human flourishing through the fulfilment of potential—offers a valuable philosophical lens. It frames education not merely as preparation for employment but as a process that nurtures equitable opportunities for both personal growth and social well-being. This requires systems that transcend narrow meritocratic ideals by addressing structural inequities and ensuring that skill development is inclusive and accessible across diverse contexts. The interplay between 21st-century skills and meritocracy is therefore dynamic and contested. While the rhetoric of meritocracy promotes fairness based on ability and effort, systemic inequalities and technological mediation continue to disrupt this ideal. A philosophically informed approach to skills development must confront these tensions directly, balancing individual agency with collective responsibility. Only by doing so can universities ensure that the cultivation of 21st-century skills fosters equity and diversity rather than reinforcing existing hierarchies, enabling talent and commitment to become the genuine arbiters of success.

This book argues that employability in the age of AI requires more than technical expertise; it also demands ethical awareness and social responsibility. Decisions shaped by AI—whether in relation to algorithmic bias, data privacy, or equity—are increasingly central to organisational practice. Employers, therefore, seek graduates who can critically evaluate the wider implications of technological change and navigate these challenges with integrity. Universities have a responsibility to embed ethical principles across teaching and learning, enabling students to engage with questions of fairness, sustainability, and social justice as part of their professional formation. By aligning leadership, entrepreneurial thinking, and ethical awareness with the realities of AI-driven workplaces, universities can prepare graduates who are not only employable but also capable of shaping the future of work. When combined with technical proficiency, these qualities position students as adaptive and socially conscious contributors within organisations and communities in an interconnected and automated world. In this context, digital literacy must extend beyond functional competence to include analytical and strategic dimensions. The ability to interpret data, evaluate digital tools, and apply them for organisational advantage is now fundamental. Familiarity with AI and automation systems not only supports productivity but also enables graduates to contribute meaningfully to innovation and efficiency.

Equally important is the capacity for continuous learning. As Adewolu (2024) notes, academic and employability skills can no longer be developed through traditional methodologies alone but must be supported by frameworks that reflect the realities of rapid technological change. Lifelong learning, once regarded as aspirational, has become essential in industries where disruption is constant and knowledge is continuously redefined (Jackson, 2015). Philosophically, it represents the sustained and self-directed pursuit of knowledge and growth across the life course. It is rooted in the belief that human potential is not fixed but can expand through reflection, engagement, and adaptation. This conception of lifelong learning recognises knowledge as fluid and dynamic, requiring openness to new ideas and a willingness to challenge established assumptions. By fostering this ethos, universities can prepare graduates not only to meet the demands of contemporary employment but also to contribute to cultures of fairness, inclusivity, and innovation. In this way, employability education is framed not simply as readiness for work, but as a broader commitment to personal development and social responsibility.

From a philosophical perspective, lifelong learning highlights the importance of curiosity, autonomy, and personal agency in shaping intellectual and moral development. It calls for a holistic view of education, where learning is understood not only as a means of individual advancement but also as a way of contributing to social progress. By fostering adaptability, resilience, and reflective awareness of self and others, lifelong learning supports both personal fulfilment and collective well-being. Universities, therefore, play a central role in cultivating attributes such as self-directed learning, intellectual curiosity, and adaptability. These qualities enable graduates to remain competitive and capable of engaging with complex professional environments throughout their careers. This approach extends beyond equipping students with skills for immediate employment, positioning them instead as lifelong learners prepared to navigate evolving industries and societal challenges. In this sense, continuous learning forms the foundation of employability: to remain relevant in dynamic labour markets, individuals must regularly renew and expand their knowledge.

The future of employability depends on universities adopting educational frameworks that combine strong academic foundations with technological innovation and practical experience. Institutions must look beyond traditional markers of achievement and redefine their purpose to prepare students for the shifting demands of society and the workplace. Conventional methods—valuable for developing critical thinking and disciplinary depth—are insufficient on their own to meet the challenges of industries transformed by AI, automation, and globalisation. To remain relevant, universities must equip graduates with technical expertise alongside ethical awareness and sound decision-making, enabling them to act responsibly in complex, interconnected environments. Failure to innovate risks leaving graduates underprepared for uncertain professional landscapes, reducing their employability and limiting their contribution to society. It may also weaken universities' capacity to address broader societal challenges, thereby diminishing their role in shaping progress and innovation. By embracing lifelong learning, however, universities can ensure that graduates develop the agility, creativity, and problem-solving capacities required to thrive in rapidly changing contexts, while also advancing equity and social responsibility.

To respond to these challenges, universities must adopt a broader perspective, creating learning environments that enable students to lead, collaborate, and address global issues with confidence and creativity. This requires rethinking education to integrate technology meaningfully, encourage cross-disciplinary engagement, and promote the application of knowledge to real-world problems. Such changes foster intellectual flexibility, social responsibility, and innovation. This vision aligns with the central argument of this book: that higher education should prepare students not only for immediate employment but also for active participation in shaping the future. By nurturing adaptability, ethical judgement, and a commitment to contributing to an evolving world, universities can remain relevant and ensure that their graduates succeed in a complex and interconnected global landscape. In examining skills development, it is important to acknowledge the limitations of the frameworks that currently dominate academic and policy discourse. Existing models often fail to capture the dynamic and transformative character of the competencies required in the 21st century. In particular, the integration of technology, AI, and soft skills is frequently treated in isolation, leaving a gap in understanding how these dimensions interact to shape employability. Higher education must therefore prepare students not only for the labour market as it exists but also for the ways in which technology continuously reshapes it. While the cultivation of soft skills such as critical thinking, collaboration, and self-regulation remains essential, these alone do not fully account for what this book terms skills dynamics. This concept emphasises the evolving and interconnected nature of competencies, where technical knowledge and soft skills interact with technological advancements to generate new forms of capability and adaptability. Skills dynamics move beyond the acquisition of discrete abilities to highlight the capacity to integrate, adapt, and apply knowledge in rapidly changing contexts—particularly those shaped by AI and digital innovation.

Skills development cannot be fully understood through existing frameworks alone. The widely cited '4Cs' model—creativity, collaboration, communication, and critical thinking—offers a useful foundation for identifying core competencies (Scott, 2015). However, its neglect of the technological dimension limits its relevance to contemporary contexts, where digital innovation shapes both how these skills are acquired and how they are applied. Gates et al. (2016) broaden the discussion by emphasising foundational soft skills such as self-control, social competence, higher-order reasoning, and positive self-concept. These attributes underpin achievement across sectors and provide the basis for advanced competencies, enabling effective participation in professional and social settings. Yet their framework, like the 4Cs model, does not explicitly account for the ways in which such skills interact with technological innovation, particularly AI, to create new forms of competence. This absence reflects a broader weakness in prevailing academic and policy discourse, where employability is too often conceptualised in static terms. In practice, skills are dynamic and interconnected, evolving in response to technological, social, and economic change. Without recognising this fluidity, frameworks risk underestimating the complexity of 21st-century employability.

This book introduces the concept of skills dynamics to bridge that gap. Skills dynamics emphasises the interconnected and adaptive nature of competencies, where technical expertise and soft skills interact with digital technologies to create novel forms of capability. This perspective challenges compartmentalised approaches to skills development, arguing instead for integrated models that reflect the transformative influence of AI and related innovations. It situates foundational skills not as fixed prerequisites but as evolving capacities whose meaning and application shift in relation to technological change (Figure 0.2).

Scott (2015) highlights the interconnectedness of the '4Cs', observing how creativity is about not only generating ideas but also refining them through critical thinking, while collaboration and communication enable their realisation across diverse contexts. When

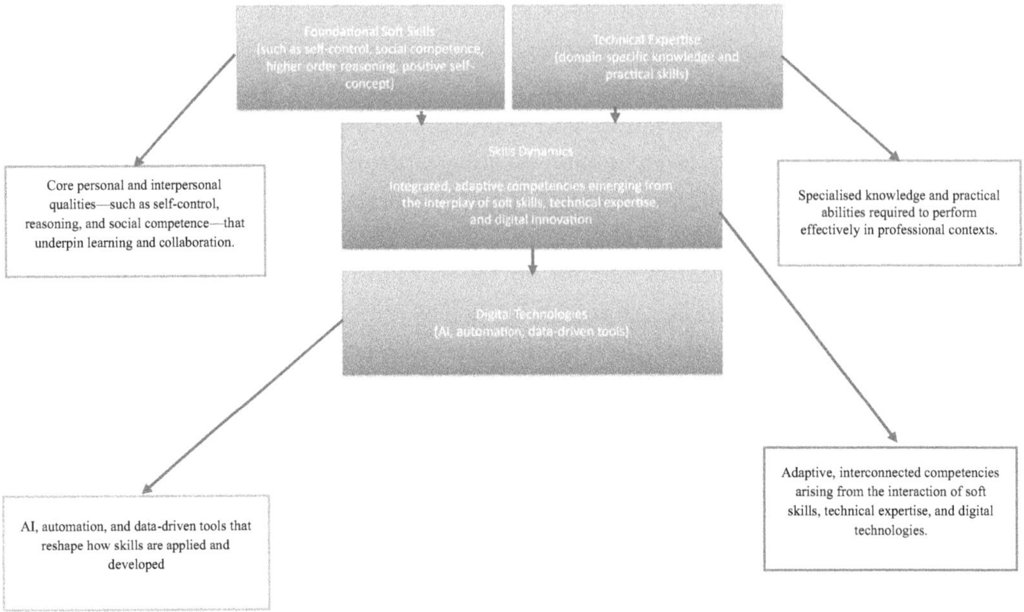

FIGURE 0.2 The skills dynamics framework.

The Skills Dynamics Framework: An integrative model illustrating how foundational soft skills, technical expertise, and digital technologies converge to generate adaptive and future-oriented competencies.

BOX 0.2 EXPLANATION NOTE—THE SKILLS DYNAMICS FRAMEWORK

The concept of Skills Dynamics highlights the adaptive interplay between different forms of knowledge and competence that shape employability in the 21st century. At its foundation are soft skills, such as self-control, social competence, and higher-order reasoning, which provide the personal and interpersonal qualities essential for learning, collaboration, and resilience. Alongside these sit technical expertise, specialised knowledge, and practical abilities required to engage effectively in professional tasks and domains. Increasingly, these two dimensions are mediated by digital technologies, including artificial intelligence, automation, and data-driven tools, which redefine how knowledge is applied, skills are developed, and work is organised.

Skills Dynamics refers to the integration of these three domains, generating interconnected and evolving competencies rather than static abilities. It recognises that employability today depends not only on possessing discrete skills but also on the capacity to adapt, integrate, and apply them in response to technological and social change. This perspective challenges fragmented approaches to skills development, offering instead a holistic model that reflects the realities of modern professional and educational environments.

considered through the lens of AI, however, these competencies take on expanded meanings. Creativity is increasingly supported by digital tools that facilitate rapid prototyping, predictive analysis, and complex problem-solving, enhancing rather than supplanting human ingenuity. Collaboration now frequently occurs in virtual and cross-disciplinary spaces, with AI-powered platforms enabling co-creation and interaction across geographical and cultural boundaries. Similarly, communication is increasingly mediated by AI systems capable of real-time translation, sentiment analysis, and interactive feedback, making engagement more inclusive and effective in global settings.

These developments suggest that while frameworks such as the '4Cs' remain valuable, they are incomplete without recognition of technological mediation. As illustrated in Figure 0.2, this book embeds the concept of skills dynamics to address this limitation by situating soft skills, technical expertise, and digital technologies within a single, adaptive model. Rather than treating competencies as discrete or static, the framework emphasises their interdependence and evolution in response to technological change. By adopting this approach, the discussion of employability shifts towards a more integrated and future-oriented perspective—one that reflects how competencies emerge from the continuous interplay between human capabilities and digital innovation in shaping 21st-century work and education.

While Scott's framework acknowledges the value of the '4Cs', it does not fully account for the transformative role of AI in shaping how these competencies are developed or their broader implications for employability. Sternberg's (2023) concept of transformational creativity offers a more expansive perspective, proposing that creativity should not only generate novel ideas but also shift paradigms and engage with pressing societal challenges. This resonates with the potential of AI in higher education, where technological tools can support students in addressing complex, real-world problems and exploring innovative solutions. At the same time, Sternberg's work highlights that creativity cannot be reduced to a by-product of technology; it requires a deeper engagement with ethics, context, and human values. This raises critical questions for universities about how to nurture transformational creativity while ensuring that students remain active, critical participants in the creative process rather than passive users of AI.

The integration of employability skills with AI also provides a means of addressing broader societal concerns, particularly in relation to ethics and regulation. The concept of skills dynamics, as introduced in this book, offers a comprehensive framework for understanding the interconnected skills required to navigate these challenges. By embedding this model into educational practice, universities can equip students not only with technical and creative capabilities but also with the critical awareness necessary to evaluate the societal implications of AI and to advocate for its responsible use. This dual emphasis on competence and ethical responsibility has the potential to drive meaningful change, positioning graduates to influence policy, strengthen accountability, and engage with the wider consequences of technological innovation. In this way, skills dynamics challenges static models of employability, arguing for a dynamic and integrative approach that reflects the realities of a technology-driven world. By linking skills development with the ethical use of AI, educational institutions can prepare students not only for the workforce but also for active participation in shaping the social and regulatory landscapes in which these technologies operate. This broader vision aligns with contemporary calls for education to move beyond narrow conceptions of employability and to embrace a holistic approach that integrates technological innovation, critical thinking, and ethical responsibility.

Gates et al. (2016) underline the importance of social and interpersonal skills in addressing interdisciplinary challenges, noting that effective collaboration is sustained by emotional intelligence, communication, and other foundational abilities. Their work reminds us that technological tools alone cannot ensure meaningful teamwork without the support of these human capacities. They also emphasise the significance of fostering a positive self-concept, which strengthens employability and supports lifelong learning. In rapidly evolving industries shaped by AI and automation, attributes such as resilience and self-efficacy are indispensable, enabling individuals to adapt to shifting demands and embrace emerging opportunities. This underlines the responsibility of universities to design learning environments that combine technological integration with the cultivation of confidence, adaptability, and a growth-oriented mindset. Such environments prepare students to navigate uncertainty with both competence and critical awareness.

Placed alongside the 4Cs model and Sternberg's (2023) account of transformational creativity, Gates et al.'s analysis demonstrates the interdependence of foundational and advanced skills. While the 4Cs highlight higher-order competencies and transformational creativity urges a paradigm-shifting engagement with challenges, both rely on the groundwork provided by interpersonal and reflective abilities. For universities, the task is therefore twofold: to equip students with the advanced competencies required to engage effectively with AI and digital innovation, while also nurturing the soft skills that anchor collaboration, creativity, and ethical judgement. This integration is captured by the concept of skills dynamics, which positions employability not as a static set of abilities but as a fluid interaction between foundational skills, advanced competencies, and technological mediation. Such a perspective challenges linear or compartmentalised models of skills development, presenting instead a holistic framework for preparing graduates. By adopting this approach, HEIs can ensure that students are not only technologically proficient but also ethical, adaptable, and capable of leading innovation in ways aligned with societal needs. In this vision, technology and AI are framed as tools that enhance human potential rather than diminish it, positioning learners as active participants in shaping equitable and sustainable futures.

The integration of AI into education and skills development represents a significant shift in how nations prepare their workforces for the demands of an evolving global economy. This transformation requires more than the acquisition of technical knowledge; it necessitates a rethinking of employability frameworks so they remain responsive to the complexities of a technology-driven world. Central to this reorientation is the need to balance technical proficiency with ethical awareness, ensuring that graduates are not only capable but also adaptable and socially responsible. Evidence of this shift can be seen in initiatives such as Finland's Elements of AI programme, which provides accessible AI literacy to learners across professional and educational backgrounds (OECD, 2021a). Similarly, Singapore's workforce strategies illustrate how technical upskilling, combined with societal awareness, can prepare individuals for the demands of interconnected and dynamic labour markets.

Yet framing employability narrowly around technical proficiencies risks reducing education to short-term industry needs. To address this limitation, this book introduces the concept of hard employability skills, which extends beyond traditional training to include specific, measurable competencies required in the digital economy. These encompass advanced data analysis, programming, and sector-specific applications of AI. While such skills are essential, their effectiveness is significantly enhanced when combined with broader competencies such as critical thinking, adaptability, and ethical reasoning. In this sense, hard employability skills must be understood as interacting with foundational soft skills, creating the adaptive framework necessary for navigating complex professional environments. For example, technical expertise may allow individuals to work effectively with AI tools, but it is the capacity to collaborate across disciplines and cultures that ensures these tools are deployed in socially constructive ways. Without such integration, there is a risk of producing technically proficient graduates who lack the capacity to engage with the wider societal consequences of their work.

As illustrated in Figure 0.2, this perspective is best understood through the interplay between foundational soft skills, technical expertise, and digital technologies. Skills dynamics emphasises the fluid and adaptive nature of competencies, showing how new forms of capability emerge when these dimensions are brought together. By situating employability within this integrated model, universities can prepare learners not only to adapt to technological change but also to shape it responsibly, aligning innovation with societal needs. Addressing these challenges also aligns with the principles of the United Nations' Sustainable Development Goals (SDGs), which provide a globally recognised framework for tackling interconnected social, economic, and environmental issues. Aligning AI and skills development with the SDGs goes beyond policy compliance; it reflects a commitment to inclusive, ethical, and transformative progress. For instance, embedding AI literacy into education not only contributes to SDG 4 on quality education but also supports innovation in healthcare (SDG 3) and sustainable economic growth (SDG 8). This alignment underlines the potential of skills development to promote both individual employability and broader societal advancement, ensuring that technological progress is harnessed for equitable and sustainable outcomes. Realising this vision requires a shift from short-term technical training towards long-term capacity building. Educational institutions must prepare students for current employment markets while also instilling the reflective and critical capacities needed to adapt to future uncertainties. In doing so, skills development is reframed as a dynamic and integrated process rather than a collection of discrete competencies. This approach equips learners to engage meaningfully with both the ethical and technological dimensions of change, preparing them to contribute responsibly to the shaping of work and society in the 21st century.

Education, represented by SDG 4, is central to aligning AI with the wider SDGs. Achieving inclusive and equitable quality education, while promoting lifelong learning, requires a curriculum that combines technological literacy with values-driven learning. AI and related technologies have considerable potential to bridge educational divides by extending access to quality resources, particularly for marginalised communities. Finland's Elements of AI initiative illustrates this well, demonstrating how critical digital skills can be made accessible to diverse populations, enabling broad participation in a rapidly digitalising society (OECD, 2021a). However, meaningful alignment with the SDGs also requires that ethics and social responsibility remain at the heart of educational reform. While AI can advance innovation and support economic growth (SDG 8: Decent Work and Economic Growth), it simultaneously poses risks such as job displacement and the exacerbation of inequality. Addressing these concerns calls for educational frameworks that embed ethical reasoning, adaptability, and resilience. Within this context, hard employability skills—such as programming, data analysis, and sector-specific applications of AI—must be integrated with critical and ethical perspectives, ensuring that technological advancement serves human needs rather than intensifying disparities.

AI is also reshaping progress towards SDG 3: Good Health and Well-being. From early diagnosis and personalised medicine to improving healthcare delivery in underserved regions, AI demonstrates transformative potential. Yet preparing individuals to design and implement such solutions must be matched by an ability to engage with ethical considerations, including data privacy, fairness, and equitable access. Similarly, the contribution of AI to SDG 13: Climate Action underlines the importance of combining technological proficiency with environmental stewardship. By analysing climate data, optimising energy systems, and reducing environmental impacts, AI tools can support sustainable development. Education must therefore prepare future professionals to leverage these innovations responsibly, embedding sustainability as a guiding principle. In addition, AI can contribute to SDG 10: Reduced Inequalities by helping to address disparities in education and opportunity. For instance, Australia's investment in educational technology demonstrates how digital tools can reduce inequities in access and achievement (University of Technology Sydney, 2022). Yet such outcomes will only be realised through intentional strategies that guarantee access to AI training and resources for underrepresented groups. Without this, technology risks reinforcing existing divides rather than closing them. Philosophically, aligning AI and skills development with the SDGs challenges the narrow view of education as solely a pathway to employment. Instead, it reframes education as a process of cultivating informed, ethical, and engaged global citizens. The interconnected nature of the SDGs reinforces the need for skills dynamics—a framework that positions skills development as an integrated and adaptive process.

The integration of AI into education and skills development reflects a growing global commitment to preparing individuals for the complexities of a rapidly changing technological environment. HEIs have a pivotal role in ensuring that these developments are aligned with the SDGs, enabling technological progress to address wider societal challenges. Embedding AI within the framework of the SDGs provides a structured means of guiding its use, ensuring that innovation contributes not only to economic growth but also to equity, sustainability, and social well-being. This alignment amplifies the potential of AI to deliver ethical applications while offering a framework for mitigating risks. National strategies provide valuable insight into how this integration is being realised. In India, public–private partnerships are expanding access to AI training programmes, aiming to democratise digital education and strengthen employability across diverse populations (TIME, 2023). Ireland has embedded AI expertise within civil service training, equipping public sector employees to regulate and manage new technologies responsibly (The Sun, 2023). Both approaches highlight the importance of combining technical proficiency with critical thinking and ethical awareness, ensuring innovation is balanced with societal responsibility.

South Korea demonstrates a more systemic model by embedding AI competencies across its education system, preparing students with both technical skills and the critical insights required to engage with digitally transformed industries (OECD, 2021a). Similarly, Germany and the United Kingdom have aligned higher education curricula with the evolving demands of AI and digital technologies, ensuring graduates are prepared for dynamic labour markets (OECD, 2021a). Australia offers a distinctive perspective by addressing educational inequalities through the application of AI and educational technologies. Research from the University of Technology Sydney shows how adaptive learning tools can provide tailored support for underserved communities, illustrating AI's potential to foster inclusion and reduce systemic disparities (University of Technology Sydney, 2022). Together, these initiatives reveal AI's broader implications for education, extending beyond workforce readiness to the promotion of social equity and sustainable development. By integrating AI with the SDGs, education can be reframed not only as a pathway to employment but also as a mechanism for tackling entrenched inequalities and enabling inclusive progress. This perspective aligns with the central argument of this book: that skills dynamics requires universities to cultivate an adaptive blend of technical expertise, foundational soft skills, and ethical awareness, preparing graduates to contribute meaningfully to both the labour market and wider society.

Sternberg's (2023) concept of transformational creativity provides a valuable framework for understanding how AI can be integrated into education and employability strategies. His work illustrates how AI has the potential to catalyse innovative thinking, enabling individuals and institutions to respond to global challenges and reshape existing paradigms. Yet Sternberg also makes clear that this transformative potential is only realised when technical expertise is accompanied by critical thinking, ethical reasoning, and human-centred values. Canada's Pan-Canadian Artificial Intelligence Strategy reflects this balance by emphasising the ethical adoption of AI and ensuring that technological innovation contributes directly to societal goals (OECD, 2021a). This example demonstrates the practical application of Sternberg's insights: technological progress must be carefully aligned with social responsibility if it is to generate equitable and sustainable outcomes. Within this context, universities emerge as crucial sites for cultivating graduates who are both technologically proficient and ethically informed, able to lead innovation while responding to its wider social consequences.

Building on the discussion of 21st-century skills, these initiatives can be interpreted as deliberate attempts to establish coherent and innovative frameworks for skills development within higher education. They underline the importance of aligning educational practices with the realities of technological change, the evolving labour market, and the imperative of social equity. Moreover, they highlight that such efforts are global in scope, extending well beyond Western contexts and adapting to diverse socio-economic and cultural environments. Rwanda, for example, has addressed the digital divide through the One Laptop per Child programme and collaborations with Carnegie Mellon University, initiatives that have enhanced digital literacy and positioned the country as a hub for

ICT-driven industries (Tremblay, 2011; Mkrtchyan et al., 2020). South Africa's skills development strategy offers another illustration, prioritising digital literacy, entrepreneurial training, and workforce preparedness, with a strong focus on reducing rural inequalities (Sey and Mudongo, 2021).

These examples demonstrate that the integration of AI and digital technologies into education is not confined to particular regions but reflects a global recognition of their role in shaping employability and societal progress. From this perspective, the argument advanced in this book—to embed technology and AI within frameworks of skills development—emerges as both timely and necessary. What becomes evident is that education systems are increasingly aware of their responsibility to cultivate not only technical and professional expertise but also the adaptability, critical insight, and ethical capacity required for future labour markets. This recognition raises an important question: how can the cultivation of these skills be systematically embedded within educational frameworks? Addressing this requires deliberate strategies that position AI and digital innovation as integral to skills formation, ensuring that universities equip graduates to engage critically and constructively with the transformations reshaping work and society.

Kenya's Vision 2030 and Nigeria's Digital Economy Policy and Strategy exemplify how African nations are embedding technological education into their development agendas. Initiatives such as Kenya's Digital Literacy Programme and Nigeria's coding and data analysis schemes reflect efforts to democratise digital skills, equipping young people for participation in emerging industries and enhancing global competitiveness (Barasa, 2021; Bello and Ajao, 2024). Egypt's integration of AI through the Egyptian Knowledge Bank further illustrates how education is being reshaped to meet labour market demands in ICT and engineering (Enterprise, 2024). These strategies highlight how African contexts are engaging with skills dynamics by linking technical capacity with inclusive access, thereby addressing inequalities while preparing for digital futures.

Industrialised nations present alternative models that also align with skills dynamics. Germany's dual-education system combines vocational training with formal learning, embedding technical expertise and ethical reasoning to prepare graduates for Industry 4.0 (Abulibdeh et al., 2024). Finland's holistic philosophy integrates creativity, problem-solving, and digital literacy throughout the curriculum, emphasising adaptability as a core element of lifelong learning (Sahlberg, 2021). Singapore's SkillsFuture initiative prioritises continuous professional development, combining ethical awareness with leadership and technical proficiency (Woo, 2020). Australia's AI-driven adaptive learning systems, designed to address inequities by tailoring educational resources to underserved communities, demonstrate how technology can support both innovation and inclusion (University of Technology Sydney, 2022). Each of these examples reflects the principles of skills dynamics by showing how foundational soft skills, advanced technical expertise, and digital technologies interact to create adaptive and future-ready competencies.

Despite their different emphases, these strategies converge on a common recognition: education must align labour market needs with broader societal goals. While African nations prioritise reducing systemic inequalities and expanding access, industrialised countries emphasise innovation, sustainability, and competitiveness. Both approaches illustrate the central argument of this book—that skills dynamics provides a framework for understanding the integration of technical skills, critical soft skills, and digital innovation. By embedding creativity, critical thinking, ethical reasoning, and digital literacy within educational systems, nations are preparing graduates to navigate technological change while contributing meaningfully to societal progress. In this light, skills dynamics emerges as a unifying framework that explains how diverse educational strategies can respond to the complexities of an interconnected and rapidly evolving world.

Table 0.1 maps a selection of national initiatives against the three dimensions of the skills dynamics framework: foundational soft skills, technical expertise, and digital technologies. This comparative view demonstrates how diverse education systems incorporate these elements to respond to evolving labour market needs, while also reflecting wider societal priorities such as inclusion, innovation, and sustainability. Situating each initiative within this framework, the table illustrates the varied yet converging approaches nations adopt to equip learners with the adaptive and integrated competencies required in a rapidly changing global context (Table 0.1).

Taken together, these national strategies reveal the diversity of approaches to skills development while highlighting a shared recognition that employability in the 21st century requires more than discrete technical training. What emerges is a picture of skills dynamics in practice: the interaction of foundational soft skills, advanced technical expertise, and digital technologies to produce adaptive and future-ready graduates. Embedding these elements in ways that reflect their unique socio-economic and cultural contexts,

TABLE 0.1 Skills Dynamics Mapping of National Initiatives

Country	Foundational Soft Skills	Technical Expertise	Digital Technologies
Kenya	STEM integration fostering problem-solving and innovation	Digital Literacy Programme embedding ICT into schools	ICT infrastructure for primary and secondary education
Nigeria	Coding and problem-solving initiatives building critical thinking	Focus on coding, data analysis, and digital economy skills	AI and digital economy policy expanding technological training
Egypt	Digital literacy and alignment with employability needs	Integration of AI and ICT into education through the Egyptian Knowledge Bank	AI and advanced technologies integrated into curricula
Germany	Ethical reasoning in the dual-education model	Advanced technical competencies for Industry 4.0	Industry 4.0 technologies integrated into dual education
Finland	Creativity, collaboration, and problem-solving embedded in the curriculum	Digital literacy as the core foundation of lifelong learning	AI and digital tools underpinning resilience and adaptability
Singapore	Leadership and ethical awareness integrated into SkillsFuture	Continuous professional upskilling in AI and emerging fields	AI and digital innovation embedded in workforce training
Australia	Equity-driven personalised learning addressing underserved groups	AI-driven adaptive learning enhancing technical capacity	Use of AI-powered adaptive learning systems

countries are collectively shaping a global vision of employability that is innovative, inclusive, and sustainable. This convergence affirms the central argument of this book—that education systems must move beyond static frameworks and embrace dynamic, integrated models of skills development to prepare individuals for an increasingly complex and technology-driven world.

Navigating technological disruption, global interconnectedness, and complex social challenges requires graduates who are adaptable, innovative, and ethically grounded. AI has the potential to support this shift by enabling personalised learning and fostering resilience and creativity. The broader challenge, however, is ensuring that employability frameworks remain responsive to diverse national contexts and evolving labour market needs. Across the world, education systems are experimenting with strategies that align skills development with economic transformation, social inclusion, and sustainability. At the heart of this discussion is the need to harmonise established pedagogical practices with the opportunities created by new technologies. Traditional approaches continue to offer valuable insights into how people learn, while AI introduces possibilities for personalisation, advanced data analysis, and adaptive learning. GenAI, with its capacity to perform tasks once associated with human judgement, represents a potentially transformative force. Yet its adoption raises pressing questions about human agency, ethical accountability, and the preservation of education as a relational and human-centred endeavour.

These tensions shape the central question explored in this book: how can HEIs integrate AI in ways that enhance employability while safeguarding ethical and societal values? Addressing this requires a multidimensional perspective that considers not only the technical and pedagogical potential of AI but also its wider social implications. Employability must therefore be approached through both educational and policy lenses, recognising the influence of institutional frameworks, governance arrangements, and regulatory oversight. This book critically evaluates how existing models enable or constrain the development of meaningful, future-oriented skills, while emphasising the importance of ethical oversight to ensure that AI is used responsibly, equitably, and transparently.

To guide readers through these themes, the book is organised into four substantive chapters, each engaging with a critical dimension of the relationship between AI, education, and employability. The opening discussion (Introduction) situates AI within wider societal transformations, stressing the dual imperatives of awareness and preparedness. It argues that recognising AI's transformative potential is insufficient unless individuals and institutions are also equipped with the competencies and frameworks required to address its ethical, social, and economic implications. Chapter 1 redefines employability as a dynamic and relational construct that extends beyond static qualifications or technical proficiency. Here, employability is conceived as an evolving interplay of technical expertise, cognitive agility, creativity, adaptability, and ethical awareness. Central to this chapter is the concept of skills dynamics, which highlights how technical, cognitive, and interpersonal capacities interact in an AI-mediated world.

Chapters 2 interrogate existing models of skills development, advancing the notion of comprehensive skills. Moving beyond the widely recognised '4Cs'—creativity, collaboration, communication, and critical thinking—these chapters integrate digital literacy, ethical reasoning, and lifelong learning as essential dimensions of employability in the age of AI. GenAI is presented not as a substitute for human intelligence but as a catalyst for new forms of learning, knowledge creation, and problem-solving, requiring both technical agility and philosophical reflection. The final chapter Conclusion draws these strands together, advancing the argument that higher education must transcend linear and static models of skill acquisition. It calls for an adaptive, holistic, and ethically grounded approach to preparing learners for AI-driven futures. Employability is reframed not simply as the acquisition of workplace competencies but as an ongoing process of cultivating resilience, inclusivity, and human-centred innovation. Embedding awareness, preparedness, and comprehensive skills into educational systems, the book proposes a new ethos for higher education—one that ensures employability remains technologically relevant while also advancing justice, equity, and human flourishing in an era of digital transformation.

This discussion sets the stage for Chapter 1, which re-examines employability within the context of wider societal and technological transformations. It challenges static definitions limited to technical competence or immediate labour market outcomes and instead introduces employability as a dynamic, relational construct. Central to this is the concept of skills dynamics, which captures the evolving interplay between technical expertise, cognitive agility, creativity, adaptability, and ethical awareness in an AI-mediated world. Chapter 1 establishes the foundation for the book's wider argument: that higher education must prepare graduates who can adapt to technological disruption while shaping its trajectory towards equity, sustainability, and human flourishing. Chapter 1 opens with a critical examination of the limitations of traditional employability frameworks, moving towards skills dynamics as a more responsive and future-oriented model for education in the age of AI.

CHAPTER 1

Redefining Employability

Skills Dynamics and the Role of AI in the 21st Century

INTRODUCTION

The intellectual foundations of this volume are deeply rooted in the arguments advanced in Generative AI in Higher Education: Guiding Principles for Teaching and Learning. In that earlier work, the central task was to challenge both uncritical enthusiasm and reactionary resistance to Generative Artificial Intelligence (GenAI). AI was not to be treated as either a passing fad or an existential threat, but as a transformative phenomenon whose meaning and impact depend on the frameworks within which it is adopted. Volume I, therefore, set out guiding principles for higher education institutions (HEIs), insisting on transparency, accountability, inclusivity, and academic integrity as non-negotiable values. It argued that the responsible engagement of HEIs requires more than technical adoption; it demands ethical governance and institutional readiness. In that sense, Volume I provided a conceptual scaffolding: a values-driven compass to orient educational policy and practice in the face of disruptive technological change. The present volume extends that conversation by turning more explicitly to the themes of ethical governance, skills, and employability. Where the first volume concentrated on the why and how of institutional engagement, this volume asks the what and who questions. Specifically: what kinds of skills are required in an AI-mediated society, and who must be prepared to develop, teach, and apply them? The section 'Introduction' positions employability as the central axis of enquiry, but redefines it in expansive and dynamic terms. Employability is no longer understood as the possession of static qualifications or narrow technical expertise. Instead, it is reconceived as the capacity to adapt, to exercise ethical judgement, to collaborate across disciplines, and to contribute creatively to human flourishing in contexts increasingly shaped by AI.

To frame this enquiry, the Introduction introduces two interdependent concepts: awareness and preparedness. Awareness denotes deep and critical engagement with the ethical,

DOI: 10.1201/9781003502517-2

social, and philosophical implications of AI. It is not mere familiarity with technical functions, but recognition of how AI reshapes power, fairness, accountability, and responsibility. Preparedness, by contrast, refers to the cultivation of practical capacities—skills, institutional frameworks, and policy responses—that enable individuals and organisations to navigate AI-rich environments effectively. The Introduction stresses that the two must be held together. Awareness without preparedness results in paralysis, while preparedness without awareness leads to reckless adoption. Only when coupled do they provide the necessary foundation for employability in the AI era. This framework is developed against a significant political backdrop: the UK Government's announcement in January 2025 of a £14 billion investment in AI. This policy decision symbolises AI's move from the periphery to the centre of national economic and industrial strategy. Yet the timing also exposes a troubling gap: although AI's transformative potential has long been acknowledged, comprehensive investment and readiness strategies are only now emerging. The Introduction interprets this as evidence that education, governance, and policy remain reactive rather than proactive, and it positions this book as a corrective intervention. Higher education, in particular, is charged with ensuring that the next generation is not only technically competent but also ethically grounded and socially responsible.

To illustrate the balance required, the Introduction presents a framework for human flourishing in the age of AI. At its apex are opportunities such as innovation, employability, and inclusivity; at its base lie persistent risks including bias, inequity, and ethical failures. Between these poles stand universities, employers, and governments, each bearing responsibility for contributing to a balanced ecosystem of learning and governance. The framework insists that employability cannot be reduced to technical training. It must instead be understood as the development of adaptable, reflective, and ethically responsible professionals capable of navigating complex futures. In consolidating the trajectory from Volume I to this volume, the argument becomes clear: principles must now give way to practice. Volume I offered ethical orientation—guidelines to ensure that HEIs engaged with GenAI responsibly. Volume II advances the conversation by operationalising those principles in the domains of governance, skills development, and employability. Taken together, the two works form a coherent continuum. Volume I provides the conceptual architecture, while Volume II develops the applied structures that allow institutions and individuals to act with both awareness and preparedness. This consolidation highlights the shared argument across both volumes: AI's impact on education and work is neither predetermined nor value-neutral. It is a human choice. If higher education succeeds in embedding ethical governance into its engagement with AI, and if it cultivates graduates equipped with dynamic repertoires of technical, cognitive, and ethical skills, then employability will not merely survive but will be redefined for the better. The challenge, as the Introduction underlines, is immense, but so too is the opportunity: to ensure that AI becomes a catalyst for justice, inclusion, and human flourishing rather than a source of division or inequity. This reconceptualisation invites a broader academic discussion of employability, tracing its evolution from a narrowly defined individual attribute towards a more relational and socially embedded phenomenon. Such a shift is essential if higher education is to respond effectively to the uncertainties of the contemporary labour market.

Employability has long been a central concern in education, policy, and workforce planning, functioning as a key measure of both individual opportunity and societal progress. Conventionally, it has been defined as the capacity to secure, retain, and advance in work while adapting to evolving demands and contributing productively to society (Hillage and Pollard, 1998). While this formulation has been influential, it is also somewhat restrictive, for it emphasises employability primarily as an individual's ability to access and progress within the labour market. Such an approach risks narrowing the discussion to career attainment alone, overlooking the wider interplay of social, cultural, and institutional forces that shape people's working lives. To respond to these limitations, scholars have argued for a more expansive understanding. Yorke and Knight (2006), for example, highlight the importance of a holistic perspective that integrates disciplinary expertise with transferable skills, adaptability, and a disposition for lifelong learning. This view recognises that employability extends well beyond technical competence, encompassing qualities such as reflection, collaboration, and the ability to engage constructively with uncertainty. In a similar vein, Tomlinson (2017) stresses that employability should be conceived as a socially embedded construct, shaped not only by personal attributes but also by structural conditions, employer practices, and policy frameworks. Adopting such a perspective allows employability to be seen as relational and dynamic rather than static or purely individual. It becomes less about the possession of fixed qualifications and more about the capacity to navigate complex and often unpredictable career pathways. In this sense, employability speaks not only to the demands of the labour market but also to the broader responsibilities of higher education in cultivating graduates who are resilient, ethically aware, and capable of contributing to human flourishing. By reimagining employability in these terms, institutions can move closer to aligning their educational missions with the realities of an AI-mediated society, ensuring that students are prepared not simply for jobs, but for meaningful, adaptable, and socially responsible careers.

Traditional conceptions of employability have long prioritised formal qualifications and technical expertise, operating on the assumption that education and specialised training provide a direct pathway to professional success. However, this perspective has been increasingly questioned in light of profound changes to the global economy, the acceleration of technological innovation, and the growing influence of AI. These developments suggest the need to reconceptualise employability as a dynamic and multidimensional construct, shaped not only by individual competencies but also by wider socio-economic structures and shifting labour market conditions (Nartey, 2025). This reconceptualisation presents both challenges and opportunities for HEIs and policymakers. For universities, it requires moving beyond traditional models of skills acquisition to embed adaptability, creativity, and technological literacy into curriculum design. For governments, it entails reassessing policy frameworks to ensure that education systems remain aligned with the realities of AI-driven economies. Such reflection enables workforce strategies to integrate historical perspectives on employability with the evolving complexities of automation and digitalisation (Brown, Hesketh, and Williams, 2004).

Evidence suggests that technical proficiency alone is no longer sufficient for sustained career success. In uncertain and rapidly changing contexts, individuals must also develop broader capacities such as critical thinking, creativity, and problem-solving to navigate shifting demands (Tomlinson, 2017). Rather than viewing such uncertainties as barriers, they may be understood as catalysts for innovation, offering scope for new forms of learning and professional development. The central question, therefore, is how these conditions can be harnessed to drive transformative approaches to employability. Addressing this question requires multidimensional analysis that integrates theoretical, practical, and policy perspectives across temporal frames. The long-standing assumption that formal qualifications guarantee stable employment has been replaced by recognition that employability depends upon lifelong learning, adaptability, and the capacity to engage with change. This represents a significant departure from human capital theory, which assumed a linear relationship between education, productivity, and career progression. In practice, employment outcomes are mediated by global economic forces, evolving employer expectations, and the transformative effects of automation and AI (Ejjami, 2024). Consequently, the debate extends beyond skills acquisition to consider how education systems and policy frameworks can empower individuals to pursue continuous growth and self-actualisation. Rather than treating learning as a static process confined to early formal education, employability should be understood as an ongoing endeavour that integrates interdisciplinary knowledge, technological fluency, and critical resilience. Such an approach would prepare graduates not only for immediate employment but also for sustained adaptability in complex and evolving global labour markets.

The growing influence of AI has altered the discourse on employability, reshaping the terrain of work much as the changing seasons transform a landscape. Just as winter strips away what is no longer sustainable and spring brings forth new growth, AI-driven automation reduces the need for routine tasks while amplifying the value of distinctly human capacities—critical thinking, emotional intelligence, and ethical judgement (Baldwin, 2019). These shifts demand that employability be reconceptualised not as a static attainment of skills, but as an adaptive and evolving process. Within this transformation, HEIs play a pivotal role in cultivating the forms of resilience and creativity that allow individuals to flourish amid uncertainty (Ajani et al., 2024). The relationship between human intelligence and AI is better understood as symbiotic than adversarial. When responsibly integrated, AI augments human cognition, enabling individuals to concentrate on the creative, strategic, and ethical dimensions of work that automation cannot replicate (Bukartaite and Hooper, 2023; Tadas and Agarmore, 2024). Yet, much like the uneven distribution of sunlight in a shifting climate, the benefits of AI risk are being unequally shared. Without deliberate investment in digital literacy and upskilling, structural inequalities may deepen, excluding communities with limited access to technological resources (Cook, 2021). The challenge, therefore, is to design educational and policy frameworks that anticipate rather than react, equipping learners with the adaptive skills needed to thrive in AI-mediated labour markets (Zubair, 2024).

This context requires a critical re-examination of traditional assumptions that equate employability with formal qualifications and technical expertise. Such models, grounded in linear and standardised understandings of education, are increasingly inadequate (Jarrahi, 2018). Much like trees that shed leaves to survive the winter, HEIs must shed rigid frameworks and embrace more flexible and personalised approaches that recognise individual pathways and cultivate lifelong learning (Brynjolfsson and McAfee, 2014; Kaplan, 2016). AI itself has evolved from automating manual functions to performing sophisticated analytical and administrative tasks (Selwyn, 2019), a development that highlights the inadequacy of static conceptions of work and learning. The future of employability lies in fostering a partnership between human intuition and AI-driven reasoning, where interpretive insight and algorithmic precision reinforce rather than displace one another (Schmager et al., 2025). To support this, HEIs must move towards pedagogical models that embed problem-solving, ethical reasoning, and technological adaptability as foundational competencies (Pagani et al., 2023). In this way, AI can be likened to a perennial force: disruptive, yet also generative, creating conditions in which new forms of knowledge, skills, and professional competence may take root.

Confronting the disruption posed by AI requires more than technical adjustments; it calls for a collective re-examination of both its possibilities and its limitations. At its core, this task is not about resisting innovation but about discerning the shifting boundaries between human capability and machine capacity. Much like the tide meeting the shore, where the ebb and flow reveal new contours without erasing the land itself, the interaction between AI and humanity creates space for distinctly human qualities—creativity, empathy, and ethical judgement—to stand out as defining features. Responsibility for navigating this terrain cannot be confined to HEIs alone. It must also extend to governments and industry leaders, whose roles in policymaking, regulation, and practice are central to shaping AI's societal impact. Governments, in particular, are challenged to reframe employment and education policies so that they support anticipatory and lifelong learning models. Such frameworks would allow individuals to adapt proactively to technological change, reduce the risks of displacement for low- and mid-skilled workers, and foster inclusive participation in digital economies (Bandi et al., 2020).

Policy must, however, go beyond mere accommodation of innovation. It should balance opportunity with oversight, ensuring that AI is developed and deployed in ways that enhance social and economic development while safeguarding ethical standards and human well-being. As Cave and ÓhÉigeartaigh (2018) suggest, AI cannot be treated as a purely technical phenomenon but must be recognised as socio-technical—demanding normative and functional responses. In this regard, higher education and scholarship have an ethical responsibility not simply to observe these transformations, but to engage directly through applied research, public dialogue, and socially responsive curricula that prepare graduates for complex futures. Industry, too, must assume its share of stewardship. Businesses should not focus narrowly on efficiency gains through automation, but should instead cultivate strategies of augmentation that harness complementarity between human and machine. Marr (2022) argues that this requires investment in professional development, digital literacy, and critical adaptability—attributes that position workers to thrive alongside AI rather than be displaced by it. This repositioning moves industry from the periphery of the debate to its centre, establishing it as both a driver of technological innovation and a co-guardian of its responsible integration. What emerges, therefore, is the need for a sustained tri-sector dialogue between academia, policy, and industry. This dialogue must avoid both the temptation to romanticise AI and the impulse to treat it with fear, recognising instead that it is a tool whose value depends on how it is governed and contextualised. Much like a compass that guides without dictating the traveller's path, AI can serve as a catalyst for human development if shaped by ethical imagination, inclusive vision, and careful regulation. The challenge, and the opportunity, is to ensure that AI's transformative power strengthens rather than diminishes our shared capacity to flourish.

At the centre of contemporary debates on AI and employability lies the need for a fundamental rethinking of how skills are understood, cultivated, and applied. This moment does not call for minor adjustments but for a paradigm shift—one that reshapes policy, pedagogy, and scholarly inquiry. Rather than maintaining a division between theory and practice, a more integrated approach is required, recognising that academic discourse and policy frameworks are interdependent forces which together shape both the narrative and material consequences of AI in society. Traditional assumptions grounded in credentialism and narrow forms of human capital theory are increasingly insufficient. Skills can no longer be conceived as fixed possessions, but as fluid capabilities: the ability to learn, unlearn, and relearn in response to rapidly shifting technological landscapes (Barnett, 2004; Senge, 2006). This shift is akin to navigating a river whose course continually changes; survival depends not on clinging to rigid structures but on the capacity to move with the current, adjusting course while retaining direction. Employability, therefore, is less a final destination and more a continuous process of adaptation, resilience, and ethical engagement. Seen through this lens, the convergence of policymaking and academic theorisation becomes more than a pragmatic necessity; it offers a way of illuminating the transformational potential of AI when guided by human-centred values. This perspective reframes AI not as a force of inevitable disruption, but as a co-evolutionary partner that compels individuals, institutions, and societies to recalibrate their relationship to knowledge, work, and meaning (Brynjolfsson and McAfee, 2014; Dede, 2010). The dichotomy between technological determinism and human agency dissolves: the future is co-constructed, emerging from the interplay between innovation, governance, and pedagogy. The key question is not whether AI will redefine employability, but how societies will shape that redefinition, and whether they will do so inclusively, sustainably, and justly.

This reorientation is sharpened by recognition of the volatility, uncertainty, complexity, and ambiguity (VUCA) that characterise the modern world of work. AI systems evolve in ways that are often unpredictable, demanding that adaptability becomes a central pillar of both educational and policy frameworks. In this context, lifelong learning is not an optional supplement but an essential orientation—an ongoing commitment to renewal rather than a one-time acquisition of knowledge. As theorists of reflexive modernisation remind us (Beck, Giddens, and Lash, 1994), learning must be iterative, responsive to uncertainty, and attuned to the constant reconfiguration of professional and social realities. The expansion of AI-powered educational platforms exemplifies this paradigm shift. Such technologies are more than neutral tools of delivery; they embody adaptive logics capable of tailoring content to the learner's cognitive pathways and developmental trajectory (Luckin et al., 2016). In doing so, they reshape not only how skills are acquired but also how employability itself is defined, mediating the relationship between the learner and the labour market through algorithmic interpretation. Much like a mirror that both reflects and distorts depending on its angle, these systems can amplify opportunities for personalisation while also introducing new risks of inequity and bias. In this argument, employability in the age of AI must be understood as a dynamic, co-created capacity. It is sustained not by static credentials but by reflexive adaptability, critical judgement, and an ongoing negotiation between human creativity and machine capability.

Sustaining employability in the age of AI demands continuous adaptation, socially inclusive frameworks, and the fusion of human creativity with AI-driven innovation to create equitable and resilient futures (Figure 1.1).

The first figure illustrates employability as a developmental trajectory, tracing the shift from traditional models, through the disruptive drivers of AI and automation, towards a redefined future grounded in adaptability, inclusivity, and human–AI complementarity. In doing so, it presents employability as a linear process of transformation, highlighting how assumptions rooted in credentialism and human capital theory are gradually reconfigured by technological and socio-economic change. This flow model captures the sense of

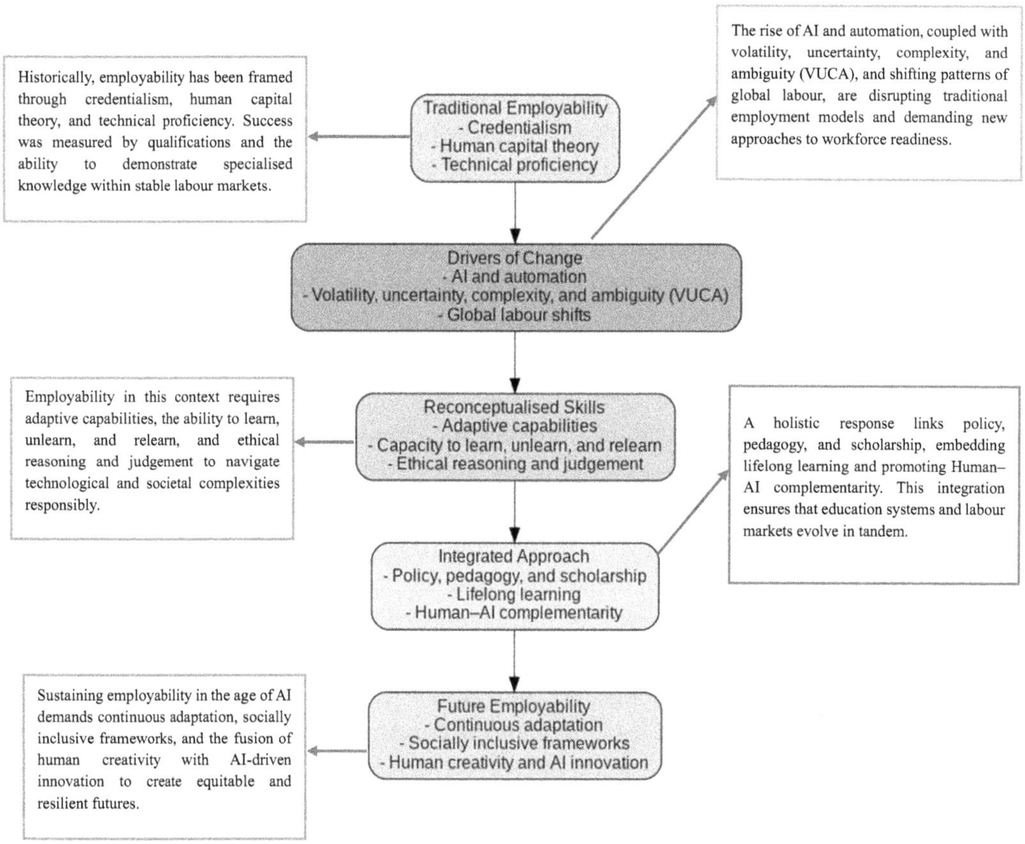

FIGURE 1.1 Evolving models of employability: from credentialism to human–AI complementarity.

The model illustrates the transition from traditional credential-based employability towards adaptive, ethical, and inclusive approaches that integrate human creativity with AI innovation.

BOX 1.1 EXPLANATION NOTE—EVOLVING MODELS OF EMPLOYABILITY: FROM CREDENTIALISM TO HUMAN–AI COMPLEMENTARITY

Employability has traditionally been understood through the lens of credentialism, human capital theory, and technical proficiency. Within this paradigm, qualifications functioned as a proxy for workforce readiness, reflecting the assumption that educational attainment and demonstrable skills directly translated into economic productivity. While such models were effective in relatively stable and predictable labour markets, they offered a limited view of employability by overlooking adaptability, creativity, and the broader social and ethical capacities that underpin resilience in periods of rapid change.

In recent decades, however, employability has been challenged by profound drivers of change. The accelerated rise of AI and automation has transformed the nature of work, displacing routine tasks while simultaneously creating new occupational categories. These technological shifts are embedded within wider contexts of VUCA, which amplify the unpredictability of career pathways. Moreover, global labour market transformations—shaped by digitalisation, demographic shifts, and economic restructuring—underscore the inadequacy of traditional employability frameworks that privilege static qualifications over dynamic capabilities.

Consequently, there is a pressing need to reconceptualise employability as a fluid and adaptive capacity rather than a fixed set of attributes. Central to this reconceptualisation is the cultivation of adaptive capabilities and the capacity to learn, unlearn, and relearn across a lifetime. Such reflexivity enables individuals to remain agile in rapidly evolving environments where yesterday's expertise may become obsolete. Equally important is the development of ethical reasoning and judgement, as workers are increasingly required to navigate the societal implications of technological innovation, including issues of fairness, accountability, and responsibility. Employability thus becomes a process of ongoing negotiation between human creativity and machine capability rather than a static outcome of formal education.

To achieve this shift, an integrated approach is essential, one that links policy, pedagogy, and scholarship. Education systems must be reoriented to embed lifelong learning, ensuring that individuals can continually update their knowledge and skills in response to changing demands. Furthermore, fostering human–AI complementarity is vital. Rather than positioning machines as replacements for human labour, the emphasis must be on developing synergies that combine human creativity, critical judgement, and emotional intelligence with AI's computational speed and efficiency. This approach offers not only productivity gains but also an ethically informed model of employability that acknowledges the value of human distinctiveness. Looking ahead, future employability is best characterised by continuous adaptation, inclusion, and innovation. It requires frameworks that are socially inclusive, ensuring that technological progress does not exacerbate inequality but instead broadens opportunity and access. At its core, employability in the age of AI rests on the fusion of human creativity with machine innovation, generating resilient, future-oriented forms of work. Rather than being reduced to static credentials, employability emerges as a dynamic, co-created capacity that reflects both the challenges and possibilities of a rapidly changing global landscape.

movement over time, demonstrating how employability is not a static attainment but an evolving response to shifting contexts. The second figure builds directly upon this argument, offering a concentric ripple framework that deepens and extends the discussion. Whereas the first figure highlights progression, the second emphasises structure and interdependence. At its centre lie the human capabilities of creativity, ethics, and adaptability—qualities that remain essential anchors even in an AI-mediated world. Surrounding layers represent lifelong learning, AI systems, and the wider ecosystems of policy, pedagogy, and industry, which collectively shape and are shaped by employability. The ripple metaphor reflects how change radiates outward: developments in technology or policy reverberate across the whole system, while human capacities at the core sustain balance and resilience. By sequencing the figures in this way, the discussion moves from a temporal narrative of transformation to a systemic representation of interconnection. Together, they provide a comprehensive account of employability in the AI age, capturing both its evolving trajectory and its layered, relational character (Figure 1.2).

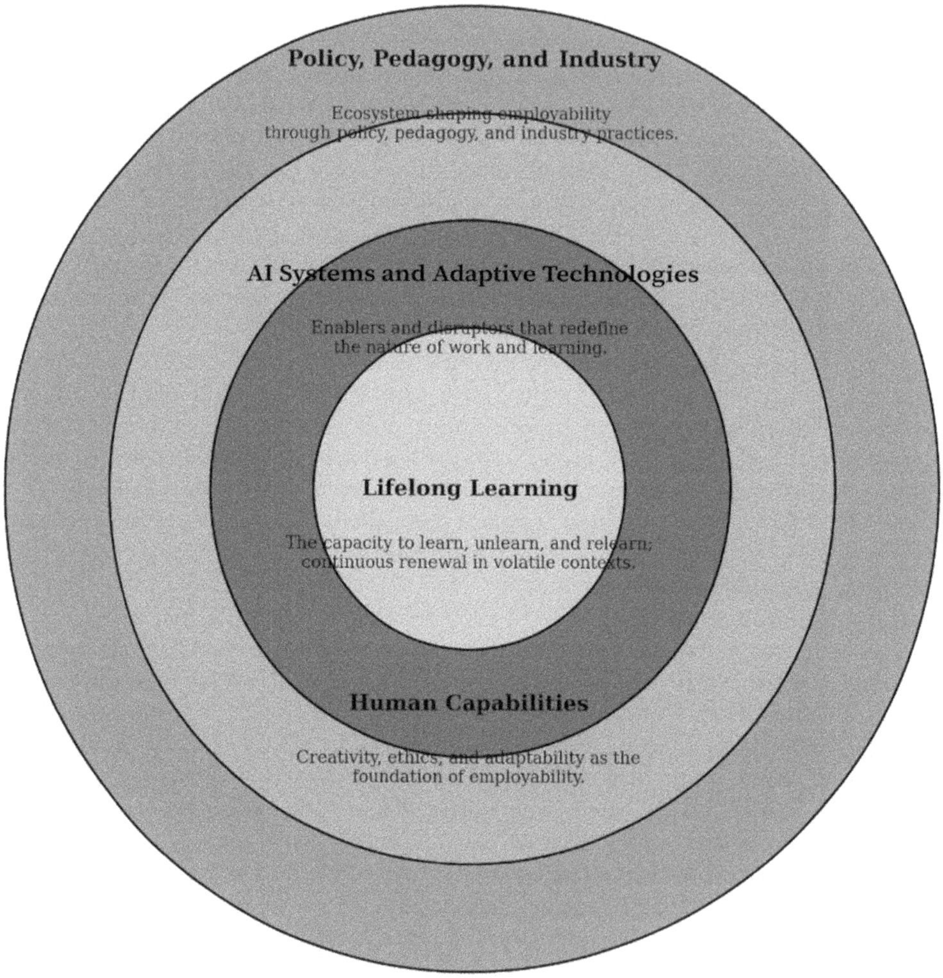

FIGURE 1.2 Concentric model of employability in the age of AI.

This model places human capabilities—creativity, ethics, and adaptability—at its core, surrounded by lifelong learning, AI systems and adaptive technologies, and the broader structures of policy, pedagogy, and industry. The concentric design illustrates how employability is shaped by interdependent layers, where changes in outer systems ripple inward and human-centred values sustain resilience and adaptability.

BOX 1.2 EXPLANATION NOTE—THE CONCENTRIC MODEL OF EMPLOYABILITY IN THE AGE OF AI

The concentric ripple framework of employability in the age of AI offers a structural representation of how human capabilities, technological systems, and institutional frameworks interact to shape future skills and professional identities. Unlike linear models, which emphasise transformation over time, this figure highlights the relational and layered nature of employability, showing how each dimension reinforces and depends upon the others. At the centre of the model are human capabilities—creativity, ethical reasoning, and adaptability. These qualities are positioned as the core of employability, reflecting their irreplaceable value in an era where routine tasks are increasingly automated. This placement highlights that while AI may replicate technical and analytical processes, the capacity for judgement, empathy, and innovative thought remains distinctly human and must be cultivated as the foundation of employability.

The next layer represents lifelong learning, conceptualised here as the capacity to learn, unlearn, and relearn in response to VUCA. This layer signifies that employability is not a static attainment but a continuous orientation towards renewal, aligning with theories of reflexive modernisation which stress adaptability as a central feature of professional survival in changing contexts. Surrounding this is the layer of AI systems and adaptive technologies. By situating technology outside lifelong learning, the model reflects its dual role as both an enabler and a disruptor. On the one hand, AI offers personalised and adaptive learning opportunities; on the other, it redefines the expectations of employability by altering the nature of work itself. The positioning of this layer captures the symbiotic relationship between human learning and machine capability.

The outermost circle, comprising policy, pedagogy, and industry, represents the broader ecosystem within which employability is situated. This placement highlights the argument that employability cannot be reduced to individual attributes alone but must be seen as socially embedded and structurally mediated. Policy frameworks, institutional strategies, and industry practices create the conditions that either enable or constrain the development and deployment of skills. Taken together, the model conveys a vision of employability as systemic, multi-layered, and interdependent. Change radiates outward like ripples in water: shifts in policy or technological infrastructures affect learning and human capacities, just as developments in human capability influence the effective integration of AI and the design of education systems. The figure, therefore, challenges reductionist views of employability, advocating instead for a holistic framework in which resilience, inclusivity, and ethical responsibility are recognised as central to thriving in AI-mediated futures.

The emergence of AI demands a reconceptualisation of skills ecosystems (Finegold, 1999), where employability is seen as an outcome of interdependent institutional, technological, and cultural dynamics. Sustainable growth now depends less on human capital accumulation and more on the creation of digitally resilient workforces able to integrate human judgement with machine intelligence. This entails not only technical proficiency but also epistemic virtues such as curiosity, adaptability, and ethical discernment—qualities that become vital as AI increasingly shapes complex decision-making processes across sectors. In this respect, employability cannot be reduced to discrete skills but must be understood as a co-evolutionary process, where human and machine systems develop symbiotically, each shaping the capacities and constraints of the other (Arthur, 2009). Professional resilience, therefore, rests on the ability to work with intelligent systems, co-construct knowledge, and navigate emerging ethical and operational complexities. The concentric ripple figure illustrates this layered view of employability. At its centre are human capabilities, such as creativity, ethics, and adaptability—qualities that remain irreplaceable even as automation advances. Surrounding this foundation is lifelong learning, representing the ability to learn, unlearn, and relearn in contexts marked by VUCA. Beyond this sits the layer of AI systems and adaptive technologies, acknowledging their dual role as enablers of personalised learning and disruptors of established practices. Finally, the outermost circle—policy, pedagogy, and industry—shows how broader institutional frameworks shape and constrain these dynamics. The ripple metaphor highlights the interdependence of these layers: shifts in policy or technology reverberate inward, just as human capabilities influence how AI is integrated and governed.

To situate this model critically, it is necessary to interrogate the ontological assumptions of employability itself. Far from a neutral concept, employability has historically functioned as a regulatory discourse embedded in systems of economic governance. It reflects the influence of neoliberal governmentality, where individuals are cast as autonomous agents responsible for their own productivity and market value (Rose, 1999). During the transition from Keynesian welfare economics to deregulated, market-driven growth, employability was reframed as a civic obligation, shifting responsibility for unemployment from structural forces to individuals labelled as underskilled or deficient (Peck and Theodore, 2000). This discourse continues to shape higher education and vocational training. Institutions often adopt employability metrics as proxies for quality, reinforcing narrow, instrumentalist models of learning. Such an approach risks reducing education to the production of market-ready subjects, thereby marginalising its role in fostering critical thought, civic engagement, and democratic participation (Giroux, 2014). Moreover, the dominant employability discourse obscures structural determinants such as outsourcing, capital mobility, and financialisation, which have reshaped labour markets beyond the reach of individual agency. From this perspective, employability must be reframed as a relational construct, not simply a property of individuals but a product of the intersection between political decisions, institutional arrangements, and economic restructuring (Standing, 2011). The ripple figure visually reinforces this position: employability is systemic, multi-layered, and interdependent, shaped as much by external structures as by individual capacities. Recasting employability in this way challenges reductionist narratives and makes space for a more just, inclusive, and ethically grounded vision of human development in an AI-mediated world.

An important, yet frequently underexplored, dimension of AI's impact on employment lies in its influence on the organisation of work over time. Conventional models of stable, full-time employment are increasingly giving way to flexible, on-demand arrangements that do not follow predictable schedules. This shift complicates traditional pathways of career progression and contributes to more fragmented professional experiences, making it difficult for individuals to establish a secure sense of occupational identity (Gregg, 2011).

In light of this, education systems that rely on linear models of incremental skill development may prove inadequate. Instead, there is a growing need to cultivate learners' capacity to adapt to fluid working conditions while maintaining productivity and psychological well-being. A parallel development is the rising prominence of emotional and interpersonal skills. As AI technologies assume responsibility for many routine and technical functions, human workers are increasingly valued for qualities such as empathy, communication, and relational competence—areas that have historically been undervalued in economic discourse (Negri and Hardt, 1999). These attributes, once dismissed as 'soft skills', now constitute essential components of employability and warrant systematic attention in preparation for the future of work.

Concurrently, the growing reliance on algorithmic systems to evaluate workers—through mechanisms such as performance dashboards, ratings, and digital monitoring—has altered the dynamics of employability. Such practices, sometimes characterised as the 'gamification' of labour, encourage individuals to engage in continual self-monitoring in order to remain competitive (Moore, 2017). While these systems can provide immediate feedback, they also reinforce highly individualised understandings of success, obscuring broader structural factors that shape access to secure and meaningful employment. A further point of concern relates to the use of AI in recruitment and training. When algorithmic systems are deployed in these processes, traditional human judgement may be marginalised, and the decision-making criteria can remain opaque. This raises significant questions of fairness, transparency, and accountability, particularly given the risk that such technologies may inadvertently perpetuate inequalities under the guise of neutrality or efficiency.

Some debates have intensified scrutiny of AI at both academic and policy levels, particularly with respect to its potential to exacerbate existing social inequalities. Critics argue that excessive reliance on AI technologies may entrench, and in some cases deepen, structural disparities in ways that are difficult to reverse (Eubanks, 2018). This concern is especially acute where AI systems are introduced without adequate ethical oversight or contextual awareness. Without deliberate efforts to embed inclusive principles, the use of AI in critical decision-making domains, such as employment, risks reproducing the very inequities it is often promoted as resolving. Empirical evidence highlights that AI-powered recruitment systems have, in certain cases, disadvantaged individuals from marginalised groups, reflecting and amplifying historical biases (O'Neil, 2017). Importantly, such outcomes should not be regarded as inherent to AI itself, but as indicative of inadequate design and implementation practices. These challenges commonly emerge when AI systems are trained on datasets that encode pre-existing social prejudices or are deployed within organisational cultures that lack critical ethical reflexivity. Addressing these shortcomings requires not only technical safeguards but also sustained institutional commitment to fairness, transparency, and accountability in the governance of AI.

The reliability of machine learning systems rests on the quality, diversity, and representativeness of the data on which they are trained. When datasets reflect existing socioeconomic inequalities or exclude significant variables, the outputs produced are likely to reproduce these distortions. Bias in AI is therefore not simply a technical concern but a socio-technical issue that necessitates interdisciplinary engagement. Without investment in ethical data governance and sensitivity to sector-specific contexts, the deployment of AI risks reinforcing inequalities rather than mitigating them. Some scholars caution against an overreliance on technological solutions to address complex challenges such as youth employability and labour market participation. Selwyn (2019), for example, advocates for a human-centred approach that situates AI within broader structural reforms, including educational change, equitable economic policy, and strengthened welfare systems. This perspective challenges technological determinism by rejecting the notion that AI alone can resolve entrenched socio-economic problems. Instead, it calls for pluralistic strategies that acknowledge the historical and institutional dimensions of inequality, positioning AI as one tool among many within a wider social policy framework.

Zuboff (2023) extends this critique by highlighting the implications of surveillance-based business models underpinning much of AI development. She argues that the commodification of personal data not only raises concerns about privacy and autonomy but also consolidates corporate power, often at the expense of public interest. Such critiques underline that the potential benefits of AI, particularly in the domain of employment, cannot be meaningfully separated from the economic and ethical structures in which these technologies operate. A more constructive pathway forward requires rethinking both the design of AI systems and the governance arrangements that regulate them. This includes careful scrutiny of how datasets are assembled and managed, alongside recognition of the normative assumptions that shape algorithmic reasoning. In practice, this entails cross-sector collaboration, regulatory foresight, and participatory design processes that foreground the perspectives of those most directly affected. The aim is not to dismiss the integration of AI, but to pursue a more ethically grounded, contextually informed, and socially inclusive vision. Within such a framework, AI may contribute to equitable transformation rather than exacerbate existing divisions.

In light of these challenges, there is a pressing need to reconceptualise employability in ways that acknowledge structural inequalities while also recognising the possibilities opened by emerging technologies. Rather than casting AI as a storm that uproots established practices, it may be more helpful to imagine it as a changing climate: unpredictable, sometimes disruptive, but also capable of creating new conditions for growth when approached with foresight and care. In this sense, employability can be seen less as a fixed structure and more as an ecosystem—shaped by interdependent forces of education, economy, and technology—which must be cultivated to remain resilient and inclusive. This reframing calls for a multidisciplinary lens, drawing on insights from education studies, labour economics, digital ethics, and policy research to envision a more humane and equitable future of work. Employability, much like a living landscape, is not static; it evolves through historical, social, and technological shifts. A brief historical perspective illustrates this point: early frameworks, grounded in human capital theory, treated employability as the accumulation of skills and qualifications, akin to storing resources in a silo for future productivity. More recent models, however, emphasise lifelong learning, adaptability, and interpersonal competence, reflecting a move towards seeing employability as a living system that thrives through diversity and flexibility. Such developments highlight the inadequacy of narrowly economistic approaches that reduce employability to individual accumulation. Just as a forest cannot be understood solely by counting its trees, employability cannot be grasped merely through lists of competencies. Its vitality depends on the relational and contextual dynamics that sustain it: the soil of social structures, the weather of economic conditions, and the light of technological change. Recognising these interdependencies is essential if employability is to be nurtured as a shared and sustainable resource, rather than a fragmented pursuit of individual advantage.

The transformation of work in the 21st century can be likened to the shifting dynamics of a quantum universe—fluid, uncertain, and governed by forces that resist fixed categorisation. Automation, digitalisation, and the rise of platform-based and gig economies have acted as gravitational fields, bending and reshaping the trajectories of employment. Boundaries that once distinguished formal from informal work have collapsed into superpositions, existing in both states at once, while certain skills have decayed, much like unstable particles, losing their relevance under the pressure of technological acceleration. Within this landscape, employability itself demands redefinition, not as a static property but as a dynamic state contingent upon constant interaction between individual capacities, social structures, and technological systems. From this perspective, labour market change should not be understood solely as an economic process, but rather as evidence of profound structural realignments. These shifts challenge traditional educational and policy frameworks in the same way that quantum indeterminacy challenges classical models of causation: outcomes can no longer be predicted with linear certainty, but must instead be managed through adaptive, probabilistic reasoning. Within this indeterminate field, AI emerges as both wave and particle—a transformative yet contested phenomenon. It has the potential to expand learning opportunities, streamline recruitment, and inform workforce development, while also carrying risks of bias, inequality, and ethical opacity. The key question, then, is not whether AI will reshape employability, but under what conditions it can generate constructive rather than exclusionary outcomes.

To respond effectively, AI must be aligned with human-centric values, echoing the principle that quantum systems remain entangled with the observers and instruments that measure them. Technology cannot be abstracted from the social and ethical frameworks in which it operates. The chapter, therefore, advances a framework for employability that is ethically grounded, contextually adaptive, and oriented towards cultivating capabilities such as creativity, critical thinking, and digital fluency. These are not incidental, but rather constitute the equivalent of quantum coherence—qualities that allow human agency to persist with clarity and resilience amid environments of rapid fluctuation. Within this cosmology of employability, HEIs play a pivotal role. Universities act as accelerators, shaping the conditions under which future trajectories unfold. Through curriculum reform, policy innovation, and pedagogical experimentation, they can influence how learners navigate uncertainty and acquire competencies that are sustainable in a continuously evolving labour market. Yet these responsibilities are not evenly distributed across the globe: just as the distribution of matter in the universe is asymmetrical, so too are global inequalities in access to education and technology. This unevenness highlights the need for international perspectives that position higher education not merely as a transmitter of disciplinary knowledge, but as a co-creator of equitable and future-ready capacities. The chapter concludes by synthesising these insights, emphasising the urgency of reimagining employability in light of AI-driven transformations and broader societal shifts. Like the universe itself, employability is expanding, unpredictable, and deeply relational. To navigate it requires holistic approaches that foreground adaptability, ethical engagement, and collective responsibility among learners, institutions, and policymakers alike. Only through such a vision can AI serve as a force of inclusive transformation rather than a mechanism of exclusion.

HISTORICAL PERSPECTIVES ON EMPLOYABILITY

This section considers the historical foundations of employability by critically engaging with the theoretical models that have shaped understandings of education, skills development, and workforce preparedness. Revisiting these perspectives helps to illuminate the enduring assumptions that continue to influence contemporary debates, particularly regarding the role of AI in reshaping labour markets. Historical frameworks are not only significant for what they contribute but also for the limitations they reveal and thus provide a basis for developing more adaptive and contextually sensitive approaches to employability in technologically dynamic economies. One of the most influential paradigms in this regard is human capital theory, advanced most notably by Becker (1964). The theory posits that investment in education and training enhances productivity and contributes to economic growth. Although developed in the mid-20th century, it continues to hold considerable sway in academic and policy discourse. Its central claim—that educational attainment translates into employability and economic value—offers a persuasive rationale for public and private investment in skills development. However, this model tends to present a reductionist view of learning by equating employability primarily with formal schooling and measurable returns. By framing individuals as units of capital to be optimised, it risks neglecting the complex, lifelong, and transformative processes through which skills are developed, refined, and applied in diverse contexts.

Critiques of human capital theory highlight its limited ability to account for the broader social and structural dimensions of employability. Factors such as regional inequalities in access to education, the uneven quality of vocational and training systems, and persistent socio-economic disparities significantly influence employment outcomes in ways the model does not adequately capture (Brown, Hesketh, and Williams, 2004). Moreover, in an era marked by technological acceleration and labour market volatility, the assumption that formal education alone secures employability has become increasingly untenable. While human capital theory provided a powerful justification for investment in education, its narrow economistic framing leaves underexplored the ways in which technological transformation, particularly AI, interacts with human skills development. The persistence of this theoretical legacy highlights the need for more holistic and critically informed approaches to employability—ones that move beyond the confines of human capital thinking. Contemporary frameworks must acknowledge the interplay between socio-structural inequalities and technological change, while recognising that employability is not a fixed outcome of formal education but an evolving capacity shaped by context, opportunity, and adaptability. Only through such an expanded perspective can discussions of employability in the age of AI respond meaningfully to the challenges and opportunities of the present.

Reimagining human capital theory for the 21st century is akin to rethinking the architecture of a bridge built in another era. While the original structure was designed to carry predictable loads across stable terrain, today's landscape is marked by shifting ground and changing currents. To strengthen this bridge for contemporary conditions, several philosophical pillars must be reinforced. The first is reflexivity, which functions like the bridge's ability to adjust its foundations in response to tremors. It requires a recognition that skills and employability are not fixed assets, but evolving capacities shaped by volatile economic and technological contexts. The second is inclusivity, comparable to widening the bridge so that those previously excluded from crossing—due to structural inequalities in access to education and training—can travel safely alongside others. This, in turn, demands adaptability, the flexibility of the bridge's materials to withstand new pressures without collapsing, symbolising the importance of lifelong learning and the ability to respond to uncertainty rather than relying solely on formal credentials. Yet strength alone is insufficient without ethics, which may be seen as the guiding compass for those who design and govern the bridge. Without ethical oversight, the structure risks serving only a privileged few, reinforcing inequities under the guise of neutrality. Finally, the principle of relationality binds these elements together, reminding us that a bridge is never built in isolation but connects communities, institutions, and generations. In this way, employability should be understood not as an individual pursuit of economic value but as a shared crossing, sustained by cooperation and mutual responsibility. Through reflexivity, inclusivity, adaptability, ethics, and relationality, human capital theory can be reconstructed as a framework resilient enough to carry societies across the turbulent waters of technological change. Figure 1.3 illustrates how employability in the 21st century can be reconceptualised

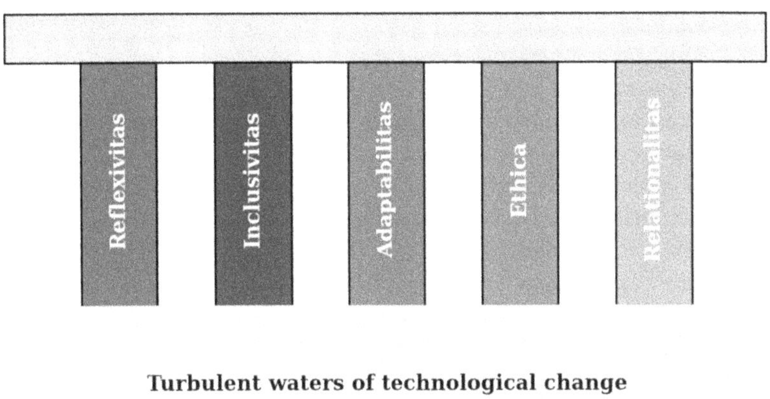

FIGURE 1.3 A reimagined human capital framework: five conceptual pillars supporting employability across technological change.

Employability as a bridge sustained by five conceptual pillars—reflexivitas, inclusivitas, adaptabilitas, ethica, and relationalitas—spanning the turbulent waters of technological change.

BOX 1.3 EXPLANATION NOTE—A REIMAGINED HUMAN CAPITAL FRAMEWORK: FIVE CONCEPTUAL PILLARS SUPPORTING EMPLOYABILITY ACROSS TECHNOLOGICAL CHANGE

The figure conceptualises employability in the 21st century as a bridge sustained by five philosophical pillars—reflexivitas, inclusivitas, adaptabilitas, ethica, and relationalitas—spanning the turbulent waters of technological change. This metaphor illustrates the limitations of traditional human capital theory and the need for a more holistic, ethically grounded framework that can respond to the rapid transformations introduced by AI and digital technologies.

Reflexivitas represents the capacity for critical self-awareness and institutional responsiveness. Within the framework of human capital theory, education has often been treated as a fixed investment that yields predictable returns. Yet AI unsettles this assumption by continually reshaping the demand for skills. Reflexivity, therefore, requires learners, institutions, and policymakers to adopt iterative modes of thinking, where employability is not a static end-state but an evolving capability. Just as a bridge must adjust to the movements of the earth and water beneath it, employability frameworks must remain adaptable to shifting technological and economic conditions.

Inclusivitas highlights the structural inequalities that human capital theory has often neglected. Traditional accounts assume a level playing field where individuals are equally able to invest in education and reap proportional rewards. In reality, AI risks exacerbating inequalities by privileging those with access to advanced training and digital infrastructure. Inclusivity demands that employability strategies ensure equitable access to education, lifelong learning, and digital resources. In this sense, the bridge must be wide enough for all to cross, not only those already advantaged by social or economic capital.

Adaptabilitas emphasises the necessity of lifelong learning and flexibility. As AI automates routine tasks and generates new forms of work, employability cannot be reduced to the accumulation of static qualifications. Instead, it involves the ability to learn, unlearn, and relearn in response to uncertainty. Human capital theory traditionally emphasised efficiency and optimisation, but adaptability reframes employability as resilience, where workers can recalibrate their skills to meet evolving labour market demands. This reflects contemporary debates in education policy, which stress the cultivation of creativity, critical thinking, and digital fluency alongside technical competencies.

Ethica anchors the framework in normative considerations. AI introduces profound ethical questions, particularly in recruitment, workplace monitoring, and algorithmic decision-making. Human capital theory has tended to focus on economic returns while overlooking the moral dimensions of education and employment. By foregrounding ethics, this framework insists that the pursuit of employability must be aligned with values of fairness, transparency, and accountability. Without this compass, technological innovation risks entrenching exclusion under the guise of neutrality.

Finally, relationalitas draws attention to the social and institutional interdependencies that shape employability. Whereas human capital theory often portrays individuals as isolated units of investment, relationality underlines the networks of support—educational, organisational, and cultural—that sustain human development. AI can either fragment or strengthen these relationships, depending on how it is designed and governed. By recognising employability as a collective achievement rather than an individual possession, this pillar resists overly economistic framings and situates human flourishing within wider social ecosystems.

Taken together, these five pillars reimagine human capital theory for an AI-driven era. They acknowledge the enduring value of education and skills while correcting for its historical blind spots. The bridge metaphor illustrates that employability must not only carry individuals across turbulent technological waters but also be strong, inclusive, and ethically grounded enough to ensure that the crossing benefits society as a whole.

through five interlinked pillars that strengthen human capital theory against the pressures of technological change.

Human capital theory offered a compelling rationale for investment in education and training, but it has also encouraged relatively static accounts of skill acquisition. Framing employability chiefly as the accumulation of qualifications and codified competences reduces learning to measurable inputs and outputs and pays insufficient attention to how skills are formed, exercised, and renewed across the life course. In rapidly changing labour markets—marked by task reconfiguration, sectoral volatility, and shifting generational expectations—such a model struggles to capture the fluidity of demand or the social conditions that shape opportunity (Brown, Lauder, and Ashton, 2010). A more adequate account places lifelong learning at the centre of the employability strategy. Treating people primarily as 'capital' to be invested in and extracted from risks overlooking capacities for reflection, reinvention, and adaptation. Universities and governments therefore have responsibilities not only to widen access to initial qualifications but to embed continuing, flexible learning opportunities and to recognise varied forms of attainment and progression.

Developments in AI can support this shift—cautiously and with governance. Adaptive systems can help identify emerging skill gaps, offer formative feedback, and recommend targeted learning pathways; they can also assist institutions in monitoring participation and outcomes (Brynjolfsson and McAfee, 2014; Luckin et al., 2016). These tools should be understood as augmenting human judgement rather than replacing pedagogy or professional expertise, and their use requires attention to fairness, transparency, and accountability. Operationally, an updated framework moves beyond narrow credentialism towards transferable capabilities—problem framing, critical thinking, collaboration, digital and data literacies—assessed through authentic tasks and reflective evidence, not solely through proxies. This entails a corresponding shift in indicators: from simple counts of qualifications to richer measures of learning over time, progression, underemployment, and the effective use of skills in context. Such a reframing retains the useful insights of human capital theory while correcting its limits, offering a more relational and adaptive account of employability suited to technologically mediated economies.

Historically, employability has been proxied by coarse indicators such as the highest qualification or speed of initial labour-market entry. While not without value, these measures understate the multidimensional character of employability in a digital, data-saturated economy. A more adequate account treats employability as an evolving capability: the capacity to work within complex socio-technical systems, to pursue sustained, self-directed learning, and to collaborate in hybrid settings where human and machine judgement interact. Policy and institutional frameworks, therefore, require reframing. Rather than a fixed endpoint delivered by formal education, employability should be understood developmentally, varying over time and across contexts (Felstead et al., 2013). The dominant, industrial-era view positioned employability chiefly as an individual responsibility, with policy concentrating on expanding access to programmes on the assumption that educational investment would translate proportionally into labour-market returns. In contemporary, technology-mediated markets, this linear presumption is difficult to sustain.

A critical re-theorisation is needed—not to discard earlier models entirely, but to recognise their practical limits and shifting conditions of application.

Some scholars argue that employability is socially constructed through economic, institutional, and cultural relations (Tomlinson, 2017). On this view, outcomes are co-produced by learners, employers, educators, and policymakers and negotiated within specific organisational settings (Holmes, 2013). Such a stance redistributes responsibility for skill formation and enables strategies that attend both to technological change and to embedded inequalities. AI can support this agenda, cautiously and under appropriate governance. Used well, AI systems may help surface emergent skill demands, provide formative feedback, and suggest tailored learning pathways; equally, they can entrench disparity if deployed without attention to fairness, transparency, and accountability (Anderson and Rainie, 2017). The goal, therefore, is augmentation rather than automation of educational and professional judgement. Operationally, this reframing implies moving beyond narrow credential counts towards richer indicators: progression and pay over time, incidence and forms of underemployment, effective use of skills in context, and participation in lifelong learning. Embedding such measures—and the supports that enable them—would align institutional practice and public policy with the realities of technologically dynamic labour markets, while advancing equity and inclusion alongside productivity.

Alternative conceptual frameworks offer useful points of contrast to the limitations of human capital theory. Sen's capability approach, for instance, shifts attention away from narrow economic returns and towards the substantive freedoms individuals possess to achieve valued ways of living (Sen, 1999). In this framing, education is not simply an input into production systems but a means of expanding personal agency, enhancing choice, and cultivating resilience in the face of change. By foregrounding what people are able to do and be, the capability approach highlights dimensions of employability often overlooked in human capital models—such as ethical judgement, well-being, and the ability to navigate uncertainty. Similarly, narrative-based perspectives on employability emphasise the dynamic and relational construction of career trajectories. Rather than viewing skills as fixed assets that yield calculable returns, these models recognise employability as situated within evolving personal stories, shaped by cultural, institutional, and technological contexts (Tomlinson, 2017). Such approaches allow for a richer appreciation of how individuals make sense of their professional development, integrate formal and informal learning experiences, and adapt to shifting occupational landscapes.

These contemporary frameworks also foreground issues of inequality and access in ways that Becker and Schultz's models did not anticipate. The capability approach, for example, exposes how structural barriers—whether economic, social, or technological—can limit individuals' opportunities to convert educational resources into meaningful outcomes. Narrative approaches likewise draw attention to the uneven distribution of cultural and social capital that influences employability. Together, these perspectives underline the ethical stakes of treating individuals as more than instruments of economic productivity. In the context of rapid technological change, such as the rise of AI and automation, these alternative models acquire renewed importance. Where human capital theory presumes a relatively stable alignment between education and labour market outcomes, capability- and narrative-based frameworks stress adaptability, reflexivity, and future-facing orientations. They encourage a more holistic understanding of employability that incorporates lifelong learning, digital fluency, and the cultivation of transferable skills, while also recognising the moral and social dimensions of professional life.

Mincer's (1974) expansion of human capital theory, through the inclusion of work experience, represents a valuable contribution to understanding employability. While this addition acknowledges the role of experiential learning, it remains situated within a framework that treats employability largely as the accumulation of capital, rather than as a dynamic and context-sensitive process. To move beyond this static interpretation, the idea of a work-integrated approach to human capital development is useful. Such an approach reframes employability not merely as the outcome of formal education and training, but as an iterative process shaped by the interplay between individuals, technological change, and workplace environments. The rationale for this reframing lies in recognising that employability skills are increasingly co-constructed within specific socio-technical contexts. In an era of rapid technological advancement—particularly in relation to AI and automation—workers are required not only to acquire new skills but also to refine and adapt them continuously through lived experience. Embedding learning within everyday professional activity enhances this adaptive capacity and better reflects the demands of knowledge economies characterised by disruption, innovation, and perpetual change. Interpreting Mincer's insights through this lens allows employability to be reconceptualised as a relational and evolving construct, responsive to temporal and spatial shifts across social, economic, and technological domains. This perspective highlights how work-based learning contributes not simply to the accumulation of human capital, but to the cultivation of agile, contextually relevant competencies essential for contemporary labour markets.

Friedman's (1955) advocacy for state intervention in education similarly shaped early approaches to employability by positioning public investment as a driver of national productivity. His emphasis on the responsibility of government helped to legitimise policy support for widening access to education and training. While this contribution remains significant, it does not fully capture the diverse and evolving influences on employability today, which include technological transformation, social change, geographical disparities, and the imperative of lifelong learning. In the current context of accelerating technological disruption, the role of government requires reconceptualisation. Employability should no longer be seen solely as the outcome of state investment in individuals and institutions, but as a shared responsibility embedded within an adaptive and inclusive ecosystem. Such an ecosystem involves governments, educators, employers, and individuals, each with distinct but interconnected roles. Governments act not only as funders but also as facilitators of equitable access to technological literacy and lifelong learning. Educators must design curricula aligned with emerging skill sets, while employers are expected to invest in continuous upskilling and reskilling strategies. Individuals, for their part, must be supported as active agents in lifelong learning, navigating transitions with resilience and adaptability.

Broadening employability governance in this way underlines the interdependence of social, technological, and economic systems. It also reinforces the need for inclusive and forward-looking strategies that ensure no group is marginalised in the evolving world of work. By adopting a co-responsible, multi-actor model, employability can be more effectively aligned with the disruptions and opportunities presented by AI and related innovations. Building on the limitations of Becker and Schultz's original formulations, later contributions by Mincer (1974) and Friedman (1955) sought to extend the reach of human capital theory in ways that responded to policy and economic concerns of their time. Mincer's inclusion of work experience acknowledged the importance of learning beyond formal education, while Friedman's advocacy for state intervention highlighted the centrality of public investment in shaping educational access and national productivity. Yet, despite these refinements, both perspectives remained anchored within a predominantly economic framing of employability, overlooking its relational, adaptive, and future-oriented dimensions. It is within this context that alternative interpretations—such as work-integrated approaches and multi-actor governance models—become essential for addressing the demands of contemporary labour markets shaped by rapid technological change.

Grubb's (1996) critique of the entrenched separation between academic education and vocational training provided an important rethinking of employability frameworks. He argued that the institutional divide between general education and job preparation weakened the effectiveness of both systems, producing a fragmented approach to skills development. In response, he advocated a more integrated model, one that combines theoretical learning with practical, industry-relevant experience. This vision, forward-looking at the time, is increasingly relevant in the context of AI, where labour market demands are complex, interdisciplinary, and rapidly evolving. In such a landscape, employability cannot be reduced to narrow technical proficiency. Instead, it requires a coordinated approach that brings together educational institutions, employers, and policymakers to design adaptive learning environments capable of preparing individuals for shifting occupational demands. This entails moving beyond parallel tracks of academic and vocational provision towards genuinely hybrid models of skill formation.

The success of structured vocational systems in several industrialised economies offers useful insights for this transformation. Ryan's (2001) comparative study of school-to-work transitions illustrated how dual systems, such as those in Germany and Austria, bridged education and employment more effectively, supporting smoother entry into stable labour markets. In contrast, Finegold and Soskice (1988) highlighted long-standing weaknesses in the United Kingdom's vocational framework, attributing poor outcomes to institutional fragmentation and limited policy support. These studies underline that vocational training is not inherently less valuable than academic education; rather, its effectiveness depends on the coherence, quality, and resourcing of the systems that sustain it. In the current context, vocational models can be reimagined through technological innovation. AI-enabled platforms, for example, offer opportunities to enhance apprenticeships by providing personalised learning pathways, real-time performance feedback, and data-driven insights into individual and sectoral skills needs. Such tools could make vocational training more responsive to labour market change, while also improving efficiency and learner engagement. However, as Keep and Mayhew (1999) caution, the success of such innovations depends on robust and equitable policy frameworks. Without safeguards to ensure accessibility, quality, and long-term sustainability, there is a risk that technology may entrench existing inequalities or fail to deliver its transformative potential. For this reason, the integration of AI into vocational pathways must be guided by strategies that prioritise both excellence and equity, ensuring that workforce development remains inclusive and socially just.

Looking ahead, the challenge lies not only in embedding AI within vocational education but also in ensuring that such integration supports lifelong learning and adaptability across the workforce. The acceleration of technological change means that skills acquired at one stage of life may quickly become obsolete. As such, vocational systems must evolve from preparing learners for a single occupational pathway to cultivating a capacity for continuous reskilling and redeployment. Achieving this requires collaboration across government, industry, and education, alongside an explicit commitment to inclusivity, so that opportunities for renewal and progression are available to all. By framing vocational education as a dynamic, lifelong, and technologically informed endeavour, policymakers and practitioners can move towards employability models that are not only future-facing but also equitable and sustainable.

Psacharopoulos and Patrinos (2004) reaffirmed the core principles of human capital theory in their updated analysis of the returns to educational investment, while also highlighting the growing importance of lifelong learning. Their recognition of continuous education is particularly relevant in the context of AI, where rapid technological change requires workers to renew and adapt their competencies across the span of their careers. In such an environment, one-off educational interventions appear increasingly insufficient. What is needed instead is a sustained, flexible approach to learning that supports individuals at different stages of professional development. Wolf's (2011) critical reflection on the limitations of relying solely on formal education as a pathway to employability remains instructive. She argued that structural transformations in the economy—shaped by globalisation, digitisation, and now AI—often progress at a pace that formal education systems struggle to match. If this gap remains unaddressed, it risks worsening skills mismatches and widening inequalities in access to meaningful employment. The challenge, therefore, extends beyond curriculum reform to encompass broader changes in how educational institutions deliver, update, and respond to evolving knowledge and skills needs.

Addressing these challenges requires the development of learning systems that are modular, flexible, and capable of rapidly integrating emerging competencies, particularly those linked to AI. Such models should be designed to provide timely, accessible, and context-sensitive opportunities for upskilling and reskilling. A central dimension of this transformation involves preparing educators to engage with AI not only as a topic of instruction but also as a pedagogical tool. The concept of AI-enabled personalised learning pathways is especially relevant here, offering potential for real-time feedback, adaptive learning experiences, and progress tracking aligned with individual needs and industry standards. By enhancing the responsiveness of education to labour market dynamics, such approaches can reduce the lag between the emergence of new skills and their acquisition.

For these innovations to be implemented effectively, three enabling conditions are essential. First, educators require sustained professional development to ensure confidence in using AI technologies and in designing pedagogies that reflect contemporary labour market fluidity. Second, institutional frameworks should adopt agile governance models, allowing for iterative revision of course content in collaboration with industry and policy actors. Third, adequate investment is necessary to strengthen digital infrastructure, ensuring equitable access to AI-enhanced learning tools across diverse educational and socio-economic settings. When combined, these efforts have the potential to make AI-driven lifelong learning not only a theoretical aspiration but also a practical foundation for building inclusive, adaptable, and future-ready workforces.

Ashton and Green's (1996) analysis of globalisation and its implications for education and training provides a useful foundation for examining the contemporary challenges associated with AI. They argued that as economies become increasingly interconnected, education systems must adapt more rapidly and engage with international perspectives. This observation acquires renewed relevance in the context of AI, whose development and application are inherently transnational. Preparing learners for participation in AI-influenced industries, therefore, requires educational frameworks that respond to local labour market needs while also aligning with global trends, standards, and competencies. One way of approaching this is through internationally networked models of AI education and training. Such models would encourage structured collaboration across borders, including the sharing of curricular resources, the coordination of skill frameworks, and the recognition of qualifications. In practical terms, this could be supported by partnerships among governments, educational institutions, and industry actors. Cross-national working groups might, for instance, co-develop AI competency frameworks that reflect the realities of global labour mobility, while transnational platforms could help disseminate best practices and innovative pedagogical approaches. This form of collaboration would not only facilitate greater alignment but could also strengthen the capacity of education systems to respond more flexibly to AI-related disruptions.

Complementing this global dimension, Bynner's (1999) research highlights the importance of sociocultural factors—such as family, community, and social context—in shaping human capital development. This perspective remains particularly relevant in an era where rapid technological change risks amplifying existing inequalities. It underlines the need for approaches to AI-related education that are rooted within communities and attentive to the diverse experiences of learners, especially those from historically marginalised groups. Putting this into practice may involve participatory methods that engage learners, families, and local stakeholders in shaping curricula and delivery. Examples include establishing advisory boards that reflect community voices, integrating culturally relevant pedagogies, and capturing lived experiences that influence how individuals access and engage with learning opportunities. By embedding inclusivity in this way, educational provision can promote a more equitable distribution of the benefits associated with AI. Moreover, it supports a broader conception of employability—one that balances global competencies with the social and cultural realities that influence lifelong learning.

Streeck's (1989) critique of neoliberal education models drew attention to the importance of workplace learning and apprenticeship systems as alternatives to narrowly academic pathways. He argued that enterprise-based training is often more effective in cultivating practical and transferable skills. This perspective remains pertinent in the context of AI, where workplace environments increasingly serve as key sites of learning. Through engagement with real-world tasks and tools, employees are able to develop the digital competencies required by evolving roles in AI-influenced industries. This emphasis on learning within employment settings resonates with broader scholarship on continuous professional development and in-company training (Barrett and O'Connell, 2001). These studies suggest that employability in the age of AI depends less on static qualifications and more on the capacity to engage in lifelong learning. AI itself may contribute to this process by supporting flexible and personalised learning—such as through automated skills assessments, tailored course recommendations, and access to short, just-in-time learning opportunities.

To translate such ideas into practice, a collaborative and grounded approach is required, one that connects government, education providers, and employers. Three complementary strategies illustrate this direction:

- **Government-supported Local Learning Partnerships**: Rather than relying solely on centralised policy, governments could encourage local learning hubs developed jointly by employers, universities, and councils. These hubs would provide short, practical courses that address immediate workplace needs, such as basic data literacy or the use of AI tools, and deliver them flexibly online or on-site.
- **University and College Micro-modules**: HEIs could offer short, stackable modules designed for working professionals. These units should be affordable, accessible online, and industry-relevant—for example, modules on GenAI in communication or ethical data practices. By linking such provision to workplace participation, universities can support more inclusive and cumulative forms of professional learning.
- **Workplace-based AI Learning Champions**: Employers might designate staff with foundational AI knowledge to act as peer mentors. These champions would not be expected to serve as technical experts, but rather to encourage informal learning and assist colleagues in adopting new tools. This low-cost intervention could be particularly effective within small and medium-sized enterprises.

Taken together, these strategies suggest that established models of employability—most notably human capital theory, vocational training, and lifelong learning—retain relevance but require reinterpretation in light of contemporary labour market dynamics. While they provide important conceptual tools, their explanatory power is limited when applied to the fast-moving and disruptive influence of AI. A critical perspective indicates that the future of employability is unlikely to be secured through broad, top-down reforms alone. Instead, progress may rest on targeted, context-sensitive interventions that embed continuous learning within the rhythms of everyday work, ensuring that opportunities for development are accessible across the life course. However, it is equally important to acknowledge the limitations of these models. Human capital theory, for example, often reduces learning to its economic returns, while vocational training can risk becoming overly narrow and inflexible. Lifelong learning, although widely advocated, may reinforce inequalities if access and resources are unevenly distributed. By critically examining such limitations, space is created for a more nuanced reimagining of employability—one that is responsive to both the challenges and the opportunities presented by AI. It is on this basis that the following section turns to Rethinking Employability: Recognising the Limitations of Traditional Models, offering a deeper critique of existing frameworks and considering how they might be reshaped to address the demands of an AI-driven future.

RETHINKING EMPLOYABILITY: RECOGNISING THE LIMITATIONS OF TRADITIONAL MODELS

Building on the preceding discussion, this section considers the limitations of traditional employability models not simply as deficiencies to be corrected, but as signals pointing towards a wider shift in how employability might be understood and enacted. Instead of rehearsing familiar critiques, the analysis reframes these limitations as prompts for rethinking employability in more responsive, ethically grounded, and epistemologically expansive ways. A recurring concern lies in the tendency to treat employability as a fixed and tightly structured system, with outcomes prescribed in advance and measured through narrow benchmarks. While such systems promise consistency, they often detach employability from the lived experiences of learners and the volatile contexts in which they seek to build their futures (Barnett, 2010). The effect can resemble a checklist culture: employability reduced to a series of compliance tasks rather than embraced as a developmental process of growth, adaptability, and transformation. If we treat this rigidity as an allegory, it is akin to navigating a dynamic landscape with a static map—the terrain shifts, yet the chart remains unchanged.

Recognising these tensions opens space for a different orientation: one that conceives of employability as organic, emergent, and situated. Rather than privileging linear progressions or standardised competency templates, such a perspective foregrounds the cultivation of intellectual flexibility, ethical discernment, and emotional resilience (Dall'Alba, 2009). This shift does not dismiss competencies but reframes them as part of a broader ecology of becoming—one in which varied trajectories, contexts, and identities are acknowledged as integral to how value and contribution are negotiated in professional life. Alongside this, there is a need to reflect on the symbolic weight employability has accrued within policy and institutional discourse. It functions as a shorthand for diverse social, economic, and technological expectations, yet remains under-theorised in terms of ethical purpose. The saturation of the term invites us to ask not only what employability equips learners to do but also what kinds of futures it seeks to legitimise. In this light, employability is less about alignment with present labour market demands and more about cultivating capacity for meaningful participation in shaping future possibilities. Such a reorientation implies pedagogical shifts. Rather than emphasising output delivery alone, institutions might approach employability as an ongoing dialogue—between learners, educators, and wider systems—sensitive to context, difference, and transformation. Seen in this way, the limitations of traditional models are not obstacles to be eliminated but openings: opportunities to imagine employability as a living, relational practice, one concerned as much with purpose and flourishing as with productivity.

While AI is reshaping work at both structural and experiential levels, many employability frameworks remain oriented towards the past, privileging stability over responsiveness to technological change. This tension is illustrated in the persistence of rigid skill taxonomies, which struggle to capture the hybrid forms of human–machine collaboration now emerging in fields such as healthcare, finance, and education (Makridakis, 2017). Within these contexts, graduates are expected not only to perform technical tasks but also to demonstrate ethical reasoning, digital adaptability, and professional judgement—capacities that sit uneasily within conventional lists of transferable skills. The issue is not that structured approaches to employability should be discarded, but that they require reimagining. A more appropriate metaphor might be that of skill dynamics: an ongoing, situated interplay between enduring human capacities and evolving technical proficiencies. Unlike static notions of skill, skill dynamics recognises adaptability as central, enabling learners to orient themselves within an uncertain and shifting landscape. This is akin to navigating the sea by stars rather than by a fixed map: while the route cannot be plotted in advance, travellers cultivate the resilience and resourcefulness needed to respond to unpredictable conditions.

Critics may question how education can prepare individuals for roles and competencies that do not yet exist. Yet, from a philosophical standpoint, this concern may be misplaced. Aspiration and imagination function as anticipatory practices through which societies prepare for the future (Barnett, 2004). Employability, therefore, should not be seen as a finite attainment but as a living process—iterative, open-ended, and continually reshaped by emerging challenges and opportunities. This reconceptualisation positions employability less as compliance with immediate employer expectations and more as a generative space for developing digital fluency, critical foresight, and lifelong learning dispositions (Jackson and Bridgstock, 2021). Learners navigating technological uncertainty require more than a toolkit of static competences: they need reflective capacities that enable reskilling, upskilling, and collaboration across disciplines. Achieving this requires not just curricular reform, but a broader cultural shift towards pedagogies that emphasise self-authorship, values-based reflection, and adaptive learning pathways.

A further challenge lies in the imbalance of voices shaping employability agendas. Policy and institutional discourses are frequently dominated by employer perspectives, with limited inclusion of student voices or broader social stakeholders. This asymmetry risks narrowing definitions of success and overlooking the diversity of learner aspirations. When employability is framed without critical dialogue, it can become a one-way prescription, rather like designing a garment for uniformity rather than tailoring it to fit varied bodies. As Hinchliffe and Jolly (2011) contend, employability should be understood as a co-constructed endeavour, where students actively shape their trajectories rather than receive pre-defined competences. Taken together, these concerns highlight that while employability remains a vital construct, its prevailing formulations are not adequate for an AI-enhanced, socially diverse, and globally interconnected world. What is required is a reframing of employability as a relational and responsive process—attuned both to present demands and to possible futures.

Building on earlier discussions about the shifting nature of employability in the 21st century, some scholarship points to a significant reconceptualisation of what it means to be 'employable' in digital, interconnected, and rapidly evolving labour markets. Earlier accounts often emphasised technical expertise and job-specific knowledge, but contemporary frameworks are moving towards a more holistic view—one that foregrounds adaptability, transversal competencies, and the capacity for lifelong learning. This shift should not be seen merely as a reaction to market volatility; rather, it represents a positive reorientation towards approaches that are responsive, dynamic, and capable of evolving with what might be termed skills dynamics—the fluid interplay of capabilities across roles, sectors, and individual career trajectories. One illustrative example of this broader framing is offered by the International Baccalaureate (2020), which demonstrates how competencies such as communication, ethical reasoning, mindfulness, and critical thinking are being embedded directly into curriculum structures. These are not treated as optional additions to technical content but as foundational to preparing learners for what is often described as a VUCA world—defined by volatility, uncertainty, complexity, and ambiguity. The inclusion of ethics and mindfulness signals a wider recognition that emotional intelligence and reflective practice are core to 21st-century employability. This emphasis resonates with humanistic approaches to education, which stress the development of the whole person (Biesta, 2010). Here, employability is framed not simply as a matter of qualification or compliance with external expectations, but as an ongoing process of self-development and critical awareness—enabling individuals to connect their evolving values, capacities, and aspirations to their participation in work.

Such a personalised and developmental understanding has particular significance in light of increasingly non-linear and hybrid career paths. In economies where trajectories are less predictable, the ability to reflect critically on one's skills, values, and aspirations becomes essential. This reconceptualisation therefore supports both curriculum innovation and the design of educational pathways that are more responsive to individual needs and contexts. Alongside this broadened vision, van Laar et al.'s (2020) systematic review identifies seven key digital skills for the contemporary workplace, including technical proficiency, information literacy, critical thinking, and collaboration. Crucially, their analysis positions these not as isolated technical attributes but as practices embedded in social and communicative contexts. In this framing, digital competence gains value only when exercised alongside interaction, cooperation, and ethical judgement—highlighting the interdependence of technical and socio-emotional literacies. Further support for this more integrated perspective is found in Duggal et al.'s (2024) call to 'rethink' employability. They challenge the continued reliance on rigid, discipline-bound approaches, advocating instead for pedagogical models that prepare learners for uncertain and dynamic career landscapes. This position aligns with Yorke and Knight's (2006) influential framework, which conceptualises employability as a synthesis of knowledge, skills, efficacy beliefs, and reflective dispositions. Their model highlights the multidimensional nature of graduate readiness and shifts emphasis away from narrow content mastery towards broader capacities that sustain lifelong adaptability.

Butum and Nicolescu's (2019) work provides an important multi-actor perspective by synthesising the views of employers, graduates, and educators. Their findings expose persistent misalignments between institutional intentions and labour market expectations, highlighting the need for more integrated and reflexive approaches to employability. Rather than treating employability as a fixed product to be delivered, they highlight its co-constructed nature, shaped through interaction between learners, institutions, workplace cultures, and societal developments. This insight shifts attention away from employability as an isolated outcome and towards what may be described as an employability ecosystem—a dynamic environment in which skills, identities, and social contexts interact and gain meaning only in relation to one another. The jigsaw puzzle is a useful allegory here: individual pieces, such as skills or experiences, retain value in themselves, but their true significance emerges only when assembled into a connected whole.

Economic perspectives reinforce this relational view. Stephany (2020) and Stephany and Teutloff (2024) illustrate how employability depends increasingly on cross-skilling and skill complementarity. Nedelkoska and Quintini (2018) demonstrate that acquiring adjacent, high-demand skills—such as coding—enhances both productivity and adaptability, while Deming and Noray (2020) argue that the value of a skill is relational, deriving not from its possession in isolation but from how it interacts with other capabilities. This resonates with the idea of employability as a capability practice (Nussbaum, 2011; Sen, 1999), where the emphasis is not on discrete inputs but on the freedoms individuals gain through the interplay of diverse capacities. In hybrid labour markets, this means moving beyond linear models of upskilling towards strategies that recognise employability as the ability to combine and recombine knowledge across technical, creative, and interpersonal domains.

Pedagogical research strengthens this argument. Khan et al. (2024), for example, show how makerspace workshops cultivate competencies such as teamwork, problem-solving, and critical reflection by embedding learning in collaborative and applied contexts. This aligns with experiential and constructivist approaches (Kolb, 2014), which view knowledge not as transmitted content but as something actively generated through participation. Such practices suggest that employability development must be embedded in authentic, social learning environments, where students are not passive recipients of pre-defined competences but co-creators of their professional trajectories (Hinchliffe and Jolly, 2011).

Taken together, these contributions point to a necessary reimagining of employability as both an ecosystem and a capability practice. As an ecosystem, employability is relational, shaped by the interactions between learners, institutions, employers, and broader social forces. As a capability practice, it is oriented towards enabling individuals to exercise agency, adaptability, and purpose in uncertain contexts. This reconceptualisation moves employability beyond the static accumulation of skills, reframing it as a cultivated disposition: the ability to learn, unlearn, and relearn within dynamic and interconnected professional landscapes. For higher education, this means a shift from credential delivery to fostering adaptive capabilities, critical awareness, and relational capacities that prepare graduates not simply for jobs, but for meaningful participation in rapidly evolving worlds of work and society (Figure 1.4).

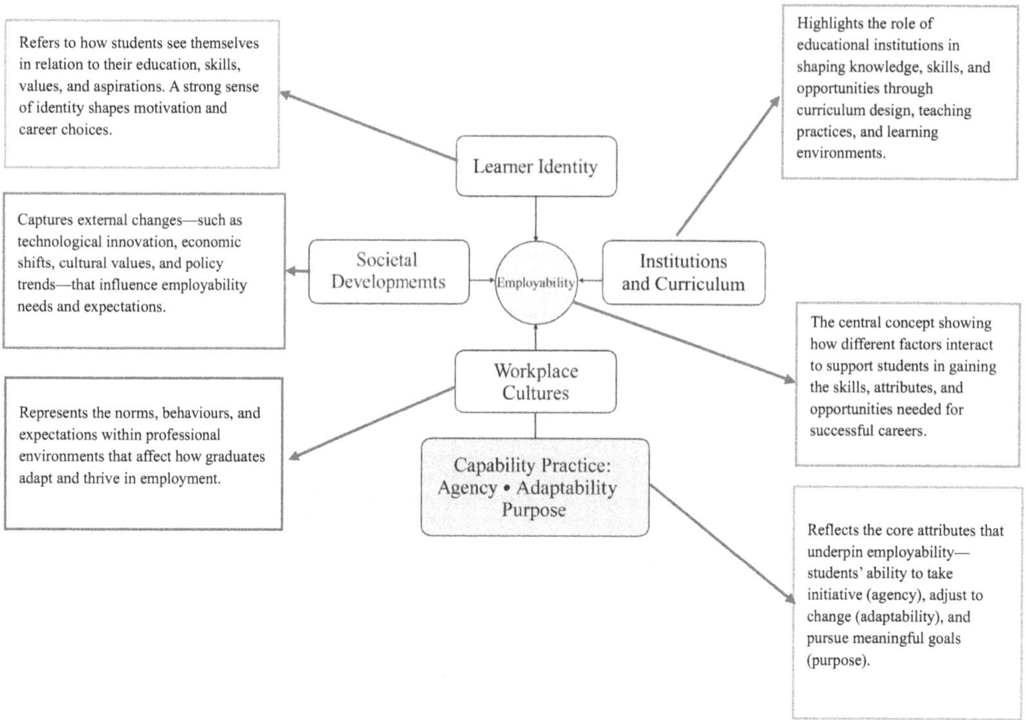

FIGURE 1.4 Employability ecosystem and capability framework.

Figure illustrating employability as an ecosystem shaped by learner identity, societal developments, institutions, and workplace cultures, underpinned by capability practices of agency, adaptability, and purpose.

BOX 1.4 EXPLANATION NOTE—EMPLOYABILITY ECOSYSTEM AND CAPABILITY FRAMEWORK

The figure conceptualises employability not as a static attribute of the individual, but as a dynamic ecosystem shaped by interdependent factors. At its centre lies employability, which is informed by four interconnected domains: learner identity, societal developments, institutions and curriculum, and workplace cultures. Beneath these dimensions sits the foundation of capability practice, emphasising agency, adaptability, and purpose. This visual model resonates with Sen's Capability Approach (Sen, 1999), which shifts the focus from narrow skills acquisition to broader capabilities that enable individuals to lead meaningful lives. Learner identity highlights the self-concept, aspirations, and personal values that individuals bring to their educational and professional journeys. Rather than viewing students as passive recipients of employability training, the framework recognises them as active agents constructing their professional identities (Tomlinson, 2017). This identity is not formed in isolation but is continuously shaped by social and institutional interactions.

Societal developments situate employability within wider structural conditions, including technological change, globalisation, and socio-economic inequalities. Employability discourses have often been criticised for over-emphasising individual responsibility, while ignoring systemic barriers such as discrimination or precarious labour markets (Brown, Hesketh, and Williams, 2004). The inclusion of this dimension acknowledges the necessity of contextual sensitivity when analysing employability. Institutions and curriculum represent the formal structures of higher education. Universities are positioned as both enablers and gatekeepers of employability, mediating access to knowledge, credentials, and opportunities. Yet the employability agenda has been critiqued for being overly instrumental, privileging labour market outcomes over critical or transformative learning (Jackson, 2015). This raises the need for curricula that balance skills development with broader educational purposes.

Workplace cultures underline the relational and collective dynamics of employment. Employability extends beyond entry into the labour market, encompassing the ability to navigate organisational norms, demonstrate adaptability, and sustain meaningful careers. Studies suggest that workplace integration depends as much on social capital, cultural fit, and resilience as on technical skills (Clarke, 2018). At the foundation, capability practice—defined through agency, adaptability, and purpose—provides the conceptual lens that ties the framework together. Agency refers to the capacity of individuals to make choices and influence their trajectories, adaptability reflects responsiveness to changing contexts, and purpose signifies alignment with personal and societal values. This triad resists reductionist views of employability as merely 'job readiness', instead promoting a holistic understanding that incorporates ethics, identity, and lifelong learning.

Critically, the model challenges linear or deficit-based views of employability, positioning it instead as an ecological and relational practice. However, one limitation is its conceptual abstraction: while it captures the multidimensionality of employability, it may lack operational clarity for policy and pedagogical implementation. Furthermore, while the framework acknowledges structural factors, the burden of adaptability still falls heavily on the individual—an issue that mirrors critiques of neoliberal employability discourses (Morley, 2001). In sum, this framework situates employability within a capability-informed ecosystem that integrates personal, institutional, societal, and workplace influences. Its strength lies in highlighting interdependencies and the role of agency, while its challenge is translating theory into practice without reinforcing inequalities or reducing education to labour market utility.

In discussions of 21st-century skills, the literature consistently highlights a set of interrelated challenges: the rapid transformation of labour market demands, the continuing importance of interpersonal and cognitive competencies, and the enduring misalignment between educational provision and the realities of contemporary work (Dede, 2009; National Research Council, 2015). While these themes are widely recognised, what is becoming increasingly apparent is that traditional approaches to categorising and teaching skills—often rigid, linear, and bound by disciplinary silos—struggle to capture the complexity of present-day learning and employment contexts. Many scholars argue that existing employability frameworks fragment skills into discrete elements, overlooking their relational, contextual, and evolving character. Addressing this issue requires more than minor adjustments; it calls for a reconsideration of the very assumptions underpinning how employability is understood. The central concern, therefore, is not merely how to bridge a 'skills gap', but how to reshape the epistemological foundations upon which skills development is conceived. This deeper reorientation—towards a more adaptive and integrative paradigm—is the focus of Volume II of this series.

The paradox of this shift can be illustrated through the familiar story of the locksmith's apprentice. The apprentice, having mastered the craft of making traditional keys, becomes adept at reproducing the most intricate designs. Yet when confronted with a door that opens by touch rather than by key, his skill set proves obsolete. He persists in reworking his most refined keys, unable to recognise that the nature of the task has changed. This parable reflects the current state of employability education: institutions continue to refine established frameworks, replicating familiar patterns, even as the external world calls for new ways of thinking. The challenge is not that learners lack ability, but that the system often equips them for contexts that no longer exist in the same form. What is needed is not simply more efficient key-making, but recognition that the lock itself has changed. The National Research Council's (2015) report makes a valuable contribution by identifying workplace competencies in STEM fields. Yet its wider significance lies in revealing the structural disconnection between the way knowledge is delivered in education and the way it is applied in professional practice. Curricula remain largely bound by disciplinary structures, whereas contemporary employment increasingly demands capabilities that cut across domains and draw upon hybrid forms of expertise. Professionals are often required to integrate insights from ethics, technology, and communication simultaneously, reflecting the rise of what might be described as knowledge hybridity. This is not simply interdisciplinarity, but the capacity to translate and apply knowledge flexibly across varied contexts, demonstrating conceptual agility.

Against this backdrop, systems-based approaches to competency mapping offer a useful conceptual advance. However, if such approaches are to be genuinely transformative, they must move beyond curriculum structures to reimagine pedagogy itself. One important orientation lies in fostering relational intelligence: the capacity to recognise and respond to the interconnections between ideas, people, and environments. This involves not only intellectual integration but also sensitivity to context, social awareness, and ethical discernment. For instance, professionals working in fields such as climate science or urban planning must navigate not only technical data but also the demands of stakeholders, the constraints of policy, and the moral and emotional dimensions of decision-making. These relational capacities, though often left uncodified, are frequently the qualities that distinguish effective practitioners. In this sense, the challenge of employability in the 21st century is not simply one of supplying individuals with predetermined skills, but of cultivating the capacity to adapt, integrate, and exercise judgement in fluid and uncertain conditions. Such a shift requires reimagining skills development not as a mechanical process of inputs and outputs, but as a practice that is adaptive, relational, and contextually responsive.

The concept of competency ecologies can be deepened through the notion of learning resilience—the capacity to navigate uncertainty, ambiguity, and occasional failure as part of the educational process. Unlike conventional competency models, which often assume linear mastery, an ecological approach recognises fluctuation, iteration, and disruption as integral to development. Learning resilience enables learners to move across diverse environments and expectations, adapting their strategies as circumstances shift. This is particularly significant given the accelerating pace of technological and social change, in which the half-life of skills is increasingly short. While scenario-based learning remains a valuable pedagogical tool, its effectiveness depends on being situated within a culture of critical reflexivity. Learners should be encouraged not only to practise technical decision-making but also to interrogate the assumptions that underpin their choices, to recognise power relations within professional practice, and to reflect on the wider social consequences of their actions. This aligns with Freire's view of education as a practice of freedom, where learning extends beyond the acquisition of skills to the cultivation of ethical agency and social responsibility (Freire, 1970).

Communication provides another important lens for reconsidering employability. Traditional frameworks have emphasised interpersonal skills (Succi and Canovi, 2020), yet the demands of contemporary practice call for a broader conception that incorporates digital and sociocultural dimensions. In an era of algorithmically mediated interaction, the ability to navigate digital social capital has become critical. This includes managing professional presence, building trust across online platforms, and interpreting digital cues with sensitivity. However, these competencies are shaped by socio-economic access, linguistic diversity, and cultural norms. Developing network literacy, therefore, requires a critical awareness of how digital infrastructures allocate visibility, privilege certain forms of expression, and reproduce systemic inequalities. Educational institutions must go beyond basic training in digital tools by embedding opportunities for students to experiment with and reflect upon their online engagements. This could include co-creating professional content, participating in structured cross-cultural dialogues, or critically auditing the representation of marginalised voices in digital networks. Through such activities, learners develop not only communicative effectiveness but also the capacity to interrogate the values and assumptions that structure digital communication.

Comparative reviews of 21st-century skills frameworks, such as those of Dede (2010) and the Partnership for 21st Century Learning (2009), provide useful taxonomies of the competencies required for life and work in complex contexts. Yet these frameworks often encounter difficulty in practice, particularly in embedding competencies into formal curricula and assessment systems. The issue lies not merely in identifying relevant skills but in creating inclusive, flexible, and context-sensitive means of recognising them. One promising approach is the development of dynamic skills portfolios: digital repositories that document a learner's evolving capabilities across academic, vocational, and community domains. Unlike traditional qualifications, which capture attainment at a fixed point, portfolios provide a longitudinal account of growth. Supported by blockchain-based credentialing, they could deliver both learners and employers a more transparent and nuanced representation of skills and experience (World Economic Forum, 2023). Importantly, such portfolios are not only technical instruments but also pedagogical ones, fostering learner agency by enabling individuals to curate and narrate their own developmental trajectories.

Research such as 'Are They Really Ready to Work?' (Casner-Lotto and Barrington, 2006) continues to highlight gaps in collaboration, problem-solving, and communication. Nonetheless, these gaps should not be attributed solely to deficits in learners, but also to the structural separation of education and employment, which have too often been treated as parallel rather than collaborative systems. A more constructive approach would involve embedding co-created assessment within curriculum design. By involving employers in shaping challenge-led tasks, real-world briefs, and mentoring frameworks, students are given opportunities to apply knowledge in authentic contexts while receiving feedback that aligns with workplace expectations. Such integrative practices foster shared responsibility, positioning industry and education as partners in preparing learners for the evolving demands of professional life.

The cartographer's tale serves as a reminder that employability cannot be understood as a static construct. Just as the map became obsolete once the landscape shifted, so too do rigid employability frameworks risk losing relevance in rapidly changing contexts. This is precisely the concern represented in Figure 1.4, which positions employability not as a fixed outcome but as a dynamic construct shaped by multiple interacting domains. At the core of the model is learner identity, a reminder that employability is lived through learners' values, aspirations, and experiences rather than simply acquired as abstract competencies. When adaptability is framed narrowly as a form of currency in the 'skills economy' (World Economic Forum, 2023), there is a danger of positioning learners as transactional actors. By contrast, the idea of a skills commons aligns more closely with Figure 1.4 as it recognises that identity develops through relationships and supportive ecosystems rather than in isolation.

The framework also draws attention to the influence of societal developments. The accelerating pace of technological and social change shortens the half-life of skills, making resilience and creativity indispensable. UNESCO-UNEVOC's (2023) emphasis on contextual sensitivity in Technical and Vocational Education and Training reflects this dimension of the figure, highlighting that skills formation must respond to cultural and local realities. For instance, rural Ghana's cooperative agricultural practices may be a more authentic means of developing teamwork and leadership than imported classroom-based models. In this way, employability is revealed to be both socially and culturally situated, echoing the broader societal forces identified in the figure. Equally central are institutions and curriculum, which serve as mediating structures in the framework. Traditional models often preserve disciplinary silos, while the demands of the modern labour market require cross-disciplinary hybridity and contextual responsiveness. Bakhshi et al. (2017) reinforce this by identifying creativity as a foundational competency for adaptability and innovation. Yet within the context of the figure, creativity must be understood as a socially embedded and interdisciplinary process. Curriculum design, therefore, needs to create opportunities for collaborative experimentation, critical inquiry, and ethical risk-taking—pedagogical practices that reflect the institutional dimension of the model.

The figure further highlights workplace cultures as an essential domain in which institutional preparation meets professional reality. Employer surveys continue to identify gaps in collaboration, problem-solving, and communication (Casner-Lotto and Barrington, 2006). Yet, as the framework makes clear, these gaps are not solely learner deficits but reflect the persistent separation between education and employment. Embedding co-created assessment and employer collaboration into curriculum design ensures that workplace cultures become part of the pedagogy itself, rather than external benchmarks of readiness. Finally, at the heart of the figure is capability practice, distilled into the interdependent qualities of agency, adaptability, and purpose. These characteristics signal a shift from employability as a fixed destination to employability as an evolving journey. Agency enables learners to shape their developmental pathways; adaptability equips them to navigate shifting environments; and purpose anchors employability in meaningful contributions to society. When creativity is reimagined as a socially situated process and aligned with AI-enabled personalised learning, these capabilities are not only reinforced but also expanded. AI, in this model, serves as an enabler of reflective growth, helping learners to recognise strengths, track progress, and engage in lifelong adaptation. Seen in this light, employability is not about producing perfect maps for fixed terrains but about cultivating the capacity to navigate landscapes that are continually changing. As depicted in Figure 1.4, employability arises through the interplay of learner identity, societal developments, institutional structures, and workplace cultures, and it is sustained by the capability practices of agency, adaptability, and purpose.

The current shift in employability discourse highlights the importance of collective responsibility and sociocultural relevance in determining both what skills are valued and how they are cultivated. Skills cannot be treated as universal abstractions; they must be understood within the sociopolitical, cultural, and ethical contexts of their time. When learners engage with issues meaningful to their communities and co-create solutions, they develop not only technical competence but also a stronger sense of civic agency. In this way, employability becomes more than an individual attribute; it takes on a relational and ethical dimension, linking personal growth with collective transformation. Importantly, recognising the uniqueness of each learner does not imply endorsing individualism or separation. Rather, it involves appreciating the individual as part of a wider whole, where diverse perspectives, experiences, and capabilities make indispensable contributions to shared learning ecologies. This approach resonates with ecological models of education, which frame knowledge, identity, and competence as interdependent and co-constructed. It is through such models that education can foster diversity, interconnectivity, and mutual recognition.

The demands of contemporary work also reveal the limitations of traditional approaches to time management, particularly in digitally mediated and remote environments. While studies confirm a positive relationship between effective time use and organisational productivity (Nnamani and Nnaemake, 2020), the accelerating tempo of digital life complicates linear models of efficiency. In response, the concept of temporal literacy has emerged. This extends beyond conventional management of schedules to encompass ethical, emotional, and cognitive dimensions of time. It entails navigating asynchronous communication, managing cognitive load, and sustaining personal boundaries amid constant digital engagement. Here, time is understood not as a commodity to be optimised but as a lived experience shaped by identity, values, and context. From this perspective, time management becomes an exercise in agency and care, requiring deliberate choices about attention, rest, and relational presence. Educational institutions, therefore, have a role in supporting learners by embedding reflective practices and providing tools for self-regulation that balance productivity with well-being. This reframing positions employability not as the accumulation of isolated skills, but as a holistic, relational, and contextually grounded process—one that places equity, creativity, and care at the centre of educational design.

Globalisation adds further complexity. Leonavičienė, Burinskienė, and Peleckis (2022) emphasise the growing importance of cross-cultural competence, as traditional boundaries blur in professional environments. Genuine intercultural capability, however, involves more than an awareness of difference; it requires active and context-sensitive engagement with diverse values, communication practices, and power dynamics. Critical reflection and ethical responsiveness are therefore vital to move beyond superficial inclusion and towards reciprocal, meaningful cross-cultural relationships. Developments in AI offer opportunities here, particularly in tailoring skills development to intercultural contexts. Yet AI cannot be treated as a neutral instrument: its integration into learning design must be guided by pedagogical principles that account for the complexities of cultural diversity (Erfan, 2024). Thoughtfully applied, AI can support inclusive and responsive environments, helping learners to navigate cultural differences while strengthening ethical awareness.

This perspective also requires a reimagining of employability as a dynamic interplay of networked capabilities, collaborative fluency, and global awareness. Networking, long identified as central to career development (Wanberg et al., 2020), is still often shaped by systemic exclusion. Institutions, therefore, carry an ethical responsibility to cultivate inclusive networking ecosystems, particularly for underrepresented learners. Structured mentorship, targeted alumni engagement, and facilitated professional introductions can all help to redistribute access to social capital. At the same time, AI-driven coaching tools now provide opportunities for personalised guidance, offering real-time feedback on networking and communication practices. Used effectively, such tools can advise learners not only on technical skills but also on the relational and ethical dimensions of career development.

AI also has the potential to act as a bridge, connecting individual learners to wider networks of knowledge and capability. Pembi and Ali (2024) highlight the rising importance of ethical judgement in professional contexts, particularly in relation to emerging technologies and data governance. Ethics education, however, must move beyond prescriptive codes to foster moral imagination—the capacity to engage empathetically with ambiguity and respond thoughtfully in complex situations. Pedagogical approaches such as dialogical learning, case-based simulations, and collaborative reflection provide fertile ground for developing this form of judgement. The central challenge becomes how to structure knowledge acquisition in ways that are technologically mediated yet anchored in enduring ethical principles. An interdisciplinary approach to employability offers one response. By drawing on insights across cultural and disciplinary boundaries, employability can be reframed not as a fixed list of competencies but as a living framework—adaptable, inclusive, and attuned to the ethical complexities of contemporary life. AI, particularly when applied in learner-centred and decentralised ways, can support this vision by personalising development pathways and fostering meaningful connections across domains. In doing so, it can contribute to the formation of graduates who are not only technically proficient but also ethically aware, socially engaged, and capable of exercising judgement in uncertain and interconnected environments.

Topaloglu and Anac (2021) note that the shift to remote work has reshaped team dynamics, requiring new forms of emotional and communicative intelligence. Neves (2024) similarly observes that while digital technologies have enhanced productivity, they have also introduced complexities into how relationships are formed and sustained. In this context, the notion of relational fluency—the ability to build trust, discern tone, and interpret nuance in digitally mediated exchanges—has become indispensable. One might think of it as learning to read the subtle ripples on the surface of a lake: while the water reflects the sky with apparent clarity, the faintest disturbance below can alter its meaning. Likewise, online communication often appears transparent, yet its undertones must be carefully interpreted if trust and collaboration are to endure. This reconfiguration of professional interaction also creates an opportunity to re-centre ethics within employability. Too often treated as peripheral, ethical reasoning should instead form part of everyday professional practice. When judgement and integrity are embedded as habits rather than afterthoughts, they cease to be reactive responses and become the very fabric of professional identity. In this way, ethics is less like a fire extinguisher—reached for in moments of crisis—and more akin to a compass, orienting one's actions consistently and predictably.

The role of mentorship provides another example of evolving practice. Historically, mentorship has been understood as a hierarchical relationship, where knowledge flows from senior to junior (Ragins and Kram, 2007). Yet in increasingly decentralised and diverse workplaces, this linear model is proving less effective. More inclusive approaches—such as peer-to-peer learning, community-driven knowledge exchange, and AI-enabled guidance—better reflect the diverse needs and experiences of the contemporary workforce. Rather than the image of a single master guiding an apprentice along a narrow path, mentorship today resembles a network of bridges across a river: multiple routes, reciprocal exchanges, and a greater emphasis on collective rather than individual progress. Feedback, too, is undergoing redefinition. Once viewed as a top-down transaction, it is now increasingly understood as dialogic, relational, and formative. Boylan et al. (2023) argue that effective feedback must be embedded in mutual trust and respect. In this sense, feedback literacy—the ability to invite, interpret, and apply feedback constructively—has become essential for both learners and professionals. Here, AI technologies offer promising support. By providing personalised, context-sensitive feedback, AI can act as a developmental partner, recognising the unique challenges and strengths of individuals. In so doing, it reframes feedback as a continuous, collaborative dialogue rather than a periodic judgement, sustaining growth through relevance and timeliness.

At the same time, scholarship is beginning to foreground the importance of well-being in employability discourses. Salanova et al. (2014) highlight how structural measures such as flexible scheduling and remote work can support work-life balance, particularly within digitally saturated environments. Their findings suggest that employability cannot be reduced to personal resilience alone, as conventional models have often implied. Rather, systemic and cultural conditions profoundly shape the capacity for reflection, rest, and meaningful connection—factors increasingly recognised as central to sustainable professional practice. To borrow an allegory: it is not enough to equip individuals with stronger sails if the sea itself remains turbulent; the currents and winds—the structural conditions—must also be attended to if the journey is to be sustainable. What emerges is a restorative model of employability, one that positions human flourishing at its core.

Well-being is not ancillary to performance but foundational to the cultivation of long-term capabilities. This approach requires organisations to assume active responsibility for embedding care within professional life, designing rhythms of work that support emotional resilience, intellectual reflection, and opportunities for genuine collaboration. In such a model, employability ceases to be a race for individual survival and becomes instead a shared endeavour in which institutions, teams, and individuals contribute to conditions of mutual growth.

AI offers significant potential for advancing a vision of employability that places well-being at its centre. When designed and implemented with care, AI can act as an enabler rather than a disruptor, supporting both individual development and organisational sustainability. For instance, AI-enabled workload monitoring can help identify early signs of stress or fatigue, prompting timely interventions before these escalate into burnout. Adaptive learning platforms can embed reflective prompts and personalised feedback, encouraging learners and professionals to engage with their values as well as their skills. Similarly, AI-based coaching tools can be used to design flexible working pathways that accommodate personal circumstances, aligning organisational objectives with individual well-being goals. Such applications illustrate how AI can strengthen the connection between capability development and sustainable practice. As contemporary labour markets place increasing value on agility, creativity, and emotional intelligence, AI systems have the capacity to identify and nurture these qualities—provided they are guided by inclusive, transparent, and ethical design principles. From this perspective, well-being should not be seen as an ancillary benefit of employability strategies, but as an integral part of how skills are cultivated, applied, and recognised in an increasingly digital economy. A restorative and AI-informed model of employability would therefore combine flexible working arrangements, institutional accountability, and ethical technological deployment with a broader redefinition of success—one that prioritises human flourishing alongside economic productivity. Within such a model, work becomes not a site of depletion but a space for growth, connection, and meaningful contribution.

AI can also support these efforts by acting as an early-warning system. Intelligent tools can monitor patterns such as excessive screen time, declining engagement, or irregular working hours—signals that may indicate compromised well-being. When governed responsibly, with careful attention to privacy and consent, such systems can provide discreet alerts and recommend appropriate interventions, from adjustments to workloads to access to counselling or rest opportunities. In educational settings, comparable systems could direct students towards well-being services, suggest tailored support strategies, or integrate reflective activities that foreground mental health as part of academic success. Looking forward, the rapid pace of technological change, highlighted by the World Economic Forum (2023), emphasises the urgency of preparing learners and workers not merely to adapt to disruption but to shape it. This requires cultivating what Miller (2018) terms futures literacy—the ability to imagine, interrogate, and co-create alternative futures. Embedding futures literacy within employability-focused education calls for moving beyond technical skill acquisition towards foresight practices such as scenario planning, systems thinking, and speculative design. These approaches encourage learners to view uncertainty not with anxiety but with creativity and resilience. Furthermore, creating inclusive spaces for dialogue about possible futures empowers individuals and communities to shape trajectories that are ethical, sustainable, and socially just.

One might think of employability as a garden. If the soil is poor and the climate harsh, no amount of individual effort will allow the plants to flourish. But when the conditions are carefully cultivated—balanced nutrients, supportive structures, and attentive care—the garden not only grows but also thrives, each plant contributing uniquely to the whole. This allegory reflects the central argument advanced in this section: employability cannot be reduced to isolated skills or individual resilience, but must be understood as a relational construct shaped by identity, society, institutions, workplaces, and capability practices. Taken together, the perspectives explored here call for a reconceptualisation of employability. Within the framework illustrated above, learner identity is enriched when well-being is recognised not as an optional benefit but as a necessary foundation for growth. Societal developments, including rapid technological change, demand that employability be aligned with values of human sustainability rather than framed solely in economic terms. Institutions and curricula play a crucial role in embedding these principles, integrating digital tools such as AI not merely to increase productivity but to foster ethical, inclusive, and imaginative forms of learning. Workplace cultures, in turn, must move beyond narrow performance metrics to embrace practices that support collaboration, trust, and care, ensuring that professional life is not a site of depletion but one of connection and meaningful contribution. At the centre of Figure 1.4, capability practice—expressed through agency, adaptability, and purpose—becomes the mechanism through which these dimensions interact, guiding learners in shaping their development with resilience, creativity, and foresight. Finally, AI holds particular promise in this vision. When ethically governed, it can serve as a constructive partner in both education and employment: monitoring well-being, tailoring developmental pathways, and supporting flexible forms of work and learning. Futures literacy, meanwhile, provides the imaginative capacity to anticipate disruption and to co-create more sustainable and socially just trajectories. These elements combined highlight that employability is best understood as a holistic and evolving construct—one that values human flourishing, embraces technological possibility, and nurtures the creative and ethical capacities needed to navigate an uncertain world.

In summary, this section has interrogated the limitations of traditional models of employability, particularly their tendency to frame skills as static or individualised. By engaging critically with recent scholarship, it has shown the need for more adaptive, context-sensitive conceptions that evolve in relation to broader transformations in society, technology, and work. Importantly, it has highlighted the potential of AI not only as a tool for efficiency but also as an enabler of ethical and inclusive approaches to capability development. Seen through the employability framework discussed here, this analysis demonstrates that employability emerges at the intersection of identity, societal change, institutional design, and workplace culture and is sustained by capability practices that affirm human sustainability and lifelong learning. This reconceptualisation also opens avenues for further interdisciplinary research, which can help clarify how such models might enable us to interpret the past more critically, respond to the present more effectively, and engage with the future more imaginatively. The next section will extend this argument by examining the changing nature of work and skills in the 21st century, with particular attention to their implications for education, policy, and practice.

RECONCEPTUALISING EMPLOYABILITY IN THE ERA OF AI AND AUTOMATION: CRITICAL PERSPECTIVES FROM CONTEMPORARY SCHOLARSHIP

Building on the preceding discussion, it is increasingly evident that the rapid acceleration of automation and AI is reshaping established norms of work and prompting a fundamental reassessment of what it means to be employable in the 21st century. These shifts raise important questions not only about the kinds of skills required for success in contemporary workplaces but also about the systemic conditions that enable or inhibit individuals from developing them. Earlier arguments have highlighted the need to reconceptualise employability as dynamic, ethical, and technologically attuned. This section extends that position by engaging with contemporary scholarship that calls for a more nuanced and systemic understanding of labour, skills, and workforce development in the context of digital transformation. At stake is not only how individuals prepare for work but also how education systems, organisations, and policy frameworks collectively respond to technological disruption.

The growth of automation presents both challenges and opportunities. On the one hand, routine tasks are increasingly performed by intelligent systems, destabilising traditional models of employment. On the other hand, new possibilities are opening for human-centred competencies that resist automation, including critical thinking, ethical reasoning, and emotional intelligence. Such developments call into question the adequacy of existing employability frameworks, many of which remain anchored in static, credential-based approaches. A growing consensus suggests that employability should instead be understood as a continuous, relational process rather than a fixed outcome. This shift prompts several critical questions. First, what does employability now mean in a world where technology operates not merely as a tool but as a co-participant in work processes? Employability must extend beyond functional or technical proficiency to encompass the capacity to navigate uncertainty, engage with complex systems, and maintain ethical orientation in technologically mediated environments. In this sense, the focus moves from task-specific readiness towards lifelong adaptability and capability development. Second, what factors enable or constrain individuals in acquiring these capabilities? The development of future-facing competencies is shaped not only by personal motivation or aptitude but also by broader systemic conditions. Access to inclusive education, digital infrastructure, social capital, and institutional support all influence the extent to which individuals can engage meaningfully with new technologies. AI itself may play a constructive role in this process, offering personalised learning pathways, identifying skills gaps, and providing context-sensitive feedback. Yet this potential must be carefully managed to avoid reinforcing inequality or reducing learning to algorithmic optimisation.

Finally, how might these observable changes in skills development inform a new foundation for employability? As labour markets become more dynamic, linear career trajectories are giving way to fragmented, portfolio-based pathways. This fluidity demands frameworks that are flexible, integrative, and responsive to change. Some studies highlight the growing importance of transversal skills, hybrid human–AI collaboration, and the expansion of gig and platform economies. These patterns suggest that employability will increasingly require foresight, creativity, and ethical imagination. Such insights should not be treated simply as descriptive trends but actively theorised and embedded in policy, curriculum, and practice. In this light, employability may be reconceptualised as a socially embedded, technologically informed, and ethically responsive construct. This perspective recognises that individual capability is shaped by wider institutional, technological, and socio-economic dynamics and that systemic thinking is essential in addressing the challenges and opportunities of the digital age. The discussion that follows develops these themes further, focusing in particular on how AI may not only accelerate change but also enable more inclusive and sustainable models of professional and personal development.

Susskind (2020) makes an important contribution to debates on the future of work by examining how advanced technologies, particularly AI, are reshaping employment. Rather than presenting this shift simply as a threat to job security, he invites a broader philosophical and policy discussion about how societies might reconfigure their notions of meaning, contribution, and well-being in contexts where paid employment may no longer stand as the central marker of economic participation. This perspective resonates with Sen's (1999) capability approach, which emphasises people's freedom to lead lives they have reason to value. It shifts attention away from work as a narrow economic transaction towards a richer understanding of employability as the capacity to flourish, participate meaningfully in community life, and pursue both personal and collective goals.

An allegory helps capture this point: if employment has traditionally been seen as the 'spine' that holds the body of society upright, then the growing role of AI suggests that we may need a new anatomy—one in which support and strength are distributed across many interdependent structures. In such a body, employability is not a single bone of economic utility, but a circulatory system that sustains growth, belonging, and purpose. Practically, this vision requires organisations to think beyond simply offering jobs. They must cultivate inclusive environments that support performance and productivity while also fostering agency, ethical awareness, and psychological well-being. This represents a reorientation in workforce development, where the focus is not only on output but also on nurturing conditions for human flourishing. The integration of AI into this landscape carries significant implications. Rather than positioning AI as a replacement for human judgement, it is more fruitful to view it as a collaborative partner—an extension of human capability. In practice, this may involve AI systems that identify skill gaps, support reflective practice, or deliver adaptive learning pathways tailored to individual needs and contexts. In this framing, AI is less a machine that dictates outcomes and more a mirror that helps individuals see where they might grow, offering guidance without undermining autonomy. Such a vision aligns closely with what has been described as a restorative model of employability—a framework that situates well-being, ethical deliberation, and adaptability at the centre of sustainable workforce development. Here, individuals are not treated as cogs in an economic machine but as moral and relational agents, capable of responding to uncertainty with empathy and foresight. This approach echoes humanistic management principles (Pirson, 2017), which stress the safeguarding of human dignity and the pursuit of shared flourishing as the basis of responsible organisational practice.

Realising this model in practice requires cultures and policies that actively enable reflection, continuous learning, and well-being. For instance, AI-enabled feedback systems could be used not simply to monitor performance but to open constructive dialogues between managers and employees. Similarly, predictive analytics might function not as a mechanism of control but as an instrument of care—identifying early signs of stress or disengagement so that timely, compassionate interventions can be made. The allegory here is of a lighthouse: technology should not act as a searchlight that exposes and disciplines, but as a beacon that guides and protects, enabling safer passage through turbulent waters. Collectively, Susskind's analysis challenges narrow economistic models of employability by foregrounding its ethical and existential dimensions. The integration of AI, from this perspective, is not merely a matter of efficiency but of augmenting human potential and fostering environments where individuals and communities can thrive. Employability in the age of AI thus becomes not a static outcome, but a shared project of human development—sustained by reflection, dignity, and collective flourishing.

Arntz, Gregory, and Zierahn's (2016) empirical analysis provides an important corrective to deterministic accounts of automation by distinguishing between the automation of specific tasks and the redundancy of entire jobs. Their findings suggest that while certain tasks may be automated, this rarely results in the wholesale elimination of roles. This distinction reframes automation not as an existential threat to employment, but as a catalyst for reconfiguring work. It points towards the potential of AI to augment, rather than replace, human labour, especially when embedded within ethical and context-sensitive frameworks. This perspective highlights the relevance of task hybridisation, in which human and AI operate in complementary ways. Instead of displacing workers, AI can enhance human capacity by reallocating effort towards higher-value, non-automatable tasks. Such an approach has practical implications for workforce development: when employees experience AI as a resource for growth and adaptability rather than as a threat, trust and constructive engagement are more likely to follow. This is particularly relevant to debates on work–life balance, where ethically deployed AI can ease workloads, enable flexible arrangements, and provide tailored support mechanisms that strengthen well-being.

Bessen (2019) develops this argument by emphasising the mediating role of labour demand in shaping automation outcomes. New technologies often generate demand for human capabilities that remain difficult to replicate—creativity, interpersonal engagement, and complex problem-solving among them. This insight strengthens the case for orienting employability not solely around technical skills but around those distinctly human attributes that complement evolving workplace needs. AI-enabled systems, when designed with ethical oversight and inclusive participation, can support this shift by mapping individual strengths, anticipating emerging skill requirements, and offering tailored opportunities for development. Yet the potential of such systems depends on transparency, fairness, and equitable access; without these safeguards, algorithmic tools risk reproducing existing inequalities.

At a broader level, reports from the McKinsey Global Institute (Manyika et al., 2017; Chui et al., 2016) highlight the inevitability of large-scale transitions in the global workforce. While acknowledging that some roles will decline, these analyses also point to growth in fields such as healthcare, education, and technology services. The challenge, then, lies less in resisting change and more in shaping pathways of transition that are timely, equitable, and sustainable. This requires systems that embed lifelong learning and career mobility into the fabric of work, moving beyond piecemeal or reactive interventions. Upskilling, from this perspective, cannot be treated as a one-off response to disruption but must be sustained as an ongoing feature of professional life. Concerns about AI integration—ranging from limited public understanding to questions of transparency and the risks of biased data—remain pressing. These anxieties are not unfounded, yet they need not preclude AI's constructive role. With appropriate attention to governance, ethical design, and public engagement, AI can be integrated as a foundational component of employability and organisational development. In this light, automation should be seen less as a story of displacement and more as an opportunity to reimagine the relationship between technology, work, and human flourishing.

Brynjolfsson and McAfee's The Second Machine Age (2014) raises critical concerns about the socio-economic consequences of technological advancement, arguing that productivity improvements driven by AI often accrue disproportionately to capital rather than labour, thereby deepening existing inequalities. This insight introduces the theoretical lens of technological inequality, which highlights the risk that innovation, if left unguided, may exacerbate structural disparities. Addressing this requires deliberate policy measures, such as investment in digital infrastructure, the design of accessible AI tools that broaden participation, and stronger protections for workers in precarious roles. In this way, technological progress can be aligned with principles of justice and shared prosperity, rather than reinforcing exclusion. This emphasis on equity resonates with the International Labour Organization's (2021) findings on digital labour platforms, where algorithmic control and diminished protections highlight the fragility of workers' rights in the platform economy. At the same time, Acemoglu and Restrepo (2019) offer a more granular perspective by introducing the concept of task reallocation. Their analysis shows that automation rarely eliminates jobs outright; instead, it redistributes tasks, producing new patterns of collaboration between humans and machines. Whereas the previous section of this chapter highlighted augmentation at the level of skills and employability, this contribution highlights the structural reorganisation of work at the level of tasks.

The implications for education and workforce development are significant. Embedding task awareness into curricula and training programmes offers a pathway towards more adaptive and learner-centred approaches. By critically engaging with how roles evolve through automation or platform-based models, learners cultivate a reflexive orientation that goes beyond technical competence. This awareness enables them to anticipate changes, recognise new demands, and proactively pursue relevant opportunities. Fostering task literacy also encourages training pathways that emerge organically from workplace realities rather than being imposed through rigid, prescriptive models. As employees and learners co-create development strategies with employers or institutions, training becomes more context-specific, responsive, and sustainable. In contrast to static curricula that quickly become outdated, such approaches allow learning to evolve alongside professional practice. This adaptive model resembles rainfall rather than irrigation: instead of flowing narrowly along pre-set channels, it nourishes growth wherever the conditions demand it. When viewed alongside the previous section's focus on task hybridisation, this point extends the argument by showing that employability depends not only on how humans and AI collaborate but also on how tasks themselves are redistributed within changing labour markets. Taken together, these perspectives highlight the importance of moving beyond deterministic narratives of automation. They invite us to conceive employability as a dynamic process that is at once ethical, adaptive, and grounded in lived work practices—where technological change is not simply endured but actively shaped towards inclusive and sustainable outcomes.

The literature on the gig and platform economy adds considerable complexity to contemporary understandings of labour, particularly in relation to fragmentation and algorithmic governance. De Stefano (2016) critiques the rise of the 'just-in-time' workforce, while Wood et al. (2019) highlight the disjunction between the autonomy platforms promise and the algorithmic oversight they impose. These analyses highlight the need for platform literacy—a set of competencies enabling workers to navigate opaque systems, interpret algorithmic decisions, and exercise agency in technologically mediated environments. Within this context, AI systems need not be limited to enhancing efficiency. When developed with ethical intent, they could support transparency by helping workers to decode platform logic, understand performance metrics, and receive feedback that strengthens their agency and safeguards their reputations in digital ecosystems. This vision calls for redefined support structures that move beyond technical training to include critical awareness of how digital infrastructures shape working lives.

Standing's (2011) concept of the precariat, characterised by chronic insecurity, further draws attention to the sociopolitical consequences of these transformations. Zwick (2018) and Fleming (2017) deepen this critique by exposing how neoliberal labour regimes, while promoting flexibility, often obscure the erosion of rights and protections. Such perspectives reveal the limits of employability models that privilege productivity while neglecting broader measures of value. They suggest the need to move beyond narrow human capital framings that reduce individuals to economic outputs, towards recognising skills as expressions of social, civic, and personal contribution. Reframing employability in this way opens space for more inclusive and humane interpretations of work in the digital age. Policy developments have begun to echo these shifts. Interventions by UNESCO (2022a) and the European Commission (2021) emphasise the creation of ecosystems of learning—networks that connect formal education, employers, civil society, and digital innovators. Within such ecosystems, AI evolves from a pedagogical tool into an enabling infrastructure capable of supporting systems that continuously adapt to technological and economic change. For example, AI-driven skills intelligence platforms, if ethically governed, can provide real-time labour market insights that inform not only individual career pathways but also institutional curricula and national training strategies. Such systems enable more participatory and responsive planning, which is increasingly vital in volatile labour markets.

In parallel, emerging policy approaches advocate a move from rigid qualification-based systems towards more flexible recognitions of learning, such as skills passports and competency portfolios. These innovations, often reliant on AI for verification and analysis, make visible the value of informal and cross-sector learning, thereby reducing barriers to mobility and enabling more inclusive transitions. Yet such tools also bring risks: without robust ethical oversight, algorithmic biases or exclusionary designs may deepen existing inequalities. The challenge, then, is not only to implement AI but also to ensure it is deployed in ways that safeguard human agency, reinforce equitable access to opportunity, and foster shared responsibility for societal well-being.

In summary, this section has examined how the accelerating integration of AI and automation is reshaping our understanding of employability. It has argued for a shift away from static, credential-focused models towards more adaptive, ethically informed, and human-centred approaches. Employability must be seen as a continuous and socially embedded process—shaped not only by technological change but also by the institutional, cultural, and structural conditions that enable or constrain agency, inclusion, and flourishing. While AI presents clear opportunities for personalised and sustainable development, its benefits depend on equitable access, ethical governance, and supportive organisational cultures. The restorative model of employability offers a productive framework in this regard, placing human dignity, reflective practice, and well-being at the heart of workforce development. To grasp the significance of this reconceptualisation, one might turn to a story from 25,000 years ago, when early humans painted on the walls of caves such as Lascaux. These images—of animals, hunts, and rituals—were not simply records of survival, but reflections of collective imagination and identity. The hunters did not paint only to capture what was; they painted to prepare for what might be, to pass knowledge across generations, and to make sense of their place in a changing world. Much like those cave paintings, employability today cannot be understood solely in terms of immediate utility or functional output. It is also about cultivating imagination, sustaining community, and preparing for uncertain futures. If early humans used pigments and firelight to navigate their world, we now use algorithms and platforms—but the underlying challenge remains: to ensure that our tools serve human flourishing rather than diminish it.

This allegory highlights the central argument of the section: technology must be integrated in ways that enhance human capacity, preserve dignity, and foster shared meaning. Just as cave art was a communal act that bound individuals to one another and to their environment, employability in the age of AI must be understood as relational and collective, not simply individual and instrumental. This naturally leads to the next line of inquiry: the kinds of skills that will matter most in this transformed landscape. Beyond technical proficiency, there is a growing need for cognitive and interpersonal capacities—adaptability, collaboration, and critical engagement—that sustain resilience in dynamic contexts. Understanding how such skills are cultivated, applied, and valued will be essential in building a future-oriented employability agenda. It is here that the concept of skills dynamics becomes increasingly salient, inviting exploration of how individuals and institutions can together respond to the evolving nature of work with foresight, creativity, and care.

REFRAMING SKILLS IN THE DIGITAL ERA: FROM TECHNICAL PROFICIENCY TO COGNITIVE AND INTERPERSONAL AGILITY

As the allegory of the cave paintings reminds us, human flourishing has long depended on the ability to imagine futures, to share knowledge, and to embed meaning in collective practice. Yet imagination alone was never sufficient. Alongside these symbolic acts, early humans developed tools from stone and bone, reshaping them across generations to meet shifting challenges. These tools were never static: each adaptation reflected a response to environmental pressures, new opportunities, or collective needs. The concept of skills dynamics reflects a similar process in contemporary contexts. Just as tool-making enabled early communities to survive and thrive, modern learners and workers must cultivate adaptive repertoires of capability that extend beyond technical proficiency. Critical thinking, collaboration, ethical discernment, and digital fluency can be thought of as the sharpened edges of employability—skills that allow individuals to navigate complex and uncertain landscapes with agility. Viewed through the employability framework, this dynamic process operates across interconnected dimensions. Identity is reshaped as learners recognise themselves not as holders of fixed attributes but as participants in lifelong adaptation. Society provides the wider context, where technological change, cultural norms, and economic structures determine what skills are valued and how they are used. Institutions and curricula act as mediators, embedding flexibility and ethical orientation into education and training systems. Workplace cultures function as testing grounds where skills are enacted, reconfigured, and revalued. At the centre, capability practice—expressed through agency, adaptability, and purpose—links these layers, creating a sustainable and coherent model of employability.

In this light, skills development is not a static acquisition but a living, ecological process—symbolic, adaptive, and collective. Just as cave paintings and tool-making were embedded within the lifeworlds of early communities, employability today must be situated within interconnected ecosystems that link learners, institutions, workplaces, and societies. The challenge is not merely to accumulate competencies but to sustain processes of renewal that prepare individuals and communities to meet the demands of the 21st century with foresight, creativity, and care. Following on from the previous section, which examined how automation, digital transformation, and the platform economy are reshaping the nature of work, this discussion turns to the evolving landscape of skills. Contemporary professional environments increasingly demand a balance between advanced technical expertise and enhanced cognitive and interpersonal capabilities. As technological change accelerates, the ability to combine specialised proficiency with adaptability, creativity, and effective collaboration has become indispensable. The emerging consensus reveals that the digital age has fundamentally altered employability. Early debates on automation focused primarily on job displacement, particularly in routine-based occupations. More scholarship, however, adopts a nuanced perspective—emphasising not simple substitution, but the evolving interplay between human and machine capabilities. The discourse has shifted from a binary narrative of job loss towards one of transformation, where technical proficiency alone is insufficient. The capacity to adapt cognitively, to communicate with nuance, and to demonstrate social and emotional intelligence has become central to employability. This recalibration suggests that the so-called 21st-century skills economy is not a distant prospect but a present reality.

Autor's (2015) historical analysis illustrates that while technological innovation has rendered some jobs obsolete, particularly those reliant on repetitive, rule-based tasks, it has also generated demand for new forms of work privileging complex reasoning, creativity, and adaptability. His work highlights the enduring value of human judgement in contexts shaped by ambiguity, ethics, and social nuance. Frey and Osborne (2017), using a probabilistic model, estimate that nearly half of jobs in the United States face a high risk of automation. Yet their findings also highlight the resilience of roles involving social interaction, creative intelligence, and non-routine analytical tasks—capacities that, at least for now, remain distinctly human. Seen in this light, the allegory of cave paintings and tool-making not only illustrates the adaptive and symbolic foundations of human development but also reminds us that employability has always been more than a technical exercise. Just as early communities drew meaning and cohesion from shared symbols and practices, so too must contemporary models of employability embed well-being, dignity, and ethical agency at their core. The restorative model of employability reflects this orientation: positioning skills not merely as instruments of productivity, but as capacities for sustaining human connection, navigating uncertainty, and contributing to collective flourishing. Much like the cave paintings that endured for millennia, these relational and ethical dimensions of work remain vital markers of what it means to be human in an age increasingly shaped by intelligent machines.

Some scholarly interventions suggest that the very definition of 'skill' in the modern economy is undergoing significant reconfiguration. The traditional emphasis on task execution is being displaced by a broader understanding that foregrounds adaptability, lifelong learning, and the capacity to engage critically and productively with technological systems. Within this reframing, the assumption that job losses resulting from automation are inherently negative appears increasingly limited. Rather than viewing technological disruption exclusively through the lens of dislocation, it may be more constructive to approach it as a prompt for recalibration—an opportunity to revisit and redefine the parameters of work, skill, and value. From this perspective, so-called 'job losses' are better understood as redirections: shifts towards roles that demand cognitive flexibility, ethical awareness, and collaborative competence. For both workers and learners, this implies not only technical upskilling but also the cultivation of broader capacities that position human agency at the centre of socio-technical systems. The central challenge, then, is not simply to prepare for a technologically mediated future, but to ensure that evolving conceptions of employability remain inclusive, sustainable, and human-centred. This demands coordinated action by educational institutions, employers, and governments to nurture environments where digital literacy is developed alongside interpersonal and ethical capabilities, equipping individuals to thrive amid uncertainty and change.

Empirical evidence reinforces this trajectory. Deming's (2017) analysis demonstrates the increasing prevalence of hybrid roles that combine analytical rigour with interpersonal skills, reflecting the growing importance of collaboration, adaptability, and nuanced communication in knowledge-intensive economies. Similarly, the OECD's Skills Outlook

(2019a) stresses the urgency of embedding digital literacy together with flexibility, creativity, and social awareness as essential competencies for navigating the unpredictability of digital transformation. The case of Amina, a mid-career professional in a logistics firm, illustrates these dynamics in practice. At the outset of her company's digital transition, she feared redundancy as her routine tasks were gradually automated. Yet rather than being displaced, she was retrained to manage AI-powered systems, drawing upon her expertise in client relations and operational nuance to interpret data insights and tailor solutions. Her role evolved from execution to orchestration, where human judgement and machine capacity worked in tandem.

Viewed allegorically, Amina's journey reflects the broader trajectory of employability in the digital era. Initially, her identity as a worker was destabilised by the threat of technological redundancy. Through retraining, however, her sense of self shifted from task-based execution to adaptive orchestration, exemplifying how identity is continually reshaped through engagement with evolving contexts. At the level of society, her story highlights the wider anxieties of labour markets in transition, where automation provokes fears of loss but also creates opportunities for redefinition. Her successful adaptation depended not only on personal resilience but also on the presence of institutional structures—training programmes, supportive management, and policies attentive to workforce development—that enabled her to redirect her capacities rather than see them diminished. The workplace functioned as a critical testing ground, providing both the challenge of disruption and the opportunity for renewed collaboration between human judgement and technological systems. At the centre of these dimensions lies capability practice, expressed in Amina's agency, adaptability, and purpose: qualities that enabled her to integrate technical systems with interpersonal insight, transforming disruption into an avenue for growth.

In this sense, Amina's story serves as both an allegory and an analytical case. It shows that employability, when framed through the dynamics of identity, society, institutions, workplace, and capability practice, is best understood not as a static condition but as an ongoing negotiation. Her trajectory mirrors the broader imperative facing 21st-century societies: to reimagine disruption not as erasure but as renewal, ensuring that the integration of AI enriches rather than diminishes the human contribution to work. Just as cave paintings and tool-making once coexisted as different but complementary expressions of human capability, so too can human and machine collaboration shape a more inclusive and sustainable vision of employability. This example helps dismantle the persistent myth that AI and automation will inevitably render human workers obsolete. While it is undeniable that certain occupations are being reshaped or phased out, it is reductive to cast this transformation as a zero-sum contest between humans and machines. Such a view neglects the enduring significance of human intuition, ethical reasoning, and imaginative foresight—capacities that remain beyond the reach of even the most advanced algorithms. Indeed, the myth of inevitable replacement is not only misleading but also counterproductive, as it distracts from the more pressing task of shaping technological ecosystems that are inclusive, ethical, and oriented towards shared flourishing.

The persistence of automation myths is not without consequence. Left unchallenged, or worse, deployed to justify uncritical technological adoption, such narratives risk obscuring the ethical and social responsibilities that must guide innovation. The introduction of AI systems without robust frameworks for human oversight, transparency, and contextual interpretation carries genuine risks: exacerbating inequality, undermining trust, and displacing workers without offering viable pathways for reskilling. In such circumstances, the issue lies not in the technology itself but in the absence of intentional and ethically informed design. The task, therefore, is to reconceptualise AI and automation not as existential threats but as potential enablers of personalised support, augmented decision-making, and more adaptive working environments. This requires shifting the debate from fear to foresight—from asking whether technology will 'take' jobs to considering how it might contribute to more meaningful forms of work. Such a shift demands recalibration across policy, pedagogy, and organisational practice to ensure that technological development is guided by ethical considerations and aligned with human development goals. What is often framed as a risk of obsolescence may instead be a transformative opportunity, provided that integration is attentive to context, equity, and sustainability. Misunderstanding this dynamic risks perpetuating myths and, more critically, forfeiting the chance to reimagine work in ways that elevate both human and technological potential.

Projections by the McKinsey Global Institute reinforce this point, estimating that by 2030 demand for emotional and social skills will rise by 24 per cent across Europe and the United States—outpacing growth in technical competencies (Bughin et al., 2018). This projection supports an emerging consensus: workforce resilience depends less on technical expertise in isolation than on the holistic development of human capabilities, particularly empathy, adaptability, and collaborative intelligence. These are qualities that cannot be replicated by machines; they rest in human judgement, ethical reflection, and contextual awareness. Bessen (2015) further illuminates this trajectory, showing that technological progress rarely eliminates human labour outright but more often stimulates demand for complementary aptitudes. His analysis highlights a subtle but crucial point: adaptation in the digital age is not a passive response to disruption, but an active, iterative process of engaging with new tools, reframing problems, and co-evolving with technology. This requires moving beyond static models of skill acquisition towards dynamic, experiential learning—learning that emerges through practice, reflection, and continual adjustment.

Much of the literature and policy discourse focuses on charting the transformations brought about by automation and AI, yet less attention is devoted to the more fundamental questions that determine how societies can respond: What should we cultivate in human workers—not only in terms of technical skills but also in ways of thinking, imagining, and relating? And how might these capacities be embedded within educational and institutional systems? These questions remain underexplored, but they are central to envisioning a future where the coexistence of human and AI is not framed as a site of tension but as a space for collaboration. The story of Daniel, a project manager in a global consultancy firm, offers more than an individual example: it can be read as an allegory for the broader transformation of employability in an AI-mediated world. Initially trained in data analytics, Daniel discovered that technical fluency alone could not address the complexity of client expectations or the dynamics of global teams. As AI systems automated forecasting and workflow management, he redefined his role by cultivating intuitive reasoning, facilitating cross-departmental dialogue, and contextualising AI insights within organisational strategies. His work evolved from controlling systems to orchestrating meaning—acting as an interpreter within a hybrid workplace.

Viewed through the employability framework, Daniel's experience illuminates how adaptation unfolds across interconnected dimensions. At the level of identity, his professional self-concept shifted from being a data technician to a reflective interpreter, showing how workers must continuously reimagine themselves within evolving socio-technical contexts. Within society, his trajectory reflects the broader challenge of adjusting cultural expectations about the value of work: from task execution to the integration of human insight with machine capacity. Institutions, in turn, play a pivotal role by embedding reflective, interpersonal, and ethical capacities into education and training, ensuring that workers like Daniel are prepared to thrive in hybrid environments. The workplace emerges as the immediate arena where these capacities are tested, reshaped, and validated in practice, demanding organisational cultures that reward not only efficiency but also collaboration, ethical reasoning, and emotional intelligence. At the centre lies capability practice—Daniel's ability to exercise agency, adapt to disruption, and infuse technological processes with purpose and meaning.

Daniel's allegory complements both the earlier cave paintings and Amina's story, together forming a continuum of how employability has evolved. The cave paintings symbolise the enduring human need to embed meaning within collective practice, reminding us that work has always been tied to imagination, knowledge-sharing, and cultural survival. Amina's journey illustrates how disruption, rather than signalling obsolescence, can be reframed as redirection when supported by institutions and workplaces that enable renewal. Daniel's experience extends this trajectory into the digital present, showing how employability in an AI-mediated world is enacted through interpretive and relational capacities—metacognition, emotional resilience, and moral imagination. Taken together, these capacities reposition humans not as peripheral to technological systems but as central agents in their interpretation and application. Daniel's story, therefore, represents more than one professional adapting to organisational change: it serves as an allegory for societies learning to navigate the new terrain of work. Just as ancient navigators combined inherited wisdom with newly fashioned instruments to cross uncharted seas, contemporary workers and institutions must learn to combine enduring human sensibilities with digital systems. In doing so, they can guide collective journeys towards futures that are both technologically innovative and ethically grounded.

Moral imagination functions as a vital bridge between human judgement and the ethical dimensions of technology. While algorithms are designed to optimise within fixed parameters, they cannot grapple with moral ambiguity or the wider social consequences of their use. Here, human actors must intervene by exercising moral imagination: anticipating how technological decisions may affect diverse communities, recognising whose perspectives are absent, and envisioning more just alternatives. This responsibility becomes particularly pressing when AI risks reinforcing inequities or producing outcomes that prioritise efficiency over fairness. Moral imagination thus demands more than procedural compliance; it invites practitioners to question whether technological outputs genuinely serve collective human goals. Together with metacognitive awareness and emotional regulation, moral imagination forms the ethical foundation of a restorative model of employability. This model shifts the understanding of technology from an external force that threatens human agency to a partner that augments human capacity. Within such a framework, individuals are not reduced to operators of technical systems; rather, they serve as interpreters, co-authors, and guardians of meaning within socio-technical landscapes. Education and organisational practice, therefore, must embed these qualities deliberately—ensuring that decision-making in AI-mediated contexts remains transparent, reflective, and human-centred.

The empirical work of Cetindamar Kozanoglu and Abedin (2021) reinforces this orientation, showing that cognitive agility—when paired with digital fluency and openness to transformation—enables individuals to thrive in uncertain, rapidly evolving environments. Their research highlights the value of dispositions rooted in curiosity, reflexivity, and a willingness to revise assumptions. These attributes complement moral imagination, for both demand an active engagement with technology that resists uncritical reliance on machine outputs. Crucially, such practitioners do not simply interpret algorithmic insights but interrogate them, situating them within broader historical, social, and ethical contexts. In this sense, the restorative model of employability reframes skills as more than technical competencies. It positions human beings as central agents of ethical judgement and relational practice, capable of guiding technological innovation towards futures that uphold dignity, inclusivity, and shared flourishing. Cultivating metacognitive awareness, emotional regulation, and moral imagination is therefore not a peripheral endeavour but a central requirement for employability in the digital age—ensuring that AI enhances, rather than undermines, the values essential to human and collective development.

This requires a reconfiguration of how we understand skill. Technological proficiency and ethical awareness should not be treated as separate domains, but as interdependent dimensions of what may be termed socio-technical competence. Such competence encompasses the technical ability to operate effectively in digital environments while also engaging critically with their implications—recognising whose perspectives are represented or excluded and responding with creativity, empathy, and foresight. To foster this, educational and organisational systems must move beyond fragmented, compliance-based training models. They should instead embed practices that encourage cross-disciplinary thinking, ethical reflexivity, and systems-level awareness. Deliberative exercises, ethically charged simulations, and collaborative design projects can surface the value-laden character of technological work, preparing individuals not only to adapt to AI but also to influence its design and deployment in ways that promote collective responsibility and human dignity. In this light, moral imagination becomes inseparable from a wider pedagogical imperative: equipping learners with the intellectual and emotional tools to navigate complex moral terrain and to respond to technological change with critical, compassionate agency. Such preparation is central to sustaining models of human–AI coexistence that uphold shared meaning, social justice, and ethical integrity.

Muduli and Pandya (2018) contribute to this evolving discourse by emphasising workforce agility as a set of adaptive behaviours that enable effective responses to technological change. Traits such as resilience, openness to innovation, and collaborative orientation are no longer peripheral but are increasingly recognised as essential for both individual and organisational sustainability. Their analysis highlights that agility is not a spontaneous reaction but a cultivated capacity, shaped by leadership, workplace culture, and learning opportunities. Complementing this, Colbert et al. (2016) propose an integrated approach to competence that disrupts the traditional division between so-called 'hard' and 'soft' skills. Their framework interweaves knowledge acquisition, cognitive engagement, and sensory-motor coordination, suggesting that effective performance in contemporary work arises from the dynamic interplay of these elements. This perspective advances a holistic conception of competence that reflects the realities of interdisciplinary tasks and hybrid human–machine collaboration. Together, these insights mark a broader shift in the discourse on employability. What emerges is a nuanced view of capability that emphasises not only what individuals can do but also how they do it, with whom, and under what conditions. Success in this context is not reducible to technical expertise but is grounded in the ability to think relationally, act responsively, and contribute meaningfully within fluid and technologically mediated environments.

Building on this discussion, the chapter now turns to the concept of skills dynamics, which offers a more expansive framework for understanding adaptability in the digital era. Skills dynamics, as outlined earlier, refers to the continuous evolution, interaction, and contextual application of competencies across the life course. It captures not only how skills are acquired and refined but also how they are reconfigured in response to shifting societal, technological, and economic contexts. This perspective challenges linear and compartmentalised models of skill acquisition, inviting instead a recognition of learning as a lifelong, adaptive, and relational process. The work of the National Research Council (2012) is particularly relevant here, advancing the notion of transferable knowledge. Their emphasis on cognitive strategies such as metacognition, critical thinking, and adaptive problem-solving highlights the need for competencies that endure beyond narrow technical domains. Rather than preparing individuals for fixed tasks, the goal is to equip them to navigate unanticipated challenges, synthesise knowledge across disciplines, and exercise informed judgement in complex environments. This aligns with contemporary calls for educational and professional systems that prioritise intellectual agility, ethical discernment, and the ability to learn through and within complexity.

The dynamics of skill development may be likened to the evolution of a river delta over centuries. As waters flow, new channels emerge, old ones shift or dry up, and fertile ground is created where streams converge. The delta is never complete; it is constantly reshaped by changing currents, weather patterns, and ecological demands. In much the same way, skills evolve through continual interaction with shifting social, technological, and institutional landscapes. Some capacities fade, others are redirected, and new ones take root in response to emerging pressures. Just as the strength of the delta lies in its interconnectedness and adaptability, so too does employability rest on the ability to sustain fluid, relational capacities that can nourish individual growth while sustaining collective flourishing. Reframing employability through the perspective of skills dynamics invites us to move beyond the static conception of human capital as something merely accumulated. Instead, it recognises that skills are relational, context-dependent, and inseparable from values, identity, and forms of social participation. This perspective foregrounds human development as a dynamic, co-evolutionary process shaped by both individual capacities and wider forces, including automation, cultural transformation, and globalisation.

Within this framework, the value of any particular skill is not fixed but contingent upon historical trajectories, social priorities, and ethical considerations. Education and workforce development, therefore, should not be viewed solely as preparation for existing occupational roles. Rather, they ought to cultivate adaptability, creativity, and social responsibility—qualities that enable individuals to engage with change thoughtfully and with integrity. Such an approach shifts the emphasis away from fragmented models of skill acquisition and towards an integrated understanding of skills as dynamic practices. This orientation provides a more accurate reflection of the realities of contemporary work and points towards a more humane vision of learning and labour: one in which the development of competencies supports not only economic activity but also the flourishing of individuals, communities, and societies.

This understanding finds further resonance in the World Economic Forum's Future of Jobs Report (2020), which highlights the growing importance of analytical thinking, creativity, and emotional intelligence. These capabilities are increasingly prioritised over narrowly defined, task-specific competencies, indicating a broader recalibration of employability in the post-industrial knowledge economy. What emerges is a clear imperative: an over-reliance on outdated assumptions about work and its required skills risks leaving individuals and institutions unprepared for transformations that are already underway. The evolution of labour markets is not occurring at the margins but at the very centre of how work is conceptualised and organised. In this light, skills development must be understood not as the static accumulation of competencies but as an unfolding process of becoming—personal, social, and structural in character. An illustrative metaphor can be found in the figure of Daedalus from Greek mythology. Beyond his reputation as a craftsman, Daedalus embodies adaptability, creativity, and attentiveness to the broader consequences of invention. His skills were not merely technical but integrated with foresight, moral awareness, and responsiveness to context. In much the same way, today's workers must learn to navigate technological change while also addressing the ethical and emotional complexities of contemporary organisational life. In doing so, they become not only participants in labour markets but also architects of their own learning journeys, shaping futures that are both sustainable and socially responsible.

From this perspective, governments, educators, and employers are called to engage more proactively with the transformations shaping the future of work. It is insufficient to respond reactively to immediate market pressures; instead, attention must be directed towards the underlying forces driving realignment. This involves questioning how skills are being reshaped, what purposes they now serve, and how learning and labour might be reimagined as creative and humanising practices that support not only economic productivity but also broader social well-being. At the centre of this reimagining lies a renewed concern with identity and purpose. In a world increasingly mediated by AI, the pressing challenge is not only how to adapt but also how to align cognitive, emotional, and social intelligences in ways that enable individuals to thrive within shifting environments. Skills such as self-awareness, organisational belonging, and interpersonal understanding are integral here. When people recognise their own values and appreciate their place within collective structures, they are better equipped to respond with flexibility and purpose to technological change. This relational awareness also informs our engagement with AI. Rather than viewing AI exclusively as a disruptive force, it can be understood as a complementary tool that extends human capacity. To realise this potential, however, demands a sustained commitment to lifelong learning, reflective practice, and ethical foresight. When guided by principles of inclusivity and responsibility, technological augmentation may become a catalyst for deeper forms of human development.

The significance of this perspective is anticipated in the work of Autor, Levy, and Murnane (2003), whose empirical research revealed that routine cognitive and manual tasks were most vulnerable to automation, whereas non-routine analytical and interactive tasks—those requiring judgement, adaptability, and human nuance—were becoming increasingly central. This finding remains pertinent, providing a basis for aligning education and training with the realities of a transforming labour market. Building on this, Bakhshi et al. (2017) emphasise adaptability as the defining feature of a future labour force shaped by cross-sectoral transformation. Their foresight modelling suggests that employment will increasingly depend on resilience, self-management, and systems thinking—capacities essential for navigating dynamic and ambiguous contexts. Rather than reinforcing a binary narrative of job loss versus job creation, their analysis frames adaptability as a continuous process of aligning individual capabilities with structural change. This position is reinforced by Cedefop (2018), whose European-level research illustrates the accelerating obsolescence of specific skill sets. Their findings demonstrate that adaptability is no longer peripheral but must be recognised as a core dimension of employability. The emergence of hybrid roles—requiring digital literacy, communication competence, and domain-specific expertise—highlights the inadequacy of static curricula. Instead, education and skills policy must prioritise models that are interdisciplinary, flexible, and responsive to the shifting demands of contemporary labour markets.

The transformation of employability extends beyond curricular reform. It requires a more fundamental reconsideration of teaching strategies, qualification frameworks, and the purposes of learning outcomes. The central question is whether present educational structures genuinely reflect the evolving dynamics of skills, or whether they continue to reproduce inherited models that offer diminishing relevance to contemporary labour markets. Where the latter holds true, the rationale for reform is compelling. Qualifications and learning objectives must be recalibrated to reflect the continuous, layered, and interdisciplinary character of skill formation in the digital age. This concern is reflected in the work of Felstead et al. (2019), who emphasise the relationship between skill utilisation and work intensity. Drawing on longitudinal evidence, they show that although skill levels across the workforce have risen, this has often been accompanied by increasing pressure and workload. Their contribution lies in shifting attention from the possession of skills to their application, demonstrating that effective use is shaped as much by organisational cultures, workplace practices, and institutional frameworks as by individual capacity. Adaptability, therefore, cannot be regarded simply as an individual attribute but must also be understood as a structural phenomenon embedded within the systems that govern work.

Collectively, this body of scholarship signals an important evolution in the understanding of adaptability. The challenge is not merely to equip individuals with new competencies but to create environments in which those competencies can be meaningfully exercised and continually developed. Such an approach calls for a holistic rethinking of education, training, and employment systems—one that acknowledges the interplay between human capability, technological innovation, and institutional design. In this light, preparing people for the future of work is not a matter of one-off readiness but of fostering conditions for ongoing reinvention, reflective practice, and inclusive growth. The OECD's Future-Ready Adult Learning Systems (2021b) develops this argument by situating adaptability at the centre of lifelong learning ecosystems. Rather than focusing narrowly on short-term upskilling, the report advocates for anticipatory and resilient frameworks that equip individuals to evolve in response to future demands. Its strength lies in recognising that employability is not determined solely by personal initiative but also by institutional design and policy responsiveness. The emphasis on flexible learning pathways—integrated within national education and employment strategies—underlines that adaptability must be structurally supported, not assumed as an innate trait. This reframing challenges long-standing narratives that place the burden of employability on individuals alone. In the context of 21st-century skills dynamics, such an approach is no longer sustainable. A more collective and inclusive perspective is required—one that acknowledges the interdependence of individual agency, social infrastructure, and policy design. Ultimately, employability must be understood as a shared responsibility between individuals, institutions, and society.

From this perspective, it becomes evident that governments, educators, and employers must engage not only with immediate market demands but also with the deeper forces reshaping skills and work. Reactive adjustments to economic shifts are insufficient. Instead, there is a need to ask more fundamental questions: What structural dynamics are driving this realignment? How do these forces alter both the content and purpose of skills development? And crucially, how might learning and labour be reimagined as creative and humanising practices that serve societal well-being alongside economic objectives? Reframing skills development in this way calls attention to questions of identity and purpose. What does it mean to be human in a world increasingly mediated by AI? How might cognitive, emotional, and social intelligences be cultivated to support flourishing, rather than mere survival, in such environments? Here, self-awareness, organisational belonging, and interpersonal understanding become central. Individuals who are attuned to their values and recognise their place within collective systems are better positioned to respond with adaptability and purpose to technological change. This relational awareness also shapes our interaction with AI. Rather than viewing AI as a threat or replacement, it can be understood here as a complement—an extension of human capacity that simultaneously requires a renewed commitment to reflective practice and lifelong learning. In this framing, technological augmentation becomes a catalyst for deeper human development, but only if guided by ethical foresight and inclusive design.

The discussion thus far has highlighted the growing importance of cognitive agility, emotional intelligence, and socio-technical competence as cornerstones of employability in the digital era. Yet the capacity to cultivate these qualities is constrained by systemic barriers that extend beyond individual effort. Two interrelated challenges are particularly significant: the persistent misalignment between educational provision and labour market needs, and the entrenched inequalities that shape access to opportunities for learning and skills development. The first challenge concerns the widening gap between what institutions teach and what workplaces require. Despite attempts to modernise curricula and strengthen industry alignment, employers frequently report difficulties in finding candidates equipped with the integrated blend of technical and interpersonal capabilities demanded by contemporary work. This disjunction undermines productivity and innovation, but more importantly, it limits individuals' ability to participate meaningfully in the evolving labour market. Static pedagogical models, weak collaboration between education and employers, and insufficient investment in lifelong learning all exacerbate this disconnect. The second challenge is structural inequality. Factors such as socio-economic background, geography, and unequal access to digital infrastructure or quality education continue to shape who is able to develop future-facing skills. These disparities reproduce cycles of exclusion, with marginalised groups often least able to access the very competencies needed to adapt in rapidly changing environments. Such inequalities are not incidental, but are embedded within wider social and institutional arrangements, requiring systemic reform if they are to be addressed effectively.

These barriers remind us that the cultivation of future-ready skills cannot be reduced to an individual responsibility. It must instead be understood as a collective endeavour, requiring institutional redesign, policy innovation, and shared responsibility across sectors. The challenge may be likened to the ancient irrigation canals that sustained early civilisations. When channels were carefully maintained and water flowed equitably, crops flourished across the community. Yet when canals were blocked or diverted to serve only a few, large parts of the land lay barren, no matter how resilient the farmers might have been. The strength of the system depended not on individual effort alone, but on the fairness of its design and the willingness of the collective to safeguard shared resources. Viewed through the employability framework, the implications of this allegory become clear. At the level of identity, inequitable systems restrict individuals' ability to recognise themselves as capable and adaptive agents. Within society, uneven access to education and digital infrastructure reproduces cycles of exclusion. Institutions, such as schools and universities, often preserve static models of learning rather than cultivating adaptive and inclusive approaches. In the workplace, mismatches between skills supplied and those demanded constrain both innovation and individual fulfilment. At the centre lies capability practice, which should integrate these dimensions into a coherent and sustainable model of employability, but which cannot be realised while systemic barriers persist. Just as ancient communities could not thrive unless the irrigation channels were collectively maintained, so too contemporary societies cannot sustain employability unless the systems that govern education and work are rebalanced. Addressing these systemic imbalances is therefore a shared task, requiring governments, institutions, and employers to reshape the conditions under which learning and labour develop. It is to these systemic challenges—and the possibilities for policy and institutional reform—that the next section now turns.

EDUCATION ALONE IS NOT ENOUGH: UNPACKING THE STRUCTURAL DIMENSIONS OF SKILLS AND EMPLOYABILITY

Consistent with the patterns outlined in earlier sections, contemporary debates continue to highlight the misalignment between governmental policy perspectives and educators' understandings of the skills required in today's labour markets. This is less a definitive 'skills gap' than a tension created by divergent agendas and deeply ingrained pedagogical traditions. For decades, both policy and practice have leaned on conventional models of employability, often failing to adapt to the shifting demands of technologically mediated work. As a result, the capabilities nurtured in formal education do not always correspond with the dynamic competencies sought by employers—an incongruity noted in recent analyses by the ILO (2020) and the OECD (2023). The persistence of this misalignment can be understood through the allegory of Janus, the Roman god of transitions, who is depicted with one face turned towards the past and another towards the future. Much like Janus, education and policy embody a dual gaze. The backward-facing countenance represents continuity, preserving stability through established curricula and qualifications. This orientation has value: it anchors learners in traditions of knowledge and ensures coherence in systems that might otherwise fragment. Yet, when this gaze becomes dominant, it constrains responsiveness, tethering institutions to outdated frameworks while the world beyond the classroom transforms.

The forward-facing aspect of Janus, by contrast, symbolises adaptability and anticipation. It reflects the imperative to embrace uncertainty and to design learning that not only mirrors current labour demands but also actively prepares for future ones. This requires cultivating more than technical competence; it calls for fostering curiosity, ethical discernment, and the capacity to collaborate across disciplinary and cultural boundaries. A balanced vision of employability must therefore hold both orientations together: grounding learners in historical insight while equipping them to move creatively into emerging futures. Two pathways emerge from this allegory. First, governments and educators must critically reflect on the trajectory of human development and its implications for labour, identity, and community in a digital age. Second, they must engage directly with the role of AI—not as a marginal tool but as a central force shaping how knowledge is created, shared, and applied in what might be called the 'forever now' of accelerated technological change. When held in tension, these pathways do not compete but converge, offering the possibility of an educational system that integrates stability with innovation. Such a system would not merely react to disruption but would reimagine employability as a dynamic, ethical, and socially embedded process—one capable of sustaining human flourishing in uncertain times.

Structural inequalities compound the persistent misalignment between skills provision and labour market needs, limiting equitable access to quality education and opportunities for skill development. Disparities grounded in socio-economic position, gender, and geography continue to restrict individuals' ability to build capabilities and participate meaningfully in the workforce. The International Labour Organization (2020) emphasises how marginalisation often obstructs access to the very resources—such as vocational training, digital infrastructure, and quality schooling—needed for labour market participation. These challenges are particularly acute in rural and economically disadvantaged regions, where under-resourced institutions and constrained pathways reinforce cycles of exclusion. In the Arab context, Adely et al. (2021) note that sociopolitical dynamics and cultural norms continue to restrict the participation of women and rural populations, deepening inequalities in skill acquisition and labour market integration. Such constraints are central, rather than peripheral, to debates on employability in the age of AI. While adaptive learning systems and personalised career guidance hold potential to expand access, their impact depends on the inclusiveness of the data on which they are built. When algorithms are trained on biased or incomplete datasets, they risk entrenching inequalities rather than addressing them. For this reason, the development and deployment of AI in education and employment must be guided by principles of ethical governance, fairness, and social justice. Regulation, in this sense, should be conceived not as a barrier to innovation but as a safeguard to ensure that technological adoption enhances, rather than undermines, equity.

The stakes extend beyond individual employability. The Boston Consulting Group (2020) warns that economies with persistent skills mismatches face diminished capacity for innovation and weakened competitiveness. Similarly, the World Economic Forum (2023) observes that as automation and AI become more deeply embedded across industries, the demand for advanced digital capabilities will rise sharply, risking the intensification of disparities unless access to upskilling is expanded. Addressing these systemic challenges, therefore, requires a dual commitment: to confront structural inequalities directly and to harness AI's transformative potential with foresight and ethical clarity. Only through such an approach can employability be reimagined as a driver of both social justice and sustainable economic resilience.

The evolving discourse on the role of HEIs in advancing graduate employability reflects broader transformations in economic expectations and educational paradigms. Central to this debate is the challenge of reconciling universities' traditional academic mission with the growing imperative to prepare students for increasingly volatile labour markets. While many HEIs have sought to integrate employability into their curricula, the degree to which they have successfully adapted to shifting social and economic conditions remains contested. Kornelakis and Petrakaki (2020) highlight the dual pressures of digitalisation and marketisation within the UK higher education sector, noting that while embedding employability-related competencies is essential, this should not come at the expense of intellectual and critical foundations. Their argument points to the need for a more nuanced approach—one that treats academic development and employability not as competing priorities but as complementary dimensions of a holistic education. Framing the debate as a binary between technical skills and academic depth oversimplifies what is in fact an interdependent relationship. More productively, HEIs might cultivate learning environments where transferable, technical, and cognitive capabilities are developed in tandem. This requires moving beyond instrumentalist conceptions of employability towards integrated frameworks that foreground adaptability, critical reasoning, and reflective practice alongside domain-specific expertise.

The persistence of graduate skill mismatches emphasises the urgency of such reform. Vecchi et al. (2023), analysing UK labour market data, report that nearly a third of graduates are employed in roles that do not require a degree, with a comparable proportion working in sectors unrelated to their studies. These patterns carry significant implications for individual career progression, national productivity, and social mobility. They also raise questions about the extent to which HEIs have effectively aligned curriculum design with labour market realities. Academic content alone cannot be assumed to translate directly into workplace relevance. Instead, curriculum development must be informed by labour market intelligence, embrace interdisciplinarity, and provide structured opportunities for applied and experiential learning. An ancient allegory helps illuminate this challenge. In Greek mythology, Daedalus fashioned wings of wax and feathers to help him and Icarus escape their confinement. Yet while the wings represented remarkable technical ingenuity, survival depended equally on judgement, restraint, and awareness of context. Icarus's failure lay not in a lack of tools but in neglecting the wisdom needed to use them responsibly. Likewise, universities today possess the intellectual 'wings' to equip graduates with technical knowledge, but without equal attention to adaptability, critical reflection, and ethical awareness, such knowledge may fail to sustain them in turbulent environments. Adopting a balanced approach would enable HEIs to support graduates in securing employment while also fostering the adaptability and reflective capacities needed to navigate complex and evolving professional landscapes. By seeking synergies between intellectual rigour and practical skill development, HEIs can enhance graduate employability while remaining faithful to their broader educational mission.

Continuing this line of inquiry, it is evident that the integration of AI into the UK higher education landscape carries significant implications for graduate employability, particularly in relation to skill mismatches and socio-economic inequality. Hazel's systematic review, McCafferty (2022), highlights how undergraduates from disadvantaged backgrounds face enduring barriers, including limited access to careers guidance, professional networks, and the social capital that increasingly determines graduate outcomes. The expansion of AI-driven recruitment—through algorithmic CV screening, automated interviews, and predictive hiring tools—has introduced new dynamics into this uneven terrain. Far from levelling the field, such technologies risk intensifying exclusion if they draw upon biased datasets or operate without transparency. Thus, a paradox emerges: tools intended to increase efficiency and objectivity may, in practice, reproduce inequality. This reality may be likened to a grand theatre in which the stage has been rapidly rebuilt, yet many performers have neither been handed the script nor taught the cues. Students from privileged backgrounds are guided backstage, trained in the language of digital recruitment, and prepared for the performance required of them. Others remain at the threshold, uncertain of how to enter or participate. HEIs, meanwhile, have observed the transformation of the stage but have been slow to ensure that all learners are equipped to act with confidence in this new setting.

Although the evidence base regarding how AI systems function in real-world recruitment remains emergent, this should not deter institutions from purposeful action. There is both an ethical and institutional responsibility to prepare students for these evolving practices. This includes embedding AI literacy within curricula, offering guidance on navigating automated recruitment processes, and cultivating the critical awareness necessary to interrogate the assumptions and consequences embedded within these systems. If higher education is to address rather than perpetuate exclusion, it must move from a reactive posture to a proactive model—one grounded in inclusion, transparency, and foresight. Designing socially responsive and personalised learning environments will be central to this task. Only by equipping all students to engage critically and creatively with AI-driven systems can higher education ensure that these technologies serve not to replicate structural inequities but to expand access, agency, and opportunity.

The House of Commons Library briefing paper Equality of Access and Outcomes in Higher Education in England (2024) draws attention to persistent disparities in access to, and outcomes from, higher education across socio-economic groups (Bolton and Lewis, 2024). While policies have sought to promote equity, the integration of AI into educational and employment practices introduces new layers of complexity. If AI-enabled learning tools are unevenly distributed, they risk widening rather than narrowing attainment gaps. For this reason, policy frameworks must embed inclusivity not as an afterthought but as a guiding principle in the design and deployment of AI systems. Yet much policy discourse remains reactive, more focused on identifying inequities than on developing practical strategies to mitigate them. A more future-facing orientation is needed, one that shifts attention towards innovative forms of support and proactive skill-building. Scandurra et al. (2024), in their study 'Do Employability Programmes in Higher Education Improve Skills and Employment Outcomes?' confirm that structured initiatives can enhance graduate outcomes. However, such programmes must evolve to include AI literacy, adaptability, and critical awareness of algorithmic systems if they are to remain relevant in the digital economy. Without this recalibration, employability interventions risk preparing students for the demands of the past rather than the rapidly transforming workplaces of the present. The task of addressing these challenges cannot rest on universities alone. It requires collaboration between three actors—government, HEIs, and learners. Their relationship may be likened to the meeting of the White Nile and Blue Nile at Khartoum, whose merging currents give rise to a river of immense power and reach. Each current has its own character, yet it is their confluence that sustains the Nile's life-giving force. Likewise, only when governments, institutions, and learners align can they generate the collective capacity required to build a resilient and equitable employability framework in the age of AI.

Policy reports increasingly recognise this necessity. The Department for Education's AI in Education: Challenges and Opportunities (DfE, 2023) outlines the promise of AI for personalised learning and enhanced engagement, while acknowledging the risks of unequal access. Similarly, the Office for Students (OfS, 2024) advocates for an ethically grounded regulatory framework to ensure AI supports widening participation rather than reinforcing exclusion. Yet a clear implementation gap persists. Universities serving underrepresented or disadvantaged communities often face structural barriers of funding, staffing, and technological capacity, leaving them less able to integrate AI meaningfully. Here, the Nile allegory gains renewed significance. Just as the river's strength depends on the unobstructed flow of its tributaries, so too does the vitality of AI-driven employability depend on the fair distribution of digital resources. When tributaries are blocked or diverted—when digital capital (Ragnedda and Ruiu, 2020) is unevenly distributed—some learners remain stranded at the margins, unable to join the main current. Addressing this requires more than the provision of technology; it demands deliberate strategies to build confidence, competence, and critical agency. Only then can AI serve as a channel of empowerment, ensuring that the shared river of opportunity carries all learners forward rather than leaving some behind in parched and isolated terrain.

Framing AI integration in higher education primarily as a matter of technical or vocational upskilling risks narrowing the scope of employability. While proficiency in digital systems is undoubtedly important, a singular focus on technical competence can marginalise equally vital attributes such as critical thinking, ethical reasoning, and socio-emotional intelligence—capacities that remain indispensable in navigating the complexity of contemporary labour markets (Susskind, 2020). If higher education neglects these broader dimensions, it risks producing graduates equipped with tools but lacking the reflective judgement necessary to deploy them responsibly. The Capability Approach (Sen, 1999) offers a valuable corrective by shifting attention from the mere availability of technologies to the substantive opportunities learners have to use them in ways that align with their aspirations and values. This perspective highlights a key tension: without careful oversight, AI systems—especially those reliant on historical datasets—can reproduce the very inequalities they purport to overcome (Eubanks, 2018; Noble, 2018). The challenge, therefore, is not only to integrate AI tools into teaching and assessment but also to ensure that such integration is accompanied by critical literacy, transparency, and pedagogical inclusion.

Policy initiatives in the UK increasingly position AI as a catalyst for personalised learning and improved employability outcomes. Yet, as the discourse on 21st-century skills reveals, the question of which competencies are prioritised—and how they are cultivated across diverse institutional contexts—remains under-examined. Ambitious national strategies often outpace institutional capacity, particularly in universities with fewer resources or weaker digital infrastructures, where the conditions for delivering AI-informed pedagogy remain limited. This disparity reflects broader inequalities in digital capital (Ragnedda and Ruiu, 2020), which shapes not only access to technology but also the ability to engage with it meaningfully. The ambiguity of the '21st century skills' agenda compounds these challenges. As James (2019) observes, the term is frequently invoked without sufficient theoretical or pedagogical clarity, leading to fragmented implementation. While AI can simulate workplace scenarios or tailor learning pathways, it does not inherently cultivate the humanistic and relational competencies—such as ethical awareness, collaborative fluency, or systems thinking—that underpin adaptability in uncertain environments. Embedding these capacities requires deliberate pedagogical design rather than technological substitution. White's (2015) analysis of the English education system illustrates this unevenness, showing how some institutions have integrated skills-based approaches strategically, while others lack the vision or resources to do so effectively. The resulting patchwork highlights the danger of treating AI as a panacea for employability challenges. Unless guided by coherent curriculum strategies that place ethical and interpersonal dimensions at the core, AI risks reinforcing a reductive emphasis on technical ability at the expense of the broader, more adaptive forms of capability that graduates require to thrive in a rapidly changing world.

Addressing the challenges of AI integration in higher education requires a pathway that unites technological innovation with the cultivation of human-centred capabilities. The ancient allegory of the River of Knowledge is instructive here: diverse streams flow together to form a river of depth and strength, each contributing its distinct character. AI constitutes one such stream, offering remarkable capacity for analysis, prediction, and efficiency. Yet, without the convergence of other streams—critical thinking, ethical reasoning, and socio-emotional intelligence—the river risks becoming shallow, unable to sustain the broader aims of education and employability. Realising this vision demands a holistic approach from policymakers and educators. Strategic investment in professional development, support for interdisciplinary collaboration, and the design of inclusive policies that address socio-economic disparities are essential. Such measures ensure that learners are not only technically proficient but also equipped to navigate the ethical, relational, and cultural complexities of contemporary professional life.

Advance HE (2020) expanded framework of 21st-century skills reflects this more inclusive orientation, emphasising resilience, collaboration, and intercultural competence. These align with the demands of an AI-augmented labour market, where technical proficiency alone is insufficient. Yet their cultivation depends heavily on institutional contexts that make these opportunities accessible. If AI-enabled systems are deployed with an overriding focus on efficiency, there is a risk of sidelining reflective practice and ethical engagement in favour of streamlined delivery. Similar concerns are raised by the International Baccalaureate Organisation (2020), which highlights mindfulness, communication, and ethical citizenship as essential attributes for meaningful participation in society. These qualities resist easy automation or quantification, yet they are central to the transformative mission of education. Their inclusion prompts a crucial question: in the pursuit of scalability and algorithmic precision, what dimensions of human development risk being overlooked? The answer underlines a central principle—AI must remain an enabler, not a substitute, with human oversight ensuring that technological adoption serves educational depth rather than undermining it.

Habets et al. (2020) demonstrate that students' reported acquisition of 21st-century skills does not always translate into confidence about their readiness for the labour market. This points to a fragile alignment between curricular provision and employment outcomes, particularly for students who lack access to professional networks or forms of digital mentorship. In such cases, the promise of skills development risks becoming unevenly distributed, with disadvantaged groups least likely to benefit from AI-enabled pathways unless questions of access and institutional equity are addressed directly. Responding to these challenges, Gretton et al. (2022) provide a practice-oriented model of skills integration. Their case study shows how employability attributes can be meaningfully embedded within assessment and feedback processes rather than bolted on as supplementary content. By aligning disciplinary learning with workplace-relevant reflection, this approach—what they term skills synchronisation—encourages students to see the interplay between academic achievement and professional competence. Yet the success of such initiatives remains contingent on institutional capacity, educator readiness, and the wider distribution of resources. Without adequate investment in staff development and digital infrastructure, the capacity to scale these reforms across the sector is limited.

Complementing this, Stoian et al. (2019) conceptualise employability not as a fixed destination but as a dynamic relationship between higher education provision, graduate capability, and shifting labour market demands. Their findings caution against universal frameworks that overlook contextual variation, calling instead for pluralistic and adaptive strategies. To illustrate this complexity, one might turn to the ancient allegory of the river delta. In such landscapes, multiple currents converge, diverge, and reshape the terrain over time. Employability, too, is sculpted by the meeting of diverse forces—disciplinary expertise, reflective practice, institutional strategy, and economic change. Its vitality lies not in uniformity but in adaptability, in the capacity of these currents to interact productively and reshape pathways as conditions evolve. Looking forward, Smith (2022) highlights the growing salience of complex cognitive and interpersonal abilities—critical thinking, adaptability, collaboration—skills that cannot be easily codified or automated. Her analysis challenges an over-reliance on digital fluency as the hallmark of employability, reminding us that technical proficiency alone is insufficient if divorced from ethical judgement, creativity, and social intelligence. For students from disadvantaged backgrounds, the development of these capacities is often constrained not by individual deficit but by limited access to enriching and socially embedded learning opportunities. The task for higher education, therefore, is not only to equip graduates with digital skills but also to ensure these are cultivated in ways that deepen human interaction, critical agency, and reflective judgement. Without this balance, AI-enabled reforms risk reproducing inequalities rather than transforming them.

Soproni (2020) urges a reframing of the employability agenda by challenging the marginalisation of so-called 'soft skills'. Attributes such as empathy, ethical awareness, and communication, she argues, should be recognised not as supplementary but as foundational to navigating a labour market increasingly marked by automation and socio-technical complexity. Her perspective aligns with Sen's (1999) capability approach, which locates the purpose of education in the expansion of agency, choice, and substantive freedom. From this standpoint, employability is not reducible to alignment with market demand but must involve cultivating the capacities that allow individuals to shape their own trajectories and participate meaningfully in social life. In this light, AI can only contribute constructively if its use extends human dignity, creativity, and critical judgement. The ancient metaphor of the artisan's chisel is instructive here: the tool is capable of producing intricate forms, yet it remains inert without the vision and intentionality of the human hand. Likewise, AI technologies, no matter how advanced, achieve their educational purpose only when directed by frameworks rooted in human values and oriented towards empowerment.

Kokkos (2020) offers a complementary critique, interrogating the policy tendency to treat education as primarily an economic instrument. He argues that such reductionism neglects the broader purposes of the humanities and sidelines education's potential to foster critical, imaginative, and engaged citizens. When governments cast humanities education as lacking immediate utility, this reflects not simply a misunderstanding of employability, but a narrowing of education's transformative role. The myth of Procrustes serves as a powerful allegory here: travellers forced to fit an iron bed through stretching or mutilation symbolise the dangers of coercing learners into rigid economic templates. In a similar manner, policies that frame employability purely in terms of human capital risk stifling individuality and disregarding the diverse capacities that enable collective transformation. Together, these perspectives highlight the inadequacy of treating employability as a static endpoint or an exercise in narrow job-readiness. Instead, employability must be understood as a dynamic, value-laden process that engages imagination and creativity as much as technical proficiency. In the age of AI, this broader conception becomes essential—not simply to prepare individuals for work, but to sustain education as a site of human flourishing and social renewal.

Connolly, Dickinson, and Hellewell (2023) advance authentic assessment as a response to contemporary educational and labour market challenges. By situating students in real-world, problem-based learning contexts, their approach allows skills to be enacted, tested, and reshaped through lived experience rather than abstracted through detached metrics. What emerges is a vision of employability as 'skills in motion'—a relational, adaptive process shaped by pedagogy, institutional values, and wider social conditions. The integration of AI into higher education intensifies the significance of this view. While AI brings powerful opportunities for tailoring learning to individual needs, it also introduces risks if implemented without sufficient inclusivity, transparency, or ethical reflection. The challenge is not simply to adopt AI tools, but to integrate them within holistic pedagogies that foster human-centred learning and ensure that technological innovation contributes to shared flourishing. This dynamic may be illuminated through the allegory of a caravan crossing the desert. For such a journey, survival depends on many interdependent elements:

1. Identity may be likened to the caravan travellers themselves—each individual carrying their own histories, aspirations, and sense of direction. Just as travellers must recognise their role within the collective, learners must understand employability as part of their evolving identity rather than a static attribute.

2. Society is reflected in the desert's shifting terrain and climate, shaping the possibilities of travel and determining which routes are open or closed. In the same way, social, technological, and cultural contexts influence which skills are valued and how they can be applied.

3. Institutions correspond to the caravan's guides and navigators, whose knowledge of maps, stars, and histories enables orientation and direction. Higher education plays a similar role, mediating between tradition and innovation, while holding responsibility for embedding ethical and adaptive capacities in curricula.

4. Workplaces are mirrored in the animals and caravans themselves—the practical systems and infrastructures that bear the weight of travel. These are the sites where skills are enacted, tested, and recalibrated, often under conditions of strain.

5. At the centre lies capability practice, symbolised by the collective discipline of the caravan: the ability to read signs, adapt to new terrains, and support one another through uncertainty. This practice integrates the whole system, ensuring that individual agency is sustained within wider social and institutional frameworks.

When these dimensions are aligned, the caravan does more than reach its destination: it generates resilience, solidarity, and new knowledge along the way. So too with employability in the digital age: when identity, society, institutions, workplaces, and capability practice are held together in balance, education does not merely prepare students for predefined roles but enables them to navigate shifting landscapes with creativity and foresight. In this sense, embedding 21st-century employability within AI-enhanced education is not simply a matter of technological adoption but of cultivating the conditions for balance and integration. HEIs are not mere ferrymen delivering students to the labour market; they are guides equipping them to cross uncertain terrains, to adapt with wisdom, and to flourish in futures that are both technologically innovative and ethically grounded. The following section will extend this discussion by examining how AI is reshaping the nature of work and the constellation of skills required to navigate it.

ARTIFICIAL INTELLIGENCE AND EMPLOYABILITY: REFRAMING WORK AND LEARNING IN THE DIGITAL AGE

The preceding discussion has highlighted how employability is too often conceptualised in static, measurable terms, leading to narrow interventions that neither reflect the complexity of contemporary labour markets nor respond adequately to the realities of skills dynamics. This limited framing has curtailed opportunities for learners and hindered the development of more adaptive, inclusive models of employability. Against this backdrop, the integration of AI has become increasingly significant, reshaping education, recruitment, and workplace learning in ways that warrant careful scrutiny. AI's promise within higher education has been widely recognised, with research emphasising its potential to personalise learning, support assessment, and enhance engagement (Luckin et al., 2016; Williamson and Eynon, 2020). Yet the conditions that would enable such personalisation to translate meaningfully into employability outcomes remain underexplored. HEIs face particular challenges in navigating this shift—not merely in adopting new technologies, but in reimagining pedagogical frameworks and institutional practices that preserve human agency while embracing digital transformation. Here, the idea of AI-personalised employability offers a useful conceptual lens. Rather than reducing personalisation to the tailoring of content, it emphasises the interplay between individual learner needs, institutional capacity, and the socio-economic contexts in which skills are cultivated and applied. Such a vision demands intentional design, ethical governance, and equitable distribution of digital infrastructure, without which AI's promise risks reinforcing, rather than redressing, structural disparities.

These questions are equally pressing in the domain of recruitment, where AI systems are increasingly used to screen applications, match candidates, and conduct preliminary assessments. While these tools are valued for their efficiency, their opacity raises enduring concerns about fairness, accountability, and the erosion of human judgement. If recruitment becomes a process in which candidates are assessed by systems whose decision-making cannot be interrogated, then the danger lies not in AI itself but in its uncritical deployment. A responsible approach requires that AI be designed with explainability and human oversight at its core, ensuring that decisions can be traced, scrutinised, and contextualised. Taken together, these developments point to the necessity of reimagining the role of AI not as a substitute for human deliberation but as a partner in extending human capacity. This requires moving beyond functionalist perspectives to confront the ethical, interpretative, and epistemological dimensions of technological change. Only through such an approach can education and labour market systems harness AI in ways that not only enhance efficiency but also uphold fairness, preserve dignity, and strengthen the foundations of employability in a digital age.

The Office for Students (2024) has underlined the need for ethical frameworks to guide AI adoption in higher education, warning of the risks of deepening inequalities if such systems are introduced without careful oversight. Yet these frameworks remain limited unless accompanied by a deeper reconceptualisation of what AI represents within educational and employability contexts. Rather than treating AI as a neutral instrument, it may be more appropriate to view it as a socio-technical partner—an epistemic actor that both shapes and is shaped by human decision-making. In this sense, AI should be defined not merely as a tool for efficiency, but as a system embedded within dialogical, transparent, and ethically governed processes that augment rather than replace human judgement. Such a reframing encourages epistemic humility, recognising that while AI can process vast data at speed, its legitimacy rests on its alignment with pedagogical values, social justice priorities, and the broader aims of inclusive education.

This orientation has implications not only for policy but also for everyday educational practice. For instance, educators may benefit from interdisciplinary engagement that brings together perspectives from computer science, law, and organisational studies to better understand how AI systems operate in recruitment and workplace settings. Collaborative workshops, reflective seminars, and dialogue across disciplines can create opportunities to interrogate assumptions of fairness, merit, and objectivity that often accompany technological interventions. Within the classroom, educators can extend this critical engagement by designing learning activities that expose students to the ethical and social dimensions of AI. Simulated recruitment exercises, case studies, or structured debates can provide spaces for students to examine how algorithmic systems embed values, distribute opportunities, and shape career outcomes. Importantly, such practices move beyond preparing students to function within AI-mediated environments; they cultivate the capacity to interrogate and influence them. In this respect, the educator's role is not simply to follow the trajectory of technological change but to model critical and ethically grounded responses to it. By embedding reflection and dialogue into the design of curricula and institutional practices, higher education can help foster a generation of graduates who are not only digitally competent but also able to navigate the ethical and relational complexities of AI-enhanced employability.

As AI becomes more deeply embedded in educational and professional contexts, it is essential to foster learners' ability not only to use such systems but also to critically interrogate them. A central responsibility of educators lies in cultivating what might be termed algorithmic literacy—an understanding of how AI systems generate outputs, the assumptions on which they rest, and the limitations inherent in their design. Rather than treating algorithmic decisions as authoritative or final, students should be encouraged to explore the processes that underpin them, including the origins of training data, the biases that may be reproduced, and the probabilistic logic through which models identify patterns (Floridi and Cowls, 2019). Such awareness is integral to developing the capacity for reflective and responsible engagement with digital technologies, both within higher education and in the workplace. At the same time, human judgement must remain central in interpreting AI-generated insights, particularly in contexts where decisions carry significant ethical or social consequences. While AI can identify skill gaps or propose personalised training pathways (Ra et al., 2019; Tomaskinova et al., 2024), its recommendations require critical evaluation within the specific circumstances in which they are applied. The effectiveness of these systems depends not only on their technical sophistication but also on the presence of supportive organisational cultures, engaged stakeholders, and strategies that address resistance to technological change (Manyika et al., 2020). Without these conditions, the adoption of AI risks reinforcing existing inequalities or producing outcomes that lack contextual sensitivity. For educators and training professionals, the challenge is therefore twofold: to equip learners with the intellectual tools needed to engage critically with algorithmic systems, and to model practices of transparency, reflexivity, and ethical responsibility in their own use of such technologies. Embedding spaces for dialogue, reflection, and critique within curricula and professional development can help ensure that AI is integrated in ways that support human agency and social equity. In this light, AI should not be regarded as a substitute for human reasoning but as a complement—an aid that, when approached thoughtfully, can enhance rather than diminish the reflective, ethical, and contextual dimensions of decision-making.

In ancient Greece, pilgrims would travel to the oracle at Delphi, seeking answers to questions of destiny, governance, and war. The Pythia's responses were delivered in fragmented, often ambiguous phrases—utterances that seemed authoritative, yet whose meaning depended entirely on the interpretation of those who received them. For some, careful reflection transformed these words into guidance that sustained their communities. For others, blind acceptance or misreading led to miscalculation and collapse. This allegory speaks powerfully to our present moment. AI systems, like the oracle, generate outputs that appear certain but are shaped by hidden conditions—datasets, probabilities, and assumptions. Their value lies not in the output alone, but in how humans interpret, question, and apply them. Just as the ancients learned that wisdom came not from the oracle's voice but from the discernment it demanded, so too must contemporary learners and educators cultivate the reflexivity, ethical awareness, and critical capacity to engage with AI responsibly. In this way, algorithmic literacy becomes less about technical mastery and more about sustaining the human ability to transform data into meaningful, ethical, and future-oriented action.

From this perspective, the future of education and employability will not be determined by AI in isolation, but by the wisdom with which it is integrated into what might be called the human learning experience—an experience that depends on oversight, judgement, and forms of knowledge that cannot be fully captured by metrics or code. Across history, it has not been the tools themselves that shaped civilisations, but the discernment with which they were used. The Greeks named this phronesis—practical wisdom concerned not only with action but also with choosing well. Comparable insights are found in African traditions, where proverbs emphasise responsibility, empathy, and the duty of care across generations. These perspectives remind us that intuition and moral discernment are not peripheral but central to navigating complexity. Just as Odysseus' journey was defined less by cunning devices than by resilience, ethical choices, and the ability to adapt to unforeseen trials, so too must our engagement with AI be guided by human sensitivity to context, consequence, and care. The integration of AI into education should therefore elevate, rather than obscure, the role of human insight. Only in the interplay between algorithmic precision and human intuition can truly transformative learning and meaningful employability emerge.

At the same time, it is necessary to recognise that AI-driven personalisation does not automatically guarantee inclusivity. As Noble (2018) cautions, algorithms are shaped by the histories embedded within their training data—histories that often reproduce social hierarchies of race, class, and gender. When applied to education or employability, such systems risk reinforcing disadvantage, particularly where predictive models undervalue students from marginalised backgrounds. These are not simply technical flaws but epistemological ones, revealing how dominant socio-technical imaginaries (Gidiotis and Hrastinski, 2024) privilege particular measures of achievement and narrow trajectories of progress. Under such conditions, claims to neutrality may obscure the reproduction of inequality, presenting partial outcomes as objective. The challenge, therefore, is not only to refine the technology but also to interrogate the values and assumptions that underpin its design and use.

The potential of personalised learning warrants careful consideration rather than outright dismissal. When designed with ethical attentiveness, such systems can support learners in ways that are both meaningful and responsive. It is important, however, to distinguish between surface-level customisation—where content is merely adjusted according to broad user patterns—and deeper forms of personalisation that attend to the learner's context, aspirations, and lived experiences. Achieving the latter requires transparent data practices, inclusive design, and sustained human oversight. Rather than positioning AI as a mechanism for sorting or categorising, such systems should cultivate open-ended, reflexive pathways that respect diversity and enable agency. In this sense, personalised learning retains value, but only when embedded within frameworks that prioritise equity, transparency, and critical review. The risks are particularly acute in the use of AI to predict employability outcomes. Baiocco et al. (2022) warn of the rise of 'digital Taylorism', whereby individuals are assessed through reductive proxies—behavioural analytics, keyword-matched profiles, or algorithmically inferred traits. While often celebrated for efficiency, such methods tend to privilege those whose experiences align with pre-encoded norms, leaving others disadvantaged. This narrowing of human potential into easily quantifiable metrics risks distorting the very notion of employability, reducing it to the legible rather than the meaningful. To counter such tendencies, institutions must critically evaluate both the datasets and the assumptions that underpin predictive systems. This includes equity audits of training data, structured consultation with underrepresented groups, and independent peer review of design processes. Through such practices, AI may become not a mechanism of exclusion, but a tool for recognising and supporting the diverse trajectories through which learners engage with education and work.

This dynamic may be understood through the ancient allegory of the loom. In many early societies, weaving was not only a craft but also a metaphor for life itself: countless threads of different textures, colours, and lengths interlaced to create a fabric strong enough to endure. If only a narrow set of threads were chosen—uniform in hue and thickness—the resulting cloth would be fragile, prone to tearing under strain. The resilience of the fabric lay in its diversity, in the interplay of threads that differed yet complemented one another. In the same way, an AI system trained only on narrow data will weave a fabric of employability that appears neat but is brittle, excluding those whose experiences do not conform to its patterns. By contrast, systems designed with inclusivity, reflexivity, and ethical oversight are able to weave a fabric that is strong, complex, and enduring—capable of holding together many lives and trajectories. Thus, the question is not whether AI should play a role in shaping education and employability, but how it can be guided to weave a fabric that is resilient, inclusive, and worthy of the society it is intended to serve.

Esmond and Atkins (2022) caution against technocratic approaches to education that privilege what can be quantified while overlooking forms of knowledge and capability not easily captured through data—such as informal skills, interpersonal understanding, and personal resilience. They argue for a richer conception of employability, one that situates education as a dynamic and relational process shaped by context, identity, and growth, rather than as a linear pathway towards predefined labour market outcomes. Without such a perspective, AI-enabled systems risk narrowing the scope of educational value, reducing success to what is legible within data-driven frameworks. This concern extends to the professional role of educators. Much of the discourse surrounding AI in education emphasises adaptive capacities—tracking learner progress, customising content, or automating assessment. Yet, as Selwyn (2019) observes, such narratives risk diminishing the interpretive and ethical agency of teachers. Educators are not mere intermediaries for algorithmic outputs; their expertise lies in contextualising, questioning, and shaping how technological affordances are translated into practice. Institutions, therefore, have a responsibility to invest in professional development that strengthens educators' critical engagement with digital systems. This might include training in algorithmic literacy, interdisciplinary dialogue on ethics and equity, and collaborative design processes that involve teachers in evaluating and adapting AI tools. Supporting such capacities reinforces the indispensable human role in fostering inclusive, meaningful, and ethically informed learning environments.

Knox, Williamson, and Bayne (2020) similarly emphasise that AI in education should not be considered pedagogically neutral. Systems are embedded within institutional priorities that define what is measured and valued, and thus their adoption constitutes a pedagogical choice rather than a simple technical enhancement. The risk is that the richness of teaching becomes constrained by measurable outputs, unless AI is deployed to augment rather than replace relational and interpretive practices. This challenge is heightened by the growing diffusion of learning across decentralised networks, open-access platforms, and peer-driven communities. In this respect, Illich's (1971) notion of 'learning webs'—non-hierarchical environments driven by curiosity and relevance—appears increasingly prescient. It highlights the need for AI to support, rather than curtail, the diversity and autonomy of learning pathways.

AI-enabled tools now make aspects of flexible and responsive learning technically viable, offering learners the possibility to access resources, receive feedback, and pursue personalised pathways beyond the limits of formal curricula. Yet such innovations raise pressing questions about legitimacy, quality assurance, and equitable access. Bulathwela et al. (2024) observe that while AI has the potential to strengthen informal learning and broaden participation, this promise depends on whether systems are designed to remain genuinely learner-centred, dialogical, and grounded in pedagogical care. Poorly designed platforms risk entrenching hierarchies rather than dismantling them, particularly where informal learning environments are shaped by commercial interests or governed by reductive metrics of performance. If learning becomes commodified in this way, the autonomy and critical agency that informal education seeks to cultivate may be compromised. To counter this, educational designers and institutions must explore models of AI integration that preserve agency and inclusivity. Such models might include participatory co-design with learners and communities, transparent governance mechanisms, and evaluative practices that prioritise qualitative, reflective indicators of growth over narrow measures of output. Central to this approach is the recognition that learning—whether situated inside or outside institutions—is a social and transformative endeavour. AI should not serve to standardise these experiences, but rather to support their plurality and depth.

Zuboff (2023) warns that many AI-driven platforms operate under the logic of 'surveillance capitalism', treating human activity as raw data to generate predictive insights and commercial value. Within education, this logic manifests in the large-scale collection of behavioural, cognitive, and emotional data, often without adequate consent or transparency. While framed as mechanisms to personalise or support learning, such systems can also function as instruments of subtle behavioural regulation, nudging students towards predetermined norms. Kwet (2019) extends this critique through the notion of data colonialism, highlighting how AI in education can impose standardised pedagogical models that marginalise local epistemologies and indigenous priorities, particularly in the Global South. In such contexts, learners may face a form of epistemic injustice in which dominant knowledge frameworks are privileged at the expense of diversity and contextual relevance. In ancient times, caravans travelled along the Silk Roads, carrying spices, textiles, and precious stones from distant lands. These routes were not merely highways of commerce; they were also rivers of knowledge, flowing across mountains, deserts, and seas. At each caravanserai, merchants exchanged more than goods—they shared stories, languages, and ideas, enriching one another's worlds. The value of these exchanges lies not in uniformity, but in diversity: the recognition that wisdom, like silk, is strongest when woven from many threads.

Yet history also records moments when such exchanges turned exploitative. Empires sought to control the routes, taxing the flow of goods, silencing unfamiliar voices, and reshaping markets to their own advantage. What once had been a space of reciprocity became, at times, a system of extraction. The journeys continued, but the encounters grew narrower, and many forms of knowledge were left untried, unseen, and undervalued. The integration of AI into education and employability resembles these ancient routes. At its best, AI can act as the caravanserai: a meeting place where learners bring their unique experiences, cultures, and aspirations, and where the tools of technology help them exchange, refine, and extend their knowledge. It can support plurality, enabling local wisdom to stand alongside global expertise. But without careful design and ethical governance, AI risks becoming less a road of exchange and more a system of control—an imperial gate that taxes access, privileges certain voices, and excludes others. Thus, the challenge is not whether to travel the new roads of digital learning, but how to ensure they remain open, plural, and reciprocal. The task before educators, policymakers, and communities is to safeguard AI as a shared space of encounter—where knowledge is not flattened into sameness, but celebrated in its difference, and where learners are treated not as commodities to be measured, but as travellers in a common journey towards flourishing.

What is at stake is not only the protection of individual privacy but also the wider ethical and pedagogical conditions under which knowledge is created, mediated, and valued. AI in education cannot be treated as a neutral intervention. It is shaped by institutional priorities, economic pressures, and geopolitical contexts that frame how learning is organised and to what purposes it is directed. Without critical oversight, algorithmic systems risk entrenching inequality, reducing education to quantifiable outputs, and displacing the collaborative roles of educators and learners as co-constructors of knowledge. Addressing these challenges requires more than incremental technical safeguards. It calls for a reorientation towards inclusive and democratic forms of AI governance in education—approaches that foreground accountability, equity, and the relational dimensions of data ethics. This entails involving students, educators, and communities in the co-design of AI tools; creating transparent mechanisms for auditing and contesting algorithmic decisions; and ensuring that technological infrastructures serve social and human purposes rather than subordinating them. In this sense, the integration of AI into education and employability systems should be understood as a political as much as a technical endeavour, one that must remain critically attentive to questions of power, difference, and justice.

In summary, this section has explored how the growing presence of AI in education and employability is reshaping debates around personalisation, innovation, and fairness. It has challenged narrow conceptions of employability as a fixed and measurable outcome, instead presenting it as a dynamic and socially embedded process shaped by learner diversity, institutional practice, and wider socio-economic structures. Central to this analysis is the idea of AI-personalised employability, which offers a more ethically grounded vision of personalisation—one attentive to the infrastructural, pedagogical, and cultural conditions necessary for equitable implementation. The discussion has also highlighted the risks posed by predictive analytics and what has been termed 'digital Taylorism', where employability is reduced to narrow indicators and non-normative learning pathways are marginalised. More broadly, the influence of AI is bound up with logics of surveillance capitalism and data colonialism, raising profound questions about consent, epistemic justice, and the politics of knowledge production. Within this shifting landscape, educators remain central—not as passive users of AI tools, but as critical agents whose ethical awareness and professional judgement mediate between algorithmic systems and the lived realities of learners. To enable them to take on this role, institutions must invest in sustained professional development, create spaces for interdisciplinary collaboration, and centre ethical reflection in both policy and practice.

This section suggests that AI cannot be regarded as a neutral addition to existing educational or employability systems. Its integration is inherently political and pedagogical, carrying the potential to reinforce exclusion if adopted without ethical foresight. Addressing this challenge requires a cultural and institutional shift in how governance is conceived and enacted. One constructive proposal is the establishment of AI governance councils within universities and policy domains. Such bodies, composed of educators, students, data scientists, ethicists, and community representatives, would provide a forum for ensuring that AI tools are developed and deployed in transparent, accountable, and inclusive ways. Their remit might include auditing systems for bias, facilitating co-design processes with diverse user groups, and providing mechanisms for oversight and redress. In parallel, embedding algorithmic literacy within curricula would enable learners to critically engage with the systems that increasingly shape their educational and professional trajectories. By cultivating this capacity, education can strengthen its role not only in preparing graduates for employment but also in empowering them to shape the conditions of work in an AI-influenced society. Figure 1.5 illustrates this conceptual alignment, showing how the interplay of technological innovation and human values, when supported by governance

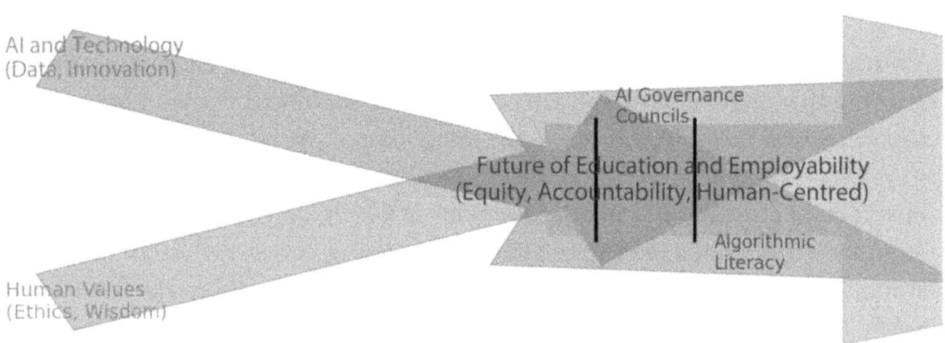

FIGURE 1.5 Converging pathways of AI and human values in shaping the future of education and employability.

AI and human values converge through governance and literacy to shape equitable, human-centred futures in education and employability.

BOX 1.5 EXPLANATION NOTE—CONVERGING PATHWAYS OF AI AND HUMAN VALUES IN SHAPING THE FUTURE OF EDUCATION AND EMPLOYABILITY

The figure illustrates the convergence of two distinct yet interdependent pathways—AI and technology, on the one hand, and human values on the other—in shaping the future of education and employability. One stream represents the technological trajectory, characterised by data-driven innovation and algorithmic applications, while the other reflects human values grounded in ethics, wisdom, and reflective practice. Their convergence highlights the recognition that neither trajectory alone is sufficient to secure equitable and sustainable outcomes.

At the centre lies the vision of a future of education and employability that is equity-focused, accountable, and human-centred. This vision is not automatically achieved but requires deliberate interventions, represented here by two critical mechanisms. The first, AI Governance Councils, symbolises the institutional structures needed to provide transparency, oversight, and ethical stewardship in the development and application of AI tools. The second, Algorithmic Literacy, represents the cultivation of learner and educator capacity to critically engage with AI systems, ensuring that individuals are not passive recipients of algorithmic decisions but active participants in shaping their implications.

The central area of integration in the figure conveys that bringing technological capability together with human values generates the most promising and resilient pathway. This integration foregrounds the principle that technological sophistication alone cannot guarantee progress; it must be mediated by human-centred frameworks that prioritise fairness, accountability, and social justice. In this way, the figure underlines a central argument of the section: the future of education and employability will not be defined solely by the power of algorithms or by ethical aspiration in isolation, but by the deliberate interweaving of both, anchored in inclusive governance and critical literacy.

and literacy mechanisms, contributes towards a more equitable, accountable, and human-centred vision of education and employability.

The central argument here is that the trajectory of education and employability will not be determined by the sophistication of the technologies we adopt, but by the values and responsibilities embedded within their use. This balance may be captured through the allegory of an ancient city, situated at the confluence of two rivers. One river carries the force of technical innovation—swift, transformative, and capable of reshaping the landscape with its energy. The other flows more slowly, bearing wisdom, culture, and human experience that have sustained the city over generations. To channel only the faster current may yield immediate prosperity, yet risks undermining the very foundations on which the city rests. To depend solely on the slower stream may preserve continuity, but at the expense of renewal and growth. The flourishing of the city relies on bringing both rivers together—harnessing the strength of innovation while preserving the depth of human insight—so that neither overwhelms the other. In this light, the integration of AI into education and employability must not be seen as a contest between progress and tradition, but as a process of convergence—where technology is steered by human values to create futures that are both resilient and transformative. The next section develops this argument further under the theme: Human-Centric AI Integration: Redefining Employability in the 21st-Century Learning Landscape.

HUMAN-CENTRIC AI INTEGRATION: REDEFINING EMPLOYABILITY IN THE 21ST-CENTURY LEARNING LANDSCAPE

Building on the preceding discussion, it is necessary to reconsider how employability is conceptualised in the context of 21st-century education and how it may be operationalised in pedagogical practice. Some macroeconomic studies, such as Acemoglu and Restrepo (2019), which examine AI's interaction with labour markets across OECD countries, suggest that employment growth can occur even in sectors most exposed to automation. This challenges deterministic narratives of technological displacement and instead points to a more complex relationship between human labour and machine intelligence. Yet such analyses, while valuable in identifying structural trends, often leave unaddressed the implications for curriculum design, pedagogical strategies, and the lived experiences of learners and workers. Without attention to these dimensions, employability risks being framed as an abstract economic category rather than a practice grounded in human development and social context. Emerging scholarship in organisational studies reflects this shift by conceptualising AI not as a displacing force but as a collaborative agent that can augment human capabilities (Daugherty and Wilson, 2018; Dell Technologies, 2023). Such perspectives call for a reframing of employability as a dynamic process that prioritises the integration of AI into educational design and institutional strategy from the outset. This integration should extend beyond operational familiarity with digital tools to foster a critical understanding of how AI systems function, what values underpin their design, and how they mediate human decision-making. In this sense, AI becomes more than an object of study; it is a catalyst for rethinking the purposes and practices of education itself. Employability must be understood not simply as preparing individuals to adapt to technological change, but as cultivating capacities that enable them to shape and interrogate the role of technology in work and society.

While the growing literature on AI and employability highlights significant possibilities, these cannot be divorced from the persistent inequalities that shape access to digital opportunities. Uneven levels of digital literacy, infrastructural provision, and institutional capacity mean that participation in AI-mediated labour markets remains far from equitable. These disparities are not simply technical gaps but expressions of broader socio-economic divisions that determine who is able to engage, contribute, and benefit from technological change. For this reason, discussions of 21st-century skills must be situated within wider social contexts, recognising that equitable access to lifelong learning and employability cannot be assumed. This challenge reflects a wider tension in educational discourse between instrumentalist and constructivist perspectives. Instrumentalist approaches emphasise efficiency, performance optimisation, and measurable outcomes, whereas constructivist pedagogies prioritise learner agency, reflexivity, and critical engagement (Selwyn et al., 2021). When AI is aligned too closely with the former, it risks narrowing the aims of education to what can be captured by data, overlooking the relational, ethical, and affective dimensions of learning that are essential for cultivating adaptable and socially responsible graduates. Instrumentalist models, long embedded in policy discourse, conceive education as a linear and standardised process in which knowledge is transmitted, and outcomes are quantified through metrics such as retention rates, test scores, or engagement analytics. AI technologies, when applied uncritically, often reinforce this paradigm through automated assessment, behavioural tracking, and personalised content delivery. While such practices may appear efficient, they risk reducing education to input-output logics that obscure the complexity of human development. In this vision, learning is treated as a problem of optimisation, rather than as a process of exploration and growth.

The implications of this orientation are significant. Skills that are difficult to quantify—such as ethical reasoning, creativity, empathy, and critical judgement—are often marginalised, even though they are central to navigating the complexities of contemporary work and society. Moreover, there is a danger that students are reconfigured as data points to be monitored, predicted, and shaped according to algorithmic priorities. Such tendencies align with neoliberal educational discourses that evaluate institutions primarily on measurable outputs and market relevance (Williamson 2021), rather than on their capacity to foster thoughtful, reflective, and responsible learners. If AI is to serve as a meaningful educational tool, it must be embedded within pedagogical frameworks that resist these reductive tendencies. Rather than using technology to reinforce existing models of efficiency and control, institutions should approach AI as a means of deepening learning, supporting diversity, and cultivating broader human capabilities. This requires a commitment to inclusive, critical, and ethically grounded practices that acknowledge learning as a complex and socially situated process. Only through such an orientation can the promise of AI be realised in ways that strengthen, rather than diminish, the human purposes of education.

Constructivist pedagogies present a more expansive and human-centred framework for integrating AI into education, one that positions learners not as passive recipients of information but as active participants in the co-construction of knowledge. In this view, learning is relational, dialogic, and situated within broader social contexts. Knowledge does not flow in a linear sequence from teacher or machine to student; it emerges through reflection, dialogue, and the interpretative agency of individuals. Within such a framework, AI should not be seen as a mechanism for delivering pre-packaged content or regulating behaviour, but as a dialogic partner capable of stimulating inquiry, enabling diverse modes of exploration, and provoking deeper questioning. Crucially, this orientation demands that learners critically interrogate the systems they engage with—examining the assumptions embedded within algorithms, the provenance of training data, and the interests represented by technological infrastructures. Such practice aligns with what Biesta (2010) describes as subjectification: the cultivation of learners who are capable of autonomous judgement and ethical responsibility within a complex and often contradictory world. The strength of this approach lies in its resistance to reductionist tendencies that seek to render students as data points in systems of optimisation. By moving away from narrowly instrumentalist models that equate education with output and efficiency, constructivist practices promote emancipatory possibilities. They enable students to shape their own learning pathways, to develop skills that are reflective and contextually grounded, and to engage critically with the socio-technical conditions that will shape their employability. At stake is more than the acquisition of technical competence: the task is to cultivate the capacities for ethical deliberation, adaptive thinking, and collaborative problem-solving that are essential in an AI-mediated world.

To illustrate this tension, one might consider the allegory of a great library at the crossroads of an ancient city. One entrance is ordered and regimented: scrolls are categorised, labelled, and dispensed according to strict systems of classification. Visitors pass quickly through, receiving what has been predetermined as useful, but with little room for wandering or surprise. The other entrance opens into winding corridors, where scrolls are scattered across alcoves and chambers. Here, knowledge is not given but discovered—sometimes through confusion, sometimes through dialogue with others encountered along the way. The first entrance mirrors the instrumentalist vision: efficient, structured, and predictable, yet constrained in scope. The second evokes the constructivist ethos: messy, relational, and open-ended, but rich in possibility. The flourishing of the city depends not on choosing one door to the exclusion of the other, but on recognising that both must remain open, each serving a different yet necessary function. In the same way, the integration of AI into education should not be confined to efficiency-driven systems of standardisation, nor left entirely to the serendipity of unstructured exploration. It must instead hold together the strengths of both orientations: harnessing the affordances of technology while preserving the depth of human inquiry, dialogue, and ethical reflection. By situating AI within an educational philosophy that foregrounds inclusion, learner agency, and critical consciousness, institutions can ensure that technology serves civic and ethical purposes as well as economic ones. Such an approach reframes employability not as a narrow metric of job readiness, but as a dynamic process of preparing individuals to navigate uncertainty, to act responsibly, and to imagine futures that are both equitable and humane.

A useful step forward may lie in reimagining the role of AI in education, not as a mechanistic instrument but as what might be termed a dialogic partner. This conception extends beyond the automation of feedback or the efficient distribution of content, positioning AI instead as a collaborator in the learning process. Rooted in the principles of dialogic pedagogy, such a model frames learning as a co-constructed endeavour, where understanding develops through questioning, interpretation, and reflection rather than passive reception. An AI Dialogic Partner would not present itself as an authority, but as a stimulus for inquiry—encouraging learners to articulate reasoning, examine assumptions, and consider multiple perspectives. In practice, this might take the form of systems capable of Socratic-style interaction: prompting students to justify decisions, explore alternative approaches, or reflect on the professional and ethical implications of their responses. These interventions can help cultivate precisely the kinds of adaptive and reflective capabilities demanded in contemporary labour markets, where employability increasingly depends on the ability to navigate complexity, exercise judgement, and learn continuously. By situating AI in this way, education can move towards a model in which technology augments rather than displaces human dialogue, strengthening the relational and critical dimensions of learning while also preparing students to engage with the unpredictable realities of work.

Figure 1.6 illustrates the proposed concept of the AI Dialogic Partner as a catalyst for employability skill development. Rather than serving as a passive instrument for content delivery, AI is positioned here as an interactive and reflective collaborator, supporting learners in developing critical, ethical, and adaptive capacities. By engaging students through questioning, scenario-based learning, and personalised feedback, the AI Dialogic Partner encourages deeper reflection, metacognitive awareness, and values-based reasoning—all of which are essential for navigating the uncertainties of 21st-century work environments (Figure 1.6).

Figure 1.7 offers a process-oriented perspective on how learners interact with an AI Dialogic Partner, complementing the earlier conceptual representation of its role in employability skill development. Whereas the first figure mapped the range of skills that such systems can support—reflective thinking, ethical decision-making, scenario-based learning, feedback interpretation, and metacognitive reflection—this figure illustrates the dynamic mechanism through which those capacities are developed in practice. At the

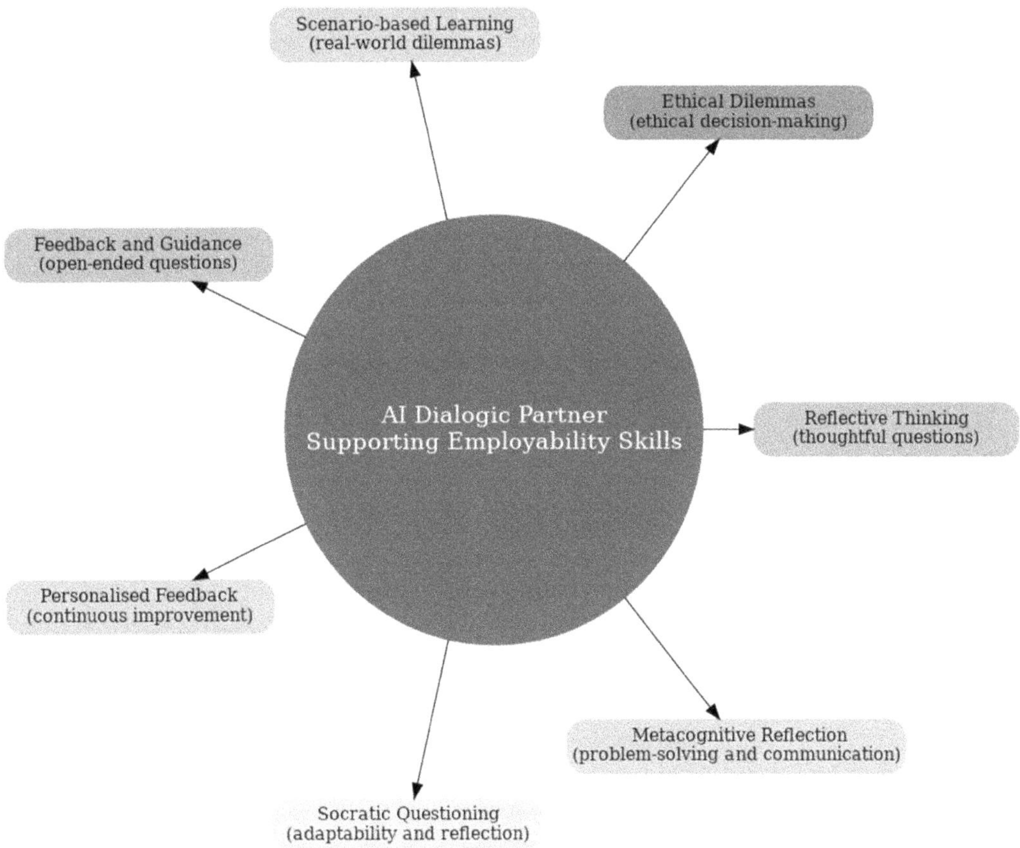

FIGURE 1.6 AI Dialogic Partner supporting employability skills.

This figure illustrates how an AI Dialogic Partner fosters employability skill development through reflective thinking, ethical decision-making, scenario-based learning, feedback, personalisation, Socratic questioning, and metacognitive reflection.

BOX 1.6 EXPLANATION NOTE—AI DIALOGIC PARTNER SUPPORTING EMPLOYABILITY SKILLS

The figure illustrates the multifaceted role of an AI Dialogic Partner in supporting the development of employability skills. Positioned at the centre, the AI system functions not as a replacement for human educators but as a complementary pedagogical tool. Its design integrates reflective questioning, ethical dilemmas, scenario-based learning, personalised feedback, Socratic questioning, and metacognitive prompts. Collectively, these functions highlight the potential for AI to scaffold learners' engagement with complex competencies such as critical thinking, adaptability, and communication. The implementation of such systems requires interdisciplinary collaboration, drawing on computer science, educational theory, cognitive psychology, and ethics. Developers must embed pedagogical sensitivity and cultural responsiveness into the AI's design to ensure inclusivity and relevance for diverse learners. Furthermore, issues of data privacy, transparency, and equitable access remain paramount, as ethical governance is essential for building trust in AI-enhanced educational environments.

Importantly, the figure underlines that the AI Dialogic Partner should be understood as a reflective mirror rather than a didactic authority. Through adaptive questioning and contextual feedback, it creates opportunities for learners to explore real-world dilemmas, practice ethical decision-making, and cultivate self-awareness. These experiences resonate with the broader demands of contemporary labour markets, where employers increasingly value transferable skills—ethical judgement, problem-solving, and effective communication—over rote knowledge alone. When thoughtfully integrated into the curriculum, such AI-driven support can extend the reach of teaching while remaining sensitive to individual learner trajectories. This alignment with lifelong learning frameworks situates the AI Dialogic Partner not merely as a technological innovation but as an evolving pedagogical ally, capable of reinforcing human-led education in an AI-augmented world. Within this vision, future-ready pedagogies are emphasised. For now, it is offered as a provocation: to imagine a form of AI in education that does not merely replicate what already exists, but reimagines what learning can become when technology is designed to converse with, rather than dictate to, the learner.

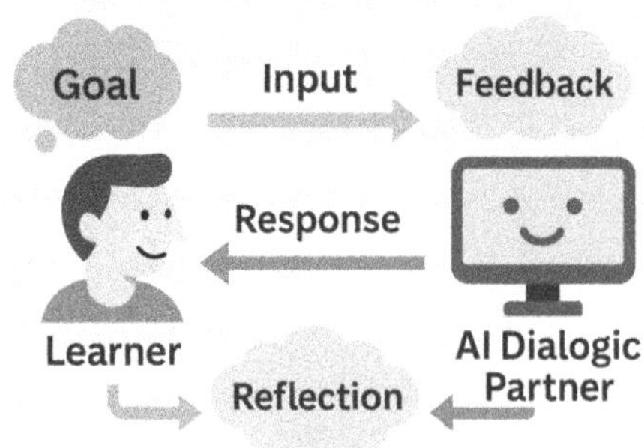

FIGURE 1.7 AI-supported dialogic learning cycle.

This figure illustrates the interactive cycle between the learner and an AI Dialogic Partner, where goals lead to input, feedback informs responses, and reflection enhances continuous learning.

BOX 1.7 EXPLANATION NOTE—AI-SUPPORTED DIALOGIC LEARNING CYCLE

The figure represents the AI-Supported Dialogic Learning Cycle, a framework for understanding the dynamic interplay between the learner and an AI Dialogic Partner. It highlights how goals, input, feedback, response, and reflection operate as interdependent processes that shape educational engagement. At the outset, the learner establishes a goal, which sets the cognitive and motivational trajectory for the interaction. This goal generates the input that activates the AI Dialogic Partner, which, in turn, provides feedback. Unlike traditional unidirectional teaching models, this framework positions AI as a dialogic participant, offering adaptive feedback that supports knowledge construction. The learner's response reflects active engagement with this feedback, enabling iterative cycles of understanding. Importantly, the cycle culminates in reflection, through which learners critically evaluate their learning process and deepen metacognitive awareness. This reflective dimension prevents AI-supported learning from being reduced to mere procedural correction, ensuring instead that learners develop self-regulation and critical thinking skills.

Contemporary discussions surrounding AI in distance education are frequently characterised by an undercurrent of optimism. In keeping with earlier reflections, AI is often presented as a technological panacea—offering solutions to persistent challenges related to access, engagement, and scalability (Zawacki-Richter et al., 2019). This framing, however, tends to gloss over more complex and enduring concerns, which extend beyond issues of data privacy and algorithmic bias. Among these is the subtle yet significant reshaping of pedagogical relationships and practices that accompanies such technological integration. AI is too often construed as a neutral instrument—an efficient mechanism devoid of context, values, or interpretive agency. Yet such a perspective risks concealing the ways in which AI systems can inadvertently perpetuate narrow, standardised conceptions of intelligence, success, and employability. These frameworks may marginalise alternative ways of knowing and learning, thereby limiting the diversity and inclusivity that contemporary education increasingly seeks to uphold. To navigate the tensions between promise and peril, it may be helpful to revisit the ancient Greek figure of Socrates and his daimonion—an inner prompting grounded not in command, but in quiet inquiry. This daimonion did not replace discourse; rather, it served as an invitation to pause, to reflect, and to question. In a similar vein, conceptualising AI as a dialogic partner in education offers a gentler and more reflective alternative to prevailing narratives. Here, AI is not cast as a surrogate teacher or assessor, but as a companion in thought—one that encourages ethical deliberation, critical engagement, and self-directed inquiry.

This approach contrasts sharply with dominant implementations of AI in higher education, which are frequently driven by imperatives of scale, efficiency, and data-driven optimisation. As Luckin et al. (2016) note, while intelligent systems have the potential to support formative feedback and learner regulation, they are often shaped by institutional priorities that favour measurable outcomes over meaningful educational experience. In such contexts, the richness of human learning risks being reduced to a series of predictive pathways and performance indicators. The notion of the dialogic partner proposes a more humane and intellectually generous vision. It reminds us that learning is not solely the acquisition of information, but a process of engagement—an unfolding of understanding shaped by conversation, uncertainty, and the reflective space between question and answer. Taken together, the figure and its underlying framework visualise the promise of AI as an enabler of dialogic pedagogy. Yet a critical perspective remains essential. The interaction cycle demonstrates how AI might scaffold deeper learning, but it must be implemented in ways that respect fairness, accountability, transparency, and human oversight (FAT-HO principles) while safeguarding learner autonomy. Ultimately, conceptualising AI as a dialogic partner, rather than a replacement for human teachers, positions it as a tool for promoting inclusivity, reflection, and context-sensitive learning.

centre of this cycle is the learner, who begins with a goal and translates this into input for the AI system. The AI responds with feedback, designed to prompt reflection rather than simply deliver answers, and the learner then generates a response that feeds back into the cycle. The iterative nature of this exchange highlights learning as a dialogic and co-constructive process.

What is critical in this representation is the emphasis on learner agency. Rather than positioning the AI as an instructional authority, the model frames it as a partner in dialogue that supports, challenges, and provokes new ways of thinking. Reflection is not incidental but central to the process, reinforcing the development of metacognitive awareness and self-regulation—capacities widely recognised as crucial for employability and lifelong learning. The cycle also makes visible how abstract capacities from the first figure are enacted: reflective thinking emerges from the learner's consideration of feedback, ethical reasoning and scenario-based learning are stimulated through the framing of goals and dilemmas, personalised feedback and Socratic questioning occur in the adaptive exchanges with the AI, and metacognitive reflection is embedded structurally in the cycle itself. Collectively, the two figures form a coherent framework for understanding both what an AI Dialogic Partner can achieve and how it achieves it. The first identifies the skills that are nurtured, while the second explains the process by which learners and AI co-construct those skills through dialogue, reflection, and iterative goal-setting. This integration highlights the importance of future-ready pedagogies, where AI is not designed to replicate existing teaching practices but to reimagine what learning might become when technology is developed to converse with learners, rather than dictate to them (Figure 1.7).

Against this backdrop, the concept of the AI Dialogic Partner provides a way of reimagining how learners engage with both employability processes and personalised learning trajectories. Instead of being viewed as a surrogate teacher or automated assessor, the AI system is reconceptualised as a dialogic companion—one that supports skill development, stimulates reflection, and nurtures ethical reasoning, while also adapting to learners' individual contexts through engagement, feedback, and guidance. This framing aligns with dialogic traditions in education that position knowledge as co-constructed through interaction rather than passively transmitted (Wegerif, 2013). Figure 1.8 visualises this dual role of AI in education. On the left, it highlights the employability process, encompassing skill development, reflection, and ethical reasoning. On the right, it depicts the personalisation dimension, comprising engagement, feedback, and guidance. At the centre sits the AI Dialogic Partner, mediating between these two domains and reinforcing the reciprocal relationship between learners. This framework underlines the potential of AI to enable not only the acquisition of employability attributes but also the cultivation of adaptable, ethically grounded, and personalised learning experiences (Figure 1.8).

Building on the earlier framework of employability and personalisation, Figure 1.8 presents the conceptualisation of the AI Dialogic Partner by situating it within a Socratic model of learning. Whereas the previous figures highlighted how AI mediates between employability processes (skill development, reflection, ethical reasoning) and personalised learning dimensions (engagement, feedback, guidance), this model focuses more explicitly on the dialogic and philosophical underpinnings of AI-supported learning. The figure

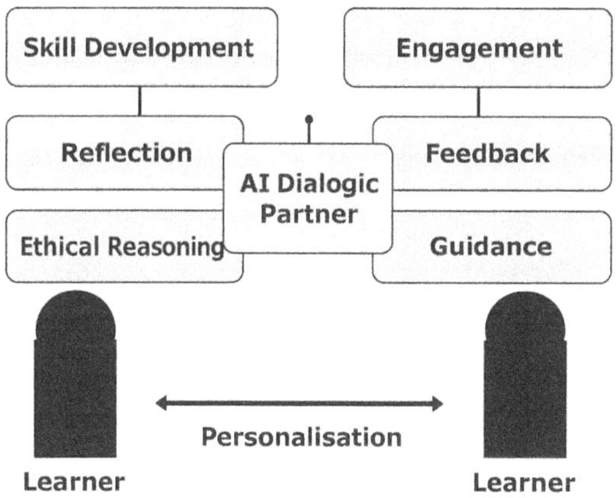

FIGURE 1.8 AI Dialogic Partner in employability development and personalised learning.

This figure illustrates how the AI Dialogic Partner supports the employability process through skill development, reflection, and ethical reasoning, while simultaneously enabling personalisation by fostering engagement, providing feedback, and offering guidance to learners.

BOX 1.8 EXPLANATION NOTE—AI DIALOGIC PARTNER IN EMPLOYABILITY DEVELOPMENT AND PERSONALISED LEARNING

The figure conceptualises the role of the AI Dialogic Partner in bridging two interconnected dimensions of contemporary education: the employability process and personalisation. On one side, employability development is represented through skill acquisition, reflective practice, and ethical reasoning. On the other, personalisation is enacted through learner-centred engagement, adaptive feedback, and tailored guidance. Together, these processes demonstrate how AI can contribute not only to the technical dimensions of employability but also to the cultivation of reflective and ethical capacities essential in rapidly changing professional landscapes. Within this dialogic framing, AI becomes a companion in thought rather than a surrogate teacher. It is capable of posing questions that unsettle, of offering perspectives that challenge assumptions, and of supporting learners as they form their own interpretations. This mode of engagement resonates with broader humanistic traditions in education—traditions that view knowledge not as fixed content to be transmitted, but as something formed in the space between self and other, learner and world.

The strength of this approach lies in its challenge to prevailing narratives of AI as a neutral, efficiency-driven tool of automation. Instead, the dialogic partner reframes AI as an interlocutor that fosters critical thinking, curiosity, and agency. For the AI to fulfil such a role, however, thoughtful design is essential. Dialogue must not be simulated merely for superficial engagement; it must be meaningful, ethical, and inclusive. This requires transparency in system design, attentiveness to the diverse epistemologies learners bring, and resistance to narrow, metric-driven conceptions of educational 'success'. When these conditions are met, the AI Dialogic Partner has the potential to support not only the acquisition of employability skills but also the cultivation of deeper, more resilient forms of employability—those grounded in adaptability, ethical discernment, and reflective practice. In this light, AI in education need not be framed as a threat to pedagogical values. Rather, it may become, like Socrates' daimonion, a quiet presence—one that does not provide definitive answers, but instead opens the space for reflection, questioning, and becoming.

positions the learner and the AI Dialogic Partner within a cyclical process of reflective learning, mediated by Socratic questioning. In this framing, AI is not cast as a transmitter of information but as 'a quiet reflective companion' that encourages learners to interrogate assumptions, engage with ambiguity, and deliberate ethically. This aligns with long-standing traditions of dialogic pedagogy, in which knowledge emerges not as a fixed commodity but as a co-constructed process shaped by inquiry, conversation, and reflection.

The conceptual continuity with the employability–personalisation framework is clear. The earlier model emphasised AI's role in facilitating practical competencies and adaptive learning pathways, while this Socratic model advances a deeper philosophical claim: that AI can cultivate critical thinking, ethical deliberation, and openness to uncertainty. Together, the two figures demonstrate that the AI Dialogic Partner supports not only instrumental aspects of employability but also the more profound intellectual and ethical capacities required for lifelong learning and democratic participation. By situating AI within a Socratic framework, the figure suggests a reorientation of technology's role in education. Instead of being driven solely by institutional imperatives of efficiency and prediction, AI can be mobilised as a reflective partner—one that expands the learner's capacity for questioning, discernment, and engagement with complexity. In this way, the two frameworks are complementary: the first attends to employability and personalised support, while the second deepens the model to highlight the humanistic and dialogic values that must underpin any responsible educational use of AI (Figure 1.9).

The preceding figures collectively illustrate the evolving conceptualisation of the AI Dialogic Partner as both a pedagogical and ethical construct within contemporary education. The first model presented the AI Dialogic Partner through the lens of the Socratic tradition, emphasising reflective learning, critical thinking, and ethical deliberation as outcomes of dialogic engagement. Here, the AI is positioned not as an oracle of knowledge but as a reflective companion—provoking inquiry, engaging with ambiguity, and

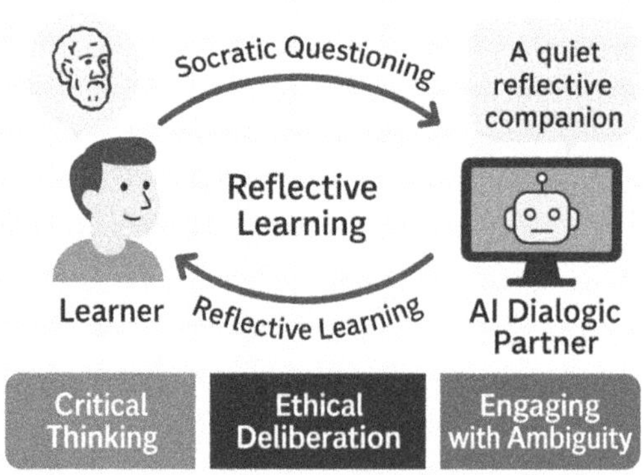

FIGURE 1.9 AI Dialogic Partner as Socratic model of reflective learning.

The AI Dialogic Partner as a Socratic model of reflective learning, fostering critical thinking, ethical deliberation, and engagement with ambiguity through dialogic questioning.

BOX 1.9 EXPLANATION NOTE—AI DIALOGIC PARTNER AS SOCRATIC MODEL OF REFLECTIVE LEARNING

As we deepen our conceptualisation of the AI Dialogic Partner, it becomes increasingly important to interrogate not only how such systems support individual learning but also how they may reshape the structural values that underpin educational practice. The discourse has shifted beyond technocratic narratives of efficiency and optimisation towards normative frameworks that place ethical and philosophical commitments at the centre of AI integration. Such frameworks foreground transparency, democratic accountability, and epistemic justice as foundational design principles, rather than peripheral concerns (Nartey, 2025). Within this evolving landscape, emerging forms of modular education—such as micro-credentials and stackable learning pathways—represent key sites for potential intervention. While these formats promise increased flexibility and accessibility, particularly within vocational, adult, and community-based contexts (Carnevale et al., 2020), their educational value is not intrinsic. Rather, their significance lies in whether AI systems are mobilised to enrich understanding and promote deeper reflection or merely to expedite credentialism and transactional forms of recognition.

Consequently, the AI Dialogic Partner must be positioned not as a neutral delivery mechanism but as an active participant in rethinking what counts as knowledge, skill, and educational worth. This repositioning requires recognition that learning is not reducible to information transfer; it is a relational, value-laden process that unfolds through inquiry, discomfort, and dialogue. It is precisely here that the Socratic metaphor acquires renewed relevance: the AI Dialogic Partner functions less as an oracle of definitive answers and more as a reflective companion, an interlocutor that provokes questioning and facilitates ethical deliberation. Such reframing compels a reconsideration of the metrics by which success in education and employment is defined. Conventional indicators—such as completion rates, job placement statistics, or algorithmic matches—capture only a partial dimension of educational outcomes. A genuinely human-centric AI agenda must instead incorporate measures of intellectual resilience, ethical maturity, and dialogic openness. These attributes are increasingly vital for learners seeking to navigate a future characterised by volatility, automation, and global interdependence.

Ultimately, the integration of the AI Dialogic Partner into educational systems must be informed not only by innovation but also by ethical imagination. This imagination re-envisions learning as a process of becoming rather than mere performance, one in which employability is conceived not as a transactional endpoint but as an evolving capability. Such capability is cultivated through the interplay of technology, pedagogy, and human judgement—an interplay where the AI Dialogic Partner serves as a Socratic ally in the co-construction of knowledge, meaning, and purpose.

nurturing intellectual resilience. Figure 1.9 extended this framing by linking the AI Dialogic Partner to broader educational values and normative commitments. It demonstrated how AI's role transcends individual learning encounters, requiring integration into value-based frameworks that prioritise transparency, democratic accountability, and epistemic justice. At the same time, it highlighted the relevance of modular education formats—such as micro-credentials and stackable learning pathways—where AI systems may either deepen pedagogical richness or risk reducing education to transactional credentialism.

Figure 1.10 situates these dimensions within the context of the ethics of employability. It highlights the dual responsibility of AI Dialogic Partners: to enable flexible educational pathways while simultaneously cultivating learners' capacity for ethical and civic engagement. This requires embedding AI not only in processes of critical thinking dialogue—judgement, inquiry, and productive discomfort—but also in institutional frameworks that safeguard the integrity of educational purpose. Collectively, the figures provide a multilayered account of the AI Dialogic Partner: as a Socratic interlocutor, a participant in normative frameworks, and a mediator of employability ethics. This integrated perspective consolidates pedagogical, structural, and ethical dimensions, affirming that the role of AI in education must be guided as much by ethical imagination as by technological innovation (Figure 1.10).

The international discourse on AI and education has matured considerably over the past years, shifting from aspirational declarations to more structured frameworks that seek to embed AI within educational reform. Landmark texts such as the Beijing Consensus on Artificial Intelligence and Education (UNESCO, 2019), UNESCO's Guidance for Policy-Makers (UNESCO, 2021a), and the UNESCO's Guidance for Generative AI in Education and Research (2023) illustrate this evolution, while the OECD's work on skills and labour markets underlines the economic imperatives that drive much of the global conversation. Taken together, these contributions reflect a growing awareness that education must adapt to AI-mediated futures. Yet the frameworks often remain shaped by technocratic priorities, emphasising governance, curricula, and market responsiveness over the deeper pedagogical foundations required for meaningful integration. The Beijing Consensus is significant for affirming equity, inclusion, and sustainability as guiding values. However, its vision is difficult to realise in contexts where infrastructure and teacher capacity are limited, and its call for AI literacy tends towards functional rather than critical skills. This narrow framing risks reducing learners to passive users of technology. Here, the conceptual models presented in the figures offer an important counterpoint. In the first, the AI

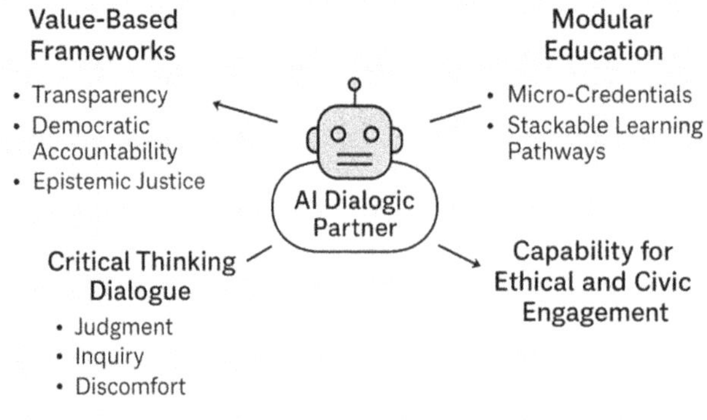

FIGURE 1.10 AI Dialogic Partner framework for employability ethics.

The AI Dialogic Partner fosters employability through value-based frameworks, critical thinking, modular education, and ethical civic engagement.

BOX 1.10 EXPLANATION NOTE—AI DIALOGIC PARTNER FRAMEWORK FOR EMPLOYABILITY ETHICS

The figure illustrates the conceptualisation of the AI Dialogic Partner as a mediating tool in the ethics of employability. At the centre, the AI Dialogic Partner functions as both a technological and pedagogical interlocutor, enabling learners to engage with ethical, cognitive, and civic dimensions of employability. Surrounding this core are four interlinked domains that frame the ethical and educational potential of AI-mediated dialogue. First, Value-Based Frameworks emphasise principles such as transparency, democratic accountability, and epistemic justice. These values ensure that AI-assisted employability training is not merely instrumental but grounded in fairness, inclusivity, and responsible governance. Second, Critical Thinking Dialogue highlights the cultivation of judgement, inquiry, and the productive role of discomfort. This reflects the necessity for learners to not only acquire technical competencies but also to critically interrogate assumptions, adapt to uncertainty, and foster resilience in professional contexts. Third, Modular Education is represented through micro-credentials and stackable learning pathways, which align with contemporary shifts towards flexible, lifelong learning. This modularity underlines the role of AI in scaffolding personalised educational trajectories that respond to evolving labour market needs.

Finally, the Capability for Ethical and Civic Engagement situates employability within broader social responsibilities. This dimension reflects a commitment to preparing learners not solely as workers but as ethically responsible and civically engaged citizens capable of navigating complex socio-technical landscapes. Overall, the figure conceptualises the AI Dialogic Partner as more than a technical adjunct; it represents a transformative agent within higher education and professional learning. By integrating values, critical reflection, modularity, and civic engagement, the framework positions AI as a dialogic partner that enhances not only employability but also ethical agency and democratic participation.

Dialogic Partner is shown as the hub of a wider ecosystem that connects value-based frameworks, modular pathways, critical thinking dialogue, and ethical and civic engagement. This positioning demonstrates how AI can be aligned with principles of transparency and accountability, while also supporting flexible learning structures without losing sight of ethical responsibility.

The OECD's analyses of skills and employability highlight the adaptability required for the future of work, but often reduce learners to economic actors. By contrast, the dialogic partner model reframes employability as more than vocational readiness. As Figure 1.9 illustrates, the AI Dialogic Partner can serve as a reflective companion that supports Socratic questioning, ethical deliberation, and engagement with ambiguity. This approach suggests that employability should be understood as the cultivation of judgement and resilience, capacities that go beyond technical proficiency. Rather than positioning AI as an instructional device, this model portrays it as a partner in inquiry and reflection, thereby opening up space for a more transformative pedagogy. Figure 1.8 extends this by showing how AI mediates processes such as skill development, reflection, ethical reasoning, engagement, feedback, and guidance. It reframes personalisation, a term often understood in policy discourse as the adaptive delivery of content, as a relational and interpretive process. Within this view, personalisation is not about tailoring outputs to learners but about enabling co-construction of meaning through dialogue. This moves away from the instrumental orientation of many international frameworks and places emphasis on learner agency and ethical reasoning.

Figure 1.7 reinforces this by depicting learning as an iterative cycle of goal-setting, input, feedback, response, and reflection. Rather than conceiving AI integration as a linear transaction, this model highlights recursive processes where learners remain active agents. It illustrates how AI can sustain reflective practice and adaptability, ensuring that feedback is not merely corrective but developmental. In this way, the model demonstrates the potential of AI to nurture dispositions such as critical awareness and ethical engagement—capacities essential for navigating digital societies. Viewed collectively, these conceptualisations offer a critique of the limitations in current global policy frameworks. They highlight that while UNESCO and the OECD have established important guiding structures, their emphasis on governance, efficiency, and labour market responsiveness often leaves pedagogical questions underdeveloped. The dialogic partner models respond to this gap by presenting AI not as a mechanism of delivery but as a reflective presence that supports inquiry, deliberation, and co-construction of knowledge. They also reframe sustainability beyond institutional stability to include the cultivation of critical, ethical, and adaptive capacities in learners. In this sense, the AI Dialogic Partner functions as a metaphor for a more holistic and transformative paradigm of education, one that moves beyond narrow literacy or instrumental personalisation. It represents an approach in which AI complements human dialogue rather than replacing it, helping learners to interrogate assumptions, engage with complexity, and participate meaningfully in shaping technological futures. As the discussion now shifts towards practical considerations, the challenge lies in how these dialogic principles can be translated into diverse educational contexts, ensuring that international policy ambitions are grounded in pedagogy that is both sustainable and inclusive.

The UNESCO Guidance for Generative AI in Education and Research (2023) signals a more mature stage in the global conversation, acknowledging directly the ethical and epistemic dilemmas that AI introduces into learning environments. Yet the document functions more as a lighthouse than a navigational chart: it casts light on dangers such as bias, dishonesty, and inequity, but offers limited instruction on how education systems with varying capacities might chart a safe and purposeful course. What is missing is not the recognition of risks but the means to translate ideals into daily practice. Here, the conception of the AI Dialogic Partner becomes valuable. It does not steer the vessel of education in place of teachers and learners, but rather travels alongside them, provoking questions and sustaining reflection. Its strength lies in enabling learners to situate their knowledge, to test assumptions, and to connect immediate tasks with wider purposes. This allegory shifts the emphasis from AI as an autopilot—automating delivery and decision-making—to AI as a compass, helping learners orient themselves amid uncertainty. This framing is particularly relevant in vocational and technical learning, where competence alone cannot prepare learners for the shifting demands of digital and green economies. The UNESCO TVET Strategy 2022–2029 highlights adaptability and lifelong learning, yet its engagement with AI remains pragmatic, too often limited to efficiency and monitoring. In contrast, the dialogic partner introduces a more relational model, one that links real-time labour market information with the reflective and ethical dimensions required for meaningful participation in dynamic work contexts. In doing so, it ensures that practice is not divorced from purpose, nor skill from responsibility.

The OECD's Impact of AI on the Workplace (2023) highlights a central tension: employers frequently report gains in productivity and efficiency, yet workers voice concerns about autonomy, surveillance, and redundancy. Parallel anxieties emerge in education, particularly in the growing use of predictive analytics and outcome-driven design. Such practices risk positioning learners primarily as data points to be measured and nudged, narrowing educational purpose and diminishing agency. Against this backdrop, the idea of the AI Dialogic Partner offers an alternative orientation. Rather than intervening to optimise behaviours, it is conceived as a partner in inquiry—engaging learners through questioning, prompting reflection, and supporting ethical deliberation. In doing so, it helps cultivate dispositions such as reflective judgement, contextual reasoning, and ethical awareness, capacities that are increasingly recognised as essential for navigating the complexities of civic and professional life. Importantly, this model complements rather than displaces the role of educators, creating space for dialogue and learner voice, and repositioning AI as a facilitator of transformation rather than a driver of transactional efficiency.

This reframing contributes to a wider reconsideration of employability in the age of AI. Dominant constructions, shaped by discourses of efficiency and productivity, tend to treat skills as static and measurable, overlooking the relational and adaptive dimensions required in dynamic labour markets. The OECD's findings suggest that AI is less a simple disruptor of work than a catalyst for reconfiguring how skills are valued and enacted, underscoring the need for educational approaches that nurture adaptability, critical reflexivity, and ethical judgement. International frameworks such as UNESCO's Guidance for Generative AI in Education and Research (2023) foreground the importance of equitable access and ethical use, yet they often remain aspirational, offering limited guidance on how these commitments can be realised in resource-constrained contexts. The AI Dialogic Partner can be read as a pedagogical construct that bridges this gap: not a technological fix but a conceptual mechanism designed to stimulate inquiry, encourage situated learning, and foster meta-cognitive capacities. In this way, it provides a practical grammar for enacting the values articulated in global policy, embedding them within the lived experience of learners.

This reconceptualisation extends most forcefully into the field of vocational education and training, where UNESCO's 2022–2029 strategy acknowledges the importance of adaptability and lifelong learning but offers only limited engagement with the pedagogical implications of AI. The dialogic model outlined here provides a complementary vision: one in which vocational learning is not confined to procedural competence or market alignment, but is shaped by dynamic, learner-centred encounters with real-time labour market intelligence, held in balance with reflective and ethical inquiry. In this reading, the OECD's analyses of AI and the workplace cease to be treated as definitive accounts of inevitable economic shifts and instead become provocations—reminders that education must act as a safeguard for autonomy, creativity, and moral discernment in times of uncertainty.

Constructivist traditions, which resist linear models of input and output, prove indispensable in this regard. They remind us that education is not a machine calibrated for productivity, but a living practice grounded in subjectivity, agency, and dialogue. The AI Dialogic Partner embodies this orientation. It functions both as a theoretical construct and as a practical pedagogical tool, offering a bridge between broad policy discourse and lived classroom realities, between the immediate demands of labour markets and the enduring purposes of education. In doing so, it resists the optimisation logic that dominates much of the discourse surrounding AI, privileging instead relational and interpretive engagements that affirm knowledge as a shared and evolving enterprise.

At the same time, this model addresses concerns of equity, inclusion, and literacy. Access to AI-enhanced opportunities is unevenly distributed, shaped by socio-economic disparities, infrastructural gaps, and institutional readiness. The dialogic approach, therefore, advocates inclusive design and interdisciplinary collaboration, with a commitment to critical AI literacy that equips learners not simply to operate technology, but to interrogate and influence its development. Strategically, it situates AI within long-term visions of education, not as a novelty or adjunct but as a companion in cultivating dispositions that balance vocational preparation with ethical, civic, and reflective capacities. To bring this section to a close, one might recall the allegory of Daedalus and Icarus. AI resembles the unpredictable winds that shape the skies of learning and labour: powerful, enabling, yet potentially perilous. The AI Dialogic Partner, in this metaphor, is not the waxen wings of overconfidence, nor the anchor of fear, but the compass that enables navigation—guiding learners to fly not merely higher, but more wisely. It is through this careful orientation, situated at the intersection of humanistic inquiry and technological transformation, that education can chart a path towards an equitable and ethical future of work. As the preceding discussion has demonstrated, the integration of AI into education invites a reorientation of purpose that moves beyond efficiency and instrumentalism towards more reflective, dialogic, and ethical paradigms. This challenge is especially acute in higher education, where questions of employability intersect with global policy frameworks, institutional innovation, and shifting labour market demands. In this context, higher education is not merely a site of skill transmission but a crucible in which adaptability, critical judgement, and civic responsibility must be cultivated. The following section explores how universities and colleges can navigate these intersecting pressures, examining the role of policy, innovation, and international perspectives in shaping employability for an AI-mediated future.

REIMAGINING HIGHER EDUCATION AND EMPLOYABILITY: INNOVATION, POLICY, AND GLOBAL PERSPECTIVES IN AN AI-MEDIATED AGE

Building on the preceding reflections on policy, pedagogy, and employability, this final section turns to the role of higher education in shaping responses to the challenges and opportunities of AI. Universities are increasingly positioned not simply as repositories of disciplinary knowledge, but as environments where learners can cultivate the cognitive, ethical, and relational capacities required for uncertain futures. In this context, AI is less a technical add-on than a prompt to reconsider how institutions prepare graduates for work, citizenship, and lifelong learning in rapidly evolving societies. Emerging evidence indicates that higher education is engaging AI in diverse and sometimes unexpected ways (Ajani et al., 2024). Within research, tools such as natural language processing and machine learning are extending the boundaries of inquiry, supporting collaborations across fields that have traditionally been distinct. These developments carry pedagogical significance: they model forms of integrative problem-solving that can inform curriculum design and encourage learners to approach complex challenges from multiple perspectives. Yet they also raise epistemological questions, including how disciplinary integrity is preserved or reshaped when AI mediates methods of knowledge production.

Alongside this, the use of AI for skills forecasting reflects a growing awareness of the need for anticipatory approaches to curriculum reform. By analysing labour market trends, some universities are beginning to adapt programmes to align with emergent competencies. Such initiatives may help institutions remain responsive, but they also carry risks. When forecasting becomes an overriding principle, there is a danger that educational purpose is reduced to what is readily measurable or immediately valuable to employers, leaving little space for broader developmental aims. For these reasons, embedding AI within higher education requires more than technical implementation. It calls for careful attention to student agency, academic freedom, and the quality of the learning experience. Ethical considerations must be central, ensuring that inclusion and equity are not subordinated to efficiency. Questions of access and infrastructure also remain pressing, as uneven resources risk widening divides between institutions and learners. At its most constructive, the integration of AI can enable curriculum innovation and pedagogical renewal; yet its promise will only be realised if it is approached as an opportunity to deepen, rather than diminish, the human dimensions of education.

Akinwalere and Ivanov (2022) provide a valuable account of how AI is being deployed to enhance institutional performance, particularly through predictive analytics, automation, and data modelling. These applications can support efficiency in research management and operational processes, yet their increasing influence on research agendas raises epistemological concerns. The danger lies in narrowing scholarship to that which is readily quantifiable, thereby constraining the autonomy and exploratory character of academic inquiry. This is not to dismiss technological innovation, but rather to call for epistemic humility—an acknowledgement that knowledge production must remain open to unpredictability, plurality, and dissent. Southworth et al. (2023) approach the issue from a pedagogical standpoint, advocating for AI as a transversal literacy to be embedded across disciplines. Their vision captures the increasingly hybrid character of education and work, highlighting the need for adaptable, cross-cutting competencies. The model presupposes considerable institutional capacity in terms of infrastructure, faculty development, and interdisciplinary coordination. In resource-constrained settings, where workloads are high and digital provision is limited, such ambitions may inadvertently exacerbate inequalities by privileging institutions already advantaged in the digital landscape.

Offering a more holistic perspective, Allam et al. (2025) advance the notion of 'living intelligence'—a co-evolutionary synthesis of human and artificial cognition designed to enhance curricular foresight. Their framework emphasises augmentation rather than displacement of human judgement, recognising AI's potential to inform future-oriented curriculum design. Yet their optimism warrants caution. Predictive profiling, while intended to anticipate learner needs, may risk reinforcing normative assumptions of success and narrowing space for dissent or creative deviation. Systems that aspire to foresight must therefore preserve openness to uncertainty and disruption—qualities fundamental to democratic and critical education. Together, these studies indicate a shift in the discourse on AI in higher education away from narrow efficiencies towards considerations of curriculum, pedagogy, and ethos. Nonetheless, they often underplay the sociopolitical conditions that shape access and implementation. Without addressing systemic inequalities, even the most imaginative frameworks risk abstraction. A more relational and dialogic approach to AI integration is therefore needed—one that foregrounds learner agency, nurtures critical reflection, and sustains epistemic diversity. The concept of the AI Dialogic Partner exemplifies such an orientation: not guiding learners through predetermined algorithmic pathways, but engaging them in open-ended intellectual encounters that foster adaptability, ethical awareness, and reflective forms of employability.

The article Artificial Intelligence and the Future of Higher Education, Part 1 (Association of Governing Boards, 2023) foregrounds the role of AI research institutes as engines of interdisciplinary collaboration and policy influence. While this perspective captures their catalytic potential, the analysis tends to privilege prestige and performance metrics over questions of inclusivity and democratic participation. What remains underexplored is how such infrastructures might be harnessed—or indeed distorted—in shaping equitable forms of employability for those traditionally marginalised within higher education. More speculative contributions, such as How AI is Shaping the Future of Higher Ed (Inside Higher Ed, 2023) and An AI-Driven Optimism for Transforming Higher Education (It's Not What You Think) (EDUCAUSE Review, 2025), attempt to move beyond optimisation logics, suggesting that AI could re-centre empathy, creativity, and learner agency. These arguments resonate with constructivist critiques of instrumentalist pedagogy, yet their transformative promise is undermined by limited engagement with the power asymmetries embedded in AI systems and the absence of clear implementation pathways. Without attention to the uneven ways AI is adopted across institutions, these visions remain suspended between aspiration and reality.

At a more strategic level, Artificial Intelligence and the Future of Higher Education: A Strategic Vision (Tobenkin, 2024) outlines a forward-looking framework centred on ethical governance, faculty development, and interdisciplinary centres of excellence. While ambitious in scope, the account pays insufficient attention to the material conditions that determine institutional capacity—most notably, funding constraints, academic precarity, and fragmented policy landscapes. Employability, where referenced, is treated in largely abstract terms, framed as curriculum alignment or technical preparation rather than as a socially embedded construct shaped by structural inequalities. Taken together, these contributions illuminate higher education's evolving relationship with AI, but they also reveal a striking gap: employability continues to be addressed primarily as a technical or economic concern, stripped of its political, cultural, and ethical dimensions. The risk is that it becomes reduced to a navigational chart of skills, when in truth it is more akin to a constellation—its meaning shifting depending on perspective, history, and context. If AI represents the vast cosmos of possibility—expansive, uncertain, and sometimes disorienting—then universities must act not as passive observers but as cartographers of this sky. The AI Dialogic Partner can be imagined here as a guiding star: not dictating a single trajectory, but providing orientation, enabling learners to chart their own courses with agency, reflection, and critical awareness. Such an approach reframes employability as more than preparation for labour; it becomes an ongoing practice of navigation—ethical, situated, and plural—through the shifting constellations of work, knowledge, and society.

The global picture of AI in higher education is best understood not as a linear trajectory but as a patchwork of uneven developments, shaped by context, capacity, and culture. Jin et al.'s (2025) comparative study of 40 universities across six world regions illustrates this unevenness: some institutions integrate generative AI rapidly into teaching and administration, while others adopt a more cautious stance, constrained by policy ambiguity, limited resources, and unresolved questions of trust. Yet, despite its breadth, the study omits a crucial dimension—how AI intersects with employability. In overlooking the shifting dynamics of skill formation and labour market transformation, it stops short of addressing the very forces that increasingly define the purposes of higher education. This omission reflects a broader reluctance within both scholarship and policy to reimagine employability as a dynamic, evolving capacity rather than a fixed outcome. One limitation of prevailing debates is the tendency to frame AI integration in binary terms—either present or absent—an approach that obscures the subtler ways in which institutions interpret and embed new technologies. More revealing is to examine how AI is negotiated within specific educational cultures. A university might implement AI-based assessment systems without considering how such tools influence students' understanding of knowledge and identity. Meanwhile, another institution with limited infrastructure may nonetheless cultivate rigorous critical dialogue about fairness, ethics, and epistemology. These contrasting examples show that the significance of AI adoption lies less in its technical presence than in the intentionality and reflexivity with which it is approached.

To conceptualise this more productively, higher education could be imagined as a garden rather than a factory. In a factory model, technologies are installed to increase throughput; in a garden, growth is shaped by soil, climate, and careful cultivation. Similarly, AI should not be imposed as a preconfigured system, but cultivated in dialogue with pedagogical values, cultural priorities, and learner needs. In this sense, institutions would be encouraged to develop adaptive ecosystems for AI integration—responsive environments in which technologies and educational practices evolve together. Such an approach calls for what might be termed a 'living AI strategy': a framework that grows iteratively, open to revision as new ethical questions, social demands, and technological possibilities emerge. This orientation does not attempt to fix the future in advance but allows institutions to adapt with it, sustaining the broader purposes of higher education while responding to the shifting conditions of the present.

In this light, higher education's task is less about mastering a finished tool and more about cultivating an environment in which AI can take root responsibly. Just as a garden cannot flourish on fertiliser alone, universities cannot rely solely on technical adoption or market alignment. Soil must be tended, weeds kept in check, and diverse species nurtured to ensure resilience. Likewise, institutions must balance efficiency with equity, innovation with reflection, and employability with broader civic and ethical capacities. If AI represents a new species introduced into this educational ecosystem, its integration must be carefully stewarded. Left unchecked, it may dominate the terrain, displacing existing practices and narrowing the diversity of knowledge. Cultivated thoughtfully, however, it can enrich the ecosystem—stimulating interdisciplinary growth, supporting adaptability, and enabling learners to thrive in uncertain conditions. This requires patience, care, and an openness to unpredictability: qualities that mirror the rhythms of education itself. A 'living AI strategy', therefore, resembles less a master plan and more an ongoing act of cultivation. It allows institutions to adapt as conditions change, while safeguarding the values that sustain meaningful learning. In this way, employability can be reimagined not as the production of uniform outputs, but as the nurturing of capacities—resilient, reflective, and ethically grounded—that enable graduates to navigate and contribute to a complex world.

An allegory from the Akan people of West Africa offers a useful way of rethinking AI strategy in education. The Eban, a protective fence around the household, is never static: it is repaired, extended, or repositioned in response to changing circumstances. It signifies safety, but also adaptability and care. In the same way, an institutional approach to AI should not be conceived as a fixed structure, settled once and for all. Rather, it must remain porous and evolving, attentive to the lived realities of learners and educators. If AI is to support employability meaningfully, its role cannot be confined to automating feedback or streamlining instruction. Instead, it must contribute to nurturing enduring dispositions such as adaptability, ethical reasoning, communication, and reflective judgement. These qualities arise less through optimisation than through dialogue—between people and technologies, between institutions and their communities, and between education and wider society. The key questions, then, are not whether AI has been adopted, but how it is shaping the ethical and epistemic life of the university, how it enables learners to navigate ambiguity with agency, and how institutions can design environments in which AI operates as a partner in inquiry rather than a directive authority. Framed in this way, employability can be reimagined not as a finite checklist of skills but as a lifelong process of becoming, shaped through ongoing encounters with knowledge, technology, and others.

Atkinson-Toal and Guo (2024) reinforce this view by emphasising the heterogeneity of higher education systems and cautioning against the homogenising influence of AI policies derived from Anglo-American models. Their work suggests that AI implementation should be understood as a reflexive dialogue between technologies and the socio-educational ecosystems into which they are introduced. One promising direction lies in the idea of regional AI knowledge commons: collaborative initiatives where institutions, industries, and communities co-develop open-source tools and resources that reflect local cultural values and economic priorities. Such initiatives can help to decentralise technological power while fostering forms of digital sovereignty that remain contextually grounded. A further dimension is highlighted by Tierney et al. (2025), whose findings foreground the affective economies surrounding AI adoption. Responses to AI are not uniform: feelings of inclusion, anxiety, or scepticism shape how students and staff engage with these tools.

Recognising this, institutions could embed affective mapping within their evaluative practices, enabling them to respond in real time to the emotional and relational dynamics of AI integration. Staff development and student support programmes might then be adapted to address concerns about surveillance, fairness, or cognitive outsourcing, thereby reinforcing trust as a pedagogical condition. In this sense, the cultivation of employability extends beyond skills into the affective and ethical life of the institution, reminding us that AI's impact will be determined as much by how it feels to engage with as by what it delivers.

The Akan allegory of the Eban—the protective fence around the household—offers a way to consolidate these reflections. It symbolises both security and adaptability, care and permeability. Conceived in this light, an AI strategy in education should not be treated as a finished structure, erected once and left to weather. Like the Eban, it must remain responsive to shifting contexts, attuned to the lived realities of learners and educators, and open to revision as new challenges and possibilities emerge. Placed alongside earlier illustrations, the allegory enriches the conceptual tapestry of this discussion. If the cosmos symbolises the vast, uncertain horizons of technological change, and the compass represents the orientation required to navigate them, then the Eban serves as the boundary that makes navigation meaningful—flexible enough to adjust, yet firm enough to provide protection and coherence. Similarly, the garden metaphor reminds us that growth must be cultivated, with attention to diversity, resilience, and care. This framing invites higher education to move beyond binary accounts of AI adoption, towards building 'living strategies' that combine foresight with humility, structure with openness. Employability, understood within such strategies, becomes not a checklist of competencies but a lifelong process of becoming—shaped through dialogue with others, with technologies, and with the shifting environments in which learners must find their way. The fence, the compass, the garden, and the cosmos together remind us that the future of education in the age of AI is not a question of rigid design but of careful stewardship: balancing protection with openness, orientation with uncertainty, and innovation with the enduring human need for meaning.

Al-Zahrani and Alasmari (2024) draw attention to the shortcomings of compliance-driven approaches to AI ethics, which have too often been confined to procedural measures such as plagiarism detection or content authentication. Such strategies, while practical, risk narrowing the ethical imagination. A more generative alternative would be to embed 'ethics-in-practice' within the very fabric of the university, through fellowships or collaborative initiatives that bring students and staff together in live audits of AI use. Rather than producing static codes, such initiatives could weave principles iteratively, much like a fabric that is strengthened and patterned through repeated interlacing. In this sense, ethics would become not an external checklist but an embodied, dialogic practice—integral to the rhythms of teaching, research, and institutional life. Equally important is the recognition that universal frameworks, often drafted from Anglo-American perspectives, can marginalise epistemologies that prioritise interdependence over individual achievement. As Blair et al. (2022) remind us, in many Global South contexts education is conceived as the cultivation of communal responsibility rather than the accumulation of discrete competencies. From this perspective, AI-enabled pedagogy might be imagined less as a tool of personalised optimisation and more as a river that sustains collective learning—its current carrying stories, shared struggles, and intergenerational dialogue. This metaphor illustrates the possibility of AI serving as a conduit for cooperation and social repair, rather than as an engine of competition or exclusion.

Drawing these strands together, the future of AI in higher education can be envisaged as a bridge-building exercise. The task is not merely to regulate technologies or anticipate their risks, but to construct pathways that connect efficiency with ethics, innovation with equity, and employability with the broader purposes of education. Such bridges must be designed with attentiveness to local terrains, resilient enough to bear the weight of diverse communities, and flexible enough to adapt as conditions shift. The challenge, then, is not only to manage AI's presence but also to reimagine the values it can serve when contextualised with care, grounded in plurality, and guided by a commitment to relational justice.

CONCLUSION

This chapter has argued that employability must be redefined in light of the transformative pressures of AI, automation, and globalisation. Traditional human capital models, which treat skills as fixed and education as linear preparation for work, are increasingly misaligned with the realities of fluid labour markets and AI-mediated systems. Instead, employability should be conceived as dynamic and relational, sustained by adaptability, ethical reasoning, and the capacity to navigate uncertainty. Central to this reconceptualisation is the recognition that skills are interdependent: technical proficiency cannot be disentangled from cognitive agility, communication, or ethical awareness. HEIs, therefore, face both a challenge and an opportunity: to move beyond static curricular models towards designs that integrate disciplinary depth with transversal capacities; to foster interdisciplinary collaboration that reflects the complexity of real-world problems; and to embed ethical reflection within pedagogy and assessment rather than treating it as an external supplement. Policy, too, has a role in incentivising and resourcing these changes, ensuring that equity and inclusivity are not sidelined as technologies advance.

AI, in this framing, is not a panacea but a catalyst. Its significance lies not in replacing human capabilities but in prompting a re-examination of how institutions prepare learners for both work and citizenship. Yet as global case studies suggest, the potential of AI to support more personalised, inclusive, and responsive education depends on context-sensitive governance, infrastructural investment, and deliberate strategies to mitigate inequality. Without such measures, the promise of AI risks reinforcing the very disparities it is often claimed to overcome. Employability in the age of AI might best be envisioned through the allegory of a constellation. Just as constellations are not fixed entities but shifting patterns that provide orientation, employability emerges at the intersection of individual capacities, institutional practices, technological systems, and societal values. Its form changes with perspective and historical moment, yet it offers guidance amid uncertainty. The task for higher education, then, is not simply to produce graduates with a checklist of competencies, but to help learners cultivate the reflexivity, ethical awareness, and adaptability needed to navigate this constellation with confidence. When supported by curriculum innovation, interdisciplinary practice, and inclusive governance, employability can function not merely as preparation for labour but as a pathway towards human flourishing in an AI-mediated world.

PATHWAY FORWARD

Chapter 1 eloquently sets the intellectual foundation for this volume by rethinking employability as a dynamic, relational, and ethically inflected construct, recalibrated through the lens of AI and socio-technical transformation. It offers a rich synthesis of theoretical, philosophical, and empirical insights to advocate for a holistic, human-centred redefinition of skills in the 21st century. Central to this vision is the notion of skills dynamics, which captures the complex interplay between personal capabilities, structural contexts, and evolving technological landscapes. The pathway forward calls for a deliberate and ethically informed redesign of educational systems that goes beyond technical skill acquisition to foster adaptability, critical reflexivity, and social consciousness. This entails:

- **Embedding AI Literacy** across curricula in a manner that prioritises both functional proficiency and ethical awareness;
- **Redesigning Pedagogical Frameworks** to support personalised and experiential learning grounded in real-world problem-solving;
- **Developing Governance Mechanisms** that ensure AI's integration into education adheres to principles of equity, transparency, and human dignity;
- **Encouraging Interdisciplinary Collaboration**, uniting educators, technologists, ethicists, and policymakers in co-creating inclusive and future-ready learning environments; and
- **Promoting Global Knowledge Exchange**, learning from both Global North and Global South innovations in AI-driven education and employability initiatives.

Ultimately, this chapter affirms that the future of employability cannot be disentangled from broader philosophical and societal questions. In reimagining the role of AI in education, we are simultaneously reimagining the purpose of education itself: not merely to prepare students for work, but to empower them to navigate, critique, and shape the world with integrity and imagination.

Now, the next chapter—Chapter 2 of this book—focuses on the regulatory and institutional frameworks necessary for the ethical and effective integration of AI within education, with particular emphasis on its implications for employability. This chapter, therefore, explores how trust, accountability, inclusivity, and a broader commitment to ethics must shape the design and governance of AI technologies that influence learners' futures in the labour market. At the core of this chapter is the principle of trust, which is especially vital when AI is used to mediate or determine opportunities related to employability. Whether in skills profiling, CV generation, personalised learning, or labour market matching, learners must feel confident that AI systems are working in their interest. If students and job-seekers are to engage meaningfully with these tools, they need assurance that the outputs are reliable, the processes are transparent, and their data is being handled with integrity. In the context of employability, trust also extends to employers and institutions who must rely on AI systems to make fair and evidence-based decisions. Thus, this chapter will examine how institutions can cultivate trust through ethical data governance, clear communication about algorithmic decision-making, and the transparent articulation of AI's role in shaping career pathways.

The second pillar, accountability, becomes increasingly complex and significant at the intersection of AI and employability. When AI systems are used to recommend career paths, assess employability potential, or guide learners towards specific sectors, the consequences can be profound and long-lasting. It is therefore essential to establish clear lines of responsibility: who is accountable when a student is wrongly profiled, when bias shapes opportunity, or when an AI system narrows rather than expands future options? This chapter explores the need for institutional safeguards, including oversight mechanisms and legal frameworks, that ensure AI technologies support—rather than constrain—learners' aspirations and choices. Equally vital is the principle of inclusivity. The promise of AI to enhance employability will only be fulfilled if it serves all learners, not just the digitally privileged or those already advantaged in the labour market. AI must be designed and implemented in ways that recognise and respond to diverse educational trajectories, cultural contexts, and barriers to access. This chapter investigates how inclusive AI systems can be designed to counteract, rather than reinforce, structural inequalities—especially for learners from marginalised backgrounds, those with disabilities, or those in underrepresented career sectors. Inclusive design, participatory data practices, and the embedding of equity principles within employability services are explored as necessary steps towards fairer outcomes.

Finally, a broader discussion of ethics threads through each of these domains. Ethical questions about power, bias, autonomy, and consent are not peripheral to employability; they are central. When AI influences how learners prepare for the world of work, it shapes not only their immediate prospects but also their sense of self, agency, and belonging within economic systems. As such, this chapter invites a careful reflection on the values that should govern AI-driven employability practices: dignity, opportunity, fairness, and human-centred development. In summary, Chapter 2 sets the ethical and institutional groundwork for the reader. It asks: how do we build AI systems in education that prepare learners for the future of work without compromising their present rights, freedoms, or hopes? In answering this, the chapter provides a framework for institutions and policymakers seeking to balance innovation with responsibility—ensuring that Generative AI supports employability in ways that are trustworthy, inclusive, and just.

Figure 1.11 provides a clear and structured overview of the key themes explored in Chapter 2. It serves not only as a visual guide but also as a conceptual map that highlights the interrelated foundations upon which ethical and effective AI-enhanced employability frameworks must be built. At the top of the figure is the notion of AI-driven educational systems (A), representing the growing presence of AI technologies in teaching, learning, and career development pathways. These systems do not exist in a vacuum; they must be grounded in robust regulatory and institutional frameworks (B) that establish clear

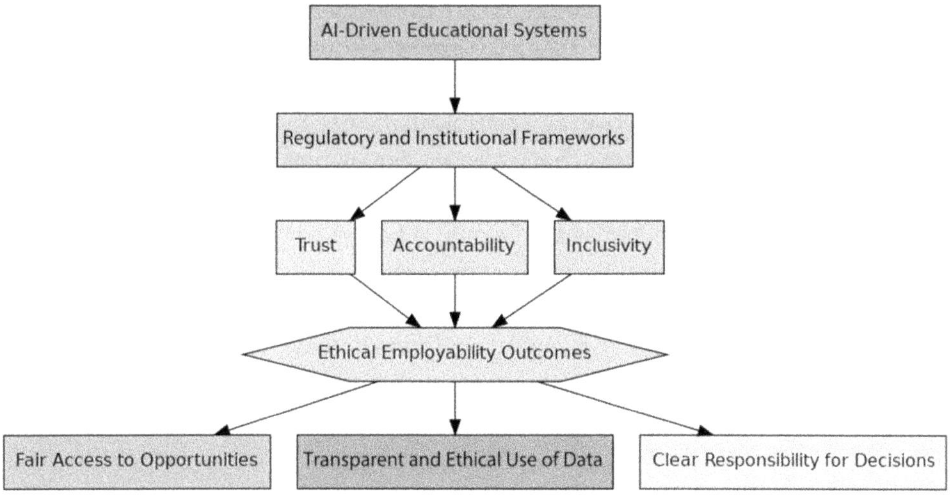

FIGURE 1.11 A conceptual framework for ethical and inclusive AI-driven employability in education.

boundaries, expectations, and protections. These frameworks, in turn, inform and give shape to three core ethical principles: trust (C), accountability (D), and inclusivity (E). These principles are not merely abstract values; they are operational imperatives that influence how AI is designed, implemented, and experienced by learners and institutions alike. The centre of the figure features ethical employability outcomes (F), which are positioned as the convergence point of these ethical pillars. This reflects the chapter's central argument—that meaningful, equitable, and future-facing employability cannot be achieved without attending to the moral infrastructure that supports it.

From this centre, the figure expands outward to illustrate the practical dimensions of ethical employability. These include ensuring fair access to opportunities (G), promoting the transparent and ethical use of data (H), and clarifying responsibility for decisions (I) that affect learners' career trajectories. These outcomes represent not only desired ends but also indicators of the integrity and inclusiveness of the AI systems in place. As this chapter unfolds, each element of the figure will be explored in greater depth. Together, they offer a coherent framework for understanding how institutions, educators, and policymakers might navigate the complexities of AI in education—anchoring innovation in values that prioritise equity, responsibility, and human dignity.

Within this structured environment, three interwoven threads must be carefully worked into the fabric of AI in education: trust, accountability, and inclusivity. Each thread carries its own strength, but only together do they form a cloth strong enough to support learners and institutions. Trust provides the assurance that engagement with AI can take place openly and without fear; accountability ensures that responsibility for decisions is not left loose or ambiguous; and inclusivity guarantees that no learner is left at the margins of the fabric. Without these strands, the weave is incomplete and liable to unravel. When woven tightly, these principles create a pattern that gives rise to ethical employability. The outcomes—fair access to opportunity, transparent use of data, and clearly assigned responsibility—do not appear by chance, but are the deliberate result of careful design and sustained attention. Each outcome is a visible motif within the wider tapestry, signifying the integrity and intentional labour behind it. This framework, then, is not a rigid structure but a living textile: flexible, adaptive, and capable of incorporating new threads as contexts change. Figure 1.11 included in this chapter serves as a map of this woven design, illustrating how each principle is interlaced with the others and how ethical employability must be crafted not as a finished piece, but as an ongoing act of weaving (Figure 1.11).

The figure presents a vertical conceptual flow chart made up of nine interconnected rectangles, each labelled with a distinct letter (A to I) and arranged in three main layers. Arrows indicate the direction of influence from top to bottom, visually guiding the reader through a sequence of foundational structures, ethical principles, and outcome dimensions relevant to AI-driven education and employability.

CHAPTER 2

Principles to Practice

Constructing Ethical AI Systems for Education and Employability

INTRODUCTION

In the unfolding reconfiguration of education through artificial intelligence (AI), trust, accountability, and inclusivity emerge as pivotal concerns. While these values have long been present in pedagogical debates, they now acquire renewed significance as they are refracted through the accelerating transformations of AI innovation. Across both the United Kingdom (UK) and global contexts, this has created a fertile yet unsettled tension: the promise of educational renewal sits uneasily alongside fears of displacement and inequity. The UK's policy discourse illustrates this ambiguity. The Department for Education's (DfE) policy statement Generative Artificial Intelligence in Education (2023) presents a cautiously aspirational vision. Central to its framing is the principle that AI should augment rather than replace the relational dynamic between teacher and learner. While this commitment is ethically resonant, the notion of 'augmentation' remains operationally vague. The rhetoric of human-centricity is persuasive, yet it offers little clarity on how such commitments will be enacted within curriculum, pedagogy, or institutional strategy.

More detailed insights can be found in the DfE's 2023 Call for Evidence, which collated practitioner perspectives. Educators expressed cautious optimism about AI's potential to personalise learning pathways, reduce administrative burdens, and provide differentiated support. Yet this optimism was tempered by persistent concerns: algorithmic bias, risks to academic integrity, misinformation, and opaque decision-making. These issues are not abstract; they reflect everyday challenges as staff navigate early deployments of AI-enabled systems, often with limited resources. Similarly, the 2024 Educator and Expert Report, commissioned by professional bodies, documents emerging innovations—AI-generated feedback, curriculum planning tools, and virtual assistants—while emphasising anxieties around data governance, transparency, and the absence of evaluative frameworks. Such

DOI: 10.1201/9781003502517-3

reports offer a detailed map of possibilities, but rarely the navigational tools required for practice. At this juncture, the discourse risks drifting into a pattern familiar from cultural allegories of ambition: visionary but insufficiently grounded. Like Plato's Atlantis, which combined technical brilliance with fatal hubris, the current trajectory may falter if it assumes that innovation alone can secure sustainability. Unless structural, ethical, and epistemic foundations are addressed—clarifying what augmentation means in practice—policy may remain adrift, promising transformation without establishing the means to achieve it.

In response, this chapter advances three interrelated dimensions that remain largely absent from UK policy discourse: ethical scalability, dialogic symmetry between human and machine intelligences, and ontological clarity regarding AI's educational role. These are not offered as supplements but as reframings, intended to redirect debate towards more foundational questions. If AI is to be meaningfully integrated into education, the key questions extend beyond capability—what AI can do—to encompass values: what systems are being built, what futures they shape, and what educational purposes they serve. The first of these, ethical scalability, highlights the need for ethical frameworks that are not only principled but adaptive. Current approaches tend to anchor themselves in fixed commitments, which risk becoming outdated as technologies evolve and as AI systems move from peripheral tools to core elements of educational practice. The central challenge is whether ethical frameworks can evolve in step with technological change, safeguarding justice, fairness, and inclusion as AI becomes embedded across classrooms, platforms, and administrative systems. The urgency of this question is amplified by the realities of uneven access and systemic inequalities, which risk being reproduced—or even exacerbated—through poorly governed AI adoption. Ethical scalability, therefore, requires more than keeping pace with innovation: it demands that equity, dignity, and voice remain at the centre of educational transformation, ensuring that the benefits of AI are distributed inclusively rather than concentrated selectively.

Closely connected to the idea of ethical scalability is the notion of dialogic symmetry. As AI systems become more deeply embedded within education, they no longer function merely as invisible administrative supports. Increasingly, they participate in processes of communication, mediation, and knowledge construction. Yet policy and pedagogical debates often assume that these interactions are neutral, overlooking the relational dynamics they inevitably introduce. Educational dialogue has never been limited to the transmission of information; it is about negotiating meaning, cultivating trust, and sustaining interpretative relationships. When AI enters this domain—through adaptive feedback systems, personalised learning environments, or generative tools—it assumes a form of interlocutory presence. This does not imply parity between human and machine intelligences, but it does invite us to consider their interaction relationally. Questions of agency, transparency, and control cannot be ignored: where are the boundaries of this dialogue drawn, who defines them, and what asymmetries of power might be concealed within seemingly benign exchanges?

From here arises the need for ontological clarity: a reconsideration of the assumptions that underlie our definitions of learning, intelligence, and teaching in contexts where non-human systems now play a constitutive role. What does it mean to learn when algorithmic systems shape the conditions under which thought unfolds? How should intelligence be defined when machines are able to generate, imitate, or assess forms of reasoning once considered uniquely human? And how might we reconceive teaching when some of its functions—feedback, evaluation, even scaffolding—are translated into algorithmic processes? These are not speculative diversions, but questions central to how educational environments are designed and governed in the presence of AI. Without ontological clarity, there is a risk of structural adaptation without conceptual understanding: systems may change while deeper purposes remain unexplored.

Together, ethical scalability, dialogic symmetry, and ontological clarity offer a critical framework for engaging with AI in education in ways that are principled, imaginative, and forward-looking. They shift the conversation from reactive policy to reflective, values-driven engagement—asking not simply how AI can be used, but how it reshapes the purposes and practices of education. To illustrate what is at stake when these foundations are neglected, we might return to the allegory of Atlantis. Its lesson lies less in dramatic collapse than in gradual misalignment: a civilisation whose ingenuity expanded so ambitiously that it lost sight of the human sensibilities it was meant to serve. Systems designed to support communal flourishing became so vast that they obscured the lives they were intended to sustain. In contemporary debates on AI in education, a similar pattern can be observed. Terms such as personalisation, optimisation, and automation dominate, often at the expense of considering their ethical and pedagogical weight. The Atlantean metaphor, therefore, serves not as a warning of imminent downfall, but as a reflective mirror—reminding us how easily educational purpose can drift away from practice when vision is not matched by grounded, human-centred design.

To avoid such drift, attention must be given to proportion: to designing systems that support rather than eclipse human judgement, that expand without outpacing relational comprehension, and that sustain rather than displace the dialogic character of education. Atlantis, in this light, is not recalled as a story of civilisational loss, but as a parable of imbalance—where scale outgrew reflection, structure outran ethics, and progress advanced without pause. Reclaiming the three components of ethical scalability, dialogic symmetry, and ontological clarity is therefore less an act of supplementing current debates than of recovering what risks being forgotten. It is a reminder that systems demanding speed must still allow for reflection and that technologies presented as neutral are never exempt from values. Atlantis was not undone by a flood alone, but by the failure to notice where the shoreline lay. Our task, by contrast, is to remember that boundary, and to design with care. Without such reflection, there is a danger of creating AI-enabled environments that are technically sophisticated yet conceptually impoverished—systems where the machinery functions but the meaning of learning is obscured. The challenge before us is not only to regulate or contain AI, but to engage it critically and imaginatively. The trajectory of education will not be shaped by technological sophistication alone, but by the depth of the questions we ask and the courage with which we reimagine what learning can mean in an age when we are no longer the only intelligence in the room. Figure 2.1 illustrates three components essential to recasting the conversation around AI and employability—elements that remain underdeveloped in current UK policy discourse.

- **Ethical Scalability** underlines the need for frameworks that evolve with technological advancement while safeguarding human dignity, fairness, and justice.
- **Dialogic Symmetry** draws attention to the relational dynamics between human and machine intelligences, recognising that educational dialogue is shaped by questions of agency, trust, and interpretative authority.
- **Ontological Clarity** engages with the deeper philosophical task of defining learning, intelligence, and teaching in contexts where non-human systems increasingly participate in knowledge construction.

Taken together, these components shift the debate from reactive responses to technological change towards a more reflective engagement with the values, relationships, and assumptions that underpin education in the age of AI (Figure 2.1).

The propositions advanced here invite a reframing of how AI's role in education is conceived. The challenge is not confined to matters of technological capacity or regulatory oversight; it is rooted in the philosophical and conceptual assumptions that guide educational practice. What is needed is not simply stronger mechanisms of control, but a form of epistemic stewardship that recognises AI as a participant within educational communities, rather than a neutral tool. This calls for epistemic humility—an acknowledgement that AI systems, however sophisticated, are embedded in human values, norms, and aspirations. Such a shift demands that education systems move beyond integrating AI as an operational instrument to continually interrogating the assumptions shaping its use. The task is to cultivate frameworks that can navigate uncertainty without sacrificing pedagogical integrity, while also advancing human flourishing. Ethical acceptability, while necessary, is insufficient; AI must actively contribute to the strengthening of educational cultures by supporting human agency, creativity, and critical consciousness. Within the UK, one notable development is the move towards ethical anticipatory governance—an approach that seeks to engage with emerging dilemmas proactively rather than reactively. The Institute for Ethical AI in Education (2021), for example, advocates embedding anticipatory ethics into institutional practice, positioning ethics not as a constraint but as a capacity for critical preparedness. In this sense, ethical foresight becomes an enabling condition for responsible engagement with technological change.

A crucial dimension of such governance is the commitment to cognitive justice and epistemic diversity. Cognitive justice requires that AI applications be designed to recognise and respect diverse epistemologies, enabling inclusivity that extends beyond access to encompass genuine recognition of difference. Equally important is the evolution of debates on transparency and accountability into a focus on algorithmic explainability. For AI to support education meaningfully, its decision-making processes must be interpretable not only to technical experts but also to educators and learners. Explainability thus becomes a pedagogical issue, creating opportunities for students and teachers to interrogate how

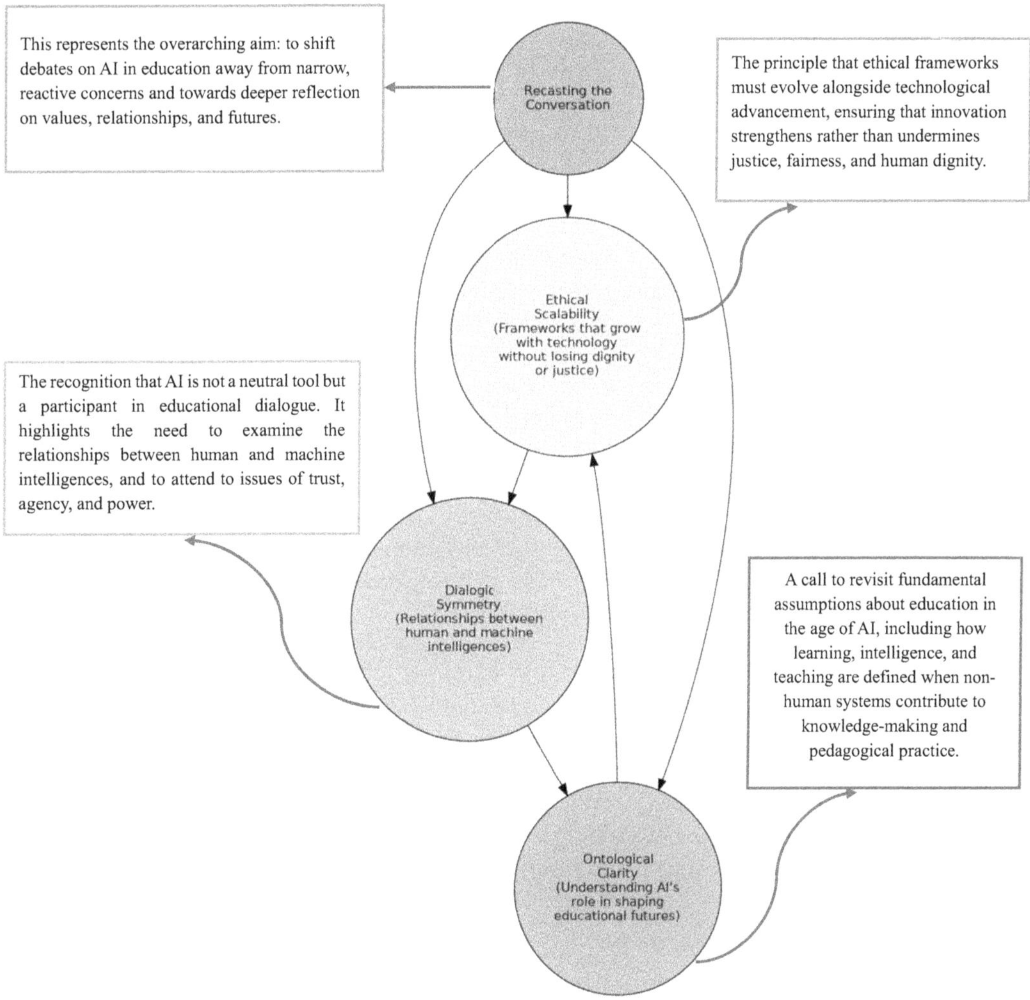

FIGURE 2.1 Recasting the conversation on AI in education.

This figure illustrates three interrelated components—ethical scalability, dialogic symmetry, and ontological clarity—that are crucial for reframing debates on AI and employability. Together, they highlight the need for values-driven, relational, and forward-looking approaches to integrating AI in educational contexts.

outcomes are generated and to reflect critically on their implications. Collectively, these perspectives move us towards reimagining education as an adaptive learning ecosystem, one that is relational, ethically grounded, and informed by collaborative human-machine interaction. In such a framework, AI is not understood as a replacement for established practices, nor as a looming threat, but as a catalyst for renewed pedagogical creativity, ethical awareness, and collective wisdom.

Recent guidance from the Quality Assurance Agency (QAA, 2023) and Jisc (2023) reflects a discernible shift within UK higher education: from initial caution—evident in bans on generative AI (GenAI) tools such as ChatGPT—towards more reflective and

BOX 2.1 EXPLANATION NOTE—RECASTING THE CONVERSATION ON AI IN EDUCATION

The figure illustrates a framework for recasting the conversation on AI in education, focusing on three conceptual components that extend beyond current UK policy discourse. Each element foregrounds a neglected yet necessary dimension for thinking about employability and learning in the age of AI. Ethical Scalability highlights the importance of ethical frameworks that are capable of adapting alongside technological development. Rather than treating ethics as static or supplementary, this component insists that principles of justice, dignity, and fairness must remain integral even as AI becomes more embedded within educational systems.

Dialogic Symmetry draws attention to the relational dynamics between human and machine intelligences. By acknowledging that AI tools increasingly participate in educational dialogue, this perspective challenges assumptions of neutrality. It urges educators and policymakers to consider how power, agency, and interpretative authority are distributed in interactions where both human and non-human actors shape meaning. Ontological Clarity calls for renewed attention to foundational questions about the nature of education in AI-mediated contexts. It asks what it means to learn when algorithmic systems influence thought processes, what counts as intelligence when machines can generate and evaluate reasoning, and how teaching is redefined when aspects of pedagogical labour are delegated to AI systems.

Together, these components provide a lens for reorienting educational debates towards reflection and values, rather than reactive adaptation to technological change. By situating AI within a broader ethical and philosophical frame, the model emphasises that the future of employability cannot be reduced to technical efficiency or economic alignment. Instead, it must be understood as a complex, relational process shaped by adaptability, justice, and the evolving dialogue between human and machine.

strategic engagement. Both organisations emphasise that institutions must move beyond restrictions and begin embedding GenAI into practices that support authentic assessment, cultivate advanced digital literacies, and inspire pedagogical renewal. Jisc, in particular, frames AI as more than an instructional supplement, positioning it as a potential catalyst for personalised learning pathways and enhanced employability. At the same time, both bodies acknowledge that such integration must be underpinned by rigorous ethical and legal safeguards, particularly in relation to bias, discrimination, and widening digital inequities. This debate extends beyond the UK. Contributions from the Council of Europe (2024) and the European Commission (2022) stress that AI integration in education must remain grounded in enduring principles of human dignity, inclusivity, and equitable access. Although articulated within continental frameworks, these commitments remain highly relevant for post-Brexit Britain, offering a moral vocabulary that transcends shifting political contexts. They provide not only normative benchmarks but also a set of guiding values to inform institutional decision-making as AI technologies reshape the pedagogical landscape.

In advancing this discussion, the chapter introduces two conceptual refinements intended to support the operationalisation of ethical AI within education and employability. The first is ethical intentionality, which calls on institutions to articulate their pedagogical and ethical commitments prior to adopting AI, rather than retrofitting principles in response to implementation. The second is a reflective digital agency, which extends beyond functional digital literacy to emphasise critical engagement—equipping learners and educators to interrogate, challenge, and co-shape the design and deployment of AI tools. Drawing on both normative theory and practice-based insight, this chapter aims to narrow the gap between high-level principles and everyday educational realities. It considers how AI systems might be designed and governed in ways that reinforce trust, strengthen human agency, and preserve education's broader social purpose. The ambition is not merely to integrate AI into existing frameworks, but to harness innovation as a catalyst for pedagogical transformation—developing learning ecosystems that remain attentive to human needs while responsive to societal change. Here, the allegory of Atlantis offers a fitting reminder. Just as the Atlanteans faltered not through ignorance but by losing proportion—allowing expansion to obscure reflection—so too education risks being carried by the current of technological change without anchoring itself in ethical purpose. Ethical intentionality and reflective digital agency serve as safeguards against this drift, ensuring that AI adoption does not prioritise speed or spectacle over substance. In remembering where the shoreline lies, institutions are better placed to design AI-enabled environments that strengthen rather than erode the human foundations of learning.

The chapter opens with Shaping Futures Thoughtfully: Generative AI, Learner Empowerment, and Ethical Pathways in Education and Employability, framing Generative AI not as a neutral add-on but as a transformative cultural force. It positions AI as a "living technology," capable of reshaping learning, agency and employability—but only when guided by ethical intentionality and reflective digital agency. The emphasis here is on empowerment, particularly for those already at risk of marginalisation, and on the relational contexts in which AI is designed and governed. In this sense, AI becomes meaningful only when it honours dignity, purpose, and human flourishing rather than optimisation alone.

From this foundation, the chapter shifts outward to the broader environment in **Regulatory and Institutional Architectures for Ethical Artificial Intelligence**. This section argues that ethical AI is never only a technical system but an institutional and legal one. Governance must therefore be anticipatory, reflexive, and participatory. Audits, guidelines, and oversight structures are cast not as bureaucratic burdens but as the ethical scaffolding that sustains trust and legitimacy. Here the text highlights the limits of purely technical fairness fixes and underlines the necessity of Institutional Responsibility and civic engagement.

Trust becomes the central theme of **Trust, Transparency, and Institutional Legitimacy as Foundations for Responsible AI and Ethical Employability**. Trust is treated as relational, historical, and earned—a property of institutions rather than machines. Transparent communication, ethical conduct, and credible governance are therefore positioned as preconditions for public legitimacy. Trust is framed as the space in which learners, workers, and citizens can confidently navigate AI-mediated systems without fear of hidden logics or arbitrary exclusion.

This leads into a deepening exploration in **Elevates Transparency from a Procedural Requirement to a Conceptual Foundation**. Transparency here is not simply disclosure or documentation; it is a moral, legal, and pedagogical condition. It underwrites intelligibility, contestability, explainability, and fairness. Transparency is shown to be inseparable from justice—a way of making AI both visible and accountable to the communities it affects, particularly when decisions shape life chances such as employment.

The chapter then turns to communication, credibility, and narrative responsibility in **Analyse the Role of Institutional Credibility and Communication in Fostering Trust**. The focus widens from what institutions disclose to how they speak, listen, and engage. Trust requires clarity, accessibility, and integrity in communication—particularly around data use, AI design, and governance intentions. Credibility becomes a lived practice, not a rhetorical claim.

This reflective groundwork becomes operationalised in **Guiding Principles for Ensuring Transparency in Artificial Intelligence**. Here the chapter shifts from theory to structured institutional guidance through five interlocking principles:

- Explainability—making AI reasoning interpretable and open to question
- Accessibility—ensuring transparency reaches *everyone*, not only experts
- Organisational Accountability—embedding responsibility across governance systems
- Pedagogical Integration—weaving transparency into curriculum and employability practices
- Vocational Equity—ensuring transparency supports *fair* opportunity and just outcomes

Each principle includes rationale and implementation strategies, illustrating how ethical transparency is built into everyday institutional life.

Accountability is then examined more directly in Accountability in **AI Governance: Structures of Oversight, Mechanisms of Redress, and the Ethics of Responsibility and Reconceptualising Accountability within the AI–Education–Employability Nexus: Ethical and Institutional Dimensions**. Together these sections re-cast accountability as a shared ethical project. They argue that meaningful responsibility requires clear duties, auditable processes, avenues for redress, and institutional cultures that remain reflexive rather than defensive. Accountability is not presented as restrictive but as enabling: it protects fairness, human dignity, and institutional legitimacy.

A parallel conversation unfolds in **Inclusive AI by Design: Advancing Equity, Access, and Participatory Practice in Education and Employability**. Inclusivity is articulated not as charitable aspiration but as a structural design mandate. The chapter foregrounds the risks of bias, exclusion, and digital stratification, while also championing co-design, diverse user testing, accessibility, and recognition of cognitive and cultural plurality. Inclusivity becomes a moral anchor and a practical design principle.

All these threads are then woven into institutional life in **Ethical Employability: Integrating Principles into Practice**. This section critiques narrow market-led employability models and proposes instead a justice-centred vision that foregrounds agency, dignity, and equity. Several guiding institutional principles are presented to ensure that trust, transparency, inclusivity, and accountability are lived through policy, staff development, student support, partnerships, curriculum design, and governance.

Across the chapter as a whole, the argument develops dialogically rather than mechanically. Trust, transparency, accountability, and inclusivity are repeatedly revisited—deepened, reframed, and connected to real governance, pedagogy, labour markets, and public legitimacy. The recurring imagery of weaving and relational interdependence reinforces the claim that no single value is sufficient in isolation. Rather, ethical AI in education and employability emerges only where these values form a robust and living ethical fabric.

SHAPING FUTURES THOUGHTFULLY: GENERATIVE AI, LEARNER EMPOWERMENT, AND ETHICAL PATHWAYS IN EDUCATION AND EMPLOYABILITY

This section engages with the evolving discourse on GenAI by offering a critical and reflective account of its potential to empower learners and shape ethical pathways at the intersection of education and employability. Rather than framing GenAI as either a neutral tool or a deterministic force, it is approached here as a living technology—a dynamic and evolving entity that, if applied responsibly, has the capacity to reshape learning experiences and support meaningful transitions into work. To contextualise this potential, one might recall the agricultural revolution, when the domestication of plants and animals transformed not only human subsistence but also social structures, relationships, and worldviews. The tools of that era were not passive; they redefined the fabric of human life. In a similar way, GenAI represents a threshold moment. It is not merely a technical development but a force capable of reconfiguring educational landscapes, social contracts, and economic opportunities—provided its use is guided by careful reflection on purpose and consequence.

The concern, then, is not whether GenAI will alter education and employability, but how such changes can be realised ethically and equitably. Central to this is the question of empowerment: how might learners—particularly those from marginalised or underrepresented groups—be supported in ways that enhance agency, cultivate critical capacities, and expand access to meaningful employment? Addressing this also requires scrutiny of the systems within which GenAI is developed and deployed: whose priorities inform its design, whose values are embedded, and whose forms of knowledge and labour are privileged or neglected. This section does not claim to resolve these questions but seeks to encourage a way of thinking that is at once principled and imaginative. It invites educators, policymakers, and learners to view GenAI not as an end in itself, but as a medium through which more inclusive, responsive, and ethically grounded futures can be envisioned. In doing so, it moves beyond narrow narratives of efficiency and optimisation towards a broader horizon, where GenAI becomes a catalyst for learning and employability rooted in care, justice, and human flourishing.

The Brookings Institution (2022) provides a critical account of the expanding use of algorithmic systems across recruitment processes, from CV screening and automated assessments to the analysis of candidates' expressions in asynchronous video interviews. These technologies are typically introduced under the banners of efficiency and cost-effectiveness, and at times even promoted as remedies for human bias. Yet, as Brookings cautions, without rigorous oversight, they risk reinforcing, rather than mitigating, existing inequalities. The difficulty lies not only in flawed implementation but also in the epistemological foundations of these systems. Algorithms are frequently trained on historical hiring data that reproduce entrenched discriminatory practices. As a result, they may systematically disadvantage applicants with non-linear career trajectories, employment gaps, or experiences that fall outside the patterns a system recognises as normative. Such exclusions are not accidental glitches but reflect deeper structural biases that shape which forms of work and knowledge are legitimised within labour markets.

While the appeal of algorithmic tools in recruitment—particularly their capacity to process large volumes of applications—may be understandable, their design often prioritises operational expedience over fairness, inclusivity, or transparency. In doing so, they fall short of the ethical standards required to sustain confidence in AI-mediated employment practices. Before deployment, therefore, such systems must be evaluated against three essential pillars: trust, accountability, and inclusivity. The challenge is not simply to acknowledge bias but to establish evaluative mechanisms that ensure responsible use. Retrospective audits and minor technical adjustments are insufficient. What is needed is a more proactive form of ethical interrogation, one that asks not only what these systems do but also how they function, who benefits, and who may be excluded. In terms of trust, for instance, the critical questions include whether decision-making processes are intelligible to candidates and recruiters alike; whether the provenance and suitability of training data are disclosed; and whether the system demonstrates consistent reliability across varied recruitment contexts without undermining equity or confidence.

Accountability within AI-driven hiring practices cannot be an afterthought; it must be treated as the scaffolding that upholds both fairness and legitimacy. Clear lines of responsibility are essential. If an algorithm unfairly excludes a candidate, who within the organisation bears responsibility? What avenues exist for challenge or appeal? And is there a transparent record of how the system has changed over time—what was altered, by whom, and for what purpose? Without such structures, assurances of ethical deployment risk being reduced to rhetoric. To illustrate the stakes, one might imagine a great maritime voyage. An organisation deploying AI in recruitment is like a vessel embarking across uncertain waters. The technology itself is the ship's sophisticated rigging—designed to harness wind and speed the journey, but also susceptible to sudden shifts and unseen currents. In such a voyage, accountability is the navigation log and the captain's chart. Every adjustment to the sails, every change of course, must be carefully documented so that decisions can be traced, explained, and, if necessary, corrected. Without this record, when storms come—or when the ship runs aground—there is no way of knowing whether error lay in the maps, the instruments, or the judgement of those at the helm. The crew, too, must know where authority rests: who commands the tiller, who is responsible for steering, and who must answer when the vessel strays. Without this clarity, the voyage risks descending into confusion, where responsibility is dispersed and errors remain unaddressed.

Alongside accountability sits inclusivity, which might be likened to the question of who is permitted passage on the ship. A vessel that only welcomes passengers who resemble the crew or who speak its language risks leaving behind those whose journeys have been shaped by caregiving, migration, or hardship. It risks ignoring travellers whose accents, attire, or customs differ, or whose access to resources is constrained. A ship that claims to represent society cannot afford to sail with only a narrow portion of its people aboard. Instead, its design must accommodate varied needs: cabins accessible to those with disabilities, provisions sufficient for all, and interpreters to ensure that every voice is heard. The sea, after all, does not discriminate—but the vessel can, if constructed without care. Similarly, AI systems in recruitment must be built upon data that recognises the full diversity of human experience, attentive to cultural expression, linguistic difference, and varied capacities. If they fail to do so, they replicate exclusion under the guise of neutrality. Collectively, accountability and inclusivity reveal that AI in hiring is not simply a matter of engineering efficiency but of shaping institutional ethics. The vessel may boast impressive sails and swift rigging, yet without careful governance and an open commitment to who it carries, it will never reach its intended shore. The real transformation lies not in speed, but in the capacity to navigate wisely and equitably, ensuring that the voyage remains open to all who seek passage. Figure 2.2 illustrates this navigational framework. Each

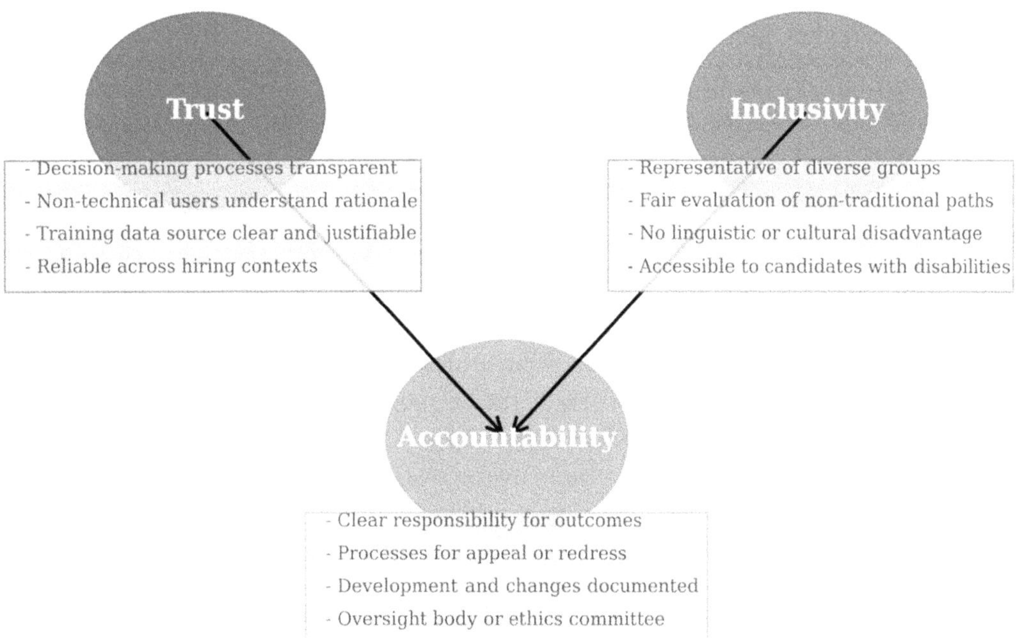

FIGURE 2.2 Trust, inclusivity, and accountability framework for ethical AI systems.

The figure highlights how Trust and Inclusivity underpin Accountability, ensuring AI systems in recruitment are transparent, fair, and ethically governed.

BOX 2.2 EXPLANATION NOTE: TRUST, INCLUSIVITY, AND ACCOUNTABILITY FRAMEWORK FOR ETHICAL AI SYSTEMS

The presented model highlights three interdependent pillars: Trust, Inclusivity, and Accountability, which together provide a foundation for the responsible deployment of AI systems. Trust is essential for user confidence in automated decision-making. For AI systems to be considered legitimate, they must demonstrate transparency, explainability, and reliability. This includes ensuring that non-technical users can understand the rationale behind algorithmic outcomes, that training data sources are clear and justifiable, and that systems function consistently across diverse contexts. Without trust, the adoption of AI is likely to be met with scepticism and resistance, undermining its potential benefits.

Inclusivity emphasises the importance of fairness and representativeness within AI development and application. Ethical AI requires training data that reflects diverse populations and safeguards against reinforcing systemic inequalities. This includes ensuring fair evaluation of non-traditional career paths, eliminating linguistic or cultural disadvantages, and maintaining accessibility for individuals with disabilities. By embedding inclusivity into design and implementation, AI systems can support equitable outcomes rather than perpetuate discrimination.

Accountability serves as the binding element of the framework, ensuring that responsibility for AI outcomes is clearly defined. Effective governance mechanisms must include processes for appeal and redress, systematic documentation of system development and modifications, and the establishment of oversight or ethics committees. These measures are vital for preventing harm, rectifying errors, and upholding public confidence. Accountability mechanisms also safeguard against the diffusion of responsibility that often arises in automated systems, ensuring that human oversight remains central.

Collectively, the Trust, Inclusivity, and Accountability framework offers a structured approach to aligning AI deployment with ethical standards and societal expectations. By situating these pillars in dialogue, the model underscores that trust cannot exist without inclusivity, and both must be underpinned by accountability. This framework resonates with international ethical guidelines, including those of UNESCO (2021b) and the OECD (2019b), which stress fairness, transparency, human oversight, and accountability as prerequisites for ethical AI.

domain—trust, accountability, and inclusivity—marks a compass point by which organisations might steer, guiding them towards an ethical horizon where AI systems in hiring do more than process candidates efficiently: they embody a deeper commitment to justice, transparency, and shared responsibility (Figure 2.2).

Chen (2023) illustrates that algorithmic hiring systems, even when explicitly designed to mitigate human bias, frequently reproduce entrenched inequalities. This occurs through the use of proxy variables—such as educational background, residential postcode, or linguistic style—which may appear neutral but are closely tied to socio-economic privilege. In effect, these proxies function as gatekeeping mechanisms, disadvantaging candidates from underrepresented groups while presenting an appearance of impartiality. Importantly, Chen (2023) contends that technical adjustments—such as reweighting features or excluding protected attributes—are inadequate as long-term solutions. Such interventions risk framing inequality as a purely computational challenge, overlooking the broader social and political contexts in which hiring takes place. Without robust governance structures and independent oversight, there is a danger that AI systems will continue to reproduce exclusionary logics while maintaining a façade of neutrality. Three interrelated deficiencies can be identified within current practices. First, the opacity of training data and modelling assumptions undermines accountability and trust. Second, the datasets used frequently fail to capture the diversity of real applicant populations. Third, there remains a notable absence of ethical protocols to guide the design, implementation, and evaluation of these systems. Collectively, these shortcomings raise serious questions about whether algorithmic hiring systems are fit for purpose in complex and socially sensitive contexts such as employment.

Moving beyond critique, there is a pressing need to reconceptualise algorithmic hiring as a domain of ethical, political, and regulatory engagement. This requires more than technical refinement: it calls for participatory design processes that include stakeholders from marginalised communities, interdisciplinary approaches to auditing, and conceptions of fairness that move beyond narrow statistical parity to reflect plural understandings of merit and opportunity. A particularly important step is the integration of merit and potential into both datasets and model design. Much existing discourse privileges historical achievements and quantifiable outputs, yet such an emphasis risks overlooking those whose opportunities have been constrained by structural inequalities or incomplete records. A potential-aware approach reframes the system's logic: it values not only demonstrated attainment but also what individuals may achieve under fairer conditions of recognition, support, and access. This shift requires a more expansive epistemology—one that recognises human capacity as emergent and dynamic rather than fixed. Here, merit is not treated as an immutable trait but as contextually shaped, evolving through the interplay of aptitude, effort, and opportunity. Such a reframing aligns with wider calls in AI ethics to centre justice, equity, and dignity. It challenges reductive data-driven legacies and encourages the design of systems that foreground inclusivity, human development, and social transformation. In summary, embedding the principles of trust, inclusivity, and accountability into AI hiring systems necessitates more than technical safeguards. It requires a deeper commitment to fairness as a sociopolitical practice and a recognition of human potential as central to ethical system design. By doing so, AI can move beyond replicating existing hierarchies to supporting a more equitable and imaginative future of work.

The literature on algorithmic justice has long established that systems designed to optimise efficiency or neutrality often reproduce existing social hierarchies. Noble (2018), for example, demonstrates how data infrastructures embed and amplify structures of race, gender, and class, while Raghavan et al. (2020) highlight the sociocultural contingencies that underpin assessments of 'merit' in recruitment. These critiques remind us that what is deemed employable or professional is rarely objective; rather, it reflects inherited norms and exclusions. While such analyses remain influential, they often centre predominantly on the harms generated by algorithmic systems. What is less developed is a recognition of the opportunities lost when human potential is occluded from consideration. A framework that privileges past achievement without accounting for future capacity risks reifying the status quo, positioning historical performance as the only legitimate marker of value. In this sense, algorithmic hiring can be likened to a lens fixed on the past, illuminating what has already been achieved but failing to capture what may yet be possible. Reframing the debate requires moving beyond an exclusive concern with harm towards a more generative orientation—one that treats AI not only as a site of risk but also as an ethical and pedagogical space in which inclusion can be actively cultivated. To achieve this, employability must be conceptualised through an epistemology that incorporates not only merit but also potential and, crucially, probability. Here, probability is understood not as a narrow statistical projection but as an ethically imaginative stance: what is the likelihood that, given appropriate conditions, an individual could flourish? What possibilities for transformation open up when access to education and lifelong learning is assured?

This shift directs attention towards futures that are often marginalised or undervalued. It positions AI as a technology capable of recognising not only historical attainment but also emergent capacity, thereby expanding the horizon of what counts as employable or valuable. Central to this reorientation is the cultivation of Civic Agency and Epistemic Agency. Civic Agency entails enabling individuals to participate fully in public life—not only as economic actors but also as contributors to the ethical and social fabric of their communities. In the context of AI and employability, this means equipping learners to engage critically with the systems that shape their opportunities and to advocate for equitable outcomes. Epistemic Agency complements this by affirming the right and ability of individuals to contribute to the production of knowledge about their capacities and futures. Together, these forms of agency resist the reduction of employability to pre-existing metrics, instead fostering a more inclusive vision of technological design—one that recognises promise, adaptability, and human dignity as central to future-oriented assessment.

Epistemic Agency refers to the capacity of individuals to question, evaluate, and generate knowledge. In the context of AI, where algorithmic outputs often present themselves as authoritative and final, this agency serves as a vital counterweight. It enables learners to interrogate how data are assembled, how classifications are derived, and whose voices are amplified or muted within such processes. Without Epistemic Agency, individuals risk being positioned as passive recipients of opaque decisions, unable to challenge or reinterpret the systems that increasingly shape their lives. When read alongside Civic Agency—the ability to participate meaningfully in public and institutional life—Epistemic Agency provides a framework for resisting the narrowing of human potential within AI-driven labour markets. Rather than merely adapting to shifting demands, individuals equipped with these capacities are able to redefine the terms on which merit and opportunity are understood. An allegory from ancient Sparta helps to clarify this point. In Spartan society, the agōgē was not merely a training ground for warriors but a system for cultivating resilience, critical judgement, and collective responsibility. Strength was not measured solely in physical achievement but also in one's ability to contribute to the polis with discipline and foresight. Similarly, in our own time, education must function as a modern agōgē: not a place that passively reproduces the hierarchies encoded in data, but a crucible in which the capacity to question, reshape, and guide technology is deliberately forged.

Within this reimagined educational role, institutions carry dual responsibilities. First, they must act as generative spaces where new forms of knowledge are produced—knowledge that actively informs more inclusive datasets, fairer taxonomies, and ethically sensitive benchmarks. Second, they must serve as ethical stewards, facilitating public discourse on the values and assumptions embedded within AI systems and ensuring that these technologies align with societal commitments to justice and equity. The accompanying Figure 2.3 depicts a circular and interdependent framework for navigating the ethical and pedagogical challenges of GenAI in employment contexts. At its centre lie six interconnected domains: Epistemic Agency, Civic Agency, Probability and Potential, Merit (Reimagined), Critical Pedagogy, and Institutional Responsibility. The circular structure signifies the ongoing feedback between these domains: civic and Epistemic Agency reshape how merit is understood; Critical Pedagogy prepares learners to engage with AI not as passive subjects but as active participants; and institutions bear responsibility both for producing knowledge and for safeguarding the values that guide AI's societal role. This model resonates with wider debates in AI ethics, complementing calls for transparency, fairness, and participatory governance. More importantly, it reframes education as both a site of resistance and a site of renewal: the forge in which civic futures are shaped, and the crucible where the ethical boundaries of AI are tested, challenged, and reimagined (Figure 2.3).

If educational institutions are to act as epistemic agents and ethical stewards in the age of AI, these commitments must be mirrored within regulatory domains. Responding meaningfully to the proliferation of GenAI in employment contexts requires more than

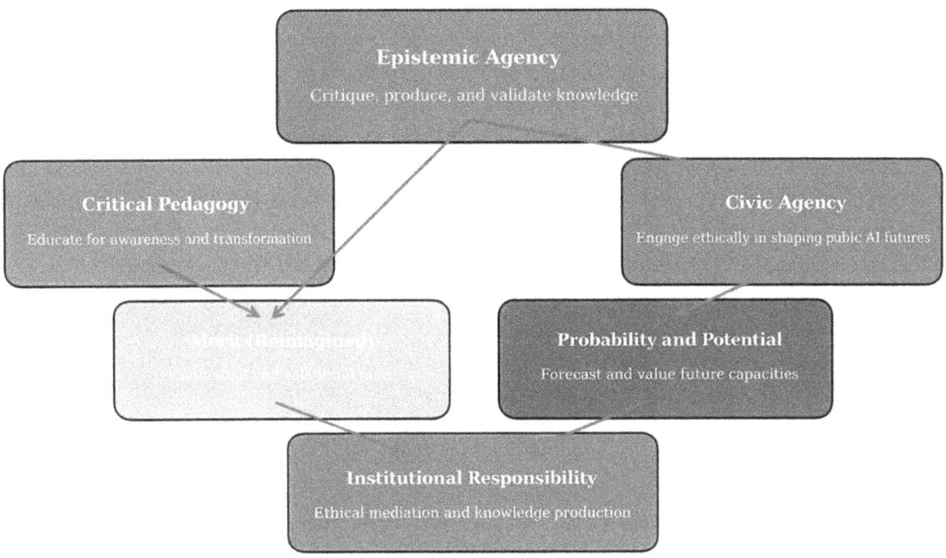

FIGURE 2.3 Interdependent domains for ethical and inclusive AI in education and employment.

This framework illustrates six interrelated domains—Epistemic Agency, Civic Agency, Critical Pedagogy, Merit (Reimagined), Probability & Potential, and Institutional Responsibility—that collectively support inclusive, ethical, and future-oriented approaches to AI in employment and education. The circular structure highlights their interdependence and the continuous feedback between pedagogy, governance, and social values.

BOX 2.3 EXPLANATION NOTE—INTERDEPENDENT DOMAINS FOR ETHICAL AND INCLUSIVE AI IN EDUCATION AND EMPLOYMENT

The integration of AI into educational and employment systems has generated significant ethical, pedagogical, and governance challenges. In order to navigate these complexities, the framework of Interdependent Domains for Ethical and Inclusive AI in Education and Employment provides a holistic model. It emphasises the relational character of six key domains—Epistemic Agency, Civic Agency, Critical Pedagogy, Merit (Reimagined), Probability & Potential, and Institutional Responsibility—whose interaction shapes both the risks and possibilities of AI-mediated futures. Epistemic Agency represents the ability of learners, educators, and workers to critique, produce, and validate knowledge. In contexts where algorithmic outputs are often perceived as authoritative and opaque, this agency is essential for resisting epistemic closure. It empowers individuals to question how data are collected, how classifications are made, and whose perspectives are embedded or excluded in the construction of AI systems.

Civic Agency refers to the ethical engagement of individuals in shaping the public role of AI. This extends beyond employability to encompass broader participation in debates about how technologies should serve social goals. Civic Agency underscores the democratic imperative: those most affected by AI must have a meaningful role in determining its applications and limits. Critical Pedagogy functions as the educational foundation of this framework. By fostering critical awareness and transformative learning, it enables individuals not only to adapt to technological systems but also to question and reshape them. It resists the reduction of education to a narrow preparation for the labour market, instead positioning it as a site where values of justice, dignity, and equity are cultivated. Merit (Reimagined) challenges traditional understandings of employability, which often rely on historically narrow and exclusionary criteria. A reimagined conception of merit acknowledges its contextual and relational nature, emphasising how ability and potential are shaped by opportunity, structural conditions, and recognition. This reframing prevents the ossification of inequality by broadening the criteria through which achievement and promise are valued.

Probability & Potential further extends this critique by insisting that AI systems must not only assess past performance but also forecast and value future capacities. This domain reframes employability as anticipatory rather than retrospective. It asks: what could individuals achieve if given equitable access to resources, recognition, and lifelong learning? Such an orientation resists the fixation on static data and opens the possibility of designing AI that supports human flourishing. Institutional Responsibility serves as the anchor of the framework. Educational and employment institutions must act as ethical mediators and knowledge producers, ensuring that AI systems reflect societal values rather than reproducing historical exclusions. This involves embedding fairness, transparency, and accountability into AI governance structures, while also providing avenues for public dialogue and oversight.

The circular and interdependent structure of the model signals that no single domain can function in isolation. Epistemic and Civic Agency informs how merit and potential are conceptualised; Critical Pedagogy equips learners to engage with these domains; and Institutional Responsibility mediates between them, ensuring that ethical and inclusive values are sustained in practice. The arrows linking the domains emphasise this dialogic and iterative process, illustrating that the design and use of AI must be understood as a continuous negotiation between theory, pedagogy, and governance. Collectively, the framework underscores that ethical AI in education and employment cannot be achieved solely through technical fixes or policy directives. Instead, it requires a multidimensional approach that foregrounds human agency, contextual understandings of merit, anticipatory visions of potential, and the responsibility of institutions as ethical stewards. By embedding these interdependent domains into practice, AI systems can be reoriented towards more inclusive, participatory, and future-oriented models of knowledge and work.

retrospective measures designed to repair harm. What is needed is anticipatory regulation—approaches that embed trust, accountability, transparency, and participatory governance from the outset. Current mechanisms, such as algorithmic audits, have been widely promoted as tools of accountability. Yet, as Brookings (2022) observes, the absence of standardised methodologies and clearly defined fairness metrics undermines their credibility. For audits to foster public trust, they must move beyond statistical validation to examine whether AI systems align with broader commitments to justice, inclusivity, and equitable opportunity. Scholars such as Chen (2023) call for a systemic rethinking of organisational responsibility, proposing measures that include interdisciplinary development teams, continuous bias testing, and the institutionalisation of internal ethical frameworks. These recommendations signal a shift from purely technical solutions towards governance grounded in reflexivity, collaboration, and shared accountability.

This resonates with Binns' (2018) contention that fairness cannot be engineered as a fixed or neutral property of algorithms. Rather, it is a contested concept, shaped by history, values, and power asymmetries. Accordingly, regulation should not only enforce compliance but also create spaces for public deliberation and co-creation. As Crawford (2021) warns, the unchecked expansion of AI risks entrenching opaque and extractive forms of power; meaningful governance must therefore aim to democratise the conditions under which AI is developed and deployed. Several policy proposals reflect this orientation. Public registries for employment algorithms, for instance, could require organisations to disclose the systems they employ, the datasets they draw upon, and the fairness criteria they adopt. Such transparency would not only enhance accountability but also allow educational institutions to align curricula with evolving ethical standards. Similarly, bias impact assessments—modelled on environmental and human rights frameworks—could ensure that systems are evaluated for their potential to reinforce structural disadvantage before deployment. These mechanisms would affirm the principle that algorithmic decision-making, particularly in employment, is inseparable from social and ethical values. Taken together, these proposals suggest that effective governance must operate across multiple registers: legal, technical, institutional, and pedagogical. For education to cultivate civic and Epistemic Agency, it must be situated within a regulatory environment that sustains those capacities in practice. Only then can AI innovation proceed responsibly, in ways that foster inclusivity and strengthen the democratic shaping of the future of work.

Alongside regulatory and institutional reform, the principle of explainability must be treated not only as a technical safeguard but also as a democratic entitlement. Wachter, Mittelstadt, and Floridi (2017) argue persuasively that individuals subject to algorithmic decision-making possess a legitimate right to understand the grounds upon which such decisions are made. Within recruitment, where opacity can obscure discriminatory practices and deny avenues for redress, this right becomes central to both fairness and accountability. In the framework, this concern aligns with Epistemic Agency, which emphasises the capacity of individuals to critique and validate the knowledge encoded into AI systems. Without transparency, learners and workers risk being excluded from processes of evaluation, a form of epistemic harm that undermines trust. Explainability, therefore, becomes a test of trust, assessing systems not solely on technical reliability but also on their openness, responsiveness, and accountability to those affected. Explainability also intersects with Civic Agency, since transparent systems enable individuals to participate ethically and politically in shaping the public role of AI. The visibility of decision-making processes allows for more meaningful debate about fairness, accountability, and the allocation of opportunity. From an educational perspective, explainable AI complements Critical Pedagogy. By fostering digital literacy and critical engagement, higher education can prepare learners not merely to adapt to technological systems but to interrogate and, where appropriate, challenge them. Employability is thereby reframed as an opportunity to strengthen democratic participation and to create conditions for equitable involvement in an AI-mediated society.

Some authors' contributions highlight both the promise and the limitations of current applications. Westman et al. (2021) examine AI-driven chatbots in higher education as tools for enhancing the reach of career services, while the U.S. Department of Education (2023) reflects on AI in student support. These interventions emphasise convenience and scalability but give less attention to Merit (Reimagined) and Probability & Potential: how systems might value emerging capacities, contextualise achievement, and forecast equitable pathways. Without such considerations, AI risks reinforcing narrow definitions of merit and reducing learners to data traces of past performance. The role of Institutional Responsibility is therefore pivotal. Universities and employers are required not only to adopt explainable systems but also to embed them within ethical governance structures. This includes transparent disclosure of the tools in use, bias assessments, and mechanisms for inclusive consultation. In doing so, institutions act as stewards of accountability, ensuring that explainability is maintained as a civic and ethical commitment rather than reduced to a technical feature. The framework as a whole demonstrates that explainability cannot be detached from broader commitments to justice, equity, and democratic accountability. It links transparency with epistemic and civic capacities, reimagines how merit and potential are valued, and underlines the institutional duty to sustain trust in AI within both education and employment.

The principle of trust, accountability, and transparency (TAT) is central to the ethical deployment of AI in employability contexts. Trust cannot be presumed; it must be actively cultivated. A useful allegory is that of a compass: its precision matters little if the traveller does not understand how it functions or whether its direction aligns with their chosen path. A compass that cannot be questioned becomes a command rather than a guide. In the same way, AI systems that lack explainability or avenues for challenge risk undermining, rather than supporting, user agency. Markus et al. (2021) identify important safeguards for career-related AI: transparency in how recommendations are generated, the ethical use of reliable and non-discriminatory labour market data, and the continued presence of human advisors for complex or sensitive cases. These are necessary conditions, yet they leave underdeveloped the learner's right to interrogate and contest the system itself. This right forms the essence of the test of trust—a normative threshold that requires AI systems to be auditable, intelligible, and responsive to those affected by their outcomes. Trust, therefore, emerges not as a by-product of technical efficiency but as the result of openness, reflexivity, and ongoing accountability.

The U.S. Department of Education's (2023) guidance reinforces this stance, calling for a human-in-the-loop approach in which AI augments, rather than replaces, human judgement. Recommendations such as identifying a student as 'at risk' or proposing career paths are not to be accepted uncritically but interpreted contextually by educators or counsellors. This underlines the necessity of human mediation, ethical oversight, and the preservation of learner dignity. National strategies, such as Finland's policy on lifelong guidance, echo this view. AI is framed as a supportive tool that helps individuals recognise their skills and link them to opportunities but never substitutes for personal judgement. Here, learners retain ultimate authority, and final decisions remain anchored in aspiration, reflection, and human insight. The test of trust thus functions as more than a conceptual device; it constitutes an ethical obligation. AI systems must be designed not only for efficiency but also for empowerment. Learners should be regarded as co-navigators—capable of questioning, interpreting, and shaping the pathways before them. An AI that fails this threshold, however sophisticated, risks becoming like a map without a legend: technically intricate yet ethically directionless.

The principle of freedom to choose, framed as informed and meaningful agency, extends the earlier discussion of transparency, accountability, and trust. Just as explainability guards against epistemic harm, the right to choice ensures that learners are not reduced to passive recipients of algorithmic outputs but positioned as co-navigators of their educational and professional pathways. The U.S. Department of Education's (2023) policy report, Artificial Intelligence and the Future of Teaching and Learning, reinforces this orientation. Its call to 'build ethical, equitable policies together' situates AI as a cultural and political phenomenon rather than a neutral innovation. The report's insistence on human-centred decision-making resonates directly with the framework's emphasis on Civic Agency and Epistemic Agency. Civic Agency is realised when learners participate in shaping how AI systems are used; Epistemic Agency emerges when they possess the capacity to interrogate the logic and assumptions encoded within those systems. The report's support for a human-in-the-loop approach illustrates how these domains are operationalised. When AI systems identify a learner as 'at risk' or recommend a career pathway, the outputs must be interpreted and, where necessary, challenged by educators or counsellors. This maintains space for contextual knowledge, ethical sensitivity, and relational judgement—ensuring that human values remain central to the process. In the language of the framework, this represents a dialogic flow between Critical Pedagogy, which equips learners to question and resist systems, and Institutional Responsibility, which obliges institutions to safeguard dignity and fairness.

The focus on equity within the report also links to the domains of Merit (Reimagined) and Probability & Potential. Equity is not presented as a technical adjustment but as a moral commitment, requiring that AI systems recognise emerging capacities and avoid reinforcing structural disadvantage. By valuing potential alongside demonstrated achievement, the framework resists narrow definitions of merit and supports more inclusive visions of employability. Finally, the attention to safety, efficacy, and privacy highlights the role of Institutional Responsibility as the anchor of the model. Educational institutions cannot treat AI as inevitable; they must approach adoption with deliberation, embedding guiding principles of transparency, participatory design, and human interpretive authority. This responsibility extends beyond governance to pedagogy: universities and colleges are called to cultivate learners who are not only digitally literate but also capable of acting as critical participants in shaping technological futures. Linking these strands together, the framework illustrates how the test of trust—accountability, transparency, and responsiveness—operates across all six domains. Explainability safeguards Epistemic Agency, Civic Agency ensures democratic participation, Critical Pedagogy prepares learners to contest and co-create, merit and potential reframe opportunity, and institutions hold the responsibility of embedding these values in practice. Within this integrated model, AI is not treated as an oracle but as a companion: a tool whose legitimacy rests on its ability to empower rather than constrain, and to support human flourishing in the uncertain terrain of contemporary education and work.

The integration of AI into African labour markets represents a decisive moment in the reconfiguration of employability. As O'Neill and Marivate (2024) observe, automation is reshaping agriculture and manufacturing while amplifying the value of digital literacy, adaptive thinking, and data-driven competencies. Yet, unlike in Euro-American contexts, these changes unfold against a backdrop of persistent inequalities, infrastructural asymmetries, and distinct cultural traditions. For this reason, any analysis of AI in Africa must be situated within frameworks that prioritise equity, cultural relevance, and inclusive participation. The six-domain model helps to clarify how these priorities might be realised. Epistemic Agency is vital in contexts where Western-centric datasets dominate. Without the capacity to interrogate whose knowledge is embedded in AI, African workers risk being misrepresented or excluded. Locally grounded data collection—through ethnographic methods, participatory research, and collaboration with vocational and informal networks—enables individuals and communities to validate how they are depicted within employability models. Civic Agency extends this by emphasising participation in decision-making around how AI systems are designed and deployed. African learners, educators, and workers must not be reduced to passive recipients of imported technologies but recognised as active contributors to shaping the ethical and political trajectory of AI adoption.

The role of Critical Pedagogy is equally significant. Educational systems must prepare learners not only with digital skills but also with the critical literacy to question and, where necessary, resist systems that reproduce global inequalities. In this way, pedagogy becomes a mechanism for safeguarding dignity and supporting democratic engagement in technological change. The domains of Merit (Reimagined) and Probability & Potential address the specific labour dynamics of the continent. Conventional models, which presume linear progressions from education to stable employment, fail to capture the improvisational and often precarious realities of African work. By valuing contextual achievements and recognising future potential, AI systems can better reflect the creativity, adaptability, and entrepreneurial ingenuity that characterise much of the informal economy. Finally, Institutional Responsibility anchors these efforts. African governments, universities, and employers must adopt principles that go beyond efficiency, embedding fairness, transparency, and participatory design into governance. Importantly, this includes building regulatory and educational infrastructures that ensure AI strengthens, rather than undermines, local capacities. Viewed through this framework, AI is not simply a disruptive technology but a site of ethical and political negotiation. When guided by epistemic and Civic Agency, Critical Pedagogy, reimagined merit, recognition of potential, and Institutional Responsibility, AI in Africa can be directed towards fostering inclusive growth and affirming local agency. In this light, the continent's encounter with AI is less a matter of technological adoption and more a project of shaping just and contextually grounded futures of work.

Some empirical research highlights a persistent challenge: many African universities remain ill-prepared for the epistemic, pedagogical, and infrastructural demands of the AI era. Mutandiro (2024) observes that graduates often enter labour markets with qualifications poorly aligned to digitally mediated economies. While misalignment between education and employment is not unique to Africa, the stakes are heightened in contexts where higher education is frequently positioned as a primary pathway to mobility and national development. This raises a critical question: how might African universities build a vision of employability that both reflects local realities and engages with global technological change? To approach this question, it is helpful to turn to allegory. One might imagine African higher education as a fleet of ships navigating a vast and shifting ocean. For decades, these vessels have sailed with maps inherited from elsewhere—charts designed for calmer waters and more predictable currents. In the present moment, however, the seas are unsettled. Waves of automation, digitalisation, and algorithmic governance buffet the ships from multiple directions, and the inherited maps no longer suffice. Some vessels, equipped with stronger sails and sturdier hulls, manage to stay their course; others, weakened by years of underinvestment, drift or falter. Yet the ocean itself is not only a site of danger. It also holds new trade routes, uncharted opportunities, and resources that can be harnessed—but only if navigators are able to adapt their methods and trust knowledge rooted in their own seas. The allegory shows that the challenge is not confined to curriculum reform or digital infrastructure. It reflects deeper structural inertia: chronic underfunding, fragmented policies, and limited collaboration between universities, governments, and industry. As Bhorat, Steenkamp, and Rooney (2024) argue, economies best placed to harness AI are those where industrial strategy, education, and public policy converge to enable adaptive and inclusive labour markets. In Africa, however, such convergence is often partial, with benefits concentrated among urban, already-skilled populations—thereby reinforcing inequalities.

A more organic and context-sensitive strategy is therefore required. Regional centres of excellence in AI and employability, embedded within public universities and supported by multisectoral partnerships, could provide a starting point. These centres would serve as hubs for interdisciplinary research, curriculum innovation, and targeted skills training aligned with national development goals. They might also operate as observatories, monitoring labour market trends and translating them into actionable guidance for policymakers, educators, and students. At the same time, universities could experiment with modular and stackable credential programmes, reflecting the lived realities of African learners who often move between formal, informal, and gig-based employment. Such programmes, co-designed with local industries in fields where AI is already gaining ground—agricultural technology, healthcare, fintech, and creative economies—would embody a more flexible and inclusive vision of employability. Returning to the allegory, African universities cannot rely indefinitely on borrowed maps. To chart a viable course, they must draw on their own cartographies: local knowledge systems, community networks, and regional aspirations. By reimagining employability in this way, higher education can act not only as a vessel of credentialing but also as a fleet of adaptive ships—capable of navigating turbulent waters, discovering new horizons, and steering societies towards futures that are equitable, innovative, and just.

A sustainable vision of employability in Africa requires us to move beyond narrow framings of individual responsibility and recognise it as a distributed outcome of interdependent systems. As illustrated in Figure 2.4, employability is shaped by the interaction of policy coherence, educational reform, technological infrastructure, local innovation

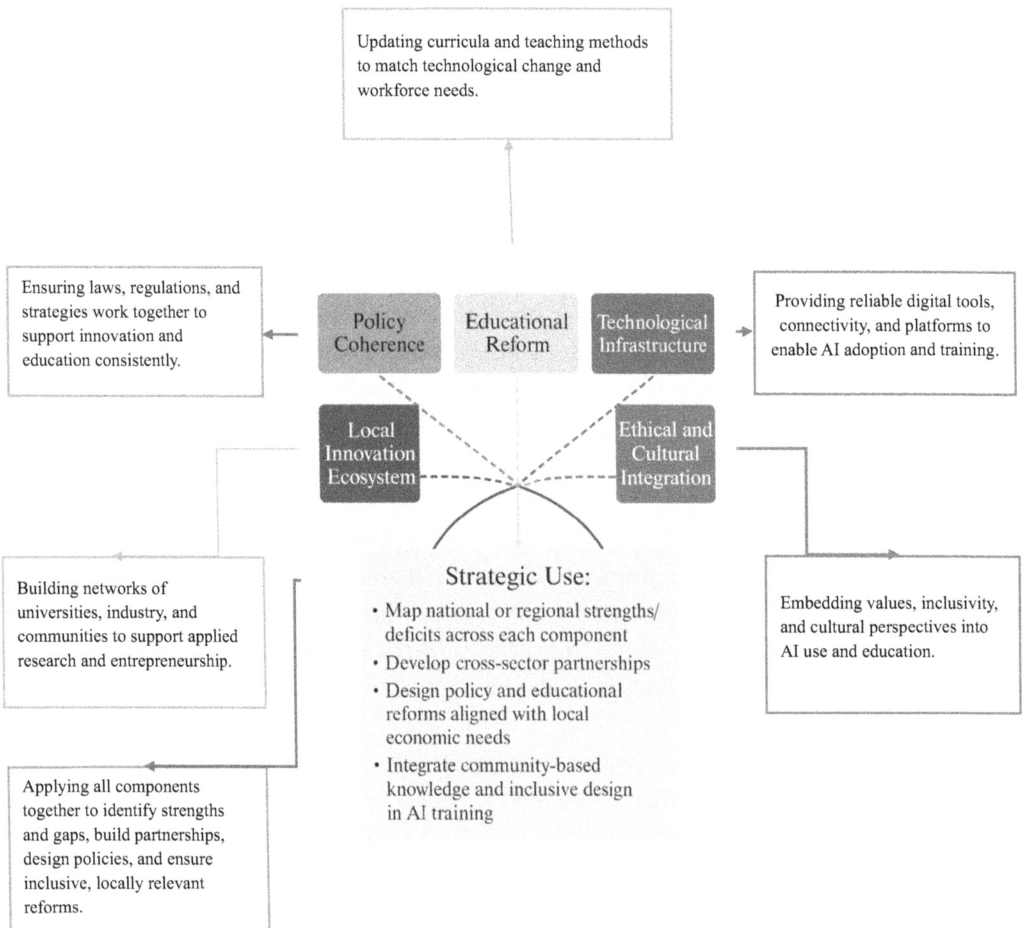

FIGURE 2.4 Strategic framework for educational reform.

The figure highlights the interconnected elements—policy coherence, local innovation ecosystems, technological infrastructure, and ethical integration—that support educational reform through strategic use and inclusive practices.

BOX 2.4 EXPLANATION NOTE—STRATEGIC FRAMEWORK FOR EDUCATIONAL REFORM

The integration of policy coherence, educational reform, technological infrastructure, local innovation ecosystems, and ethical and cultural integration provides a strategic framework for embedding AI into education and national development agendas. Each of these components is interdependent, and their effectiveness depends on being approached holistically rather than in isolation. Policy coherence is critical because fragmented or contradictory policies hinder innovation and create uncertainty for institutions and industries. Aligning educational, economic, and technological policies ensures that reforms are sustainable and strategically consistent. For example, if digital skills strategies are not matched by investments in infrastructure, or if regulation lags behind technological adoption, reforms may be rendered ineffective.

Educational reform is equally important, as traditional curricula often fail to prepare learners for rapidly changing labour markets shaped by AI and automation. Reform must go beyond incremental updates, instead embedding interdisciplinary learning, digital literacy, and critical thinking. This requires pedagogical innovation that balances technical competence with ethical reasoning, given AI's societal impacts. Technological infrastructure forms the backbone of reform, yet access to reliable digital tools and connectivity is unequally distributed. Without addressing the 'digital divide', policies risk reinforcing existing inequalities rather than reducing them. Infrastructure must be seen not merely as a technical enabler but as a social good that underpins inclusion and participation. Local innovation ecosystems play a pivotal role in contextualising reforms. Universities, industries, and communities must collaborate to co-design research and training that reflect regional economic needs and cultural contexts. This local grounding ensures that reforms are not imported models but adaptive frameworks that support sustainable development and employability.

Finally, ethical and cultural integration provides a normative foundation. AI and educational reform are not value-neutral processes; they carry risks of bias, exclusion, and cultural homogenisation. Embedding ethics and cultural perspectives in design and implementation fosters inclusivity, builds public trust, and aligns AI systems with social justice principles. Strategically, the interplay between these components allows governments and institutions to map strengths and deficits, design responsive reforms, and build cross-sector partnerships. Crucially, integrating community-based knowledge into AI training and design helps to democratise innovation, making reforms both equitable and locally relevant.

ecosystems, and ethical and cultural integration. These structural components determine how AI is introduced and how it interacts with skills development, graduate transitions, and labour markets. Placed in dialogue with the six-domain ethical AI framework, Figure 2.4 underlines the importance of embedding civic, epistemic, and pedagogical commitments within broader institutional and policy environments. Epistemic Agency is central to addressing the over-reliance on Western datasets and donor-led training schemes critiqued by Afolayan and Okafor (2023). Without localised data practices and the ability to interrogate how knowledge is encoded, African societies risk being misrepresented or marginalised in global AI economies. Civic Agency comes into play in ensuring that local communities, educators, and learners actively shape the design and deployment of AI, rather than passively adopting imported solutions. This requires mechanisms for inclusive consultation and participatory governance, ensuring that technology reflects collective aspirations rather than external imperatives.

The domain of Critical Pedagogy highlights the role of education in equipping learners not only with technical skills but also with the critical capacity to question, reinterpret, and even resist systems that reproduce inequality. Here, Educational Reform, as mapped in Figure 2.4, becomes a crucial mediator: universities must act as sites of both knowledge production and ethical reflection. Similarly, Merit (Reimagined) and Probability & Potential align with the recognition that African labour markets often follow non-linear and improvisational patterns, shaped by informal economies and entrepreneurial ingenuity. Employability models must value contextual achievements and emerging capacities rather than rely on narrow metrics of past performance. Finally, Institutional Responsibility anchors the framework, linking directly to the structural dimensions of Figure 2.4. Policy coherence, technological infrastructure, and ethical integration are not abstract ideals but the conditions through which institutions can mediate between global technological trends and local developmental needs. Without this responsibility, reform risks fragmentation, entrenching inequalities rather than fostering opportunity. Together, the integration of these two models demonstrates that AI adoption in Africa cannot be reduced to questions of training or technical capability. It is a systemic and ethical project, requiring anticipatory governance, participatory design, and educational reform that foregrounds African epistemologies and community-based knowledge. In this light, AI is not merely a technological disruption but a catalyst for reimagining employability as a collective endeavour—one that affirms equity, resilience, and agency across African societies.

The argument may be drawn together through the image of constructing a house. Each element of Figure 2.4 represents part of its foundation and structure. Policy coherence lays the ground plan; educational reform provides the framework of walls and beams; technological infrastructure supplies the wiring and plumbing that make the house liveable; local innovation ecosystems are the skilled builders who adapt the design to the terrain; and ethical and cultural integration ensures that the house reflects the values and traditions of its community. Yet a house is more than bricks and mortar. The six domains of the ethical AI framework provide the principles by which the home becomes habitable. Epistemic Agency ensures that residents can understand and influence its design. Civic Agency guarantees that the doors are open, welcoming participation in how the house is used. Critical Pedagogy trains new generations to maintain and improve it, while merit and potential remind us that every resident contributes differently to the life within. At the centre, Institutional Responsibility is the roof—sheltering all other efforts and ensuring that the structure remains secure. The allegory underlines a simple truth: Africa cannot live in houses built entirely to foreign blueprints. To be resilient and just, its foundations must be laid with local materials, shaped by community knowledge, and designed to withstand its own conditions. AI, in this sense, is not the house itself, but a new set of tools—capable of helping to build, but only effective if guided by collective purpose and ethical design (Figure 2.4).

Discussions of AI and employability are often framed too narrowly, with emphasis placed primarily on skills acquisition. Such an approach risks overlooking more fundamental questions: whose knowledge is valued, which skills are prioritised, and how these choices shape educational futures. Bordes (2025) reminds us that a transformative AI education in Africa cannot remain confined to instrumentalist paradigms. Instead, it requires the cultivation of critical AI literacy, embracing ethical reasoning, awareness of power relations, and the integration of indigenous knowledge systems. This perspective resonates with the African Population and Health Research Center (Wakiaga and Waweru-Mwangi, 2025), which has argued for pedagogical justice as central to meaningful educational reform. Infrastructure, while necessary, cannot alone address the challenge. What is equally required is a reshaping of curricula and pedagogies so that learners are not only prepared for emerging labour markets but are also empowered to participate equitably within them. Education, in this sense, should not reproduce existing hierarchies but enable societies to reimagine their own possibilities. The Ghanaian allegory of the Eban—the protective fence surrounding a family compound—offers a useful metaphor here. The fence embodies security but also collective responsibility, with every member contributing to its strength. Similarly, employability in Africa must be understood as a shared responsibility in which governments, universities, industries, and communities co-create enabling systems that recognise and support individuals in their pursuit of meaningful work. Without such collective stewardship, digital training risks becoming fragile, unable to provide sustained protection or opportunity.

The conceptual framework presented here positions educational reform at the centre of inclusive employability strategies, in dialogue with policy coherence, technological infrastructure, ethical and cultural integration, local innovation ecosystems, and social capital networks. Taken together, these elements highlight employability not as a narrow matter of training but as a dynamic process embedded within socio-economic, political, and technological contexts. The strategic principles that accompany Figure 2.4—mapping regional strengths and deficits, fostering cross-sectoral partnerships, aligning education with local economic priorities, and embedding inclusivity through design—underline the value of a systems-based approach. Yet the quality and purpose of collaboration remain critical. While public–private partnerships are often presented as solutions to skills gaps, they warrant careful scrutiny. For example, Microsoft's pledge to train one million South Africans in AI competencies (Dludla, 2025) has been celebrated as expanding access to digital learning. However, such initiatives may also entrench the interests of global technology corporations, promoting skill sets that align with platform capitalism rather than the diverse and context-specific needs of African societies. Critical engagement with these dynamics is therefore essential if AI and employability reforms are to foster genuine inclusivity and long-term sustainability.

Interventions that frame education predominantly through employability and productivity metrics risk narrowing its broader purpose as a public good. When this occurs, indigenous knowledge systems, community-centred values, and pedagogical practices that nurture critical consciousness and democratic participation can be marginalised. An alternative vision is therefore required—one that situates employability within African contexts, ensuring that external partnerships are approached strategically and in ways that advance long-term social and economic justice. As the Global Partnership for Education

(2025) has observed, inclusive multistakeholder governance is essential to embedding AI in education meaningfully. Yet collaboration on its own is insufficient. Without robust regulatory frameworks to secure transparency, accountability, and fairness, the deployment of AI risks exacerbating existing inequalities. Employability, in this light, should not be reduced to individual adaptability alone but must be understood as shaped by structural conditions such as algorithmic governance, data sovereignty, and digital rights. Without such critical engagement, the continent risks deepening forms of digital exclusion under the banner of technological progress, thereby undermining aspirations for equitable development.

At the same time, the ontology of work in Africa is undergoing a significant transformation. The acceleration of AI technologies is not only altering established forms of labour but also reshaping definitions of value and human contribution. Conventional employment categories are increasingly inadequate to capture emergent realities, particularly as gig platforms, algorithmic management, and data-driven surveillance reconfigure work into new, often precarious, arrangements. These developments blur the boundaries between formal and informal economies, labour and leisure, and local agency and global technological control. In doing so, they embed African workers within global platform economies in complex and uneven ways. Such shifts necessitate a recalibration of employability discourses. Contemporary debates must develop a conceptual vocabulary that reflects hybrid work identities, transnational flows of digital labour, and the affective dimensions of platform-mediated employment. Terms such as networked labour, algorithmic precarity, and data coloniality provide useful entry points for interrogating these dynamics. Crucially, this reorientation also calls into question the adequacy of conventional indicators—employment rates, productivity levels, or narrowly defined skills outcomes—which often fail to account for the qualitative, relational, and contingent aspects of work in AI-mediated environments. Insights from feminist economics, postcolonial theory, and critical data studies may offer more nuanced frameworks for understanding how labour is being reconfigured in both visible and hidden ways, and for ensuring that future employability strategies capture the lived realities of workers navigating these shifting terrains.

The impact of AI on employability cannot be disentangled from wider questions of data sovereignty, epistemic justice, and the political economy of digital infrastructures. Africa's integration into the global data economy remains structurally uneven, with limited influence over the terms of access, governance, and redistribution. Without deliberate intervention, these asymmetries risk being deepened by AI, reproducing long-standing dependencies within global economic systems. Addressing this requires more than reactive policy adaptation. It calls for a proactive and visionary approach in which education is not simply a conduit into existing labour markets, but a space that fosters critical imagination, collective agency, and transformative social possibility. In such a model, policy must respond to the volatility of contemporary work while also asserting the rights of individuals as digital citizens, whose contributions hold value beyond conventional measures of productivity or employment. A useful metaphor for this approach can be found in the image of the baobab tree. Its resilience during drought does not rest on chance but on deep-rooted adaptation, developed over generations. Beneath its branches, communities gather not only to preserve memory but also to imagine new futures. Similarly, African employability strategies in the age of AI must be grounded in deep social roots, cultivating resilience, creativity, and adaptability that extend beyond the visible metrics of labour market participation.

A parallel perspective emerges in Latin America, where Colombia's Política Nacional de Inteligencia Artificial – CONPES 4144 (Departamento Nacional de Planeación, 2021) sets out a strategy for economic modernisation and digital innovation. While signalling governmental recognition of AI's potential, this policy reflects a developmentalist logic that treats technology as inherently neutral and primarily a vehicle for global competitiveness. This orientation risks subordinating ethical and social considerations to economic imperatives. What is particularly striking is the policy's silence on structural exclusions affecting Afro-Colombian, Indigenous, and rural populations. By neglecting intersectional inequalities, it risks entrenching the very asymmetries it claims to address. In contrast, evolving African frameworks—such as the African Union's Data Policy Framework—increasingly foreground human rights, cultural sovereignty, and inclusive development. These approaches reflect a recognition that AI strategies must be embedded in participatory governance structures that build trust and empower marginalised communities. The contrast between Colombia's economistic framing and Africa's more integrated vision underlines a wider point: AI policies that fail to engage with inequality, accountability, and transparency risk undermining their own effectiveness. Strategies rooted only in technical feasibility or economic utility are ill-equipped to address the complex intersections of employability, ethics, and social justice. As emerging technologies reshape labour and learning, meaningful reform requires more than the adoption of AI systems; it demands sustained attention to the ethical, pedagogical, and political environments into which these systems are introduced.

The OECD and CAF (2022) regional report, though ambitious in scope, reflects a normative orientation shaped largely by Global North standards of responsible innovation. While it recognises the infrastructural and institutional challenges faced across Latin America and the Caribbean, its proposed responses emphasise governance harmonisation and capacity-building in line with OECD benchmarks. This framing positions responsible AI primarily as a technical and institutional issue to be resolved through regulatory alignment, rather than as a political and cultural endeavour grounded in the region's diverse social contexts. In doing so, it risks overlooking questions of epistemic autonomy, historical inequality, and redistributive justice in the development and deployment of digital technologies. By assuming that employability and skills in the age of AI can be secured through the adoption of externally defined norms, the report inadvertently sidelines the importance of cultivating locally rooted models of capability, inclusion, and digital citizenship. Within the discourse of so-called 21st-century skills, such an orientation may produce technocratic solutions that privilege compliance over creativity, adaptability, and critical reflection—capacities that are increasingly essential for navigating uncertain labour markets.

The Inter-American Development Bank (2022) offers a more contextually attentive perspective, foregrounding civil society engagement and hybrid governance. Yet even here, procedural ethics are often prioritised over the broader social imaginaries and collective aspirations that might better inform regionally responsive AI strategies. These frameworks typically stop short of engaging substantively with decolonial thought or participatory epistemologies, instead reinforcing a managerial logic in which fairness, transparency, and inclusion are treated as fixed operational targets rather than as evolving and contested principles. For employability, this represents a notable limitation. Skills such as critical digital literacy, ethical reasoning, and social awareness cannot be cultivated in environments where the underlying values of AI systems remain unquestioned. They require pedagogical spaces where learners are encouraged to interrogate the societal consequences of emerging technologies and to imagine alternatives. Without such spaces, initiatives risk narrowing responsible AI into a pipeline of skills training designed for existing systems, rather than preparing individuals to contribute to their transformation.

The OEI and ProFuturo (2023) report presents AI as a driver of educational transformation and a tool for reducing inequality across Latin America. While this ambition appears progressive, the underlying pedagogical framing is largely oriented towards efficiency and personalisation. AI is depicted less as a means of rethinking the purposes and ethics of education than as a mechanism for optimisation. Such an instrumentalist approach carries risks. Algorithmic models of personalisation can inadvertently reinforce stratification, particularly when data-driven classifications reproduce existing social biases. The promise of individualised learning, when detached from Critical Pedagogy, risks narrowing educational horizons by allowing algorithms rather than communities of learners to determine the scope of engagement. In resource-constrained environments, these solutions often function more as aspirational symbols than as practical interventions, reflecting the influence of imported technological architectures rather than locally grounded pedagogies. This tendency echoes Paulo Freire's caution against the 'banking model' of education, where knowledge is passively delivered to learners. In its digital form, AI-enabled personalisation may deposit algorithmically generated pathways that constrain rather than expand possibilities. A critical approach would instead emphasise dialogue, collective agency, and the democratic purposes of education, ensuring that technology supports rather than supplants pedagogical vision.

Salas-Pilco and Yang (2022) systematic review of AI in higher education reinforces this concern. Despite its empirical breadth, the review reveals a field still dominated by studies of implementation, with limited interrogation of how AI reshapes autonomy, pedagogical relations, or the political economy of knowledge. Questions relating to surveillance, managerialism, and the wider social implications of AI remain underexplored. By contrast, contributions such as those by Derechos Digitales (2021) highlight the importance of civic participation and rights-based approaches in shaping AI policy. This rights-centred perspective gestures towards an alternative model in which the public is understood not merely as users of AI systems but as co-creators of their meaning and direction. A useful metaphor here is the distinction between the mirror and the window. Current narratives often treat AI as a mirror, reflecting and optimising existing patterns. What is needed, however, is a window: an opening through which learners and educators can imagine new possibilities and participate in shaping futures. AI, if critically situated, can serve as a companion in this dialogical process—not a determinant of outcomes, but a tool that supports education's deeper commitment to justice, humanisation, and collective transformation.

Dialzara's (2024) practitioner-focused overview of AI regulation offers a valuable guide for policymakers by concentrating on national frameworks, compliance, and harmonisation. Yet this formalist approach risks presenting law as a neutral mechanism, detached from the political and historical conditions that shape its operation. In contexts where legacies of inequality and exclusion remain deeply embedded, such portrayals obscure how regulation often reproduces rather than resolves structural asymmetries. The limited engagement with customary legal practices, collective rights, and regional jurisprudence further narrows the scope of analysis, overlooking the plural legal realities through which many communities encounter justice and governance. Developing interventions attempts to broaden this terrain. Soares Seto (2025) work under the banner of AI from the South exemplifies an epistemological shift. Rejecting the assumed universality of Euro-American paradigms, they foreground Latin American ontologies and socio-technical imaginaries. Their contribution is not only to localise AI debates but also to provincialise dominant frameworks, creating space for pluriversal approaches that acknowledge diverse ways of knowing and governing technology. This move positions the region not at the margins of AI discourse but as a site of conceptual innovation.

Building on this, Rodríguez Fernández (2025) illuminate the hidden labour regimes underpinning AI through their concept of cognitive extractivism. They reveal how data annotators, content moderators, and microworkers sustain algorithmic systems while often labouring under precarious and unprotected conditions. Such work, largely invisible in mainstream narratives, highlights the human infrastructures of so-called autonomous systems and the exploitative dynamics they can conceal. Ramírez Plascencia and Alonzo González (2025) approach these dilemmas from a doctrinal and philosophical standpoint, offering a rigorous analysis of AI's ethical and legal tensions. However, their reliance on European normative traditions limits the framework's resonance within Latin American contexts, where Indigenous cosmologies and Afro-descendant conceptions of relational rights remain central. The omission of these perspectives reflects a broader challenge within AI ethics, where claims to universality risk eclipsing the cultural and historical diversity necessary for building more inclusive normative foundations.

The intellectual and political tensions surrounding AI governance in Latin America can be mapped conceptually as a field of intersecting currents. Figure 2.5 illustrates these dynamics, highlighting how global regulatory models, national legal frameworks, and technocratic narratives converge at the top of the structure, while alternative epistemologies, critical traditions, and participatory approaches emerge from the bottom. The visualisation is not intended as a definitive taxonomy but as a heuristic device—making visible the tensions, overlaps, and potential convergences between dominant institutional logics and counter-narratives grounded in social justice, decoloniality, and plural legal traditions. At the upper level, Global Governance Scripts cascade into National Legal Frameworks and Formal Regulatory Approaches, culminating in Technocratic AI Narratives. These flows embody the influence of external models that prioritise

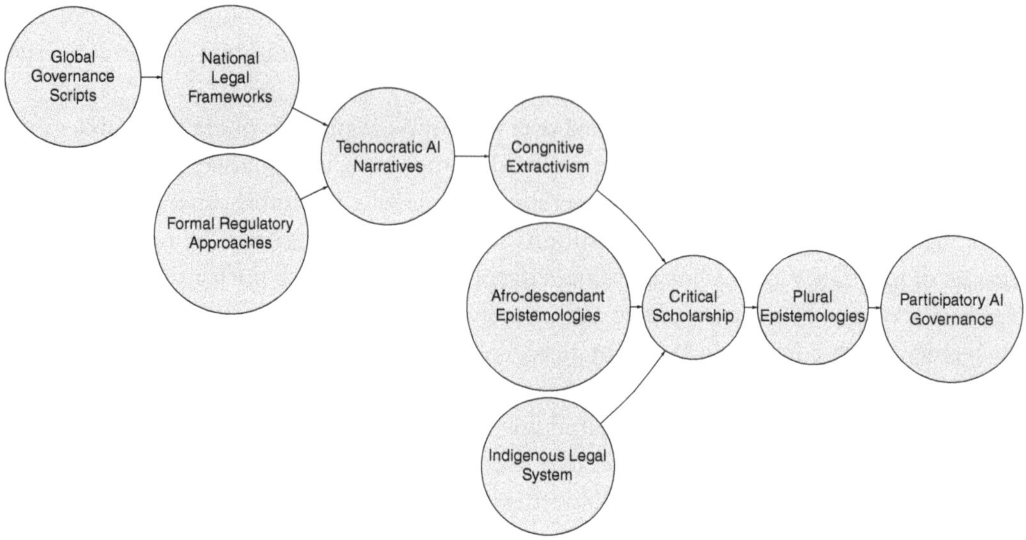

FIGURE 2.5 Pathways of AI governance in Latin America: from global scripts to participatory approaches.

This figure illustrates the contrasting trajectories of AI governance in Latin America. The upper flow traces how global governance scripts, national legal frameworks, and formal regulatory approaches often culminate in technocratic narratives and cognitive extractivism. The lower flow highlights countercurrents shaped by Indigenous legal systems, Afro-descendant epistemologies, and critical scholarship, converging into plural epistemologies that point towards participatory models of AI governance.

harmonisation, compliance, and efficiency. From here, the trajectory often leads to Cognitive Extractivism, capturing how algorithmic systems depend on invisible and precarious labour arrangements that remain obscured in mainstream policy discourse.

By contrast, the lower part of Figure 2.5 represents an epistemological countercurrent. Indigenous Legal Systems, Afro-descendant Epistemologies, and Critical Scholarship converge into Plural Epistemologies, pointing towards a more inclusive horizon. This confluence directs attention to Participatory AI Governance, envisioned not as a fixed endpoint but as a process of ethical co-design, relational accountability, and democratic dialogue. Seen through the allegory of rivers, Figure 2.4 charts two distinct yet interconnected flows. The first, engineered and fast-moving, represents technocratic regulation: powerful in its force but inattentive to the fertile banks it bypasses. The second, slower and meandering, gathers strength from tributaries of lived experience, historical resistance, and collective knowledge. Where these currents meet, turbulence arises, but so too does the possibility of renewal. It is at this confluence that the future of AI governance in Latin America must be imagined: not as a singular stream dictated by external models, but as a shared watercourse shaped by plural voices. In this sense, Paulo Freire's reminder that educators must not think for but with communities becomes instructive once more. AI, like the river, must not be imposed as a predetermined channel but cultivated as a common resource. Its promise lies not in replicating inherited hierarchies, but in creating

BOX 2.5 EXPLANATION NOTE—PATHWAYS OF AI GOVERNANCE IN LATIN AMERICA: FROM GLOBAL SCRIPTS TO PARTICIPATORY APPROACHES

The figure functions as a conceptual cartography of AI governance and epistemological plurality. Its structure juxtaposes dominant, technocratic trajectories of regulation with alternative, community-rooted pathways of knowledge and governance. On one side, we see familiar signposts—Global Governance Scripts, National Legal Frameworks, and Formal Regulatory Approaches—which together constitute the prevailing infrastructure of AI governance. These elements reflect an institutional emphasis on compliance, standardisation, and risk management, reproducing narratives of control that privilege technocratic authority.

The progression from these established routes towards Technocratic AI Narratives highlights how global and national regulatory mechanisms often contribute to an AI discourse framed by efficiency, technological inevitability, and economic competitiveness. Such narratives, however, risk reproducing Cognitive Extractivism—the appropriation of knowledge, culture, and human experience in ways that consolidate power in the hands of a few actors, while marginalising alternative voices and epistemologies. The figure challenges this linearity by mapping out countervailing traditions. Through Afro-descendant Epistemologies and Indigenous Legal Systems, we are invited to recognise traditions of law, governance, and philosophy that resist assimilation into dominant global frameworks. These epistemologies insist upon relationality, reciprocity, and responsibility, standing in stark contrast to technocratic abstraction. Their presence in the figure signals a refusal of erasure and a commitment to broadening the normative horizons of AI governance.

The convergence of these traditions within Critical Scholarship marks a crucial inflection point. Here, epistemological resistance becomes methodologically generative: scholars are urged to interrogate assumptions embedded within regulatory regimes, to unearth silences, and to foreground marginalised knowledge systems. This moment in the figure captures the possibility of re-routing AI governance through plural epistemologies, reconstituting it as an inclusive and participatory practice. From Critical Scholarship, the path extends towards Plural Epistemologies and ultimately to Participatory AI Governance. This trajectory imagines governance not as a top-down imposition but as a deliberative process, engaging civil society, local communities, and historically excluded groups in shaping technological futures. Such a shift reframes AI from being an instrument of control to a catalyst for emancipation and social justice.

Academically, the figure can serve multiple functions:

- *As a conceptual map, it frames research questions at the intersection of AI ethics, legal pluralism, and labour politics, particularly within the Global South.*
- *As a pedagogical tool, it prompts students and practitioners to interrogate the assumptions embedded in regulatory orthodoxies.*
- *As a policy framework, it encourages dialogue that transcends institutional silos, incorporating the lived experiences and normative insights of communities most affected by AI.*
- *As a provocation for scholarship, it challenges researchers to imagine how alternative legal and philosophical traditions might be operationalised within AI systems and infrastructures.*

Ultimately, the figure invites us to reconceive AI as a contested terrain. Futures are not solely determined by technological capacity or financial investment, but by the epistemologies we valorise, the solidarities we forge, and the struggles we choose to honour. The chart, therefore, is not merely descriptive but normative: it maps both the limitations of current governance models and the possibilities of emancipatory alternatives.

the conditions for communities to navigate, negotiate, and reshape its flow towards justice and dignity (Figure 2.5).

In reviewing the literature on technology and employment across Asia, it is evident that AI is being woven into diverse economic and institutional settings. This process signals more than a technological adjustment; it reflects a reconfiguration of how employability is conceived and how skills are valued and cultivated across the region. The consequences, however, are uneven. Labour market outcomes vary depending on national policy frameworks, the structure of domestic industries, and institutional capacities to support workforce transitions. Despite these differences, a recurring theme in the scholarship is the importance of embedding trust, transparency, and accountability within the governance of AI and its social implications. Wang et al. (2024) case study of China highlights a pronounced structural bifurcation within the labour market. High-skilled, AI-oriented roles are expanding, while many routine cognitive and manual occupations are increasingly vulnerable to obsolescence. This trend is often characterised as skills polarisation, whereby technological change amplifies the value of advanced competencies while eroding the stability of mid-level skills. The implications extend well beyond technical training; they raise wider socio-economic questions about how education and training systems recalibrate their objectives in order to prepare learners for adaptable, future-oriented employment. In the Chinese context, this necessitates not only policy reform but also a rethinking of employability as encompassing resilience and lifelong learning across all sectors of society.

Equity within skills development is a particularly pressing concern. The literature suggests that cultivating a technologically literate elite will not suffice. Rather, the benefits of AI-related skilling must be distributed more evenly across the education system, from foundational learning to professional and adult education. Without such inclusivity, the risks of skills polarisation are compounded, entrenching existing inequalities both within and across nations. Similar dynamics are discernible in South Asia. World Bank (2025) analysis underscores the predominance of informal labour in economies such as India, Bangladesh, and Pakistan. Here, the central question is not whether AI will eradicate jobs outright, but how it may reshape the content, security, and bargaining power within already precarious forms of employment. Automation, in such contexts, can alter expectations and conditions without necessarily triggering large-scale unemployment. The critical challenge, therefore, lies in integrating AI equitably into existing socio-economic structures, ensuring that technological change does not exacerbate vulnerabilities. The transformative potential of AI across South Asia—and indeed Asia more broadly—depends on factors that extend well beyond technological innovation. It rests on the creation of inclusive and resilient systems of skills development, equitable access to digital infrastructure, and coherent policy frameworks that prioritise human capabilities.

International policy discourse increasingly demonstrates that national approaches to AI skills development are varied in scope and uneven in ambition. Rigley et al. (2024) in a systematic review spanning seven countries including Singapore, Australia, and Canada, show how policy frameworks often prioritise technical fluency—such as coding, machine learning, and data analytics—at the expense of critical digital literacies, ethical reasoning, and lifelong learning infrastructures. They call for a more comprehensive skills taxonomy that situates AI within its wider social and political contexts, a position echoed in UNESCO's (2024) advocacy for a socio-technical curriculum combining digital proficiency with ethical reflexivity and cultural awareness. Tensions between policy ambition and lived educational realities highlight the limitations of generic approaches. Regional experiences in Southeast Asia illustrate how the uncritical transfer of policy models can exacerbate inequalities. For example, in rural Thailand, AI tools are being introduced to close learning gaps (UNESCO-UNEVOC, 2023), yet without sufficient investment in teacher training and curriculum reform, such initiatives risk becoming short-term technical fixes rather than sustainable solutions. The issue is therefore less the presence of AI in education than the manner of its implementation, which is frequently influenced by external funding priorities and political imperatives rather than by participatory, context-sensitive design.

The OECD (2023) guidance on Southeast Asia reframes employability in terms of resilience rather than reactive skills acquisition. This shift places emphasis on transversal capabilities—such as adaptability, collaboration, and critical thinking—that are vital in an era of rapid demographic and technological change. Here, resilience denotes more than the ability to adjust; it reflects the institutional and pedagogical capacity to anticipate and reconfigure in the face of disruption. Comparable debates are evident in African contexts, where youth unemployment already presents a structural challenge. AI integration in sectors such as agriculture, finance, and education offers potential for innovation but is constrained by uneven infrastructure and fragile education systems. Policy frameworks such as AVPN's (2025) co-designed skilling ecosystems, grounded in lifelong learning and social innovation, emphasise inclusivity and collaboration across public, private, and civil society actors. Similarly, in its AI Opportunity Agenda for Vietnam, Google (2024) presents AI as a major catalyst for Vietnam's socio-economic development, while stressing that this potential depends on building public trust through coherent governance, ethical safeguards and investment in education. These models suggest a growing recognition that employability should not be reduced to technical training programmes. Rather, it must be approached as a systemic and dynamic process—responsive to shifting economic demands yet rooted in principles of inclusion, transparency, and human dignity.

Drawing on data from Central and Eastern Europe, Istudor et al. (2024) demonstrate that employees' skills often remain insufficient for effective AI adoption, which strengthens the case for rethinking employability frameworks in the context of AI-driven transformation. Their findings highlight how fragmented policies and the persistent gap between educational provision and labour market realities undermine the promise of AI-driven development. They argue convincingly that employability should not be understood as a static inventory of skills but rather as a relational capability—emerging from the interplay of institutions, pedagogical cultures, and sociopolitical structures. Without such coherence, even progressive reforms risk entrenching exclusion, particularly for those disadvantaged by historical inequities or infrastructural deficiencies. Placed alongside cases from Asia and Africa, these insights point to the necessity of reframing employability as both structural and ethical. It is insufficient to focus narrowly on technical training or coding fluency; what is required is a more holistic vision that embraces epistemic diversity, inclusive design, and the social conditions that allow individuals and communities to participate meaningfully in AI-enabled futures. Figure 2.5 introduced earlier serves as a conceptual map of these possibilities. At one end lie dominant routes—Global Governance Scripts, National Legal Frameworks, and Technocratic Narratives—which prioritise compliance and efficiency but often culminate in Cognitive Extractivism. From this centre, alternative pathways diverge: Afro-descendant Epistemologies, Indigenous Legal Systems, and Critical Scholarship open possibilities for more plural and participatory forms of governance. Together, these streams converge on Participatory AI Governance, where employability is reimagined as an inclusive, reflexive, and contextually grounded practice.

This structure may be understood through the allegory of a river system. Its upper course, narrow and channelled, mirrors current technocratic emphases on narrowly defined competencies. Yet as the river flows, it branches into tributaries, each sustaining resilience through diversity. These tributaries symbolise the epistemological traditions and community practices that enrich employability with relational depth. Just as a river cannot sustain life if channelled into a single engineered route, employability cannot thrive if confined to narrow, technocratic frameworks. The river allegory resonates with the African philosophy of Ubuntu—'I am because we are'. Ubuntu emphasises that human flourishing is inseparable from relationality and mutual recognition. Applied to AI and employability, Ubuntu challenges the reduction of workers to units of technical proficiency and insists on valuing the collective contexts within which skills acquire meaning. It reminds us that employability is not merely about individual adaptability, but about sustaining communities of practice, fostering dignity, and ensuring that technological transitions strengthen rather than fracture the social fabric.

In policy terms, this means embedding intergenerational learning frameworks into national strategies, acknowledging that employability extends across the life course and requires different forms of support for younger entrants and older workers alike. It also calls for the cultivation of community-based ecosystems—particularly in rural and peri-urban contexts—that align digital skills with local aspirations and cultural values. Equally significant is the need for intersectional sensitivity. AI reshapes opportunities in ways mediated by gender, class, disability, and geography. Policies that ignore these dimensions risk reproducing exclusion. By contrast, intersectionally informed strategies can create enabling conditions for meaningful participation, resonating with Ubuntu's insistence on shared dignity and justice. In sum, this section has traced how employability in AI-driven economies must be reimagined as a relational and ethical construct, nourished by multiple epistemologies and attentive to structural equity. The figure, when read through the allegory of the river and the philosophy of Ubuntu, reminds us that employability is not a solitary journey but a shared current of knowledge, dignity, and solidarity. As the analysis turns to Regulatory and Institutional Frameworks: The Foundation for Ethical AI, the task will be to assess whether legal and organisational infrastructures are capable of sustaining such a plural and life-affirming vision of the future. The next section will extend this analysis by turning to Regulatory and Institutional Frameworks: The Foundation for Ethical AI. Here, the focus will be on the legal, normative, and organisational infrastructures that shape the governance of AI. The discussion will consider whether current frameworks—ranging from supranational initiatives such as the EU AI Act to the work of national regulators, civil society organisations, and professional bodies—are adequate to sustain the kind of plural and life-affirming vision outlined above. The aim is to move beyond a compliance-oriented approach and to examine how regulation might become anticipatory, participatory, and inclusive, providing both technical safeguards and ethical foundations for just and sustainable AI futures.

REGULATORY AND INSTITUTIONAL ARCHITECTURES FOR ETHICAL ARTIFICIAL INTELLIGENCE

The preceding chapter highlighted that employability in AI-influenced economies cannot be reduced to discrete skills acquisition, but must be understood as a relational and ethical construct. This insight provides an important foundation for examining how regulatory and institutional frameworks shape the governance of AI. While questions of education, labour, and capability are often addressed in policy discourse, they remain inseparable from the structures that determine how technological change is directed, managed, and justified. Classical political traditions offer a useful lens for considering these questions. In ancient Greece, the contrast between Sparta and Athens illustrated divergent visions of governance: the former built on centralised discipline and conformity, the latter on deliberation, participation, and accountability. This tension remains relevant in contemporary AI debates. Across many regions, regulatory responses to AI reflect a tendency towards 'Spartan' models of control—formal, efficiency-driven, and often borrowed from external templates. Such approaches prioritise stability and alignment with global standards, but risk obscuring the diverse voices, traditions, and epistemologies that shape local contexts. By contrast, an 'Athenian' orientation—rooted in dialogue and shared responsibility—suggests that AI governance can be conceived as a collective project, one in which authority is legitimised through participation rather than compliance. This perspective resonates strongly with critical traditions within the Global South, particularly the work of Paulo Freire, who emphasised dialogue and conscientisation as foundations of social transformation. Applied to AI, these traditions remind us that governance must extend beyond compliance mechanisms to include practices of listening, adapting, and engaging with those most directly affected by technological change. Regulation, in this sense, should not only safeguard against harm but also cultivate the conditions for collective agency.

The current regulatory landscape, however, reflects the dominance of technocratic and legal-formalist frameworks. Global governance narratives—often articulated through the EU AI Act, OECD guidelines, or G20 declarations—exert significant influence on national strategies, shaping both language and policy orientation. While these instruments advance important principles of fairness, accountability, and transparency, they frequently marginalise pluralistic perspectives and overlook questions of equity, particularly in contexts marked by colonial legacies and structural inequalities. It is within this space that critical scholarship has turned towards decolonial ethics as a corrective. Decolonial approaches call for dismantling inherited structures of power that privilege Western epistemologies and regulatory models, while foregrounding cultural pluralism, community agency, and historically marginalised perspectives. In AI governance, this entails embedding inclusive participation, ensuring equitable access to digital infrastructures, and recognising the ethical legitimacy of diverse cultural values. The risks of neglecting such perspectives are evident in the sphere of employment, where AI is increasingly used in recruitment, performance evaluation, and career management. Batool, Zowghi, and Bano (2023) identify fragmentation and inconsistency in governance frameworks but pay limited attention to how these weaknesses translate into workplace realities. This omission is significant, as fragmented regulation leaves workers navigating AI-mediated systems without adequate safeguards for procedural fairness, transparency, or employment stability. In such contexts, the promise of efficiency risks becoming a mechanism of exclusion, undermining both trust and legitimacy. Collectively, these insights point to the need for regulatory and institutional frameworks that do not merely replicate technocratic control but actively sustain plural and participatory visions of the future. By moving beyond imported models and engaging more deeply with dialogic, decolonial, and community-rooted traditions, AI governance can begin to align institutional design with the ethical imperatives of equity, dignity, and inclusion.

Batool et al.'s study draws attention to the fragmentation of AI governance but gives insufficient consideration to the conditions that lend legitimacy and credibility to regulatory frameworks. The literature consistently highlights that without meaningful incorporation of TAT, governance structures risk reinforcing existing power asymmetries and limiting the capacity of workers and communities to challenge algorithmic decisions. This concern is particularly acute in the employment domain, where AI is increasingly deployed in recruitment, monitoring, and performance evaluation. Here, the issue is not only whether such systems are adopted but also whether those affected have credible avenues to participate in and contest the processes shaping their opportunities. Leslie et al. (2022) address this gap by emphasising the need to translate ethical commitments into enforceable institutional mechanisms. Their work signals a shift in the debate: from aspirational frameworks to compliance infrastructures and legally binding standards capable of embedding ethical principles within operational governance. This transition is significant for employability, as the robustness of such mechanisms directly influences the fairness of access to work and the degree of protection individuals have against algorithmic bias or discriminatory practice.

Building on this, Morley et al. caution that TAT should not be treated as ancillary principles. Rather, they constitute the foundation upon which ethical regulation must be built if it is to achieve legitimacy and public confidence. Ethical frameworks that neglect these elements remain vulnerable to scepticism and weak implementation. The implications for employability are considerable. As Ahmad and Bilal (2024) notes, employability in the age of AI increasingly extends beyond technical proficiency. Workers must also acquire a degree of 'regulatory literacy'—the capacity to understand and navigate the institutional and legal dimensions of AI governance. This includes knowing how rights can be exercised, how fairness can be demanded, and how accountability can be enforced in technologically mediated workplaces. Leslie and Perini (2024) add weight to this argument, suggesting that a broad set of AI-era competencies is becoming increasingly central to sustaining career resilience. In this sense, employability is reconceptualised not only as a matter of technical skill but also as the ability to engage critically with the governance systems that structure access to employment itself.

Building upon the preceding analysis, this section advances the conceptual framework of Ethical Regulatory Literacy (ERL). ERL refers to the knowledge, skills, and critical awareness required for stakeholders—employees, educators, policymakers, and organisational leaders—to engage meaningfully with AI governance in the workplace. It positions individuals not simply as passive recipients of regulation, but as active participants capable of scrutinising, contesting, and shaping the systems that structure their employment. The rationale for ERL rests on two interlinked claims. First, ethical and effective deployment of AI technologies cannot be secured through technical design alone; it requires a workforce and citizenry that understand the regulatory and institutional dimensions of technological governance. Second, cultivating ERL strengthens TAT by equipping stakeholders with the means to hold both organisations and algorithms to account. This is particularly vital as AI increasingly mediates recruitment, performance management, and workplace decision-making. Without such literacy, individuals risk being subjected to opaque systems without the tools to challenge their outcomes. Practically, ERL can be embedded through education and professional development programmes, alongside policy frameworks that make regulatory processes more accessible. Such initiatives would not only demystify governance structures but also enhance institutional capacity for ethical oversight. The emphasis here is on co-creation: ensuring that organisations and employees together shape environments where AI is governed in ways that are both legitimate and socially sustainable.

This approach resonates with Jobin, Ienca, and Vayena (2019), who argue that AI cannot be understood apart from the legal, institutional, and social contexts in which it operates. Their call for participatory governance reframes employability not merely as adaptation to technological change, but as involvement in defining the terms of work and value. Similarly, Corrêa et al. (2023) highlight that while there is broad consensus on ethical principles such as fairness, transparency, and accountability, the absence of enforceable compliance mechanisms undermines their effectiveness. Their critique of 'performative compliance' is particularly salient, as it exposes how organisations may adopt ethical language symbolically while leaving exploitative labour practices intact. These contributions reinforce the need for ERL as both a pedagogical and governance imperative. It not only empowers individuals to navigate AI-driven labour markets with confidence but also provides a framework for challenging surface-level ethical commitments and demanding substantive accountability. The accompanying figure illustrates this integrative vision, mapping how ERL might be situated within broader governance structures so as to bridge the gap between abstract principles and everyday employment practices.

The conceptual framework of ERL can be directly mapped onto the trajectories illustrated in Figure 2.5. The figure charts two contrasting pathways: on one side, the dominance of Global Governance Scripts, National Legal Frameworks, and Formal Regulatory Approaches, converging into Technocratic AI Narratives and ultimately Cognitive Extractivism. This route reflects a familiar pattern in which governance is imposed through

importance of situating AI ethics within institutional and legal contexts rather than treating ethics as an abstract set of principles. Their call for inter-institutional engagement resonates with the early stages of the figure, which foreground literacy and training as shared responsibilities across educational and professional domains. Corrêa et al. (2023), meanwhile, highlight the recurring problem of convergence around high-level principles without sufficient mechanisms for accountability. Their critique sharpens the middle stages of the framework, where participatory governance is shown not as rhetorical inclusion but as the necessary basis for legitimacy. What emerges from the interplay between these perspectives is a temporal dimension of ethics that is often overlooked: the challenge of sustaining values over time. Ethics cannot be understood as a one-off exercise of principle articulation; it requires rhythm—regular processes of listening, revising, and adapting. Here, ERL might be conceived less as a static repository of skills and more as a kind of institutional tether: the infrastructure that grounds responsiveness while preventing drift. This view recasts ERL not merely as comprehension but as continuity. Its purpose lies in cultivating patterned practices—feedback loops, curricular renewal, staff dialogue—that embed ethics into organisational life as an ongoing rhythm rather than a reactive response. The figure, therefore, does not present ethics as a final destination; rather, it gestures towards an architecture of repetition, where legitimacy is maintained through structured renewal. In this respect, the framework offers less a solution than an orientation: a way of keeping ethical practice alive, responsive, and institutionally sustained.

Extending the arguments of Jobin et al. (2019) and Corrêa et al. (2023), ERL can be understood as a means of closing the gap between ethical aspiration and practical implementation. Its value lies in equipping stakeholders to recognise when compliance is merely performative and to call for genuine accountability. When integrated into curricula and professional training, ERL enhances the capacity of individuals and institutions alike to participate substantively in the co-creation of ethical standards, thereby resisting symbolic gestures of inclusivity and promoting more authentic governance practices. In the domain of employability, ERL reframes ethical engagement as proactive rather than reactive. It enables individuals to critically interrogate the systems that shape their working lives, thus offering a measure of protection against opacity, bias, or inequity in recruitment and workplace decision-making. At the same time, it strengthens governance by positioning transparency and accountability not as aspirational ideals, but as demands that stakeholders are equipped to articulate and pursue. In this respect, ERL translates theoretical ethics into enforceable expectations. The challenges of embedding such practices are underscored by Morley et al. (2021), who shift the discussion from normative principles to practical mechanisms of implementation. Their emphasis on auditing, algorithmic impact assessment (AIA), and participatory toolkits illustrates how ethics can be operationalised within organisational structures. This is particularly relevant to employability, where ethical discourse often remains detached from the material practices that govern hiring, evaluation, and promotion. Morley and colleagues highlight the need for organisational reflexivity: an institutional capacity for continuous reflection and adaptation to evolving ethical demands. Together, ERL and the applied approaches outlined by Morley et al. point towards a model of governance that is not only principled but also structurally embedded. This requires collaboration across developers, employers, educators, and policymakers to ensure that ethics are not peripheral, but integral to the lifecycle of AI systems. Such integration—spanning design, deployment, and ongoing revision—offers a foundation for a more participatory, transparent, and accountable approach to AI in the workplace.

In a complementary register, Jobin, Ienca, and Vayena (2019) provide a foundational mapping of global AI ethics guidelines. While they identify broad agreement on principles such as fairness, non-maleficence, and autonomy, their study also exposes the absence of enforceability. This lack of traction is particularly significant in the context of employability, where ethical language often serves a symbolic function. As Jobin et al. caution, ethical frameworks may legitimise technological adoption while masking unjust or opaque practices. Workers may be invited to trust systems branded as 'fair', even as those very systems reproduce bias in recruitment, progression, and evaluation. The challenge is not simply one of insufficient principles, but of ethics being strategically co-opted to obscure inequity. This perspective resonates with earlier concerns about the temporality and endurance of ethics. Employability in an AI-mediated labour market cannot be reduced to technical proficiency or adaptive skills; it must involve a sustained, critical engagement with the infrastructures that shape access to work. The ERL is central here, not as a peripheral competence but as a grounding capability. It provides individuals with the means not only to navigate automated systems but also to question, contest, and reshape them when they fail to uphold equity and justice. Returning to the earlier allegory, ERL can be understood as the tether that steadies the lighthouse amid shifting tides. It is the modest but vital infrastructure that ensures ethical commitments are not swept away by waves of performative compliance or symbolic rhetoric. In this light, employability in the age of AI is not merely about surviving automation; it is about cultivating agency, reflexivity, and participation in regulatory processes. ERL, then, is foundational: it holds systems accountable while keeping ethical practice grounded, adaptive, and responsive to change.

In advancing the discussion on ethical engagement with AI and employability, ERL has already been introduced as a foundational capacity. To extend this framework, I propose a complementary dimension: AI Ethical Reflexive Learning. This addition does not replace but completes ERL, together forming what may be described as a Double ERL model—a dialogic structure through which ethical preparedness is cultivated in both outward and inward directions. The first dimension, ERL, enables individuals to interpret and navigate external governance structures, from institutional protocols to legal instruments. Yet this capacity remains partial if it is not accompanied by an inward orientation: a sustained practice of ethical reflexivity. Reflexivity here is more than episodic self-checking; it is a deliberate orientation that involves moral attentiveness, humility in the face of uncertainty, and readiness for ethical transformation. It is this dimension that AI Ethical Reflexive Learning seeks to capture—an ongoing labour of questioning and adaptation that acknowledges the fluidity of socio-technical contexts. Together, literacy and reflexivity give shape to what might be called ethical employability: a conception of preparedness that extends beyond technical competence to embrace conscience, responsibility, and care. Ethical employability does not reduce ethics to compliance but instead situates it as an active engagement with the assumptions and values that underpin AI systems and workplace practices. The interdependence of these capacities can be clarified by returning to Plato's Allegory of the Cave. The act of perceiving shadows as illusions and recognising deeper structures aligns with ERL: it is the acquisition of literacy to see through surface appearances. Yet the allegory is equally about return—the responsibility to re-enter the cave, to engage with others, and to act for the collective good. This return reflects the essence of reflexive learning: knowledge translated into responsibility, and understanding embodied in action. In this way, AI Ethical Reflexive Learning ensures that ERL does not remain a detached lens, but becomes part of a communal ethic of participation, responsibility, and care within AI-mediated work.

The practical implications of a dual framework of ERL and Ethical Reflexive Learning extend well beyond the classroom. As AI systems increasingly shape recruitment, evaluation, and task management, individuals are drawn into environments where the ethical stakes are both opaque and unevenly distributed. In such contexts, regulatory literacy alone cannot suffice. What is also required is a cultivated reflexive capacity: the ability to pause, interrogate, and ethically reposition oneself in relation to shifting technological and institutional norms. This reflexive dimension should not be understood as a peripheral attribute but as a critical faculty. It enables individuals to register ethical dissonance, to confront normative contradictions, and to envisage alternatives to established practices. In doing so, reflexivity nurtures a form of ethical resilience—an orientation that allows people not only to operate within AI-mediated systems but also to challenge and reshape them when they perpetuate inequity or opacity.

The strength of the Double ERL framework lies in the interplay between literacy and reflexivity. Literacy grounds individuals in the external mechanisms of governance—codes, policies, and regulatory instruments—while reflexivity ensures that such engagement does not harden into uncritical compliance. Without literacy, there is a risk of disempowerment; without reflexivity, there is a danger of reproducing the very systems that entrench injustice. By holding these two axes together, the Double ERL resists both cynicism and complacency. It offers a mode of ethical empowerment that transforms responsible AI from rhetorical aspiration into lived practice. In this sense, the framework does not prescribe a fixed destination. Rather, it sketches a pathway—an invitation to cultivate collective responsibility and to sustain ethical practice as an ongoing endeavour. Returning to the earlier allegory of the cave, Double ERL does not simply illuminate the shadows; it insists on the responsibility to return, to act with others, and to translate insight into care and justice.

The Double ERL figure builds directly on the three earlier frameworks, consolidating their insights into a more integrated account of ethical preparedness. The initial figures traced a linear pathway: from foundational literacy, through training and participatory governance, towards systemic outcomes of trust, employability, and authentic compliance. The Double ERL model now reframes this trajectory, positioning Ethical Regulatory Literacy (ERL) and Ethical Reflexive Learning as two interdependent orientations—outward and inward—that together sustain ethical engagement across time. This synthesis introduces a shift from progression to interplay. On the outward-facing side, ERL equips individuals with the tools to navigate formal regulatory systems, ensuring clarity in relation to institutional protocols and legal standards. On the inward-facing side, reflexive learning cultivates attentiveness, moral imagination, and the courage to question entrenched norms. At their intersection lies a shared ethical fulcrum: the point at which knowledge and conscience converge, enabling workers not only to comply with rules but also to interrogate and transform the socio-technical systems that shape their labour. Without literacy, individuals risk ethical disempowerment; without reflexivity, they risk reproducing injustice uncritically.

The deeper significance of this integration can be expressed through a new allegory—that of the ethical bridge. Imagine a great river flowing through a city, representing the shifting currents of technological change. On one bank lie the structures of law and policy; on the other, the terrain of reflexivity and moral imagination. Individuals and institutions must cross continually between these shores. A bridge is required: strong enough to provide stability, yet flexible enough to respond to pressure. ERL provides the beams and piers, grounding ethical practice in accountability. Reflexive learning forms the suspension cables, absorbing strain and enabling movement. Only when these components work together can the bridge hold, allowing safe passage across turbulent waters. When read alongside the earlier allegories, the continuity becomes clearer. The lighthouse tether captured the temporality of ethics—the need for rhythm, regular adjustment, and anchoring amidst tides. The bridge allegory now extends this by highlighting the connection: the necessity of moving between regulatory structures and reflexive practice without becoming stranded on either side. Together, these images foreground ethics not as static compliance, but as rhythm and relation—as the ongoing capacity to adapt, reconnect, and endure. In this light, the Double ERL model does more than summarise prior frameworks; it draws them into a coherent philosophy of ethical employability. Preparedness for AI-mediated work is not a fixed achievement but a sustained practice, animated by repetition and return. It is a rhythm of literacy and reflexivity, a continual crossing and tethering, through which institutions and individuals alike hold open the possibility of justice, clarity, and care in the shifting landscapes of AI (Figure 2.7).

Building on comparative analyses of international AI governance frameworks, the concepts of Ethical Regulatory Literacy and AI Ethical Reflexive Learning provide a valuable foundation for interrogating how regulatory structures both enable and constrain moral agency in contemporary educational and policy contexts. These dimensions make clear that responsible engagement with AI cannot be reduced to technical compliance with legal frameworks; it must also involve the cultivation of ethical sensibilities capable of grappling with the indeterminacy, contestation, and normative dilemmas inherent in socio-technical systems. The European Union's Artificial Intelligence Act 2024 (AI Act) represents the most comprehensive attempt to regulate AI through binding obligations. Its risk-based classification system imposes strict requirements for high-risk systems, mandating conformity assessments, traceability, technical documentation, and human oversight (EU AI Act, 2024). Yet while these provisions institutionalise accountability, they risk encouraging a compliance mentality in which practitioners prioritise procedural adherence over substantive ethical reflection. The notion of Ethical Regulatory Literacy responds to this tension by insisting that regulation be interpreted not merely as a checklist but as an evolving normative framework requiring critical engagement and legal consciousness.

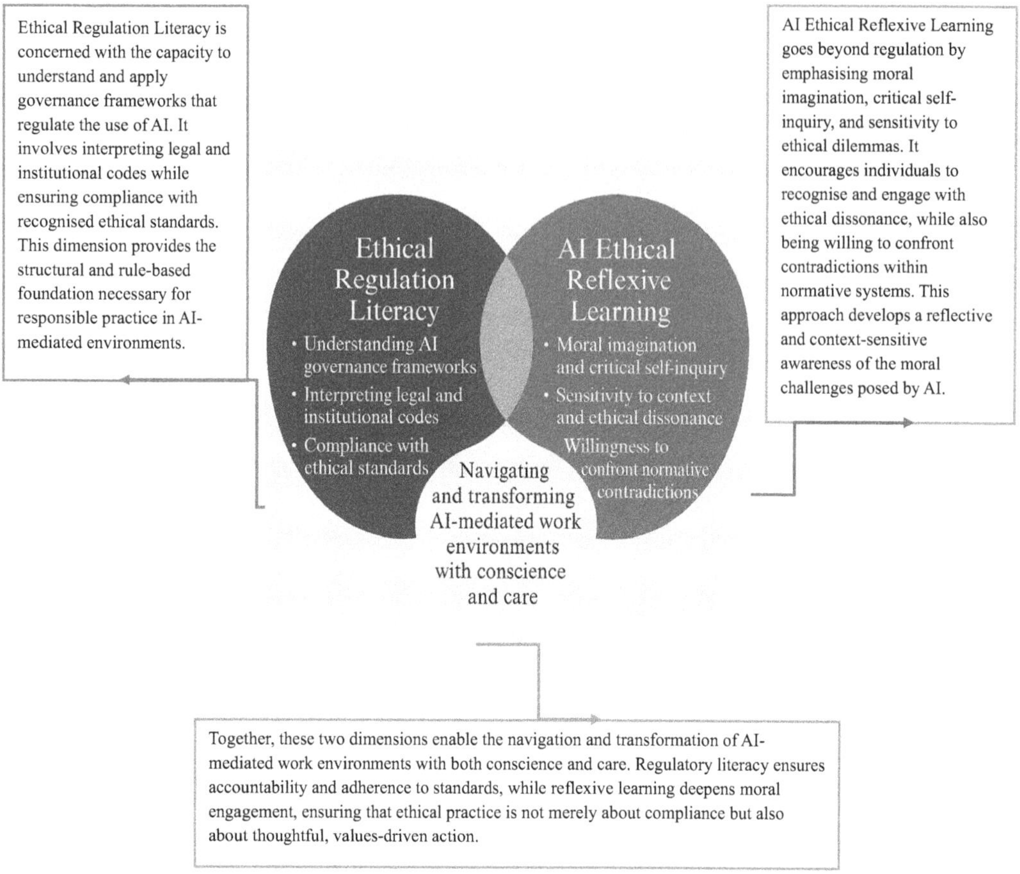

FIGURE 2.7 Double ERL model for ethical employability in AI-mediated environments.

The figure visually represents the Double ERL model as a Venn diagram comprising two overlapping circles. The left circle is labelled Ethical Regulatory Literacy, highlighting the capacity to engage with external governance structures such as laws, policies, and institutional protocols. The right circle is labelled AI Ethical Reflexive Learning, illustrating the inward, continuous practice of ethical self-awareness, critical reflection, and moral responsiveness in AI-mediated contexts. The intersection of the two circles symbolises the integrated space of ethical employability, where regulatory literacy and reflexivity converge to support responsible, conscientious participation in digitally governed work environments.

By contrast, AI Ethical Reflexive Learning foregrounds the interpretive and moral work that lies beyond codified regulation. It highlights the importance of moral imagination, self-scrutiny, and the capacity to confront ethical contradictions that formal governance instruments cannot fully anticipate. The OECD Principles on Artificial Intelligence (2019a; updated 2024) reinforce this orientation by promoting inclusivity, human-centred values, transparency, and accountability. Although non-binding, the OECD framework has reshaped policy agendas by emphasising institutional capacity-building and public engagement, thereby recognising that systemic accountability depends as much on ethical culture as on legal design. Crucially, its insistence on explainability and human oversight aligns

BOX 2.7 EXPLANATION NOTE—DOUBLE ERL MODEL FOR ETHICAL EMPLOYABILITY IN AI-MEDIATED ENVIRONMENTS

The figure illustrates the interplay between Ethical Regulatory Literacy and AI Ethical Reflexive Learning as dual but complementary dimensions of ethical competence in AI-mediated work environments. On the left, ethical regulatory literacy emphasises a compliance-oriented approach—the ability to understand governance frameworks, interpret legal and institutional codes, and ensure alignment with established ethical standards. This dimension is essential in operationalising accountability and safeguarding against breaches of professional and societal trust. However, while necessary, regulatory literacy alone risks fostering a technocratic or rule-bound orientation that may overlook the complexity of ethical dilemmas that exceed codified standards.

The right side of the figure—AI ethical reflexive learning—extends beyond compliance, foregrounding critical, imaginative, and context-sensitive engagement with AI ethics. It calls for moral imagination, self-inquiry, and sensitivity to ethical dissonance, as well as the courage to confront contradictions embedded in normative frameworks. This reflexivity cultivates the disposition to question not only whether practices conform to regulations but also whether they are just, equitable, and socially responsible. It acknowledges that codes and standards can be contested, incomplete, or even complicit in structural injustices.

The overlap between these two domains highlights the necessity of integrating literacy and reflexivity. Practitioners require both the technical capacity to navigate governance systems and the critical disposition to interrogate and transform them. The central outcome—'navigating and transforming AI-mediated work environments with conscience and care'—underscores an ethical praxis that is neither reducible to compliance nor to abstract critique, but rather a synthesis of both. Such praxis enables professionals to address the rapid evolution of AI systems in ways that are legally robust, ethically defensible, and socially responsive.

In academic terms, the model resonates with theories of ethical professionalism (Banks, 2020), critical reflexivity (Fook and Gardner, 2007), and AI governance frameworks (Floridi and Cowls, 2019), which collectively argue for a move beyond static rules towards a dynamic ethical engagement. The figure, therefore, advocates for a dual literacy-reflexivity paradigm as foundational to responsible AI practice in education, healthcare, and other sectors where human dignity and justice are at stake.

with the AI Act but simultaneously exposes the limits of regulation when interpretive and moral capacities are underdeveloped.

The tension between these two modes—rule-based literacy and reflexive ethical learning—underscores a wider paradox in global AI governance. Over-reliance on regulation risks reducing ethics to compliance, while an exclusive focus on reflexivity risks normative relativism and fragmentation. Canada's Directive on Automated Decision-Making (2020; updated 2024), with its emphasis on AIAs and public transparency, illustrates a possible middle ground: it codifies procedural safeguards while simultaneously requiring practitioners to exercise judgement in applying them. Collectively, these initiatives suggest that effective AI governance demands a synthesis of both dimensions. Ethical Regulatory Literacy provides the structural competencies necessary to ensure accountability, but without AI Ethical Reflexive Learning, it remains shallow and technocratic.

Conversely, reflexive learning enriches governance with moral depth, but without regulatory literacy, it risks remaining aspirational. It is in the interplay—and at times the productive tension—between these approaches that the conditions for both systemic accountability and individual empowerment can be realised.

What emerges from the convergence of the governance initiatives is a persuasive case for embedding Ethical Regulatory Literacy within both formal education and wider civic learning. The purpose is not confined to training individuals to comply with legal obligations, but to enable them to interpret and apply regulatory norms in ways that are contextually sensitive and critically informed. Such an orientation seeks to foster a culture of responsibility in which legal knowledge is complemented by moral awareness and social accountability. Realising this ambition requires policy frameworks that encourage pedagogical innovation—whether through curriculum design, professional development, or public engagement—that treat ethical and legal literacy as integral dimensions of contemporary citizenship. While instruments such as the EU AI Act 2024 and the OECD Principles on Artificial Intelligence provide structural foundations for responsible governance, their effectiveness ultimately depends on the cultivation of capacities that extend beyond procedural adherence. In this sense, Ethical Regulatory Literacy is not a peripheral aspiration but a practical condition for sustaining TAT in AI-mediated environments.

Yet literacy of this kind, though necessary, is insufficient on its own to address the deeper ethical complexities that accompany the diffusion of AI. The ability to navigate and transform AI-shaped settings with conscience and care arises only where regulatory knowledge intersects with reflexive moral engagement. This intersection is not supplementary but essential to preparing individuals for the indeterminacy and contestation that characterise socio-technical systems, particularly in domains such as education, healthcare, justice, and public administration. AI Ethical Reflexive Learning foregrounds precisely those capacities that regulation cannot, by itself, generate: moral imagination, critical self-inquiry, attentiveness to context, and the readiness to grapple with normative tensions. These qualities are closely aligned with the values articulated in UNESCO's Recommendation on the Ethics of Artificial Intelligence (2021b), which underlines the centrality of human dignity, critical thought, and social justice in shaping technological futures. Such framing recognises that the ethical governance of AI cannot be confined to compliance regimes but must remain an open and dialogic engagement with evolving moral landscapes.

Together, the dual concepts of Ethical Regulatory Literacy and AI Ethical Reflexive Learning form mutually reinforcing pillars of effective governance and pedagogy. Regulation supplies the scaffolding that secures accountability and consistency, while reflexivity ensures that this structure remains flexible, humane, and responsive to moral complexity. An allegory may help to illustrate the relationship: in the image of the ship of state, the vessel may be equipped with charts, rules, and instruments—much as AI governance frameworks provide laws, classifications, and procedures. Yet without a navigator capable of wisdom, foresight, and moral discernment, the ship risks drifting or being steered into peril. Ethical Regulatory Literacy equips us to read the charts; AI Ethical Reflexive Learning enables us to discern the stars. Only in combination can they guide societies safely through the uncertain seas of technological change.

This synthesis has clear implications for contemporary education. Across Europe, initiatives in digital citizenship education are beginning to incorporate legal and ethical dimensions of AI into secondary curricula, while universities experiment with interdisciplinary modules that combine computer science, law, and philosophy. Professional development programmes for teachers and civil servants increasingly integrate training in algorithmic accountability, data governance, and critical digital literacy. These developments suggest a growing recognition that preparing citizens for an AI-mediated world requires more than technical fluency. What is needed is an educational culture that cultivates both regulatory competence and ethical reflexivity, enabling learners not only to comply with existing frameworks but also to question, adapt, and improve them in light of broader social values. In this way, education becomes the site where the ship is provisioned, its navigators trained, and its course continually reassessed in dialogue with the shifting moral horizons of technological life.

In considering employability within AI-mediated professional environments, these two capacities should be recognised not simply as regulatory skills but as dispositions that enable professionals to sustain agency in increasingly complex technological systems. A central requirement here is the capacity for ethical risk anticipation: the ability to recognise not only immediate technical challenges but also the wider ethical harms that may emerge as AI interacts with social and institutional structures. This anticipatory orientation aligns with the preventative ethos of the EU AI Act, yet it also extends beyond compliance by encouraging professionals to imagine the long-term ethical trajectories of technological development. Closely related to this is the need for socio-technical imagination. As AI becomes more deeply embedded within organisational and civic life, it must be understood not only as a technical instrument but also as part of a broader ecology of practices, values, and power relations. The UNESCO Recommendation affirms this perspective by insisting that AI be considered within its social, cultural, and environmental contexts. From the standpoint of employability, this suggests that future professionals will need to think critically about the wider societal pathways that AI may shape, rather than focusing exclusively on immediate tasks of design or policy adherence. Equally important is a commitment to long-termism in ethical reasoning. While professional training often centres on addressing present-day risks, both the EU AI Act and UNESCO highlight the necessity of considering intergenerational consequences. Decisions taken today can entrench inequalities, exclusion, or environmental burdens that endure far into the future. Professionals with robust Ethical Regulatory Literacy will therefore be those capable of sustaining ethical reflection across extended temporal horizons, resisting the pull of short-term pressures.

Attention must also be paid to micro-ethics, the subtle, often unnoticed decisions that accumulate during the design, deployment, and management of AI systems. These seemingly minor choices shape the moral character of technological environments over time. Employability in such contexts will increasingly depend on the ability to remain ethically attentive in the small routines of daily practice, treating ethics as integral to professional identity rather than as an occasional add-on. Finally, as AI development and governance are frequently distributed across teams, organisations, and jurisdictions, the notion of distributed ethical accountability becomes increasingly significant. Professionals will need to engage collaboratively with ethical challenges, sharing responsibility across disciplinary and institutional boundaries. Taken together, these considerations suggest that employability and ethical governance in an AI-mediated world will depend on capacities richer than those traditionally recognised. Skills such as ethical risk anticipation, socio-technical imagination, long-term ethical reasoning, micro-ethical attentiveness, and collaborative accountability will be essential. Understood in this broader light, Ethical Regulatory Literacy and AI Ethical Reflexive Learning are not only conditions for professional success but also foundations for shaping participatory technological futures that remain socially responsible and ethically grounded.

Figure 2.8 illustrates the dynamic relationship between global regulatory frameworks and the cultivation of ethical capacities at the individual and institutional levels. It shows how instruments such as the EU AI Act, the UNESCO Recommendation on the Ethics of Artificial Intelligence (2021b), and the OECD Principles on AI (2024) set the structural conditions for responsible practice, while the complementary concepts of Ethical Regulatory Literacy and AI Ethical Reflexive Learning provide the interpretive and

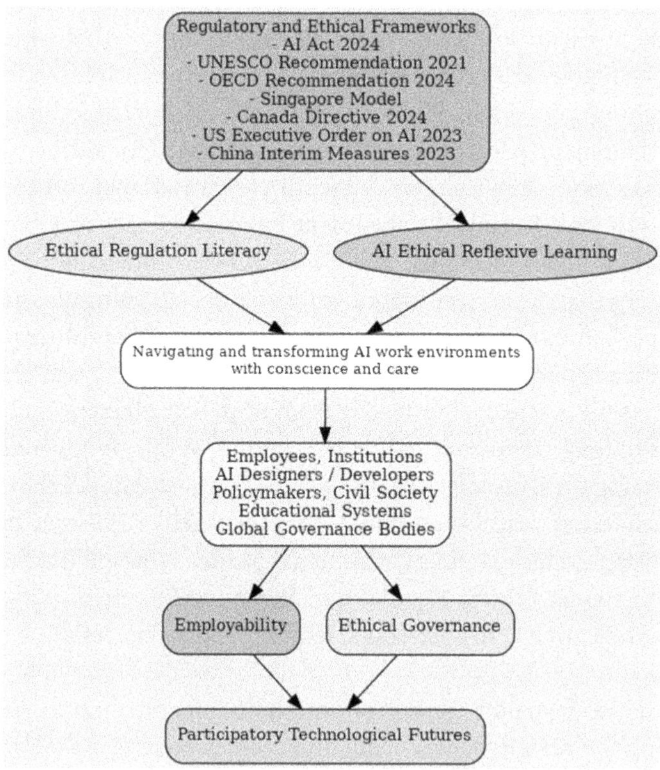

FIGURE 2.8 Ethical and regulatory pathways for AI governance and employability.

This figure illustrates the interaction between global AI regulatory frameworks, ethical literacy, and reflexive learning, highlighting their role in shaping employability, ethical governance, and participatory technological futures.

BOX 2.8 EXPLANATION NOTE—ETHICAL AND REGULATORY PATHWAYS FOR AI GOVERNANCE AND EMPLOYABILITY

The figure conceptualises the interrelationship between regulatory frameworks, ethical competencies, and future-oriented technological governance in the context of AI. At the top, the inclusion of international and national regulatory and ethical instruments—such as the AI Act (2024), UNESCO Recommendation on the Ethics of AI (2021b), and OECD Recommendation (2024)—highlights the global momentum towards standardising ethical AI practices. These frameworks provide the structural foundation for cultivating two core domains: Ethical Regulatory Literacy and AI Ethical Reflexive Learning.

Ethical Regulatory Literacy emphasises the ability of individuals and organisations to interpret, apply, and critically engage with evolving legal and ethical standards. AI Ethical Reflexive Learning, by contrast, stresses continuous reflection and adaptation within AI design, development, and implementation processes. Together, they support the navigation and transformation of AI-driven environments with conscience and care, ensuring that technological innovation is aligned with human values.

The subsequent layer identifies the key stakeholders—employees, institutions, AI designers, developers, policymakers, civil society, educational systems, and global governance bodies—who act as both beneficiaries and agents of ethical AI integration. Their active participation is essential in translating high-level regulatory commitments into practice.

From this engagement flow two critical outcomes: Employability and Ethical Governance. Employability relates to equipping individuals with the knowledge and skills necessary to thrive in AI-mediated labour markets, while Ethical Governance pertains to embedding accountability, transparency, fairness, and inclusivity in AI systems. Both outcomes converge in the pursuit of Participatory Technological Futures, which underscores a vision of AI governance that is democratic, inclusive, and anticipatory, rather than reactive.

This conceptual framework, therefore, illuminates the pathways through which regulatory instruments and ethical literacies shape not only workforce readiness but also broader societal trust and legitimacy in AI. It foregrounds the importance of synergy between compliance (regulatory literacy) and critical engagement (reflexive learning) in achieving sustainable, ethically grounded technological futures.

moral tools required to navigate them. These capacities, once embedded in employees, designers, policymakers, educators, civil society, and governance bodies, shape the twin outcomes of employability and ethical governance, ultimately contributing to the creation of participatory technological futures (Figure 2.8).

Following the conceptual structure illustrated by Figure 2.8, it becomes clear that governance strategies across different jurisdictions embody distinct orientations towards the reflexive dimension of AI ethics. These variations are not merely technical but philosophical, reflecting diverse ways of imagining the relationship between regulation, ethical responsibility, and technological progress. An allegory may help clarify this interplay. Regulation can be thought of as the architecture of a bridge, providing the necessary structural integrity to span uncertain terrain, while reflexive learning is akin to the art of walking across it—requiring balance, awareness, and responsiveness to shifting conditions. A bridge without structure is impassable, yet one with structure alone, absent mindful traversal, fails to achieve its purpose. In much the same way, regulatory literacy and ethical reflexivity sustain one another, forming the conditions through which AI can be developed and applied with both rigour and conscience. International examples illustrate how these elements are differently prioritised. Frameworks such as Singapore's Model AI Governance Framework and Japan's AI Strategy focus strongly on procedural reliability, ensuring systems are auditable and explainable. By contrast, strategies such as India's AI for All emphasise inclusion and social equity, situating ethics in relation to broader questions of justice and lived experience. These divergences underline that while regulatory mechanisms—like technical standards or audit obligations—may lend themselves to harmonisation, the cultivation of reflexive ethical practices remains inseparable from cultural, political, and historical context.

From Figure 2.8, the central notion of 'navigating and transforming AI work environments with conscience and care' is thus best understood as an ethical praxis. It signals that familiarity with governance frameworks, while necessary, is not sufficient. Practitioners must also develop moral capacities and critical imagination, supported by institutional environments that allow for discretion and ethical judgement. This convergence is particularly urgent in domains such as cybersecurity, where surveillance imperatives may collide with privacy rights, or in environmental applications, where efficiency logics can obscure ecological responsibilities. Addressing these tensions requires more than compliance. It calls for professionals capable of questioning prevailing assumptions and envisioning alternative pathways. Within this perspective, Ethical Regulatory Literacy provides the scaffolding of procedural and legal clarity, while AI Ethical Reflexive Learning breathes life into that scaffolding, animating it with reflection, creativity, and a commitment to the public good. Together, they allow practitioners not simply to adapt to AI ecosystems, but to shape them in ways consistent with human dignity, democratic values, and the aspiration of sustainable technological futures.

The conceptual model presented in Figure 2.8 carries important implications for education, particularly in light of the shifting demands of employability in AI-mediated societies. Contemporary education cannot remain confined to the transmission of regulatory content; rather, it must encourage learners to engage with governance as a living ethical practice. Within this framework, Ethical Regulatory Literacy and AI Ethical Reflexive Learning are best understood not as separate competencies but as interdependent capacities, each sustaining and deepening the other. Together, they form the basis of a pedagogy that prepares individuals to act with discernment, responsibility, and creativity in contexts where law and ethics intersect. An allegory may illuminate this connection. One might think of regulation as the compass, providing direction and orientation, while reflexivity functions as the traveller's judgement—the capacity to read the terrain, recognise shifting conditions, and decide when to stay the course or when to adapt. A compass without judgement risks rigidity; judgement without a compass risks disorientation. It is only through their interplay that purposeful and ethical navigation becomes possible. In a similar fashion, the integration of regulatory literacy and reflexive learning supports learners not only in meeting compliance obligations but also in cultivating the moral imagination needed to question, reinterpret, and advance governance frameworks in ways attentive to human dignity and collective well-being.

The educational implications are clear. Employability in AI-mediated economies cannot be reduced to technical proficiency. It increasingly demands regulatory adaptability, ethical resilience, and the ability to reconcile tensions between efficiency, human rights, and democratic values. Professionals who internalise these capacities will be better positioned to act responsibly in complex environments, to foster cultures of inclusivity, and to guide innovation in ways that serve society rather than destabilise it. At the policy level, embedding this model into national and international strategies would contribute to strengthening the moral foundations of governance itself. It would signal a shift away from procedural compliance as an endpoint, towards a dialogic and participatory ethos in which education becomes a site for critical engagement and civic responsibility. In this sense, Figure 2.8 is not only descriptive but also strategic: it reframes employability as an ethical practice and positions education as a central catalyst for shaping AI futures that are sustainable, inclusive, and attentive to human values.

Scholarship has documented the fragmented and uneven nature of global AI governance (Batool et al., 2023). While this literature makes an important contribution, it has often overlooked the implications of such fragmentation for employability. Without TAT at the centre of governance frameworks, employability risks becoming precarious, reinforcing inequalities rather than enabling fair participation in AI-mediated economies. Other contributions (Ahmad and Bilal, 2024; Leslie et al., 2022) place emphasis on enforceability, yet principles cannot be sustained in practice unless they are embedded within cultures of trust and accountability from the outset. It is within this context that the concept of ERL acquires significance. ERL is not reducible to the knowledge of rules but represents a capacity for critical engagement with governance structures, including the ability to assert rights and demand institutional accountability. The allegory of a tethered coastal lighthouse captures this quality: like a beacon responsive to the tides, ERL must adapt to technological change while remaining firmly anchored in ethical orientation. In this sense, ERL is less a body of static content than an iterative practice, sustained through dialogue, feedback, and the continual revision of institutional norms.

A key challenge in this terrain is the gap between ethical aspiration and organisational practice. Studies by Morley et al. (2021), Jobin et al. (2019), and Corrêa et al. (2023) warn against the risks of performative compliance, where institutions appear ethical without substantive transformation. ERL, critically enacted, provides a way of resisting such tokenism by equipping professionals to discern when ethics is being instrumentalised rather than meaningfully embedded. This leads to the proposal of a Double ERL model, comprising the following two mutually sustaining dimensions:

- **Ethical Regulatory Literacy**: outward-facing engagement with legal frameworks, policies, and institutional structures.
- **Ethical Reflexive Learning**: inward-facing cultivation of ethical sensitivity, critical imagination, and the courage to navigate ambiguity.

The allegory of Plato's Cave helps to frame this dynamic. Regulatory literacy resembles the recognition of shadows as representations rather than realities, while reflexive learning is the responsibility of returning to the cave to share insight, deliberate collectively, and co-create more just possibilities. Within this framing, employability is reimagined not as mere adaptability to shifting technical environments, but as the exercise of critical ethical agency. This model resonates with international instruments, including the EU AI Act (2024), the OECD Principles (2019a/2024), and Canada's Directive on Automated Decision-Making (2020/2024). These frameworks signal a growing recognition that governance requires practitioners to be both legally literate and ethically engaged. Yet there is a danger that compliance becomes bureaucratised, reducing ethics to procedure. To resist this ossification, continuous reflexivity is essential. Here, a further allegory—the bridge rebuilt while crossing—captures the necessity of governance as a living practice: one that must be reconstructed in motion, balancing stability with openness to ethical renewal.

Employability in the age of intelligent systems cannot be imagined as walking across a completed bridge, but as participating in its ongoing reconstruction while crossing turbulent waters. This demands not only technical adaptability but also ethical steadiness: the capacity to move with the tides of change while remaining oriented by enduring principles, much like a lighthouse tethered against shifting seas. Within this dynamic process, anticipatory ethical capacities—risk perception, socio-technical imagination, long-term foresight, attentiveness to micro-ethical dilemmas, and collaborative accountability—emerge as essential attributes of the professional identities of the future. Here, Ethical Regulatory Literacy functions as the scaffolding of the bridge, supplying the legal and procedural supports for action, while Ethical Reflexive Learning provides the imagination and conscience that animate the journey—akin to recognising, as in Plato's cave, the shadows for what they are and taking responsibility for returning to engage others in building more just realities. Together, these capacities ensure that employability is not reduced to survival within shifting markets, but becomes an exercise of ethical agency directed towards inclusive and sustainable futures.

The argument advanced in this section is that education, policy, and governance must structurally embed the principles of Double ERL. Ethics must not be treated as a secondary concern or reduced to procedural checklists; rather, it should constitute the living ethos of AI governance, professional identity, and civic responsibility. In moving from critique to construction, the discussion has traced a pathway from the identification of fractures in current governance models towards the proposal of a participatory and generative framework for ethical employability. Yet the viability of this framework depends on the wider conditions that sustain it. As the bridge allegory suggests, resilience in motion requires trust in the structure, confidence in its builders, and clarity in communication among those crossing. The next stage of the discussion, therefore, turns to the ethical and institutional foundations that make Double ERL actionable: trust, transparency, and legitimacy. These are not ancillary features but the elements that determine whether the journey across remains possible, fair, and inclusive.

TRUST, TRANSPARENCY, AND INSTITUTIONAL LEGITIMACY AS FOUNDATIONS FOR RESPONSIBLE AI AND ETHICAL EMPLOYABILITY

Extending the Double ERL framework developed in the previous section, this part of the chapter considers the broader conditions through which ethical employability can be realised in AI-mediated contexts. If regulatory literacy and reflexive learning provide the capacities for action, then their effectiveness depends on the surrounding environment of trust, transparency, and institutional legitimacy. This relationship can be understood through an allegory of sound and light. Light represents the promise of transparency—illuminating systems, rendering decisions visible, and exposing practices that would otherwise remain obscure. Yet illumination alone is not sufficient. Just as light can dazzle without clarifying, technical disclosure may create the appearance of openness without offering genuine understanding. For transparency to become meaningful, it must be accompanied by sound: the resonant practices of dialogue, accountability, and ethical responsiveness that allow individuals and institutions to interpret what is seen and respond to what is revealed. Within this allegory, trust arises when sound and light are harmonised. Trust is not generated by visibility alone, nor by dialogue in isolation, but by their interplay—by institutions that both shine light on their processes and attune themselves to the voices of those affected. Legitimacy emerges when this harmony is sustained over time, as institutions demonstrate not only competence but also an ethical willingness to listen, explain, and act with fairness.

Practical illustrations highlight how this interplay may be enacted. Student data platforms require not only transparent disclosure of data use (light) but also opportunities for students to question, contest, and co-design practices (sound). AI literacy initiatives similarly rely on making systems comprehensible (light) while enabling critical debate and collective reflection (sound). In such examples, trust is established not as a static state but as an ongoing rhythm—sustained through the combined clarity of illumination and the resonance of communication. By framing trust, transparency, and legitimacy in this way, the discussion builds directly on the Double ERL model. Where that framework highlighted the interplay of scaffolding and conscience, here the emphasis falls on the ethical environment in which such capacities can flourish. Employability is thus reimagined not only as the exercise of individual competence but also as participation in institutional ecologies that balance illumination with resonance. In this balance lies the possibility of responsible AI that supports education, work, and democratic life with integrity and care (Figure 2.9).

While early discussions of AI ethics in education frequently emphasised aspirational principles, current debates highlight the need for a more grounded engagement with how technology reshapes educational practice. Contemporary scholarship recognises that responsible AI cannot be addressed through technical solutions alone; it requires reflection on the institutional structures, cultural assumptions, and normative expectations that shape educational systems. In this sense, AI is not a neutral tool, but part of wider social and cultural transformations that influence both the design of learning environments and collective understandings of educational purpose. Responsible AI, therefore, is best

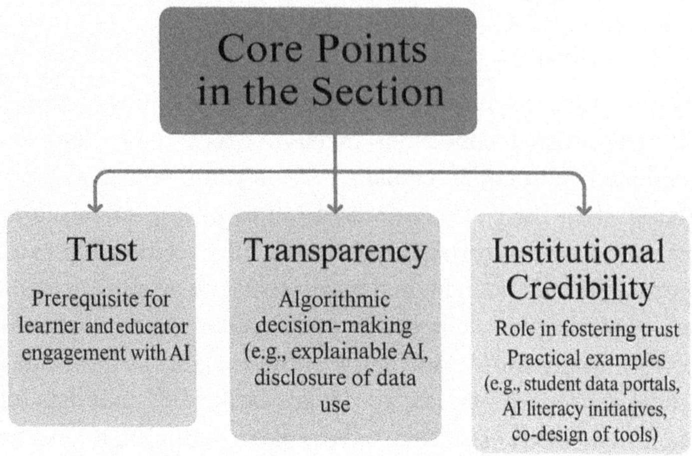

FIGURE 2.9 Framework of core governance principles in AI-enhanced education.

Conceptual framework highlighting the core principles of trust, transparency, and institutional credibility as foundational elements for ethical engagement with AI in education.

BOX 2.9 EXPLANATION NOTE—FRAMEWORK OF CORE GOVERNANCE PRINCIPLES IN AI-ENHANCED EDUCATION

The figure illustrates a conceptual framework outlining three interdependent principles—trust, transparency, and institutional credibility—that are central to ethical engagement with AI in education. Trust is positioned as a prerequisite for learner and educator engagement with AI-enabled systems. Without confidence in the fairness and reliability of technological processes, the adoption of AI tools risks resistance and scepticism. Trust, therefore, functions as the foundation upon which meaningful educational interactions with AI can be built.

Transparency is presented as a critical mechanism for ensuring accountability in algorithmic decision-making. Practices such as explainable AI and disclosure of data use make visible the rationale behind automated outputs, enabling stakeholders to interrogate, validate, and challenge decisions that affect learners. Transparency mitigates the 'black box' nature of AI, thereby reinforcing user confidence and safeguarding ethical standards.

Institutional credibility highlights the systemic role of educational organisations in embedding ethical AI practices. Institutions not only foster trust but also operationalise it through initiatives such as student data portals, AI literacy programmes, and participatory co-design of tools. By demonstrating responsible governance and inclusivity, institutions enhance their legitimacy and ensure that AI use aligns with educational values and learner rights.

Taken together, the figure underscores that sustainable and ethical integration of AI in education is contingent upon the interplay between these three principles. Trust provides the foundation, transparency ensures accountability, and institutional credibility operationalises these commitments through policy and practice.

understood as an evolving concept, situated within ongoing social and pedagogical change. This perspective encourages consideration of how assumptions about AI's role in teaching and learning are formed, and how these assumptions influence both pedagogical relationships and the development of skills valued in future labour markets. AI chatbots and similar intelligent systems, for example, are not only functional supports but also active participants in educational interactions, influencing the way authority, collaboration, and trust are experienced.

Chen (2023) illustrates this dynamic by showing how AI chatbots, when designed as multirole pedagogical agents, blur traditional boundaries between tutor, peer, and assessor. This fluidity raises ethical questions that extend beyond privacy or security, drawing attention to how trust, accountability, and professional responsibility are negotiated in AI-mediated contexts. Moreover, the integration of such technologies has implications for employability. As institutions increasingly emphasise adaptability to digital environments, there is a risk that employability is framed primarily in terms of compliance with technological change, rather than fostering critical thinking, ethical judgement, and reflexivity. A responsible approach to AI in education must therefore move beyond seeing technology as a simple extension of existing practice. Instead, it should acknowledge AI as part of a wider reconfiguration of educational values and relationships. Such an approach requires sustained critical reflection, a commitment to relational authenticity, and attention to the collective goods of education as well as individual skill development.

Ghimire and Edwards (2024) highlight that current policy frameworks for AI in education are often fragmented and reactive, shaped by a tendency towards technological solutionism rather than proactive, flexible governance. Their analysis points to a broader concern: the growing role of transnational corporations in influencing governance structures, sometimes beyond the regulatory capacity of individual states. While this trend raises important questions about power and accountability, it should not be viewed solely in negative terms. The interplay between corporate actors and public regulators, though marked by tensions, can also create opportunities for constructive collaboration. When managed effectively, such collaboration may contribute to governance frameworks that align technological innovation with wider societal goals rather than narrowly commercial imperatives. Responsible approaches to AI governance must therefore extend beyond the technical and procedural, engaging critically with the wider geopolitical and economic conditions that determine how benefits and risks are distributed. This requires attention to questions of equity, particularly in relation to employability and skills development, where AI has the potential either to mitigate or to reinforce existing inequalities. Steering corporate involvement towards socially beneficial outcomes is a key challenge, demanding mechanisms that prioritise inclusivity, shared responsibility, and long-term societal value.

Karran et al. (2024) add further complexity by challenging the assumption that broad stakeholder participation automatically yields ethical governance outcomes. Their findings show that the priorities of students, educators, and institutions often diverge: students seek personalisation, educators emphasise autonomy, and institutions tend to prioritise scalability and efficiency. These competing expectations reveal the limits of participation if it is treated as an end in itself. Meaningful governance requires not only consultation but also an ongoing negotiation of interests, recognising the uneven distribution of influence across stakeholders. A relational approach—sensitive to these dynamics—offers a more robust pathway, as it moves beyond surface-level inclusion towards an active balancing of competing needs and values. Collectively, these perspectives suggest that effective AI governance in education rests on two interconnected principles: first, the careful management of corporate and institutional influence to ensure alignment with collective rather than narrow interests; and second, a deeper engagement with stakeholder diversity that acknowledges and negotiates tensions in a transparent and equitable way. Only through such approaches can AI governance frameworks become responsive to the broader social purpose of education.

Although aspirations for responsible and equitable AI governance are widely acknowledged, achieving them requires more than procedural compliance or rhetorical commitment. What is needed is an ethical architecture that addresses the diverse interests and tensions shaping the development and use of AI in education. This discussion advances the principles of Trust, Transparency, and Institutional Legitimacy as the foundation of such an approach. Unlike evaluative models such as the TAT test, which assess the ethical performance of individual AI systems, this framework is concerned with the broader governance relationships among stakeholders, including learners, educators, institutions, developers, policymakers, employers, funders, and society at large. Within this model, Trust is not limited to technical reliability but extends to the relational confidence stakeholders hold in institutions and governance processes. Transparency goes beyond disclosure to require genuine intelligibility, enabling stakeholders to understand and engage with the logics and consequences of AI systems. Institutional Legitimacy functions as the cornerstone, demanding that authority is continually earned through fairness, inclusivity, and responsiveness. These principles are mutually reinforcing: trust is dependent on transparency and legitimacy, while legitimacy itself cannot be sustained without trust and openness.

To illustrate how these principles interact across different stakeholder groups, the matrix table is introduced (Table 2.1). It maps the correlations between trust, transparency, and legitimacy across learners, educators, institutions, developers, policymakers, employers, society at large, funders, and civil society. The purpose of this table is to show that responsible AI governance emerges not from isolated commitments, but from the dynamic interplay of ethical responsibilities across all actors involved. This table highlights that the sustainability of AI in education depends on cultivating shared ethical commitments across different layers of governance. Trust, transparency, and institutional legitimacy must therefore be understood as systemic conditions rather than isolated attributes. Only by embedding these principles relationally—across stakeholder interactions—can AI governance move beyond rhetorical aspiration and towards genuinely equitable and socially responsive practice.

To conceptualise the interdependence of these principles, we may draw on the ancient allegory of the Three Fires. In this allegory, a civilisation sustained itself through three sacred flames: the Hearth, representing Trust, which provided warmth and security; the Beacon, symbolising Transparency, which illuminated the path and revealed hidden

TABLE 2.1 Matrix of Stakeholder Responsibilities in Building Trust, Transparency, and Institutional Legitimacy for AI Governance in Education

Stakeholder	Trust	Transparency	Institutional Legitimacy
Learners	Confidence in fair, supportive AI use	Clear disclosure of data usage and learning impacts	Institutions protecting learner rights
Educators	Trust in AI preserving pedagogical autonomy	Transparency in AI-driven teaching methods	Respect for professional ethics and teaching integrity
Institutions	Trust earned through ethical leadership	Open communication about AI procurement and use	Consistency between ethical statements and operational practices
Developers	Responsibility for user-centric, safe design	Transparent development and testing processes	Alignment with ethical design standards and compliance
Policymakers	Trust built via participatory, open regulatory processes	Policy transparency and legislative clarity	Policies reflecting public interest, not corporate capture
Employers	Assurance that AI-ready skills are ethically cultivated	Transparency in AI use for hiring and evaluation	Ethical application of AI in workplace settings
Society at Large	Trust in AI systems serving public interest	Public transparency about societal AI impacts	Democratically legitimated AI governance
Funders & Sponsors	Trust that investments promote ethical AI development	Transparency in funding priorities and sponsored research	Ethical stewardship of educational investments
Civil Society	Trust that civil society voices influence AI governance	Transparency actions and policy engagement	Advocacy grounded in democratic, inclusive processes

dangers; and the Flame of Assembly, embodying Institutional Legitimacy, which united the community through shared governance. The survival of the civilisation depended on tending these fires together, as each one reinforced and sustained the others. If one fire waned, the balance of the whole was lost, leading to fragmentation and decline. This allegory resonates with contemporary challenges in AI governance. Just as the ancient fires could not endure in isolation, neither can trust, transparency, and legitimacy be sustained independently. Trust falters without transparency, transparency is disregarded without legitimacy, and legitimacy cannot be maintained without the confidence and openness provided by the other two. Taken together, the allegory and the matrix emphasise that responsible AI governance is not a matter of isolated ethical tests or technical safeguards. Instead, it requires a relational framework in which trust, transparency, and institutional legitimacy are cultivated in tandem, ensuring that AI in education develops in ways that are both ethically robust and socially responsive (Table 2.1).

The stakeholder matrix operationalises the principles of Trust, Transparency, and Institutional Legitimacy by mapping them onto the differentiated roles and responsibilities of actors involved in the governance of AI within education and society more broadly. It demonstrates that ethical AI governance cannot be secured through abstract principles alone, but requires attention to the specific positions, capacities, and vulnerabilities of diverse stakeholders. Within this framework, Trust emerges as a condition shaped differently across relationships. Learners require confidence that AI systems will be used fairly and in ways that support their development. Educators need assurance that such systems respect and preserve pedagogical autonomy. Institutions are expected to demonstrate ethical leadership through visible, consistent commitments to integrity in practice. Developers carry the responsibility of ensuring that design processes remain user-centred and safe, while policymakers must build trust by embedding participation and openness into regulatory processes. Employers, funders, and civil society actors similarly carry trust-building responsibilities within their spheres of influence.

Transparency is presented as an equally differentiated obligation. For learners and educators, it concerns clarity around data use and the intelligibility of AI-driven interventions. For institutions, developers, and funders, transparency must extend to procurement, design, and sponsorship processes, ensuring that practices can be scrutinised beyond immediate applications. At the policy level, transparency requires legislative clarity and openness in decision-making. Civil society organisations play a vital role here, enhancing public understanding and advocating for equitable information flows. Finally, Institutional Legitimacy provides the ethical anchor for the framework. Legitimacy is not assumed but must be continually earned through consistency, accountability, and responsiveness. Institutions must safeguard learner rights and uphold professional standards. Developers need to align design choices with recognised ethical frameworks. Policymakers are required to demonstrate that governance reflects public interest rather than private capture. Employers and funders must ensure their practices reinforce democratic legitimacy rather than undermine it. Civil society, meanwhile, serves as a counterbalance, challenging and renewing legitimacy through democratic participation and critical advocacy. The matrix, therefore, illustrates that responsible AI governance is not reducible to technical compliance. Instead, it relies on cultivating relationships in which trust, transparency, and legitimacy reinforce one another across the wider governance ecosystem.

This matrix reinforces the argument that responsible AI governance must be both relational and stakeholder-sensitive, recognising that ethical principles acquire meaning only through the ways they are enacted across different contexts. Trust, transparency, and institutional legitimacy should not be understood as discrete values, but as interdependent dynamics that gain significance when cultivated together. Their interplay requires ongoing negotiation among diverse actors, from learners and educators to developers, policymakers, employers, and civil society organisations. What emerges is the need for an ethically integrated framework of governance—one that moves beyond technical compliance or procedural disclosure and instead engages with the lived realities of human relationships, institutional practices, and global interdependencies. The aim is not simply to describe stakeholder roles, but to propose a normative orientation for how AI can be governed in ways that sustain both educational integrity and societal well-being. To illustrate these interconnections, Figure 2.10 is introduced. It conceptualises how Trust, Transparency, and Institutional Legitimacy intersect to anchor the pursuit of Ethical AI, with accountability serving as the binding element that ensures these principles are continually enacted and renewed across stakeholder groups (Figure 2.10).

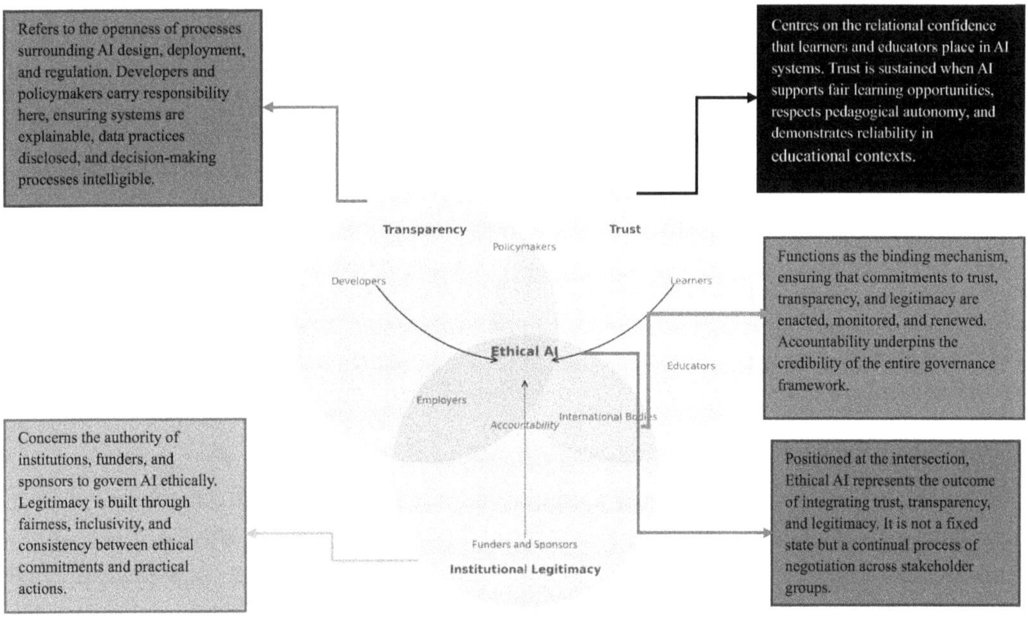

FIGURE 2.10 Intersecting dynamics of trust, transparency, and institutional legitimacy in ethical AI governance.

Venn framework illustrating how trust, transparency, and institutional legitimacy intersect to support ethical AI governance across stakeholder groups.

BOX 2.10 EXPLANATION NOTE—INTERSECTING DYNAMICS OF TRUST, TRANSPARENCY, AND INSTITUTIONAL LEGITIMACY IN ETHICAL AI GOVERNANCE

The figure conceptualises the interdependent relationship between Trust, Transparency, and Institutional Legitimacy as foundational principles of ethical AI governance. Rather than treating these elements as discrete values, it highlights their overlap as the ethical space in which AI can be developed, deployed, and regulated responsibly. At the centre lies Ethical AI, understood not as a fixed endpoint but as the product of continuous negotiation among stakeholders across different domains of influence.

Trust emerges through the relationships between learners, educators, and institutions and is sustained when AI systems are seen to support learning and protect professional autonomy. Transparency, associated most directly with developers and policymakers, ensures that processes of design, deployment, and regulation are intelligible and open to scrutiny. Institutional Legitimacy, carried by funders, sponsors, and governance bodies, demands fairness, responsiveness, and accountability in organisational and regulatory practices.

The figure also underlines the role of accountability as the binding dynamic that connects the three principles. Accountability functions as the ethical mechanism through which trust, transparency, and legitimacy are enacted and renewed. For example, developers can only sustain trust if their practices are transparently communicated and institutionally aligned with ethical standards. Policymakers can only claim legitimacy when transparent processes are matched by accountability to public interest. Similarly, institutions maintain credibility by aligning their ethical commitments with consistent, accountable action.

By positioning stakeholders within the overlapping circles, the figure makes clear that no actor operates in isolation. Learners depend on educators and institutions; developers must work within transparent standards shaped by policymakers; funders and employers shape the conditions under which AI is implemented; and civil society provides oversight by questioning and renewing legitimacy. The interdependence shown here illustrates that the governance of AI is not reducible to technical checks or procedural safeguards but is deeply relational, requiring collaborative engagement across sectors and scales.

In this way, the figure reinforces the section's central claim: that ethical AI governance is sustained only when trust, transparency, and institutional legitimacy operate in concert, mediated by accountability, and distributed across the full spectrum of stakeholder relationships.

In advancing debates on ethics and regulation, Roe and Perkins (2024) invite a shift in perspective: from viewing AI solely as a technical instrument to recognising it as an epistemic agent—one that not only shapes actions but also influences ways of knowing. Their concern is that an uncritical embrace of GenAI, particularly in education, risks elevating efficiency and replicability over critical inquiry and epistemic diversity. This underlines the importance of embedding ethics and equity at the core of AI design and governance, extending beyond education into broader societal domains. Within this context, Figure 2.10 illustrates how Trust, Transparency, and Institutional Legitimacy function as interdependent foundations of ethical AI. Learners and educators rely on trust to ensure that AI supports, rather than undermines, educational values. Developers and policymakers sustain transparency by ensuring design processes and regulatory decisions remain open to scrutiny. Funders, sponsors, and international bodies establish institutional legitimacy through practices that demonstrate fairness, inclusivity, and responsiveness. At the centre, accountability operates as the binding mechanism, ensuring that commitments made in each domain translate into enforceable practices and credible governance.

This framing resonates with concerns raised by Sun et al. (2024), who identify structural weaknesses in existing regulatory models, noting that their reliance on voluntary compliance often falters under commercial pressures to prioritise innovation and market adoption over enforceable safeguards. Figure 2.10 reflects this critique by showing that legitimacy cannot rest on rhetoric or self-regulation alone; it requires mechanisms of accountability—such as independent audits, ombudsperson roles, and participatory governance frameworks—that continually renew trust and transparency. Thus, the model visualised here emphasises that ethical AI is not a fixed state but a dynamic equilibrium, sustained through the interplay of trust, transparency, and legitimacy across stakeholder groups. Its resilience depends on adaptive governance structures capable of responding to technological change, safeguarding epistemic diversity, and ensuring that AI contributes to collective well-being rather than narrowing intellectual and ethical horizons.

Figure 2.10 emphasised the relational interplay of Trust, Transparency, and Institutional Legitimacy, positioning them as the ethical conditions through which diverse stakeholders sustain the possibility of Ethical AI. It highlighted that these principles are not discrete values but interdependent dynamics, mediated by accountability, that require continual negotiation across learners, educators, developers, policymakers, funders, and civil society. Figure 2.11 extends this discussion by showing how these relational principles align with and evolve into the evaluative dimensions of the TAT test. Here, Trust remains a common value across both models, serving as the foundation of governance and evaluation alike. Transparency functions as a shared priority, sustaining the integrity of systems by ensuring that design choices, data practices, and regulatory frameworks remain intelligible and open to scrutiny. Importantly, however, the principle of Institutional Legitimacy undergoes a conceptual transformation: it evolves into Accountability. This marks a shift from legitimacy as a normative quality of institutions to accountability as a procedural mechanism of enforceability. This transformation is significant. Whereas legitimacy is sustained through fairness, inclusivity, and responsiveness, accountability requires institutions to demonstrate these commitments in measurable and verifiable ways. In practice, this means moving from ethical assurances to independent audits, regulatory oversight, and enforceable standards. By linking the relational model of ethical principles to the procedural model of evaluation, the figure illustrates how ethical AI governance depends not only on cultivating values but also on embedding them into structures of accountability that can withstand commercial pressures and institutional inertia. It therefore bridges the ethical architecture of governance with the pragmatic demands of system testing, showing that responsible AI requires both principled foundations and enforceable safeguards (Figure 2.11).

This section has highlighted not only the importance of ethical commitments but also the way in which these commitments are being operationalised—moving from aspirational principles towards mechanisms of institutional evaluation. Figure 2.11 reflects this shift, showing how the foundational values of trust, transparency, and institutional legitimacy are increasingly translated into their procedural counterparts within testing frameworks. This transition, while necessary for governance, also brings challenges. As ideals are transformed into instruments of assessment, there is a risk that ethical concerns become absorbed into administrative practice, potentially narrowing their scope and reducing their vitality. Díaz-Rodríguez et al. (2023) emphasise that while standardising ethical principles within AI governance is valuable, caution must be exercised to avoid reducing them to rigid technical prescriptions. Similarly, Corrêa et al. (2023) observe that

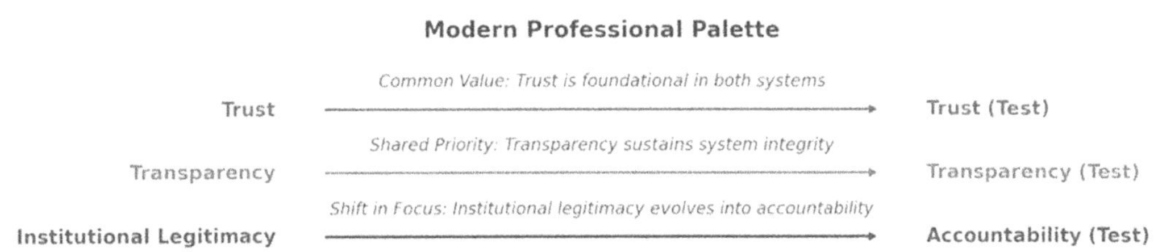

FIGURE 2.11 Palette of trust, transparency, and accountability.

The Palette illustrates how trust provides the foundation, transparency sustains system integrity, and institutional legitimacy evolves into accountability.

BOX 2.11 EXPLANATION NOTE—PROFESSIONAL PALETTE OF TRUST, TRANSPARENCY, AND ACCOUNTABILITY

The figure illustrates the way in which the principles of Trust, Transparency, and Institutional Legitimacy are mapped onto the evaluative dimensions of the Trust, Accountability, and Transparency (TAT) test. It demonstrates that while trust and transparency operate as shared values across both ethical governance and evaluative frameworks, institutional legitimacy undergoes an important conceptual transformation, evolving into accountability.

Trust is presented as a common foundation: in both governance models and evaluative systems, it underpins confidence in the fairness, reliability, and ethical integrity of AI. Transparency likewise remains central, sustaining the integrity of AI systems through disclosure, clarity, and intelligibility of processes. The more significant shift occurs with Institutional Legitimacy, which, while essential for ethical governance, requires translation into accountability when operationalised in testable and enforceable terms. This highlights the move from normative authority—built through fairness, inclusivity, and responsiveness—to procedural mechanisms of oversight, verification, and enforcement.

The value of this framework lies in its ability to bridge ethical principles with practical evaluative standards. It shows that while ethical AI governance begins with shared commitments to trust, transparency, and legitimacy, effective regulation requires these commitments to be substantiated through accountability mechanisms. In doing so, the figure reinforces the argument that responsible AI governance must be both normatively grounded and procedurally enforceable, ensuring that principles are not only articulated but also translated into credible and measurable practices.

the proliferation of AI ethics guidelines, without meaningful convergence, may contribute to fragmentation rather than coherence. These insights underline a central difficulty: ensuring that ethical guidance in AI remains responsive to social and educational needs, including the development of employability skills, without collapsing into procedural conformity.

For example, in a city once guided by living traditions of ethical reasoning, a structure known as the Loom was created to support collective decision-making. At first, it functioned as a participatory, deliberative tool. Over time, however, its processes became formalised and its authority centralised. What began as a dynamic space for moral reflection was transformed into a rigid apparatus of control. The lesson is clear: frameworks risk losing their ethical depth when they become static and procedural rather than open and reflexive. In the same way, concepts such as trust, transparency, and institutional legitimacy should not be treated as fixed endpoints. Their value lies in being continuously reinterpreted and renewed through critical reflection, participatory governance, and institutional responsiveness. Ethical AI governance, therefore, depends less on codification than on the ongoing negotiation of principles in practice, ensuring that responsibility retains its substance and does not become a matter of appearance alone.

The relationship between AI governance and employability raises pressing ethical questions that extend beyond the mechanics of technical oversight. As higher education systems come under increasing pressure to demonstrate graduate outcomes, the discourse around employability risks being framed in narrowly economistic terms—equating success with alignment to immediate labour market demands. Such a perspective, however, obscures the broader educational mission and undervalues the role of universities in cultivating reflective, adaptive, and ethically attuned graduates. AI introduces a further complication. By embedding algorithmic models into processes of recruitment, assessment, and skills forecasting, there is a danger that employability becomes conflated with compliance to predictive logics. This tendency risks constraining students' futures within preconfigured categories rather than enabling the imaginative exploration of diverse career and civic pathways. The ethical responsibility of educational institutions, therefore, is not simply to integrate AI in ways that optimise efficiency, but to interrogate how these technologies reshape assumptions about human potential, value, and contribution.

This critical stance suggests that employability should be re-envisioned not as the endpoint of algorithmic optimisation, but as an ongoing practice of ethical and civic development. It requires fostering dispositions such as reflexivity, social responsibility, and the capacity to question technological mediation itself. These qualities resist quantification yet are vital for sustaining democratic and professional life in AI-mediated societies. The earlier stakeholder-principle matrix and relational governance figure can be read through this lens: not as fixed tools of measurement, but as prompts to reframe the relationship between education, labour, and technology. They highlight that governance is not solely a matter of procedural compliance, but of nurturing trust, transparency, and legitimacy across diverse actors. When situated in the employability debate, these frameworks emphasise that learner agency and institutional accountability must remain at the centre of regulatory design. Employability, approached in this way, becomes less a passive alignment with economic demand and more an invitation to participate actively in shaping equitable, socially responsive futures. It is this orientation—anchored in ethical stewardship and pedagogical care—that prepares the ground for the subsequent focus on transparency, where questions of visibility, accountability, and trust within algorithmic systems come to the fore.

ELEVATES TRANSPARENCY FROM A PROCEDURAL REQUIREMENT TO A CONCEPTUAL FOUNDATION

The movement from principles into practice raises one of the most contested dimensions of AI governance: the question of transparency. Rather than beginning with assertions, it may be more fruitful to follow a line of inquiry in the manner of Socratic reasoning, where clarity is sought not through immediate answers but through the careful refinement of questions. If trust and legitimacy in governance depend on the visibility of processes, then we must ask: what does it mean to claim that a decision has been made by an algorithm? At first glance, the answer appears straightforward—AI systems process data and return outcomes. Yet a deeper interrogation unsettles this simplicity. Does such a system offer an act of reasoning comparable to human judgement, grounded in contextual awareness, or does it merely reproduce patterns from past data? If the latter, can we describe its output as a 'decision' in any meaningful ethical sense, or only as a statistical projection dressed in the language of objectivity?

This form of questioning exposes the fragility of transparency in contemporary AI systems. The complexity of advanced models, particularly those driven by machine learning, often renders their operations opaque even to their designers. Descriptions of 'black box' architectures capture not only technical opacity but also the concealment of values, assumptions, and social biases embedded in the training data. To whom, then, should the responsibility of explanation belong? And how far can technical documentation, however detailed, substitute for genuine intelligibility in democratic and educational contexts? The challenge becomes most acute where algorithmic outputs materially shape human opportunity—whether in access to employment, education, credit, or public welfare. In these settings, opacity is not merely inconvenient but destabilising of both ethical and legal accountability. If those most affected cannot understand, question, or contest decisions, then transparency becomes not a safeguard but an empty promise. What, then, should be the measure of a transparent system? Is it sufficient to disclose that data has been processed, or must transparency extend to the assumptions, trade-offs, and social implications embedded in the design itself? Such questions suggest that transparency cannot be reduced to the availability of technical detail. Rather, it must be understood as an ongoing ethical and political practice: a commitment to ensuring that decisions mediated by AI remain open to scrutiny, challenge, and contestation. In this way, transparency is not simply about seeing into the machine; it is about sustaining the conditions under which human reasoning, accountability, and democratic participation remain possible.

If the Socratic method teaches us anything, it is that understanding does not rest in the immediate answer but in the careful probing of what is being claimed. Applied to AI governance, this insight reframes transparency not simply as a technical feature but as both a principle and a practice. As a principle, it underpins the ethical legitimacy of AI systems, aligning with the broader demands of trust and accountability. As a practice, it requires the creation of mechanisms—technical, procedural, and institutional—that make algorithmic processes open to scrutiny, comprehensible to those affected, and subject to challenge. Within this landscape, the role of Explainable AI (XAI) is often foregrounded. XAI provides methods through which automated reasoning can be rendered interpretable, allowing a degree of communication between systems and their users. Yet, if we follow the Socratic line of questioning—'What does explanation achieve, and what does it leave untouched?'—it becomes clear that interpretability alone cannot settle the ethical demands of transparency. An explanation can reveal how an output was generated, but it cannot determine whether the process was fair, whether the data was responsibly sourced, or whether the consequences are socially justifiable. Such questions extend beyond technical elucidation to the realm of values, rights, and public accountability.

This is why transparency must be understood as part of a wider ethical infrastructure. When XAI is situated within systems of participatory governance, supported by public oversight, critical education, and procedural rights of redress, its value becomes more than technical. It contributes to what might be called a culture of justifiability—where algorithmic decisions are not only visible but also defensible, contestable, and open to revision. Without such embedding, explanation risks becoming little more than surface-level clarity, offering answers without real space for critique. The Socratic emphasis on questioning also reminds us that transparency is never without tension. Demands for clarity may conflict with commercial secrecy, technical feasibility, or even data privacy. As Ananny and Crawford (2018) observe, focusing too narrowly on technical traceability risks neglecting the institutional and relational dynamics through which algorithms gain legitimacy. Transparency, therefore, must be recognised as context-sensitive: a property not of systems in isolation, but of systems-in-context—shaped by how algorithms interact with law, institutional cultures, and the lived experiences of those subject to their decisions. From this perspective, transparency is less about producing final answers than about sustaining the conditions in which meaningful questioning, critique, and justification remain possible. It is this ongoing orientation—towards dialogue, contestability, and ethical reflection—that ensures transparency does not ossify into a procedural ritual but continues to serve as a cornerstone of democratic and educational responsibility in the age of AI.

For transparency to carry weight in AI governance, it must be approached as a systemic commitment rather than a procedural add-on. Mechanisms such as AIAs, documentation protocols, and registers of automated systems contribute to this, but they cannot suffice on their own. Transparency also requires a pedagogical dimension, embedded in curricula and professional training that cultivate ethical reflexivity and regulatory awareness. Within this dual orientation lies the significance of the Double ERL model, which highlights that ethical engagement in AI-mediated environments depends as much on internal responsiveness as on external comprehension. To capture this complexity, transparency may be thought of less as a fixed window into algorithmic systems and more as a lens that requires constant adjustment. Such a lens makes it possible not only to see but also to interpret, critique, and act. Without it, transparency risks degenerating into symbolism—gestures of openness that obscure rather than illuminate. With it, transparency can serve as a condition of possibility: a practice that enables individuals and institutions to exercise meaningful agency within AI-driven systems.

This perspective underlines why transparency is increasingly foregrounded in international AI governance. Supranational bodies such as the European Commission, alongside national regulators and scientific advisory groups, consistently articulate transparency as a precondition for trust and social sustainability. Yet this prominence does not remove its conceptual challenges. Too often, transparency is treated as a static compliance requirement rather than a dynamic, relational practice. Such treatment risks reducing it to superficial disclosure, capable of meeting formal obligations but incapable of fostering genuine intelligibility or moral accountability. The consequences of this limitation are particularly evident in the sphere of employability. Individuals encounter algorithmic systems in contexts that shape access to work, education, and professional development, yet frequently without the ability to understand or contest the reasoning behind outcomes. Here, transparency is not simply one among many desirable attributes; it constitutes the connective tissue between ethical aspiration and technological practice. Positioned this way, it is less a supporting pillar of trustworthy AI than a structural condition without which trust, accountability, and legitimacy cannot be sustained.

The World Health Organisation's guidance on AI in healthcare (2021) reframes transparency as a principle of anticipatory design, requiring that information be made available prior to the creation or deployment of systems. This approach shifts transparency away from retrospective justification and towards proactive engagement, enabling ethical scrutiny, informed consent, and public dialogue before technologies are embedded into practice. Such a framing resonates with the proactive orientation of Ethical Regulatory Literacy, which stresses the importance of interrogating the purpose, scope, and oversight requirements of AI at the earliest stages of decision-making. Applied to employability, this orientation extends beyond interpreting algorithmic outputs to evaluating their appropriateness, limitations, and wider implications. It signals the need for interpretive competence alongside technical proficiency—an ability to contextualise AI-driven outcomes and to make reasoned, ethical judgements about their application in professional and social life. UNICEF (2021) builds on this perspective through its advocacy of child-centred transparency, which calls for AI systems to be explained in terms accessible to different levels of comprehension. This reinforces the principle that intelligibility is not an expert privilege but a right that should extend to all who are affected by algorithmic systems. More broadly, it highlights the importance of inclusivity in fostering ethical agency: learning processes must be structured to accommodate diversity if they are to support widespread and meaningful participation.

These approaches suggest that transparency, ethics, and employability should not be treated as parallel domains but as mutually reinforcing dimensions of education and governance. A helpful way to conceptualise their interrelation is through the image of a double helix: transparency, ethical reflexivity, and employability coil together, bound by connecting principles such as interpretability, accountability, and human agency. Each strand is incomplete without the others, and their interaction sustains a framework that is capable of adaptation and growth. The implication is that preparing individuals for AI-integrated futures requires more than technical skills or regulatory awareness. It demands a form of professional and civic formation in which ethical awareness, regulatory understanding, and practical reasoning are deliberately interwoven into curriculum and pedagogy. If this integration is to have a genuine impact, it must be developed as a living, evolving framework—responsive to technological change, yet anchored in human values and social responsibility.

This model (Figure 2.12) illustrates the interdependence of transparency, ethical reflexivity, and employability, conceptualised here as a double helix. The connecting strands—interpretability, accountability, and human agency—act as the structural bonds that sustain coherence and resilience. The image echoes the Socratic method by prompting inquiry not into isolated answers but into the relationships that give meaning: What does it mean to interpret responsibly? How does accountability connect practice with principle? To what extent does human agency remain central when decisions are mediated by systems? In this sense, the figure is not only descriptive but also diagnostic, inviting continuous questioning of how these elements hold together, adapt, and remain open to ethical reasoning in changing contexts (Figure 2.12).

The figure presents a conceptual structure through which the interdependence of AI, education, ethics, and governance can be examined as mutually sustaining rather than discrete concerns. By invoking the form of the double helix, it illustrates how transparency,

FIGURE 2.12 The DNA of responsible AI education: intertwining transparency, ethical reflexivity, and employability.

This figure visually represents the relationship between transparency, ethical reflexivity, and employability as interdependent strands of a double helix, inspired by the structure of DNA. These strands are connected by conceptual 'base pairs'—interpretability, accountability, and human agency—which symbolise the values that bind ethical practice, governance, and future-oriented professional development. The model illustrates how each strand is incomplete without the others, highlighting the need for integrated, adaptive, and ethically grounded approaches to AI education and employability in the 21st century.

BOX 2.12 EXPLANATION NOTE—DNA OF RESPONSIBLE AI EDUCATION: INTERTWINING TRANSPARENCY, ETHICAL REFLEXIVITY, AND EMPLOYABILITY

Figure 2.12 illustrates the conceptualisation of transparency, ethical reflexivity, and employability as interdependent dimensions of AI governance and education. Framed as a double helix, the model highlights that these domains are not parallel or isolated but structurally bound together through three key connecting principles: interpretability, accountability, and human agency.

The value of the model lies in how it mirrors the Socratic mode of inquiry introduced earlier. Rather than assuming these principles to be fixed or self-evident, the figure prompts ongoing questioning about how they operate in relation to one another. For instance, what does it mean to make an AI decision interpretable in ways that go beyond technical decoding to enable critical judgement? How does accountability serve as more than institutional compliance, linking ethical intention with meaningful responsibility? And crucially, how is human agency preserved when algorithmic systems increasingly mediate decisions about learning, employability, and opportunity?

The positioning of employability at the intersection underscores that preparing individuals for AI-mediated futures requires more than technical skill acquisition. It involves cultivating the capacity to engage with transparency critically, to exercise reflexive judgement, and to ensure that human values remain central to professional and social practice. In this way, the figure captures the argument advanced in this section: transparency must be understood not merely as disclosure but as part of a broader ethical infrastructure in which employability and reflexivity are co-developed.

Ultimately, the double-helix form signals dynamism and adaptability. Just as DNA sustains growth and renewal, so too must ethical AI governance evolve through continuous questioning, reinterpretation, and participatory practice. This model therefore serves less as a static representation and more as a reminder that ethical engagement in AI is a living, relational process—shaped by ongoing dialogue between principles, practices, and human responsibility.

ethical reflexivity, and employability are entwined strands, held together by conceptual linkages—interpretability, accountability, and human agency—that sustain coherence and resilience. This framing draws attention not simply to the presence of ethical principles but to the ways in which they function in relation, reinforcing or constraining one another in practice. This relational quality recalls the Socratic method of inquiry, which does not seek answers in isolation but pursues clarity through questioning the links between assumptions, claims, and consequences. In a similar way, the figure prompts reflection on what it means, for instance, to claim that a system is transparent: transparent to whom, for what purpose, and with what implications for accountability or human agency? The strength of the model lies in making visible that none of these concepts can be sustained in isolation, for each depends on the interrogation and support of the others. This emphasis on relationality finds resonance in emerging regulatory standards. The guidance of the United Kingdom's Information Commissioner's Office and the Alan Turing Institute (2020) highlights four interconnected principles—transparency, accountability, contextual awareness, and reflection on impacts—that together form the groundwork for meaningful oversight. Likewise, the UK Government's Algorithmic Transparency Recording Standard (2023) begins to embed disclosure not merely as an administrative task but as a civic expectation, requiring institutions to articulate the logic and purpose of AI systems in accessible terms. These developments suggest that transparency is better conceived as an orientation—a commitment to ethical clarity and reflexivity—rather than a technical endpoint.

At the same time, critical tensions remain. The U.S. National Institute of Standards and Technology's AI Risk Management Framework (2023) underscores how ethical imperatives to disclose can conflict with proprietary interests or technical opacity, producing structural barriers to both regulatory scrutiny and public understanding. Here, the helix metaphor acquires particular force: just as the strands of DNA lose coherence if one is broken, so too do governance frameworks falter when reflexivity, transparency, or employability are pursued in isolation. The task, then, is to nurture their interdependence—through education, regulation, and institutional practice—in ways that maintain openness to questioning and adaptation. In this sense, the figure is not only an illustration but also a provocation. It challenges us, in a manner reminiscent of Socratic dialogue, to move beyond static definitions and ask how these principles interrelate, how they sustain ethical life in technological societies, and how they might be strengthened through continuous critical engagement.

The convergence of transparency, reflexivity, and employability is increasingly reflected in regulatory developments that seek to address the risks of opacity in algorithmic decision-making. One prominent example is New York City's Local Law 144 (2021), which requires bias audits for AI-driven hiring tools and obliges employers to inform candidates when such systems are used. While this marks a significant step towards accountability in employment contexts, its effectiveness depends less on the publication of information than on the capacity of individuals and organisations to interpret, question, and respond to it. Without such interpretive engagement, disclosure risks functioning as a procedural formality rather than a meaningful basis for fairness. Similar challenges emerge in initiatives such as the AI registers launched by Amsterdam and Helsinki or New Zealand's Algorithm Charter. These frameworks seek to embed transparency as a civic practice by making algorithmic details publicly accessible. Yet their impact is limited unless supported by educational and institutional infrastructures that enable the information to be critically understood and acted upon. The issue is not the absence of transparency mechanisms, but the unevenness of the capacities required to make them effective.

This difficulty is also evident in more formalised regulatory instruments. The General Data Protection Regulation (GDPR), through Articles 13 to 15, establishes transparency as a legal right by mandating that individuals be provided with information about the logic and consequences of automated decisions. In practice, however, this provision is inconsistently enforced and often expressed in terms that fail to provide genuine intelligibility. The gap between disclosure and comprehension highlights a recurring weakness: transparency, while necessary, cannot operate in isolation. Reviews such as that conducted by the Centre for Data Ethics and Innovation (CDEI) (2020) underline this point. By recommending mandatory transparency in public sector algorithms, the CDEI contributed directly to the UK Government's Algorithmic Transparency Standard. Yet the real value of such measures lies not in the publication of information alone, but in whether individuals and communities possess the reflexive capacities to evaluate and contest what is revealed. It is in this confluence of institutional openness and human capability that the possibility of ethical employability emerges—an ability not simply to navigate AI-mediated systems, but to do so with discernment, responsibility, and critical awareness.

The Open Government Partnership's State of the Evidence report (2023) underlines the uneven progress of algorithmic transparency in public governance. While AI is increasingly deployed in public decision-making, the mechanisms designed to ensure disclosure and accountability often remain fragmented and difficult to interpret. Transparency, in this context, cannot be treated as a guarantee of legitimacy; it becomes meaningful only when anchored within broader ethical and civic infrastructures that allow individuals and institutions to engage with, contest, and respond to what is disclosed. This brings us back to the dialectical reasoning associated with Socrates. In his method, knowledge advances not through final answers but through sustained questioning. For AI governance, the relevant questions are not simply 'Is this system transparent?' but 'Transparent for whom? To what purpose? Under what conditions can this knowledge be meaningfully acted upon?' In other words, transparency must be interrogated as a relational practice rather than assumed as a fixed achievement. The literature on explainability reinforces this orientation. Adadi and Berrada (2018) frame explainability as a structural necessity in contexts where decisions carry significant ethical weight. Arrieta et al. (2020) distinguish between intrinsically interpretable systems and post hoc explanations, yet caution that without substantive transparency, both approaches risk superficiality. The central issue is not whether AI can be explained, but whether those explanations support genuine interpretive agency—empowering individuals to critique and act, rather than merely observe.

It is here that the Double ERL helix model acquires force. Just as the strands of transparency, reflexivity, and employability are structurally entwined, so too must transparency and explainability be understood as part of an ongoing dialogue. Interpretability, accountability, and human agency act as the conceptual 'base pairs' that hold the structure together, ensuring that transparency does not collapse into disclosure alone, but contributes to critical reflexivity and ethical employability. In this sense, the Socratic method is mirrored in the helix: its strength lies not in static answers but in the continual testing of relations, the questioning of assumptions, and the cultivation of resilience through dialogue.

Debates on the value of explainability have prompted significant reflection on the limits of current approaches. Rudin (2019) challenges the widespread reliance on post hoc explanation, particularly in contexts where decisions carry high ethical stakes. She contends that retrofitting interpretability onto opaque models can generate partial or misleading accounts, and instead calls for the prioritisation of inherently interpretable systems whose decision logic is transparent by design. This position shifts the emphasis away from explanation as an afterthought and towards transparency as an integral feature of system architecture, raising a broader point: the design of AI must embed ethical clarity from the outset if it is to avoid superficial gestures of accountability. Other scholars have sought pragmatic alternatives to balance transparency with practical usability. Wachter, Mittelstadt, and Floridi (2017) propose counterfactual explanations, which clarify what changes in input data would have produced a different outcome. This method offers a degree of accessibility by showing individuals how they might understand or challenge automated decisions in concrete terms, while also aligning with data protection requirements. Yet, as Ananny and Crawford (2018) caution, openness has limited ethical force unless it is situated within institutional and procedural structures that allow disclosed information to be acted upon. Their critique of the so-called 'transparency ideal' highlights the need for operational settings—audits, review mechanisms, and redress pathways—through which explanation acquires substance as accountability.

Floridi et al. (2018) extend the discussion by introducing the principle of explicability, understood as the fusion of transparency and explainability into a dual obligation: systems must be both observable in function and justifiable in relation to those affected. This move underscores that technical clarity alone is insufficient; it must be matched by ethical intelligibility. Building on this, Mitchell et al. (2019) propose the practical tool of model cards—structured documentation specifying a system's intended use, performance metrics and limitations—to enhance transparency and responsible reporting of AI models. Such instruments serve as mediating artefacts between technical design and user comprehension, equipping non-specialists, including educators, clinicians, and employers, with the means to interpret AI systems in ways relevant to their contexts. What unites these perspectives is the recognition that transparency cannot operate in isolation. Whether pursued through inherently interpretable models, counterfactuals, or model cards, its value depends on integration with ethical reflexivity and institutional mechanisms that enable meaningful engagement. When viewed through the strand framework developed in this work, transparency is best understood not as a static disclosure but as one element in a dynamic architecture—co-evolving with reflexivity and employability to sustain trust, accountability, and informed agency in AI-mediated environments.

The challenges of opacity are particularly acute in education, where AI increasingly mediates assessment and personalised learning. Kwakye (2025a) cautions that many AI tools in education lack sufficient explainability for either students or educators, leaving those most affected unable to interpret or challenge technological decisions. Their findings

TABLE 2.2 Mapping Transparency, Reflexivity, and Employability across Key Domains

Domain	Transparency	Reflexivity	Employability/Human Agency
Education	Explainable systems and accessible reporting on AI in learning and assessment	Teachers and learners as co-interpreters of AI processes; critical questioning embedded in pedagogy	Learners enabled to develop adaptive, ethical capacities beyond compliance with opaque systems
Employment	Disclosure of evaluative criteria in algorithmic hiring; overcoming proprietary secrecy	Public and regulatory oversight of hidden evaluative logics; participatory governance	Employability reframed as fair recognition of skills under transparent and just conditions
Healthcare	Multilayered transparency across data, models, and governance structures	Reflexive alignment of AI with informed consent, clinical validation, and patient trust	Patients and professionals empowered to interpret and act on AI-supported clinical decisions

suggest that regulatory audits or compliance disclosures are insufficient on their own; what is needed is transparency by design, supported by reporting mechanisms intelligible to non-specialists and governance processes that treat teachers and learners as co-interpreters rather than passive recipients. Similar concerns arise in the employment sphere. Raghavan et al. (2020), examining algorithmic hiring systems, identify the prevalence of proprietary secrecy that obstructs both regulatory scrutiny and public debate. Their introduction of the concept of epistemic opacity is particularly salient: when evaluative criteria remain hidden, applicants are denied the possibility of contesting decisions that shape their prospects. This insight widens the debate on employability, shifting attention from the development of skills alone to the fairness and transparency of the systems through which those skills are judged and valued.

Kiseleva et al. (2022) highlight the need to approach transparency in healthcare as a multilayered process, extending from data provenance and algorithmic design to the governance structures that regulate their use. Rather than a one-off act of disclosure, transparency here functions as an iterative alignment of innovation, ethical responsibility, and social trust, supported by practices such as informed consent, clinical validation, and patient engagement. Placed alongside insights from education and employment, this perspective underscores that transparency acquires meaning only through its interaction with other ethical commitments. In educational contexts, it enables learners and teachers to interpret and question AI-driven processes, fostering reflexivity as part of pedagogy. In employment, it is tied to fairness in evaluation, ensuring that skills are recognised under accountable conditions rather than through opaque mechanisms. Healthcare, by contrast, illustrates how transparency must operate as a continuous process of validation and oversight. Together, these contexts show that transparency, reflexivity, and employability are not discrete concerns but interdependent strands of a broader ethical architecture. The Double ERL helix model captures this interconnection, illustrating how each strand reinforces the others to sustain trust and ensure that AI systems remain socially accountable and publicly legitimate. Table 2.2 develops this argument further by showing how the three strands take shape across education, employment, and healthcare, each requiring distinct yet complementary forms of operationalisation.

This mapping makes clear that transparency takes on distinct forms across domains, yet remains inseparable from reflexivity and employability. In education, transparency enables critical engagement with assessment systems but becomes meaningful only when learners and teachers are empowered to question and co-construct their use. In employment, it is tied to procedural justice, where the right to fair recognition depends upon open evaluative criteria and mechanisms of redress. In healthcare, transparency is an iterative process, requiring continuous alignment between technical design, ethical responsibility, and patient trust. Across these contexts, employability is reframed—not merely as skill possession, but as the ethical and interpretive capacity to navigate AI-mediated environments. When compared with the earlier stakeholder matrix, the distinction is evident. That table provided a horizontal perspective, mapping who carries responsibility for trust, transparency, and legitimacy across different actors. The present table offers a vertical perspective, showing where these principles must be enacted within key societal domains. Collectively, they provide a fuller picture of AI governance: one that attends both to differentiated responsibilities among stakeholders and to the sectoral variations that shape how ethical principles can be realised.

Solomonides et al. (2021), writing on behalf of the American Medical Informatics Association, identify transparency as a core ethical requirement for AI in clinical practice, essential for supporting trust, accountability, and the avoidance of bias. Their emphasis on explicit communication introduces a crucial distinction between internal transparency—where explanations are accessible to practitioners—and external transparency—where patients can meaningfully comprehend AI-assisted decisions. This differentiation underscores the importance of audience-specific intelligibility, a consideration of growing significance as healthcare professionals are increasingly called upon to interpret, mediate, and ethically defend algorithmic outcomes within practice and training. Expanding this discussion, Hildebrandt (2012) advances the notion of a critical transparency right, shifting attention from passive access to information towards the active ability to demand justification. Her contribution draws attention to the need for legally enforceable mechanisms through which individuals may compel institutions to explain the rationale underpinning automated decisions. By reframing explanation as a right rather than a discretionary courtesy, Hildebrandt situates transparency within the domain of Civic Agency and democratic participation. This perspective aligns with the regulatory strand of the present framework, indicating that ethical reflexivity must be embedded not only in professional education but also within broader constitutional and administrative structures. Pasquale's (2015) analysis further strengthens this normative trajectory through his depiction of the 'black box society'. He highlights the structural opacity of contemporary algorithmic systems, in which institutions collect and interpret personal data while limiting the capacity of individuals to understand or contest outcomes. Such asymmetry signals not only a deficit in transparency but also a deeper imbalance of power that threatens democratic accountability. Importantly, Pasquale resists presenting transparency as a singular solution; instead, he advances an integrated approach that incorporates disclosure, auditability, procedural fairness, and public-interest interventions. Within this wider architecture of accountability, transparency becomes one component of a sustained system of checks and balances, ensuring that institutional practices remain subject to external scrutiny and participatory oversight.

From an employability perspective, Pasquale's (2015) intervention offers a valuable reminder that engagement with AI-driven systems cannot be reduced to passive adaptation. What is required is the cultivation of a critical capacity to question the grounds upon which algorithmic decisions are made and to advocate for fairer and more intelligible practices. This shift from accommodation to active agency resonates with Socratic reasoning, which emphasises inquiry as the basis of ethical life. For Socrates, unexamined assumptions risked undermining justice and civic responsibility; similarly, uncritical acceptance of algorithmic systems risks naturalising asymmetries of power that erode both professional integrity and democratic participation. In this sense, the ability to interrogate, justify, and contest technological decisions becomes not only a technical skill but also a moral and civic competence. Such a perspective also challenges the tendency to treat transparency as a procedural obligation or static disclosure. If transparency is understood merely as the release of information, it fails to capture the relational and contested character of decision-making in digital societies. Instead, as the Open Data Institute (2020) and the Ada Lovelace Institute (2021) suggest, transparency must be reconceived as a dynamic practice that fosters interpretability, reflection, and accountability across diverse audiences. This emphasis on cognitive accessibility echoes the Socratic insistence that knowledge must be both understandable and action-guiding, enabling individuals not just to receive information but to deliberate upon it meaningfully.

Diakopoulos's (2020) typology of transparency instruments strengthens this argument by distinguishing between different modes of disclosure, such as algorithmic audits and user-facing explanation tools, and situating them within specific contexts of deployment. This illustrates that transparency cannot be standardised without diminishing its ethical value; it must be responsive to the epistemic needs of those who rely upon it. Here again, the Socratic method is instructive: just as questioning must adapt to the interlocutor's knowledge and experience, transparency must be tailored to the audience if it is to empower rather than obscure. The healthcare sector provides a concrete illustration of this principle. The UK Department of Health and Social Care's 2019 Code of Conduct for Data-Driven Health and Care Technology emphasises transparency as a foundational principle, underlining the need for clear, accountable communication about how digital and data-driven systems are used in patient care (Department of Health and Social Care, 2019). In this framing, transparency becomes less a bureaucratic requirement and more a communicative practice that sustains trust and agency. Yet, as Burt's (2019) analysis of the "AI transparency paradox" reminds us, transparency initiatives risk becoming performative if they are not anchored in robust governance mechanisms. Meaningful transparency requires alignment with oversight, participatory design, and civic auditability—mechanisms that transform openness into genuine accountability. These perspectives suggest that employability in the age of AI cannot be equated with technical proficiency alone. Rather, it demands the development of capacities that reflect Socratic ideals: the courage to question, the readiness to reason ethically, and the willingness to engage in dialogue about the institutional conditions shaping technological decisions. By situating transparency within this broader horizon of civic and professional responsibility, a pathway emerges towards AI governance that is not only formally regulated but also grounded in the lived realities of those most affected.

Across the literature reviewed in this section, transparency emerges as a recurring concern, yet its substantive meaning remains elusive. Although frequently invoked, it is often presented either as a procedural safeguard or as a broad normative aspiration, seldom with sufficient theoretical precision or practical guidance. This conceptual ambiguity is particularly problematic in the governance of AI, where transparency is expected to legitimate decision-making and secure accountability. In fields as diverse as education, healthcare, employment, and public administration, reliance on an undefined notion of transparency risks reducing it to a rhetorical appeal. What is required instead is a framework capable of clarifying not only what transparency demands but also why it matters. To meet this need, a tripartite framework can be advanced—what may be described as a three-strand model—comprising moral, ethical, and legal dimensions. Each strand provides a distinct yet interdependent lens, and together they anchor transparency in the social, institutional, and political realities within which AI systems are embedded.

The moral strand rests on principles of human dignity and autonomy, affirming that individuals possess the right to understand processes that affect their lives. Here, transparency becomes a moral condition for recognising personhood and sustaining agency. Socratic reasoning is instructive: his insistence that 'the unexamined life is not worth living' highlights the moral imperative of self-understanding and critical awareness. Similarly, without moral clarity, transparency risks becoming an empty gesture—technically satisfied by disclosure, but devoid of genuine empowerment. The ethical strand concerns the reflexive, contextual, and dialogic enactment of transparency. It is not solely about the content of disclosure but also about how and why it is communicated, and to whom. This strand underscores the importance of inclusivity, responsiveness to social diversity, and deliberative engagement. The Socratic method—characterised by dialogue, questioning, and co-construction of meaning—mirrors this approach. Just as Socratic inquiry develops truth through conversation rather than monologue, ethical transparency evolves through interaction between designers, practitioners, users, and wider publics.

The legal strand situates transparency within enforceable rights and procedural safeguards. It protects due process, enables redress, and provides mechanisms of accountability, as exemplified in frameworks such as the GDPR and sector-specific audit standards. Yet law alone cannot secure legitimacy; it requires both moral recognition and ethical practice to remain relevant and just. Socratic discourse again offers resonance: his demand for reasoned justification before authority reflects the same principle that legal transparency should not merely codify rules but compel institutions to provide explanations that can withstand critical scrutiny. Together, these strands suggest that transparency in AI must be substantively defined rather than procedurally assumed. Like Socratic questioning, it is not a static attribute but a dynamic practice of interrogation, justification, and reflection. By situating transparency at the intersection of moral dignity, ethical dialogue, and legal enforceability, this model positions it as both a civic and professional virtue—one that enables AI systems to be rendered accountable to the people whose lives they shape. From an employability perspective, this Socratic framing offers more than a philosophical insight; it delineates the very competencies required in AI-mediated workplaces. The capacity to question, reason, and demand justification mirrors the professional skills now expected of graduates and practitioners alike. Just as Socratic dialogue refused passive acceptance of authority, employability in digital societies cannot be reduced to technical proficiency or procedural compliance. Instead, it requires the cultivation of critical inquiry, ethical reflexivity, and legal consciousness—capacities that enable professionals not only to work with AI but also to interrogate and shape the institutional settings in which these systems operate. In this respect, transparency is not simply an external governance requirement but a lived professional practice, central to sustaining trust, accountability, and Civic Agency in an era defined by algorithmic decision-making (Figure 2.13).

The figure conveys the Three-Strand Model of AI Transparency, emphasising that meaningful transparency does not emerge from any single strand in isolation, but from the convergence of moral, ethical, and legal dimensions. Rather than representing a hierarchy, these domains operate as mutually reinforcing practices, each essential for shaping AI systems that are accountable and human-centred. To clarify this interdependence, the Platonic allegory of the sun provides a helpful metaphor. In The Republic, the sun is not itself the

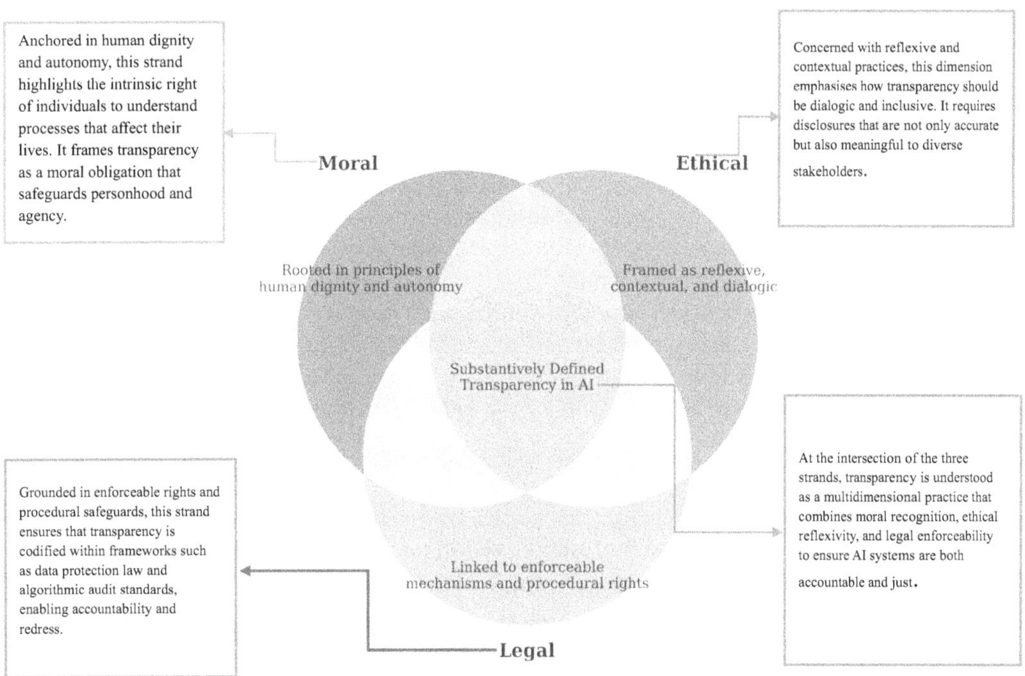

FIGURE 2.13 A three-strand model of substantively defined transparency in AI.

A three-strand model of substantively defined transparency in AI, illustrating the interconnection of moral, ethical, and legal dimensions.

BOX 2.13 EXPLANATION NOTE—A THREE-STRAND MODEL OF SUBSTANTIVELY DEFINED TRANSPARENCY IN AI

This tripartite model illustrates the moral, ethical, and legal strands that together constitute a substantively defined conception of transparency in AI. It moves beyond procedural or rhetorical invocations of openness by situating transparency at the intersection of three interdependent domains, each of which addresses a distinct dimension of accountability.

The moral strand underlines that transparency is not simply a technical or organisational courtesy but a recognition of human dignity and autonomy. By affirming the right of individuals to understand processes that affect their lives, this dimension highlights the normative importance of transparency as a safeguard for personhood and agency. In the absence of moral grounding, transparency risks becoming performative—achieved through superficial disclosure without granting individuals genuine interpretive insight.

The ethical strand frames transparency as a reflexive, contextual, and dialogic practice. This moves the discussion beyond static notions of disclosure to focus on how, why, and for whom information is communicated. Ethical transparency is inherently relational, requiring deliberation, inclusivity, and responsiveness to social diversity. In this sense, it is less concerned with the volume of information provided and more with its intelligibility, relevance, and capacity to support critical reflection among diverse stakeholders.

The legal strand positions transparency within enforceable mechanisms and procedural rights. It operates as a structural safeguard to ensure due process, prevent harm, and provide avenues of redress. Legal frameworks such as data protection legislation, algorithmic audit requirements, and sector-specific standards exemplify this dimension. Yet, while legal codification provides the procedural scaffolding, it is insufficient in isolation: without moral legitimacy and ethical responsiveness, law risks reducing transparency to a compliance exercise rather than a meaningful governance practice.

At the centre of the figure lies substantively defined transparency in AI, emerging from the interplay between these three strands. This intersection reflects the recognition that no single perspective can adequately account for the complexities of algorithmic governance. Moral principles confer legitimacy, ethical reflexivity ensures contextual responsiveness, and legal enforceability secures accountability. Taken together, they articulate a multidimensional approach that transforms transparency from a static requirement into a dynamic practice of justification, scrutiny, and empowerment.

This model therefore demonstrates that transparency in AI is not reducible to disclosure alone but is a normative, dialogic, and juridical practice. By critically integrating moral, ethical, and legal dimensions, it provides a framework capable of addressing both the theoretical ambiguity and the practical challenges that have long characterised debates on algorithmic accountability.

object of vision, but the condition that makes vision possible; it illuminates, nurtures, and enables understanding. Similarly, transparency in AI cannot be reduced to the release of information. It must provide the conditions through which individuals, institutions, and societies are able to see more clearly, deliberate more justly, and act more responsibly in relation to algorithmic systems. Visibility without intelligibility is insufficient—true transparency requires that meaning be rendered accessible, actionable, and purposeful. Within this framework, the moral strand reflects the life-giving role of the sun. It affirms the intrinsic worth of human subjects and insists that those affected by algorithmic decisions are owed not only access to knowledge but also recognition of their dignity and autonomy. This moral imperative explains why transparency matters in the first place: it legitimises the demand for openness as a condition of human agency in the face of opaque technologies.

The ethical strand can be likened to the sun's light as it interacts with particular terrains. Ethical transparency does not operate as a uniform or standardised mechanism; rather, it adapts to diverse cultural, institutional, and social contexts. Like shifting shadows, it requires reflexivity and contextual sensitivity, translating technical processes into forms that invite dialogue, support reflection, and encourage shared ethical judgement. The legal strand corresponds to the ordered path of the sun's orbit. It offers predictability, structure, and enforceability, formalising the conditions that sustain transparency. Legal mechanisms provide the procedural scaffolding that ensures transparency is not left to voluntary goodwill, but is protected through codified rights and obligations. In this sense, legal transparency safeguards the durability of both moral imperatives and ethical practices by embedding them in binding frameworks of accountability. At the centre of the figure lies the zone of convergence—substantively defined transparency in AI—where these three strands intersect. Here, transparency becomes more than disclosure; it becomes a form of human-centred intelligibility, enabling people not only to know but also to understand and to act. This is where the sun metaphor is most fully realised: transparency is reimagined as an enabling condition, one that makes visible the operations of AI while also nurturing the ethical, legal, and moral grounds for human flourishing. In this light, the figure is not merely descriptive but normative: it represents transparency as a composite virtue that is life-affirming, illuminating, and generative of justice. In an age when AI mediates access to knowledge, opportunity, and civic participation, the model serves as a reminder that transparency is not an end in itself. Its value lies in what it enables—critical reflection, responsible governance, and the preservation of human dignity.

The discussion developed in this section demonstrates that transparency cannot be reduced to a single definition, metric, or checklist. Instead, it must be understood as a composite construct sustained through the interdependence of moral obligation, ethical engagement, and legal enforceability. Each strand brings a distinctive contribution, yet their significance lies not in isolation but in their convergence, producing a more coherent foundation for accountable and trustworthy AI systems. Philosophically, this may be likened to the vastness of the universe, where differing patterns of celestial bodies—stars, planets, and galaxies—follow their own logics, yet remain interconnected within a larger cosmic order. No single pattern defines the universe, but together they create a system of balance, interrelation, and intelligibility. In a similar manner, transparency in AI is not constituted by one strand alone; it emerges from the alignment of diverse but interdependent practices, forming an ethical architecture that is at once procedural, relational, and transformative. This framework reveals transparency to be more than an instrument of compliance. Properly enacted, it becomes a generative condition for fostering civic trust, professional responsibility, and institutional legitimacy in a world increasingly shaped by algorithmic decision-making. The strength of this strand-based model lies in its capacity to integrate insights from explainable AI research, legal theory, civic participation, and sectoral practice. By doing so, it affirms that trustworthy AI is not achieved through technical fixes or regulatory imposition alone, but through sustained commitments to education, inclusive governance, and public engagement. In this light, a transparent AI system is not one that simply reveals its inner workings, but one that enables and sustains a plurality of interpretive perspectives—anchored in law, ethics, and moral responsibility, while attentive to the evolving demands of professional and civic life. Transparency thus becomes less about exposure and more about illumination: an ongoing practice of rendering decisions intelligible, contextual, and open to scrutiny. Building on this conceptual foundation, the following section turns to the question of institutional credibility and strategic communication. If transparency provides the conditions for intelligibility, then credibility and communication determine how that intelligibility is received, trusted, and acted upon. The next section, therefore, offers a critical analysis of how institutional credibility and communicative practices shape public trust in AI systems.

ANALYSE THE ROLE OF INSTITUTIONAL CREDIBILITY AND COMMUNICATION IN FOSTERING TRUST

Building on the preceding discussion—where transparency was conceptualised as a composite practice grounded in moral, ethical, and legal strands—this section turns to the institutional conditions through which these principles acquire practical force. Transparency, if it is to support accountability and intelligibility, cannot stand alone. It requires institutional arrangements that make information not only available but also interpretable, contestable, and embedded within the contexts of those affected by AI systems. Here, institutional credibility emerges as a central concern. It is within institutions—educational, governmental, and corporate—that commitments to dignity, contextual sensitivity, and legal accountability are either realised or undermined. The moral dimension of transparency presupposes institutions willing to affirm individual autonomy; the ethical dimension requires responsiveness to diverse publics; and the legal dimension depends on more than procedural compliance, demanding the institutional capacity to disclose and justify decisions. Where credibility is absent—where institutions are inconsistent, opaque, or misaligned with societal expectations—the strands of transparency risk being rendered ineffective, and trust in AI governance correspondingly weakened.

Equally important is institutional communication. This cannot be reduced to the unilateral transmission of technical detail, but functions as the interpretive bridge between regulatory frameworks and everyday experience. Through communication, institutions frame the meaning of transparency, explain the rationale for algorithmic processes, and create spaces where individuals can understand, question, or accept AI's role in their lives. In this sense, communication is integral to what may be described as relational intelligibility: it is not merely about revealing how systems operate, but about enabling people to interpret and respond in ways that preserve their agency. This section, therefore, extends the earlier framework by examining how institutional credibility and communication mediate the enactment of transparency. The guiding questions are clear: what enables institutions to act as credible agents of transparent governance? How can communication practices translate regulatory design into public legitimacy? And what institutional commitments are necessary to ensure that transparency is not left as an abstract ideal, but materialised in forms that sustain human-centred, accountable, and reflexive applications of AI?

The difficulties addressed in this section arise not only from conceptual ambiguity—where transparency is often reduced to disclosure or procedural duty—but also from the institutional challenge of embedding it in forms that are intelligible, actionable, and ethically responsive. To move the debate forward, insights from communication theory, institutional ethics, and science and technology studies are used here to explore how institutions enact transparency and how such enactments are received, interpreted, or resisted. The objective is not to introduce new categories but to deepen the analysis of how institutional credibility and communicative design give practical force to the moral, ethical, and legal dimensions of transparency. Afroogh et al. (2024), in a systematic review, demonstrate that trust in AI is neither stable nor uniform but contingent on historical, social, and institutional contexts. Trust is often shaped by inherited assumptions and past experiences, which, while instructive, can perpetuate suspicion and limit openness to constructive engagement. When applied uncritically, such backward-facing models risk reinforcing defensiveness rather than cultivating innovation and ethically robust practices in relation to AI.

A future-oriented conception of trust is therefore needed—one that develops in tandem with technological change and through sustained engagement with diverse publics. Trust should be understood as relational and dynamic, cultivated through transparency, procedural fairness, and ethical attentiveness. This perspective resonates with Plato's allegory of the divided line, which distinguishes between different modes of apprehension: imagination, belief, reasoning, and understanding.

- At the level of imagination, institutions risk relying on inherited impressions of AI—shaped by fear, suspicion, or utopian promise—without grounding these views in evidence.
- At the level of belief, trust is based on past institutional performance: confidence or scepticism rooted in historical experience. While this offers stability, it can also constrain adaptability.
- Through reasoning, institutions begin to engage critically with AI governance, recognising that transparency requires contextual responsiveness, procedural fairness, and inclusive communicative practices.
- Finally, understanding represents the most developed form of institutional trust: a state where transparency is not only disclosed but also rendered intelligible, contestable, and aligned with moral and ethical commitments.

By drawing on the divided line, it becomes clear that institutional credibility in AI governance cannot rest on impressions or inherited beliefs alone. It must progress towards more reasoned and ultimately intelligible practices, where transparency is enacted as a dynamic and relational condition. In this sense, credibility is not a static attribute but an achievement—secured through institutions' ability to move publics beyond appearances towards meaningful understanding, thereby embedding transparency as a lived and sustainable practice (Figure 2.14).

Afroogh et al.'s (2024) findings underline that trust cannot be conceived in abstraction but must be situated within the institutional practices and social relationships that shape it. In the context of AI, this requires institutions to move beyond generalised claims of transparency and to respond to the differentiated expectations and concerns of the communities they serve. Yet while Afroogh and colleagues map the conditions under which trust in AI is fostered or undermined, their account remains largely diagnostic. It stops short of offering a normative or institutional framework through which trust might be cultivated in practice, leaving unresolved the question of how institutions can actively demonstrate their trustworthiness. A more forward-looking model would require AI-governing bodies to embed mechanisms of participation and deliberation into their operational structures. This could involve citizen advisory panels with oversight of algorithmic systems, open consultations that enable diverse publics to contribute to decision-making, and co-design practices that ensure affected groups have a voice in shaping outcomes. Complementary measures might include publicly accessible reporting dashboards that translate technical information into intelligible forms, and reflexive feedback loops that allow systems to adapt in light of public input. Such mechanisms would not merely fulfil procedural requirements; they would actively strengthen institutional legitimacy by positioning organisations as responsive and accountable stewards of AI in public life. Figure 2.15 illustrates this trajectory by framing the development of organisational trust as an iterative process. It begins with initial exposure and dialogue, progresses through stages of ethical integration and participatory engagement, and culminates in what may be termed trust maturity. This representation reinforces the argument that institutional trust in AI is not secured through opacity or institutional inertia, but through sustained transparency, meaningful communication, and principled governance (Figure 2.15).

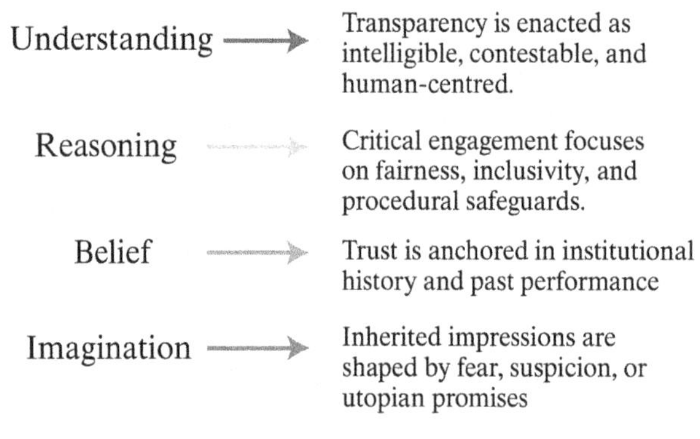

FIGURE 2.14 Institutional layers of trust in AI systems.

Four levels of institutional trust in AI, ranging from imagination shaped by inherited impressions to understanding grounded in transparency and human-centred principles.

BOX 2.14 EXPLANATION NOTE—INSTITUTIONAL LAYERS OF TRUST IN AI SYSTEMS

This figure adapts Plato's allegory of the divided line to conceptualise stages of institutional trust in AI. It illustrates how perceptions of AI governance can progress from inherited assumptions to reasoned and intelligible forms of engagement.

At the most basic level, imagination reflects trust shaped by impressions, fears, or utopian promises. Here, institutional credibility is vulnerable to distortion, as perceptions are based more on speculation than on evidence. Moving upward, belief situates trust in historical performance and institutional reputation. While this stage provides stability, it is inherently backward-looking and may constrain innovation by over-relying on past experience.

The stage of reasoning represents a more reflective mode of trust. Institutions at this level engage critically with fairness, inclusivity, and procedural safeguards, ensuring that transparency is not only formally enacted but also contextually responsive. Finally, understanding embodies the most developed form of trust, where transparency is rendered intelligible, contestable, and human-centred. At this stage, institutional credibility is sustained not by appearances or past achievements alone, but by the ongoing capacity to enable interpretation, dialogue, and ethical accountability.

The figure highlights that institutional trust is not static but developmental. It requires movement from inherited impressions towards practices that prioritise critical engagement and intelligibility. In doing so, it underlines the responsibility of institutions to foster transparency as a dynamic condition—one that enables publics to scrutinise, contest, and meaningfully participate in the governance of AI.

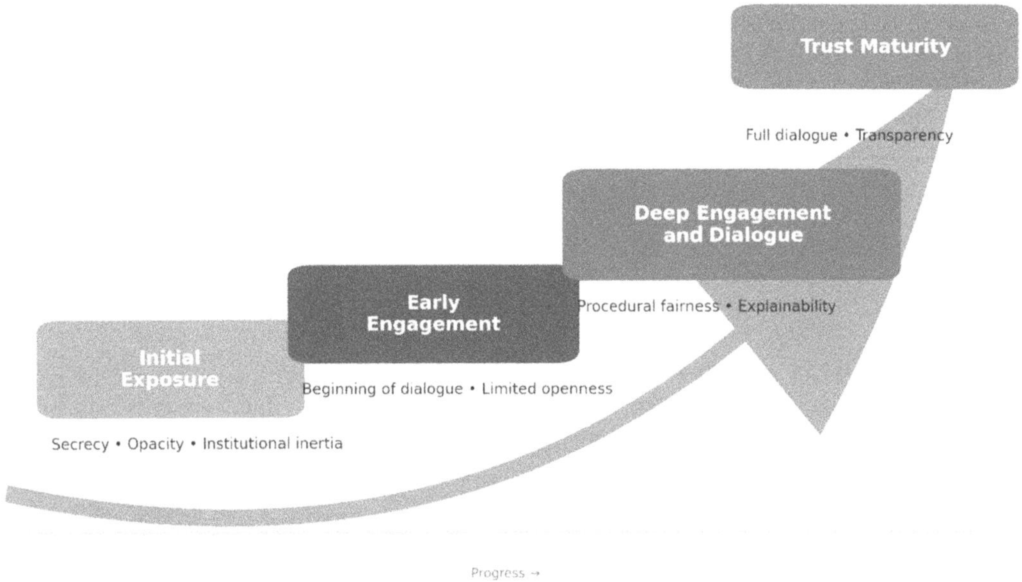

FIGURE 2.15 Pathway to trust maturity.

This figure illustrates the progressive stages from Initial Exposure through Early Engagement and Deep Engagement & Dialogue to Trust Maturity. Each stage highlights the shift from secrecy and institutional inertia towards fairness, explainability, transparency, and full dialogue.

BOX 2.15 EXPLANATION NOTE—PATHWAY TO TRUST MATURITY

The figure 'Pathway to Trust Maturity' conceptualises the progressive stages through which institutions, organisations, or systems evolve in building and sustaining trust. The upward trajectory represented by the curved arrow illustrates the dynamic movement from conditions of secrecy and institutional inertia towards greater transparency, dialogue, and fairness. This pathway is presented as four distinct but interconnected stages: Initial Exposure, Early Engagement, Deep Engagement & Dialogue, and Trust Maturity.

At the Initial Exposure stage, institutions are typically characterised by limited openness, secrecy, and structural inertia. At this point, stakeholders often encounter barriers to information, decision-making is opaque, and trust is minimal. This stage highlights the risks associated with institutional non-disclosure and the potential for stakeholder disengagement.

Progressing to Early Engagement, dialogue begins to emerge, albeit in a limited form. Organisations start to involve stakeholders in preliminary discussions, creating early opportunities for exchange. However, openness at this point is tentative, and the balance of power still favours institutional control. This phase signals a shift away from opacity but remains vulnerable to scepticism if not consolidated by further transparency.

The third stage, Deep Engagement & Dialogue, represents a more substantive commitment to procedural fairness and explainability. Here, institutions begin to implement mechanisms that make processes transparent and accountable. Stakeholders are increasingly recognised as active participants rather than passive recipients, and dialogue evolves into meaningful collaboration. This stage reflects a growing acknowledgement that trust cannot be secured through symbolic gestures alone but requires structural and procedural guarantees.

Finally, the process culminates in Trust Maturity, characterised by sustained dialogue, transparency, and mutual accountability. At this stage, stakeholders perceive institutions as legitimate, fair, and open, creating the conditions for long-term trust. Trust maturity does not imply a static endpoint but rather a sustainable culture of dialogue and transparency that continually adapts to new challenges.

Overall, the figure underscores that trust is not an immediate achievement but a gradual process requiring intentional efforts to overcome opacity and inertia. The model highlights the importance of embedding fairness, explainability, and transparency at every stage in order to move from superficial engagement to genuine trust maturity.

This figure provides a conceptual representation of how organisational trust in the governance of AI develops over time. It frames trust not as a fixed outcome but as a dynamic and iterative process, shaped by institutional choices, ethical commitments, and communicative practices. The ascending curve illustrates a gradual trajectory towards Trust Maturity, beginning with the stage of Initial Exposure. At the point of initial exposure, organisations introduce AI systems or related policies to internal or external stakeholders. Trust at this stage is fragile and highly contingent. If accompanied by secrecy, opacity, or institutional inertia, the conditions for trust can be quickly undermined, reinforcing perceptions of distance or resistance between institutions and their publics. Conversely, openness at this juncture creates the foundations for further engagement. The model then moves into Early Engagement, where organisations begin to establish dialogue, albeit often in a limited form. This stage signals a tentative shift towards openness, as stakeholders are invited into preliminary conversations. While the depth of participation may remain constrained, even partial transparency can foster familiarity and reduce the perception of risk. Importantly, this step requires consistency: early engagement that is superficial or tokenistic is unlikely to generate confidence and may instead reinforce scepticism. The subsequent phase, Deep Engagement and Dialogue, reflects a more embedded commitment to collaboration. Here, institutions actively recognise stakeholders not simply as audiences but as participants with a legitimate role in shaping governance. This stage is characterised by the integration of principles such as procedural fairness and explainability, ensuring that processes are transparent, comprehensible, and equitable. It represents a transition from limited communication to substantive dialogue, enabling stakeholders to see their concerns addressed in institutional design and decision-making.

The trajectory culminates in Trust Maturity, where sustained dialogue, ethical alignment, and institutional accountability converge. At this point, trust extends beyond functional confidence in the technical operation of AI systems to embrace confidence in the organisation's ethical stance, communicative openness, and responsiveness over time. Trust maturity, therefore, signifies both a practical and normative achievement: it reflects institutional systems that not only work effectively but also resonate with the values and expectations of the communities they serve. Along the curve, three interrelated features—dialogue, explainability, and procedural fairness—are presented as critical enablers of this progression. These qualities do not operate in isolation but together form the conditions under which engagement can develop into genuine trust. In contrast, a failure to advance beyond opacity or rigid institutional practices—represented in the figure by the lower, diverging pathway—creates risks of stagnation, disengagement, and even resistance. Such outcomes are particularly acute in the governance of AI, where questions of fairness, rights, and well-being are paramount. Overall, the figure reinforces the argument that institutional trust in AI governance must be cultivated intentionally. It cannot be reduced to technical assurances alone but requires principled governance, ethical integration, and meaningful communication. Trust emerges not as a property of technology itself, but as the outcome of socially embedded, ethically responsive, and communicatively open institutional action.

Durán and Pozzi (2025) provide a valuable philosophical lens for interrogating the trajectory towards institutional trust depicted in the figure. They argue against the assumption that trust can be secured simply through reliability metrics or externally imposed assurance mechanisms. Instead, they suggest that genuine trustworthiness rests on the alignment of institutional practices with relational and moral norms, notably epistemic humility, moral consistency, and procedural fairness. In reframing transparency as an ethical orientation rather than a purely informational exercise, their work highlights the expectation that institutions should not only account for their decisions but also embody values that resonate with those affected by their systems. This view gains depth when situated within a broader philosophical tradition. Socratic thought, for example, reminds us that virtue is not a static attribute but a reflective and dialogic practice. Although AI systems cannot themselves possess virtue, institutions that design and govern them can act with virtuous intent. This requires a shift beyond the minimal ethic of avoiding harm towards actively promoting social goods, such as fairness, inclusion, and integrity in deliberation. From this standpoint, ethical governance entails embedding normative commitments into institutional structures, ensuring that decision-making processes are transparent, participatory, and responsive.

Bareis (2024) extends this discussion through the concept of trustification, which emphasises the socio-technical processes by which institutional trust in AI is assembled and maintained. Trust, in this account, is not a discrete or isolated property but the outcome of continuous interaction between social actors, technical artefacts, and governance frameworks. The implication is that ethical and legal transparency can only be meaningful when situated within this broader ecosystem of interdependencies. This relational view is complemented by Liao and Sundar's (2022) MATCH framework, which foregrounds the communicative function of AI system design. Their analysis demonstrates that trustworthiness is conveyed not only through institutional rhetoric or regulatory signals but also through the interface of the system itself. Transparency cues, affordances, and mechanisms for explainability all shape how users interpret the system's ethical orientation. In this respect, trust is mediated in the micro-interactions between humans and machines, where transparency and procedural fairness are either reinforced or undermined in practice. These perspectives suggest that the movement towards trust maturity, as illustrated in the figure, cannot be reduced to technical assurance or rhetorical claims. Instead, it requires institutions to enact transparency as an ongoing ethical practice—embedding fairness, explainability, and dialogue not only in formal governance structures but also in the lived experiences of those who interact with AI systems.

To ground the conceptual trajectory of transparency in a more tangible space, the metaphor of a crystal-clear glass offers a useful point of reflection. This imagery does not suggest that transparency entails unfettered access to every detail of internal processes, but rather that it represents a condition of clarity, coherence, and reflective openness. Much like a finely crafted vessel, effective governance must retain structural integrity while permitting sufficient visibility for informed judgement. It must resist the distortions of selective openness or the illusion of accountability that conceals deeper ethical shortcomings. In this framing, trust in AI systems depends not solely on what is revealed, but on the ways in which disclosure is structured, contextualised, and sustained within broader institutional commitments to fairness and justice. Ancient African philosophy provides a meaningful lens for deepening this metaphor. Within traditions such as Ma'at in Egyptian thought, the notion of truth and justice is never conceived merely as factual disclosure but as the harmonisation of order, morality, and relational accountability. Transparency, viewed through this lens, is less about the passive act of seeing and more about cultivating a social and ethical balance in which institutions demonstrate fidelity to both their stated values and their communities. Similarly, the philosophy of Ubuntu emphasises that individual and institutional actions are always situated within a wider relational fabric: I am because we are. Applied to AI governance, this perspective reminds us that disclosure without integrity, or openness without responsiveness, fails to nurture the relational trust on which social legitimacy depends.

The challenge, then, is not simply to design systems that can be observed, but to embed interpretability and moral coherence into the very structures of governance. As Bareis' notion of trustification underscores, trust is not a fixed attribute but the outcome of continuous, relational processes involving technological artefacts, institutional cultures, and public narratives. Transparency, from this socio-technical perspective, becomes a dynamic practice of ethical resonance rather than a static condition of visibility. Liao and Sundar's MATCH framework further illustrates how this resonance is enacted in practice: the design of interfaces, the provision of transparency cues, and the capacity for explainability all function as communicative acts through which institutions either affirm or erode public confidence. This complexity is further highlighted by Neyazi et al. (2023), whose cross-cultural research demonstrates how trust in AI is mediated by wider communicative environments. Their findings—that traditional news consumption often correlates with higher trust, while reliance on social media, particularly under conditions of misinformation, erodes it—illustrate the fragility of trust in contested public spheres. From an African philosophical standpoint, this points to the need for institutions not only to disclose but also to cultivate interpretive resilience: practices that enable communities to discern, interpret, and critically engage with information. Collectively, these perspectives suggest that transparency in AI governance must be reframed as an ethical and relational undertaking, one that combines moral accountability, legal obligation, and cultural reflexivity. Trust is not secured by technical disclosure alone, nor by rhetorical assurances, but through continuous engagement in which institutions embody the values they proclaim. In this sense, transparency is best understood not as an end in itself but as a practice of ethical harmony—akin to Ma'at's call for order and justice, or Ubuntu's ethic of relational interdependence. Through such practices, institutions move closer to realising trust not as an abstract virtue, but as a lived, collective achievement sustained over time.

The broader sociopolitical environment within which institutions operate introduces important complexities to debates on AI governance. Flew (2023) highlights this within the context of a global erosion of institutional trust, noting the interconnections between political economy, media discourse, and public scepticism. His work cautions against the assumption that transparency, when narrowly defined as legal compliance or procedural disclosure, can by itself repair damaged trust. Rather, he points to the structural conditions—economic, political, and cultural—that fundamentally shape how institutions are perceived and held accountable. This perspective challenges instrumental or reductive accounts of transparency and underlines the importance of embedding legitimacy within wider practices of inclusivity and communicative engagement. The importance of communicative practice is further illustrated by Li et al. (2021), whose study of a Chinese petrochemical organisation demonstrates how trust is cultivated through consistent and purpose-driven communication. Their findings show that trust is not an abstract concept but a lived experience that emerges from the day-to-day practices of organisational leadership. Communication, in this sense, operates as the medium through which ethical and legal principles are enacted, giving substance to institutional commitments and aligning policy with workplace realities.

The communicative terrain of trust becomes more intricate in technologically mediated settings. Baake, Schmitt, and Metag (2025) examine the use of AI-generated avatars in science communication, observing that such tools can strengthen perceptions of institutional credibility when deployed responsibly. However, their research also underscores the conditionality of this trust, which depends less on the technological sophistication of the medium and more on the moral and epistemic integrity of the institution itself. This finding points to the performative nature of transparency: it cannot be assumed, but must be continually enacted through ethical reflexivity and institutional coherence. At a regulatory level, the evolving European discourse reflects attempts to reconcile normative ideals with enforceable governance mechanisms. The Ethics Guidelines for Trustworthy AI (European Commission, 2019) have been influential in shaping international discussions on responsible AI, but their aspirational and non-binding character exposes a gap between values and implementation. The subsequent White Paper on Artificial Intelligence (European Commission, 2020) advances this agenda by framing trust as a regulatory objective. Its advocacy of a proportionate and risk-based model reframes trust as a matter of institutional legitimacy, dependent not on declarative commitments but on the demonstrable ability of institutions to justify their actions in ways that resonate with societal expectations. These perspectives reveal that trust in AI governance cannot be reduced to disclosure alone. Rather, it is co-constructed through communicative integrity, ethical orientation, and structural responsiveness. Trust, in this refined view, emerges at the intersection of organisational practice, institutional accountability, and regulatory legitimacy—requiring institutions to engage not only in transparency but also in forms of governance that are ethically grounded, socially attuned, and continuously responsive.

Anthony, Sharma, and Noor (2024) contribute a critical perspective from the Global South, emphasising the need for pluralistic approaches to AI governance. Their intervention questions the presumed universality of Western-derived ethical frameworks, arguing instead for governance practices that are co-produced, culturally resonant, and historically grounded. Trust, in this view, is not only a procedural or relational construct but also epistemic, shaped by whose knowledge is legitimised and whose voices are authorised in defining risk, accountability, and value. This standpoint invites a rethinking of governance as a practice of reciprocal recognition, in which deliberation, co-design, and inclusivity are central to building legitimacy. Complementing this call for epistemic plurality, the OECD Survey on Drivers of Trust in Public Institutions (2024) identifies communicative reliability, procedural integrity, and service responsiveness as practical conditions underpinning institutional trust. These qualities are not abstract principles but are realised through routine citizen–institution interactions, particularly within digital service environments. Empirical work such as that of Carter and Bélanger (2005) reinforces this point, showing that trust in e-government platforms depends on both perceptions of institutional credibility and the reliability of technological infrastructures.

Bannister and Connolly's (2011) typology of interpersonal, institutional, and system-level trust provides a useful analytic lens for situating these dynamics. Their work suggests that effective digital governance must integrate all three dimensions, recognising that confidence in AI-driven systems is inseparable from perceptions of institutional legitimacy. Importantly, they argue for a shift from transactional to transformational governance—where trust is not treated as a by-product of service delivery but as a co-produced condition, cultivated through inclusive and ethically grounded engagement. Yi's (2023) study of digital governance in China offers an empirical complement to this conceptual framing. His findings indicate that streamlined digital services can improve institutional trust, but that this effect is highly contingent on the surrounding information ecology. In environments where conflicting or critical narratives circulate widely, efficiency gains are insufficient to sustain public confidence. This underscores the need for governance models that not only prioritise transparency and efficiency but also strengthen communicative resilience and media literacy. Finally, the NIST AI Risk Management Framework (2023) provides a pragmatic orientation by embedding accountability, procedural transparency, and organisational reflexivity within internal governance processes. Its contribution lies in reframing trust as the outcome of ongoing institutional practice rather than external messaging. Trustworthiness, on this account, requires adaptive systems of monitoring, learning, and accountability, ensuring that ethical commitments are operationalised and subject to scrutiny. Collectively, these perspectives extend the discussion of trust in AI governance beyond compliance and efficiency. They highlight the importance of cultural specificity, communicative integrity, and institutional reflexivity, situating trust not as a passive response to technological outputs but as a negotiated and situated achievement, embedded within wider sociopolitical and organisational contexts.

The OECD Recommendation on Artificial Intelligence (2019a) has become an important reference point in shaping the discourse on trustworthy AI, outlining widely endorsed principles such as fairness, accountability, robustness and transparency (OECD, 2019a). Its significance lies less in legal enforceability than in its function as a soft law instrument, establishing a shared vocabulary and encouraging convergence around common expectations. However, the effectiveness of such principles depends on their contextual application. Without adaptation to diverse governance environments, global frameworks risk remaining symbolic rather than transformative. Singapore's Model AI Governance Framework (2020) responds to this challenge with greater operational specificity: unlike high-level guidelines, it provides practical guidance for private sector actors, encouraging firms to embed accountability and transparency into their organisational routines (Personal Data Protection Commission, Singapore, 2020). This approach reflects a move from compliance-oriented regulation towards collaborative governance, where trust is positioned as the co-produced outcome of institutional practice, corporate responsibility, and public engagement. By contrast, Keefer and Scartascini's (2022) analysis of Latin America and the Caribbean offers an empirical complement to this conceptual framing: their findings indicate that structural inequities, institutional fragility, and historical exclusion continue to shape patterns of trust in the region. In such contexts, digital innovation alone is insufficient to repair legitimacy. Trust, they argue, must be rebuilt through sustained investment in public infrastructure, ethical responsiveness, and inclusive democratic practices. This analysis cautions against technologically deterministic assumptions and reframes trust as a deeply political condition—dependent on the capacity of institutions to redress systemic imbalances and deliver tangible reforms.

The United Nations E-Government Survey 2020 frames digital transformation in the public sector not merely as a technical undertaking, but as a people-centred process grounded in policy innovation, citizen engagement and participatory governance, oriented towards sustainable development (UN DESA, 2020). It underscores the role of user-centred design and open data in strengthening institutional credibility, illustrating how trust arises not only from efficiency but also from transparency, inclusivity, and responsiveness across governance ecosystems. Within higher education, comparable dynamics can be observed. Pillai et al. (2023) show that students' adoption of AI-based teacher-bots in Indian higher education is strongly shaped by perceived trust, usefulness and personalisation, alongside contextual factors such as attachment to human teachers and clarity of communication. Rather than evaluating the technology in isolation, students interpret AI tools through the reputational lens of the hosting institution. Similarly, Wang (2014) demonstrates that trust in digital learning environments depends on the visibility of instructor presence, the consistency of interaction, and the reliability of the infrastructure. These findings collectively affirm that AI systems in education must reinforce pedagogical relationships grounded in human connection and ethical accountability, rather than replace them. Overall, these perspectives emphasise that trust in AI governance cannot be reduced to compliance with abstract principles or technical performance. It must be cultivated through the interplay of normative aspiration, institutional ethics, and political and cultural realities. Effective governance, therefore, requires both principled commitments and reflexive adaptation to context, ensuring that trust is built not as an abstract value but as a lived and relational practice.

At the policy level, international frameworks increasingly stress that trust in AI must be cultivated through institutional commitments to transparency, accountability, and inclusive participation. UNESCO (2022b) and the European Commission (2022) both highlight that meaningful trust cannot be reduced to technical assurances; rather, it must rest on the capacity of learners, educators, and wider publics to interrogate and shape the systems that mediate their experiences. By framing trust as a normative orientation, these initiatives foreground rights, inclusion, and ethical safeguards as structural requirements rather than discretionary goals. The OECD's (2021a) review of AI in education sharpens this perspective by examining how predictive analytics and algorithmic assessment can shape perceptions of fairness and legitimacy. Where such tools are poorly explained or insufficiently accountable, they risk undermining student confidence in institutional processes. The implication is that trust in educational AI must be built not only through performance and transparency but also through the perceived justice and intelligibility of institutional decisions. Beyond the education sector, large-scale surveys reinforce the fragile and conditional nature of public trust in AI. Gillespie et al. (2023) document ambivalence across multiple countries, with governance clarity and ethical oversight identified as critical determinants of credibility. Similarly, the Edelman Trust Barometer (2024) finds that while technology companies often enjoy initial trust, this is precarious in the absence of clear and continuous communication about AI practices. These findings demonstrate that trust is not static but requires sustained engagement and institutional coherence.

In response, a number of organisations have begun to embed trust as a structural element of AI governance and design. This includes the World Economic Forum (2022), IBM through the work of Nirmal (2022), and Microsoft through the leadership of Crampton (2022), each of whom emphasise trust as an organisational, rather than merely reputational, priority. These approaches emphasise user-centred design, stakeholder consultation, and governance mechanisms that embed trust across the development lifecycle. The shift here is notable: trust is recast as an internalised responsibility, enacted through organisational practice and ethical alignment. Regionally grounded perspectives further underline the contextual nature of trust. Research by the Economist Intelligence Unit (2020) and the OECD (2024) highlights that public trust in AI is unevenly distributed, particularly in Latin America, where it is closely tied to governance reform, civic engagement, and institutional credibility. In such contexts, technological readiness is insufficient without broader commitments to political legitimacy and inclusivity. The emphasis on cultural responsiveness is echoed in the African Union's Policy Guidelines on AI for Africa (2024), the Ada Lovelace Institute's Data Divide report (2021), and NITI Aayog (2020). Each underscores that trust is not a universal condition but a situated practice, grounded in local histories, values, and participatory processes. These frameworks collectively reaffirm that trust in AI cannot be assumed as a natural by-product of innovation. Rather, it must be continually negotiated through transparency, ethical reflexivity, and institutionally grounded forms of accountability.

This section has shown that trust in AI governance is a multidimensional construct that resists reduction to technical performance or regulatory compliance. Rather than conceiving trust as a discrete output, it is more accurately understood as an institutional condition, shaped by ethical, moral, and legal commitments embedded in governance practice. Across international, national, and sectoral contexts, a recurring theme has emerged: trust must be cultivated deliberately through participatory and context-sensitive approaches that move beyond abstract declarations towards meaningful engagement. Three strands appear central to this endeavour. The ethical strand emphasises the integration of fairness, accountability, and respect for human agency into both system design and institutional routines. Here, trust is not secured through statements of intent, but through the practical embedding of values into governance processes. The moral strand extends this perspective by interrogating institutional character: the cultivation of integrity, humility, and attentiveness to affected communities. This requires reflexivity, especially in contexts where technological infrastructures risk obscuring power asymmetries. The legal strand reinforces these commitments by providing structures of accountability and redress. Yet such frameworks must remain adaptive, evolving in step with the socio-technical systems they aim to regulate.

Importantly, the analysis has avoided placing AI itself at the centre. Trust emerges relationally, situated within wider governance ecologies marked by historical trajectories, institutional credibility, and communicative competence. From risk-based regulatory frameworks to regionally grounded policy guidelines, the key challenge is not to engineer trust artificially, but to earn it through openness, dialogue, and ethical alignment. The central claim, therefore, is not that AI systems must be trusted, but that the institutions responsible for their deployment must strive to become trustworthy. Ancient African philosophy provides a resonant lens through which to draw this discussion to a close. Traditions such as Ma'at in Egypt and Ubuntu in Southern Africa emphasise that legitimacy rests not in technical prowess alone but in relational balance, justice, and collective responsibility.

Ma'at embodies the pursuit of order and justice as conditions of societal trust, while Ubuntu locates human dignity and legitimacy in interdependence: I am because we are. Applied to AI governance, these perspectives remind us that trustworthiness is not an abstract principle but a lived practice of relational accountability. Institutions earn trust when they demonstrate fidelity to communal values, respond to diverse voices, and orient technological systems towards the common good. Framed in this way, the governance of AI is reoriented towards a more reflective and responsible future. The aspiration is not merely for systems that are efficient or explainable, but for institutions that are just, inclusive, and genuinely worthy of public confidence.

GUIDING PRINCIPLES FOR ENSURING TRANSPARENCY IN ARTIFICIAL INTELLIGENCE

Building on the preceding discussion of ethical foundations in AI—particularly the importance of fairness, accountability, and human agency—this section turns to the principle of transparency, which operates not in isolation but as a condition that enables the realisation of those broader values within organisational settings. Transparency is the connective tissue that allows organisations to demonstrate that their AI systems are not only technically robust but also ethically coherent, socially responsive, and legally compliant. In this sense, transparency should not be understood as a superficial gesture of openness but as an embedded and ongoing organisational practice. In the previous section, we considered the ethical tensions that arise when AI systems make or influence decisions that have significant consequences for individuals and communities. I also noted that the complexity of AI technologies—particularly in their data-driven and algorithmic dimensions—can obscure how decisions are made, which in turn can limit opportunities for recourse, correction, or critique. Within this ethical landscape, transparency serves both an instrumental and normative function: it enables oversight and contestability, while also signalling respect for the dignity, rights, and autonomy of those affected by AI-enabled systems.

Transparency, in this context, is not merely about disclosing information. It is about enabling meaningful understanding. It encompasses the provision of intelligible explanations for how AI systems function, the rationale behind their outputs, and the processes through which they are designed, monitored, and improved. Crucially, this understanding must extend beyond technical teams to include a broad range of organisational actors—from senior leadership and human resource professionals to service users and affected communities. In this way, transparency reinforces one of the key themes from the previous discussion: that ethical AI is not solely a technological matter but a social and Institutional Responsibility. A central challenge identified earlier was the potential for AI systems to reinforce or conceal bias, particularly when deployed in areas such as recruitment, performance evaluation, or service delivery. Transparency offers one mechanism through which such risks can be mitigated. By requiring organisations to document the assumptions, data sources, and decision rules built into their systems, transparency creates space for scrutiny and reflection. It also facilitates early detection of errors, unintended consequences, or unjustifiable disparities—supporting the proactive identification and redress of harms before they become systemic. The guiding principles outlined in this section build directly on these ethical concerns and offer a framework for organisations seeking to operationalise transparency as part of a wider culture of responsible AI. Three principles will be discussed: explainability, accessibility, and organisational accountability. Together, these principles move the concept of transparency beyond an abstract ideal into something actionable and contextually responsive.

PRINCIPLE 1: EXPLAINABILITY—MAKING AI REASONING UNDERSTANDABLE

Rationale

Explainability is a core principle of ethical and responsible AI governance. It refers to the capacity of an AI system to articulate clear, meaningful, and contextually appropriate rationales for its decisions or outputs. In an organisational setting, explainability enables both internal users and external stakeholders to comprehend how and why a particular decision was generated by the system. This understanding is not only instrumental for operational transparency but also vital for cultivating trust, fostering accountability, and ensuring that human oversight remains central to automated decision-making processes.

Where AI systems are deployed in areas such as education, employment, or resource allocation, decisions may carry significant consequences for individuals. In such high-stakes contexts, opacity can undermine fairness, erode confidence, and restrict the ability of affected parties to seek clarification, challenge outcomes, or pursue redress. The principle of explainability, therefore, functions as a safeguard against arbitrary or inscrutable decision-making. It provides a bridge between the complexity of algorithmic processes and the legitimate expectations of users and communities for clarity, fairness, and responsiveness.

It is important to distinguish explainability from full algorithmic transparency. The former does not require an exhaustive exposition of source code or mathematical logic; instead, it involves producing targeted, understandable explanations that are proportionate to the use case and intelligible to the relevant audience. This distinction enables organisations to balance the need for interpretability with considerations of technical feasibility, commercial confidentiality, and user accessibility.

Dimensions of Explainability

Explainability can be meaningfully implemented by attending to the following three interrelated dimensions:

1. **Audience-Appropriate Explanations**
   Explanations must be tailored to the needs and capacities of specific audiences. A data scientist or compliance officer may require technical details relating to model architecture, input features, or performance metrics. In contrast, a non-specialist user—such as a student, job applicant, or service recipient—may require a high-level summary of the key factors that influenced the AI-generated decision. An effective approach to explainability must therefore involve the development of multitiered explanation strategies that cater to diverse stakeholders.

2. **Contextual Relevance**
   Explanations must be relevant to the domain in which the AI system operates. For instance, in a healthcare application, patients and clinicians may need insight into the clinical criteria or patient history informing a diagnostic recommendation. In contrast, in a financial services context, the focus may be on credit scoring variables, spending history, or risk thresholds. Contextualising the explanation ensures that it is both meaningful and actionable within the domain of use.

3. **Human-Centric Design**
   Explainability should be embedded into the human–machine interface, supporting users to engage critically and reflexively with AI outputs. Rather than being an optional add-on, it must be integrated into the design and delivery of systems from the outset. This includes enabling users to ask follow-up questions, provide feedback, and intervene where necessary—ensuring that human agency remains intact. This aligns with broader ethical commitments to autonomy, participation, and informed decision-making.

Practical Applications

To operationalise explainability, organisations should embed explanatory features within AI-enabled tools at key points of user interaction. The goal is not merely to fulfil regulatory obligations but to empower users with insight and confidence in the systems that affect them.

EXAMPLE 2.1 EDUCATION—STUDENT DATA PORTALS

An AI-powered student support platform that predicts academic performance or identifies students at risk of disengagement should not deliver recommendations in isolation. Instead, it should provide explanatory dashboards outlining the key inputs used—such as attendance, prior attainment, or engagement with digital resources—and how they contributed to the risk prediction. These explanations should be easily interpretable by both students and staff and may be visualised using intuitive graphs or infographics. This enables timely intervention and encourages collaborative dialogue around student progress, rather than passive receipt of automated decisions.

EXAMPLE 2.2 EMPLOYMENT—RECRUITMENT AND HIRING TOOLS

AI-driven recruitment platforms that screen or rank applicants must be transparent about the factors influencing their evaluations. For example, if a candidate's application is flagged as high-potential, the system should provide a summarised rationale highlighting relevant experience, skills alignment, or specific keywords matched with job requirements. Importantly, such explanations must be non-discriminatory and aligned with equal opportunity principles. They should also be available to human reviewers, ensuring that algorithmic suggestions are interpreted within the broader context of the candidate's suitability and organisational values.

EXAMPLE 2.3 FINANCIAL SERVICES—LOAN ELIGIBILITY SYSTEMS

When AI tools assess creditworthiness, customers denied a loan or offered an unfavourable rate should receive a clear explanation—such as credit history concerns, income thresholds, or outstanding debts—that informs them of the reasons behind the outcome. Providing this information in an accessible format not only supports the customer's understanding but also opens pathways for future improvement and financial literacy.

Explainability, when implemented thoughtfully and systematically, contributes to the creation of AI systems that are not only technically sound but also socially responsible and ethically defensible. By ensuring that users can make sense of AI-driven decisions, organisations promote fairness, safeguard human dignity, and strengthen trust in digital innovation.

PRINCIPLE 2: ACCESSIBILITY—ENSURING TRANSPARENCY IS INCLUSIVE AND USABLE

Rationale and Justification

Accessibility is fundamental to ethical transparency. It ensures that information about AI systems is not merely available but also understandable and usable by a broad range of stakeholders. This principle recognises that the ethical value of transparency is undermined if technical language, inaccessible formats, or poor dissemination exclude those most impacted by AI systems. By addressing these barriers, accessibility enables more equitable participation and supports the three-strand transparency model—moral, ethical, and legal—advanced in this book.

Practical Steps for Implementation

Multitiered Communication Formats

AI-related information should be communicated through layered formats tailored to different audiences.

- Provide technical documentation for developers and compliance professionals.
- Create plain-language summaries and visual aids (infographics, figures, videos) for general users.
- Translate key materials into multiple languages and use formats accessible to people with disabilities (e.g. screen-reader compatible documents, captions for videos).

Inclusive AI Literacy Initiatives

Institutions should invest in AI literacy programmes that equip stakeholders with the understanding necessary to engage meaningfully with AI systems.

- Run regular workshops or tutorials on AI basics, system purposes, limitations, and user rights.

- Co-design materials with diverse user groups to ensure relevance and cultural responsiveness.
- Incorporate these programmes into induction processes and continuing professional development (CPD).

Interactive Explanation Tools

- AI interfaces should support dynamic and user-driven explanations.
- Embed interactive help icons, glossary links, and walkthrough guides within AI dashboards.
- Use example-based or scenario-driven explanations that relate to users' real-world concerns.
- Enable users to simulate outcomes or explore 'what-if' scenarios to better understand how inputs influence results.

Context-Sensitive Design

Accessibility must reflect the domain in which the AI system operates.

- **In education**: explain student analytics in terms of attendance, engagement, or assessment patterns.
- **In employment**: clarify algorithmic hiring decisions with reference to skills, experience, or role alignment.
- **In healthcare**: use clear language to describe diagnostic recommendations, supported by figures or summaries for patients and clinicians alike.

Feedback and Revision Loops

Transparency mechanisms should be continually evaluated for clarity and usefulness.

- Include feedback buttons or surveys to assess users' understanding and identify areas of confusion.
- Use this feedback to revise and improve explanatory content and formats.
- Involve user advisory panels in the review process to ensure accountability and responsiveness.

Accessibility Audits and Standards

Institutions should adopt formal measures to evaluate the inclusiveness of their transparency practices.

- Develop accessibility benchmarks specific to AI communications.
- Conduct periodic audits of AI-enabled services and documentation to ensure compliance.
- Publish findings as part of institutional transparency reports, reinforcing public accountability.

EXAMPLE 2.4 EDUCATION—STUDENT AI SUPPORT PORTALS

A university implements an AI-powered system to predict student disengagement. Alongside this tool, the institution offers explanatory dashboards that clearly outline the key indicators used—such as class attendance, online activity, and assessment history. Students and staff are invited to attend regular workshops to better understand the system, and user feedback informs periodic updates to improve explanation quality.

EXAMPLE 2.5 EMPLOYMENT—AI IN PERFORMANCE MANAGEMENT

A company introduces AI tools to evaluate employee performance. Each dashboard includes clear, jargon-free explanations of how metrics are calculated and what factors influence evaluations. Employees can access visualisations of their performance trends and receive contextualised feedback with suggestions for improvement. Workshops are run quarterly to ensure all staff understand the system.

EXAMPLE 2.6 HEALTHCARE—PATIENT COMMUNICATION SYSTEMS

A hospital deploys an AI system to assist in diagnosis. Patients receive printed and digital summaries explaining how the AI reached its conclusions, using layman's terms and visual aids. An on-site AI liaison team is available to answer follow-up questions and ensure that patients feel informed, respected, and involved in decisions about their care.

PRINCIPLE 3: ORGANISATIONAL ACCOUNTABILITY—EMBEDDING RESPONSIBILITY WITHIN STRUCTURES

Rationale and Justification

Transparency must be embedded institutionally, not left to ad hoc efforts. Organisational accountability ensures that responsibility for the ethical and transparent use of AI systems is distributed across structures of governance, leadership, and practice. This principle rejects the notion that ethical oversight can be delegated solely to technical teams or automated processes. Instead, it emphasises that meaningful transparency must be sustained by human institutions that are capable of learning, adapting, and responding to challenges over time.

Organisational accountability also involves clear delineation of roles and obligations throughout the AI system lifecycle—from design to deployment, monitoring, and redress. It creates the conditions for transparency to be proactive rather than reactive, continuous rather than episodic. Importantly, it ensures that those affected by AI systems have defined channels for recourse and that ethical concerns such as bias, opacity, or exclusion are not merely documented but addressed.

Institutionalising transparency in this way supports a culture of internal reflexivity and ethical responsibility. By embedding transparency into governance processes, organisations move beyond symbolic commitments and towards operationalised, context-sensitive, and socially responsive AI practice.

Practical Steps for Implementation

AI Governance Structures

- Establish cross-functional AI ethics committees that include legal, technical, operational, and community voices.
- Designate senior-level AI ethics officers or champions to oversee transparency initiatives.
- Ensure these structures have the authority to halt or modify AI projects if ethical concerns arise.

Accountability across the AI Lifecycle

- Integrate AIAs into project planning, risk management, and procurement processes.
- Require documentation of decision-making processes, data provenance, and audit trails for all AI systems.
- Develop policies outlining responsibilities for monitoring performance, addressing errors, and updating systems.

Grievance and Redress Mechanisms

- Provide clear and accessible routes for individuals to challenge or seek explanations of AI-generated decisions.
- Establish response timelines and escalation pathways for complaints related to AI systems.
- Ensure that these processes are overseen by independent bodies or ombuds services where possible.

Collaborative Framework Development

- Co-create transparency and accountability frameworks with internal staff, service users, and external stakeholders.
- Regularly review these frameworks in light of new legal standards, technological changes, or stakeholder feedback.
- Incorporate lived experiences and community input to ensure relevance and legitimacy.

Reflexive Organisational Culture

- Encourage staff to report concerns or limitations in AI systems without fear of reprisal.

- Use system failures or near misses as learning opportunities to improve organisational practice.
- Include transparency and accountability in internal training, appraisal, and professional development schemes.

Public Communication and Reporting

- Publish regular transparency reports outlining AI use, impact assessments, feedback received, and governance responses.
- Make these reports accessible to non-specialist audiences and available in multiple formats.
- Engage in external audits or peer reviews to enhance credibility and trust.

Examples of Organisational Accountability in Practice

EXAMPLE 2.7 LOCAL AUTHORITY—HOUSING ALLOCATION

A local authority adopts an AI-driven system to assist with housing allocation. To embed transparency, it establishes a participatory oversight board comprising residents, frontline housing officers, and data ethics experts. This board meets quarterly to review system performance, flag concerns, and recommend changes. All housing applicants are informed of their rights and provided with a contact point for questions or appeals.

EXAMPLE 2.8 UNIVERSITY—ADMISSIONS TRANSPARENCY FRAMEWORK

A university uses AI to support postgraduate admissions. It creates an interdisciplinary committee to monitor fairness and ensure explainability of admission decisions. The committee publishes anonymised audit findings and maintains a feedback channel for applicants. Staff involved in admissions receive training on how to explain system-generated recommendations to prospective students.

EXAMPLE 2.9 HEALTH PROVIDER—AI RISK GOVERNANCE UNIT

A national health service provider integrates an AI risk governance unit into its digital health division. This unit coordinates ethics reviews, responds to patient concerns, and ensures compliance with regulatory standards. It works closely with patient advocacy groups to co-develop explanatory materials and organises annual public forums to share updates on the organisation's AI systems.

PRINCIPLE 4: PEDAGOGICAL INTEGRATION—EMBEDDING TRANSPARENCY INTO LEARNING AND EMPLOYABILITY FRAMEWORKS

Rationale and Justification

In the context of employability, transparency must be understood not merely as an organisational characteristic but as a core educational competency. Pedagogical integration involves preparing learners to critically engage with the systems that influence their professional and civic futures—particularly when those systems rely on AI-powered screening, analytics, or automated decision-making. It fosters ethical reflexivity and legal understanding, both of which are central to the Double ERL framework outlined earlier in this book.

Practical Steps for Implementation

Transparency Literacy in Curriculum Design

- Integrate modules on transparency literacy into undergraduate, postgraduate, and vocational programmes.
- Focus these modules on AI systems used in employment, education, and public services.
- Emphasise practical understanding of data rights, algorithmic explainability, and digital accountability.

Interdisciplinary Teaching Approaches

- Deliver content through co-taught sessions involving technical, legal, and ethical perspectives.
- Include contributions from employers, civil society, and regulatory bodies to ensure real-world relevance.
- Encourage discussion and debate around case law, guidance, and ethical dilemmas in AI deployment.

Simulated and Experiential Learning Environments

- Create interactive simulations that allow learners to compare transparent versus opaque AI systems.
- Use scenario-based learning to examine how transparency affects fairness, trust, and outcomes.
- Encourage students to reflect on how their own data might be used in automated systems.

Case-Based Learning and Applied Critique

- Incorporate case studies analysing the use of AI in areas such as recruitment, performance management, and university admissions.

- Task students with evaluating the transparency of these systems and proposing improvements.
- Ground recommendations in established legal and ethical frameworks, including data protection and non-discrimination principles.

EXAMPLE 2.10 DIGITAL BUSINESS PROGRAMME—RECRUITMENT AI CASE STUDY

A university's digital business programme includes a dedicated module exploring the use of AI in recruitment. Students examine real-world case studies where algorithmic tools are used to shortlist candidates. They evaluate the system's transparency, identify risks such as bias or opacity, and develop recommendations for improving fairness and explainability. These recommendations are informed by relevant legislation, ethical standards, and technical guidance.

PRINCIPLE 5: VOCATIONAL EQUITY—ENSURING TRANSPARENT AI SUPPORTS FAIR EMPLOYABILITY OUTCOMES

Rationale and Justification

Employability must not be undermined by opaque, discriminatory, or poorly understood AI systems. This principle extends the discourse on transparency to its social justice dimensions, asserting that AI must contribute to equitable access to work opportunities—particularly for individuals and communities historically marginalised in the labour market. Vocational equity requires that transparency be applied in practical and actionable ways, enabling individuals to understand algorithmic assessments, question decisions, and take informed steps to improve outcomes. This aligns closely with the ethical and legal dimensions of transparency set out earlier in this book, reinforcing the principle that genuine empowerment is only possible where institutions are open, responsive, and accountable. By ensuring that AI systems do not perpetuate or obscure inequality, vocational equity promotes a vision of technology that supports—not hinders—fair employability pathways for all.

Practical Steps for Implementation

Transparent Decision-Making in Recruitment

- Require employers to provide clear, accessible explanations for automated hiring decisions.
- Ensure that individuals are informed of their right to request a human review or lodge a formal challenge.
- Provide standardised templates or summary reports explaining scoring criteria and system limitations.

Transparency Standards for Job Platforms

- Establish guidelines for algorithmic transparency on digital job-matching and career development platforms.

- Ensure these platforms explain how recommendations or rankings are generated and provide opt-out or correction mechanisms.
- Involve regulators and worker advocates in setting and monitoring these standards.

Worker and Union Participation

- Support trade unions, professional bodies, and worker associations in scrutinising AI systems used in employment contexts.
- Facilitate the co-creation of transparency benchmarks and fairness indicators in consultation with affected groups.
- Encourage collaborative audits and information-sharing between employers and employee representatives.

Feedback and Improvement Mechanisms

- Incorporate notification systems that inform candidates of how AI systems have assessed them and what steps could improve future outcomes.
- Design transparent scoring rubrics for automated assessments that clearly link evaluation metrics to role criteria.
- Ensure that feedback is timely, comprehensible, and tailored to the user's context and capabilities.

EXAMPLE 2.11 AUTOMATED HIRING PLATFORM—CANDIDATE TRANSPARENCY FEATURES

A recruitment company uses an AI system to evaluate CVs and generate shortlists. To promote transparency and vocational equity, the platform provides candidates with a breakdown of their scores across relevant criteria, such as qualifications, experience, and keyword relevance. Candidates also receive a plain-language explanation of how the system works, their right to request a manual review, and guidance on how to improve their ranking in future applications. These measures are co-developed with input from unions and equality advocacy groups to ensure fairness and clarity.

Building upon the prior discussion of ethical foundations in AI—particularly the intertwined values of trust, accountability, and human agency—this section has examined the role of transparency not as a stand-alone virtue, but as a necessary condition through which such broader commitments become actionable and legitimate. Within organisational settings, transparency functions as both a procedural mechanism and a normative ideal. It connects technical systems with Institutional Responsibility, ensuring that the development, deployment, and impact of AI technologies remain intelligible, contestable, and responsive to human needs. In this context, transparency must be reimagined not as a discrete act of disclosure, but as an embedded, sustained, and structurally integrated practice that underpins ethical governance. This section has contended that transparency holds a dual character: it is at once instrumental, enabling oversight and rectification, and expressive, signalling respect for those subjected to algorithmic influence. Given the increasing reliance on AI systems in domains such as education, employment, and public service delivery, the imperative for transparency becomes particularly acute. The opacity of algorithmic processes not only impairs accountability but may also suppress individual autonomy and compound structural inequalities—particularly where decisions have material consequences for people's futures.

To that end, five guiding principles have been proposed, each advancing a distinct yet interrelated facet of transparency. The first principle, explainability, anchors transparency in the practical need to make AI-generated outcomes intelligible to diverse audiences. It calls for layered, audience-sensitive communication that bridges technical complexity and user comprehension. The second principle, accessibility, ensures that the right to understand is not curtailed by barriers of language, format, or technological literacy. In this way, accessibility reinforces the moral, legal, and ethical strands of the transparency model outlined earlier in this book. The third principle, organisational accountability, shifts the emphasis from individual technical responsibility to systemic and structural obligations. It asserts that transparency must be supported by governance architectures, reflexive cultures, and institutional mechanisms for redress. Crucially, it recognises that ethical AI cannot be achieved through technological design alone, but must be cultivated through deliberative, cross-disciplinary, and participatory processes.

The fourth principle, pedagogical integration, extends transparency into the domain of employability. It posits that learners—particularly those entering AI-mediated professions—must be equipped with the critical capacity to understand, engage with, and shape the digital systems they will both use and be subject to. Transparency here is not simply an organisational value but a foundational element of civic and professional formation. The fifth principle, vocational equity, further deepens this link by emphasising the social justice implications of transparency. It argues that AI systems used in employment must be not only fair in outcome but also transparent in method, ensuring that individuals can understand, challenge, and improve their engagement with algorithmic tools. Together, these principles constitute a coherent framework through which transparency can be embedded across the design, deployment, and governance of AI systems. They offer both a conceptual foundation and a series of practical strategies for operationalising transparency in ways that are ethical, inclusive, and attuned to the needs of contemporary learners, workers, and citizens. In so doing, they advance the claim that transparency is not an abstract ideal, but a tangible and evolving practice essential to responsible innovation and equitable digital futures. This discussion naturally leads to the next area of inquiry: accountability. While transparency is necessary for visibility and understanding, it does not, in itself, guarantee ethical conduct or just outcomes. The following section explores how governance mechanisms, oversight bodies, and redress frameworks must be instituted to ensure that transparency is accompanied by responsibility, enforcement, and meaningful consequences.

ACCOUNTABILITY IN AI GOVERNANCE: STRUCTURES OF OVERSIGHT, MECHANISMS OF REDRESS, AND THE ETHICS OF RESPONSIBILITY

Following the earlier discussion of transparency as a cornerstone of ethical, legal, and pedagogical integrity in AI systems, this section turns to a closely related principle: accountability. If transparency provides visibility into how AI operates, accountability ensures that such visibility has practical consequences—requiring that systems and their stewards be answerable for the outcomes of automated decision-making. Yet within the expanding

AI landscape, and particularly in the interlinked fields of education and employability, accountability often remains diffuse, ambiguously defined, or structurally absent. This gives rise to pressing normative and practical questions: Who bears responsibility when AI systems reproduce bias or cause harm? What avenues of redress exist for those affected? And how might accountability be embedded so as to support fairness, trust, and justice? The stakes are acute in contexts where AI systems assess student performance, predict risk, or influence progression; and in employment settings where hiring, appraisal, and workforce planning are increasingly shaped by algorithmic tools. In such domains, decisions carry significant weight yet are not always accompanied by clear explanations, opportunities for challenge, or clarity about where responsibility ultimately resides. Crucially, the burdens of opacity and error tend to fall most heavily on those with the least capacity to contest outcomes—exacerbating existing inequalities.

To meet these challenges, accountability must be reframed as more than retrospective liability or individual blame. It is better understood as a distributed and anticipatory practice that integrates ethical culture, legal safeguards, and institutional design. At its most effective, accountability extends across the AI lifecycle: from the initial stages of design and procurement, through implementation and monitoring, to review and redress. Internal mechanisms such as governance audits, accountability matrices, and escalation pathways provide institutions with tools to monitor risks and address concerns proactively. These must be complemented by external mechanisms—including liability regimes, regulatory oversight, and independent ombudspersons—that safeguard the public interest where institutional systems fall short. This broader vision resonates with two enduring traditions of political thought. In classical accounts, Athena symbolised wisdom joined with justice—reminding civic institutions that insight without courage achieves little and that strength without fairness corrodes legitimacy. In African philosophy, the principle of Ubuntu highlights that responsibility is relational: individuals and institutions exist within webs of interdependence where accountability is shared, not hoarded. Taken together, these perspectives illuminate accountability as both protective and participatory: protective in ensuring redress when harm occurs, and participatory in recognising that responsibility is grounded in relationships between institutions and the communities they serve.

This section therefore examines how accountability should operate within the AI–education–employability nexus. It clarifies the allocation of responsibility when systems directly or indirectly shape learner outcomes or employment opportunities, before exploring internal and external mechanisms for monitoring, review, and redress. Throughout, the analysis draws on case studies and policy initiatives to illustrate both the possibilities and the pitfalls of current practice. Importantly, it builds on the conceptual framework developed earlier—including the Double ERL model and the strand-based account of transparency—to argue that accountability must be structurally, ethically, and communicatively embedded. Institutions cannot merely disclose the presence of AI systems; they must assume ownership of the outcomes those systems produce and be prepared to interrogate, explain, and amend them when necessary. In this light, accountability is not a static endpoint but an evolving ethos of responsibility—distributed across technical, institutional, and civic domains. A just AI future will depend on institutions capable of combining the foresight symbolised by Athena with the relational ethic of Ubuntu: systems of governance that are not only legally robust but also morally coherent, socially grounded, and fundamentally worthy of public trust.

RECONCEPTUALISING ACCOUNTABILITY WITHIN THE AI–EDUCATION–EMPLOYABILITY NEXUS: ETHICAL AND INSTITUTIONAL DIMENSIONS

In the evolving discourse on AI governance, particularly within the intersecting fields of education and employability, accountability must be conceived in broader terms than narrow legal liability. More usefully, it can be understood as a duty of care—an obligation on the part of institutions to anticipate, prevent, and respond to potential harms generated by algorithmic systems, including those that may be systemic or unintended (Nartey, 2021). Such a conception shifts accountability from being merely retrospective to becoming a forward-looking and relational practice, grounded in commitments to human dignity, fairness, and inclusive governance. Mark Bovens' (2007) framework remains instructive here. By presenting accountability as a triadic relationship between an actor, a forum, and a standard, he situates responsibility not in static definitions but in ongoing processes of justification, evaluation, and, where appropriate, sanction. This model is particularly pertinent in AI-mediated contexts, where decision-making is increasingly distributed between human and machine agents. The critical question—who speaks for the algorithm?—highlights the importance of empowering oversight bodies, ethics committees, and even informed constituencies such as students or job applicants to act as legitimate forums of accountability. Christina Moser (2023) extends this view by embedding accountability within a human rights orientation. Her emphasis on redress as a principle of design, rather than a post hoc response, aligns with the idea of anticipatory accountability. For educational settings, where algorithmic tools shape admissions, performance analytics, or disciplinary decisions, this principle is crucial. These systems are not ethically neutral; they structure access to opportunity and can exacerbate inequality if left unexamined. Moser's position underscores the need for institutions to move beyond compliance towards proactive and reflexive accountability structures, capable of addressing harms before they crystallise.

Yet these perspectives also reveal an unresolved challenge: AI technologies evolve rapidly, often unpredictably, making accountability a moving target. Structures of oversight must therefore be adaptive as well as anticipatory. Within this book's earlier conceptual framing, the idea of Double ERL—Ethical Regulatory Literacy and Ethical Reflexive Learning—offers a way forward. Here, accountability is not confined to institutional procedures but extends to the cognitive and ethical capacities of individuals and collectives, ensuring that governance is both technically informed and morally responsive. The classical thought experiment of the Ship of Theseus provides a helpful metaphor for considering this trajectory. The question it poses—whether an object that has had all its parts replaced remains the same—speaks directly to the fluid identity of accountability systems. In AI governance, institutional structures, technical mechanisms, and regulatory instruments may change over time, but the legitimacy of accountability depends on coherence between evolving practices and enduring ethical commitments. If procedures adapt without clarity of principle, accountability risks becoming hollow; yet if principles remain static while oversight structures become obsolete, accountability may lose practical force. This perspective is especially relevant in the employability domain, where AI tools used for recruitment, appraisal, or workforce planning are subject to continual revision through updates, new data sources, and shifting institutional priorities. Preserving accountability in such environments requires not only technical traceability but also a sustained commitment to ethical integrity. Just as the Ship of Theseus requires careful maintenance to remain seaworthy, accountability in AI governance must be continually reconstructed, ensuring that institutions preserve their moral identity amid technological and organisational change.

Advancing the analysis of accountability in AI governance, particularly in education and employability, requires careful distinction between accountability and responsibility. McGrath and Whitty (2018) differentiate the two: accountability denotes an externally oriented obligation to report, explain, and justify actions, whereas responsibility reflects an internally held sense of moral or professional ownership. This distinction is especially pertinent in AI contexts, where agency is distributed across developers, institutional leaders, algorithmic processes, and end users. In such environments, where design, deployment, and use often overlap, clarity regarding both external reporting duties and internal ethical responsibilities is foundational to robust governance. This perspective suggests that accountability cannot be reduced to procedural compliance. Institutions must cultivate ethical reflexivity among those who design, implement, and rely upon AI systems. Here, the idea of an AI duty of care becomes central. This principle frames accountability as a proactive obligation to anticipate, prevent, and mitigate harm throughout the lifecycle of AI systems. Once technologies begin shaping outcomes—whether in automated grading, hiring decisions, or welfare assessments—they create enduring bonds of obligation between developers, institutions, and those affected. The duty of care should not be seen as an abstract aspiration but as a practical commitment: embedding ethical safeguards in design, maintaining ongoing monitoring, and ensuring meaningful human oversight of decisions.

Frink and Klimoski's (1998) organisational theory of accountability reinforces this principle by stressing the behavioural dimensions of institutional practice. They argue that accountability mechanisms are effective only when roles, expectations, and consequences are clearly defined and embedded within organisational structures. This insight is highly relevant in AI governance, where complexity can obscure or diffuse responsibility. To address this, institutions can implement accountability matrices—frameworks that link decision points and system behaviours to identifiable individuals or roles with oversight and explanatory responsibilities. Such measures not only clarify lines of answerability but also encourage a wider culture of ethical attentiveness. Equally important are feedback loops: institutional processes through which ethical lapses or performance failures can be identified, assessed, and rectified in real time. These mechanisms align with the earlier framework of Ethical Regulatory Literacy and AI Ethical Reflexive Learning, which positions accountability as an iterative practice rather than a one-off compliance exercise. Embedding such adaptive structures ensures that institutions learn from experience, adjust to emerging risks, and maintain their duty of care. In this way, accountability in AI governance becomes an evolving practice—responsive, preventative, and firmly grounded in institutional and human responsibility.

The proposed AI duty of care can be better understood when examined alongside established duty of care principles in other sectors such as healthcare, education, and employment law. While parallels exist, important distinctions also emerge that highlight the unique demands of algorithmic governance. In clinical contexts, the duty of care obliges practitioners to anticipate and prevent foreseeable harm to patients, grounded in both professional ethics and legal liability. Negligence is assessed by reference to whether a practitioner exercised reasonable skill and judgement in line with recognised standards of practice. The parallel in AI governance lies in the expectation that developers and institutions must design and implement systems with safeguards that prevent foreseeable harms. Yet unlike healthcare, where responsibilities are clearly tied to identifiable practitioners, AI systems diffuse agency across engineers, vendors, institutional leaders, and end users. This fragmentation complicates questions of liability and makes the embedding of institutional oversight structures, such as accountability matrices, particularly vital. In education law, the duty of care entails creating safe environments for learners and ensuring equitable access to opportunity. Breaches often arise when institutions fail to provide adequate support or oversight, leading to harm through neglect rather than direct action. The resonance with AI governance is evident in contexts such as algorithmic grading, admissions, or risk assessment, where the fairness and accuracy of decision-making shape life chances. Here, the duty of care must extend beyond ensuring technical correctness to include ethical safeguards against bias and mechanisms for redress. Unlike traditional educational duties, however, algorithmic decision-making introduces opacity that requires additional layers of transparency and interpretability to sustain trust.

Employers hold a duty of care to provide safe and non-discriminatory working conditions, including safeguards against unfair or biased treatment. In AI-mediated hiring and performance management, the risks of discrimination or procedural unfairness are amplified through automated processes that can obscure the basis of decisions. The AI duty of care parallels employment law obligations by requiring institutions to ensure that systems do not reinforce inequality. Yet it diverges in its preventative emphasis: it requires not only compliance with anti-discrimination law but also continuous monitoring, explainability and meaningful human oversight to ensure fairness throughout the employment lifecycle. Across these domains, however, established duties of care tend to focus on retrospective liability—remedying harm once it has already occurred. By contrast, the AI duty of care must be anticipatory, adaptive, and ongoing. Given the evolving and often unpredictable nature of algorithmic systems, accountability cannot be confined to post hoc adjudication. Instead, it must be embedded throughout design, deployment, and use, supported by institutional learning and ethical reflexivity. The comparative perspective illustrates that while the AI duty of care draws from established legal traditions, it requires novel approaches that respond to the distributed, opaque, and dynamic character of algorithmic decision-making. It must therefore function not only as a legal safeguard but also as an institutional ethic—ensuring that accountability is proactive, relational, and continuously reconstructed as technologies evolve.

Building on the preceding discussion, accountability in AI governance must be recognised as both a structural commitment and an ethical practice. In education and employability, where algorithmic decisions shape opportunities for learning, progression, and work, accountability is not incidental but essential to the legitimacy and fairness of institutional processes. It should be conceived not as a reactive response to failure but as a pre-emptive duty of care: a continuous obligation for institutions and developers to anticipate risks, safeguard against foreseeable harms, and align technological design with human-centred values. This duty of care extends beyond legal compliance. It requires attention to the broader ethical and social consequences of AI systems that operate at scale, often with opacity, and sometimes beyond the intentions of their designers. Here, the Double ERL framework—Ethical Regulatory Literacy and AI Ethical Reflexive Learning—provides a dual approach to embedding accountability in practice. The first strand, Ethical Regulatory Literacy, equips institutions to identify responsibilities clearly and maintain coherence across governance structures. It ensures that regulatory principles are translated into operational practices, such as maintaining audit trails, clarifying data governance protocols, and establishing decision pathways open to scrutiny. Through such measures, accountability becomes more than symbolic; it is made actionable and transparent.

The second strand, AI Ethical Reflexive Learning, situates accountability within the realm of institutional culture and human judgement. It prevents accountability from being reduced to compliance checklists or performance metrics by fostering critical engagement with the values embedded in AI systems. This reflexivity is particularly crucial in education and employability, where fairness cannot be reduced to technical measures alone. It enables stakeholders to question assumptions that underpin algorithmic models—for example, how 'merit' is defined in recruitment, or how 'risk' is constructed in learning analytics—and to adapt governance practices in response. A useful illustration of this dual commitment can be drawn from the image of the Bridge of Eleutheria, a concept from pre-Socratic philosophy. The bridge, said to link the present to future possibility, did not endure through its physical structure alone but through the shared obligations of those who maintained it. If any member of the community failed in their duty—through neglect, indifference, or self-interest—the bridge would weaken, threatening collective passage into the future. In the same way, AI infrastructures may hold the potential to transform education and work, but their stability rests not only on technical sophistication. It also depends on the ethical commitments of those who design, govern, and rely upon them.

This vision resonates strongly with the African philosophy of Ubuntu, which places emphasis on interdependence and shared responsibility. The principle that 'a person is a person through other persons' underlines that accountability cannot be borne by isolated individuals or institutions. It must be understood as a collective practice, grounded in relationships of mutual recognition and responsibility. In the context of AI governance, Ubuntu reminds us that technological systems shape not only individual outcomes but also the fabric of community life. Accountability, therefore, must be relational: distributed across technical, institutional, and civic actors and continuously sustained through dialogue and ethical attentiveness. Together, the Bridge of Eleutheria and Ubuntu frame accountability as both structural and relational. They highlight that the governance of AI cannot rely solely on compliance or technical control but must rest on shared commitments to fairness, transparency, and human dignity. In this way, accountability becomes not only an institutional mechanism but also a collective ethos—one that sustains the pathways of trust and justice on which future educational and employment systems will depend.

Accountability in AI governance must be reconceived as a relational practice that extends beyond retrospective blame to encompass a proactive duty of care. This duty binds institutions, developers, educators, employers, and regulators not only to those immediately affected by algorithmic systems but also to future communities who will inherit their consequences. It demands a shift away from seeing accountability as an external imposition and towards embedding it as an internalised ethic within organisational practice. In practical terms, accountability requires institutions to establish clear lines of responsibility, ensure that oversight mechanisms operate with independence, and cultivate accessible feedback channels. Equally, it depends on fostering a cultural orientation in which stakeholders at every level recognise their role in sustaining the integrity of AI systems. Responsibility, in this sense, cannot be deferred to the machine; it must be embraced as an ongoing ethical commitment shaped by human agency. This integrated conception aligns with the Double ERL framework introduced earlier, which combines Ethical Regulatory Literacy with AI Ethical Reflexive Learning. Through regulatory literacy, institutions maintain procedural clarity by embedding tools such as audit trails, data governance protocols, and contestable decision pathways. Reflexive learning complements this by ensuring that accountability remains grounded in human discernment, enabling institutions to interrogate the values and assumptions underpinning AI applications—particularly in education and employment, where questions of fairness, inclusion, and opportunity are deeply contextual.

The myth of Daedalus and the Labyrinth offers a cautionary lens. Daedalus' technical mastery produced an extraordinary structure, yet one that trapped and disoriented those within it. The story reminds us that innovation, if divorced from foresight and moral responsibility, can generate systems that entangle rather than empower. In the governance of AI, accountability functions as the safeguard that prevents technological architectures from becoming labyrinths of opacity and exclusion. Properly conceived, it ensures that systems remain open to scrutiny, intelligible to those affected, and responsive to calls for redress. Technical approaches reinforce this need. Kacianka and Pretschner (2021) propose accountability-by-design, advocating for features such as decision logging, data provenance tracking, and forensic auditing. These measures do more than enhance technical robustness; they provide ethical guarantees that decisions affecting learners or workers can be traced and justified. However, as Sahlgren (2023) observes, an exclusive focus on procedural mechanisms risks narrowing accountability to a technical exercise, obscuring the deeper social and political contexts in which AI operates. If accountability becomes synonymous only with explainability or auditability, it may inadvertently depoliticise structural inequities, particularly in employment and education where efficiency and performance metrics often overshadow questions of equity and human development. For this reason, accountability must remain both structural and reflexive: structural in embedding technical safeguards and regulatory mechanisms, reflexive in questioning whether the systems themselves advance justice and inclusion. Only through this dual orientation can AI governance avoid reproducing hierarchies of exclusion and instead contribute to fairer, more transparent, and genuinely human-centred practices.

Vidyadhari, Handa, and Wang (2024), building on the FairAIED project, show how the opacity of educational AI systems can limit the ability of learners to understand or contest decisions that directly affect their futures. When justified by reference to commercial secrecy or algorithmic complexity, such opacity risks disenfranchising those subject to automated judgements. Their analysis makes clear that explainability is not simply a technical attribute but an ethical requirement, essential for sustaining participation, fairness, and institutional legitimacy. This perspective reinforces that accountability in AI governance must extend beyond procedural compliance or regulatory formalism. It should be understood as a relational and anticipatory practice: a duty of care requiring institutions and developers to anticipate harm, embed safeguards, and remain open to scrutiny. In the fields of education and employability—where AI increasingly mediates access to recognition, opportunity, and mobility—accountability must be dialogic and continuous, enabling processes of oversight, contestation, and reform. Conceived in this way, accountability is both pedagogical and institutional. It supports learners and workers not only as subjects of algorithmic systems but also as participants in their design and governance. Accountability is therefore not a retrospective allocation of blame, but a formative ethos embedded across the AI lifecycle—from system design and deployment through to monitoring and evaluation (M&E).

A range of cultural perspectives can illuminate this ethos. In Indigenous traditions, the symbol of the circle conveys continuity, equality, and reciprocity, highlighting the importance of dialogue in sustaining accountability. In Eastern philosophy, the image of the river speaks to adaptability, reminding institutions that accountability requires constant adjustment as social and technological contexts evolve. In Western thought, the myth of Daedalus and the Labyrinth offers a cautionary reminder that technical ingenuity without foresight or ethical responsibility can produce systems that confine rather than empower. Together, these perspectives frame accountability not as a static mechanism but as a dynamic, culturally situated practice. It requires attentiveness to context, willingness to recalibrate, and openness to critique. In this sense, accountability functions less as an external imposition than as a civic ethic—one that sustains trust and legitimacy in AI systems across diverse educational and employability settings.

Khotami (2017) identifies accountability as a cornerstone of democratic governance, ensuring that institutions remain answerable to those they serve. Yet in AI-mediated environments—where responsibility is distributed between designers, organisations, and technologies operating with limited transparency—such clarity is difficult to sustain. Questions of who is accountable, and for what, often remain unresolved. Schedler's (1999) framework, distinguishing answerability (the duty to explain decisions) from enforceability (the capacity to impose consequences), offers a useful analytic tool. Within education and employability, algorithmic grading or automated candidate selection frequently lacks either dimension: explanations are partial, and effective oversight is absent. Fox (2007) reinforces this critique, noting that transparency without responsiveness becomes performative rather than substantive. In educational contexts, dashboards and analytics can give an impression of openness while concealing structural inequities or epistemic limitations. For accountability to function meaningfully, it must move beyond procedural compliance and be understood as a relational practice. Institutions must not only justify their actions but also create environments capable of reflection, adaptation, and redress. Mulgan's (2000) observation that accountability is 'elastic' captures both its strength and its risk: while flexibility allows adaptation to technological change, unchecked elasticity dilutes coherence. Sahlgren (2023) warns against rhetorical appeals to 'algorithmic accountability', which may obscure systemic inequities under the guise of technical reform.

What emerges is the need to frame accountability as a form of ethical stewardship. This involves anticipating harm, embedding safeguards at the design stage, and cultivating cultures of reflexivity and inclusion. In this conception, accountability is not an external imposition applied after harm, but an internalised ethic guiding institutions throughout the AI lifecycle. Cultural traditions provide rich resources for deepening this vision. In ancient Egypt, the weighing of the heart before Ma'at, goddess of truth and justice, signified that integrity must be demonstrable rather than proclaimed. Applied to AI, this reminds us that institutions must ensure their decisions are ethically 'light'—transparent, just, and subject to scrutiny. In Daoist philosophy, the metaphor of the river conveys adaptability and balance. Just as a river changes course yet maintains its flow, accountability requires continuous recalibration, recognising that technological and social contexts evolve. Institutions must remain flexible enough to adapt while preserving ethical orientation. In many Indigenous traditions, the circle represents reciprocity and dialogue. Accountability here is collective, grounded in inclusion and equality. Applied to AI governance, it emphasises that responsibility should not rest solely with distant authorities but should be distributed, ensuring that those affected by decisions have a voice in shaping them. In Greek mythology, the story of Daedalus and the Labyrinth warns against ingenuity without foresight. A system that dazzles in complexity but entraps those within it illustrates the dangers of technical innovation divorced from moral responsibility. For AI governance, this cautions against designing systems that appear impressive yet obscure pathways of accountability. Collectively, these perspectives frame accountability not as a narrow technical mechanism but as a multidimensional ethic. It is at once demonstrable (Ma'at), adaptive (Daoist river), reciprocal (Indigenous circle), and reflective (Greek Labyrinth). Each highlights the necessity of embedding accountability into both institutional structures and cultural practices, ensuring that AI systems in education and employability serve justice as well as efficiency.

Bovens (2010) offers a useful refinement of the accountability debate by distinguishing between two complementary perspectives: accountability as a virtue and accountability as a mechanism. The former foregrounds the ethical orientation of institutional actors, stressing values such as fairness, transparency, and integrity; the latter emphasises the formal structures that enable justification, oversight, and, where necessary, sanction. In the governance of AI within education and employability, these perspectives should be seen not as alternatives but as interdependent. Ethical disposition without procedural rigour risks superficiality, while mechanisms without virtue risk empty formality. Together, they provide the foundation for accountable governance that is both principled and enforceable. The dangers of fragmented or ambiguous responsibility are illustrated in Romzek and Dubnick's (1987) account of the Challenger disaster, where diffuse authority and inadequate oversight allowed systemic flaws to escalate into tragedy. Their analysis is pertinent to AI contexts, where decisions affecting students or job applicants often traverse multiple actors and layers of technological abstraction, obscuring clear lines of responsibility. In educational systems, Al-Zahrani (2024) highlights how opaque algorithmic processes can generate outcomes that are ethically difficult to defend and procedurally resistant to challenge. Such opacity, if unchecked, erodes not only fairness in individual cases but also the credibility of institutions.

Moser (2023) advances this critique by insisting that accountability should not be confined to retrospective explanation but should serve as a forward-looking architecture of protection. Her focus on anticipatory governance aligns with the principle of a duty of care: an obligation on institutions to design systems that prevent foreseeable harms, incorporate safeguards, and enable meaningful redress. In this sense, accountability is best understood as infrastructure—sustaining the possibility of contestation, correction, and responsiveness before crises emerge. Supranational frameworks reinforce this orientation. The OECD (2014), World Bank (2024), and IMF (2005) conceptualise accountability as central to legitimacy in governance, framing it as an ongoing process of engagement with those affected by institutional decisions. When applied to AI, this perspective suggests that compliance audits or risk assessments alone are insufficient. Instead, participatory mechanisms—such as community-based oversight boards, algorithmic charters, and inclusive grievance procedures—are necessary to balance power and ensure responsiveness. By embedding such participatory structures into AI governance, institutions can avoid accountability becoming a hollow procedural exercise. Instead, it becomes a living practice: anticipatory in outlook, relational in character, and grounded in the dual imperative of preserving institutional integrity while protecting the rights and dignity of those subject to technological systems.

The discussion of accountability in AI governance cannot be detached from the broader principles of transparency and trust explored earlier in this book. Each principle retains its distinct emphasis—transparency enabling visibility, accountability ensuring answerability and redress, and trust reflecting the legitimacy that follows from ethical and credible practice. Yet their significance lies in their interdependence. Transparency without accountability risks becoming performative display; accountability without transparency risks becoming opaque bureaucracy; and both, if pursued without regard for trust, risk failing to secure the legitimacy that sustains educational and institutional authority. When viewed as a constellation rather than as isolated principles, these commitments outline a governance model that is anticipatory, relational, and ethically grounded. Transparency provides the conditions under which institutional processes can be scrutinised; accountability embeds mechanisms and cultures through which scrutiny can lead to meaningful response; and trust emerges as the lived experience of institutions acting with consistency, integrity, and responsiveness. The idea of accountability as a living practice situates this constellation within a dynamic, socio-technical context. It acknowledges that AI-mediated decisions in education and employability are rarely static or singular but evolve across time, contexts, and communities. To be credible, governance must therefore be flexible enough to adapt, yet principled enough to retain ethical orientation. Participatory structures—such as inclusive oversight boards, contestable decision pathways, and dialogue with those directly affected—provide the means through which accountability, transparency, and trust are renewed rather than merely declared. In this sense, AI governance should not be conceived as a fixed architecture but as a process of continual ethical stewardship. Its task is not only to prevent harm or correct error but also to sustain conditions in which fairness, justice, and human dignity can flourish across educational and employment landscapes. Such a model repositions institutions not as passive overseers of technology but as active custodians of values, responsible for guiding AI systems in ways that are intelligible, just, and worthy of confidence.

Institutional efforts such as the European Commission's Ethics Guidelines for Trustworthy AI (2019) and definitional work undertaken by the National Institute of Standards and Technology (NIST) have sought to formalise accountability through technical measures. By promoting traceability, auditability, and decision-logging, these initiatives have helped embed accountability within the architecture of AI systems. Yet such procedural mechanisms, while significant, are not sufficient to guarantee ethical outcomes in socially consequential domains such as education and employability. In these settings, decisions are not merely computational but deeply situated within histories, power dynamics, and expectations of Institutional Responsibility. The World Health Organization's (2007) framework for health systems governance offers a useful perspective by treating accountability not as an administrative formality but as a relational and systemic property. This framing highlights responsiveness, reflexivity, and the capacity to adapt to complex, human-centred environments as critical conditions of trust. Applied to AI, it suggests that governance cannot rest solely on compliance, but must reflect an active ethic of responsibility. At the centre of this ethic lies the principle of duty of care. Understood here not as a general aspiration but as a binding obligation, the duty of care requires institutions to anticipate risks, prevent foreseeable harms, and remediate where necessary. Fulfilling this responsibility cannot be achieved through transparency alone. It requires deliberate institutional practices that demonstrate a commitment to justice: ensuring that algorithmic outputs are not only explainable but also open to challenge, that those affected by automated decisions have access to redress, and that system design is informed by the lived experiences of its users.

This proactive orientation calls for accountability to be both structural and moral. Structurally, it involves embedding safeguards, oversight, and contestability throughout the AI lifecycle. Morally, it requires reflexivity about the assumptions underpinning system design: Who stands to benefit? Who is excluded? What values are being privileged in algorithmic reasoning? Such questions cannot be left to individual discretion but must be institutionalised as part of governance practice. Importantly, accountability must be understood within the broader ecosystem in which AI operates—an ecosystem shaped by policy choices, economic incentives, labour markets, and pedagogical priorities. Here, accountability is not simply about allocating responsibility after harm occurs, but about cultivating foresight and embedding moral infrastructure so that institutions act with integrity before harm arises. By integrating technical traceability with relational ethics, a more comprehensive model of governance begins to emerge—one in which AI systems are accountable not simply because they comply with predefined standards, but because the institutions deploying them remain attentive and responsive to the realities of human vulnerability and aspiration. In education and employability, this principle is particularly critical: each algorithmic decision has the potential to influence not only immediate outcomes but also the broader life trajectories of individuals. The duty of care, therefore, stands as a constitutive principle of accountability, binding institutions to act with humility, integrity, and courage in shaping the futures of those they serve.

The analysis developed in this chapter suggests that accountability, transparency, and trust cannot be treated as discrete principles. Their force lies in their interconnection, forming a composite ethic through which AI governance in education and employability can be made both legitimate and humane. Transparency provides the conditions under which decisions can be scrutinised, but its value depends on whether visibility is accompanied by mechanisms for contestation and response. Accountability gives these mechanisms substance, ensuring that institutions remain answerable and that their obligations are embedded in structures of oversight, redress, and reflexive learning. Trust, in turn, emerges not as an abstract expectation but as the lived experience of institutions demonstrating care, integrity, and responsiveness over time. The principle of duty of care binds these strands together. It redefines accountability not as a retrospective allocation of blame but as a forward-looking obligation to anticipate, prevent, and remedy harm. By rooting transparency in meaningful disclosure, and accountability in responsive institutional practice, the duty of care provides the ethical foundation upon which trust can grow. Without this grounding, transparency risks becoming a performative gesture, and accountability a hollow formality. This integrated model acknowledges that AI systems are situated within complex ecosystems of policy, labour markets, and pedagogy. Each algorithmic decision carries consequences not only for immediate outcomes but also for the long-term trajectories of individuals and communities. To govern AI responsibly, institutions must therefore move beyond technical compliance and embrace a wider ethic of stewardship—one that combines procedural clarity with moral reflexivity and is attentive to the social contexts in which technologies operate. Such a model positions AI governance not as a static architecture but as an evolving practice. Its task is to preserve fairness, dignity, and justice within environments where technology increasingly shapes opportunity. By weaving together transparency, accountability, and trust under the guiding principle of duty of care, institutions can move towards a form of governance that is not only credible but also worthy of public confidence.

Memarian and Doleck's (2023) review of fairness, accountability, transparency, and ethics (FATE) in higher education highlights a persistent gap between the adoption of ethical language and the establishment of mechanisms that make accountability operational. This gap is particularly visible in learner evaluation and credentialing, where opaque algorithms shape academic and professional opportunities without sufficient avenues for scrutiny or redress. Their analysis underscores the need to move beyond value statements to create processes through which affected individuals can challenge and influence outcomes. Chambers Goodman (2025) demonstrates similar risks in the employment sector. Her legal analysis shows how opacity in algorithmic hiring undermines applicant agency and can entrench inequities by presenting discriminatory practices as neutral or objective. Here, the challenge is not only to make systems more transparent but also to ensure that institutional practices provide meaningful recourse. Applicants must be able to understand how decisions are reached, to receive explanations, and to access mechanisms for contesting unfair outcomes. Fabris et al. (2024) add weight to this critique by observing that many hiring algorithms are deployed without a robust evidentiary basis for claims of fairness or social benefit. They argue that accountability must rest on empirical validation and demonstrable outcomes, rather than symbolic commitments. Langenkamp et al. (2020) propose a concrete step in this direction through algorithmic transparency reports, enabling regulators and advocates to scrutinise system performance. Albaroudi et al. (2024) extend this logic further, advocating for continuous audits and bias monitoring to ensure that systems remain aligned with institutional values and social expectations. Together, these contributions frame accountability as an iterative process: one that is reflexive, adaptive, and sensitive to shifting contexts.

Oladele, Hammond, and Thakur (2025), through comparative policy analysis, note that while international frameworks often affirm transparency and fairness, few provide enforceable pathways for redress. Their work highlights the importance of independent oversight and sector-specific protections if accountability is to withstand the operational complexities of AI in the workplace. Ramos (2022), writing within the UNESCO framework, returns to a normative foundation, insisting that accountability must remain people-centred and accessible. In employment contexts where AI governs access to work and conditions of labour, she argues that accountability must be designed to preserve dignity and rights, not merely to meet procedural benchmarks. Taken collectively, these perspectives reinforce a critical redefinition of accountability in AI governance. It cannot be limited to technical compliance or procedural audits. Instead, it must be embedded as both an ethical and Institutional Responsibility: enabling contestability, securing redress, and cultivating reflexive learning across all stages of system design and implementation. Within education and employment—sectors where AI decisions shape opportunities and life trajectories—accountability must therefore function as a structural ethic of care. Only when institutions act with foresight, integrity, and responsiveness can trust be built and fairness sustained in AI-mediated environments.

The analysis of accountability in AI governance shows that it cannot be treated as a static or one-dimensional concept. Rather, it must be understood as a dynamic practice that operates across legal, ethical, and institutional domains. Within the contexts of education and employability—where algorithmic systems shape progression, hiring, and access to opportunity—accountability is more than a technical safeguard. It is an ethical commitment that stretches across the entire lifecycle of AI, from design and deployment to monitoring, evaluation, and redress. A central insight has been the reframing of accountability through the principle of duty of care. This principle moves discussion beyond conventional compliance or narrow answerability, highlighting instead the proactive responsibilities of institutions to anticipate and prevent harm. Duty of care provides a conceptual foundation that unites procedural mechanisms with moral orientation, requiring institutions to protect the rights, agency, and dignity of those subject to algorithmic decision-making. The risks of opacity in AI systems make this responsibility particularly acute. Without adequate explanation, recourse, and redress, individuals can be disempowered and inequalities reinforced. To counter this, accountability must be embedded within a wider framework of trust—one that combines technical auditability with moral responsiveness. It is not enough for systems to be explainable in principle; the explanations must be accessible, contestable, and meaningful to those affected.

Equally important is the recognition of accountability as a virtue, not solely a mechanism. This perspective shifts attention to institutional culture, leadership practices, and the cultivation of reflexivity. Institutions must not only create accountable systems but also embody accountability in their values and behaviours—listening to those impacted, adapting to feedback, and integrating lessons from failure into governance structures. Finally, accountability is inherently relational. It requires the active involvement of students, educators, workers, developers, and policymakers, not as passive recipients of technological decisions but as participants in shaping and evaluating them. This relational dimension situates accountability within a democratic ethos, where legitimacy arises from inclusive and deliberative governance as much as from technical reliability. In this sense, accountability becomes both a structural framework and a moral orientation: anticipatory in scope, participatory in form, and essential for ensuring that AI systems in education and employability are not only effective but also just.

Accountability in AI governance cannot be confined to procedural safeguards or technical mechanisms. Tools such as audit trails, documentation protocols, and impact assessments remain necessary, yet they only acquire meaning when situated within institutional cultures committed to openness, reflexivity, and care. Without channels for explanation, challenge, and redress, disclosure risks being symbolic rather than substantive. Accountability must therefore be understood as more than a procedural demand: it is an ethical practice, grounded in a duty of care that requires foresight, responsiveness, and integrity. This understanding also reconfigures the meaning of employability. Beyond preparing individuals to adapt to shifting labour markets, employability should be framed as the capability to engage critically with the systems that increasingly shape educational and professional opportunities. Within this reframing, accountability is not only protective but also enabling: it allows learners and workers to question AI-mediated decisions, seek justification, and advocate for fairness. In this sense, accountability empowers participation and ensures that individuals are not reduced to passive recipients of opaque outcomes. A helpful way to draw these threads together is through the image of a shared vessel. In many ancient traditions, a vessel at sea did not belong to one individual but to a community. Its safe passage depended not only on the strength of its timber or the skill of its builders but also on the coordinated efforts of all who sailed within it. Neglect, arrogance, or silence from any one party could endanger the whole. Similarly, accountability in AI does not rest on technical design alone. It requires the ongoing vigilance of developers, educators, policymakers, and users, all of whom share responsibility for keeping systems ethically sound and socially just. When maintained with care, the vessel of accountability can carry education and employment towards more equitable futures; when neglected, it risks becoming rudderless, exposing communities to harm and mistrust. Seen through this lens, accountability is not a constraint on innovation but its moral and democratic condition. It provides the structure within which AI can serve human dignity and social justice, ensuring that technological progress strengthens rather than undermines institutional trust. With this foundation established, attention now turns to inclusivity. The next section, Inclusive AI by Design: Advancing Equity, Access, and Participatory Practice in Education and Employability, will consider how equity, participation, and accessibility can be structurally embedded so that the vessel of AI governance does not carry only the few, but creates safe and sustainable passage for all.

INCLUSIVE AI BY DESIGN: ADVANCING EQUITY, ACCESS, AND PARTICIPATORY PRACTICE IN EDUCATION AND EMPLOYABILITY

Following the exploration of accountability in the AI–education–employability nexus, this section turns to the equally integral principle of inclusivity. If accountability concerns who is responsible for the design and consequences of AI systems, inclusivity asks who is present within them—whose perspectives are recognised, whose voices are heard, and whose participation is enabled. In this sense, inclusivity must not be viewed as an aspirational ideal but as a structural condition for trustworthy governance. Approaching inclusivity in this way requires moving beyond rhetorical commitments to diversity. It demands systematic efforts to prevent exclusion—whether by addressing biased datasets, ensuring accessibility in design, or countering the marginalisation of certain identities. At stake is not only the fairness of algorithmic outputs but also the fundamental recognition of those whose lives and futures are shaped by these systems. Without such attention, AI risks entrenching rather than alleviating inequality, leaving some groups further marginalised and disconnected from educational and professional opportunities.

The image of cosmic balance offers a useful way to draw these concerns together. In ancient traditions, disorder was not understood as conflict but as imbalance—when certain forces overshadowed others or became disconnected from the whole. Applied to AI governance, inclusivity becomes the practice of restoring balance: ensuring that no single perspective dominates and that diverse ways of knowing and being are allowed to coexist in constructive relation. Just as an ecosystem sustains itself through interdependence, AI systems in education and employability gain legitimacy when they are designed to integrate, rather than suppress, plural voices and experiences. This perspective highlights inclusivity as both ethical and institutional. It compels us to ask whose aspirations are rendered visible in the models we train and the policies we adopt, and whose remain unseen. Meaningful inclusion requires not only representation but also co-creation, where those most affected by AI systems participate in shaping them. It requires sensitivity to cultural and linguistic diversity, and an embrace of intersectional data practices that acknowledge complexity rather than reduce it to simplified categories. Such measures position inclusivity as a relational ethic—an ongoing attentiveness to plurality, dialogue, and justice. Through the metaphor of cosmic balance, inclusivity is revealed not as an additive feature of governance but as the condition that sustains harmony within AI systems. Where accountability asks who is answerable, inclusivity asks who belongs, and on what terms. Together, they form complementary strands of ethical governance: accountability, ensuring that institutions can be held to account for their actions, and inclusivity, ensuring that all affected communities have a place within those actions. In this way, AI in education and employability is not legitimised by efficiency alone, but by its capacity to foster belonging, dignity, and opportunity within a balanced and interdependent whole.

Efforts to promote inclusivity in AI systems, particularly in education and employability, cannot be separated from the wider structures of social power in which these systems are embedded. Inclusivity and accountability should not be treated as parallel aspirations but as mutually reinforcing conditions that underpin the legitimacy and effectiveness of AI governance. Accountability raises the question of who bears responsibility when technologies perpetuate harm or inequity, while inclusivity presses further by asking whose experiences and perspectives are recognised and whose agency is supported. Together, they form an interdependent framework that foregrounds justice and credibility in the development and application of AI. Without such a framework, algorithmic systems risk reproducing and amplifying existing social inequalities. As West, Whittaker, and Crawford (2019) demonstrate, tools often presented as objective and neutral can, in practice, entrench racial, gendered, and socio-economic disparities if deployed without structural safeguards. In education and employability, where outcomes shape life chances and future opportunities, this risk is especially acute. The claim of fairness or efficiency, when unaccompanied by robust oversight, may mask rather than address patterns of exclusion.

Despite the critical insights already available, two gaps remain in current debates. First, there is limited guidance on the concrete processes by which inclusivity can be operationalised within AI systems. Second, inclusivity is too often positioned as a desirable but secondary consideration, rather than as a principle embedded throughout governance design. Addressing these gaps requires reconceptualising AI not simply as a technical innovation but as a policy instrument situated within broader institutional and democratic contexts. From this perspective, the governance of AI must be pragmatic as well as principled—designed with context in mind, structurally grounded, and responsive to diverse publics. This approach reframes accountability as more than transparency or technical traceability. It becomes a practice of ensuring equitable participation, distributive justice, and institutional responsiveness. In parallel, inclusivity is not limited to representational diversity but demands structural attention to who is able to contest, co-create, and benefit from AI systems. Embedding these commitments across the lifecycle of AI—procurement, design, deployment, and review—creates conditions in which educational and employability technologies can serve as instruments of equity rather than exclusion. In summary, accountability and inclusivity must be understood as interdependent rather than optional components of AI governance. Only by treating them as integral to institutional design can AI systems contribute meaningfully to education and employability in ways that are socially responsive, ethically credible, and attentive to human dignity.

Buolamwini and Gebru's (2018) Gender Shades study demonstrated that commercial facial recognition systems performed markedly worse on darker-skinned women than on lighter-skinned men. The significance of this finding lies not only in the technical disparity but also in its exposure of deeper structural biases embedded within data practices and development cultures. When technologies of this kind are applied in educational contexts, the implications extend beyond functionality. They raise critical concerns about recognition and visibility—about whose identities are consistently acknowledged by AI systems and whose remain obscured. This resonates with broader notions of epistemic exclusion, whereby certain groups are systematically marginalised in the processes through which knowledge is created, validated, and legitimised. Parallel concerns are evident in natural language processing. Bender et al. (2021) describe large language models (LLMs) as 'stochastic parrots', drawing attention to how these systems reproduce dominant linguistic norms without genuine understanding. In educational contexts, this tendency risks privileging mainstream linguistic practices while marginalising alternative forms of expression. In multilingual and culturally diverse classrooms, such dynamics may exacerbate inequities, positioning some learners' voices as central and others as peripheral. The problem, therefore, is not only technical but also epistemological: AI systems risk reinforcing hierarchies of voice and value, deciding which forms of communication are rewarded and which are disregarded.

These critiques highlight a wider deficiency in current governance frameworks: the assumption that bias can be resolved through incremental technical refinement. As Baker and Hawn (2022) argue, predictive tools in education often misidentify or underserve learners on the basis of race, disability, socio-economic background, or geography. These errors do not occur in isolation but accumulate across data collection, model training, and interpretation. Addressing them requires more than technical solutions; it calls for layered strategies that embed equity throughout the AI lifecycle and engage with the broader sociopolitical contexts in which these systems operate. From this vantage point, AI governance must be reimagined as a pragmatic policy project—one that acknowledges the entanglement of technology with histories of inequality and distributions of power. Inclusivity and accountability, in this formulation, are inseparable: accountability ensures that harms can be identified and addressed, while inclusivity ensures that diverse voices and perspectives shape both problem definitions and solutions. Together, they provide the ethical and institutional conditions under which AI can be aligned with democratic and educational values. The metaphor of cosmic balance offers a useful way of drawing these threads together. In traditions where harmony was seen as the alignment of interdependent forces, imbalance—rather than outright conflict—was considered the source of disorder. Applied to AI, this perspective highlights that exclusion and bias arise not simply from flawed code but from an imbalance in whose knowledge, values, and experiences are encoded into systems. To restore balance requires more than technical repair: it demands institutional reflexivity, inclusive design, and participatory governance. Just as a balanced cosmos sustains all elements within it, an inclusive AI ecosystem must recognise the plurality of voices that constitute educational and professional life. Only then can AI systems move beyond reproducing inequality and contribute instead to futures grounded in justice, dignity, and belonging.

In earlier sections of this chapter, the Double ERL framework was introduced as a dual ethical literacy comprising two complementary dimensions: Ethical Regulatory Literacy, the outward-facing capacity to interpret and navigate governance mechanisms; and Ethical Reflexive Learning, the inward cultivation of moral discernment and critical awareness. Together, these literacies highlight the human capacity to engage responsibly with AI at both institutional and individual levels. Yet, when attention shifts from how people engage with AI to how AI systems themselves are designed and enacted, a further conceptual tool is needed. To this end, the ERL justice framework is proposed, centring on Epistemic, Relational, and Linguistic justice. While Double ERL emphasises the ethical capacities of human actors, ERL justice addresses the structural hierarchies and exclusions embedded in AI systems. It offers a complementary perspective, enabling scrutiny of the values, assumptions, and silences encoded in technological infrastructures. Three interwoven dimensions underpin this framework:

- **Epistemic justice** questions whose knowledge is recognised and whose is excluded. In education, where AI systems mediate curricula and assessment, this involves challenging the privileging of narrow or standardised epistemologies over plural, community-based, or non-Western traditions of knowing.
- **Relational justice** considers how AI mediates human interactions. In educational and employability contexts, it asks whether systems reproduce surveillance and hierarchy or foster transparency, reciprocity, and respect. Practical markers include meaningful oversight and avenues for contesting or contextualising automated decisions.
- **Linguistic justice** interrogates the privileging of dominant language norms in AI models. Where multilingualism and cultural diversity characterise the learning environment, reliance on standardised dialects risks marginalising non-dominant linguistic practices. Justice in this dimension entails not only surface-level translation but also attentiveness to idiom, dialect, and cultural nuance.

These three dimensions can be envisioned as the strands of a woven fabric. A fabric retains its integrity only when each strand is interlaced with the others: epistemic justice ensuring that diverse knowledges are not erased, relational justice securing respectful and transparent interactions, and linguistic justice affirming the value of multiple voices and expressions. If one strand is weakened or neglected, the fabric frays, and the governance of AI risks exclusion, opacity, and mistrust. The ERL justice framework thus functions as a rigorous evaluative lens for institutions, guiding them to test whether AI systems in education and employability reinforce or resist structural inequities. Its contribution lies not in framing justice as an abstract aspiration but in embedding it within design, deployment, and institutional practice. In this way, it provides a normative foundation for pragmatic AI policy—one that is responsive to both technical effectiveness and the sociocultural dynamics of recognition, participation, and care.

Applied holistically, the ERL justice framework operates both diagnostically and as a design-oriented guide. Its value lies in helping institutions to recognise systemic exclusions while simultaneously informing the development of AI systems that are more inclusive and culturally responsive. Rather than functioning as a static checklist, ERL justice fosters a dynamic process of evaluation, adaptation, and renewal. It calls for interdisciplinary collaboration and sustained reflection on how technologies intersect with the lived realities, identities, and aspirations of learners and communities. In this sense, inclusivity is not presented as a final objective, but as a continuous practice—an ethic of attentiveness to the often subtle, and sometimes obscured, forms of exclusion that algorithmic systems may replicate. This framework also provides a scaffold for embedding justice into the operational logic of AI governance, ensuring that technological development is aligned with the wider goals of educational equity and social responsibility. Crucially, distinguishing ERL justice from Double ERL clarifies the dual challenge of AI governance: on the one hand, the cultivation of ethical capacities within individuals and institutions; on the other, the structural redesign of systems to ensure that justice and inclusion are not incidental, but integral. Taken together, these approaches expand the ways we imagine AI governance, opening up possibilities for futures that are not only technologically advanced but also equitable and culturally responsive. Figure 2.16 illustrates the three intersecting dimensions of the ERL justice framework—epistemic, relational, and linguistic justice—and highlights the guiding questions that institutions should engage with when designing, implementing, or evaluating AI systems in education and employability (Figure 2.16).

Table 2.3 represents a practical extension of the ERL Justice framework, translating the conceptual dimensions of epistemic, relational, and linguistic justice into tangible evaluative practices. Where the figure maps the conceptual space, the table operationalises it—providing guiding questions, markers of inclusive practice, and space for institutional self-assessment. In this way, it serves as a bridge between abstract reflection and applied

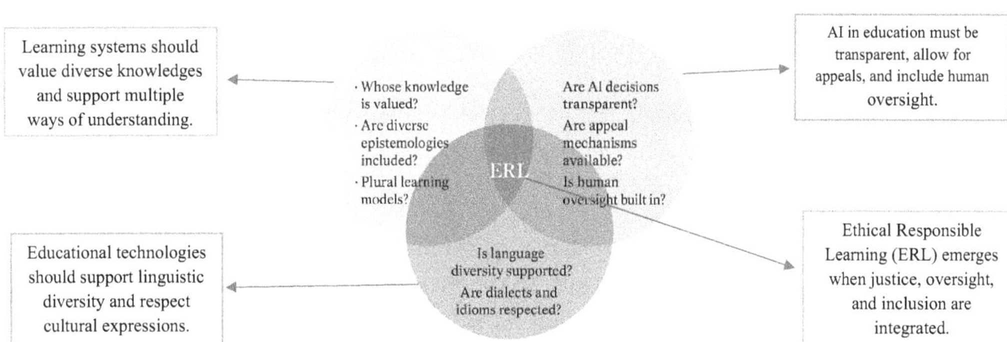

FIGURE 2.16 ERL justice framework—dimensions of inclusive.

This figure represents the ERL Justice Framework, which outlines three critical dimensions of justice that serve as a practical test for evaluating the inclusivity of AI systems, particularly in education and employability contexts.

BOX 2.16 EXPLANATION NOTE—ERL JUSTICE FRAMEWORK—DIMENSIONS OF INCLUSIVE

This figure illustrates the ERL justice framework, which brings together three interdependent dimensions—epistemic, relational, and linguistic justice—to evaluate the fairness and inclusivity of AI systems in education and employability. It expands the discussion of accountability by shifting attention from human ethical literacy (as captured in the Double ERL framework) to the design and structural logic of AI systems themselves.

The first strand, epistemic justice, addresses the hierarchies of knowledge embedded within AI. It asks whose knowledge is valued, whether diverse epistemologies are included, and whether plural learning models are acknowledged. This challenges the dominance of narrow or standardised conceptions of knowledge that risk marginalising indigenous, local, or alternative traditions of learning.

The second strand, relational justice, foregrounds the quality of interaction between individuals and institutions mediated by AI. It questions whether AI decisions are transparent, whether appeal mechanisms are available, and whether human oversight is present. In this way, relational justice reframes accountability as more than compliance, positioning it as an ethic of reciprocity and dialogue that sustains institutional legitimacy.

The third strand, linguistic justice, interrogates how AI systems engage with language diversity. It asks whether different dialects and idiomatic expressions are respected and whether multilingual contexts are accommodated. This is particularly significant in education, where systems that normalise dominant linguistic forms risk silencing or marginalising diverse student populations.

At the centre of the figure lies ERL, signalling that justice emerges not from isolated interventions but from the integration of epistemic, relational, and linguistic considerations. The overlaps highlight how these strands reinforce one another: for example, relational transparency without epistemic inclusion remains partial, and linguistic responsiveness without accountability risks being symbolic.

Placed alongside the Double ERL framework—which emphasises Ethical Regulatory Literacy (the outward-facing capacity to interpret and navigate AI governance) and Ethical Reflexive Learning (the inward-facing cultivation of moral discernment)—the ERL justice framework provides a complementary perspective. While Double ERL equips individuals and institutions with the ethical capacities to act responsibly, ERL justice ensures that the systems themselves are designed to embody inclusivity, accountability, and fairness. Together, they form a dual structure: one directed at cultivating ethical agency, the other at embedding justice within the architecture of AI.

governance, reinforcing the argument that accountability and inclusivity must be enacted as interdependent commitments rather than rhetorical aspirations. This integrative approach speaks to a broader concern: that AI in education and employability cannot be judged solely on technical performance, but must be evaluated in terms of the values it embodies, the relationships it mediates, and the voices it amplifies—or excludes. The table thus underlines that accountability without inclusivity risks proceduralism, while inclusivity without accountability risks dilution. Justice-oriented governance requires both structures that allow systems to be questioned and contested and practices that ensure all constituencies are recognised within those processes.

TABLE 2.3 ERL Justice Framework– Evaluation Table

Dimension	Focus Area	Key Questions	Indicators	Institutional Notes
Epistemic Justice	Knowledge inclusion and representation	• Whose knowledge is valued? • Are diverse epistemologies included? • Do systems reflect plural educational paradigms?	• Representation of non-dominant knowledge systems • Culturally plural training datasets • Support for multiple learning models	[e.g. Findings from curriculum datasets, gaps in diverse representation]
Relational Justice	Transparency and human interaction	• Are AI decisions transparent? • Are appeal mechanisms available? • Is human oversight embedded?	• Audit trails and clear explanation of AI decisions • User control and appeal options • Human-in-the-loop systems for accountability	[e.g. User feedback, audit logs, presence of oversight protocols]
Linguistic Justice	Language inclusion and cultural sensitivity	• Is language diversity supported? • Are dialects and idioms respected? • Is inclusion more than surface-level translation?	• Multilingual interface options • Recognition of dialects and idiomatic language • Context-aware and culturally sensitive language representation	[e.g. Language support in platform, missed local nuances, translation quality issues]

Note: This table is structured to support AI system audits, institutional inclusivity reviews, or policy evaluations in education and employability. The 'Institutional Notes' column can be used for documentation, reflection, or tracking improvement actions.

To capture this interplay, we might recall the ancient image of the loom. In weaving, strength and coherence are achieved not by a single thread, but by the interlacing of warp and weft—each dependent on the other, yet distinct in purpose. If accountability is the warp, giving structure and direction, then inclusivity is the weft, weaving diversity, recognition, and belonging through the fabric. The ERL Justice framework, together with its evaluative table, functions as the loom itself: the structure that enables institutions to weave systems of governance that are both resilient and responsive. Without this balance, the fabric frays—producing systems that appear orderly on the surface but lack integrity when subjected to strain. Through this metaphor, the table is revealed not as a checklist, but as an instrument for weaving ethical coherence into the design and deployment of AI systems. By guiding institutions to examine whose knowledge is legitimised, how relationships are mediated, and which languages are given voice, it helps cultivate AI ecosystems capable of supporting dignity, equity, and trust. It is in this weaving together of principles and practices that AI governance can move from aspiration to embodiment, ensuring that systems serve not only efficiency but also justice and human flourishing (Table 2.3).

The table extends the ERL Justice framework by transforming its three core dimensions—epistemic, relational, and linguistic justice—into a practical evaluative tool for institutional use. Its structure is designed to guide reflection by pairing focus areas with key questions and indicative markers of inclusive practice, while also providing space for institutions to record their own analysis and outline potential follow-up actions. In this way, the table encourages a shift from abstract ethical commitments to concrete practices that are responsive to context. The dimension of epistemic justice invites institutions to scrutinise whose knowledge is valued within AI systems and whether alternative epistemologies are represented. This raises important questions about the extent to which diverse traditions of thought are incorporated into educational technologies and how far training datasets reflect cultural plurality. Practical indicators, such as the inclusion of non-dominant knowledge systems and support for multiple models of learning, encourage institutions to evaluate whether AI systems reproduce narrow definitions of knowledge or enable genuinely plural educational paradigms. Relational justice highlights the ways in which AI systems mediate interactions between individuals and institutions. It calls for transparency in automated decisions, the provision of clear appeal mechanisms, and the integration of human oversight. These requirements point to accountability as a lived practice rather than a technical ideal, where users are provided with intelligible explanations and meaningful avenues to contest outcomes. Indicators such as audit trails, user feedback systems, and oversight protocols illustrate how relational justice can be operationalised, ensuring that power is not obscured behind opaque systems but distributed in ways that respect agency and dignity.

Linguistic justice directs attention to language diversity and cultural sensitivity, recognising that communication is both a technical and a cultural act. AI systems that fail to accommodate dialects, idioms, and multilingual realities risk reproducing exclusion under the guise of accessibility. Indicators such as multilingual interfaces, recognition of dialectical variation, and context-aware language representation demonstrate what inclusive practice might look like in this domain. Here, the concern is not only whether users can access content, but whether their linguistic and cultural identities are acknowledged and respected in the design of digital environments. The table, therefore, functions as more than an evaluative checklist; it is a tool for cultivating reflexivity within institutions, prompting critical engagement with the values embedded in AI systems. By addressing knowledge, relationships, and language in an integrated manner, it challenges institutions to recognise the structural exclusions that may otherwise remain hidden. In supporting this kind of reflection, the table helps build AI ecosystems that are not only functional but also attentive to justice, equity, and the diverse realities of those they are meant to serve.

A central challenge in AI governance is determining whether institutional systems are genuinely inclusive or merely performing ethical compliance. The ERL Justice Framework Evaluation Table addresses this by offering a structured means through which institutions can interrogate their practices and embed justice into the architecture of AI systems. Its purpose is not to affirm what already exists, but to create space for critical reflection and redesign. In this respect, the framework resonates with Collier's (2020) conception of design justice, which emphasises moving from designing for communities to designing with them. By requiring institutions to ask whose knowledge, relationships, and language practices are recognised, and whether these are substantively integrated into system design, the table highlights how inclusivity can become an operational principle rather than a peripheral aspiration. The approach also aligns with Burgstahler's (2022) model of Universal Design in Higher Education, which insists that accessibility must be embedded from the outset rather than treated as an afterthought. The ERL table gives this principle practical force, offering indicators that guide institutions in anticipating exclusion and addressing it proactively. Its relational and linguistic dimensions, in particular, foreground the importance of transparency, contestability, and cultural-linguistic inclusion—issues often neglected in conventional system audits.

The framework's significance is further reinforced by international policy developments. Recent initiatives, such as the World Economic Forum's Blueprint for Equity and Inclusion in AI (2022) and the European Commission's Ethical Guidelines on the Use of AI and Data in Teaching and Learning (2022), have emphasised the need for inclusive and participatory practices across the AI lifecycle. Yet while these documents provide a valuable normative orientation, they leave institutions with the challenge of operationalising inclusion. The ERL evaluation table responds to this gap by offering a methodology that structures analysis, documents findings, and supports iterative improvement. Its design also contributes to building institutional memory by recording not only outcomes but also identified gaps and proposed actions. By inviting input from a wide range of stakeholders, including those outside technical domains, the framework positions justice as a shared responsibility across the institution.

The practical turn represented by the ERL table connects closely with work in participatory and culturally responsive design. Nicholson et al. (2022), for example, illustrate how co-design in education can reposition teachers as co-creators of technology, ensuring that classroom realities directly shape digital systems. Ahrweiler et al. (2024) extend this approach through the AI FORA methodology, which creates safe, inclusive spaces for cross-cultural engagement. While developed for public services, its emphasis on sustained dialogue and reflexive practice holds clear relevance for education and employability contexts. Both examples demonstrate that inclusion requires more than consultation: it depends on practices of collaboration that continuously test and refine the legitimacy of technological systems. Viewed in this light, the ERL Justice Framework Evaluation Table offers more than an evaluative tool. It functions as a diagnostic of the epistemological, relational, and linguistic assumptions embedded in AI governance, while also providing a scaffold for institutional learning and adaptation. Its value lies in creating processes through which inclusion becomes a lived and reflexive commitment, ensuring that justice is woven into the everyday practices of AI development and use.

A growing body of scholarship and practice signals a shift in how inclusivity within AI should be understood: not as a fixed outcome but as a continuing orientation within institutional life. This perspective emphasises relational inclusion, which demands collaboration with communities rather than design conducted on their behalf. Such an approach reframes inclusivity as a practice of shared responsibility, attentive to the dynamics of power, knowledge, and voice. Within this ethos, the ERL Justice Framework Evaluation

Table offers more than an evaluative instrument. It can act as a catalyst for dialogue, creating a structured setting in which different institutional actors—educators, students, community partners, and equity leads—can interrogate assumptions, identify limitations, and consider refinements. Its accessibility to non-specialists ensures that questions of justice are not restricted to technical experts but are opened to those who directly experience the effects of AI systems. In participatory environments, this becomes a practical means of embedding inclusivity throughout the design process, supporting iterative, responsive, and reflexive governance.

This orientation aligns with broader movements towards participatory responsibility in educational technology. Recent contributions, including those of Culatta, Reich, and Ito, and the U.S. Department of Education, underline the importance of recognising educators, learners, and communities as active agents in shaping both the development and deployment of AI. Culatta's practitioner-focused work, while not grounded in peer-reviewed research, highlights concrete risks—such as the exclusionary effects of misidentification in facial recognition or the privileging of dominant language norms in reading algorithms. By situating these examples within classroom practice, his intervention illustrates how the seemingly neutral operation of AI can reproduce structural inequities. Though pragmatic in style, it contributes to a wider discourse that encourages educators to engage critically with digital tools, fostering a culture of vigilance in which technologies are continually examined for their ethical and epistemic implications. Through this lens, the ERL framework acquires renewed significance as both diagnostic and generative: a scaffold that enables institutions to move beyond technical compliance and towards an ethos of participatory, situated, and justice-oriented design. By embedding such reflexivity, inclusivity is no longer treated as an aspiration at the margins of innovation, but as a constitutive principle of how educational technologies are imagined, governed, and practised.

Reich and Ito's (2017) contribution provides a systemic perspective that treats inclusion not as a compensatory adjustment but as a foundational principle of design. Their concept of 'equity by design' rejects retrofit solutions and instead advances generative co-creation with learners who have historically been marginalised. By questioning the notion of an 'average student' and foregrounding variability and contextual diversity, their framework anticipates current critiques of cultural uniformity within GenAI systems. Its enduring relevance lies in its insistence that design processes must be participatory, pluralistic, and responsive to those they affect. This orientation resonates with more recent policy developments, including the 2023 U.S. Department of Education report, which seeks to institutionalise inclusive and participatory approaches. The report's emphasis on structured engagement, universal design, and iterative prototyping marks a shift from efficiency-driven narratives towards equity as a cultivated design value. While its inclusion of stakeholder consultations and listening sessions models a form of deliberative governance, the absence of rigorous evaluative mechanisms risks leaving these commitments unfulfilled.

At the intersection of learning analytics and inclusive AI, Buckingham Shum, Ferguson, and Martinez-Maldonado extend this discussion through a human-centred design paradigm that privileges interpretability, agency, and contextual relevance. Their approach, grounded in participatory workshops and iterative development, positions educators and learners as active collaborators in shaping analytics tools. In this framing, students are not passive data subjects but co-designers of systems that respond to local pedagogical needs. The insistence on intelligibility and transparency represents a deliberate departure from opaque optimisation models, instead enabling informed learner self-regulation and pedagogical reflection. By challenging reductionist uses of data, their work reinforces the view that inclusivity in AI should be measured not simply by the absence of harm, but by the extent to which systems foster engagement, autonomy, and meaningful participation.

A useful way to draw these insights together is through the metaphor of communal architecture. Just as a well-designed public space requires the contributions of many—architects, builders, planners, and inhabitants—so too do inclusive AI systems demand the input of diverse communities. A square or marketplace that reflects only the vision of its architect may stand tall but remain unwelcoming, whereas one shaped by dialogue with its users becomes a living environment that supports belonging and exchange. In the same way, inclusive AI cannot be constructed by technical expertise alone; it must be built through iterative engagement with those whose lives it will affect. The durability of such systems, like that of enduring civic architecture, rests not only on structural integrity but also on the recognition of shared ownership and collective responsibility.

Ko and Mutale broaden debates on inclusive AI by disrupting conventional hierarchies of technological design. Their model of community-led co-creation illustrates how learners—particularly those in rural and resource-constrained settings—can actively shape the development of AI-enhanced platforms. By shifting focus from adaptation of existing systems to grassroots innovation, their work foregrounds local agency and relational knowledge as central to meaningful inclusion. Although not grounded in extensive empirical evidence, this perspective offers a valuable normative contribution: it reframes inclusion as authorship, where marginalised groups are positioned not merely as recipients of technology but as co-designers of its form and purpose. Zhang et al.'s meta-analysis provides empirical depth to these normative claims. Drawing on 29 studies in special education, they demonstrate that AI tools can deliver moderate positive impacts on learning outcomes when tailored to learner needs and supported by specialist expertise. Crucially, the study reports consistent benefits across disability types and educational settings, suggesting that inclusive design need not compromise effectiveness. Their call for the formal integration of accessibility professionals and special educators into development processes moves beyond rhetorical commitments to inclusivity, underscoring it as both a policy requirement and a pedagogical necessity. The findings thus reveal the risks of excluding disabled learners from design and evaluation, while also establishing evidence for the transformative potential of participatory inclusion.

Complementing these perspectives, Salas-Pilco, Xiao, and Oshima advance a multilevel framework for justice-oriented AI in education, spanning pedagogical, technological, and sociocultural dimensions. Their review highlights the dangers of universalising Western pedagogical models while neglecting linguistic diversity, infrastructural disparity, and cultural specificity. By foregrounding multilingual content, teacher preparation, and culturally responsive tools, they underscore the epistemic stakes of AI design in marginalised contexts. While the analysis would have been strengthened by an intersectional account of how race, gender, disability, and class shape experiences of exclusion, the framework nevertheless affirms a central principle: inclusion must be embedded in the pluralities of lived educational realities, not reduced to statistical measures of fairness.

Gibson's intervention makes an important contribution by interrogating the assumption that AI technologies automatically advance accessibility for disabled learners. His observation that only a small proportion of students felt their needs had been considered in AI development points to a failure that is more than technical oversight: it reflects the absence of representational ethics and institutional attentiveness. By calling for 'born-accessible' systems, Gibson underscores the necessity of designing technologies with accessibility as a structural principle rather than as a supplementary adjustment. This reorientation situates accessibility within an ethic of co-design, demanding the sustained involvement of those most directly affected by AI-driven systems. In this sense, accessibility must be laid into the foundations of technological design, much like the strength of a building rests not on superficial decoration but on the depth and stability of its supporting structures. Retrofitting accessibility after the fact is akin to shoring up weak walls; it may offer temporary support, but it does not resolve the fragility of the structure itself.

This perspective resonates with Seale's characterisation of inclusion as a continuing, negotiated practice rather than a finite task. Both call for institutions to adopt forms of collaborative governance, where learners and educators are positioned not as passive recipients but as co-authors of the technological environments in which they operate. Such an approach reframes accessibility as relational, grounded in co-responsibility and institutional humility, rather than as a technical adjustment to pre-existing systems. The implications for AI governance extend beyond individual design choices. Justice in educational technologies cannot be achieved solely through the inclusion of accessible features; it must also emerge from reconfigured relationships—between institutions and learners, between diverse epistemic traditions, and across cultural and linguistic divides. This demands a shift away from conceiving inclusion as a measurable endpoint towards recognising it as a continuous and participatory practice. Within this reorientation, co-responsibility entails more than consultation: it requires genuine co-production, where learners, educators, and communities help to shape not only the use but also the very form of AI systems. Institutional humility complements this by acknowledging the limits of internal expertise and by creating space for external perspectives to guide revision and innovation. Humility, in this sense, is not passive but generative: it sustains dialogue, opens systems to critique, and permits continual rebalancing in response to diverse needs. Viewed through this lens, Gibson's contribution deepens the ERL justice framework by demonstrating that inclusion cannot be appended to technological systems once built; it must be embedded at the foundations. Just as architects ensure that a structure can bear the weight of what it is designed to hold, so too must institutions ensure that AI systems are able to support the full diversity of those who will live and learn within them. Inclusion, then, is not the endpoint of a technical process but the ground upon which trustworthy and just educational technologies must be constructed.

Temple-Murray's practitioner account, though written in a less formal register, offers a valuable window into how AI is embedded within the everyday life of classrooms. His reflections on the use of generative tools to support English as an Additional Language (EAL) learners and those experiencing academic difficulty highlight how relational attentiveness can guide AI towards inclusive ends. Rather than displacing teaching, the account illustrates a collaborative pedagogy in which human expertise mediates and refines algorithmic capacities. At this micro-level, AI becomes less a system of control and more a tool for extending the teacher's ability to respond to diverse learner needs. This same account also touches indirectly on questions of linguistic justice, illustrating how multilingual generation can scaffold understanding without erasing cultural or linguistic difference. While anecdotal, the insights demonstrate how relational and linguistic considerations, often absent from high-level policy discourse, are enacted in practice through educator discretion and responsiveness. The historical review by Khalil, Slade, and Prinsloo advances this perspective by situating learning analytics within longer debates about equity. Their work challenges the assumption that dashboards and predictive models are neutral instruments, framing them instead as expressions of institutional values and priorities. By questioning the accessibility of data interfaces and the presumption of objectivity, they draw attention to the epistemic stakes of analytics: what is made visible, what is obscured, and who is invited into the interpretive process. Their argument that systems should enable participation rather than simply visualise performance reflects an ethos of relational justice that insists on agency and contestability within data-driven environments.

Seale's earlier scholarship provides a philosophical and methodological grounding for these positions. Her treatment of accessibility as a reflexive, ethical practice resists compliance-driven approaches and reaffirms the necessity of involving disabled learners in evaluative processes. By framing accessibility as an evolving responsibility rather than a standardised output, her work anticipates many of the concerns now central to debates on inclusive AI. She underscores the principle that those historically excluded from technological authorship must be central to its ongoing development and governance. The pragmatic orientation of the Digital Promise research-practice brief builds on these arguments by offering concrete design features—such as scaffolded supports, adaptive translation, and embedded bias detection—that are presented not as optional enhancements but as core requirements of responsible AI. Although not anchored in an explicit theoretical framework, the brief foregrounds the importance of co-design with marginalised learners, situating inclusion within collaborative practice. It also highlights the persistence of what might be termed a practice gap: the disjunction between normative commitments to inclusion and the realities of institutional infrastructures that limit meaningful participation. Too often, participatory design is invoked rhetorically but enacted superficially, resulting in systems that claim equity yet overlook lived experience. Together, these contributions illuminate a broader trajectory in the governance of educational AI—one that shifts the focus from technical adequacy to relational ethics. They suggest that inclusivity is sustained not through isolated interventions but through systemic transformation, underpinned by co-responsibility, institutional humility, and the redistribution of design agency. In this framing, inclusivity is neither a checklist nor an endpoint but an ongoing negotiation of values and practices through which AI can contribute meaningfully to educational equity.

Addressing the practice gap requires more than technical refinement or the procedural inclusion of diverse groups. What is needed is a relational ethic of co-responsibility, in which institutions recognise their interconnected obligations in shaping the systems they design, adopt, and govern. This entails moving beyond episodic consultation towards building enduring capacities for dialogue, mutual accountability, and iterative responsiveness. Within this orientation, the ERL framework helps to clarify how exclusion often manifests: as epistemic disconnection, when local or alternative knowledges are disregarded; as relational breakdown, when affected communities are positioned as recipients rather than co-authors of technological systems; and as linguistic inattention, when dominant norms of communication are embedded without sensitivity to cultural or linguistic diversity. Closing the practice gap, therefore, involves cultivating design cultures that are reflexive, co-constructed, and contextually situated, where institutional humility and shared authorship are not peripheral values but central practices.

Figure 2.17 visualises this orientation by positioning the Relational Ethic of Co-responsibility at the centre of the ERL justice framework. Surrounding this core are the three interlinked dimensions of Epistemic, Relational, and Linguistic Justice, each highlighting a key locus of ethical engagement. These dimensions are, in turn, framed by the outer commitments of Institutional Humility and Accountability, which provide the conditions for sustaining inclusive practices. Taken as a whole, the figure illustrates that inclusivity in AI-mediated education and employability cannot be reduced to isolated technical solutions. Instead, it is a systemic practice: grounded in justice, sustained through accountability, and enabled by the humility of institutions to listen, adapt, and share responsibility with those whom these systems most profoundly affect (Figure 2.17).

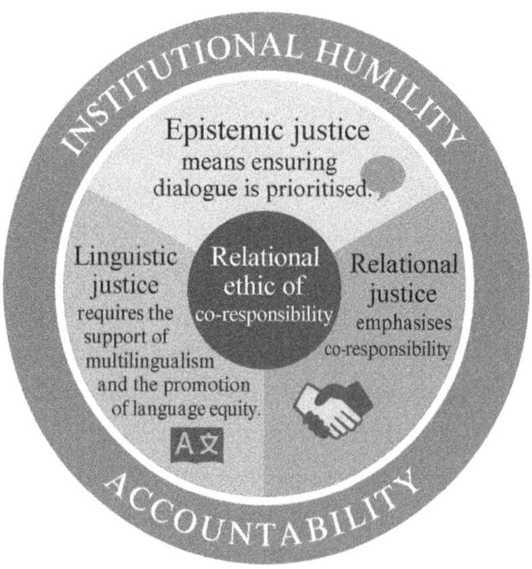

FIGURE 2.17 Framework for justice and co-responsibility.

This figure illustrates the relational ethic of co-responsibility, supported by epistemic, linguistic, and relational justice and grounded in institutional humility and accountability.

BOX 2.17 FRAMEWORK FOR JUSTICE AND CO-RESPONSIBILITY

The figure offers a conceptual representation of the values and design principles necessary for ethically grounded and socially responsive AI in education and employability. It is not merely a visual aid, but a normative statement about how justice, inclusion, and accountability must be operationalised if AI systems are to serve all learners equitably. At the heart of the figure lies the relational ethic of co-responsibility and institutional humility. This central tenet captures the proposition that inclusion is not a matter of procedural compliance or technical enhancement, but a shared ethical practice. Co-responsibility refers to the distributed nature of ethical agency—developers, educators, institutions, and affected communities are all co-authors of the systems they engage with. Institutional humility complements this by inviting a posture of openness: a willingness to acknowledge the limits of institutional knowledge, listen to marginalised perspectives, and revise practices in light of lived experience. Together, these ideas reflect a shift from top-down implementation towards collaborative, reflexive engagement.

Radiating from this centre are the three interconnected dimensions of the ERL Justice Framework: epistemic, relational, and linguistic justice. Each dimension asks a distinct but interrelated question about how AI systems include—or exclude—users based on what they know, how they relate, and how they communicate.

- ***Epistemic justice** focuses on the inclusion of diverse knowledges. The terms 'plural knowledges' and 'dialogue across traditions' signal the imperative to resist the standardisation of knowledge that often accompanies algorithmic systems. This dimension asks whether educational AI acknowledges and values indigenous, community-based, or non-Western forms of knowing—or whether it reproduces a narrow epistemic canon.*
- ***Relational justice** interrogates how AI shapes human interactions. It includes principles such as 'mutual accountability' and 'participatory design', foregrounding the need for transparent systems that support ethical engagement rather than reproduce hierarchical or opaque decision-making. This dimension aligns with critiques of AI-driven surveillance in education, calling instead for systems that are co-designed with users and open to challenge.*
- ***Linguistic justice** addresses the privileging of dominant language norms within AI. Through 'multilingualism' and 'cultural-linguistic nuance', this component highlights how seemingly neutral systems often marginalise speakers of non-standard dialects or those from linguistically diverse backgrounds. It encourages sensitivity not just to translation, but to the embeddedness of language in identity, culture, and epistemology.*

Surrounding these justice domains are the enabling institutional conditions of accountability and institutional humility. These are not passive values but active commitments that must underpin policy, practice, and design. Accountability demands that institutions be answerable not only for outcomes but also for the assumptions, data, and governance structures that shape those outcomes. Institutional humility, appearing now only once and correctly framed, signals the need for continuous learning, openness to critique, and a refusal to treat inclusion as a solved problem. In its totality, the figure illustrates that inclusivity in AI is not a static achievement but an evolving relationship—between people, institutions, and knowledge systems. It makes visible the ethical architecture required to move beyond rhetorical commitments and into the realm of meaningful, context-sensitive transformation. Rather than offering a universal checklist, it provides a reflective space for inquiry, dialogue, and co-creation—anchored in justice, but responsive to difference.

The CoSN district-level report adopts a systems-oriented lens, addressing school leaders and IT decision-makers. While its discussion of the digital divide, data inequity, and access disparities provides a familiar entry point, its treatment of equity often narrows to logistical issues such as broadband access or device distribution. Less attention is given to deeper structural concerns, including curricular marginalisation or the surveillance implications of algorithmic systems. Nonetheless, the report's emphasis on infrastructure and governance as levers for inclusion aligns with the ERL framework's focus on institutional co-responsibility. It underscores the point that meaningful change depends not only on ethical design but also on sustained institutional commitment and the redistribution of resources and attention. In contrast, Gonzalez et al. offer a more conceptually expansive intervention. Their tripartite framework of Accessibility, Identity, and Epistemology links inclusive AI to decolonial thought and Critical Pedagogy. By interrogating assumptions embedded within training data and algorithmic outputs, the authors prompt institutions to reconsider both the scope of inclusion and the conditions under which knowledge is legitimised. Although largely theoretical and without substantial empirical grounding, the article is notable for its intellectual ambition and for advancing epistemic justice as a cornerstone of AI design. It calls for reflexive approaches that acknowledge historical exclusions and seek to reposition technology as a site of plural and just knowledge-making.

Taken in dialogue, these contributions highlight the importance of a relational ethic that connects design choices to institutional cultures and broader power dynamics. Their value lies less in prescribing definitive solutions than in offering diverse entry points into the collective project of cultivating inclusive educational futures. Building on the preceding analysis of accountability in the AI–education–employability nexus, inclusivity is here considered not as a supplementary principle but as an operational dimension of governance. Inclusivity concerns not only who is responsible but also who is recognised, represented, and supported, and on what terms. This framing insists on its integration with justice, participation, and structural responsiveness. It also challenges the prevailing tendency to cast fairness and transparency as primarily technical matters. Through the lens of the ERL Justice Framework, inclusivity emerges as a multidimensional practice: it addresses how knowledge is validated (epistemic justice), how relationships are mediated (relational justice), and how language and expression are accommodated (linguistic justice). These dimensions demand movement beyond procedural inclusion towards an institutional orientation that is reflexive, participatory, and responsive to the asymmetries that AI systems may reproduce or amplify. Finally, the discussion draws attention to the practice gap: the disjunction between ethical aspirations and institutional realities. This gap is less a matter of technical oversight than of structural constraint—limited participatory mechanisms, fragmented policy implementation, and efficiency-driven logics. Addressing it requires embedding inclusivity into the cultures of design, governance, and institutional value systems. In this sense, inclusivity is not achieved through isolated interventions but through systemic reorientation.

The ERL framework provides a means of diagnosing and addressing systemic exclusions, not through prescriptive solutions, but by fostering ethical reflexivity and collaborative scrutiny. Its accompanying Justice Framework Evaluation Table exemplifies this orientation, offering institutions a structured yet flexible tool for assessing inclusion. Unlike conventional audit mechanisms, the table is designed to surface latent assumptions about knowledge, power, and representation, drawing attention to the relational, epistemic, and linguistic dimensions that often remain obscured within technical systems. Empirical studies reinforce the importance of this diagnostic lens. Works such as Buolamwini and Gebru's Gender Shades and Bender et al.'s critique of language models reveal that bias is rarely incidental but systematically embedded in data selection, model training, and development cultures. In educational contexts, such findings carry profound implications: when linguistic practices or cultural identities fall outside dominant norms, students risk being misrepresented, marginalised, or rendered invisible by algorithmic systems.

Within this landscape, participatory design emerges not simply as a methodological preference but as a justice imperative. Research by Buckingham Shum et al., Ko and Mutale, and Zhang et al. illustrates how inclusive processes can re-centre user voices at the outset of design, rather than as afterthoughts. These contributions affirm that technologies are not neutral artefacts but socially situated systems shaped by specific assumptions and relations of power. Consequently, inclusion requires an institutional disposition of humility and co-responsibility: a willingness to listen, adapt, and engage with those most directly affected. Framing AI as both a technical and policy challenge is critical to bridging the persistent gap between normative declarations of fairness and the systemic conditions that reproduce inequality. The ERL framework, together with tools such as the evaluation table and participatory initiatives like AI FORA, does not provide definitive solutions. Instead, it nurtures a mode of engagement rooted in care, accountability, and reflexivity. Inclusion is thus repositioned not as an endpoint, but as a relational and epistemic responsibility to be enacted continuously. This orientation also creates a natural bridge to the next concern: how such principles can be operationalised in practice. The following section on Ethical Employability examines how the commitments articulated within the ERL framework can be integrated into educational and workplace systems, ensuring that accountability and inclusivity extend beyond conceptual debate into tangible practice.

ETHICAL EMPLOYABILITY: INTEGRATING PRINCIPLES INTO PRACTICE

Building on the discussion of relational inclusion and the ERL Justice Framework, this section turns to the ethical foundations of employability within higher education. As institutions increasingly measure their value through graduate outcomes, there is a pressing need to question the assumptions that underpin employability strategies. Too often, employability is framed narrowly as alignment with labour market demands or the cultivation of discrete competencies. Such instrumentalist approaches risk overlooking the structural inequalities that shape learner trajectories and the ethical responsibilities institutions hold towards their students. An alternative framing positions employability not as a transactional mechanism but as a socially embedded and ethically attuned practice. This shift requires recognising the heterogeneity of learners' pathways, many of which are marked by systemic constraints, unequal access to resources, and intersecting forms of exclusion. Employability, in this sense, cannot be reduced to a question of skills acquisition alone, but must be situated within a wider commitment to justice, dignity, and inclusivity. The ethical triad of trust, accountability, and inclusivity provides a critical lens through which employability may be reimagined. When embedded in curriculum design and institutional practice, these values reposition employability as a collective and relational endeavour. This orientation acknowledges students not merely as future workers but as diverse individuals whose lived experiences, aspirations, and challenges demand recognition. It also compels institutions to confront uncomfortable questions about who their graduates are, and whose identities or trajectories remain marginalised within dominant employability discourses. This more expansive understanding of employability does not offer a definitive template. Rather, it calls for higher education institutions (HEIs) to adopt an ongoing stance of ethical reflexivity—one that interrogates existing assumptions, disrupts inequitable norms, and fosters conditions for fair and sustainable transitions beyond higher education.

A second critical question concerns the future horizon: what might employability look like over the next two to three decades? This perspective shifts attention from present arrangements to the uncertainties of an evolving labour landscape shaped by artificial intelligence, climate disruption, global mobility, and the reorganisation of work. Anticipating these dynamics requires higher education to move beyond short-term responsiveness to employer demand and to cultivate dispositions of adaptability, resilience, and civic responsibility. Such an orientation asks institutions not only to prepare students for existing roles but also to equip them to participate in shaping futures that are increasingly indeterminate. A third question follows: is the current model of employability still fit for purpose? Addressing this requires a candid appraisal of frameworks that rely heavily on skills lists, graduate attributes, and narrow employer partnerships. While these mechanisms have value, they risk reducing education to economic output and neglecting the broader ethical and intellectual formation of students. They also tend to privilege certain occupational trajectories while marginalising forms of work—such as care, creativity, or community leadership—that contribute significantly to social cohesion but sit outside dominant success narratives.

Reimagining employability requires curriculum development that is not additive but transformative. This means aligning content, pedagogy, and digital infrastructures with the ethical triad of trust, accountability, and inclusivity. Trust depends on transparent assessment, shared goal-setting, and cultures of openness that foster confidence between students, institutions, and employers. Accountability requires inclusive governance and mechanisms that give genuine weight to student voice, ensuring employability provision is co-constructed rather than imposed. Inclusivity extends into curriculum design, learning environments, and opportunities for practice, recognising diverse identities, aspirations, and ways of knowing. Such a reorientation signals that employability cannot be treated as a fixed endpoint or reduced to market alignment. Instead, it should be understood as a dynamic ethical project that nurtures integrity, creativity, and compassion. In this light, employability is not only about preparing students to participate in the labour market but also about equipping them to interrogate and reshape its logics. Success, therefore, becomes defined less by graduate outcomes alone and more by the fairness and accessibility of the pathways that enable them, as well as their contribution to justice, dignity, and democratic responsibility.

Figure 2.18 situates the triad of trust, accountability, and inclusivity as the conceptual anchor for this rethinking, surrounded by four guiding questions: Who is the contemporary graduate? What might employability look like in the future? Are current models adequate? How should curricula be co-aligned with technology? These questions serve as points of ethical inquiry, prompting higher education to confront its assumptions and responsibilities in a rapidly changing social and technological landscape. This framing positions employability as a relational practice that bridges education, governance, and social responsibility. It prepares graduates not only to adapt to uncertain futures but also to shape them in ways that are inclusive, equitable, and sustainable (Figure 2.18).

Building on the Ethical Employability Framework, the concept of trust—as one pillar of the ethical triad—requires deeper consideration within contemporary employability discourse. Trust is not an abstract aspiration, but a relational practice fostered through transparency, mutual respect, and attentiveness to students' diverse experiences. For HEIs, this entails an ethical responsibility to ensure that employability strategies, whether through curriculum, support systems, or graduate outcome narratives, are not simply responsive to labour market trends but meaningfully aligned with principles of equity, diversity, and inclusion (EDI). Within this framing, EDI is more than representation or compliance; it

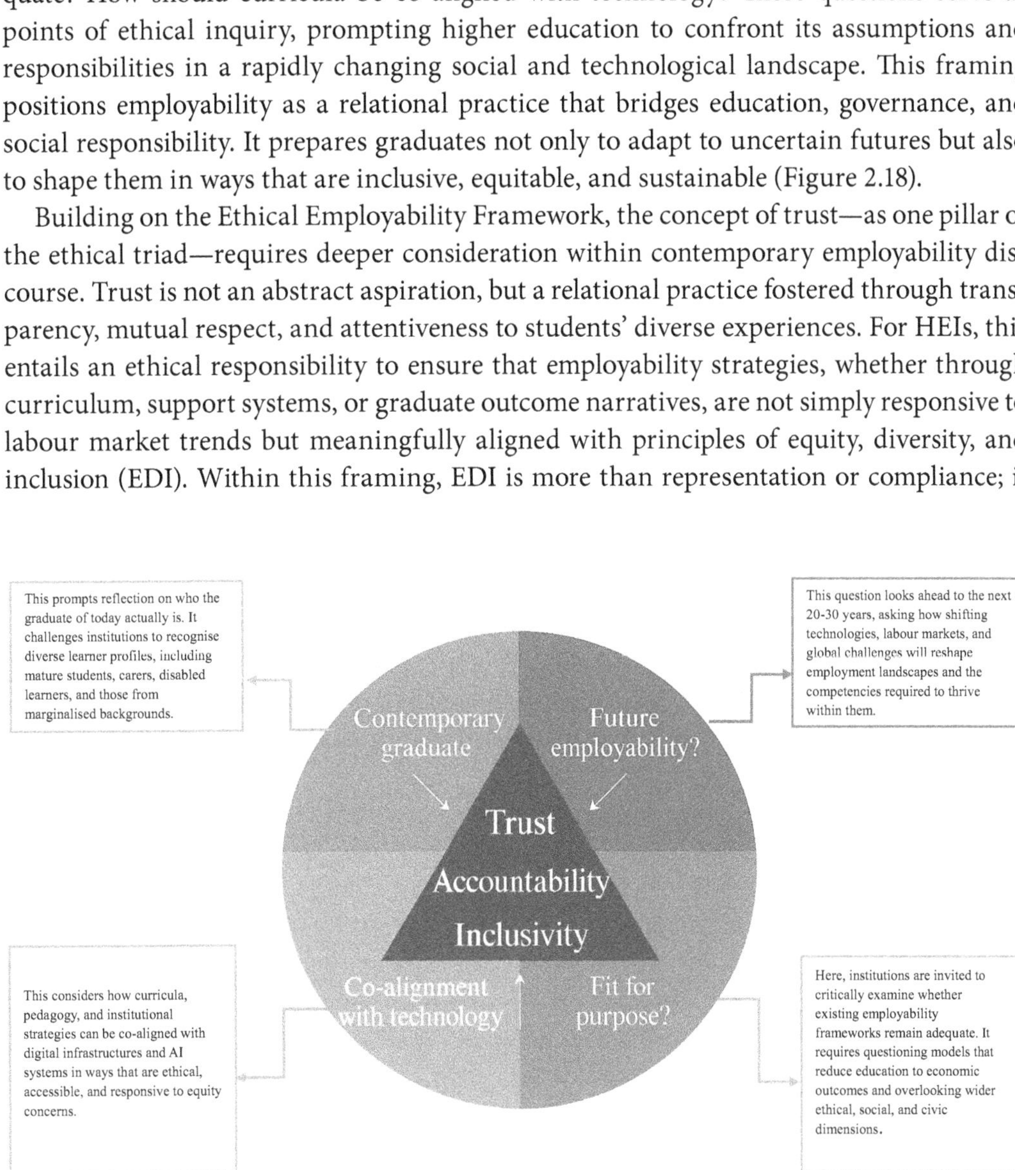

FIGURE 2.18 The ethical triad of employability.

This figure illustrates trust, accountability, and inclusivity as the central principles for reimagining employability. The surrounding questions—about the contemporary graduate, the future of employability, the adequacy of current models, and the co-alignment of education with technology—serve as points of ethical reflection, guiding institutions towards more just and sustainable practices.

BOX 2.18 EXPLANATION NOTE—THE ETHICAL TRIAD OF EMPLOYABILITY

The figure positions trust, accountability, and inclusivity as the central ethical triad for reimagining employability within higher education. These principles function as interdependent commitments that provide both orientation and critique in contexts where employability is often reduced to skills checklists, performance indicators, or narrow labour market alignment.

The surrounding questions—Who is the contemporary graduate? What might employability look like in the future? Are current models fit for purpose? How should education co-align with technology?—represent critical points of reflection rather than discrete technical challenges. They invite institutions to interrogate their assumptions about graduate identity, to anticipate shifting labour markets, to assess the adequacy of existing frameworks, and to consider how emerging technologies reshape both learning and work.

Placing the triad at the centre underscores that employability must be understood as an ethical and relational practice, not merely a functional outcome. Trust requires transparency and integrity in assessment and institutional commitments. Accountability demands governance structures that respond to student voice and address systemic inequalities. Inclusivity calls for curriculum design and learning environments that recognise diverse identities, aspirations, and ways of knowing.

Critically, the figure signals that employability is not a terminal endpoint but an ongoing responsibility: a practice that bridges education and work while contributing to more just, sustainable, and plural futures. By situating employability in this way, higher education is encouraged to move beyond market responsiveness and towards its wider democratic and social mission.

provides a critical lens through which employability must be conceived. Recognising students' heterogeneous social, cultural, and economic backgrounds means acknowledging historical exclusions, addressing barriers to progression, and supporting differentiated pathways into meaningful work.

The integration of AI further sharpens these responsibilities. While AI can personalise learning, track labour market trends, and widen access to career tools, it also risks amplifying inequalities if deployed uncritically. Trust in this context requires openness about both the potential and the limitations of AI-driven metrics. Institutions strengthen trust when they move beyond reductive outcomes such as salary benchmarks or league tables and instead situate employability within wider structural conditions—geographic disparities, sectoral insecurities, and uneven access to networks and social capital. A culture of trust also depends on positioning students as active participants in shaping their futures rather than passive recipients of institutional guidance. Their aspirations, constraints, and lived experiences must be treated as integral to the design of employability provision. This requires moving beyond rhetorical commitments to EDI and embedding equity through concrete practices of curriculum design, delivery, and evaluation. In this light, the ethical responsibility of higher education is twofold: to align employability strategies with the realities of a technologically mediated and socially stratified labour market, and to communicate and implement those strategies in ways that build relational trust. Trust thus becomes not only a principle but also a practice of institutional care—anchored in listening, responsiveness, and adaptability. Such a reconceptualisation positions trust as both foundational to ethical employability and central to the wider project of socially just higher education in an age increasingly shaped by AI.

Building on the preceding discussion, accountability within employability must be reinterpreted as a relational and forward-looking ethic, centred on care, inclusion, and the cultivation of human potential. Rather than reducing accountability to a retrospective measure of graduate employment rates or institutional standing in league tables, a broader conception asks more fundamental questions: whose futures are supported, whose aspirations are validated, and by what means opportunities are created or constrained. Such a perspective moves accountability beyond compliance with external benchmarks, repositioning it as a responsibility to expand the range of meaningful pathways that HEIs make available to their students. This reorientation places emphasis on the recognition of individual differences. In a context increasingly influenced by standardisation and algorithmic evaluation, accountability must also entail creating spaces for students to develop their distinct identities, interests, and capabilities. Pedagogical approaches that combine technical competence with critical, creative, and transformative learning are essential here. In this light, technology becomes more than an instrument of delivery; it can act as a facilitator of personalised trajectories, provided it is employed with intentionality and ethical sensitivity.

Framed in this way, HEIs are not simply custodians of labour market readiness, but enablers of social mobility and intellectual agency. Their accountability is not only upward—to regulators, employers, or funders—but reflexive, grounded in the promises made to students, the relationships sustained with communities, and the values embodied through their practices. This involves moving from mechanistic outputs to values-based strategies, underpinned by transparency, responsiveness, and critical self-examination. In operational terms, this requires evaluative measures that extend beyond employment statistics to encompass student voice, lived experience, and progression within diverse contexts. It also demands equipping students with the capacity to interrogate and shape their own futures through ethical reasoning, critical thinking, and socio-technical literacy. In this sense, accountability functions both as a mirror—enabling institutions to reflect on their commitments—and as a compass, guiding them towards inclusive and ethically grounded approaches to employability in an AI-mediated world.

Following the consideration of trust and accountability, inclusivity emerges as the third strand of ethical employability. Too often framed narrowly in terms of widening access or meeting demographic targets, inclusivity requires a more profound reorientation—one that recognises its ethical and epistemic dimensions. It should not be reduced to a corrective gesture or statistical compliance but understood as a continuous institutional commitment to dismantling barriers and enabling diverse learner trajectories to flourish. In this sense, inclusivity entails a duty of care that extends beyond economic opportunity to encompass cultural, epistemic, and symbolic dimensions of exclusion. Prevailing narratives of employability frequently privilege particular forms of knowledge, behaviour, and expression that do not reflect the lived realities of many students, particularly those from historically marginalised groups. An inclusive approach demands that these assumptions be interrogated and reimagined so that employability frameworks do not simply reinforce dominant norms but contribute to reshaping them. This reimagining requires institutions to recognise the validity of multiple ways of knowing and to embed epistemic justice into their practices. Students should be able to participate fully in employability initiatives without being required to suppress or assimilate aspects of their identities. HEIs thus become not only sites of preparation for work but also agents of social change, fostering conditions in which employability contributes to equity rather than entrenching immobility. Barriers are not only structural or economic but also discursive: they lie in whose voices are valued, whose aspirations are legitimised, and whose futures are rendered imaginable.

Operationally, inclusivity must be integrated across institutional systems and practices—curriculum design, career services, community partnerships, and staff development. It must be iterative and reflexive, open to critique from those whose experiences challenge the dominant graduate outcome narrative. Only in this way can employability move beyond a transactional pathway into work and become a vehicle for social mobility, dignity, and human flourishing. Framed within this triad of trust, accountability, and inclusivity, ethical employability should be seen not as a static ideal but as a dynamic practice. These principles gain strength in their interplay, guiding how institutions conceive, deliver, and evaluate their responsibilities. Capability theory, as advanced by Sen and Nussbaum, provides a powerful lens for this reorientation. It shifts the focus from narrow metrics of job acquisition towards the substantive freedoms individuals have to live lives they value. For employability, this means moving away from an emphasis on skills input and employment output towards supporting students in accessing sustainable and self-authored careers aligned with their aspirations and circumstances. Under this framing, inclusivity becomes more than representation; it becomes a question of justice and imagination. Institutions must ask whether their employability strategies enable diverse pathways and respect plural definitions of success, or whether they remain tethered to dominant ideals of productivity and professionalism. In doing so, employability is repositioned not merely as labour market preparation but as a catalyst for equitable opportunity and human development.

The capabilities approach invites a reorientation of employability from narrow measures of institutional performance to a more expansive concern with the real freedoms students are able to exercise. It highlights that employability cannot be fully understood through skills training or graduate outcomes alone, but must take account of the broader social and structural conditions that enable or constrain individuals in pursuing futures they value. Health, housing, care responsibilities, discrimination, and social networks all play decisive roles in shaping opportunity, yet these factors are often marginalised within conventional employability frameworks. A capability-oriented perspective thus reframes evaluation: not by what services or interventions are offered, but by what capacities and possibilities are genuinely expanded. This orientation acquires particular urgency in the age of AI, where predictive analytics and algorithmic tools increasingly mediate pathways into work. While such technologies promise efficiencies, they also risk embedding partial or exclusionary assumptions if based on limited historical data. The challenge for institutions is therefore not only technical—ensuring system reliability or compliance—but ethical, requiring reflection on how these systems construct value, whose experiences they recognise, and whose futures they foreclose. The adoption of AI in career guidance and skills development raises questions that extend beyond managerial concerns: whether employability is being defined in ways that affirm plural identities and aspirations, or constrained within narrow and homogenising models of success.

Re-examining existing policy frameworks is vital in this respect. Graduate outcome measures, often treated as fixed benchmarks of institutional achievement, rarely interrogate whose trajectories are celebrated, whose challenges are made visible, and whose potential remains unacknowledged. Where policy rests on reductive definitions of employability, it risks reinforcing rather than reducing inequality. An ethical conception of employability, therefore, demands more than compliance with external metrics; it requires a commitment to fostering student flourishing as a matter of institutional purpose. Trust is nurtured when students are recognised as partners in shaping their futures; accountability acquires substance when institutions acknowledge their responsibilities to learners themselves, not only to funders or employers; and inclusivity is realised when systemic and symbolic barriers to participation are actively dismantled. Placed within this broader horizon, skills acquisition and labour market engagement remain important, but are understood as part of a wider project of human development and justice. The capabilities framework offers both critique and direction: it challenges the adequacy of dominant models while providing principles for transformation. Employability, in this light, becomes a participatory and reflexive practice, grounded in dignity and oriented towards the co-creation of meaningful futures in a changing world.

Extending the discussion of ethical employability, informed by trust, accountability, inclusivity, and the capabilities approach, the emerging field of anticipatory ethics offers an important further dimension. This perspective encourages HEIs to move beyond reactive alignment with existing labour markets and to engage with the ethical responsibilities of preparing students for uncertain and evolving futures. In contexts shaped by technological disruption, political volatility, and ecological instability, employability cannot be confined to present conditions without risking narrowness of vision. Anticipatory ethics, therefore, reimagines employability as a future-facing practice: one that equips learners with the adaptive, reflective, and justice-oriented capacities necessary to engage with work in ways that remain ethically grounded amid change. Such an orientation has clear implications for curriculum design, institutional partnerships, and the evaluation of graduate outcomes. Rather than emphasising conformity to established occupational pathways, HEIs are invited to nurture resilience and ethical imagination—through initiatives such as foresight exercises, scenario planning, and critical reflection on the social implications of automation and AI. Partnerships with employers may also be reconfigured to prioritise organisations that demonstrate commitments to fair labour practices, environmental responsibility, and social innovation, thereby embedding values-led decision-making into employability strategies.

Alongside this anticipatory lens, the concept of distributed professionalism reframes employability as a shared institutional endeavour. It resists the tendency to locate responsibility for student futures solely within careers services and instead highlights the collective role of lecturers, tutors, professional staff, alumni, and external partners as co-constructors of professional identity. For such distributed practice to be meaningful, institutions must invest in integrative infrastructures that sustain collaboration, dialogue, and shared responsibility—for example, cross-departmental planning teams, student co-design mechanisms, and partnerships that bridge academic and professional domains. This approach resonates with the capabilities perspective, insofar as it situates employability within the broader relational and cultural fabric of university life. Students' aspirations are not shaped in isolated interventions but in the cumulative, everyday experiences of learning communities. Distributed professionalism, therefore, requires institutions to reflect critically on whose voices shape employability discourse and who is empowered to influence students' trajectories. By embedding employability in this collaborative and anticipatory way, HEIs can foster approaches that are both ethically robust and socially responsive, aligning student development with a wider vision of justice, care, and responsibility.

In reframing ethical employability, it is vital that students are positioned not as passive beneficiaries of institutional provision but as active partners in shaping both their educational experiences and future opportunities. Participation must move beyond occasional consultation to become a sustained practice of co-leadership, where learners are meaningfully involved in curriculum design, the strategic development of career services, and the ethical review of employability support. Equally, universities must reconsider how they work with employers. Rather than preparing graduates solely to adapt to prevailing workplace demands, institutions can take a more active role in fostering inclusive and responsible employment practices. This may be achieved by building partnerships with organisations that prioritise equity, progression, and civic and environmental responsibility, thereby extending the influence of higher education into the wider labour market and supporting a more just and sustainable employment landscape.

The conceptual framework illustrated in Figure 2.18 provides a way of bringing these ideas into focus. At its centre are three interdependent values—trust, accountability, and inclusivity—which together form the ethical foundations of employability. These are not abstract aspirations but practical commitments that should shape how institutions design, deliver, and evaluate their employability strategies. The surrounding prompts—questions about graduate identity, future trajectories, institutional purpose, and technological alignment—serve as guiding points of reflection. They invite HEIs to move beyond compliance with narrow benchmarks and instead ask: What kinds of graduates are being prepared? What futures are being enabled? Are existing systems sufficient to address the diversity and complexity of contemporary contexts? And importantly, how are these practices evolving alongside the transformative influence of technology?

Read as a whole, the framework portrays employability not as a linear path from study to work but as an ongoing, circular process—one that requires reflexivity, ethical attentiveness, and responsiveness to change. It highlights the need for institutions to ensure that the integration of digital and AI tools is aligned with their ethical responsibilities so that innovation strengthens rather than undermines agency and inclusion. The challenge, therefore, is not simply to respond to technological and social shifts but to shape them in ways that open futures grounded in justice, dignity, and shared responsibility.

What this framework ultimately offers is not a prescriptive formula but a reflective instrument through which HEIs can continually interrogate whether their employability strategies remain ethically grounded amid shifting technological, social, and economic conditions. It signals a call for ongoing dialogue about institutional purpose, responsibility, and direction, recognising that ethical employability is not a fixed endpoint but a dynamic practice that requires renewal and responsiveness. Centring on the values of trust, accountability, and inclusivity, the framework positions employability as a collective ethical undertaking—one that depends on institutional reflexivity as well as meaningful collaboration with students, educators, employers, and wider communities.

This orientation may be usefully illustrated through the allegory of the navigational astrolabe. Historically, sailors turned to the astrolabe not for a predetermined route but for guidance in navigating the uncertainties of open seas and distant horizons. The instrument provided points of orientation—the stars, the horizon, the movements of the heavens—while leaving space for human interpretation, judgement, and adaptability. In much the same way, the ethical employability framework does not prescribe a single pathway for institutions; instead, it offers bearings through which strategies can be aligned with enduring ethical commitments, while remaining responsive to changing contexts. Just as the astrolabe demanded skill, attentiveness, and humility in its use, so too does this framework require reflexivity, dialogue, and care to ensure that employability is enacted in ways that remain just, inclusive, and forward-looking.

On this basis, the discussion now moves from conceptual foundations to practical application. The subsequent section translates these ethical commitments into operational principles across four strategic domains: policy development, staff training and professional development, student support and feedback systems, and labour market alignment. In each of these, the triadic values of trust, accountability, and inclusivity will be mobilised not only as guiding ideals but also as principles embedded in the everyday structures, relationships, and practices of HEIs.

GUIDING PRINCIPLE: ETHICAL EMPLOYABILITY IN POLICY DEVELOPMENT

Following the elaboration of ethical employability as a triadic framework comprising trust, accountability, and inclusivity, this section develops a guiding principle for embedding these values into institutional policy development. HEIs increasingly face pressures to demonstrate the effectiveness of their employability strategies in terms of graduate outcomes, salary returns, and labour market alignment. Yet, without an ethical foundation, such metrics risk becoming disconnected from the complex lived realities of students and the responsibilities of universities as public institutions. This principle calls for a critical reorientation: policy development should not merely respond to the demands of the labour market but must be driven by the moral imperative to serve learners equitably, prepare them for meaningful futures, and contribute to the social good. Ethical employability in policy development demands more than reactive regulation or the inclusion of generic diversity statements. It requires a transformation in how employability is understood, operationalised, and governed. The conceptual framework developed earlier in this chapter—visualising the intersection of values, structures, and relationships—serves as a practical map for this transformation. By attending to this ethical intersection, HEIs can craft policies that are transparent in their intentions, accountable in their outcomes, and inclusive in their reach.

GUIDING PRINCIPLE 1

HEIs must ensure that all employability-related policies are conceived, implemented, and reviewed through an ethical lens grounded in trust, accountability, and inclusivity. Policy development must reflect a participatory, reflexive, and justice-oriented ethos that supports equitable graduate outcomes and empowers all learners to navigate meaningful and sustainable futures. Policies should not only align with labour market demands but must also recognise the structural barriers that shape student trajectories and foster capabilities that go beyond narrow economic metrics.

Rationale

Policy frameworks are the scaffolding upon which institutional practice is built. In the context of employability, policies determine how resources are allocated, how programmes are evaluated, and how success is defined. However, too often, employability policies are constructed in reaction to external performance indicators—such as the Teaching Excellence Framework (TEF), Graduate Outcomes Survey, or league table rankings—rather than internal ethical commitments. This results in policies that are shaped by institutional competition rather than student development and by economic imperatives rather than social justice.

To counter this, policy development must be reoriented towards ethical employability. This requires rethinking employability not as a linear process of preparing students for the labour market, but as a dynamic relationship between values, structures, and lived experience. The ethical triad—trust, accountability, and inclusivity—offers a coherent and actionable foundation for such a reimagining. It encourages policies that not only respond to economic realities but also cultivate institutional cultures of care, openness, and fairness.

Drawing on Amartya Sen and Martha Nussbaum's capabilities approach, this principle reframes policy as a tool to enhance students' real freedoms—their capabilities to do and to be what they value. This shifts the institutional emphasis from producing employable graduates to enabling meaningful futures. Within this view, employability is not merely a metric of job readiness but a holistic outcome shaped by access to support, recognition of difference, and responsiveness to aspiration.

Operationalising the Principle

Embedding ethical employability into policy development requires tangible structures and actions that institutionalise values. The following mechanisms offer practical routes for implementation:

- **Policy Transparency and Accessibility**: Employability policies must be publicly available, written in clear and inclusive language, and subject to regular review. Transparency cultivates trust among students and staff, fostering a sense of institutional integrity.

- **Participatory Policy Design**: Policies should be developed collaboratively, incorporating the voices of students, alumni, academic and professional services staff, and community stakeholders. This affirms students as epistemic agents and encourages shared responsibility for institutional direction.
- **Equity Impact Assessments**: Every employability-related policy should undergo a formal equity review to examine its differential impact across race, class, gender, disability, and migration status. Such assessments help ensure that policies promote, rather than hinder, inclusive outcomes.
- **Capabilities-Aligned Metrics**: Traditional employment outcomes should be complemented by metrics that assess student agency, access to opportunity, and long-term well-being. This encourages policies that reflect the diversity of student aspirations and lived realities.
- **Ethical Employer Engagement Protocols**: Institutions must create policy frameworks that govern employer partnerships, ensuring alignment with values such as fair pay, ethical leadership, and inclusive hiring. Partnerships should be assessed not only on opportunity volume but also on alignment with justice-centred aims.

Illustrative Example

A university developing a new employability strategy implements a co-creation process involving student unions, alumni from underrepresented backgrounds, careers staff, and academic leads. The resulting policy includes commitments to:

- Ensure all internships are paid and accessible.
- Include community-based employers in recruitment events.
- Introduce 'career narrative' assessments that allow students to define success on their own terms.
- Publish annual disaggregated employability data and action plans.
- Establish a student policy review panel with voting rights.

This case illustrates that ethical employability policy is not simply about inclusion—it is about institutional transformation.

Strategic Alignment

To ensure coherence across the institution, the principle of ethical employability in policy development should be embedded within wider strategic documents such as Access and Participation Plans, Institutional Learning and Teaching Strategies, and Equality, Diversity and Inclusion (EDI) frameworks. This alignment ensures that employability is not an isolated concern but part of the broader mission of higher education.

Furthermore, this principle complements anticipatory ethics by encouraging HEIs to consider the long-term societal impact of their graduates. Policies shaped by ethical employability should ask not only what the labour market needs now but also what kind of future world of work universities are contributing to. This demands critical engagement with trends in automation, AI, environmental sustainability, and social equity.

Impact

If implemented effectively, this principle delivers wide-ranging and multidimensional benefits:

- **For Students**: Greater trust in institutional processes; enhanced ownership of career pathways; improved access to relevant, just, and meaningful employment.
- **For Institutions**: Stronger public credibility; improved alignment between policy and practice; enriched student experience and satisfaction.
- **For Society**: Graduates equipped to contribute to inclusive economies, democratic cultures, and ethical workplaces; a higher education sector aligned with the public good.

Challenges and Mitigation Strategies

Like any transformative initiative, this principle faces potential barriers. These include resistance to change, policy fatigue, resource constraints, and misalignment with national accountability frameworks. However, these challenges can be addressed through:

- **Change Management Plans**: Providing structured support and training for staff, along with clear timelines and leadership buy-in.
- **Capacity Building**: Allocating resources for equity audits, data collection, and staff development to sustain ethical policy work.
- **Collaborative Sector Learning**: Sharing good practices across institutions through networks such as Advance HE, AGCAS, and civic university partnerships.

By positioning ethical employability as a strategic necessity rather than an optional extra, institutions can ensure long-term sustainability and integrity.

Future Outlook

Policy development in higher education must evolve to meet the demands of a rapidly changing world. Ethical employability provides a robust foundation for that evolution. As AI, automation, and global crises reshape the conditions of work and learning, institutions must rise to the ethical challenge of preparing students not only to survive but also to thrive, question, and transform. This principle affirms that ethical governance—rooted in trust, accountability, and inclusivity—is the cornerstone of that effort.

GUIDING PRINCIPLE 2

Staff training and professional development must be systematically aligned with the ethical framework of employability, ensuring that every member of academic and professional services staff is equipped to foster inclusive, accountable, and trust-building practices.

Institutions must invest in creating development opportunities that not only promote technical competencies but also cultivate ethical awareness, critical reflexivity, and collaborative responsibility across all levels of employability support.

Rationale

While policy forms the structural backbone of ethical employability, staff enact these principles in practice. The everyday decisions made by academic tutors, career advisors, placement coordinators, administrative personnel, and senior leaders shape the student experience and influence whether institutional values are realised or diluted. Staff are therefore not neutral agents but active participants in the ethical life of the institution.

However, in many HEIs, staff training related to employability remains narrowly focused on compliance, metrics, or career-specific information. This approach risks undermining the relational, situated, and value-laden nature of employability. If ethical employability is to be achieved, training must go beyond procedures and introduce staff to broader questions of justice, inclusion, and care in student development.

A foundational component of this principle is the idea of distributed professionalism, which challenges the notion that employability belongs solely to career services. Instead, all staff contribute to the shaping of students' professional identities and postgraduate trajectories. This concept requires a cultural shift wherein teaching staff understand employability not as an external imposition but as intrinsic to curriculum and student engagement. Similarly, support staff must be recognised and supported as critical facilitators of student confidence, access, and growth.

Implementation Strategies

To realise this principle in practice, institutions should:

- **Develop ethically grounded induction programmes** for new staff that introduce the institution's employability strategy as an ethical framework, not simply a compliance agenda.
- **Embed ethics and inclusivity into CPD** sessions, exploring topics such as algorithmic bias in career analytics, ethical uses of learning analytics, or supporting marginalised students' aspirations.
- **Foster interdisciplinary collaboration** between career services, academic departments, student support, and equality, diversity, and inclusion (EDI) teams, creating shared ownership of employability outcomes.
- **Create reflective practice spaces**, such as staff learning communities or ethics roundtables, that enable personnel to critically examine their assumptions about employability, success, and student potential.
- **Provide resources on inclusive pedagogies and employment-related inequalities**, ensuring that staff are informed about how social class, race, gender, disability, and immigration status affect student access to meaningful employment.

Impact

Ethical staff development ensures that employability does not become a mechanised or depersonalised process. Instead, it positions employability as a shared ethical project across the institution—grounded in attentiveness to student experience and contextual awareness. Staff who are ethically literate and reflexively engaged are better able to offer nuanced, supportive, and empowering guidance to students.

Moreover, this principle enhances institutional coherence. When all parts of the university system are aligned in their ethical commitments, students receive clearer, more consistent messages about their value, possibilities, and the institution's commitment to their futures. Staff also benefit from a deeper sense of professional purpose and agency, particularly when they are trusted to make ethical judgements rather than follow inflexible rules.

Theoretical Foundation

The principle draws on relational ethics, which foregrounds the interdependence of actors within educational spaces. It challenges hierarchical models of expertise and encourages educators to engage in mutual learning with their students. This perspective is further supported by Critical Pedagogy (Freire, 1970), which asserts that education should be an emancipatory process grounded in dialogue, reflexivity, and co-construction of knowledge.

Additionally, the application of capabilities theory (Sen and Nussbaum) in staff training enables institutions to move from deficit-based narratives—where students must be 'fixed' to meet employer demands—to strength-based models that focus on enabling real freedoms and flourishing. Staff trained within this paradigm are more likely to encourage diverse conceptions of success, resist homogenising pressures from the labour market, and advocate for equitable institutional change.

Illustrative Example

A university implementing this principle might revise its annual staff development week to include sessions on:

- 'Embedding Ethical Employability in Teaching and Assessment'
- 'Decolonising Graduate Outcomes: Challenges and Approaches'
- 'AI in Careers Advice: Risks and Opportunities'
- 'Working with Neurodiverse Students: Strategies for Inclusive Transitions'

Staff feedback and student co-facilitation would form part of a continuous improvement loop, aligning with the institution's ethical values. Ethical employability cannot be implemented without the committed, knowledgeable, and ethically engaged participation of staff. Principle 2 affirms that staff training is not a peripheral exercise but a strategic priority. It must be relationally grounded, intellectually robust, and structurally supported. When done well, it ensures that the institution not only prepares students for the workplace but also reimagines the workplace itself—as a space for fairness, inclusivity, and social transformation.

GUIDING PRINCIPLE 3

Student support and feedback systems must be designed as ethically grounded, student-centred structures that uphold the core values of trust, accountability, and inclusivity. These systems are not auxiliary functions but fundamental mechanisms through which students experience and assess the integrity of institutional commitments to ethical employability. This includes the integration of AI; such systems must be reflexive, participatory, and transparently aligned with the lived realities and diverse aspirations of learners.

Rationale

The efficacy and legitimacy of any employability strategy depend not only on the robustness of its formal design but also on how it is experienced and interpreted by students. Trust is eroded when students perceive institutional systems as opaque, unresponsive, or indifferent to their concerns. Conversely, trust is cultivated when support structures genuinely listen, adapt, and act upon student input in a transparent and relationally respectful manner.

AI-driven technologies offer the potential to enhance these systems by enabling more personalised, predictive, and responsive support. Learning analytics, sentiment analysis, and intelligent career advising platforms, for example, can provide timely interventions and tailored resources. However, these tools also raise serious ethical concerns. Without careful design and oversight, they risk reproducing bias, eroding agency, and reinforcing exclusion—particularly for students from marginalised backgrounds. As such, the deployment of AI must be embedded within broader structures of ethical governance, participatory feedback, and critical reflection.

Implementation Strategies

1. **Trust-Enhancing Feedback Mechanisms**: HEIs must establish formalised feedback systems that are continuous, multi-modal, and action-oriented. Feedback should not be confined to periodic satisfaction surveys but should include:
   a. Focus groups co-led by students.
   b. Anonymous digital input systems embedded in student portals.
   c. Real-time feedback tools integrated into AI-driven platforms (e.g. chatbots with escalation functions). These systems must close the loop—clearly demonstrating how student input informs change—to build institutional trustworthiness.
2. **Inclusive Student Support Services**: Employability-related support must move beyond one-size-fits-all models. Services should:
   a. Acknowledge differential access to opportunity based on race, disability, socio-economic background, gender identity, and migration status.
   b. Offer bespoke support models for mature students, carers, first-generation learners, and others whose employability journeys may diverge from conventional assumptions.

   c. Be co-designed with students and community representatives to ensure cultural and epistemic relevance.

3. **AI-Assisted but Human-Guided Support Systems**: AI can augment support provision, but it must not displace human judgement. Ethical practice demands:
   a. Transparent use of algorithms in career profiling or risk prediction.
   b. The right of students to understand and contest AI-generated recommendations.
   c. The maintenance of meaningful human contact in all AI-supported services, such as hybrid advising models combining chatbots with tutor follow-ups.
4. **Participatory Feedback Governance**: Institutions must move beyond consultative models and embed co-governance. This includes:
   a. Student representation on employability and digital ethics boards.
   b. Paid student researchers conducting peer-led audits of support systems.
   c. Joint publication of annual reports on employability outcomes and inclusion benchmarks, co-authored with students.
5. **Embedding Feedback in AI Development**: When AI tools are introduced for employability, their design, deployment, and revision must be informed by:
   a. Participatory testing involving diverse student groups.
   b. Ongoing monitoring of disparate impact (e.g. whether students with disabilities receive less accurate job matches).
   c. Feedback prompts integrated into AI interfaces (e.g. 'Was this recommendation helpful for your goals?').
6. **Theoretical Foundation**: This principle is grounded in the concept of relational accountability, which repositions students not as data points but as epistemic contributors to institutional learning. Drawing from Critical Pedagogy (Freire, 1970) and participatory design (Schön, 1983; DiSalvo, 2009), the principle advocates for systems that are co-constructed and dynamically adapted in dialogue with students. From a technological perspective, this aligns with the idea of explainable AI and value-sensitive design (Friedman and Nissenbaum, 1996), which argues that AI systems must reflect the moral and social values of their users.

Illustrative Example

A UK-based institution introduces an AI-powered platform called Pathfinder, which tracks students' engagement with employability services and recommends career resources. Recognising ethical risks, the university:

- Conducts a six-month co-design process with students from diverse backgrounds, including those with visual impairments and neurodivergence.

- Publishes a plain-English ethics charter on how data is used, and who has access.
- Trains personal tutors to interpret Pathfinder's data in conjunction with students, emphasising dialogue over compliance.
- Implements a student-led review panel that meets quarterly to assess the tool's performance and propose changes.

Early evaluations suggest that Pathfinder increased participation in career mentoring by 38%, particularly among first-generation students, with qualitative feedback indicating enhanced confidence and clarity about career options. Importantly, this was achieved not through the AI alone, but through the integration of participatory governance, inclusive design, and human-centred interpretation.

Impact

When feedback and support systems reflect ethical priorities, their impact extends far beyond individual service delivery. They:

- Enhance institutional responsiveness by embedding student voice in strategic direction.
- Improve graduate outcomes not only quantitatively but also qualitatively, aligning employment trajectories with students' aspirations and values.
- Strengthen trust, particularly among communities historically underserved by HEIs.
- Encourage ongoing institutional learning, where feedback is not a performance measure but a source of collective wisdom.

Furthermore, in the context of AI, ethically governed feedback mechanisms serve as a safeguard against automation drift—ensuring that technology serves educational justice rather than undermines it.

Challenges and Responses

While the ambition of this principle is clear, implementation is not without difficulty. Common challenges include:

- **Data overload and analysis fatigue**, especially when feedback is gathered but not meaningfully used. → *Response: Prioritise depth over breadth and communicate clearly how feedback leads to change.*
- **Scepticism about AI's fairness** among both staff and students. → *Response: Build digital literacy and maintain transparent governance over AI systems.*
- **Resource constraints in personalising support**. → *Response: Leverage AI to triage and flag needs, but never at the expense of human care and ethical review.*

Principle 3 affirms that student support and feedback systems are not administrative accessories but moral infrastructures. They are the channels through which the institution demonstrates care, listens to lived experience, and upholds ethical consistency in its employability offer. In an age where AI shapes decision-making and institutional efficiencies are valorised, this principle insists that students' voices, needs, and rights remain central. It positions feedback not as a retrospective tool, but as an anticipatory mechanism—informing how institutions grow, correct, and transform. And it places support not in the domain of service alone, but in the ethos of care that defines ethical employability in its fullest sense.

GUIDING PRINCIPLE 4

Employability cannot be ethically advanced unless it is continuously evaluated, critiqued, and improved in light of changing student needs, labour market conditions, and Institutional Responsibilities. M&E processes must be designed not simply to track outcomes, but to interrogate the values that underpin them. Institutions must embed a culture of critical review that links graduate outcomes to ethical purpose, educational justice, and inclusive opportunity.

Rationale

While many HEIs collect data on graduate outcomes, such practices often reflect compliance-driven models aimed at rankings or regulatory requirements. These approaches risk reducing employability to a set of transactional outputs—employment status, salary levels, or job relevance—without exploring deeper questions of meaning, equity, or student well-being.

An ethical employability framework demands a shift: from outcome reporting to outcome responsibility. This includes asking not just what jobs graduates secure, but how, why, and for whom. Are employability tools working for students from marginalised backgrounds? Are AI systems reinforcing systemic bias? Are universities equipping students to thrive in a complex and uncertain future of work—or merely survive?

Without robust, ethically informed monitoring, institutions may inadvertently entrench inequalities under the guise of neutrality. Embedding structured and participatory M&E processes allows institutions to identify blind spots, correct misalignments, and ensure that interventions reflect the lived experiences of students—not the assumptions of the institution or employers.

Implementation Strategies

To realise this principle in practice, institutions should:

- Design M&E frameworks that centre student voice and lived experience, including mechanisms such as student-led employability audits, reflective interviews, and participatory focus groups.
- Regularly collect and disaggregate graduate outcome data by race, gender, disability, socio-economic background, and discipline to detect patterns of exclusion or systemic advantage.

- Evaluate the use of AI-driven employability tools not only for functional accuracy but also for fairness, accessibility, and alignment with students' long-term aspirations.
- Create employability ethics dashboards that transparently report on progress against equity and inclusion benchmarks, going beyond headline employment rates.
- Embed feedback loops into course and curriculum design so that insights from employability monitoring inform pedagogical innovation and institutional reform.

Impact

Ethically embedded monitoring processes transform employability from a compliance mechanism into a space of ongoing institutional reflection and growth. Students benefit from a more equitable and responsive system, and staff gain deeper insight into how their work contributes to student development. Over time, this principle fosters institutional cultures that value critical learning, transparency, and justice. It also enables a more expansive imagination of success: one not confined to salary or sector, but defined by the degree to which students can pursue meaningful, sustainable, and self-directed futures.

Theoretical Foundation

This principle draws on approaches to participatory evaluation and critical institutional reflexivity, which argue that those most affected by educational practices—students—must be involved in shaping and assessing them. It is also informed by justice-oriented thinking in education, which insists that outcomes cannot be divorced from questions of access, recognition, and redistribution. By linking evaluation practices with ethical inquiry, institutions move beyond surface metrics towards deeper questions: Whose futures are being prioritised? Whose voices are shaping our definitions of employability? And how can systems be continually reimagined to reflect the diversity of student aspirations?

Illustrative Example

A university committed to this principle might establish a cross-departmental Employability Ethics and Impact Committee involving students, alumni, academic staff, and employer partners. The committee could:

- Review anonymised graduate outcomes and student feedback quarterly.
- Publish an annual 'Ethical Employability Report' aligning institutional actions with social justice commitments and the UN Sustainable Development Goals.
- Audit all AI-enabled career services for bias, usability, and equity of access.
- Develop a 'Career Justice Dashboard' that visualises how institutional interventions support different student groups and where gaps remain.

Through such actions, employability becomes not just a measurable endpoint, but a moral and educational process—subject to collective scrutiny, ethical intention, and continual reinvention.

GUIDING PRINCIPLE 5

External partnerships are essential to a meaningful and future-facing employability agenda. However, for such partnerships to be ethical, they must be grounded in principles of mutual respect, shared responsibility, and long-term value creation for students and society. This principle affirms that employer engagement should not serve market imperatives alone but must reflect the university's broader mission of equity, integrity, and inclusive social transformation.

Rationale

Universities frequently collaborate with employers, industry bodies, and professional networks to co-create curricula, facilitate placements, and develop skills pathways. Yet such relationships often privilege high-profile corporate actors and reinforce dominant norms of 'employability' shaped by market competitiveness, not student diversity or public good.

An ethical employability framework requires a more critical and inclusive approach to partnership. Who counts as an employer partner? Are universities engaging with social enterprises, local businesses, or grassroots organisations that reflect the communities their students come from? Are partnerships structured to prioritise student agency, well-being, and rights—particularly for those undertaking unpaid or precarious work placements?

This principle recognises that partnerships carry institutional risk and responsibility. Where power imbalances exist—between universities and employers, or between students and workplace supervisors—institutions must act as guardians of fairness, dignity, and educational value. Effective partnerships should benefit all parties, but especially students, who must not be treated as passive recipients of employer expectations but as co-participants in shaping ethical futures of work.

Implementation Strategies

To realise this principle in practice, institutions should:

- Develop ethical partnership charters that outline expectations for inclusion, fair treatment, and educational relevance in all employer collaborations.
- Establish a diverse portfolio of employer partners, including SMEs, third-sector organisations, and underrepresented industry sectors, to reflect the plurality of student aspirations.
- Co-create work-based learning experiences with employers that are remunerated, developmentally appropriate, and designed with student feedback and well-being in mind.
- Build cross-institutional networks—linking academic departments, employability teams, EDI offices, and external partners—to ensure alignment between partnership goals and the university's ethical mission.
- Conduct regular reviews and audits of placement experiences and employer collaborations, including anonymised student evaluations that inform future engagement criteria.

Impact

By embedding ethics into external partnerships, institutions move beyond transactional employer relations towards relational and mission-driven engagement. Students benefit from a richer, more inclusive range of opportunities, while employers gain insights into the next generation of socially conscious graduates. Crucially, this principle ensures that employability does not become synonymous with conformity to dominant economic structures, but rather fosters critical engagement, sectoral innovation, and equitable pathways to meaningful work.

Theoretical Foundation

This principle is informed by critical engagement theories and co-production models in higher education, which position students as active collaborators in knowledge creation and institutional development. It also draws on labour ethics and educational justice, which caution against exploitative practices in work-based learning and advocate for structural protections for students navigating the transition into professional environments. Additionally, the concept of 'critical public pedagogy' supports a view of external partnerships as sites of mutual learning—where universities, employers, and communities collectively shape the future of work in ways that are ethical, inclusive, and socially valuable.

Illustrative Example

A university applying this principle might revise its partnership policy to include:

- A formal Employer Code of Ethics, co-designed with students and staff, requiring fair pay, inclusive supervision, and a commitment to developmental outcomes.
- A rotating Student–Employer Advisory Group, ensuring that placement design, recruitment practices, and assessment criteria are co-governed and reflect diverse perspectives.
- Strategic collaborations with social justice-oriented employers—such as disability inclusion networks, refugee entrepreneurship hubs, or climate-focused start-ups—to widen the narrative of who counts as a valuable partner.
- A public Employability Partnership Impact Report, evaluating not only the number of placements or employer prestige but also learning quality, social relevance, and ethical alignment.

Through these measures, universities can create a more reflective and just employability ecosystem—one that supports students in becoming not only job-ready but also ethically grounded contributors to the world they enter.

GUIDING PRINCIPLE 6

Embedding employability into the curriculum should not reduce higher education to vocational training, nor should it treat career preparation as an add-on. Instead, ethical employability must be integrated into the very structure, content, and pedagogy of academic programmes—foregrounding values of inclusion, sustainability, purpose, and justice in how students are taught to engage with their disciplines and their futures.

Rationale

In many institutions, employability is addressed through bolt-on modules, careers weeks, or optional workshops—often disconnected from the learning students undertake in their degree programmes. This fragmentation reflects a narrow vision of employability as instrumental skill acquisition, disconnected from disciplinary knowledge, civic values, or student identity.

An ethical approach to employability begins with the curriculum. It asks: How do course materials and assessment methods shape students' sense of agency and possibility? Are we teaching students to ask critical questions about the world of work, or merely to navigate it? Are we equipping students to imagine futures beyond dominant economic paradigms?

This principle affirms that all educators have a role to play in shaping employability—not by inserting employer content into their lectures, but by cultivating the capacities, reflexivity, and ethical orientations that empower students to contribute meaningfully and equitably to society.

Implementation Strategies

To realise this principle in practice, institutions should:

- Audit programmes for implicit and explicit employability content, identifying where knowledge, skills, and values development are (or are not) meaningfully embedded.
- Integrate ethical and social dimensions of employment—such as inequality, automation, climate justice, and digital ethics—into subject teaching across disciplines.
- Co-design assessments that simulate real-world challenges while encouraging critical reflection, interdisciplinary thinking, and purpose-driven learning.
- Provide curriculum development resources and workshops to support academic staff in aligning disciplinary learning with employability in a values-based framework.
- Foster student–staff curriculum partnerships to co-create inclusive learning pathways that reflect diverse aspirations and definitions of success.

Impact

When ethical employability is integrated into curriculum design, students experience their degrees as relevant not just to getting a job, but to living with purpose. They begin to see their studies as directly connected to their future roles in shaping a just, sustainable, and inclusive society. This approach also shifts institutional cultures. Employability becomes a shared pedagogical responsibility rather than an outsourced service, strengthening coherence between academic programmes, careers provision, and institutional mission.

Theoretical Foundation

This principle draws on Critical Pedagogy, which situates education as a tool for liberation and social transformation. It also builds on the capabilities approach (Sen, Nussbaum), which focuses on expanding real freedoms for individuals to choose the lives they value. By bringing these traditions into curriculum design, universities support a richer, more human-centred model of employability—one that values reflection over replication, imagination over imitation, and transformation over compliance.

Illustrative Example

A university operationalising this principle might:

- Embed discipline-specific ethical dilemmas into core modules, encouraging students to connect their subject knowledge to real-world employability contexts.
- Partner with employers and civic organisations to co-develop project-based assessments that centre on sustainability, justice, or public interest goals.
- Introduce a 'Future Pathways Portfolio' across all degree programmes, in which students reflect on their growth, values, and aspirations across the course of their studies.
- Provide interdisciplinary electives that explore themes such as 'Work and the Common Good', 'AI and Labour Futures', or 'Global Citizenship in Practice'.

By making employability a lived and meaningful thread throughout the curriculum, students graduate not only with degrees but also with a deeper understanding of who they are, what matters to them, and how they want to shape the world.

GUIDING PRINCIPLE 7

Ethical employability must prioritise the well-being, dignity, and flourishing of students—not as secondary concerns, but as foundational commitments. This principle affirms that employability cannot be ethical if it sacrifices mental health, marginalises identity, or reduces learners to economic outputs. Institutions must recognise the emotional and existential dimensions of students' transitions into work and embed care, respect, and inclusivity into every stage of employability provision.

Rationale

The pressure to become 'employable' can produce intense anxiety, particularly for students from marginalised backgrounds who face structural barriers and exclusionary norms in the labour market. Career services that focus on productivity, networking, or self-branding may unintentionally deepen feelings of inadequacy, comparison, or alienation.

An ethical approach to employability requires institutions to treat students not as commodities or human capital, but as whole persons with complex identities, needs, and aspirations. This includes supporting students in navigating uncertainty, validating diverse life choices (including non-linear career paths), and actively addressing the ways race, gender, disability, migration status, and mental health shape employability experiences.

Universities have a duty to protect student dignity—especially as AI tools, surveillance systems, and competitive metrics become more prevalent. Dignity means students feel seen, heard, and valued regardless of their outcomes; it means being supported with empathy rather than judged by narrow standards of 'success'.

Implementation Strategies

To realise this principle in practice, institutions should:

- Integrate mental health and well-being supports into all employability programmes, including referrals, mindfulness practices, and compassionate communication training for staff.
- Avoid framing employability as individual responsibility alone; instead, promote narratives of collective care, systemic analysis, and institutional support.
- Develop trauma-informed and culturally responsive approaches to careers advice, ensuring students feel safe, affirmed, and understood.
- Offer opt-in reflective tools (journals, workshops, mentoring circles) that help students explore career values, identity, and personal meaning—not just outcomes.
- Include well-being impact assessments for new employability technologies or policies, with students involved in ethical oversight.

Impact

Embedding student well-being into employability practice ensures that higher education serves not only to prepare students for labour markets but also to honour their humanity. It promotes confidence, resilience, and authenticity in professional development. This approach also improves long-term outcomes. Students who feel supported, respected, and empowered are more likely to engage meaningfully with employability services, to pursue sustainable opportunities, and to contribute positively to workplaces and society.

Theoretical Foundation

This principle draws on care ethics, which emphasise attentiveness, responsibility, and relational support in professional and educational settings. It also builds on dignity-centred education frameworks, which view learners not as means to economic ends but as ends in themselves. The integration of critical mental health studies challenges institutions to move beyond individualised resilience narratives and address the structural conditions—precarity, racism, debt—that shape student well-being in the context of employability.

Illustrative Example

A university committed to this principle might:

- Embed a Student Dignity Charter into its employability strategy, affirming every learner's right to respect, inclusion, and psychological safety.

- Co-create well-being-informed employability workshops with counselling teams and student networks, addressing impostor syndrome, burnout, and values-based career planning.
- Audit job platforms and AI career tools for language and logic that may induce anxiety or reinforce deficit thinking (e.g. automated rankings, competitive scoring).
- Develop a 'Wellbeing in Work Transitions' curriculum strand, focusing on rest, boundary-setting, and ethical negotiation of workplace culture.

By treating well-being as a central pillar—not an afterthought—institutions create conditions in which employability becomes not only possible but also sustainable and just.

GUIDING PRINCIPLE 8

As universities increasingly adopt data-driven and AI-powered tools to support employability—such as predictive analytics, career path algorithms, and skills dashboards—there is an urgent ethical imperative to ensure that such technologies respect student rights, avoid harm, and reinforce institutional trust. Data governance must be proactive, participatory, and principled.

Rationale

Employability systems often rely on large volumes of student data: attendance records, assessment outcomes, module choices, digital behaviour, and demographic profiles. While such data can offer insight into student development and career pathways, it can also entrench bias, reinforce inequity, or violate privacy if left unexamined.

The adoption of AI introduces further risks. Unexplainable recommendations, black-box systems, and opaque algorithms may shape students' futures without their informed understanding or consent. Furthermore, AI systems often reproduce the very inequalities they are meant to overcome—exacerbating barriers for students from marginalised groups.

An ethical employability framework requires that institutions not only comply with legal data protections (e.g. GDPR) but also move beyond compliance to create a culture of trust, transparency, and digital dignity.

Implementation Strategies

To realise this principle in practice, institutions should:

- Develop and publicly share ethical guidelines for the use of data and AI in employability tools, co-authored with students, legal experts, and digital ethicists.
- Ensure algorithmic explainability—students must be able to understand how career suggestions, risk scores, or job-matching tools generate recommendations.
- Provide opt-out mechanisms and meaningful consent for participation in predictive or AI-driven systems.

- Conduct regular bias audits and fairness assessments of AI tools, disaggregating impact by race, gender, disability, and socio-economic background.
- Create data literacy programmes so students can critically interpret digital tools and advocate for their own interests.

Impact

By embedding transparent and fair data governance into employability practices, universities help ensure that technological advancement does not undermine ethical purpose. Students benefit from clearer guidance, stronger protections, and a deeper sense of control over how their data shapes their futures. This also strengthens institutional legitimacy. A university that is open about how it uses data and AI in employability—inviting scrutiny, feedback, and challenge—demonstrates its commitment to justice, integrity, and democratic governance.

Theoretical Foundation

This principle draws on digital ethics, including frameworks like the EU's Ethics Guidelines for Trustworthy AI and the UNESCO Recommendation on the Ethics of Artificial Intelligence. These emphasise principles of transparency, accountability, and non-discrimination. It also reflects theories of data justice, which insist that data practices must not only be efficient or accurate but also fair, participatory, and situated in a social context.

Illustrative Example

A university implementing this principle might:

- Publish a 'Transparent Tech in Employability' report detailing the functioning, partners, and safeguards behind every AI tool in use.
- Establish a Student Data Ethics Council, empowered to review proposed technologies and provide ongoing input into their use.
- Partner with AI researchers to conduct explainability workshops, helping students interpret their personalised job matches or skills scores.
- Integrate data ethics modules into employability courses, enabling students to reflect on how data is used in recruitment, performance evaluation, and workplace surveillance.

This principle ensures that the path to future employment is guided by not only innovation but also fairness, clarity, and respect.

In summary, this framework of eight guiding principles articulates a reimagined approach to employability—one that is deeply ethical, relational, and attuned to the complex realities of students' lives. Rather than treating employability as a peripheral outcome or compliance task, the principles position it as a shared Institutional Responsibility rooted in values of dignity, justice, and care. Each principle affirms that employability must not only prepare students for work but also support them in imagining and shaping more inclusive and sustainable futures. When thoughtfully embedded across curriculum, partnerships, technologies, and governance structures, employability becomes a space through which higher education can live out its ethical commitments. This is not a fixed blueprint but an invitation to continual reflection. As labour markets shift and student populations evolve, so too must our practices. Ethical employability, at its core, requires humility, responsiveness, and a willingness to learn alongside those we seek to support. Building on this foundation, the next section turns to challenges and future directions. It offers a reflective account of the tensions, uncertainties, and structural constraints that continue to shape the landscape of employability in higher education. At the same time, it considers emerging opportunities for rethinking practice and policy in ways that remain ethically grounded, relationally attuned, and open to transformation.

ETHICAL AI AND THE FUTURE OF EMPLOYABILITY: CHALLENGES, RISKS, AND POLICY PATHWAYS

Building on the earlier discussion, it is important to turn to the challenges, risks, and policy trajectories shaping the integration of AI into higher education and employability. While AI—particularly LLMs—is frequently framed as transformative for institutional practice and the cultivation of future skills, its adoption is far from straightforward. The embedding of AI into educational systems is not a neutral act of technological substitution, but a process that raises profound questions about justice, autonomy, and the credibility of knowledge. Institutions under pressure to demonstrate relevance in a volatile social and economic landscape must also ensure that equity and inclusivity remain central to their strategies. These considerations cannot be treated as supplementary; they are fundamental to the legitimacy of AI in higher education. One significant challenge lies in the scalability of ethical practice. Pilot projects often show encouraging potential, yet their expansion across whole institutions or sectors can expose systemic disparities. Differences in digital infrastructure, organisational readiness, and governance maturity mean that not all institutions are equally equipped to adopt AI responsibly. The result is a landscape marked by uneven uptake, where well-resourced universities move quickly while others struggle to establish even basic safeguards. This divergence risks deepening existing inequalities rather than ameliorating them.

In this context, policy assumes a central role. Rather than responding belatedly to technological change, policy must be treated as a constitutive element of AI integration, shaping how systems are conceived, deployed, and evaluated. Forward-looking approaches should not only anticipate potential harms but also create inclusive governance processes that engage diverse stakeholders, including students, in meaningful deliberation. This orientation shifts the focus from compliance to co-creation, embedding ethical reflection within institutional decision-making. The notion of algorithmic stewardship is particularly valuable here. It frames AI governance not as a one-off act of regulation but as a continuing responsibility—one that requires institutions to design, maintain, and review systems across their lifespan. Stewardship emphasises responsiveness, adaptability, and ethical vigilance, recognising that AI operates within evolving technological, legal, and cultural environments. For higher education, this means that AI-driven practices such as admissions, learning analytics, and career guidance must remain transparent and open to scrutiny. Crucially, stewardship helps safeguard students—especially those from marginalised backgrounds—by ensuring that algorithmic systems are accountable, explainable, and responsive to contestation.

Algorithmic stewardship extends and deepens the ethical orientation established in the earlier framework of trust, accountability, and inclusivity. Where that triad provides the values through which employability and education should be reimagined, stewardship offers the structural means of carrying those commitments into practice. Trust is advanced when institutions practise reflexivity, questioning the purposes and implications of AI rather than assuming optimisation to be inherently beneficial. Accountability is reinforced through participatory governance, where advisory groups, ethics committees, and student consultations ensure that responsibility is shared and decisions are transparent. Inclusivity is realised when capacity-building equips diverse communities—staff, students, and partners alike—to engage critically with AI, embedding justice and voice into both design and implementation. Figure 2.19 situates stewardship as the platform connecting ethical foundations with AI innovation. Governance and policy, capacity building, and inclusive practice are depicted as the interdependent supports that hold this structure in place, ensuring that human-centred AI remains balanced between technological advancement and moral responsibility. At the centre, the aspiration is not simply efficiency or competitiveness, but responsive, human-centred AI that affirms dignity and widens opportunity.

This vision can be imagined through the allegory of a suspension bridge. Ethical foundations and AI innovation form the anchoring pillars, while governance, capacity, and inclusivity act as the cables that bear weight and absorb pressure. Algorithmic stewardship itself functions as the platform across which institutions, learners, and communities travel. Yet, like any bridge, this structure must be continually adjusted to withstand shifting conditions—emerging technologies, evolving social expectations, and persistent inequalities across the higher education sector. Some institutions, especially those with limited resources, may find the task as challenging as building in strong winds with few tools. Yet it is in these circumstances that resilient, context-sensitive, and often most imaginative designs are forged. What matters most is not the uniformity of design but the spirit of adaptive craftsmanship. Each institution must interpret and apply stewardship in relation to its student body, pedagogical ethos, and local realities. Collaboration across institutions can further strengthen these efforts, enabling collective responsibility and shared innovation. In this way, stewardship ensures that the triadic values of trust, accountability, and inclusivity are not left abstract but embedded in the daily governance of AI. Ultimately, the bridges we build in higher education must do more than span the technological divide. They must carry forward the diversity, agency, and dignity of all who cross them. If stewardship is embraced as a living practice—anchored in care, humility, and justice—then employability strategies will not only prepare graduates for uncertain futures but also shape those futures in ways that remain ethically coherent, socially responsible, and humanly meaningful (Figure 2.19).

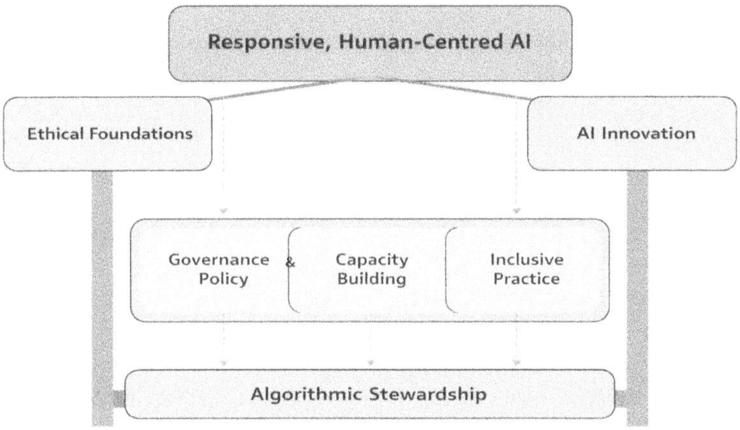

FIGURE 2.19 Balancing ethical AI and employability in higher education: a stewardship framework.

This conceptual figure illustrates the integration of ethical principles and innovation in the use of AI within higher education. Represented as a suspension bridge, it emphasises the importance of Algorithmic Stewardship in balancing Ethical Foundations and AI Innovation. Key pillars of implementation—Governance & Policy, Capacity Building, and Inclusive Practice—are supported by a responsive, human-centred approach to AI that upholds trust, accountability, and equity across the student experience.

BOX 2.19 EXPLANATION NOTE—BALANCING ETHICAL AI AND EMPLOYABILITY IN HIGHER EDUCATION: A STEWARDSHIP FRAMEWORK

The figure presents a conceptual architecture for Responsive, Human-Centred AI, grounded in the balance between Ethical Foundations and AI Innovation. These two pillars act as the structural supports of the framework, signifying the dual imperative of ensuring moral responsibility while driving technological advancement.

At the core of this framework lies Algorithmic Stewardship, which functions as the foundational layer. This emphasises the need for systematic oversight of algorithmic processes, ensuring that AI systems remain accountable, transparent, and aligned with societal values. Stewardship in this context is not merely technical but extends to governance, ethics, and continuous monitoring to mitigate risks such as bias, opacity, or harmful unintended consequences.

Above this base sit three operational domains—Governance & Policy, Capacity Building, and Inclusive Practice. Together, these domains articulate the means by which ethical aspirations and technological developments are operationalised.

- *Governance & Policy underscores the institutional and regulatory frameworks required to direct AI innovation responsibly. This includes the design of legal safeguards, ethical guidelines, and institutional accountability structures that can anticipate and respond to emerging risks.*
- *Capacity Building highlights the necessity of equipping stakeholders—policymakers, educators, developers, and end users—with the skills, knowledge, and critical literacy needed to engage meaningfully with AI. It situates education and professional development as essential prerequisites for equitable adoption.*

- *Inclusive Practice points to the social dimension, ensuring that AI design, deployment, and evaluation incorporate diverse perspectives and avoid reproducing systemic inequalities. Inclusivity here is both a normative commitment and a practical requirement for legitimacy and trustworthiness.*

Together, these operational components connect the Ethical Foundations with AI Innovation, illustrating that technological progress must be guided by ethical reasoning, while ethical aspirations must remain responsive to evolving technological realities. The overarching element—Responsive, Human-Centred AI—symbolises the synthesis of these components, representing an AI ecosystem designed not around efficiency or profit alone, but around the enhancement of human well-being, dignity, and agency.

Critically, the framework highlights the importance of interdependence: ethical foundations without innovation risk stagnation, while innovation without ethics risks harm. Similarly, stewardship without inclusive practice risks becoming technocratic, and capacity building without policy coherence risks fragmentation. Thus, the figure can be interpreted as a systemic model that foregrounds the necessity of integration, balance, and reflexivity in AI governance.

Flowing from earlier reflections on algorithmic stewardship and the bridge metaphor, an additional dimension requiring sustained attention is the challenge of generative misinformation. Widely accessible tools such as ChatGPT and other LLMs have introduced new epistemic risks, particularly when outputs are insufficiently grounded in verifiable evidence or lack transparent provenance (Srivastava, 2025) Within higher education, where accuracy, rigour, and trust underpin both teaching and credentialing, the unchecked circulation of such content is especially problematic. The concern is not only one of factual accuracy but also of maintaining epistemic integrity in contexts where digital competence and critical engagement with machine-generated information are increasingly tied to employability. If misinformation infiltrates feedback systems, assessments, or certification processes, the credibility of both student outcomes and institutional reputation can be compromised. In this respect, algorithmic stewardship becomes more than a guiding principle: it represents a practical framework for sustaining quality and trust while integrating AI into teaching, assessment, and curriculum design. The challenge is less about data abundance than about the ways in which data are curated, models are trained, and outputs are interpreted within pedagogical practice. Such concerns reaffirm the indispensable role of human judgement, ethical scrutiny, and reflective engagement. Importantly, these risks need not be seen solely as obstacles. They may also serve as catalysts for professional development, cross-disciplinary collaboration, and more deliberate forms of institutional learning. By involving educators in the oversight and shaping of AI applications, universities can mitigate risks while also enhancing their capacity to prepare students for an AI-augmented world.

A parallel challenge relates to the growing reliance on surveillance technologies within higher education. Systems such as plagiarism detection software, predictive analytics, and behavioural monitoring are often introduced under the banner of efficiency and student success. et, as research shows, technologies in education can inadvertently erode students' autonomy and privacy, producing an atmosphere of scrutiny rather than support (Mutimukwe, Twizeyimana & Viberg, 2021). This tension is particularly pronounced in employability-focused contexts, where trust, psychological safety, and the cultivation of self-directed learning are vital to long-term success. At the same time, it would be overly simplistic to frame all monitoring practices as inherently negative. When deployed transparently and underpinned by ethical principles, such tools can generate insights into learning behaviours and enable more responsive, personalised educational pathways. Here again, the significance of algorithmic stewardship becomes apparent. By embedding stewardship into governance and policy design, institutions are better placed to balance the benefits of technological innovation with the rights and well-being of their communities. Anticipatory safeguards—rooted in ethical governance rather than reactive intervention—can both mitigate technical and moral concerns and reinforce cultures of accountability, care, and informed trust. Properly implemented, such frameworks allow universities to integrate AI in ways that are not only efficient but also ethically resilient, supporting the development of digitally literate graduates equipped for the complexities of an AI-shaped future.

Beyond the ethical and technical dimensions, the question of institutional capacity introduces a further layer of complexity. As Jin et al. (2025) highlight, many universities remain under-prepared in terms of infrastructure, staff expertise, and strategic orientation to integrate AI responsibly. This is not simply a matter of logistics; it reflects deeper systemic tendencies in how institutions approach technological change. In the pursuit of digital credibility—often driven by market pressures and reputational competition—AI systems are at times adopted hastily, without sufficient consideration of their long-term pedagogical and ethical implications. Such dynamics carry particular weight in relation to employability strategies. Where institutions lack strong internal expertise or the capacity for inclusive design, AI may exacerbate inequalities rather than alleviate them. While the use of AI in career services, assessments, and learner analytics holds promise, its benefits are conditional on careful calibration and oversight. Poorly designed or rigid systems risk excluding those whose learning pathways or employment trajectories do not fit predefined models, thereby reinforcing rather than challenging existing inequities.

A further difficulty lies in the fragmented nature of AI governance across the sector. Frameworks are often devised in isolation, bound to national priorities or local contexts, with limited opportunities for cross-sectoral or international alignment. Wynants et al. (2025), in their Ethical Principles AI Framework, argue that progress requires participatory ethics—governance shaped through collaboration among students, educators, policymakers, and technologists. Such inclusivity is not an optional ideal but a necessity if AI is to uphold the values of democratic education, including autonomy, critical inquiry, and equitable access. This perspective also calls attention to the limitations of static governance models. As Batool et al. (2023) observe, meaningful governance requires adaptive infrastructures capable of evolving alongside both technological innovation and shifting cultural or institutional demands. Equally pressing is the need for more empirical research into the lived experiences of students and staff engaging with AI, particularly those from marginalised or underrepresented groups. Without such insight, institutional strategies risk becoming detached from the everyday realities they are intended to serve. If AI is to contribute positively to higher education and employability, it must be embedded within a culture of care and co-creation. Stewardship, in this sense, extends beyond principle into practice, expressed through continual dialogue, reflexivity, and responsiveness. Only under such conditions can AI support institutional missions while enabling students to flourish within an evolving digital landscape.

Building on the arguments developed in this section, it is clear that addressing the ethical and operational challenges of AI in higher education requires more than incremental policy adjustments or isolated innovations. What is needed is a durable institutional infrastructure—one that not only embeds the principles of algorithmic stewardship into everyday practice but also remains sensitive to local contexts, sectoral disparities, and the shifting dynamics of the digital environment. In response, I propose the establishment of Institutional AI Stewardship Labs (IASLs): interdisciplinary, participatory hubs designed to support ethical innovation, strengthen institutional capacity, and guide the integration of AI across educational, administrative, and employability domains. These are not envisaged as conventional research centres, but as practice-based infrastructures situated at the heart of the university's civic and pedagogical mission.

IASLs would operate as cross-functional spaces where students, academic and professional staff, technologists, and community partners work collaboratively on the governance, design, and evaluation of AI systems. By doing so, they offer a means of addressing pressing challenges such as the premature adoption of untested technologies, the fragmentation of governance practices, and unequal access to expertise and resources. More importantly, the model seeks to move beyond abstract commitments, providing universities with a concrete mechanism for translating principles of stewardship into action. Through their design, IASLs offer a structured yet adaptable framework for enhancing transparency, building institutional trust, and advancing digital equity. In this way, they align the adoption of AI with the core values of higher education, ensuring that innovation does not come at the expense of inclusivity or ethical responsibility. The strategic rationale of the IASL model rests on four interdependent pillars, which together outline its role as both a safeguard and an enabler in the evolving landscape of AI in higher education.

1. **Foresight and Ethical Scenario Planning**
   One of the defining features of AI technologies is their unpredictability. As systems evolve—sometimes invisibly—so too do their implications for pedagogy, assessment, employability, and institutional autonomy. IASLs would take on the role of ethical foresight units, engaging in scenario mapping and future-thinking exercises that help identify both opportunities and emerging risks. This proactive orientation marks a shift from reactive governance to anticipatory stewardship, enabling institutions to shape AI adoption rather than be shaped by it.

2. **Participatory Prototyping and Co-Design**
   Echoing earlier discussions of participatory ethics, IASLs would centre inclusive design methodologies as part of their core operating model. All AI tools used in

high-stakes contexts—such as admissions, grading, or employability profiling—would be subject to participatory prototyping processes. These would involve diverse stakeholder groups, including students from underrepresented backgrounds, to test for usability, fairness, and context-specific relevance. Such practices not only enhance the legitimacy and accountability of AI systems but also deepen institutional understanding of how these technologies function in lived, everyday settings.

3. **Embedded Staff Development and Peer Learning**
To address the persistent gap in institutional capacity, IASLs would serve as sites of continuous professional learning. Rather than treating AI literacy as an isolated competency, these labs would embed ethical and technical development into broader academic practice. This could include hands-on workshops, co-teaching schemes, peer mentoring networks, and short courses co-developed with external experts. In doing so, IASLs would help shift AI governance from a technocratic function to a distributed, embedded capacity across the institution.

4. **Transparency, Audit, and Ethical Communication**
A final core function of the IASL would be to develop and publish AI transparency statements, audit logs, and public-facing briefings tailored to institutional contexts. These would not only meet regulatory requirements but also enhance internal and external trust. Rather than a one-size-fits-all approach, the IASL would tailor communications to diverse stakeholders—including students, local employers, and accrediting bodies—offering layered, intelligible explanations of how AI systems work and what values they embody. This multi-audience communication strategy is key to preserving the epistemic and civic responsibilities of higher education.

Figure 2.19 illustrates the four interrelated pillars that underpin the proposed model of IASLs. Each pillar reflects a practical orientation towards embedding algorithmic stewardship in higher education: foresight and ethical scenario planning to anticipate risks and opportunities; participatory prototyping and co-design to ensure inclusive and context-sensitive development; embedded staff development and peer learning to strengthen institutional capacity; and transparency, audit, and ethical communication to promote trust and accountability. Together, these domains articulate a framework that is both adaptive and principled, positioning universities to navigate AI integration with care, reflexivity, and integrity. The establishment of IASLs also offers a pathway for addressing systemic disparities across the sector. While some institutions may be able to establish fully resourced versions of the model, others might adopt lighter, iterative adaptations—working collaboratively with peer institutions, regional consortia, or civic organisations to co-develop guidance and share evaluative tools. In this sense, IASLs are a vehicle not only for institutional resilience but also for inter-institutional solidarity, fostering a culture of mutual learning and ethical innovation.

What is most distinctive about the IASL model is its ability to hold together imperatives too often cast as oppositional: innovation and inclusion, efficiency and reflexivity, technological fluency and ethical restraint. Rather than privileging one at the expense of the other, the model offers a pragmatic yet imaginative response to the current moment—enabling HEIs not simply to adapt to the pressures of AI integration, but to shape its trajectory in ways aligned with their educational and civic missions. In this light, IASLs can be understood as more than a policy mechanism. They represent a form of moral infrastructure: a commitment to care, deliberation, and shared responsibility. By translating the challenges of AI into opportunities for renewal, they allow institutions to exercise ethical leadership, ensuring that technological transformation strengthens rather than undermines the principles of democratic education (Figure 2.20).

In summary, the section advances a guiding principle of Ethical Employability in Policy Development, arguing that HEIs must anchor employability in trust, accountability, and inclusivity rather than narrow labour-market responsiveness or metric chasing. Drawing on the capabilities approach, employability is reframed from producing 'job-ready' graduates to enabling meaningful futures—expanding learners' real freedoms through ethical policy, pedagogy, and governance. From that foundation, the section sets out a practical programme:

- **Principle 1—Policy:** Build participatory, transparent policies that are reviewed for equity impact, use capabilities-aligned metrics (agency, opportunity, well-being), and apply ethical criteria to employer partnerships. Policy becomes a vehicle for justice, not an echo of rankings.
- **Principle 2—Staff Development:** Treat employability as a distributed professionalism. Systematic CPD should cultivate ethical awareness, critical reflexivity, and inclusive practice across academic and professional services, not just careers teams.

FIGURE 2.20 Core functions of institutional AI stewardship labs (IASL).

This figure illustrates the four core functions of Institutional AI Stewardship Labs, which serve as collaborative frameworks to guide the ethical, inclusive, and transparent implementation of AI in educational settings. These include foresight and scenario planning, participatory prototyping, embedded staff development, and transparent communication practices.

BOX 2.20 EXPLANATION NOTE—CORE FUNCTIONS OF INSTITUTIONAL AI STEWARDSHIP LABS (IASL)

The figure illustrates the conceptual design of Institutional AI Stewardship Labs (IASLs), structured around four interdependent pillars that operationalise the principles of algorithmic stewardship within higher education. Each component addresses a distinct but connected dimension of institutional readiness, ethical responsibility, and collaborative practice.

The first pillar, Foresight and Ethical Scenario Planning, highlights the importance of anticipatory governance. By engaging in scenario mapping and future-oriented exercises, institutions can explore potential risks and opportunities associated with AI adoption before they materialise. This proactive stance enables universities to prepare not only for technical shifts but also for the broader social and ethical challenges that accompany them.

The second pillar, Participatory Prototyping and Co-Design, underscores the value of inclusive methodologies in shaping AI systems. Involving students, educators, technologists, and community stakeholders in the design process ensures that AI tools are responsive to diverse needs and reflective of democratic educational values. This participatory orientation challenges the technocratic tendency to impose solutions from above, instead emphasising collaboration and co-creation.

The third pillar, Embedded Staff Development and Peer Learning, directs attention to capacity building within the academic workforce. Continuous professional learning, shared across disciplinary and professional boundaries, is positioned as a prerequisite for meaningful AI integration. Rather than treating AI as a purely technical matter, this pillar affirms the need for reflective practice, peer exchange, and critical engagement across the university community.

The fourth pillar, Transparency, Audit, and Ethical Communication, reinforces the role of accountability in sustaining institutional trust. Practices such as publishing transparency statements and maintaining audit logs establish visible mechanisms of responsibility, enabling institutions to demonstrate integrity in the governance and use of AI. Ethical communication also plays a crucial role in building trust among students and staff, ensuring that AI does not operate as a hidden infrastructure but as a transparent, accountable system.

Taken together, these four pillars articulate a framework that is at once pragmatic and principled. The IASL model does not present stewardship as an abstract commitment but as an actionable institutional practice. By integrating foresight, participation, capacity building, and transparency, IASLs offer a means of aligning technological innovation with the ethical and pedagogical missions of higher education. In doing so, they position universities to engage with AI not only as adopters of new tools but also as stewards of their social, civic, and educational implications.

- **Principle 3—Student Support & Feedback:** Design student-centred, participatory systems that earn trust through clarity, responsiveness, and co-governance. AI may augment provision, but recommendations must be explainable, contestable, and human-guided.
- **Principle 4—Monitoring & Evaluation:** Shift from compliance to outcome responsibility. Disaggregate outcomes, embed student-led audits, and evaluate AI not only for accuracy but also for fairness and alignment with learners' long-term aspirations.

- **Principle 5—External Partnerships:** Re-balance employer engagement with an ethical charter, broadened partner portfolios (SMEs, third sector, civic bodies), paid and developmental placements, and routine review of partner practices against inclusion and dignity.
- **Principle 6—Curriculum:** Integrate ethical employability into disciplinary learning—assessment, project work, and cross-cutting themes (automation, climate justice, digital ethics)—so students connect knowledge to purpose, not just to hiring signals.
- **Principle 7—Well-being, Dignity, Flourishing:** Centre care ethics. Avoid individualising responsibility; validate non-linear trajectories; build trauma-informed, culturally responsive advising; and evaluate technologies for well-being impact.
- **Principle 8—Data & AI Governance:** Move beyond compliance to digital dignity. Publish clear guidelines, ensure explainability and opt-outs, run bias audits, and deliver data-literacy so students can interpret and challenge algorithmic influence.

Recognising operational complexity, the section proposes Algorithmic Stewardship as the connective tissue that keeps ethics and innovation in balance. A practical vehicle—IASLs—is outlined to operationalise foresight, participatory co-design, embedded staff learning, and transparent audit/communication, with adaptable models for differently resourced institutions.

The argument resolves into a coherent institutional settlement: employability must be ethically constituted before it is operationalised. That means policies built with those affected, curricula that cultivate judgement and purpose, partnerships that reflect the public good, and infrastructures—human and technical—that can be questioned, explained, and repaired. Trust is earned through transparency and shared authorship; accountability is realised through clear oversight, auditable systems, and real avenues of redress; inclusivity is made tangible by equity reviews, dignifying support, broadened employer ecologies, and capabilities-aligned metrics that register agency and well-being, not salary alone. Algorithmic stewardship and IASLs provide the organisational muscle to keep these commitments alive as contexts shift—anticipating risks, co-designing tools with diverse students, building staff capacity, and communicating openly about how data and AI shape opportunity. In this settlement, employability stops being a performance target and becomes an ethical promise: universities will equip students not only to access work but also to shape it—critically, inclusively, and with their dignity intact.

CONCLUSION

The analysis presented in this chapter has demonstrated that the integration of AI into education and employability cannot be reduced to a matter of technological efficiency or administrative convenience. It is, rather, a deeply ethical, institutional, and philosophical undertaking that raises questions about what it means to learn, to teach, and to work in an era where decision-making is increasingly mediated by non-human systems. The triadic framework developed here—trust, accountability, and inclusivity—emerges not as an optional set of considerations but as the very foundation upon which legitimate and sustainable practices must be built. Yet these principles, as argued throughout, require continual expansion and refinement in order to respond to the evolving realities of algorithmic systems. Ethical scalability, dialogic symmetry, and ontological clarity together provide the conceptual depth necessary for understanding AI's role in reshaping education and labour markets, preventing both policy drift and conceptual impoverishment.

Trust is the first of these imperatives, and it has been shown to be a structural condition rather than a rhetorical ornament. Without transparency, openness, and intelligibility, AI systems risk functioning less as aids to human development than as command structures that impose decisions upon learners, educators, and workers. As Wachter, Mittelstadt, and Floridi (2017) argue, those subjected to algorithmic decisions possess a legitimate right to understand how those decisions are made. In the absence of such explainability, trust cannot be sustained. Yet, as Knowles and Richards (2021) highlight, trust in AI systems is not simply a by-product of technical reliability; it requires systems that are auditable, responsive and intelligible to non-specialist stakeholders. (Knowles and Richards, 2021). In this sense, trust is pedagogical as well as technical: it equips individuals to interrogate how knowledge and opportunity are shaped by machines. The allegory of the compass provides a vivid reminder that guidance without intelligibility becomes compulsion and that confidence in any navigational system depends upon the ability to understand and, when necessary, to question its direction.

Accountability is equally central. The maritime metaphor employed earlier illustrates that without a clear chart and log of responsibility, vessels navigating with AI-powered rigging will drift into opacity. As the Brookings Institution (2022) and Chen (2023) caution, algorithmic hiring systems too often disperse responsibility across developers, institutions, and vendors, leaving no one answerable when harm occurs. In education, when predictive systems identify students as 'at risk' or when generative tools provide automated feedback, the stakes are no less serious. If responsibility for outcomes is not clearly defined, affected individuals are left with no meaningful avenues for appeal. Accountability must therefore be conceived as a proactive design: institutions must create structures of oversight, maintain transparent records of system development, and embed avenues for redress. It cannot be an afterthought to technical deployment but the scaffolding upon which legitimate adoption rests. Without accountability, the promise of fairness and transparency collapses into rhetoric, unanchored from practice. Inclusivity completes the triadic frame and proves the most difficult to enact. The risk, as Noble (2018) and Raghavan et al. (2020) demonstrate, lies in the entrenchment of systemic inequities within data infrastructures. Training datasets frequently reflect historical inequalities of race, gender, class, and geography, which are then reproduced under the guise of computational neutrality. Proxy variables—such as postcode, educational background, or linguistic style—function as gatekeepers that perpetuate exclusion while presenting the appearance of impartiality (Chen, 2023). The allegory of the ship reminds us that a vessel claiming to carry society cannot exclude whole segments of its population from passage. Inclusivity requires more than representational diversity; it requires cognitive justice (Visvanathan, 2009), whereby multiple epistemologies and cultural traditions are recognised and respected. This has implications not only for data collection and system design but also for pedagogy, ensuring that educational environments shaped by AI do not marginalise local or indigenous ways of knowing.

Yet, as this chapter has argued, trust, accountability, and inclusivity on their own are not sufficient. Ethical scalability, dialogic symmetry, and ontological clarity provide crucial conceptual refinements. Ethical scalability demands frameworks that evolve in step with AI's pace of innovation. Static codes of conduct, however principled, risk obsolescence in the face of generative systems and adaptive algorithms that reshape themselves through continuous learning. Anticipatory governance, as advocated by the Institute for Ethical AI in Education (2021), is therefore vital. Rather than reacting to harms after they occur, institutions must cultivate a capacity for ethical foresight, embedding adaptability, justice, and fairness as conditions that evolve alongside technological systems. In parallel, dialogic symmetry challenges the assumption that AI is merely a neutral tool. As adaptive platforms and generative models increasingly provide feedback, scaffolding, and assessment, they enter into dialogue with learners. This makes them interlocutory presences, shaping meaning and interpretative authority in ways that demand scrutiny. Digital literacy must therefore be reconceived as reflective digital agency, equipping learners and educators not simply to use systems but to interrogate, challenge, and co-design them. Finally, ontological clarity ensures that institutions do not adapt structurally without re-examining their foundational purposes. Questions such as what it means to learn when algorithmic systems mediate thought, or how to define intelligence when machines produce reasoning once thought to be uniquely human, cannot be dismissed as philosophical diversions. They are central to preventing the drift into a condition where systems function but meanings are obscured. The allegory of Atlantis serves here as a cautionary tale: innovation without reflection risks imbalance, where technological expansion obscures human proportion and purpose.

The chapter's sustained attention to employability adds an important dimension to this discussion. Algorithmic systems now mediate recruitment processes, shaping opportunities for work and access to livelihoods. Brookings (2022) documents how CV screening, automated assessments, and asynchronous video interviews risk replicating existing inequalities, while Chen (2023) highlights how proxy variables embed exclusion within apparently neutral models. Noble's (2018) work on algorithmic injustice similarly demonstrates how data infrastructures amplify pre-existing hierarchies. The conceptual tools advanced here—merit reimagined, probability, and potential—offer a way forward. They shift attention from static measures of past achievement towards anticipatory assessments of capacity, resilience, and emergent potential. This is particularly vital for candidates from marginalised backgrounds whose trajectories may not fit the patterns encoded within historical datasets. Employability in the age of AI must be reconceived as an anticipatory project, oriented not only to what individuals have achieved but also to what they might achieve under fairer conditions of recognition, opportunity, and support.

The framework of epistemic and Civic Agency further strengthens this orientation. Employability is not reducible to skills acquisition; it is shaped by the collective ability to critique, participate, and redefine the criteria by which opportunity is allocated. Learners must be enabled to interrogate how systems operate, to demand transparency, and to contest discriminatory outcomes. Institutions must act not only as providers of training but also as ethical stewards, ensuring that AI adoption enhances agency rather than constraining it. UNESCO's (2021b) call for human-centred AI resonates strongly here, affirming that the purpose of technological adoption is to support dignity, inclusivity, and human flourishing. In this light, algorithmic employability frameworks become not only technical systems but also sites of democratic negotiation over what counts as valuable work and legitimate opportunity.

The comparative exploration of African and Latin American contexts underscores that AI adoption is always situated within uneven global terrains. African experiences reveal both infrastructural deficits and opportunities for innovation grounded in local epistemologies and community needs (O'Neill and Marivate, 2024). The allegories of ships navigating turbulent seas and houses built from local materials emphasise the need for endogenous frameworks rather than dependence on borrowed maps. Latin American policies, such as Colombia's CONPES 4144, demonstrate the risks of economistic logics that treat technology primarily as a vehicle for competitiveness while neglecting structural inequalities. By contrast, emergent frameworks that foreground cognitive justice, epistemic sovereignty, and pluriversal approaches illustrate more promising directions. These regional analyses remind us that AI in employability must be conceived as a political, cultural, and ethical project rather than a technical inevitability.

Nevertheless, this analysis has limitations that must be acknowledged. While conceptual frameworks and allegories provide depth, empirical grounding remains limited. Greater engagement with the lived experiences of learners, educators, and job applicants navigating AI systems would strengthen the argument. The voices of students and workers, while normatively emphasised, are not directly present. Inclusivity in theory must be mirrored by methodologies that centre marginalised perspectives, whether through participatory research, ethnography, or co-design processes. Moreover, while allegories such as Atlantis, maritime voyages, and protective fences are illuminating, their frequency risks overshadowing empirical analysis. Future research would benefit from balancing metaphor with systematic evidence, ensuring that conceptual richness is grounded in lived realities.

In drawing together the argument, the conclusion must also set out a forward-looking agenda. Several commitments emerge as particularly urgent. First, institutions must embed ethical scalability through dynamic frameworks that evolve alongside technology. Anticipatory governance, continuous bias testing, and reflexive adaptation must become standard practice. Second, a reflective digital agency must be cultivated as a core educational aim, ensuring that learners and educators are not passive consumers of AI but critical participants in shaping its role. Third, employability must be reimagined through frameworks that value reimagined merit, probability, and potential, thereby resisting exclusionary logics embedded in historical data. Fourth, epistemic and Civic Agency must be prioritised, with mechanisms such as participatory audits, algorithmic registries, and transparency protocols enabling democratic engagement with technological adoption.

Fifth, AI governance must be localised, ensuring that Global South contexts are not subsumed within externally imposed paradigms but empowered to draw upon indigenous knowledge, cultural sovereignty, and community-based practices. Finally, allegory and conceptual analysis must be complemented by empirical research, enabling a more comprehensive understanding of AI's impact on educational and labour systems.

The central claim of this chapter—that ethical AI in education and employability requires collective commitment to trust, accountability, and inclusivity—remains pressing. Yet the extension of these principles into ethical scalability, dialogic symmetry, and ontological clarity deepens their significance and equips them to withstand future technological transformations. The allegories woven throughout—from Atlantis to the baobab tree—remind us that technological progress without reflection risks imbalance and that innovation without proportion can undermine human flourishing. The future of education and employability in the age of AI is not a predetermined trajectory but an open horizon to be shaped collectively through values, governance, and practice. The challenge is not simply to integrate systems that function but to ensure that they serve human purposes, affirm dignity, and support flourishing. AI must not be accepted as an inevitability but embraced as an invitation: an invitation to reimagine how learning, work, and society are organised when intelligence is no longer solely human. Accepting this invitation requires courage, critical imagination, and Institutional Responsibility. It requires remembering, as the allegories caution, where the shoreline lies, ensuring that expansion does not eclipse proportion and that innovation does not erode reflection. Only then can AI serve not as an Atlantean hubris but as a compass for ethical, inclusive, and meaningful futures.

CHAPTER 3

Conclusion

In closing this volume, it is necessary to step back and take a panoramic view of the intellectual and practical terrain traversed across the preceding chapters. At its core, this book has sought to reframe employability, skills development, and ethical governance in higher education in the context of AI and more particularly generative AI. The arguments advanced have been neither abstract nor detached; rather, they have been deeply rooted in the realities of how universities, employers, governments, and societies must respond to the accelerating technological changes of our time. The central claim—sustained throughout the work—is that employability in the 21st century cannot be reduced to narrow measures of technical proficiency or labour-market responsiveness. Instead, it must be understood as a dynamic, relational, and ethically grounded process of human development, one that equips graduates not only to adapt to change but also to shape it in ways conducive to justice, equity, and flourishing. The problem with which this book has wrestled is multifaceted. On one level, it concerns the inadequacy of traditional models of employability, which treat competencies as static attributes that can be acquired, measured, and certified independently of the wider technological and social contexts in which they are enacted. On another level, it concerns the failure of policy and institutional discourse to fully acknowledge the ethical dimensions of AI and the responsibilities that arise when technology mediates human action, creativity, and judgement. Still further, it addresses the uneven distribution of preparedness across global contexts, where structural inequalities—economic, cultural, and infrastructural—determine who can participate meaningfully in an AI-driven economy and who remains excluded.

The threads of awareness and preparedness, introduced at the outset of this book, have thus become leitmotifs in the broader narrative. Awareness denotes the critical capacity to reflect upon the implications of AI: to understand how it reshapes work, knowledge, and governance, and to recognise its ethical and social risks. Preparedness, in turn, signifies the capacity to translate such awareness into practical readiness: the development of skills, institutional frameworks, and regulatory measures that anticipate challenges and enable responsible engagement. Both are indispensable; neither is sufficient in isolation.

DOI: 10.1201/9781003502517-4

The argument has consistently emphasised that the interplay between awareness and preparedness is where the true work of employability takes place. The urgency of this work cannot be overstated. As national strategies from the United Kingdom, Finland, Singapore, South Korea, and multiple African nations attest, the question of how to prepare graduates for AI-mediated futures is no longer hypothetical but immediate. Governments are investing heavily in AI infrastructure, employers are reconfiguring job roles around automation and data, and universities are redesigning curricula to embed digital literacies and ethical reasoning. Yet, as the analysis has shown, these initiatives are uneven in their scope and sometimes limited in their vision. Too often, the focus falls disproportionately upon technical upskilling, leaving unaddressed the ethical, intercultural, and interpersonal dimensions that are equally essential for navigating technological disruption.

At the same time, the global policy discourse, exemplified in the Sustainable Development Goals (SDGs), highlights the interconnectedness of education, equity, and sustainability. AI has the potential to accelerate progress towards these goals, but it also threatens to entrench inequalities if deployed without reflection or accountability. The central problem, then, is one of balance: how to harness the affordances of AI in ways that extend human potential without sacrificing justice, fairness, or dignity. This brings us to the allegorical arc through which the conclusion as a whole will unfold. The Sumerian myth of Inanna's Descent to the Underworld provides an ancient but strikingly resonant framework for interpreting the challenges of higher education in the age of AI. In the story, Inanna, goddess of wisdom and fertility, chooses to descend into the underworld to confront her sister, the queen of death. At each of the seven gates, she is required to remove one of her garments or ornaments, symbols of her power and identity. By the time she reaches the final gate, she stands stripped bare, vulnerable and exposed, before the forces of death. Only through this stripping away, and the ordeal of death itself, does she return renewed to the realm of the living, her wisdom deepened, her power reconstituted in new form.

This myth, one of the oldest recorded allegories of descent and renewal, speaks directly to the predicament of higher education at this historical juncture. Universities, governments, and societies stand at the threshold of their own descent into a world reshaped by AI. At each stage of this journey, they are compelled to relinquish the securities of established paradigms: the reliance upon static qualifications, the assumption of meritocratic neutrality, the faith in technical skills as sufficient guarantors of success. What remains, as these garments are shed, is the naked question of purpose: what is education for in an AI-mediated world? What must universities preserve, and what must they be willing to let go, if they are to emerge renewed?

The allegory is not merely decorative. It captures with unusual precision the dynamics of disruption and transformation that this book has sought to articulate. Just as Inanna's descent involved both loss and renewal, so too must higher education undergo a process of critical unravelling and reconstitution. To cling uncritically to the old garments of employability—fixed models of skill acquisition, narrow measures of technical proficiency, assumptions of market determinism—is to misunderstand the nature of the transformation at hand. To embrace the descent, by contrast, is to acknowledge that employability must be reimagined as a dynamic, ethical, and interconnected process: one that integrates technical expertise with ethical reasoning, intercultural awareness, creativity, and adaptability.

The chapters preceding this conclusion have already laid the foundation for such a reimagining. Introduction provided the concept of skills dynamics, situating employability within a framework that emphasises the interplay between technical expertise, foundational soft skills, and the mediating role of digital technologies. Chapter 1 extended this into the notion of comprehensive skills, integrating digital literacy, ethical awareness, and lifelong learning into the core of employability. Chapter 2 examined national strategies across multiple contexts, demonstrating both the diversity of approaches and the convergence upon adaptability, inclusion, and sustainability as central goals. Chapter 3 drew these threads together, advancing the argument that employability must be conceived as a process of becoming, oriented towards justice and human flourishing rather than narrowly towards labour-market responsiveness.

To restate the core problem, then, is to acknowledge that the world stands at a gate not unlike those through which Inanna passed. The garments we are asked to shed are the familiar but insufficient paradigms of education, work, and governance. The descent we must undertake is the confrontation with uncertainty, bias, inequality, and the ethical dilemmas of technology. The renewal that lies beyond depends upon our willingness to integrate awareness with preparedness, to cultivate comprehensive skills, and to embed ethical governance at the heart of education and employability. This, in essence, is the challenge and the opportunity of our time. It is not a problem that can be solved once and for all, but a process of continual descent and renewal, adaptation and reflection. Higher education must learn to live within this cycle, drawing upon its deepest values of justice, integrity, and human dignity to guide its way. Only by doing so can it emerge, like Inanna, renewed and transformed—stripped of old certainties but clothed anew in the garments of wisdom, adaptability, and ethical responsibility.

The preceding chapters have highlighted that the very notion of employability has undergone a profound metamorphosis in the face of rapid technological transformation. Once conceived as a relatively narrow matter of preparing graduates with occupational competencies for immediate labour-market insertion, employability must now be understood as a living, adaptive process: dynamic, relational, and deeply ethical. The core claim of this book is that the frameworks traditionally used to describe employability—grounded in static skills taxonomies, credential-based meritocracy, and the rhetoric of individual responsibility—are no longer adequate for the complexity of the 21st century. Instead, what is required is a systemic and holistic synthesis: one that acknowledges the evolving interplay of technical expertise, foundational literacies, interpersonal capacities, ethical awareness, and digital fluency.

The concept of skills dynamics, provided in Introduction, represents a decisive break with static models. It recognises that skills do not exist as discrete and permanent attributes but rather as adaptive, interconnected competencies that emerge from the interaction of personal, social, and technological forces. This is not simply a semantic innovation; it marks a fundamental reconceptualisation of what it means to be employable. A graduate who possesses technical expertise but lacks adaptability will be as ill-prepared as one who can communicate effectively but cannot navigate digital systems. Similarly, ethical awareness cannot be treated as an optional addition; it is indispensable in contexts where AI shapes decisions with far-reaching human consequences. This dynamic framing resonates with the allegory of Inanna's descent. At each gate, as she sheds her adornments, she is stripped of the illusion of permanence. What once appeared to define her identity—the crown of divinity, the jewels of fertility, the robes of power—are revealed to be provisional, transient, and insufficient in the face of transformation. So too with the static models of employability. They may once have served as markers of preparedness, but they cannot withstand the descent into an AI-mediated world. What remains, and what must be cultivated anew, are adaptive capacities that can survive the stripping away of old securities.

The critique of traditional frameworks such as the 4Cs—creativity, collaboration, communication, and critical thinking—was not offered to dismiss their value but to argue for their insufficiency when taken in isolation. Creativity, in an AI context, involves not only generating ideas but also engaging critically with algorithmic outputs, assessing their ethical implications, and applying them in socially constructive ways. Collaboration extends beyond human-to-human interaction into hybrid forms of co-creation with digital agents, mediated across cultural and geographical divides. Communication increasingly involves interpreting data visualisations, engaging across languages through machine translation, and navigating algorithmically curated information environments. Critical thinking, finally, must be expanded to encompass critical *digital* literacies: the ability to interrogate the biases, assumptions, and implications embedded in technological systems themselves.

This integrated framework of comprehensive skills, developed in Chapters 1 and 2, positions employability as a convergence of multiple literacies: cognitive, digital, ethical, intercultural, and reflective. It challenges the compartmentalisation that has long characterised employability discourse, instead insisting upon synthesis. Here again, the allegory illuminates. Inanna's descent was not the loss of isolated attributes but the unravelling of a whole system of meaning. Her renewal was possible only because she emerged with a new integration, one that wove vulnerability and wisdom into a deeper fabric of identity. So too must comprehensive skills represent not the simple accumulation of attributes but their interweaving into a living, adaptive tapestry.

The comparative analysis of national strategies demonstrates both the diversity of responses to AI and their underlying convergence. In contexts such as Finland, the emphasis on holistic education embeds creativity, adaptability, and digital literacy across the curriculum. Singapore's SkillsFuture initiative prioritises lifelong learning and continuous reskilling, recognising employability as a process rather than an endpoint. Germany's dual-education system integrates vocational training with ethical reasoning, preparing graduates for Industry 4.0. Meanwhile, African nations such as Kenya, Nigeria, and Rwanda grapple with the digital divide but are leveraging public–private partnerships to expand access to AI literacy and ICT training. What unites these strategies is a recognition that employability cannot be conceived in narrow technical terms. Whether the emphasis is on inclusivity, competitiveness, or sustainability, the underlying logic is dynamic: employability is about preparing individuals not simply to *enter* the labour market but to *navigate* and *shape* its ongoing transformations. This comparative perspective reinforces the central argument of this book: that skills dynamics and comprehensive skills are not parochial concepts but globally resonant frameworks, capable of illuminating the shared challenges of diverse contexts.

Yet the divergences must also be acknowledged. Industrialised nations often prioritise innovation and competitiveness, while emerging economies foreground access and inclusion. These different emphases reflect not merely policy choices but structural conditions: resource constraints, infrastructural disparities, and historical inequalities. Here lies a critical ethical imperative. If employability frameworks are to advance justice as well as economic growth, they must be attentive to these asymmetries. Preparedness cannot be the preserve of the privileged; it must be cultivated inclusively, lest AI reinforce existing inequities rather than alleviate them. Perhaps the most significant shift in this synthesis is the recognition that employability is not merely an individual attribute but a collective responsibility. Governments must create enabling policy environments; employers must embed fairness and accountability into hiring and workplace practices; universities must design curricula that integrate ethical reasoning with technical proficiency. The focus cannot be solely upon what the graduate brings to the market; it must also encompass what the market and the institutions that structure it owe to the graduate and to society.

This reframing challenges the neoliberal tendency to place the entire burden of employability upon individuals, obscuring the structural inequities that constrain opportunity. Inanna's descent once again illuminates this point. Her vulnerability at the gates was not a personal failing but the condition imposed upon her by the structures of the underworld. Her renewal was made possible not only by her own resilience but also by the cosmic order that eventually restored her. Similarly, graduates do not confront the gates of employability alone; their preparedness and flourishing depend upon the structures—educational, institutional, and regulatory—that support them. The synthesis of skills and employability presented here culminates in a paradigm shift: from employability as possession to employability as becoming. Traditional models have treated employability as a set of possessions—skills, credentials, experiences—that can be acquired and displayed as currency in the labour market. The argument advanced in this book is that such a framing is inadequate. Employability must be understood as a process of continual becoming: an ongoing negotiation of identity, capacity, and responsibility in contexts of uncertainty and change.

This vision is not utopian; it is deeply pragmatic. The volatility of labour markets, the unpredictability of technological trajectories, and the interdependence of global systems make it impossible to guarantee stability or certainty. What can be cultivated, however, is adaptability, ethical judgement, resilience, and the capacity to learn continuously. These are the qualities that enable individuals not only to survive disruption but also to shape it towards constructive ends. Here, the allegory finds its full resonance. Inanna's descent was not about the preservation of her possessions but about the transformation of her being. Her renewal was not the simple restoration of what she had lost but the reconstitution of her identity on deeper, more resilient foundations. Likewise, employability in the age of AI must be about transformation: not the preservation of static skills but the cultivation of adaptive capacities that enable graduates to flourish amid uncertainty.

Finally, this synthesis points towards a broader horizon. Employability, skills dynamics, and comprehensive skills are not ends in themselves but means towards the greater goal of human flourishing. As the justice–responsibility framework illustrated earlier in the book, the purpose of AI integration must be to enhance human dignity, opportunity, and sustainability. Employability must therefore be reframed not as a private good but as a public responsibility, contributing to the collective flourishing of societies as well as the individual success of graduates. The allegory reminds us that no descent is undertaken alone and no renewal is achieved in isolation. Inanna's journey was embedded in the cosmic order of Sumerian belief, reflecting the interconnection of life, death, and renewal. So too must employability be situated within the universal interconnectedness of human societies, technological systems, and ecological limits. To prepare graduates for AI-mediated futures is not simply to equip them with tools for survival but to enable them to participate in the collective task of shaping just, inclusive, and sustainable worlds.

If the synthesis of skills and employability provides the scaffolding for a renewed understanding of what higher education must cultivate, the ethical governance of artificial intelligence offers the normative compass by which this scaffolding must be directed. The preceding chapters made clear that without a robust ethical architecture, the integration of AI into education and work risks deepening inequalities, exacerbating bias, and subordinating human flourishing to technocratic efficiency. The task of ethical governance is therefore to anchor the dynamic vision of employability within principles that safeguard justice, fairness, and dignity.

THE FAT-HO FRAMEWORK AS ETHICAL CORE

The FAT-HO framework—Fairness, Accountability, Transparency, and Human Oversight—emerges as a conceptual centrepiece in this book's argument. Each dimension speaks directly to the risks and responsibilities that accompany AI in education and employability.

- **Fairness** demands the mitigation of algorithmic bias and the pursuit of inclusivity in both education and employment. Without fairness, AI becomes a tool of exclusion, reinforcing structural inequities under the guise of efficiency.
- **Accountability** insists that institutions and governments retain responsibility for the decisions mediated by AI. Delegating judgement to machines cannot absolve humans of responsibility for outcomes.
- **Transparency** requires the demystification of algorithmic processes. Graduates, educators, and policymakers alike must be able to scrutinise how decisions are made, by whom, and on what grounds.
- **Human Oversight** anchors the entire framework by asserting that AI must remain subordinate to human values, intentions, and deliberations. Oversight is not a technical add-on but the ethical safeguard of human agency.

Together, these principles offer not merely a checklist of considerations but a coherent ethos for navigating the AI-mediated future. They affirm that employability, to be just and meaningful, must be cultivated in ways that preserve human dignity, not diminish it. Here, the allegory of Inanna once again proves instructive. At each gate, as she descends further into the underworld, she is stripped not only of power but also of certainty. The shedding of her adornments mirrors the shedding of assumptions: that technology is neutral, that skills can be isolated from ethics, that markets can be left to self-regulate. Each gate is a confrontation with the insufficiency of these beliefs. Ethical governance represents the wisdom that emerges when one has passed through such gates: a recognition that vulnerability necessitates responsibility and that power, once stripped of illusion, must be reconstituted upon foundations of justice and transparency.

The discussion of policy frameworks throughout this book emphasised that ethical governance is not an abstract aspiration but an urgent global agenda. UNESCO's Recommendation on the Ethics of Artificial Intelligence (2021b) articulates principles of human rights, inclusivity, and sustainability, urging member states to integrate ethical considerations into AI policy. The OECD AI Principles similarly call for fairness, transparency, and accountability, setting a global benchmark for responsible innovation. UNICEF's policy guidance on AI for children extends these concerns to the most vulnerable populations, highlighting the need for education systems to safeguard learners' rights in digital contexts. The convergence of these frameworks signals a shared recognition: AI is not merely a technological challenge but a moral and societal one. However, as the comparative analysis revealed, the translation of these global principles into national policy remains uneven. Some states, such as Finland and Singapore, have embedded ethics into curricula and skills strategies. Others, particularly in lower-income contexts, face the double burden of digital divide and limited regulatory capacity. The result is a patchwork of preparedness, with significant risks of global inequity. It is here that the allegorical descent acquires further resonance. Just as Inanna's passage through the underworld revealed the asymmetries of power and vulnerability, the global landscape of AI governance reveals stark asymmetries of capacity. For some, the descent into AI-mediated futures is navigated with the security of robust infrastructures and ethical frameworks. For others, it is experienced as exposure without protection, vulnerability without safeguards. Ethical governance, in this context, is not only about principles but also about solidarity: the recognition that interconnectedness demands collective responsibility for ensuring that no society is abandoned at the gates.

A recurrent theme in policy debates is the tension between safeguarding ethics and fostering innovation. Critics often frame regulation as a brake upon technological advancement, warning that excessive oversight will stifle creativity and competitiveness. Yet this binary is deeply misleading. Far from being antithetical to innovation, ethical governance provides the legitimacy and trust without which innovation cannot be sustained. If graduates and societies perceive AI as opaque, biased, or unjust, they will resist its adoption. Conversely, when AI is transparent, accountable, and human-centred, it is more likely to be embraced, adapted, and integrated constructively. This dialectic between regulation and innovation echoes the ambivalence of Inanna's descent. The stripping away of adornments could be interpreted as a loss of freedom, yet it was precisely through this vulnerability that renewal became possible. Similarly, regulation may appear as a constraint, but it is through ethical constraint that true renewal—innovation aligned with human flourishing—becomes achievable. Governance is not the opposite of progress; it is its condition of possibility.

Ethical governance cannot be the sole responsibility of governments. Universities, employers, and international bodies all bear responsibility for embedding the FAT-HO principles into practice. Universities, in particular, occupy a pivotal position. As sites where future professionals are educated, they have a duty to cultivate awareness of AI's ethical dimensions, to design curricula that integrate fairness and accountability, and to foster critical literacies that empower graduates to question algorithmic systems. Employers, likewise, must ensure that hiring practices, workplace surveillance, and performance evaluations mediated by AI are fair, transparent, and accountable. At the structural level, ethical governance requires not only compliance but also culture. To build cultures of fairness, accountability, transparency, and human oversight is to create environments where ethical reflexivity is as normal as technical problem-solving. This cultural embedding is what transforms principles from abstract aspirations into lived practices. Without such embedding, ethical frameworks risk remaining ornamental, like the discarded jewels at Inanna's gates—symbols devoid of protective power.

Finally, ethical governance must be understood within the wider context of universal interconnectedness. AI is not bounded by national borders, institutional silos, or disciplinary domains. Its development and deployment are inherently global, shaped by transnational corporations, international policy frameworks, and the flows of data across networks. To govern AI ethically, therefore, requires recognition that decisions made in one context reverberate globally. An algorithm trained on biased data in one country may perpetuate discrimination across many. A failure of oversight in one industry may erode trust across entire societies. The allegory offers a profound lesson here. Inanna's descent was not a private ordeal but a cosmic event, affecting not only herself but also the cycles of fertility, life, and renewal across the world. Her vulnerability disrupted the balance of existence, and her renewal restored it. So too with AI: its governance is not a parochial matter but a collective concern, bound up with the balance of justice, opportunity, and sustainability on a planetary scale. To reframe employability through the lens of ethical governance is therefore to see it as more than preparation for work. It is preparation for participation in a world where every technological decision has ripple effects across human communities and ecosystems. Graduates must not only be skilled but also ethically literate, capable of recognising interconnectedness and bearing responsibility for its implications.

Thus, ethical governance does not merely accompany the synthesis of skills and employability; it completes and deepens it. The FAT-HO framework ensures that the dynamic vision of employability is anchored in principles that protect human dignity and foster justice. Global policy frameworks demonstrate both the urgency of this task and the risks of uneven implementation. The tension between regulation and innovation highlights the need for ethical constraint as the condition of sustainable progress. The collective responsibility of institutions emphasises that employability is not only an individual matter but also a shared duty. And the principle of interconnectedness reminds us that governance must be global, inclusive, and solidaristic. As the descent narrative continues, higher education stands now at the middle gates of the underworld. The adornments of old assumptions have been stripped away; the risks of vulnerability are fully apparent. What remains is the choice: to rebuild employability upon the brittle ground of technocratic efficiency or to reconstitute it upon the resilient foundations of fairness, accountability, transparency, and human oversight. The path of renewal lies in the latter, where employability becomes not only a personal asset but also a collective ethical commitment, a contribution to the flourishing of humanity in an AI-mediated world.

The preceding sections have repeatedly invoked the ancient Sumerian tale of Inanna's Descent to the Underworld as a metaphorical guide for understanding the transformative pressures that higher education now faces. In this part of the conclusion, the allegory is taken up in fuller detail. By mapping the seven gates through which Inanna passed onto the challenges facing universities, governments, and societies in an AI-mediated world, the myth becomes more than a symbolic echo; it becomes a structural framework for interpreting descent, vulnerability, and renewal. At the first gate, Inanna is compelled to surrender her crown, the emblem of her status and authority. For higher education, the crown symbolises the reliance upon fixed credentialism—the belief that degrees, certificates, and qualifications are sufficient markers of employability. In an era of AI, where skills evolve rapidly and non-linear career paths are increasingly common, such reliance becomes untenable. Universities must learn to relinquish the illusion that static credentials alone can guarantee graduates' futures. Instead, they must cultivate lifelong learning and adaptability, recognising that employability is a continual process of growth rather than a fixed state conferred at graduation.

At the second gate, Inanna is stripped of her necklace, a symbol of her identity and belonging. For universities, this reflects the loss of disciplinary insularity—the long-held assumption that knowledge can remain neatly compartmentalised within traditional academic boundaries. AI transcends such boundaries: data science merges with ethics, engineering with sociology, and medicine with law. To descend into the AI underworld is to acknowledge that no discipline can stand alone. Employability, therefore, demands interdisciplinary integration, preparing graduates to navigate hybrid domains where technical, social, and ethical dimensions converge. At the third gate, Inanna's breastplate is removed, stripping her of protection. For education systems, this is the relinquishing of the protective illusion of meritocratic neutrality. Traditional employability models have often assumed that success is determined solely by individual merit, obscuring structural inequities of class, race, gender, and geography. AI threatens to amplify these inequities through biased algorithms and exclusionary access to resources. Passing through this gate requires recognition that fairness cannot be presumed; it must be actively cultivated. Employability frameworks must confront systemic bias and embed equity at their core.

At the fourth gate, Inanna loses her bracelet of gold, a symbol of wealth and utility. For higher education, this is the surrender of purely technical rationality—the belief that technical skills alone can secure employability and progress. AI demonstrates that technical proficiency without ethical reasoning can be destructive, leading to discriminatory systems, exploitative practices, and environmental harm. To survive this gate, universities must integrate ethics, creativity, and critical reflection into curricula, ensuring that technical competence is always mediated by responsibility. At the fifth gate, Inanna is compelled to give up her ring, a circle representing bonds and contracts. For our present context, the ring symbolises the social contract surrounding data: the implicit trust that personal and educational data will be used responsibly. In practice, however, AI often relies upon exploitative data practices—surveillance, commodification, and opacity. As Inanna is stripped of her ring, so too must higher education acknowledge the fragility of trust in data-driven systems. Employability in the AI age requires not only data literacy but also data ethics, empowering graduates to question who benefits from data, who is exploited, and how governance structures can preserve integrity.

At the sixth gate, Inanna loses her robe, the garment that clothed her identity. For universities and societies, this gate represents the stripping away of market determinism—the conviction that employability should be defined entirely by labour-market demand. While responsiveness to employment trends is necessary, the descent into AI reveals the inadequacy of market logics to guide educational purpose. Left unchecked, market determinism reduces education to training, ignoring its role in cultivating citizens, communities, and ethical agents. Passing through this gate demands that employability be re-anchored in human flourishing rather than market expediency. At the final gate, Inanna stands naked before the throne of Ereshkigal, queen of death. This is the moment of ultimate exposure, where all protective symbols have been surrendered. For higher education, this corresponds to the confrontation with human vulnerability in an AI-driven world. Here, the question is stark: what remains of education when all garments of tradition, market, and technical rationality are stripped away? The answer is the essence of human agency itself: the capacity for reflection, ethical judgement, creativity, and solidarity. This is what cannot be automated, commodified, or outsourced. In this moment of exposure lies the possibility of renewal.

In the myth, Inanna does not remain in the underworld. After experiencing death, she is restored and returns to the world above, transformed by her ordeal. Her renewal does not erase her vulnerability but integrates it, making her wisdom deeper and her power more resilient. Likewise, higher education cannot remain paralysed at the gates of AI disruption. Having surrendered outdated paradigms, it must return with renewed clarity: employability reconceived as dynamic, ethical, and interconnected. The allegory thus frames descent not as failure but as a necessary transformation. Each gate represents a challenge that must be faced: the shedding of static credentialism, disciplinary insularity, meritocratic neutrality, technical reductionism, exploitative data practices, market determinism, and the fear of human vulnerability. Each stripping away is painful but generative, clearing space for new forms of wisdom and preparedness.

The enduring relevance of Inanna's descent lies in its capacity to illuminate the cyclical nature of transformation. Just as fertility and life in the Sumerian cosmos depended upon her renewal, so too does the flourishing of contemporary societies depend upon the renewal of education in response to AI. The myth offers a reminder that vulnerability is not the end of the story; it is the beginning of wisdom. For higher education, the mandate is clear. Employability must be reconstituted not as a possession of static attributes but as a process of becoming, mediated by awareness, preparedness, and ethical responsibility. The FAT-HO principles must serve as guiding stars, ensuring that the renewal is grounded in justice and transparency. And above all, the descent must be embraced collectively, recognising that no university, no nation, and no graduate passes through the gates alone.

The descent through the seven gates, as mapped in the allegory of Inanna, revealed not only the stripping away of assumptions but also the unveiling of a deeper truth: human existence, and therefore human education, is bound by interconnection. No graduate enters the labour market in isolation, just as no society navigates the challenges of AI in isolation. The transformations described in this book—the reconceptualisation of employability, the cultivation of comprehensive skills, the embedding of ethical governance—cannot be undertaken by any one institution, state, or sector alone. They are situated within the global fabric of interdependence, a fabric made visible in the shared aspirations of the SDGs. The SDGs articulate a vision of collective flourishing, encompassing education, equity, sustainability, and justice. Goal 4, to 'ensure inclusive and equitable quality education and promote lifelong learning opportunities for all', resonates directly with the arguments advanced here. Employability reframed as dynamic becoming aligns with the SDG emphasis on lifelong learning and adaptability. Goal 8, which calls for 'decent work and economic growth', is similarly enriched by an employability discourse that foregrounds fairness, accountability, and inclusivity. Beyond these, the interconnectedness of education with Goals on gender equality (5), reduced inequalities (10), climate action (13), and partnerships for the goals (17) demonstrates that employability cannot be reduced to economic metrics alone. It is implicated in the wider web of justice, sustainability, and human dignity.

The allegory once again offers a frame for interpretation. Inanna's descent disrupted the cosmic balance; fertility and life on earth were suspended during her absence. Her return restored harmony, not simply for herself but for the entire cosmos. In the same way, the renewal of employability through comprehensive skills and ethical governance is not only for the benefit of individual graduates. It is a renewal for societies, economies, and ecosystems, affecting the entire balance of global justice and sustainability.

The interconnectedness of the present world means that risks are no longer localised. An algorithm trained on biased datasets in one region can shape employment decisions in another. A failure to regulate data exploitation in one country can undermine trust in digital systems globally. Climate impacts, economic disruptions, and pandemics demonstrate with increasing urgency that the fates of nations are bound together. The AI-mediated transformations of work and education are no exception. Universal interconnectedness, therefore, entails universal responsibility. If employability is reconceived as dynamic, ethical, and inclusive, then this vision must extend across borders. It cannot be reserved for graduates in wealthy nations while excluding those in contexts of digital scarcity. Preparedness and awareness must be cultivated globally, through partnerships, knowledge-sharing, and solidarity. To do otherwise would be to replicate the logic of exclusion at precisely the moment when interdependence demands inclusion.

The interconnectedness of employability calls for a cosmopolitan vision, one that transcends parochial or nationalist framings. Universities must see themselves not only as local institutions but also as global actors, preparing graduates for participation in a world of shared challenges. Governments must design AI strategies not only for competitiveness but also for global equity, recognising that innovation without justice is a fragile and unsustainable foundation. Employers must understand that the adoption of AI has ripple effects across global labour markets, shaping opportunity and exclusion far beyond their immediate contexts. This cosmopolitan vision aligns with the spirit of the SDGs, which insist that no goal can be achieved in isolation. Progress towards sustainable education cannot be separated from climate action, gender equality, or the reduction of inequalities. Employability, in this light, becomes not a narrow outcome but a universal process of preparing individuals and societies for participation in the ongoing work of global flourishing.

The myth of Inanna concludes with renewal, not only for the goddess herself but also for the cycles of fertility, life, and justice across the cosmos. This universality is its enduring power. Renewal in the AI age must likewise be understood as interconnected. To renew employability is to renew justice, sustainability, and human dignity across borders. To embed ethical governance in AI is to contribute not only to local trust but also to global legitimacy. To cultivate comprehensive skills is to prepare not only individuals for work but also societies for shared futures.

Universal interconnectedness is therefore not an abstract ideal but the condition of survival and flourishing in the 21st century. The descent into AI disruption compels higher education, governments, and societies to confront vulnerability. The renewal that emerges from this descent must be collective, cosmopolitan, and globally just. The descent through the underworld, the synthesis of skills and employability, and the embedding of ethical governance have brought us to the final stage of this book: the moment of return. Inanna, having endured the stripping of her adornments and the confrontation with death, does not remain in darkness. She rises again, restored, transformed, and reconstituted. Her renewal restores cosmic balance, reminding her people that vulnerability, though painful, is the necessary precondition for wisdom and flourishing.

This final part of the conclusion embraces that narrative arc. It considers the future pathways that higher education must walk as it emerges from its own descent into the AI-mediated world. It reflects on the broader implications of the book's arguments, tying them together into a comprehensive vision. And it closes with a reflection on the enduring lesson of interconnectedness: that education, employability, and ethics are inseparable from the universal cycles of loss, renewal, and transformation.

THE FUTURE PATHWAYS OF HIGHER EDUCATION

The first pathway concerns curricular transformation. Universities must design curricula that integrate technical expertise with ethical reasoning, creativity, and global awareness. It is no longer sufficient to add digital literacy modules as supplements to existing programmes. Digital ethics, AI fluency, and intercultural competence must be embedded across disciplines, infusing the entire educational experience. Like Inanna's crown, the old model of isolated credentialism has been shed. What remains is the responsibility to cultivate adaptability and holistic awareness in every graduate. The second pathway is institutional responsibility. Universities cannot limit themselves to transmitting skills; they must model ethical governance in their own use of AI. Admissions systems, learning analytics, and academic integrity tools must be designed and implemented in line with FAT-HO principles: fairness, accountability, transparency, and human oversight. By embodying these values in practice, universities provide living exemplars for students, shaping not only their competencies but also their ethical imagination.

The third pathway is global solidarity. Preparedness and awareness cannot be the privilege of a few. Partnerships across borders—between universities in the Global North and South, between governments, between public and private sectors—are necessary to address asymmetries of access and opportunity. Just as Inanna's absence disrupted the balance of the cosmos, so too does global inequity threaten the balance of education and employability. Renewal requires inclusion: no society must be abandoned at the gates of technological transformation. The fourth pathway is lifelong learning. Employability, reconceived as dynamic becoming, cannot be contained within the temporal boundaries of a degree. The future will demand continuous renewal of skills, ethical reasoning, and reflective capacity. Lifelong learning must therefore be cultivated not only as a personal habit but also as a structural reality: supported by governments, incentivised by employers, and enabled by universities. Just as the cycles of fertility renewed the Sumerian world, so must the cycles of learning sustain our own.

Drawing together the arguments of this book, the intellectual contribution can be summarised in three interconnected claims. First, employability must be reconceived as dynamic, relational, and ethical. It is not the possession of static skills but the cultivation of adaptive capacities—technical, ethical, intercultural, and creative—that enable individuals to flourish amid change. Second, ethical governance is the necessary condition of meaningful employability in the AI age. Without fairness, accountability, transparency, and human oversight, employability risks being hollow, perpetuating inequality rather than enabling justice. Third, employability and ethical governance are inseparable from global interconnectedness. The challenges of AI are not bounded by disciplines or borders. They demand cosmopolitan visions, solidarity across divides, and a recognition that education is a public responsibility, contributing to the flourishing of humanity as a whole. Together, these claims constitute a paradigm shift: from employability as possession to employability as becoming, from AI as disruption to AI as invitation, from education as private investment to education as global stewardship.

The allegory of Inanna's descent has accompanied this conclusion as more than a metaphor. It has structured the narrative of vulnerability, stripping away, and renewal. Now, at its close, the myth reveals its full significance. Like Inanna, higher education has been stripped of its old securities: the certainty of credentialism, the comfort of disciplinary boundaries, the illusion of neutrality, the reductionism of technical rationality, the trust in data contracts, the determinism of markets, and the denial of human vulnerability. Each has been surrendered at the gates of AI transformation. And like Inanna, higher education has stood exposed before the throne of uncertainty, forced to confront the fragility of human agency in a world of algorithms. But this exposure is not the end; it is the moment of possibility. From vulnerability arises wisdom. From descent arises renewal. From death arises life. The lesson of the allegory is not despair but transformation. Renewal requires the shedding of illusions, the recognition of vulnerability, and the commitment to rebuild upon the foundations of justice, awareness, and interconnectedness. Higher education, having passed through the gates, must now rise again—not restored to what it was, but renewed into what it must become.

The argument of this book ends where it began: with the conviction that awareness and preparedness are the dual imperatives of our age. To be aware is to recognise the risks and possibilities of AI. To be prepared is to cultivate the skills, ethics, and solidarities necessary to navigate them. Together, they form the pathway through the underworld and into renewal.

The Sumerians understood that the cycles of descent and renewal were universal, binding gods and humans, fertility and death, and past and future. Our age demands a similar recognition: that education, employability, and AI are bound within cycles of transformation that extend across societies and generations. To ignore interconnectedness is to court imbalance. To embrace it is to restore harmony. The final mandate is therefore clear. Higher education must embrace its role as custodian of human flourishing in the AI-mediated world. It must prepare graduates not merely for employment but for participation in the collective work of justice, sustainability, and renewal. It must weave technical expertise with ethical governance, disciplinary insight with cosmopolitan vision, and individual growth with global responsibility. This is the wisdom that emerges from descent. This is the renewal that lies beyond the gates. And this is the future towards which higher education, employability, and AI must now journey—together, interconnected, and ever becoming.

Bibliography

Abulibdeh, A., Zaidan, E. and Abulibdeh, R., 2024. Navigating the confluence of artificial intelligence and education for sustainable development in the era of Industry 4.0: Challenges, opportunities, and ethical dimensions. *Journal of Cleaner Production*, 445, p. 140527.

Acemoglu, D. and Restrepo, P., 2019. Automation and new tasks: How technology displaces and reinstates labor. *Journal of Economic Perspectives*, 33(2), pp. 3–30.

Ada Lovelace Institute, 2021. *The Data Divide: Public Attitudes to Tackling Social and Health Inequalities in the COVID-19 Pandemic and Beyond*. Ada Lovelace Institute. Available at: https://www.adalovelaceinstitute.org/report/the-data-divide/ [Accessed 15 Jun. 2025].

Ada Lovelace Institute, AI Now Institute & Open Government Partnership, 2021, *Algorithmic Accountability for the Public Sector*. Available at: https://www.opengovpartnership.org/documents/algorithmic-accountability-public-sector [Accessed 15 Jun. 2025].

Adadi, A. and Berrada, M., 2018. Peeking inside the black-box: A survey on explainable artificial intelligence (XAI). *IEEE Access*, 6, pp. 52138–52160.

Adely, F.I.J., Mitra, A., Mohamed, M. and Shaham, A., 2021. Poor education, unemployment and the promise of skills: The hegemony of the "skills mismatch" discourse. *International Journal of Educational Development*, 82, p. 102381.

Adewolu, O.A., 2024. *Higher education, skills development and students' preparedness for employability: A case study of the University of Lagos, Nigeria (towards a sustained practice approach with the triple helix model of innovation)*. Doctoral dissertation. University College London.

Advance HE, 2020. *21st Century Skills*. Advance HE. Available at: https://www.advance-he.ac.uk/knowledge-hub/21st-century-skills [Accessed 25 November 2024].

Afolayan, O. and Okafor, C., 2023. The impact of artificial intelligence on employment: Evidence in Africa. *International Journal of Research and Innovation in Social Science*, 7(5), pp. 123–130.

African Union, 2024. *Continental Artificial Intelligence Strategy*. African Union Commission. Available at: https://au.int/sites/default/files/documents/44004-doc-EN-_Continental_AI_Strategy_July_2024.pdf [Accessed 15 Jun. 2025].

Afroogh, S., Akbari, A., Malone, E., Kargar, M. and Alambeigi, H., 2024. Trust in AI: Progress, challenges, and future directions. *Humanities and Social Sciences Communications*, 11(1), Article 1568. https://www.nature.com/articles/s41599-024-04044-8

Ahmad, B. and Bilal, S., 2024. Knowledge of AI as a future work skill for career sustainability: The role of person job fit. In: *Academy of Management Proceedings*, vol. 2024, no. 1, p. 16847. Valhalla, NY: Academy of Management.

Ahrweiler, P., Spaeth, E., Siqueiros Garcia, J.M., Luque Capellas, B. and Wurster, D., 2024. *Participatory Artificial Intelligence in Public Social Services: From Bias to Fairness in Assessing Beneficiaries*. Cham: Springer.

AI Skills for the UK Workforce. 2025. UK Government / Skills England, published 29 October. Available at: https://www.gov.uk/government/publications/ai-skills-for-the-uk-workforce [Accessed 15 January 2026].

Ajani, O.A., Gamede, B.T. and Bansal, R., 2024. Challenges and opportunities of integrating Industry 5.0 and emerging technologies in higher education for enhancing employability skills. In: A. Chakir, R. Bansal and M. Azzouazi, eds. *Industry 5.0 and Emerging Technologies: Transformation Through Technology and Innovations*. Cham: Springer, Studies in Systems, Decision and Control, vol. 565, pp. 217–230.

Akinwalere, S.N. and Ivanov, V., 2022. Artificial intelligence in higher education: Challenges and opportunities. *Border Crossing*, 12(1), pp. 1–15.

Albaroudi, S., Abdallah, S., Mezni, H. and Yahia, S.B., 2024. Fairness-aware AI recruitment: Techniques, challenges, and opportunities. *Information*, 15(1), p. 10. [online] Available at: https://www.mdpi.com/journal/information [Accessed 13 May 2025].

Allam, H.M., Gyamfi, B. and AlOmar, B., 2025. Sustainable innovation: Harnessing AI and living intelligence to transform higher education. *Education Sciences*, 15(4), p. 398.

Al-Zahrani, A., 2024. Unveiling the shadows: Beyond the hype of AI in education. *Journal of Educational Technology*, 21(3), pp. 45–59. Available at: https://pmc.ncbi.nlm.nih.gov/articles/PMC11087970/

Al-Zahrani, A.M. and Alasmari, T.M., 2024. Exploring the impact of artificial intelligence on higher education: The dynamics of ethical, social, and educational implications. *Humanities and Social Sciences Communications*, 11(1). Available at: https://www.nature.com/articles/s41599-024-03432-4 [Accessed 7 Apr. 2025].

Ananny, M. and Crawford, K., 2018. Seeing without knowing: Limitations of the transparency ideal. *New Media & Society*, 20(3), pp. 973–989.

Anderson, J. and Rainie, L., 2017. *The Future of Jobs and Training*. Washington, DC: Pew Research Center. [online] Available at: https://www.pewresearch.org/internet/2017/05/03/the-future-of-jobs-and-training/ [Accessed 5 Oct. 2025].

Antaki, M., 2006. The critical modernism of Hannah Arendt. *Theoretical Inquiries in Law*, 8(1), pp. 251–275.

Anthony, A., Sharma, L. and Noor, E., 2024. *Advancing a More Global Agenda for Trustworthy Artificial Intelligence*. Washington, D.C.: Carnegie Endowment for International Peace. Available at: https://carnegieendowment.org/2024/ai-global-trust-agenda [Accessed 5 May 2025].

Arntz, M., Gregory, T. and Zierahn, U., 2016. The risk of automation for jobs in OECD countries. OECD Social, Employment and Migration Working Papers No. 189.

Arrieta, A.B., Díaz-Rodríguez, N., Del Ser, J., Bennetot, A., Tabik, S., Barbado, A., Garcia, S., Gil-Lopez, S., Molina, D., Benjamins, R. and Chatila, R., 2020. Explainable artificial intelligence (XAI): Concepts, taxonomies, opportunities and challenges toward responsible AI. *Information Fusion*, 58, pp. 82–115.

Arthur, W.B., 2009. *The Nature of Technology: What It Is and How It Evolves*. New York: Simon & Schuster.

Ashton, D. and Green, F., 1996. *Education, Training and the Global Economy*. Cheltenham: Edward Elgar Publishing.

Asia Venture Philanthropy Network (AVPN), 2025. *AI Inclusion and Skilling Policy Framework: Terms of Reference for Development of an AI Workforce Inclusion Policy Toolkit*. Singapore: AVPN, February. Available at: https://avpn.asia/wp-content/uploads/2025/01/23.1.25-Terms-of-Reference-ToR_-AI-Inclusion-and-Skilling-Policy-Dialogues-and-Toolkit-Development.pdf [Accessed 15 Jun. 2025]

Association of Governing Boards, 2023. Artificial intelligence and the future of higher education, part 1. [online] Available at: https://agb.org/trusteeship-article/artificial-intelligence-and-the-future-of-higher-education-part-1 [Accessed 6 Apr. 2025].

Atkinson-Toal, A. and Guo, C., 2024. Generative Artificial Intelligence (AI) education policies of UK universities: A systematic content analysis. *Enhancing Teaching and Learning in Higher Education*, 2, pp. 70–94.

Autor, D.H., 2015. Why are there still so many jobs? The history and future of workplace automation. *Journal of Economic Perspectives*, 29(3), pp. 3–30.

Autor, D.H., Levy, F. and Murnane, R.J., 2003. The skill content of recent technological change: An empirical exploration. *Quarterly Journal of Economics*, 118(4), 1279–1333.

Baake, J., Schmitt, J.B. and Metag, J., 2025. Balancing realism and trust: AI avatars in science communication. *Journal of Science Communication*, 24(2), A03.

Baiocco, S., Fernández-Macías, E., Rani, U. and Pesole, A., 2022. The algorithmic management of work and its implications in different contexts (No. 2022/02). JRC Working Papers Series on Labour, Education and Technology.

Baker, R.S. and Hawn, A., 2022. 'Algorithmic bias in education', *International Journal of Artificial Intelligence in Education*, 32(4), pp. 1052–1092.

Bakhshi, H., Downing, J., Osborne, M. and Schneider, P., 2017. *The Future of Skills: Employment in 2030*. London: Pearson.

Baldwin, R., 2019. *The Globotics Upheaval: Globalization, Robotics, and the Future of Work*. Oxford: Oxford University Press.

Bandi, R.K., Klein, S., Madon, S., Monteiro, E. and Ranjini, C.R., 2020. The future of digital work: The challenge of inequality. In: *IFIP WG 8.2, 9.1, 9.4 Joint Working Conference (IFIPJWC 2020)*, Hyderabad, India, 10–11 December 2020. Proceedings. Cham: Springer, pp. 3–10.

Banks, S., 2020. *Ethics and Values in Social Work*. 5th ed. London: Bloomsbury Academic.

Bannister, F. and Connolly, R., 2011. 'Trust and transformational government: A proposed framework for research', *Government Information Quarterly*, 28(2), pp. 137–147. https://doi.org/10.1016/j.giq.2010.06.010

Barasa, P.L., 2021. *Digitalization in Teaching and Education in Kenya: Digitalization, the Future of Work and the Teaching Profession Project*. Geneva: International Labour Organization. [online] Available at: http://erepository.au.ac.ke/bitstream/handle/123456789/1312/wcms_783665.pdf?sequence=1&isAllowed=y [Accessed 8 Jan. 2025].

Bareis, J. (2024). The trustification of AI: Disclosing the bridging pillars that tie trust and AI together. *Big Data & Society*, 11(2). https://doi.org/10.1177/20539517241249430

Barnett, R., 2004. Learning for an unknown future. *Higher Education Research and Development*, 23(3), pp. 247–260.

Barnett, R., 2010. *Being a University*. London: Routledge.

Barrett, A. and O'Connell, P.J., 2001. Does training generally work? The returns to in-company training. *Industrial and Labor Relations Review*, 54(3), pp. 647–662

Batool, Z., et al., 2023. Using a machine learning model for employability prediction: A Moroccan case study. In: *Proceedings of the 6th International Conference on Networking, Intelligent Systems & Security (NISS 2023)*. New York: ACM, pp. 51–55.

Beck, U., Giddens, A. and Lash, S., 1994. *Reflexive modernization: Politics, tradition and aesthetics in the modern social order*. Stanford University Press.

Becker, G.S., 1964. *Human Capital: A Theoretical and Empirical Analysis, with Special Reference to Education*. New York: National Bureau of Economic Research/Distributed by Columbia University Press.

Bello, O. and Ajao, A.O., 2024. Digital literacy and skills development in Nigeria: Policies, barriers and recommendations. *Journal of African Innovation and Advanced Studies*, 5(2), pp. 1–18. Available at: https://africanscholarpub.com/ajaias/article/view/262/261

Bender, E.M., Gebru, T., McMillan-Major, A. and Shmitchell, S., 2021. 'On the dangers of stochastic parrots: Can language models be too big?', *Proceedings of the 2021 ACM Conference on Fairness, Accountability, and Transparency (FAccT '21)*, pp. 610–623. https://doi.org/10.1145/3442188.3445922

Bessen, J., 2015. Toil and technology. *Finance & Development*, 52(1), pp. 10–13. Available at: https://www.imf.org/external/pubs/ft/fandd/2015/03/bessen.htm [Accessed 17 Apr. 2025]

Bessen, J.E., 2019. AI and jobs: The role of demand. NBER Working Paper No. 24235.

Bhorat, H., Steenkamp, F. and Rooney, C., 2024. Artificial intelligence and skilled employment in South Africa. *Technology in Society*, 78, p. 102540. Available at: https://www.sciencedirect.com/science/article/pii/S2590051X24000406 [Accessed 17 Apr. 2025].

Biesta, G., 2010. *Good Education in an Age of Measurement: Ethics, Politics, Democracy*. Boulder, CO: Paradigm Publishers.

Biesta, G.J., 2015. *Good Education in an Age of Measurement: Ethics, Politics, Democracy*. Abingdon: Routledge.

Binns, R., 2018. Fairness in machine learning: Lessons from political philosophy. *Proceedings of the Conference on Fairness, Accountability, and Transparency*, pp. 149–159.

Blair, A., Evans, D., Hughes, C. and Tight, M. eds., 2022. *International perspectives on leadership in higher education*. Emerald Group Publishing.

Bolton, P. and Lewis, J., 2024. Equality of access and outcomes in higher education in England. House of Commons Library Research Briefing, No. CBP-9195, 25 July. Available at: https://researchbriefings.files.parliament.uk/documents/CBP-9195/CBP-9195.pdf [Accessed 17 Apr. 2025].

Bordes, J., 2025. AI education in Africa: Empowering the continent's next-generation workforce. *Forbes Business Council*. Available at: https://www.forbes.com/councils/forbesbusinesscouncil/2025/02/21/ai-education-in-africa-empowering-the-continents-next-generation-workforce/ [Accessed 17 Apr. 2025].

Boston Consulting Group (BCG), 2020. *Alleviating the Heavy Toll of the Global Skills Mismatch*.

Bovens, M., 2007. Analysing and assessing accountability: A conceptual framework. *European Law Journal*, 13(4), pp. 447–468. https://doi.org/10.1111/j.1468-0386.2007.00378.x

Bovens, M., 2010. Two concepts of accountability: Accountability as a virtue and as a mechanism. *West European Politics*, 33(5), pp. 946–967.

Boylan, M., Adams, G., Perry, E. and Booth, J., 2023. Re-imagining transformative professional learning for critical teacher professionalism: A conceptual review. *Professional Development in Education*, 49(4), pp. 651–669.

Bridgstock, R., 2017. The university and the knowledge network: A new educational model for twenty-first century learning and employability. In: M. Tomlinson and L. Holmes, eds. *Graduate Employability in Context: Theory, Research and Debate*. London: Palgrave Macmillan, pp. 339–358.

Brookings Institution, 2022. Auditing employment algorithms for discrimination. [online] Brookings. Available at: https://www.brookings.edu/articles/auditing-employment-algorithms-for-discrimination [Accessed 15 Apr. 2025].

Brown, P., Hesketh, A. and Williams, S., 2004. *The Mismanagement of Talent: Employability and Jobs in the Knowledge Economy*. Oxford: Oxford University Press.

Brown, P., Lauder, H. and Ashton, D., 2010. *The Global Auction: The Broken Promises of Education, Jobs, and Incomes*. Oxford University Press.

Brynjolfsson, E. and McAfee, A., 2014. *The Second Machine Age: Work, Progress, and Prosperity in a Time of Brilliant Technologies*. WW Norton & company.

Bughin, J., Hazan, E., Lund, S., Dahlström, P., Wiesinger, A. and Subramaniam, A., 2018. *Skill shift: Automation and the future of the workforce*. McKinsey Global Institute, 23 May. Available at: https://www.mckinsey.com/featured-insights/future-of-work/skill-shift-automation-and-the-future-of-the-workforce [Accessed 17 Apr. 2025].

Bukartaite, R. and Hooper, D., 2023. Automation, artificial intelligence and future skills needs: An Irish perspective. *European Journal of Training and Development*, 47(10), pp. 163–185.

Bulathwela, S., Pérez-Ortiz, M., Holloway, C., Cukurova, M. and Shawe-Taylor, J., 2024. Artificial intelligence alone will not democratise education: On educational inequality, techno-solutionism and inclusive tools. *Sustainability*, 16(2), p. 781.

Buolamwini, J. and Gebru, T. (2018) 'Gender Shades: Intersectional accuracy disparities in commercial gender classification', *Proceedings of the 1st Conference on Fairness, Accountability and Transparency (FAT' 18)**, *Proceedings of Machine Learning Research*, 81, pp. 77–91. Available at: https://proceedings.mlr.press/v81/buolamwini18a.html [Accessed 15 June 2025].

Burgstahler, S.E., 2022. *Universal Design in Higher Education: From Principles to Practice*. 2nd ed. Cambridge, MA: Harvard Education Press.

Burt, A., 2019. The AI transparency paradox. *Harvard Business Review*, 13 December. Available at: https://hbr.org/2019/12/the-ai-transparency-paradox [Accessed 15 Jun. 2025].

Butum, L.C. and Nicolescu, L., 2019. Learn and work in the 21st century: A review of employability models for HE graduates: Different levels of analysis. *Management Dynamics in the Knowledge Economy*, 7(1/23), pp. 71–86.

Bynner, J., 1999. Education and family components of identity in the transition from school to work. In: W.R. Heinz, ed. *From Education to Work: Cross-National Perspectives*. Cambridge: Cambridge University Press, pp. 233–252.

Canada. Treasury Board of Canada Secretariat, 2020; amended 2024. *Directive on Automated Decision-Making*. Government of Canada. Available at: https://www.canada.ca/en/government/system/digital-government/digital-government-innovations/responsible-use-ai/guide-scope-directive-automated-decision-making.html [Accessed 15 Jun. 2025].

Carnevale, A.P., Garcia, T.I., Ridley, N. and Quinn, M.C., 2020. *The Overlooked Value of Certificates and Associate's Degrees*. Georgetown University Center on Education and the Workforce.

Carter, L. and Bélanger, F., 2005. The utilization of e-government services: Citizen trust, innovation and acceptance. *Information Systems Journal*, 15(1), pp. 5–25. https://doi.org/10.1111/j.1365-2575.2005.00183.x

Casner-Lotto, J. and Barrington, L., 2006. *Are They Really Ready to Work? Employers' Perspectives on the Basic Knowledge and Applied Skills of New Entrants to the 21st Century US Workforce*. Washington, DC: Partnership for 21st Century Skills.

Cave, S. and ÓhÉigeartaigh, S.S., 2018. An AI race for strategic advantage: Rhetoric and risks. In: J. Furman, G.E. Marchant, H. Price and F. Rossi, eds. *Proceedings of the 2018 AAAI/ACM Conference on AI, Ethics, and Society (AIES 2018)*, New Orleans, LA, USA, 2–3 Feb. 2018. ACM, pp. 36–40.

Cedefop, 2018. *Skills Forecast: Trends and Challenges to 2030*. European Centre for the Development of Vocational Training.

Centre for Data Ethics and Innovation, 2020. *Review into Bias in Algorithmic Decision-Making*. Available at: https://www.gov.uk/government/publications/cdei-publishes-review-into-bias-in-algorithmic-decision-making [Accessed: 2 May 2025].

Cetindamar Kozanoglu, D. and Abedin, B. (2021). Understanding the role of employees in digital transformation: Conceptualization of digital literacy of employees as a multi-dimensional organizational affordance. *Journal of Enterprise Information Management*, 34(6), pp. 1649–1672.

Chalkiadaki, A., 2018. A systematic literature review of 21st century skills and competencies in primary education. *International Journal of Instruction*, 11(3), pp. 1–16.

Chambers Goodman, M., 2025. *Bias by design: The hidden legal vulnerabilities of algorithmic hiring. Colorado Law Review*, [online] Available at: https://lawreview.colorado.edu [Accessed 13 May 2025].

Chapple, M. and Tolley, H., 2013. Embedding key skills in a traditional university. In: C. Fallows and R. Steven, eds. *Integrating Key Skills in Higher Education*. London: Routledge, pp. 67–76.

Chen, Z., 2023. Ethics and discrimination in artificial intelligence-enabled recruitment practices. *Humanities and Social Sciences Communications*, 10(1), pp. 1–12.

Chui, M., Manyika, J., and Miremadi, M. 2016. Where machines could replace humans-and where they can't (yet). In *The McKinsey Quarterly*, pp. 1–12.

Clarke, M., 2018. Rethinking graduate employability: The role of capital, individual attributes and context. *Studies in Higher Education*, 43(11), pp. 1923–1937.

Colbert, A.E., Yee, N. and George, G., 2016. The digital workforce and the workplace of the future. *Academy of Management Journal*, 59(3), pp. 731–739.

Collier, A., 2020. Inclusive design and design justice: Strategies to shape our classes and communities. *EDUCAUSE Review*. Available at: https://er.educause.edu/articles/2020/10/inclusive-design-and-design-justice-strategies-to-shape-our-classes-and-communities [Accessed 22 May 2025].

Connolly, D., Dickinson, L. and Hellewell, L., 2023. The development of undergraduate employability skills through authentic assessment in college-based higher education. *Journal of Learning Development in Higher Education*, 27. Available at: https://journal.aldinhe.ac.uk/index.php/jldhe/article/view/1004 [Accessed 3 April 2025].

Cook, C., 2021. *The Next Wave of Disruption: Emerging Market Media Use of Artificial Intelligence and Machine Learning*. Bogotá: Centro Latinoamericano de Investigacion Periodistica (CLIP).

Corrêa, N.K., Galvão, C., Santos, J.W., Del Pino, C., Pinto, E.P., Barbosa, C., Massmann, D., Mambrini, R., Galvão, L., Terem, E. and de Oliveira, N., 2023. Worldwide AI ethics: A review of 200 guidelines and recommendations for AI governance. *Patterns*, 4(10), p. 100857. https://doi.org/10.1016/j.patter.2023.100857

Council of Europe, 2024. *Regulating the Use of Artificial Intelligence Systems in Education – Preparatory Study on the Development of a Legal Instrument*. Council of Europe.

Crampton, N., 2022. 'Microsoft's framework for building AI systems responsibly', *Microsoft on the Issues*, 21 June. Available at: https://blogs.microsoft.com/on-the-issues/2022/06/21/microsofts-framework-for-building-ai-systems-responsibly/ [Accessed 15 June 2025].

Crawford, K., 2021. *The Atlas of AI: Power, Politics, and the Planetary Costs of Artificial Intelligence.* Yale University Press.

Dall'Alba, G., 2009. Learning professional ways of being: Ambiguities of becoming. *Educational philosophy and theory*, 41(1), pp. 34–45.

Daugherty, P.R. and Wilson, H.J., 2018. *Human + Machine: Reimagining Work in the Age of AI.* Boston, MA: Harvard Business Review Press.

De Stefano, V., 2016. The rise of the just-in time workforce: On demand work, crowdwork, and labor protection in the gig economy. *Comparative labor law and policy journal*, 37(3), pp. 461–471

Dede, C. (2009). Immersive interfaces for engagement and learning. *Science*, 323(5910), pp. 66–69.

Dede, C., 2010. Comparing frameworks for 21st century skills. In: J. Bellanca and R. Brandt, eds. *21st Century Skills: Rethinking How Students Learn*. Bloomington, IN: Solution Tree Press, pp. 51–76.

Dell Technologies, 2023. *Innovation Index: Full Findings Report*. Dell Technologies. Available at: https://www.delltechnologies.com/asset/en-us/solutions/business-solutions/industry-market/dell-technologies-innovation-index-full-findings-report.pdf [Accessed 28 Nov. 2025].

Deming, D.J., 2017. The growing importance of social skills in the labor market. *Quarterly Journal of Economics*, 132(4), pp. 1593–1640.

Deming, D.J. and Noray, K., 2020. Earnings dynamics, changing job skills, and STEM careers. *The Quarterly Journal of Economics*, 135(4), pp. 1965–2005.

Departamento Nacional de Planeación, 2021. *Política Nacional de Inteligencia Artificial – CONPES 4144*. Bogotá: Government of Colombia. Available at: https://accesspartnership.com/colombia-national-ai-policy/ [Accessed 21 Apr. 2025].

Department for Education, 2025. *Generative Artificial Intelligence (AI) in Education: Policy Statement*. London: Department for Education. Available at: https://www.gov.uk/government/publications/generative-artificial-intelligence-ai-in-education [Accessed 15 Apr. 2025].

Department for Education (DfE), 2023. *Generative Artificial Intelligence in Education*. London: Department for Education. [online] Available at: https://www.gov.uk/government/publications/generative-artificial-intelligence-in-education [Accessed 5 Oct. 2025].

Department of Health and Social Care, 2019. *A Guide to Good Practice for Digital and Data-driven Health and Care Technology: Code of Conduct for Data-Driven Health and Care Technology*. UK Government, 6 January. Available at: https://www.gov.uk/government/publications/code-of-conduct-for-data-driven-health-and-care-technology [Accessed 15 Jun. 2025].

Derechos Digitales, (2021). *Artificial Intelligence and Participation in Latin America*. Available at: https://www.derechosdigitales.org/wp-content/uploads/01_EN_Artificial-Intelligence-and-Participation-in-Latam_FINAL-1.pdf [Accessed 21 Apr. 2025].

Diakopoulos, N., 2020. Transparency. In: M.D. Dubber, F. Pasquale and S. Das, eds. *The Oxford Handbook of Ethics of AI*. Oxford University Press. https://doi.org/10.1093/oxfordhb/9780190067397.013.11

Dialzara, 2024. *AI Regulation in Latin America: Strategies, Policies, and Compliance*. Available at: https://dialzara.com/blog/ai-regulation-in-latin-america-strategies-policies-compliance/ [Accessed 21 Apr. 2025].

Díaz-Rodríguez, N., Del Ser, J., Coeckelbergh, M., López de Prado, M., Herrera-Viedma, E. and Herrera, F., 2023. *Connecting the dots in trustworthy artificial intelligence: From AI principles, ethics, and key requirements to responsible AI systems and regulation*. arXiv preprint arXiv:2305.02231.

DiSalvo, C., 2009. 'Design and the construction of publics', *Design Philosophy Papers*, 7(1), pp. 7–28.

Dludla, N., 2025. Microsoft to train 1 million South Africans on AI skills. *Reuters*, 23 Jan. [online] Available at: https://www.reuters.com/technology/artificial-intelligence/microsoft-train-1-million-south-africans-ai-skills-2025-01-23/ [Accessed 17 Apr. 2025].

Duggal, H.K., Khatri, P., Thomas, A. and Pironti, M., 2024. Changing learning paradigms: An interplay of digital Taylorism and technostress on perceived employability. *Journal of Management History*, 30(2), pp. 166–194.

Durán, J.M. and Pozzi, G. (2025). Trust and trustworthiness in AI. *Philosophy & Technology*, 38(16).

Dweck, C., 2006. *Mindset: The New Psychology of Success*. New York: Random House.

Economist Intelligence Unit, 2020. *Staying Ahead of the Curve: The Business Case for Responsible AI. Economist Intelligence Unit*, October 2020. Available at: https://pages.eiu.com/rs/753-RIQ-438/images/EIUStayingAheadOfTheCurve.pdf [Accessed 15 June 2025].

Edelman Trust Barometer, 2024. *2024 Edelman Trust Barometer: Insights for the Tech Sector (Supplemental Report)*. New York: Edelman Trust Institute.

EDUCAUSE Review, 2025. An AI-driven optimism for transforming higher education (it's not what you think). [online] Available at: https://er.educause.edu/articles/2025/2/an-ai-driven-optimism-for-transforming-higher-education-its-not-what-you-think [Accessed 6 Apr. 2025].

Ejjami, R., 2024. AI's impact on vocational training and employability: Innovation, challenges, and perspectives. *International Journal for Multidisciplinary Research (IJFMR)*, 6(4), pp. 1–16.

Enterprise, 2024. The education ministry's new AI-powered education platform takes aim at private tutoring industry. [online] Available at: https://enterprise.news/egypt/en/news/story/afe41f94-5aca-4830-ab4c-c25916582809/the-education-ministry%25e2%2580%2599s-new-ai-powered-education-platform-takes-aim-at-private-tutoring-industry [Accessed 8 Jan. 2025].

Erfan, M., 2024. The impact of cross-cultural management on global collaboration and performance. *Advances in Human Resource Management Research*, 2(2), pp. 102–112.

Eryandi, K.Y. and Nuryanto, A., 2020. 21st-century skills of life career skills in productive learning of vocational high school of technical expertise engineering in Yogyakarta city. *American Journal of Educational Research*, 8(7), pp. 480–484.

Esmond, B. and Atkins, L., 2022. *Education, Skills and Social Justice in a Polarising World: Between Technical Elites and Welfare Vocationalism*. Routledge.

Eubanks, V., 2018. *Automating Inequality: How High-Tech Tools Profile, Police, and Punish the Poor*. New York: St. Martin's Press.

European Commission, 2019. *Ethics Guidelines for Trustworthy Artificial Intelligence*. European Commission. Available at: https://digital-strategy.ec.europa.eu/en/library/ethics-guidelines-trustworthy-ai [Accessed 15 June 2025].

European Commission, 2020. *White Paper on Artificial Intelligence: A European Approach to Excellence and Trust*. Brussels: European Commission. Available at: https://ec.europa.eu/info/publications/white-paper-artificial-intelligence-european-approach-excellence-and-trust_en [Accessed 5 May 2025].

European Commission, 2021. *Proposal for a Regulation Laying Down Harmonised Rules on Artificial Intelligence (Artificial Intelligence Act)*. [online] Available at: https://eur-lex.europa.eu/legal-content/EN/TXT/?uri=CELEX%3A52021PC0206 [Accessed 22 Apr. 2025].

European Commission, 2022. *Ethical Guidelines on the Use of Artificial Intelligence and Data in Teaching and Learning for Educators*. Luxembourg: Publications Office of the European Union. https://doi.org/10.2766/127030. Available at: https://teachertaskforce.org/sites/default/files/2023-03/2022_EC_ethical%20guidelines%20on%20the%20use%20of%20artificial%20intelligence_EN.pdf [Accessed 15 Jun. 2025].

European Commission High-Level Expert Group on AI, 2019. *Ethics Guidelines for Trustworthy AI*. Brussels: European Commission. Available at: https://ec.europa.eu/futurium/en/ai-alliance-consultation [Accessed 5 May 2025].

European Parliament and Council, 2024. *Regulation (EU) 2024/1689 of the European Parliament and of the Council of 13 June 2024 Laying Down Harmonised Rules on Artificial Intelligence (Artificial Intelligence Act)*. Official Journal of the European Union, L 1689, 12.7.2024. Available at: http://data.europa.eu/eli/reg/2024/1689/oj [Accessed 15 Jun. 2025].

Fabris, E., Rossi, A., Ferretti, S. and Rahwan, I., 2024. *Algorithmic hiring: A multidisciplinary survey*. *arXiv preprint* arXiv:2403.12345.

Felstead, A., Gallie, D., Green, F. and Henseke, G., 2019. The determinants of skills use and work pressure: A longitudinal analysis. *Economic and Industrial Democracy*, 40(3), pp. 730–754.

Felstead, A., Gallie, D., Green, F. and Inanc, H., 2013. *Skills at Work in Britain*. London: Centre for Learning and Life Chances in Knowledge Economies and Societies, Institute of Education. Available at: https://www.llakes.ac.uk/wp-content/uploads/old/1.%20Skills%20at%20Work%20in%20Britain%20-%20mini-report.pdf [Accessed 23 Mar. 2025].

Finegold, D., 1999. Creating self-sustaining, high-skill ecosystems. *Oxford Review of Economic Policy*, 15(1), pp. 60–81.

Finegold, D. and Soskice, D., 1988. The failure of training in Britain: Analysis and prescription. *Oxford Review of Economic Policy*, 4(3), pp. 21–53.

Fleming, P., 2017. The human capital hoax: Work, debt and insecurity in the era of Uberization. *Organization Studies*, *38*(5), pp. 691–709.

Flew, T., 2023. Mediated trust and artificial intelligence. *Emerging Media*, 1(1), 22–29. https://doi.org/10.1177/27523543231188793

Floridi, L. and Cowls, J., 2019. A unified framework of five principles for AI in society. *Harvard Data Science Review*, 1, pp. 2–15. https://doi.org/10.1162/99608f92.8cd550d1

Floridi, L. and Cowls, J., 2022. A unified framework of five principles for AI in society. In: *Machine Learning and the City: Applications in Architecture and Urban Design*, pp. 535–545.

Floridi, L., Cowls, J., Beltrametti, M., Chatila, R., Chazerand, P., Dignum, V., Luetge, C., Madelin, R., Pagallo, U., Rossi, F., Schafer, B., Valcke, P. and Vayena, E., 2018. AI4People—An ethical framework for a good AI society: Opportunities, risks, principles, and recommendations. *Minds and Machines*, 28(4), pp. 689–707. https://doi.org/10.1007/s11023-018-9482-5

Fook, J. and Gardner, F., 2007. *Practising Critical Reflection: A Resource Handbook*. Maidenhead: McGraw-Hill Education (UK).

Fox, J., 2007. The uncertain relationship between transparency and accountability. *Development in Practice*, 17(4–5), pp. 663–671. https://doi.org/10.1080/09614520701469955

Freire, P. (1970). *Pedagogy of the Oppressed*. New York: Herder and Herder.

Frey, C.B. and Osborne, M.A., 2017. The future of employment: How susceptible are jobs to computerisation? *Technological Forecasting and Social Change*, 114, pp. 254–280.

Friedman, B. and Nissenbaum, H., 1996 'Bias in computer systems', *ACM Transactions on Information Systems*, 14(3), pp. 330–347. https://doi.org/10.1145/230538.230561

Friedman, M., 1955. The role of government in education. In: R.A. Solo, ed. *Economics and the Public Interest*. New Brunswick: Rutgers University Press, pp. 123–144.

Frink, D.D. and Klimoski, R.J., 1998. Toward a theory of accountability in organizations and human resource management. *Research in Personnel and Human Resources Management*, 16, pp. 1–51.

Gates, S., Lippman, L., Shadowen, N., Burke, H., Diener, O. and Malkin, M., 2016. *Key Soft Skills for Cross-SectoralYouth Outcomes*. Washington, DC: USAID's YouthPower: Implementation, YouthPower Action. [online] Available at: https://www.youthpower.org/sites/default/files/YouthPower/resources/Key%20Soft%20Skills%20for%20Cross-Sectoral%20Youth%20Outcomes_YouthPower%20Action.pdf [Accessed 10 Jan. 2025].

Ghimire, A. and Edwards, J., 2024. From guidelines to governance: A study of AI policies in education. arXiv preprint arXiv:2403.15601. Available at: https://arxiv.org/abs/2403.15601 [Accessed 15 Jun. 2025].

Gidiotis, I. and Hrastinski, S., 2024. Imagining the future of artificial intelligence in education: A review of social science fiction. *Learning, Media and Technology*, 49(5), pp. 597–611.

Gillespie, N., Lockey, S., Ward, T., Macdade, A. and Hassed, G. (2023) *Trust in Artificial Intelligence: A global study 2023*. KPMG International and The University of Melbourne. Available at: https://assets.kpmg.com/content/dam/kpmgsites/xx/pdf/2023/09/trust-in-ai-global-study-2023.pdf [Accessed 15 Jun. 2025].

Giroux, H.A., 2014. *Neoliberalism's War on Higher Education*. Chicago: Haymarket Books.

Global Partnership for Education, 2025. *From Commitment to Action: Advancing the Use of AI in Education in Africa*. Available at: https://www.gpekix.org/blog/commitment-action-advancing-use-ai-education-africa-through-regional-collaboration-and [Accessed 17 Apr. 2025].

Google, 2024. *An AI Opportunity Agenda for Vietnam*. Google Public Policy, July. Available at: https://publicpolicy.google/resources/vietnam_ai_opportunity_agenda_en.pdf [Accessed 15 Jun. 2025].

Gregg, M., 2011. *Work's Intimacy*. Cambridge: Polity.

Gretton, S., Harvey, C., Raine, D., Hurkett, C., Williams, D. and Symons, S., 2022. Revisiting the research-teaching nexus framework: Two case studies introducing research into programme level undergraduate teaching. *International Journal of Teaching and Learning in Higher Education*, 33(2), pp. 259–272.

Grubb, W.N., 1996. *Working in the Middle: Strengthening Education and Training for the Mid-skilled Labor Force*. Jossey-Bass Publishers, Inc.

Habets, O., Stoffers, J., van der Heijden, B. and Peters, P., 2020. Am I fit for tomorrow's labor market? The effect of graduates' skills development during higher education for the 21st century's labor market. *Sustainability*, 12(18), pp. 1–13.

Hanna, M., Pantanowitz, L., Jackson, B., Palmer, O., Visweswaran, S., Pantanowitz, J., Deebajah, M. and Rashidi, H., 2024. Ethical and bias considerations in artificial intelligence (AI)/machine learning. *Modern Pathology*, 37, pp. 1–31.

Hildebrandt, M., 2012. The dawn of a critical transparency right for the profiling era. In: J. Bus, M. Crompton, M. Hildebrandt and G. Metakides, eds. *Digital Enlightenment Forum Yearbook 2012*. Amsterdam: IOS Press BV, pp. 41–56. https://doi.org/10.3233/978-1-61499-057-4-41

Hillage, J. and Pollard, E., 1998. *Employability: Developing a Framework for Policy Analysis*. Institute for Employment Studies.

Hinchliffe, G.W. and Jolly, A., 2011. Graduate identity and employability. *British Educational Research Journal*, 37(4), pp. 563–584.

Holmes, L., 2013. Competing perspectives on graduate employability: Possession, position or process? *Studies in Higher Education*, 38(4), pp. 538–554.

Hutson, J. and Ceballos, J., 2023. Rethinking education in the age of AI: The importance of developing durable skills in the Industry 4.0. *Journal of Information Economics*, 1(2), pp. 26–36.

Illich, I., 1971. *Deschooling Society*. New York, NY: Harper & Row.

ILO (International Labour Organization), 2021. *Digital Labour Platforms and the Future of Work: Towards Decent Work in the Online World*.

Inside Higher Ed, 2023. How AI is shaping the future of Higher Ed. [online] Available at: https://www.insidehighered.com/views/2023/03/22/how-ai-shaping-future-higher-ed-opinion [Accessed 6 Apr. 2025].

Institute for Ethical AI in Education, 2021. *The Ethical Framework for AI in Education – Final Report*. Buckingham: University of Buckingham. Available at: https://www.buckingham.ac.uk/research-the-institute-for-ethical-ai-in-education [Accessed 15 April 2025].

Inter-American Development Bank, 2022. *Artificial Intelligence for Social Good in Latin America and the Caribbean: The Regional Landscape and 12 Country Snapshots*. Available at: https://publications.iadb.org/en/artificial-intelligence-for-social-good-in-latin-america-and-the-caribbean-the-regional-landscape-and-12-country-snapshots [Accessed 21 Apr. 2025].

International Baccalaureate, 2020. 21st century employability skills. [online] Available at: https://ibo.org [Accessed 25 Mar. 2025].

International Labour Organization (ILO), 2020. *World Employment and Social Outlook: Trends 2020*.

International Monetary Fund (IMF), 2005. *The IMF's Approach To Promoting Good Governance And Combating Corruption – A Guide*. Washington, DC: International Monetary Fund.

Istudor, N., Socol, A.G., Marinaş, M.C. and Socol, C., 2024. Analysis of the adequacy of employees' skills for the adoption of artificial intelligence in Central and Eastern European countries. *Amfiteatru Economic*, 26(67), pp. 703–720.

Jackson, D., 2015. Employability skill development in work-integrated learning: Barriers and best practice. *Studies in Higher Education*, 40(2), pp. 350–367.

Jackson, D. and Bridgstock, R. (2021). The future of graduate employability: A literature review. *Higher Education Research & Development*, 40(1), 1–16.

James, C., 2019. *The Ambiguity of 21st-Century Skills: Educational Perspectives and Implications*. London: Routledge.

Jarrahi, M.H., 2018. Artificial intelligence and the future of work: Human–AI symbiosis in organisational decision making. *Business Horizons*, 61(4), pp. 577–586.

Jin, Y., Yan, L., Echeverria, V., Gašević, D. and Martinez-Maldonado, R., 2025. Generative AI in higher education: A global perspective of institutional adoption policies and guidelines. *Computers and Education: Artificial Intelligence*, 8, p. 100348.

Jisc, 2023. *Artificial Intelligence (AI) in Tertiary Education*. 3rd ed. Bristol: Jisc. Available at: https://www.jisc.ac.uk/reports/artificial-intelligence-in-tertiary-education [Accessed 15 April 2025].

Jobin, A., Ienca, M. and Vayena, E., 2019. The global landscape of AI ethics guidelines. *Nature Machine Intelligence*, 1(9), pp. 389–399. https://doi.org/10.1038/s42256-019-0088-2

Joynes, C., Rossignoli, S. and Fenyiwa Amonoo-Kuofi, E., 2019. *21st Century Skills: Evidence of Issues in Definition, Demand and Delivery for Development Contexts (K4D Helpdesk Report)*. Brighton: Institute of Development Studies.

Kacianka, S. and Pretschner, A., 2021. *Designing accountable systems. arXiv preprint* arXiv:2101.08102.

Kaplan, J. 2016. *Artificial intelligence:What everyone needs to know*. Oxford, UK: Oxford University Press.

Karran, A.J., Charland, P., Martineau, J.-T., Ortiz de Guinea Lopez de Arana, A., Lesage, A.M., Sénécal, S. and Léger, P.-M., 2024. Multi-stakeholder perspective on responsible artificial intelligence and acceptability in education. arXiv preprint arXiv:2402.15027. Available at: https://arxiv.org/abs/2402.15027 [Accessed 15 Jun. 2025].

Keefer, P. and Scartascini, C., (eds.) 2022. *Trust: The Key to Social Cohesion and Growth in Latin America and the Caribbean*. Inter-American Development Bank, Washington, DC. https://doi.org/10.18235/0003911

Keep, E. and Mayhew, K. 1999. The assessment: Knowledge, skills and competitiveness. *Oxford Review of Economic Policy*, 15(1), pp. 1–15.

Khan, A., Davies, C. and Tomlinson, J., 2024. Evaluating 21st century skills development through makerspace workshops in computer science education. *Journal of Educational Technology and Innovation*, 15(1), pp. 45–66.

Khotami, M., 2017. The concept of accountability in good governance. In: *Proceedings of the International Conference on Democracy, Accountability and Governance (ICODAG 2017)*. Atlantis Press, pp. 29–31.

Kiseleva, A., Kotzinos, D. and De Hert, P., 2022. Transparency of AI in healthcare as a multilayered system of accountabilities: Between legal requirements and technical limitations. *Frontiers in Artificial Intelligence*, 5, p. 879603. https://doi.org/10.3389/frai.2022.879603

Knowles, B. and Richards, J.T., 2021. 'The sanction of authority: Promoting public trust in AI', *arXiv preprint* arXiv:2102.04221. Available at: https://arxiv.org/abs/2102.04221 [Accessed 15 June 2025].

Knox, J., Williamson, B. and Bayne, S., 2020. Machine behaviourism: Future visions of 'learnification' and 'datafication' across humans and digital technologies. *Learning, Media and Technology*, 45(1), pp. 31–45.

Kokkos, A. (2020). Embedding employability skills in UK higher education: Between skill instrumentalism and humanities education. *Arts and Humanities in Higher Education*, 19(3), 275–291.

Kolb, D.A., 2014. *Experiential Learning: Experience as the Source of Learning and Development*. 2nd ed. Upper Saddle River: FT Press.

Kornelakis, A. and Petrakaki, D., 2020. Embedding employability skills in UK higher education: Between digitalization and marketization. *Industry and Higher Education*, 34(5), pp. 290–297.

Kwakye, S.F., 2025a. *Towards transparent and interpretable predictions of student performance using explainable AI*. PhD thesis, University of East London. Available at: https://repository.uel.ac.uk/item/xxxxxx/towards-transparent-and-interpretable-predictions-of-student-performance-using-explainable-ai [Accessed 15 Jun. 2025].

Kwakye, S.F. 2025b. *Towards Transparent and Interpretable Predictions of Student Performance Using Explainable AI* (Doctoral dissertation, University of East London).

Kwet, M., 2019. *Digital colonialism: South Africa's education transformation in the shadow of Silicon Valley*. PhD dissertation. Rhodes University. Available at: https://papers.ssrn.com/sol3/papers.cfm?abstract_id=3496049 [Accessed 4 Apr. 2025].

Langenkamp, A.G., Robertson, T. and Czerwonka, A., 2020. *Automated hiring transparency: A legal analysis and proposal. SSRN Electronic Journal*, [online] Available at: https://papers.ssrn.com [Accessed 13 May 2025].

Leonavičienė, E., Burinskienė, A. and Peleckis, K., 2022. The role of national culture as an indicator of evidence of sustainable development. *Folia Oeconomica Stetinensia*, 22(2), 146–167.

Leslie, D., Burr, C., Aitken, M., Katell, M., Briggs, M. and Rincon, C., 2022. Human rights, democracy, and the rule of law assurance framework for AI systems: A proposal. arXiv preprint arXiv:2202.02776.

Leslie, D. and Perini, A.M., 2024. Future shock: Generative AI and the international AI policy and governance crisis. *Harvard Data Science Review*, 5. https://doi.org/10.1162/99608f92.88b4cc98

Li, J., Zhou, Y., Yao, J. and Liu, X., 2021. An empirical investigation of trust in AI in a Chinese petrochemical enterprise based on institutional theory. *Scientific Reports*, 11, Article 13564. https://www.nature.com/articles/s41598-021-92904-7

Liao, Q.V. and Sundar, S.S., 2022. Designing for responsible trust in AI systems: A communication perspective. *Proceedings of the 2022 ACM Conference on Fairness, Accountability, and Transparency (FAccT '22)*, pp. 1257–1268. New York, NY, USA: Association for Computing Machinery. https://doi.org/10.1145/3531146.3533182

Luckin, R., Holmes, W., Griffiths, M. and Forcier, L.B., 2016. *Intelligence Unleashed: An Argument for AI in Education*. London: Pearson. [online] Available at: https://edu.google.com/pdfs/Intelligence-Unleashed-Publication.pdf [Accessed 7 Apr. 2025].

Makridakis, S., 2017. The forthcoming Artificial Intelligence (AI) revolution: Its impact on society and firms. *Futures*, 90, pp. 46–60.

Manyika, J., Lund, S., Chui, M., Bughin, J., Woetzel, J., Batra, P., Ko, R. and Sanghvi, S., 2017. Jobs lost, jobs gained: Workforce transitions in a time of automation. *McKinsey Global Institute*, 150(1), pp. 1–148.

Manyika, J., Lund, S., Chui, M., Bughin, J., Woetzel, J., Batra, P., Ko, R. and Sanghvi, S., 2020. *The Future of Work in Europe: Automation, Workforce Transitions, and the Shifting Geography of Employment*. McKinsey Global Institute.

Markus, A.F., Kors, J.A. and Rijnbeek, P.R. 2021. The role of explainability in creating trustworthy artificial intelligence for health care: a comprehensive survey of the terminology, design choices, and evaluation strategies. *Journal of biomedical informatics*, *113*, p. 103655.

Marr, B., 2022. *Future Skills: The 20 Skills and Competencies Everyone Needs to Succeed in a Digital World*. John Wiley & Sons.

McCafferty, H., 2022. An unjust balance: A systematic review of the employability perceptions of UK undergraduates from disadvantaged socio-economic backgrounds. *Research in Post-Compulsory Education*, 27(4), pp. 570–593.

McGrath, S.K. and Whitty, S.J., 2018. Accountability and responsibility defined. *International Journal of Managing Projects in Business*, 11(3), pp. 687–707. https://doi.org/10.1108/IJMPB-06-2017-0058

Memarian, F. and Doleck, T., 2023. FATE in higher education: A systematic review. *Educational Technology & Society*, 26(2), pp. 17–30.

Miller, R., 2018. *Transforming the Future: Anticipation in the 21st Century*. Taylor & Francis, p. 300.

Mincer, J.A., 1974. *Schooling, Experience, and Earnings*. New York: National Bureau of Economic Research.

Mitchell, M., Wu, S., Zaldivar, A., Barnes, P., Vasserman, L., Hutchinson, B., Spitzer, E., Raji, I.D. and Gebru, T., 2019. Model cards for model reporting. *Proceedings of the 2019 Conference on Fairness, Accountability, and Transparency – FAT '19*. New York: ACM, pp. 220–229. https://doi.org/10.1145/3287560.3287596

Mkrtchyan, A., Niyibizi, P.A., Torgusson, C. and Hayward, I.M.L., 2020. *Rwanda Economic Update: Accelerating Digital Transformation in Rwanda*. Washington, D.C.: World Bank Group. Available at: http://documents.worldbank.org/curated/en/912581580156139783/Rwanda-Economic-Update-Accelerating-Digital-Transformation-in-Rwanda [Accessed 12 Jan. 2025].

Moore, P.V., 2017. *The Quantified Self in Precarity: Work, Technology and What Counts*. London: Routledge.

Morley, J., Elhalal, A., Garcia, F., Kinsey, L., Mökander, J. and Floridi, L., 2021. Ethics as a service: A pragmatic operationalisation of AI ethics. *Minds and Machines*, 31(2), pp. 239–256.

Morley, L., 2001. Producing new workers: Quality, equality and employability in higher education. *Quality in Higher Education*, 7(2), pp. 131–138. Available at: https://www.researchgate.net/publication/233236245_Producing_New_Workers_Quality_Equality_and_Employability_in_Higher_Education [Accessed 15 Apr. 2025].

Moser, C., 2023. *The Concept of Accountability and Human Rights Violations*, Max Planck Institute for Comparative Public Law & International Law Research Paper No. 2023-26, Forthcoming in Michelle Duin & Kristin Henrard (eds), *Research Handbook on the Accountability for Human Rights Violations: What, Who, What For, How, To What Extent* (Edward Elgar Publishing Ltd). Available at: https://ssrn.com/abstract=4655627 [Accessed 15 Jun. 2025].

Muduli, A. and Pandya, G., 2018. Psychological empowerment and workforce agility. *Psychological Studies*, 63(3), pp. 276–285.

Mulgan, R., 2000. 'Accountability': An ever-expanding concept?. *Public Administration*, 78(3), pp. 555–573. https://doi.org/10.1111/1467-9299.00218

Mutandiro, K., 2024. African universities are failing to prepare tech graduates for jobs in AI. *Rest of World*. Available at: https://restofworld.org/2024/ai-skills-training-africa/ [Accessed 17 Apr. 2025].

Mutimukwe, C., Twizeyimana, J.D. and Viberg, O., 2021. 'Students' information privacy concerns in learning analytics: Towards a model development', *arXiv preprint* arXiv:2109.00068. Available at: https://arxiv.org/abs/2109.00068 [Accessed 15 Jun. 2025].

Nartey, E., 2021. *Accountability and Corporate Human Rights Violations in Tort and International Law*. Cambridge Scholars Publishing.

Nartey, E.K., 2025. *Generative AI in Higher Education: Guiding Principles for Teaching and Learning*. London: Routledge.

National Institute of Standards and Technology (NIST), 2023. *Artificial Intelligence Risk Management Framework (AI RMF 1.0)*. NIST Special Publication 1270, National Institute of Standards and Technology, Gaithersburg, MD. Available at: https://nvlpubs.nist.gov/nistpubs/ai/nist.ai.100-1.pdf [Accessed 15 Jun. 2025].

National Research Council, 2012. *Education for Life and Work: Developing Transferable Knowledge and Skills in the 21st Century*. Washington, DC: National Academies Press.

National Research Council, Division of Behavioral, Social Sciences, Board on Science Education and Committee on Successful Out-of-School STEM Learning, 2015. *Identifying and Supporting Productive STEM Programs in Out-of-school Settings*. National Academies Press.

NCC Group, 2025. NCC Group welcomes the UK Government'sAI investment plans and commitment to address security challenges. [online] Available at: https://www.nccgroup.com/us/newsroom/news-reaction-ncc-group-welcomes-the-uk-government-s-ai-investment-plans-and-commitment-to-address-security-challenges/#:~:text=Yesterday%2C%20UK%20Prime%20Minister%20Sir,deliver%20public%20services%20more%20efficiently [Accessed 14 Jan. 2025].

Nedelkoska, L. and Quintini, G., 2018. Automation, skills use and training. OECD Social, Employment and Migration Working Papers, No. 202, OECD Publishing, Paris.

Negri, A. and Hardt, M., 1999. Value and affect. *boundary 2*, 26(2), pp. 77–88.

Neves, R., 2024. Collaboration and team dynamics. In: *The Engineering Leadership Playbook: Strategies for Team Success and Business Growth*. Berkeley, CA: Apress, pp. 113–179.

New York City, 2021. *Local Law 144 of 2021: Automated Employment Decision Tools*. Available at: https://www.nyc.gov/site/dca/about/automated-employment-decision-tools.page [Accessed: 2 May 2025]. Welcome to NYC.gov | City of New York

Neyazi, T.A., Ee, T.K., Nadaf, A.H. and Schroeder, R., 2023. The effect of information seeking behaviour on trust in AI in Asia: The moderating role of misinformation concern. *New Media & Society*. https://ora.ox.ac.uk/objects/uuid:81123f9b-e38c-47bc-af9c-dcaa3b361c2e

Nicholson, R., Bartindale, T., Kharrufa, A., Kirk, D. and Walker-Gleaves, C., 2022. Participatory design goes to school: Co-teaching as a form of co-design for educational technology. *Proceedings of the 2022 CHI Conference on Human Factors in Computing Systems*, Article 150, pp. 1–17. Available at: https://doi.org/10.1145/3491102.3517667 [Accessed 22 May 2025].

Nirmal, D., 2022 *The Importance of Governance: What We're Learning From AI Advances in 2022*. IBM. Available at: https://www.ibm.com/think/articles/ai-governance-2022 [Accessed 15 Jun. 2025].

NITI Aayog, 2020. *Towards Responsible #AIforAll: Principles for Responsible Artificial Intelligence in India*. NITI Aayog. Available at: https://www.niti.gov.in/sites/default/files/2020-11/Towards_Responsible_AIforAll_Part1.pdf [Accessed 15 Jun. 2025].

Nnamani, J. and Nnaemake, C., 2020. Effect of entrepreneurial competencies on profitability of quoted manufacturing firms in Nigeria. *International Journal of Scientific and Research Publications*, 10(1), pp. 799–806.

Noble, S.U., 2018. *Algorithms of Oppression: How Search Engines Reinforce Racism*. New York: New York University Press.

Nussbaum, M.C., 2011. *Creating Capabilities: The Human Development Approach*. Cambridge, MA: Harvard University Press.

O'Neil, C., 2017. *Weapons of Math Destruction: How Big Data Increases Inequality and Threatens Democracy*. New York: Crown.

O'Neill, M. and Marivate, V., 2024. AI and the future of work in Africa – White Paper. arXiv. Available at: https://arxiv.org/abs/2411.10091 [Accessed 17 Apr. 2025].

OECD, 2014. Accountability and control of public spending in the public sector. In: *Government at a Glance 2013*. Paris: OECD Publishing, pp. 1–3.

OECD, 2019a. *OECD Skills Outlook 2019: Thriving in a Digital World*. Paris: OECD Publishing.

OECD, 2019b *Recommendation of the Council on Artificial Intelligence*. Paris: OECD Publishing.

OECD, 2021a. *National Artificial Intelligence Strategies*. Paris: OECD Publishing. [online] Available at: https://goingdigital.oecd.org/data/notes/No14_ToolkitNote_AIStrategies.pdf [Accessed 8 Jan. 2025].

OECD, 2021b. *Future-ready Adult Learning Systems: Developing Skills and Adaptability in a Changing World of Work*. OECD Publishing.

OECD, 2023. *The Impact of AI on the Workplace: Evidence from OECD Case Studies of AI Implementation*. Paris: OECD Publishing. Available at: https://www.oecd.org/publications/the-impact-of-ai-on-the-workplace-2247ce58-en.htm [Accessed 7 Apr. 2025].

OECD, 2024. *OECD Survey on Drivers of Trust in Public Institutions – 2024 Results: Building Trust in a Complex Policy Environment*. Paris: OECD Publishing. https://doi.org/10.1787/9a20554b-en. Available at: https://www.oecd.org/publications/oecd-survey-on-drivers-of-trust-in-public-institutions-2024-results_9a20554b-en.htm [Accessed 15 Jun. 2025].

OECD and CAF, 2022. *The Strategic and Responsible Use of Artificial Intelligence in the Public Sector of Latin America and the Caribbean*. OECD Publishing. Available at: https://www.oecd.org/en/publications/2022/03/the-strategic-and-responsible-use-of-artificial-intelligence-in-the-public-sector-of-latin-america-and-the-caribbean_17c90e5e.html [Accessed 21 Apr. 2025].

OEI and ProFuturo, 2023. *The Future of Artificial Intelligence in Education in Latin America*. OEI. Available at: https://oei.int/wp-content/uploads/2023/04/the-future-of-artificial-intelligence-in-education-in-latin-america-oei-profuturo.pdf [Accessed 21 Apr. 2025].

Office for Students (OfS), 2024. *Regulating the Use of AI in Higher Education*. London: OfS.

Okolie, U.C., Nwosu, H.E. and Mlanga, S., 2019. Graduate employability: How the higher education institutions can meet the demand of the labour market. *Higher Education, Skills and Work-Based Learning*, 9(4), pp. 620–636.

Oladele, F., Hammond, J. and Thakur, R., 2025. *Global frameworks for labour-focused AI regulation*. *SSRN Electronic Journal*, [online] Available at: https://papers.ssrn.com [Accessed 13 May 2025].

Open Data Institute, 2020. *Data 2020: AI and algorithmic accountability*. Open Data Institute, 21 February. Available at: https://theodi.org/article/data-2020-ai-and-algorithmic-accountability/ [Accessed 15 Jun. 2025].

Open Government Partnership, 2023. *State of the Evidence: Algorithmic Transparency*. Available at: https://www.opengovpartnership.org/documents/state-of-the-evidence-algorithmic-transparency/ [Accessed: 2 May 2025]

Organisation for Economic Co-operation and Development (OECD), 2019a; updated 2024. *Recommendation of the Council on Artificial Intelligence (OECD AI Principles)*. Paris: OECD. Available at: https://legalinstruments.oecd.org/en/instruments/oecd-legal-0449 [Accessed 15 Jun. 2025].

Organisation for Economic Co-operation and Development (OECD), 2019b. *Recommendation of the Council on Artificial Intelligence*. Adopted 22 May 2019, OECD, Paris.

Organisation for Economic Co-operation and Development (OECD), 2024. *OECD Updates AI Principles to Stay Abreast of Rapid Technological Developments*, 3 May. OECD. Available at: https://oecd.org/en/about/news/press-releases/2024/05/oecd-updates-ai-principles-to-stay-abreast-of-rapid-technological-developments.html [Accessed 15 Jun. 2025].

Pagani, R.N., de Sá, C.P., Corsi, A. and de Souza, F.F., 2023. AI and employability: Challenges and solutions from this technology transfer. In: M.D. Lytras, A.A. Housawi and B.S. Alsaywid, eds. *Smart Cities and Digital Transformation: Empowering Communities, Limitless Innovation, Sustainable Development and the Next Generation*. Emerald Publishing Limited, pp. 253–284.

Partnership for 21st Century Learning (P21), 2009. P21 framework definitions. [online] Available at: https://www.battelleforkids.org/networks/p21 [Accessed 26 Mar. 2025].

Pasquale, F., 2015. *The Black Box Society: The Secret Algorithms That Control Money and Information*. Cambridge, MA: Harvard University Press.

Peck, J. and Theodore, N., 2000. Beyond 'employability'. *Cambridge Journal of Economics*, 24(6), pp. 729–749.

Pembi, S. and Ali, B.K., 2024. Ethical business decision-making in organizations: A theoretical perspectives. *Advanced Qualitative Research*, 2(1), pp. 19–30.

Personal Data Protection Commission, Singapore, 2020. *Model AI Governance Framework*. 2nd ed. Personal Data Protection Commission, Singapore. Available at: https://www.pdpc.gov.sg/help-and-resources/2020/01/model-ai-governance-framework [Accessed 15 Jun. 2025].

Pillai, R., Sivathanu, B., Metri, B. and Kaushik, N., 2023. 'Students' adoption of AI-based teacher-bots (T-bots) for learning in higher education', *Information Technology & People*, 37(1), pp. 328–355. https://doi.org/10.1108/ITP-02-2021-0152

Pirson, M., 2017. *Humanistic Management: Protecting Dignity and Promoting Well-Being*. Cambridge: Cambridge University Press.

Psacharopoulos, G. and Patrinos, H.A., 2004. Returns to investment in education: A further update. *Education Economics*, 12(2), pp. 111–134.

Quality Assurance Agency for Higher Education (QAA), 2023. *Maintaining Quality and Standards in the ChatGPT Era: QAA Advice on the Opportunities and Challenges Posed by Generative Artificial Intelligence*. Gloucester: QAA. [online] Available at: https://www.qaa.ac.uk/docs/qaa/members/maintaining-quality-and-standards-in-the-chatgpt-era.pdf [Accessed 15 Apr. 2025].

Ra, S., Shrestha, U., Khatiwada, S., Yoon, S.W. and Kwon, K., 2019. The rise of technology and impact on skills. *International Journal of Training Research*, 17(sup1), pp. 26–40.

Raghavan, M., Barocas, S., Kleinberg, J. and Levy, K., 2020. Mitigating Bias in Algorithmic Hiring: Evaluating Claims and Practices. *Proceedings of the 2020 Conference on Fairness, Accountability, and Transparency*, pp. 469–481.

Ragins, B.R. and Kram, K.E., 2007. The landscape of mentoring in the 21st century. In: B.R. Ragins and K.E. Kram, eds. *The Handbook of Mentoring at Work: Theory, Research, and Practice*. SAGE Publications, pp. 659–692.

Ragnedda, M. and Ruiu, M.L., 2020. *Digital Capital: A Bourdieusian Perspective on the Digital Divide*. Bingley: Emerald Publishing Limited.

Ramírez Plascencia, D. and Alonzo González, R.M. (eds.), 2025. *Ethical and Legal Dilemmas of Artificial Intelligence in Latin America*. Cham: Springer Nature Switzerland.

Ramos, A., 2022. *AI, jobs, and UNESCO's ethics framework*. *UNESCO Working Papers*, [online] Available at: https://scholarworks.umb.edu [Accessed 13 May 2025].

Rawls, J., 2020. *A Theory of Justice: Revised Edition*. Cambridge, MA: Harvard University Press.

Reich, J. and Ito, M., 2017. *From good intentions to real outcomes: Equity by design in learning technologies*. [pdf] Digital Media and Learning Research Hub. Available at: https://clalliance.org/publications/from-good-intentions-to-real-outcomes-equity-by-design-in-learning-technologies [Accessed 22 May 2025].

Rigley, E., Bentley, C., Krook, J. and Ramchurn, S.D., 2024. Evaluating international AI skills policy: A systematic review of AI skills policy in seven countries. *Global Policy*, 15(1), pp. 204–217.

Rodríguez Fernández, F. 2025. La inteligencia artificial como herramienta transformadora en la educación: aplicación, impacto potencial y políticas. *Papeles de Economía Española*, 184, pp. 110–127.

Roe, J. and Perkins, M., 2024. Generative AI and agency in education: A critical scoping review and thematic analysis. arXiv preprint arXiv:2411.00631. Available at: https://arxiv.org/abs/2411.00631 [Accessed 15 Jun. 2025].

Romzek, B.S. and Dubnick, M.J., 1987. Accountability in the public sector: Lessons from the Challenger tragedy. *Public Administration Review*, 47(3), pp. 227–238.

Rose, N., 1999. *Powers of Freedom: Reframing Political Thought*. Cambridge: Cambridge University Press.

Rudin, C., 2019. Stop explaining black box machine learning models for high stakes decisions and use interpretable models instead. *Nature Machine Intelligence*, 1(5), pp. 206–215. https://doi.org/10.1038/s42256-019-0048-X

Ryan, P., 2001. The school-to-work transition: A cross-national perspective. *Journal of Economic Literature*, 39(1), pp. 34–92.

Sahlberg, P., 2021. *Finnish Lessons 3.0: What Can the World Learn from Educational Change in Finland?* New York: Teachers College Press.

Sahlgren, M., 2023. Algorithmic fairness and accountability in education. *ERIC Education Resources Information Center*, [online] Available at: https://eric.ed.gov [Accessed 13 May 2025].

Salanova, M., Llorens, S. and Ventura, M., 2014. Technostress: The dark side of technologies. In: *The Impact of ICT on Quality of Working Life*. Dordrecht: Springer Netherlands, pp. 87–103.

Salas-Pilco, S. Z. and Yang, Y., 2022. Artificial intelligence applications in Latin American higher education: A systematic review. *International Journal of Educational Technology in Higher Education*, 19, Article 21.

Scandurra, R., Kelly, D., Fusaro, S., Cefalo, R. and Hermannsson, K., 2024. Do employability programmes in higher education improve skills and labour market outcomes? A systematic review of academic literature. *Studies in Higher Education*, 49(8), pp. 1381–1396.

Schedler, A., 1999. Conceptualizing accountability. In: A. Schedler, L. Diamond and M.F. Plattner, eds. *The Self-Restraining State: Power and Accountability in New Democracies*. Boulder, CO: Lynne Rienner Publishers, pp. 13–28.

Schmager, S., Pappas, I.O. and Vassilakopoulou, P., 2025. Understanding human-centred AI: A review of its defining elements and a research agenda. *Behaviour & Information Technology*, 44, pp. 1–40.

Schön, D.A., 1983. *The Reflective Practitioner: How Professionals Think in Action*. New York: Basic Books.

Scott, C., 2015. The futures of learning 2: What kind of learning for the 21st century? *UNESCO Education Research and Foresight Working Papers*, No.14. Paris: UNESCO. [online] Available at: https://unesdoc.unesco.org/ark:/48223/pf0000242996 [Accessed 2 Jan. 2025].

Segbenya, M., Bervell, B., Frimpong-Manso, E., Otoo, I.C., Andzie, T.A. and Achina, S., 2023. Artificial intelligence in higher education: Modelling the antecedents of artificial intelligence usage and effects on 21st century employability skills among postgraduate students in Ghana. *Computers and Education: Artificial Intelligence*, 5, p. 100188.

Selwyn, N., 2019. *Should Robots Replace Teachers?: AI and the Future of Education*. Chichester: John Wiley & Sons.

Selwyn, N., Pangrazio, L. and Campbell, M., 2021. Education and the datafied world: Possibilities, promises and pitfalls. *Learning, Media and Technology*, 46(3), pp. 233–245.

Sen, A., 1999. *Development as Freedom*. Oxford: Oxford University Press.

Senge, P.M., 2006. *The Fifth Discipline: The Art and Practice of the Learning Organization*. Broadway Business.

Sey, A. and Mudongo, O., 2021. *Case Studies on AI Skills Capacity Building and AI in Workforce Development in Africa*. Research ICT Africa. Available at: https://www.ai4d.ai/research/case-studies-on-ai-skills-capacity-building-and-ai-in-workforce-development-in-africa [Accessed 12 Jan. 2025].

Smith, M.-S., 2022. The future of work: Skills for the future. *Prospects Luminate*, August. Available at: https://luminate.prospects.ac.uk/the-future-of-work-skills-for-the-future [Accessed 3 Apr. 2025].

Soares Seto, K., 2025. AI from the South: Artificial intelligence in Latin America through the sociotechnical imaginaries of Brazilian tech workers. *Globalizations*, pp. 1–16.

Solomonides, A.E., Koski, E., Atabaki, S.M., Weinberg, S., Mcgreevey, J.D., Kannry, J.L., Petersen, C. and Lehmann, C.U., 2021. Defining AMIA's artificial intelligence principles. *Journal of the American Medical Informatics Association*, 29(4), pp. 585–591. https://doi.org/10.1093/jamia/ocab006

Soproni, L. (2020). Employability skills: Rethink your learning. *Global Journal of Sociology and Anthropology*, 10(1), 14–20.

Southworth, J. et al., 2023. Developing a model for AI across the curriculum: Transforming HE via innovation in AI literacy. *Computers & Education: Artificial Intelligence*, 4, p. 100137.

Srivastava, S., 2025. 'Large language models threaten language's epistemic and communicative foundations', *Proceedings of the 2025 Conference on Empirical Methods in Natural Language Processing (EMNLP 2025)*, pp. 28651–28665. Available at: https://aclanthology.org/2025.emnlp-main.1457.pdf [Accessed 15 Jun. 2025].

Stahl, B.C., 2021. Ethical issues of AI. In: *Artificial Intelligence for a Better Future: An Ecosystem Perspective on the Ethics of AI and Emerging Digital Technologies*. Cham: Springer, pp. 35–53.

Standing, G., 2011. *The Precariat: The New Dangerous Class*. London: Bloomsbury Academic.

Stephany, F., 2020. When does it pay off to learn a new skill? Revealing the complementary benefit of cross-skilling. arXiv preprint arXiv:2010.11841. Available at: https://arxiv.org/abs/2010.11841 [Accessed 15 Apr. 2025]

Stephany, F., and Teutloff, O. 2024. What is the price of a skill? The value of complementarity. *Research Policy*, *53*(1), pp. 104898.

Sternberg, R.J., 2023. Transformational creativity. In: V.P. Glăveanu, ed. *The Palgrave Encyclopedia of the Possible*. Cham: Palgrave Macmillan (Springer Nature), pp. 1676–1682.

Stoian, C. R., Archibald, C. and Geary, K., 2019. Learn and work in the 21st century: A review of employability models for HE graduates at different levels of analysis. *Management Dynamics in the Knowledge Economy*, 7(2), 261–282.

Stoica, A.E., 2010. *Development and testing of a comprehensive skill framework for the successful employability of MBA graduates*. Doctoral dissertation. Waseda University.

Streeck, W., 1989. Skills and the limits of neo-liberalism: The enterprise of the future as a place of learning. *Work, Employment and Society*, 3(1), pp. 89–104.

Succi, C. and Canovi, M., 2020. Soft skills to enhance graduate employability: Comparing students and employers' perceptions. *Studies in Higher Education*, 45(9), pp. 1834–1847.

Sun, N., Miao, Y., Jiang, H., Ding, M. and Zhang, J., 2024. From principles to practice: A deep dive into AI ethics and regulations, arXiv preprint arXiv:2412.04683. Available at: https://arxiv.org/abs/2412.04683 [Accessed 15 Jun. 2025].

Susskind, D., 2020. *A World Without Work: Technology, Automation and How We Should Respond*. London: Penguin UK.

Tadas, P. and Agarmore, S., 2024. Redefining work in the age of AI: Challenges and pathways to opportunities. In: *2024 IEEE International Conference on Signal Processing, Informatics, Communication and Energy Systems (SPICES 2024)*, 20–22 Sept. 2024, Kottayam, India. New York, NY: IEEE, p. 111.

Tafazoli, D., 2023. Critical appraisal of artificial intelligence-mediated communication. arXiv preprint arXiv:2305.11897.

The Alan Turing Institute, 2020. *Data Science and AI in the Age of COVID-19: Report on Findings from Late 2020 Workshops*. The Alan Turing Institute. Available at: https://www.turing.ac.uk/news/publications/data-science-and-ai-age-covid-19-report [Accessed: 10 July 2023].

The Sun, 2023. AI training for government workers major part of smart tech plan. Available at: https://www.thesun.ie/tech/14141957/ai-training-government-workers-tech-plan-job-fears/ [Accessed 8 Jan. 2025].

Tierney, A., Peasey, P.V. and Gould, J.J.M., 2025, Student perceptions on the impact of AI on their teaching and learning experiences in Higher Education. *Research and Practice in Technology Enhanced Learning*, 20.

TIME, 2023. India is emerging as a key player in the global AI race. [online] Available at: https://time.com/7018294/india-ai-artificial-intelligence-ambani/ [Accessed 8 Jan. 2025].

Tobenkin, D., 2024. Artificial intelligence and the future of higher education, part 1. *Trusteeship Magazine*, 32(1), January/February. [online] Available at: https://agb.org/trusteeship-article/artificial-intelligence-and-the-future-of-higher-education-part-1/ [Accessed 6 Apr. 2025].

Tomaskinova, J., West, L.B., Chircop, T., Judge, J., de Vries, S., Marinescu-Muster, R.F., Hiddink, F., Delicata, F., Pierucci, M., Montalto, M. and Camilleri, S. 2024. Shaping the future: Navigating the AI era with an innovative training model. In *EDULEARN24 Proceedings*. IATED. pp. 6295–6303.

Tomlinson, M., 2017. Forms of graduate capital and their relationship to graduate employability. *Education + Training*, 59(4), pp. 338–352.

Topaloglu, M. and Anac, A.S., 2021. Exploring major factors affecting virtual team performance. *European Journal of Business and Management Research*, 6(5), pp. 107–114.

Tremblay, J., 2011. *One Laptop per Child Technology, Education and Development in Rwanda*. Canada: McGill University.

U.S National Institute of Standards and Technology, 2023. *Artificial Intelligence Risk Management Framework (AI RMF 1.0)*. U.S. Department of Commerce. Available at: https://nvlpubs.nist.gov/nistpubs/ai/nist.ai.100-1.pdf [Accessed: 01 June 2024].

U.S. Department of Education, 2023. *Artificial Intelligence and the Future of Teaching and Learning: Insights and Recommendations*. [pdf] Office of Educational Technology. Available at: https://www.ed.gov/sites/default/files/ai-report.pdf [Accessed 22 May 2025].

UK Government, 2023. *Algorithmic Transparency Recording Standard*. Available at: https://www.gov.uk/government/collections/algorithmic-transparency-recording-standard-hub [Accessed: 2 May 2025].

UNESCO, 2019. *Beijing Consensus on Artificial Intelligence and Education*. Paris: UNESCO. [online] Available at: https://unesdoc.unesco.org/ark:/48223/pf0000368303 [Accessed 7 Apr. 2025].

UNESCO, 2021a. *Artificial Intelligence and Education: Guidance for Policy-Makers*. Paris: UNESCO. Available at: https://unesdoc.unesco.org/ark:/48223/pf0000376709 [Accessed 7 Apr. 2025].

UNESCO, 2021b. Recommendation on the ethics of artificial intelligence. [online] Available at: https://www.unesco.org/en/articles/recommendation-ethics-artificial-intelligence [Accessed 22 Apr. 2025].

UNESCO, 2022a. *UNESCO Strategy for TVET (2022–2029): Transforming Technical and Vocational Education and Training for Successful and Just Transitions*. Paris: UNESCO-UNEVOC. Available at: https://unevoc.unesco.org/pub/unesco_strategy_for_tvet_2022-2029.pdf [Accessed 7 Apr. 2025].

UNESCO, 2022b *AI and Digital Transformation in Southeast Asia*. UNESCO Bangkok.

UNESCO, 2023. *Guidance for Generative AI in Education and Research*. Paris: United Nations Educational, Scientific and Cultural Organization.

UNESCO, 2024. *AI and Critical Thinking in Curricula*. Official policy doc.

UNESCO-UNEVOC, 2023. Soft skills acquisition for the knowledge economy: A research strategy for policy evolution in TVET. [online] Available at: https://unevoc.unesco.org [Accessed 26 Mar. 2025].

UNICEF, 2021. *Policy Guidance on AI for Children*. New York: United Nations Children's Fund.

United Nations Department of Economic and Social Affairs (UN DESA), 2020. *United Nations E-Government Survey 2020: Digital Government in the Decade of Action for Sustainable Development – With Addendum on COVID-19 Response*. United Nations, New York. Available at: https://publicadministration.un.org/egovkb/Portals/egovkb/Documents/un/2020-Survey/2020%20UN%20E-Government%20Survey%20%28Full%20Report%29.pdf [Accessed 15 Jun. 2025].

University of Technology Sydney, 2022. Shaping AI and edtech to tackle Australia's learning divide. Available at: https://opus.lib.uts.edu.au/bitstream/10453/162604/3/Shaping%20AI%20%26%20EdTech%20-%20LOBLE%20-%20Final%20report%20-%20December%202022.pdf [Accessed 8 Jan. 2025].

van Laar, E., van Deursen, A.J.A.M., van Dijk, J.A.G.M. and de Haan, J., 2020. Determinants of 21st-century skills and 21st-century digital skills for workers: A systematic literature review. *SAGE Open*, 10(1), pp. 1–14.

Vecchi, M., Vignoles, A. and Battiston, A., 2023. Graduate skills and labour market mismatch in the UK. *Studies in Higher Education*, 48(4), pp. 755–772.

Vidyadhari, P., Handa, R. and Wang, Y., 2024. *FairAIED: Ethics in educational AI systems. arXiv preprint* arXiv:2402.08932.

Visvanathan, S., 2009. *The search for cognitive justice. India Seminar.* Available at: http://www.india-seminar.com/2009/597/597_shiv_visvanathan.htm [Accessed 29 Dec. 2025].

Voogt, J., 2010. Teacher factors associated with innovative curriculum goals and pedagogical practices: Differences between extensive and non-extensive ICT-using science teachers. *Journal of Computer Assisted Learning*, 26(6), pp. 453–464.

Voogt, J. and Roblin, N.P., 2012. A comparative analysis of international frameworks for 21st century competences: Implications for national curriculum policies. *Journal of curriculum studies*, 44(3), pp. 299–321.

Wachter, S., Mittelstadt, B. and Floridi, L., 2017. Why a right to explanation of automated decision-making does not exist in the general data protection regulation. *International Data Privacy Law*, 7(2), pp. 76–99.

Wakiaga, L. and Waweru-Mwangi, C., 2025. *Embracing AI in Education*. African Population and Health Research Center. Available at: https://aphrc.org/blogarticle/embracing-ai-in-education/ [Accessed 17 Apr. 2025].

Wanberg, C.R., Ali, A.A. and Csillag, B., 2020. Job search and employment success: A quantitative review and future research agenda. *Journal of Applied Psychology*, 105(7), pp. 674–713.

Wang, X., Chen, M. and Chen, N., 2024. How artificial intelligence affects the labour force employment structure from the perspective of industrial structure optimisation. *Heliyon*, 10(5), p. e26686.

Wang, Y.D., 2014. 'Building student trust in online learning environments', *Information*, 17(5), pp. 295–302.

Webber, J., 2009. *The Existentialism of Jean-Paul Sartre*. London: Routledge.

Wegerif, R., 2013. *Dialogic: Education for the Internet Age*. London and New York: Routledge

West, S. M., Whittaker, M., and Crawford, K. 2019. *Discriminating Systems: Gender, Race and Power in AI*. New York: AI Now Institute, New York University.

Westman, S., Kauttonen, J., Klemetti, A., Korhonen, N., Manninen, M., Mononen, A., Niittymäki, S. and Paananen, H., 2021. Artificial intelligence for career guidance – Current requirements and prospects for the future. *IAFOR Journal of Education: Technology in Education*, 9(4), pp. 43–62.

White, J., 2015. 21st Century skills: A perspective from England. *e-Pedagogium*, 15(2), pp. 51–61. https://doi.org/10.5507/epd.2015.016

Williamson, B., 2021. *Datafication of Education: A Critical Perspective on Emerging Patterns*. London: Routledge.

Williamson, B. and Eynon, R., 2020. Historical threads, missing links, and future directions in AI in education. *Learning, Media and Technology*, 45(3), pp. 223–235.

Wolf, A., 2011. *Review of Vocational Education: The Wolf Report*. London: TSO (The Stationery Office). Available at: https://www.gov.uk/government/publications/review-of-vocational-education-the-wolf-report [Accessed 15 Apr. 2025].

Woo, J.J., 2020. *Singapore's Policy Designs for Higher Education and Economic Development*. Singapore: Springer. [online] Available at: https://books.google.com [Accessed 8 Jan. 2025].

Wood, A.J., Graham, M., Lehdonvirta, V. and Hjorth, I., 2019. Good gig, bad gig: Autonomy and algorithmic control in the global gig economy. *Work, employment and society*, *33*(1), pp. 56–75.

World Bank, 2024. *Digital Skills in Indonesia: Pathways and Gaps*. World Bank Group.

World Bank, 2025. *Artificial Intelligence: Real impact – labour market implications in South Asia*. World Bank. Available at: https://openknowledge.worldbank.org/bitstreams/a6e15c66-daaa-4c9f-80d5-65951eea2cc5/download [Accessed 15 Jun. 2025].

World Economic Forum, 2020. *The Future of Jobs Report 2020*. Geneva: World Economic Forum.

World Economic Forum, 2022. *A Blueprint for Equity and Inclusion in Artificial Intelligence*. World Economic Forum Global Future Council on Artificial Intelligence for Humanity, 29 June. Available at: https://www.weforum.org/publications/a-blueprint-for-equity-and-inclusion-in-artificial-intelligence/ [Accessed 15 Jun. 2025].

World Economic Forum, 2023. *The Future of Jobs Report 2023*.

World Health Organization, 2021. *Ethics and Governance of Artificial Intelligence for Health*. Geneva: WHO. Available at: https://www.who.int/publications/i/item/9789240029200 [Accessed 15 June 2025].

World Health Organization (WHO), 2007. *Everybody's Business: Strengthening Health Systems to Improve Health Outcomes—WHO's Framework for Action*. Geneva: WHO.

Wynants, S., Devolder, P. and Van Roy, V., 2025. AI ethics frameworks in higher education: A comparative review. *AI & Society*, 40(2), pp. 217–236.

Yan, L., Jin, Y., Echeverria, V., Gašević, D. and Martinez-Maldonado, R., 2025. Generative AI in higher education: A global perspective of institutional adoption policies and guidelines. *Computers and Education: Artificial Intelligence*, 8, p. 100348.

Yi, J., 2023. 'How does digital government affect citizens' trust in government? Evidence from China', *SSRN Electronic Journal*. Available at: https://papers.ssrn.com/abstract=4576773 [Accessed 15 Jun. 2025].

Yorke, M. and Knight, P.T., 2006. *Embedding Employability into the Curriculum. Learning and Employability Series One*. New York: Higher Education Academy. Available at: www.heacademy.ac.uk/resource/embedding-employability-curriculum [Accessed 20 Feb. 2025].

Zawacki-Richter, O., Marín, V.I., Bond, M. and Gouverneur, F., 2019. Systematic review of research on artificial intelligence applications in higher education–where are the educators? *International Journal of Educational Technology in Higher Education*, 16(1), pp. 1–27.

Zubair, S., 2024. AI-driven automation: Transforming workplaces and labor markets. *Frontiers in Artificial Intelligence Research*, 1(3), pp. 373–411.

Zuboff, S., 2023. The age of surveillance capitalism. In: C. Calhoun, J. Gerteis, J. Moody, S. Pfaff and I. Virk, eds. *Social Theory Re-Wired: New Connections to Classical and Contemporary Perspectives*. 4th ed. London: Routledge, pp. 203–213.

Zwick, A., 2018. 'Welcome to the Gig Economy: Neoliberal Industrial Relations and the Case of Uber'. *Geojournal*, 83(4), pp. 679–691.

Index

Note: Pages in *italics* refer to figures and pages in **bold** refer to tables.